BISON
BOOKS

D0048509

Chimney Rock on the North Platte is the most famous landmark of the Great Platte River Road. This romanticized version by Alfred Lambourne conveys the sense of wonder and excitement which this strange geological specimen inspired.

—Union Pacific Railroad Museum

THE GREAT PLATTE RIVER ROAD:

The Covered Wagon Mainline
Via Fort Kearny To Fort Laramie

By

MERRILL J. MATTES

University of Nebraska Press
Lincoln and London

First Bison Book printing: 1987

Library of Congress Cataloging-in-Publication Data
Mattes, Merrill J.
  The great Platte River road.
  Reprint. Originally published: Lincoln: Nebraska
State Historical Society, c1969. Originally
published in series: Nebraska State Historical
Publications.
  Bibliography: p.
  Includes index.
  1. North Platte River Valley—History. 2. North
Platte River Valley—Description and travel.
3. Overland journeys to the Pacific. 4. Frontier
and pioneer life—North Platte River Valley.
5. Oregon Trail. I. Title.
F672.N8M38 1987   978.7'16   87-10844
ISBN 0-8032-3124-5
ISBN 0-8032-8153-6 (pbk.)

Reprinted by arrangement with the
Nebraska State Historical Society

∞

Dedicated
To my wife, Clare
and our sons, Warren, John and David

FOREWORD

This comprehensive study of pioneer trail travelers on the Great Platte River Road has resulted from a Woods Fellowship administered by the Nebraska State Historical Society from funds donated by the Woods Charitable Fund, Inc. Funds for the original publication in 1969 were provided by the Nebraska State Centennial Commission and the Nebraska State Historical Society Foundation.

Volume XXV marked the resumption of the Society's oldest series of publications. Begun in 1885 as *Transactions and Reports*, the name of the series was changed with Volume VI to *Proceedings and Collections*, with Volume XVI to *Collections*, and with Volume XVIII to*Publications*. The last volume prior to the present issue, Volume XXIV, was published in 1958.

The response to this publication was excellent, which resulted in the Society Board approving the publication of Volume XXVI *From the Missouri to the Great Salt Lake: An Account of Overland Freighting* by Professor William F. Lass in 1972 and Volume XXVII *Conquering the Great American Desert: Nebraska* by Professor Everett Dick in 1975. Funds for the republication of this book were provided by the Woods Charitable Fund, Inc. Publication Trust administered by the Nebraska State Historical Society Foundation.

MARVIN F. KIVETT, *Director*
Nebraska State Historical Society

Preface to the First Edition

There is a vast literature on the trans-Mississippi western frontier in general and the Oregon-California Trail in particular. Another book on the subject must justify itself by exploring new territory or at least by providing new interpretations or fresh syntheses of old data. Although this book covers old familiar territory, geographically speaking, it examines it first with an unfamiliar telescopic lens, then microscopically through a host of witnesses.

This is a study in depth of the eastern third of the central overland trail system from the Missouri River to the Pacific Coast, that part which followed the Platte River via Fort Kearny to Fort Laramie. It is not based on broad general impressions gleaned from secondary works, nor does it lean heavily on the writing of one particular traveler. It is distilled from the firsthand impressions of *several hundred* covered wagon emigrants, representing both sexes and all degrees of human latitude, who somehow contrived to leave something for the historical record. It is the story of their unique collective Platte River experience as it emerges from their own unvarnished journals.

In over thirty years of exposure to the subject of overland migrations, and with exceptional opportunities to read the primary sources, published and unpublished, the writer has been impressed with two remarkable facts which have not been adequately defined or fully appreciated by historians and writers of history. The first fact is that the many overland trails which funneled up the Platte and the North Platte actually comprised one immense transcontinental route of transcendent importance in American history, the grand corridor of westward expansion, which is herein labeled the Great Platte River Road. The second fact is the quite staggering number of emigrant accounts (mainly family diaries, but including also letters and reminiscences) which have survived and are now available for systematic scrutiny and analysis by the scholar.

This has been an effort to make a nation-wide search for original sources, and to work primarily from those sources. Several bibliographies of central overland narratives have been published. Among the more notably comprehensive are Camp's edition of Wagner's *The Plains and the Rockies*, the bibliography in Irene Paden's *The Wake of the Prairie Schooner*, and the 1849 checklist appended to Dale Morgan's edition of the James Pritchard journal. In the latter is an implied forecast that the total number of known narratives, published and unpublished, might be on the order of magnitude set forth in the bibliography of this work. Well over 700 overland narratives are accounted for here. Even so, it is conceded this bibliography is not all-inclusive. The 700-plus eyewitness accounts listed are only those which were accessible and which were utilized in this study.

After examining other bibliographies the writer has become aware of other accounts which were not reached. Some leads just evaporated on contact. A few items were inaccessible because of library restrictions. There are rare publications and manuscripts in eastern libraries, notably the Library of Congress and the Western Americana Collection, Yale University, which were not pursued because the writer was already overwhelmed with the process of digesting those on hand. (Microfilmed copies of some items at Yale became available through the courtesy of the Western History Research Center, University of Wyoming at Laramie.) There are many journals in Utah repositories—the Mormon church archives, Brigham Young University, and others—which were not tracked down, partly because the Mormon journals tend to be highly repetitious, but again because of sheer human limitations. Then there are those fleeting items that appear in rare book dealers' catalogs, so rarefied in price that they might as well be on the moon. If all these marginal or elusive journals were added, the total would doubtlessly exceed 800.

It is estimated at least 90 per cent of all known covered wagon testaments surviving have been examined for this work. The remaining elusive 10 per cent can be tracked down by others whose primary business it is to compile a thoroughly exhaustive bibliography rather than attempt to interpret the epic story that goes with it. Our compilation should make their cleanup project a relatively simple task.

A discussion of the character of the emigrant writings themselves is included in Chapter II. We have mentioned sources which proved elusive. More important, we make a deep bow to the libraries and repositories where the bulk of the overland narratives *were* found, the officials of which were uniformly gracious and long-suffering in making their resources available to the writer.

As might be expected of a body of literature which was largely motivated by the journalists' desires to get to the West Coast, the biggest concentration of overland narratives, published and unpublished, was found in California. The Huntington Library in San Marino, the Bancroft Library on the University of California campus at Berkeley, and the California State Library at Sacramento all have outstanding collections of manuscripts and rare books; collectively they hold well over 50 per cent of known manuscript materials. Other significant collections were found at the Newberry Library in Chicago, the Missouri Historical Society in St. Louis, and the Wisconsin Historical Society at Madison.

Most published materials, except those in the rare category, were found in the library of the Nebraska State Historical Society and in collections of the National Park Service. A high percentage of such materials is to be found in the publications of various state historical societies and pioneer associations, mainly those of Oregon, California, Utah, Colorado, Wyoming, Nebraska, Missouri, Iowa, and other trans-Mississippi states, but including also Illinois, Ohio, Indiana, and Michigan and a few surprise entries from repositories in Alabama, North Carolina, New Jersey, and West Virginia.

A few manuscripts and rare publications came to this writer's attention through the volition of individuals. In other words, while most sources had to be tracked down in libraries, a few simply drifted in through the osmosis of common interests. Two most helpful friends and Oregon Trail detectives must be mentioned—Charles W. Martin of Omaha and Paul Henderson of Bridgeport, Nebraska. To the latter a special debt is also owed, for generous assistance in providing map data and notes, as well as for volunteer service as trail guide on field trips.

It would be superfluous to identify here all individuals and institutions whose cooperation made this research possible. In the overland narrative section of the appended bibliography the search location of all primary sources is given, along with the date of the overland crossing. Our gratitude to the officials of all indicated repositories is sincere and continuing.

Particular acknowledgment is made to the University of Illinois Press for the re-use in Chapter IV of portions of the article by the present author, "The Jumping-off Places on the Overland Trail," appearing in *The Frontier Re-examined* (1967), edited by John Francis McDermott. Likewise, Chapter XV is substantially a reproduction of the author's long out-of-print booklet, *Fort Laramie and the Forty-Niners* (1949), published by the Rocky Mountain Nature Association in the year of the Fort Laramie military post centennial.

An unorthodox system of referencing is employed here. The number of quotations woven into the text, in the neighborhood of three thousand, makes impractical the usual method of footnoting. Instead, each source identified in the text may be checked as an item in the bibliography. In the case of manuscripts, which comprise a high percentage of the total sources, no page reference is apropos; and in the case of publications, the absence of a precise page identification in each instance is a minor sacrifice to gain space and simplification of format. Information not specifically referenced is the result of general knowledge built into the writer's background or obtained from materials indicated in the second part of the bibliography.

It may appear to some that in this treatment of the Platte River Road, the north, or Council Bluffs, side of the Road has been neglected. The detailed geography of the Council Bluffs Road and the incidents of covered wagon travel relating thereto are not treated extensively here for two reasons. First, the story of the Mormons who used the north bank has been told voluminously elsewhere, most recently and with eloquence by Wallace Stegner in his *Gathering of Zion*. Second, non-Mormons on the north side recounted experiences similar to those told by travelers on the south or Oregon Trail side.

If the Council Bluffs Road seems slighted, the Pike's Peak Road up the South Platte from Julesburg to Denver must seem neglected altogether. While this too is part of the Platte River Road system, it comes to a regional dead-end in Colorado. It is the transcontinental route up the main Platte and the North Platte that primarily concerns us.

Another more serious discrepancy or omission is a study of that bona fide part of the Platte River Road west of Fort Laramie, to the Sweetwater and South Pass. Suffice it to say that Fort Laramie was the logical and tangible end of the first or Plains phase of the overland journey; no one book could encompass the entire distance. The mountain or Wyoming phase of the Platte to the Continental Divide, and thence to Fort Bridger, will require an equivalent volume.

This undertaking, which is Nebraska-oriented, was made possible by a research grant from the Woods Charitable Fund, Inc., and the faith of the Nebraska State Historical Society and its selection committee in the author's knowledge of, and enthusiasm for, the history of the covered wagon migrations. The grant was inspired by the wish of the donors to produce a series of original historical monographs in commemoration of the 1967 Nebraska Statehood Centennial.

The project had the approval of the National Park Service, U.S. Department of the Interior, employer of the undersigned, on the basis that work on the book would be independent. It was understood, however, that the product would ultimately benefit the Service's research and interpretive program, as well as the cause of general scholarship.

The comprehensive research involved actually goes back two or three decades; the manuscript itself was developed during a period of some eight years of intermittent time. The result, while nearly encyclopedic in length, is neither as literary nor as definitive as the author would wish. The chief satisfaction lies in the realization that this rather massive effort may inspire scholars of this and forthcoming generations to labor further in this enormous vineyard, following its windings and tracing its dimensions far beyond the present accomplishment.

MERRILL J. MATTES
San Francisco, California
July 4, 1969

Preface to the Second Edition

It has been gratifying to observe the brisk sale of the First Edition of 7,500 copies of *Great Platte River Road*. From the standpoint of collectors of Western Americana the book has now achieved a certain distinction as being "out-of-print," and therefore commanding some scarcity value on the market. While the large number of hardcover copies now in private or public library possession may prevent it from finding its way into the "rare" category soon, stray copies handled by dealers in this field are finding a level of value substantially above the original bargain price.

Our observation on market value has nothing to do with exploitation. Far from it. The Nebraska State Historical Society reaps no profit from its publications; all the proceeds are returned to a revolving fund for new publications. Also in accordance with Society policy, the author receives no percentage royalties whatever from sales. His reward is of a more spiritual nature, if you will, the pleasure of having made some original contribution to the literature of the trans-Mississippi—primarily the Nebraska—frontier.

Monetary value is not important except as one index to something far more important, namely, the impact of *Great Platte River Road* on Nebraskans generally and scholars of Western American history nation-wide. Citizen and student understanding of Nebraska pioneer history has been enhanced by the historical and geographical unity of the new "Platte River Road" concept, and the magnifying glass placed over the myriad details of the overland migrations gleaned from hundreds of eye-witness accounts. Conspicuous evidence of this may be found, not only in heightened interest in the subject in Nebraska classrooms and newspapers, but in the adoption by the State Highway Department of the term "Great Platte River Road" on the official state highway map, as somewhat synonymous with Interstate-80, the main east-west traffic artery.

The work has become a fixture in footnotes and bibliographies found in recent scholarly books on the western scene, and its value as a standard reference work on the central overland route—including the unique 40-page bibliography—has been certified by western historians of national reputation, among them George P. Hammond, LeRoy R. Hafen, Robert M. Utley, Ray E. Billington, and James C. Olson.

A more objective test of a book's enduring merit—as distinct from appearance on ephemeral best-sellers lists—is formal recognition by cultural or academic organizations. *Great Platte River Road* met this test emphatically, with the receipt, by author and publisher, of three national awards. These were "Best Western Non-Fiction of 1969" awarded by the Heritage Foundation of the National Cowboy Hall of Fame; the Award of Merit by the American Association of State and Local History; and the Silver Spur awarded by the Western Writers of America.

The book has been influential in the historic preservation field. Several of the historic sites and landmarks illuminated in the book have been recommended for consideration as new state historic properties. The existing Fort Kearny State Park and Chimney Rock Historic Site are scheduled for improvements. Court House Rock has recently been acquired as a State Historic Site. The book has also been a factor in stimulating a Congressional proposal for a new "Western Trails National Park," to encompass the series of North Platte Valley landmarks, including the established Scotts Bluff National Monument and Fort Laramie National Historic Site.

In a work of this exceptional magnitude, utilizing nearly 1,000 sources and setting forth a multiplicity of facts on each of over 500 pages of narrative, the incidence of revealed errors of fact or typography has proved to be negligible. Even so, in this new edition every effort has been made to rectify the tiny percentage of error. While most errata proved to be picayune, one critic gleefully discovered an alleged "gold mine of errors" in the brief Kansas City jump-off section; this has been partly rewritten in an effort to achieve an even higher degree of factual purity.

Most reviewers of the First Edition had words ranging from commendation to praise. Modesty forbids direct quotation of these gems because then we would have to quote from two jaundiced reviewers—definitely exceptions—who expressed concern over alleged shortcomings of design, scope, or rhetoric. Whatever the merit, or whatever the shortcomings, of *Great Platte River Road*, 7,500 copies were bought (and presumably read) without benefit of publicity through the commercial advertising enjoyed by most histories, whether meritorious or mediocre.

Continued demand for copies of the now extinct First Edition is the warrant for this Second Edition, a step unprecedented in the long history of Society publications. The well-known ravages of inflation dictate the use of economical paperback, for the motives of the Society continue to be, not monetary gain, but the widest possible dissemination of knowledge about Nebraska's proud heritage.

MERRILL J. MATTES
Littleton, Colorado
January, 1979

Table of Contents

List of Illustrations

ILLUSTRATIONS (cont'd)

List of Maps

Great Platte River Road

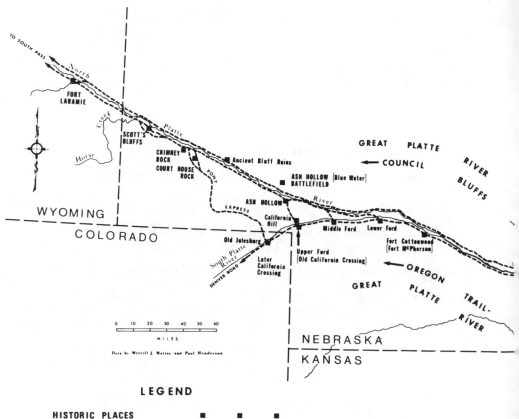

TO SOUTH PASS

North

FORT
LARAMIE

Creek

Horse

Platte

SCOTT'S
BLUFFS

CHIMNEY
ROCK
COURT HOUSE
ROCK

PONY

EXPRESS

Ancient Bluff Ruins

ASH HOLLOW

California
Hill

GREAT   PLATTE

← COUNCIL

ASH HOLLOW [Blue Water]
BATTLEFIELD

River

RIVER

BLUFFS

WYOMING

COLORADO

Old Julesburg

South Platte
River

Later
California
Crossing

DENVER ROAD

Upper Ford
[Old California Crossing]

Middle Ford

Lower Ford

Fort Cottonwood
[Fort McPherson]

← OREGON

GREAT   PLATTE   TRAIL-

RIVER

NEBRASKA

KANSAS

0   10   20   30   40   50   60
MILES

Data by Merrill J. Mattes and Paul Henderson

LEGEND

HISTORIC PLACES   ■   ■   ■

GREAT PLATTE RIVER ROAD   ------------

MODERN STATE BOUNDARIES   — — — —

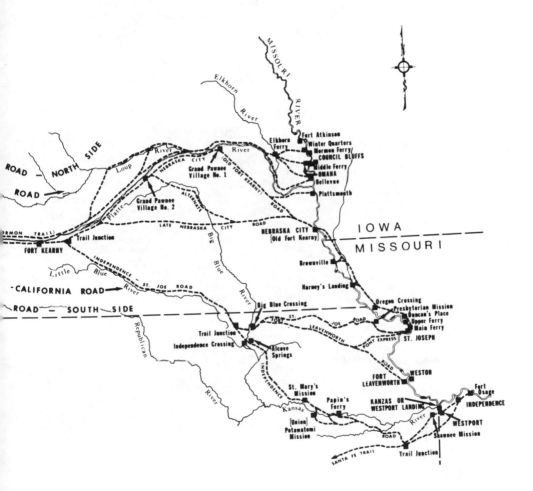

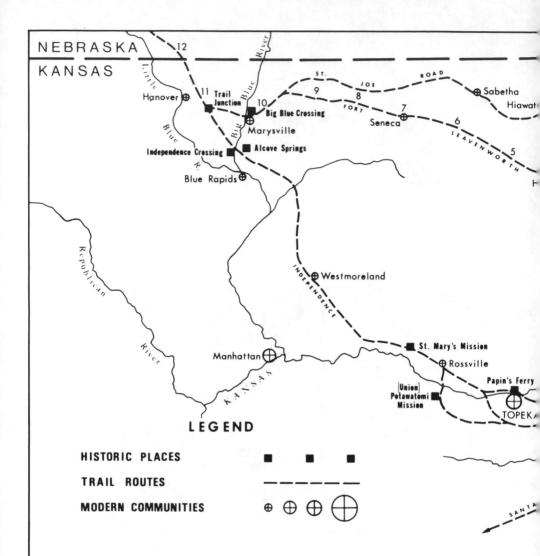

Great Platte River Road [Part 1]
Independence Road, Fort Leavenworth Road,
St. Joe Road

PONY EXPRESS/STAGE STATIONS 1860—1866

1 Elwood/Wathena
2 Troy
3 Lewis/Chain Pump
4 Kinnekuk
5 Kickapoo/Goteschall
6 Log Chain
7 Seneca
8 Ash Point
9 Guittard's/Vermillion Creek
10 Maryville/Big Blue
11 Cottonwood
12 Rock House

Oregon Crossing

Duncan's Place

Highland

Upper Ferry

Presbyterian
Mission

Troy

Main Ferry

Lancaster

St. Joseph Area

Atchison

M I S S O U R I

WESTON

FORT LEAVENWORTH

Kansas City
Area

Fort Osage

INDEPENDENCE

KANZAS OR
WESTPORT LANDING

Shawnee
Mission

WESTPORT

Lawrence

R I V E R

Olathe

N

S

0   5   10   20
        M I L E S

Gardner

Trail Junction

FE   TRAIL

Data by Merrill J. Mattes and Paul Henderson

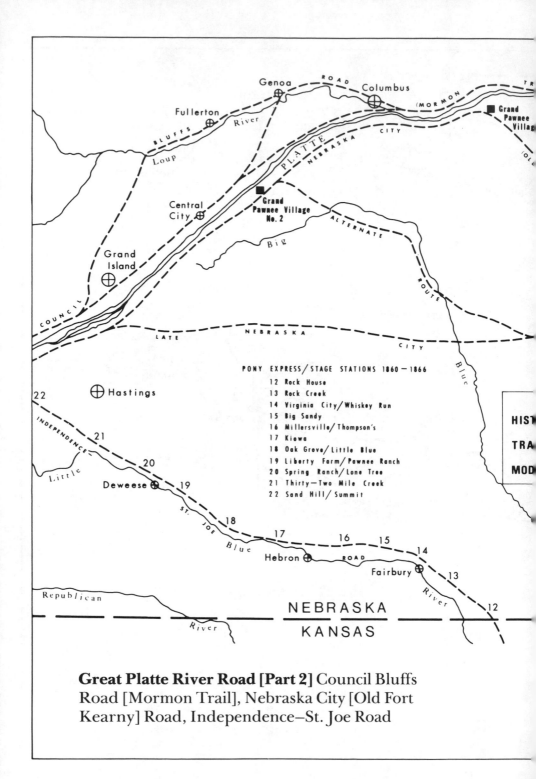

Great Platte River Road [Part 2] Council Bluffs
Road [Mormon Trail], Nebraska City [Old Fort
Kearny] Road, Independence–St. Joe Road

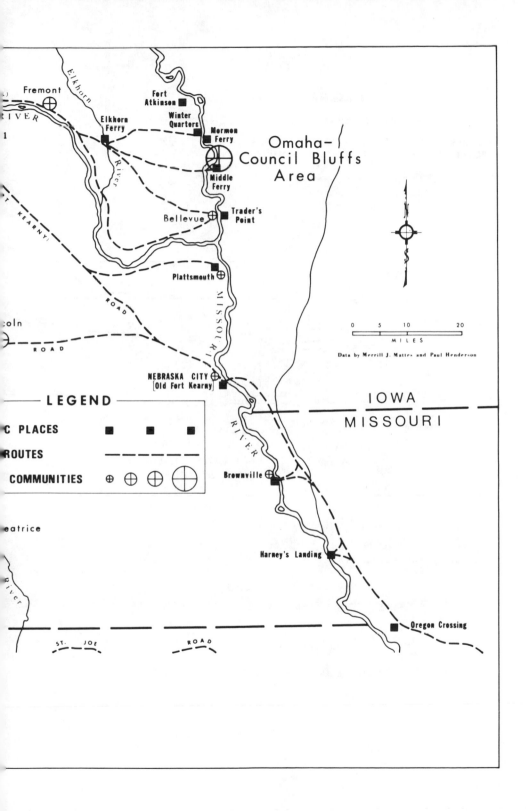

Fremont

Elkhorn

Fort
Atkinson

Winter
Quarters

Elkhorn
Ferry

Mormon
Ferry

Omaha–
Council Bluffs
Area

1

River

Middle
Ferry

KEARNY)

Trader's
Point

Bellevue

N

Plattsmouth

ROAD

MISSOURI

oln

ROAD

0   5   10   20
MILES

Data by Merrill J. Mattes and Paul Henderson

NEBRASKA CITY
[Old Fort Kearny]

RIVER

IOWA

MISSOURI

LEGEND

C PLACES

ROUTES

COMMUNITIES

Brownville

eatrice

River

Harney's Landing

Oregon Crossing

ST.   JOE   ROAD

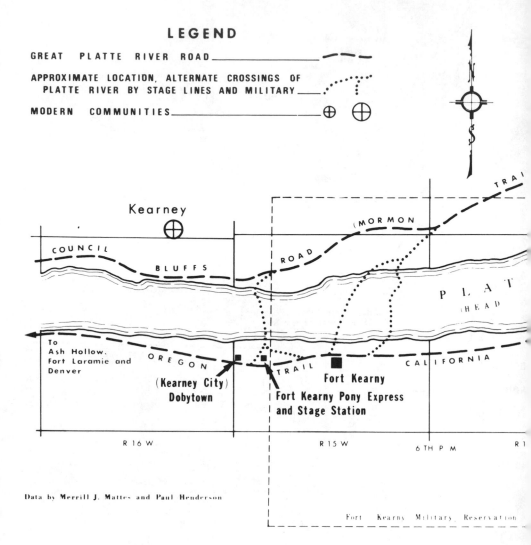

Data by Merrill J. Mattes and Paul Henderson

Great Platte River Road
Vicinity of Fort Kearny Military Reservation

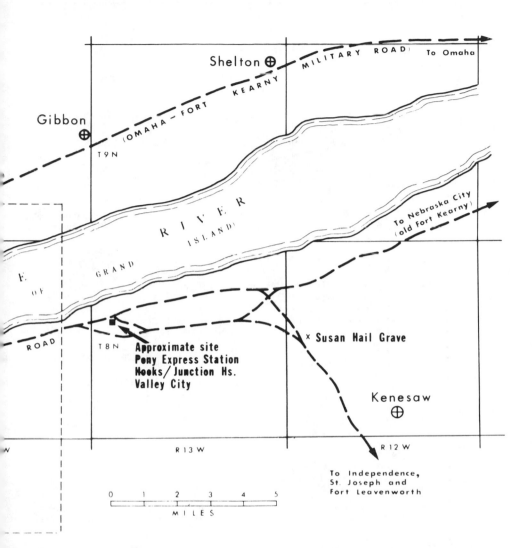

Shelton ⊕

(OMAHA — FORT   KEARNY   MILITARY ROAD)   To Omaha

Gibbon
⊕

T 9 N

G R A N D   R I V E R   ISLAND

F.
OF

G R A N D

To Nebraska City
(old Fort Kearny)

ROAD

T 8 N

■ Approximate site
Pony Express Station
Hooks/ Junction Hs.
Valley City

× Susan Hail Grave

Kenesaw
⊕

R 13 W

R 12 W

To Independence,
St. Joseph and
Fort Leavenworth

0   1   2   3   4   5
MILES

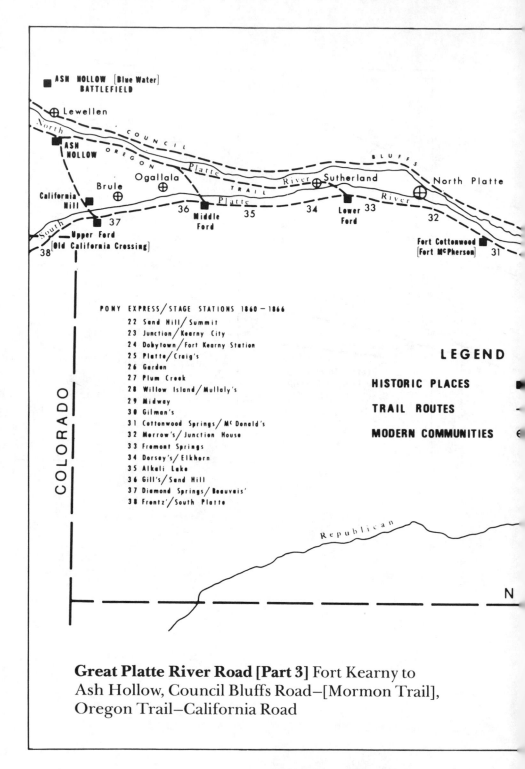

ASH HOLLOW [Blue Water]
BATTLEFIELD

Lewellen

North

COUNCIL

ASH
HOLLOW

OREGON

Platte

BLUFFS

River

Sutherland

North Platte

Brule

Ogallala

TRAIL

California
Hill

Platte

Platte

River

36

35

34

Lower
Ford

33

32

37

Middle
Ford

South

Upper Ford
[Old California Crossing]

Fort Cottonwood
[Fort McPherson]

31

38

PONY EXPRESS/STAGE STATIONS 1860—1866

22 Sand Hill/Summit
23 Junction/Kearny City
24 Dobytown/Fort Kearny Station
25 Platte/Craig's
26 Garden
27 Plum Creek
28 Willow Island/Mullaly's
29 Midway
30 Gilman's
31 Cottonwood Springs/McDonald's
32 Morrow's/Junction House
33 Fremont Springs
34 Dorsey's/Elkhorn
35 Alkali Lake
36 Gill's/Sand Hill
37 Diamond Springs/Beauvais'
38 Frontz'/South Platte

COLORADO

LEGEND

HISTORIC PLACES

TRAIL ROUTES

MODERN COMMUNITIES

Republican

River

N

Great Platte River Road [Part 3] Fort Kearny to
Ash Hollow, Council Bluffs Road–[Mormon Trail],
Oregon Trail–California Road

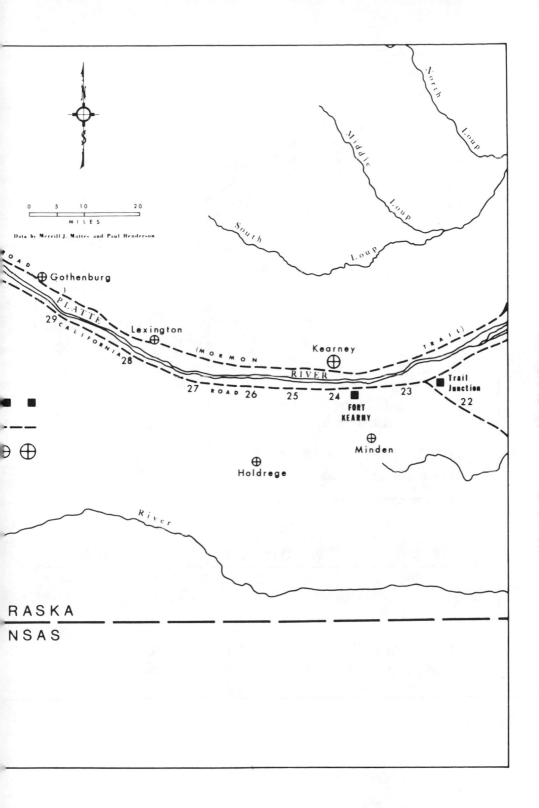

MILES

0 5 10 20

Data by Merrill J. Mattes and Paul Henderson

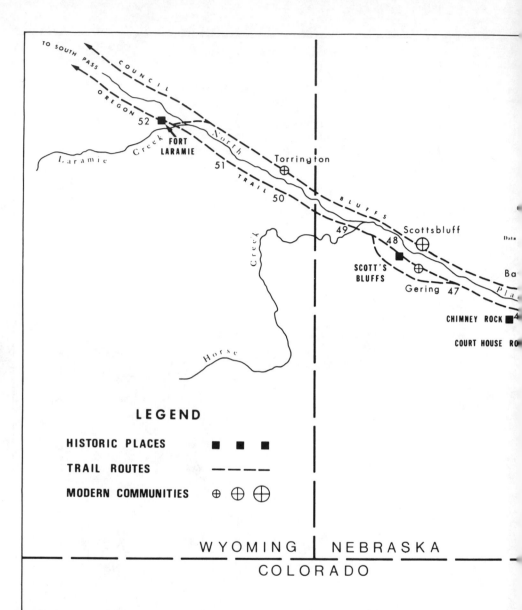

TO SOUTH PASS

COUNCIL

OREGON

Laramie Creek

52
FORT LARAMIE

North

51

TRAIL

50

Torrington

BLUFFS

49

Scottsbluff

48

Data

SCOTT'S BLUFFS

Gering 47

Ba

Pla

CHIMNEY ROCK ■

COURT HOUSE RO

Creek

Horse

LEGEND

HISTORIC PLACES ■ ■ ■

TRAIL ROUTES – – – – –

MODERN COMMUNITIES ⊕ ⊕ ⊕

W Y O M I N G | N E B R A S K A

C O L O R A D O

Great Platte River Road [Part 4] Ash Hollow to
Fort Laramie, Oregon Trail–California Road,
Council Bluffs Road–[Mormon Trail]

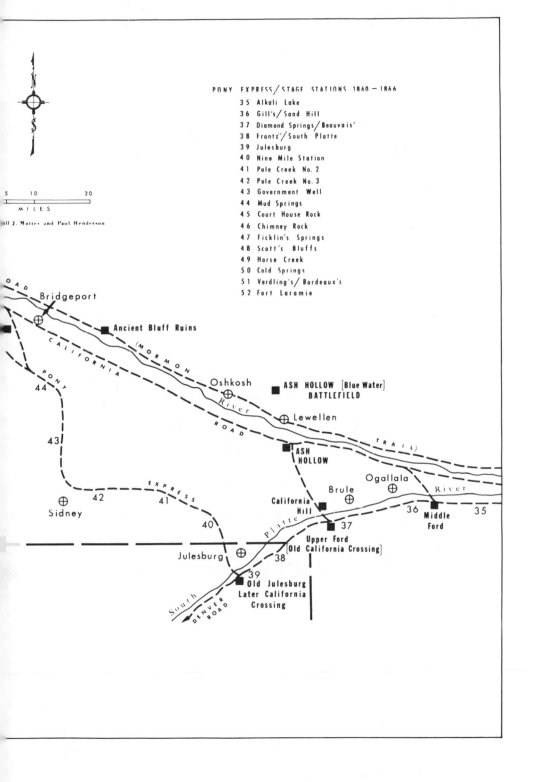

PONY EXPRESS/STAGE STATIONS 1860 — 1866

35 Alkali Lake
36 Gill's/Sand Hill
37 Diamond Springs/Beauvais'
38 Frontz'/South Platte
39 Julesburg
40 Nine Mile Station
41 Pole Creek No. 2
42 Pole Creek No. 3
43 Government Well
44 Mud Springs
45 Court House Rock
46 Chimney Rock
47 Ficklin's Springs
48 Scott's Bluffs
49 Horse Creek
50 Cold Springs
51 Verdling's/ Bordeaux's
52 Fort Laramie

5   10   20
MILES

ill J. Mattes and Paul Henderson

Bridgeport

Ancient Bluff Ruins

Oshkosh

ASH HOLLOW [Blue Water]
BATTLEFIELD

Lewellen

ASH HOLLOW

Ogallala

Brule

California Hill

Sidney

Julesburg

Upper Ford
[Old California Crossing]

Middle Ford

Old Julesburg
Later California Crossing

Great Platte River Road
Ash Hollow Vicinity

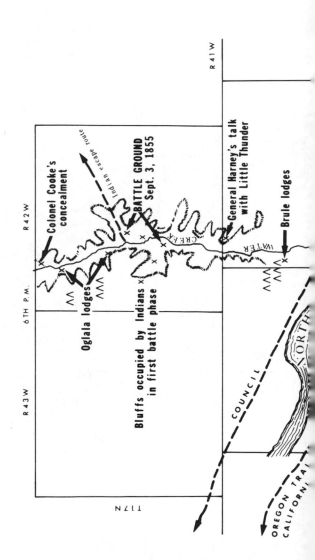

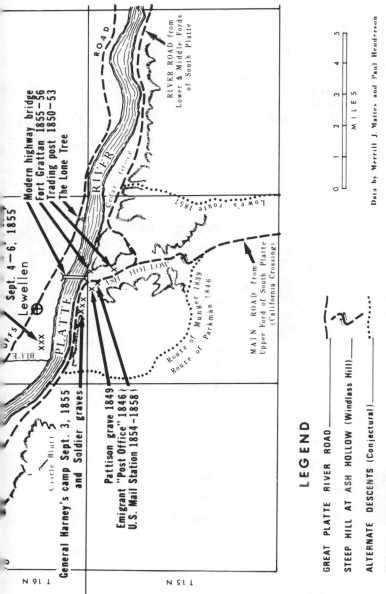

Sept. 4—6, 1855
Lewellen

Modern highway bridge
Fort Grattan 1855—56
Trading post 1850—53
The Lone Tree

General Harney's camp Sept. 3, 1855
and Soldier graves

Pattison grave 1849
Emigrant "Post Office" 1846
U.S. Mail Station 1854—1858

Castle Bluff

BLUFFS

PLATTE

RIVER

ROAD

Cedar Grove

ASH HOLLOW

Route of Munger 1839
Route of Parkman 1846

Lowe's route 1857

RIVER ROAD from
Lower & Middle Fords
of South Platte

MAIN ROAD from
Upper Ford of South Platte
(California Crossing)

T 16 N

T 15 N

LEGEND

GREAT PLATTE RIVER ROAD

STEEP HILL AT ASH HOLLOW (Windlass Hill)

ALTERNATE DESCENTS (Conjectural)

MODERN COMMUNITY

0   1   2   3   4   5
MILES

Data by Merrill J. Mattes and Paul Henderson

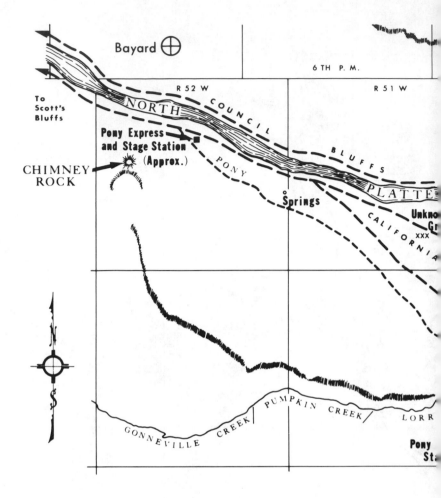

0 1 2 3 4 5
MILES

Data by Merrill J. Mattes and Paul Henderson

Great Platte River Road
**Trail Junctions at Chimney and
Court House Rocks**

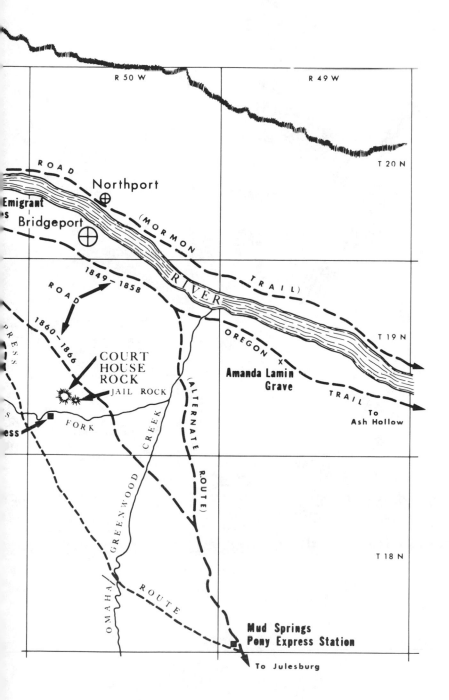

R 50 W

R 49 W

T 20 N

ROAD

Northport

Emigrant

Bridgeport

(MORMON

TRAIL)

RIVER

1849-1858

ROAD

1860-1866

COURT
HOUSE
ROCK

JAIL ROCK

OREGON

X
Amanda Lamin
Grave

TRAIL

To
Ash Hollow

T 19 N

PRESS

FORK

(ALTERNATE

ROUTE)

CREEK

GREENWOOD

OMAHA

ROUTE

T 18 N

Mud Springs
Pony Express Station

To Julesburg

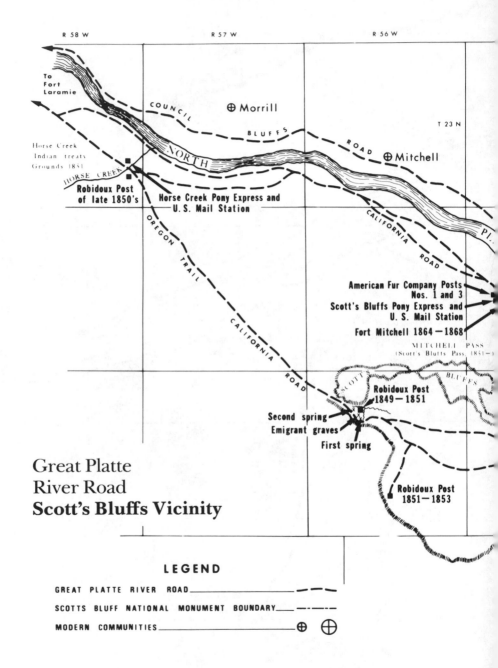

R 58 W   R 57 W   R 56 W

To
Fort
Laramie

⊕ Morrill

T 23 N

COUNCIL

BLUFFS

ROAD

⊕ Mitchell

Horse Creek
Indian treaty
Grounds 1851

NORTH

HORSE CREEK

Robidoux Post
of late 1850's

Horse Creek Pony Express and
U. S. Mail Station

CALIFORNIA
ROAD

PLA

OREGON TRAIL

CALIFORNIA

American Fur Company Posts
Nos. 1 and 3
Scott's Bluffs Pony Express and
U. S. Mail Station
Fort Mitchell 1864—1868

MITCHELL PASS
(Scott's Bluffs Pass, 1851—)

ROAD

SCOTT

BLUFFS

Robidoux Post
1849—1851

Second spring
Emigrant graves

First spring

Great Platte
River Road
Scott's Bluffs Vicinity

Robidoux Post
1851—1853

LEGEND

GREAT PLATTE RIVER ROAD_____ — — —

SCOTTS BLUFF NATIONAL MONUMENT BOUNDARY____ —··—··—

MODERN COMMUNITIES_____ ⊕   ⊕

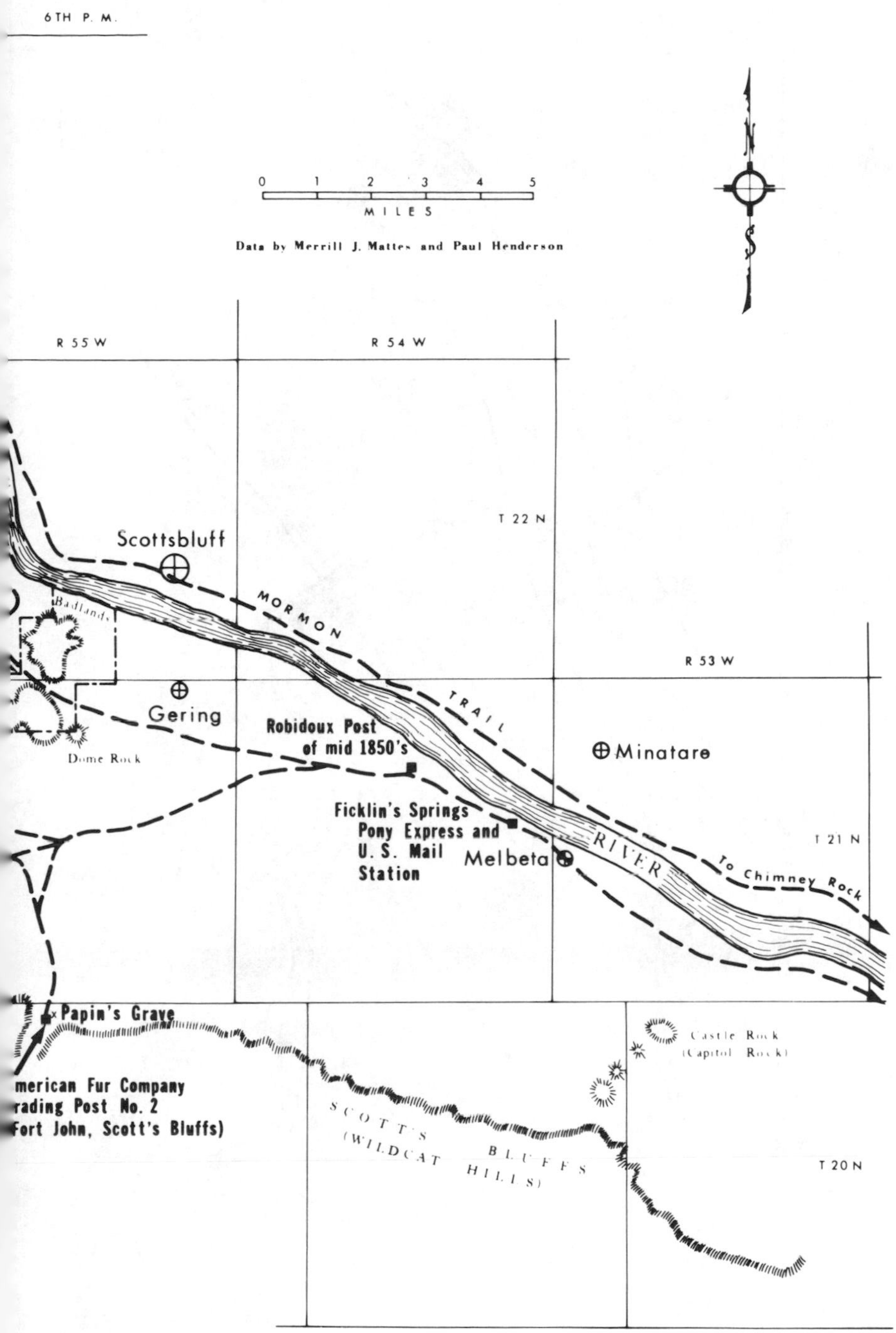

6TH P. M.

0 1 2 3 4 5
M I L E S

Data by Merrill J. Mattes and Paul Henderson

N

S

R 55 W

R 54 W

T 22 N

Scottsbluff

MORMON

Badlands

TRAIL

R 53 W

Gering

Robidoux Post
of mid 1850's

⊕ Minatare

Dome Rock

Ficklin's Springs
Pony Express and
U. S. Mail
Station

Melbeta ⊕

RIVER

T 21 N

To Chimney Rock

Papin's Grave

Castle Rock
(Capitol Rock)

merican Fur Company
rading Post No. 2
Fort John, Scott's Bluffs)

S C O T T ' S   B L U F F S
(WILDCAT HILLS)

T 20 N

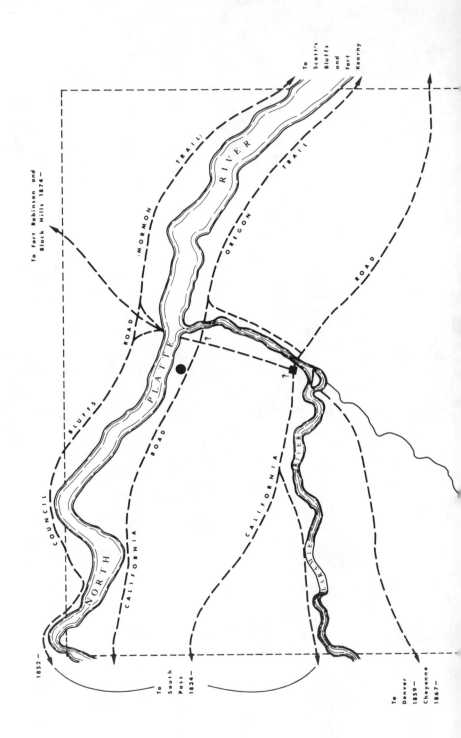

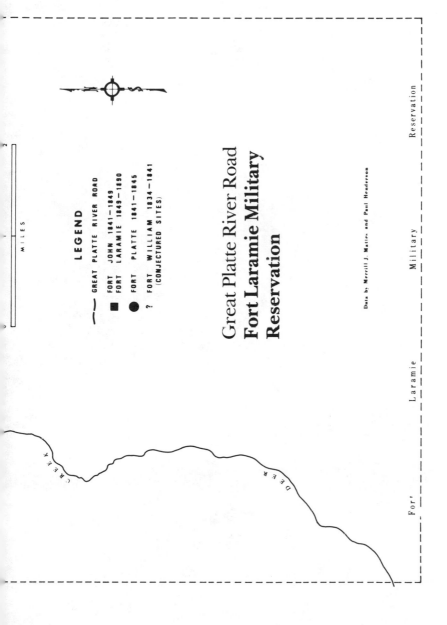

MILES

LEGEND

— GREAT PLATTE RIVER ROAD

■ FORT JOHN 1841—1849
FORT LARAMIE 1849—1890

● FORT PLATTE 1841—1845

? FORT WILLIAM 1834—1841
(CONJECTURED SITES)

Great Platte River Road
Fort Laramie Military
Reservation

Data by Merrill J. Mattes and Paul Henderson

Reservation

Military

Laramie

For'

CREEK

DEER

The Great Platte River Road

I

The Platte: Grand Corridor
of Westward Expansion

WHEN THOMAS JEFFERSON inspired the purchase of the Louisiana Territory from the Emperor Napoleon in 1803, the United States of America was an infant republic, its democratic aspirations and its uncharted wilderness the butt of royal European jokes. The eagle that would one day soar heavenward was but a fledgling, wobbly-winged. Even the visionary Jefferson was only dimly aware of the vastness of its domain and its potential power, but he was sustained by the faith eloquently expressed by his minister, Robert Livingston:

> The instrument we have signed will prepare centuries of happiness for innumerable generations of the human race. The Mississippi and the Missouri will see them prosper and increase in the midst of equality, under just laws, freed from the errors of superstition and the scourges of bad government, and truly worthy of the regard and care of Providence.

A more typical attitude toward the Louisiana Purchase was that of a certain New England congressman, who scorned that "the purchase was not only illegal but was an enormous price to pay for a worthless desert too vast to be governed."

Little did this scoffer (whose name will be charitably concealed) dream that this masterstroke of diplomacy, taking advantage of French and Spanish domestic troubles, was the key to a treasure-house of fabulous riches—the trans-Mississippi West—which would

3

become wholly ours within five decades, after further treaties with Spain, Mexico, and Great Britain. In retrospect, the Louisiana Purchase seems like the very spark which touched off the fuse culminating in the explosion of human energy which characterized America's mid-century push to the Pacific.

The westward course of empire followed three main arrow-like prongs: the Missouri River, the Santa Fe Trail, and the Great Platte River Road. The explorers Lewis and Clark blazed the arching, twisting transcontinental route offered by two great river systems, the Missouri and the Columbia. For two decades the Missouri River was the principal thoroughfare of fur traders in keelboats who exploited the animal wealth of the mountains; later, steamboats became the classic mode of travel. The Santa Fe Trail, from the great bend of the Missouri at present Kansas City, up the Arkansas River to Bent's Fort and Raton Pass (or branching at Cimarron Cut-off), was pioneered in the 1820s by merchants lured by Mexican cowhides and silver; and the route became a great highway of commerce to the Southwest.

The third and by all standards the most important "way west" was the Platte River Road, the great highway for the covered wagon migrations to Oregon, California, and Utah. It is necessary to underline the reasons for this importance. We take nothing away from the immortal Lewis and Clark and their water route; and we would not for a moment rob the early fur trappers of the glory of their exploring achievements throughout the Rocky Mountain West. Neither can we share the mistaken view, prevalent in some writings, that the Missouri River and Santa Fe routes were, after all, commercial routes, while the pioneers up the Platte were somehow more spiritually motivated. True, the Mormons sought religious freedom; but they also had a healthy interest in the things of this world. There were many Sabbath observers on the Oregon Trail, but still we can ascribe mainly basic human economic motives to the covered wagon emigrants. While the prospect of a home on the far-distant Willamette or Sacramento might have had a more romantic aura than a home back in rural Wisconsin or Ohio, the former emerges no more spiritually blessed merely because of its Pacific Coast location.

No, travelers up the Platte (including Mormons) were not demonstrably more pure than those up the Missouri or the Arkansas, even though there were more often women and children present.

(We do not have time to examine the widespread theory that women and children are necessarily repositories of good, while men—especially when traveling with other men—are more inclined toward evil.) The emigrants' primary motive, like that of the trappers and traders, was economic, whether expressed in terms of land or gold or just "freedom to pursue happiness." And, while the results of the covered wagon migration might be called patriotic, with much of the territory in Oregon and California being "conquered" through immigration, the sentiment that people migrated west and underwent hardships just to carry the flag in the parade of Manifest Destiny is of dubious validity.

To defend the view that the Platte River Road was the primary route of westward expansion, a profound moral cause is not needed—only a smattering of geography and a few statistics. Lewis and Clark made it all the way to the mouth of the Columbia, true; but they had a terrible time traversing the mountain passes, and their route never did become a transcontinental wagon road. The Mullan Road, completed in 1862, was suitable only for pack trains, and much of Lewis and Clark's route today is still an unspoiled wilderness. The fur trappers who followed them stayed in the Rockies to hunt beaver, while steamboats were often stranded on sandbars and certainly never got beyond Fort Benton, below the Great Falls. Except for Idaho and Montana gold-seekers in the 1860s, the Missouri River was not the key to a bona fide transcontinental migration route.

It is true that a few thousand California gold-seekers from the southern states did reach the Coast by desert variants or extensions of the Santa Fe Trail (such as the Gila Trail and the Yuma Trail), but for the most part the Santa Fe Trail stopped at Santa Fe. It is also true that many gold-seekers voyaged around Cape Horn or made overland connections via Panama or southern Mexico; but the great majority of those who migrated to Oregon, California, and intermediate points went directly overland up the Platte River. It is estimated that over 350,000 made this journey, welding a continent together with wagon wheels.

In the north was the Rocky Mountain barrier, and in the south was the hostile desert. If God smiled on America's credo of Manifest Destiny, he showed it most clearly in providing a geographically central corridor up the Platte, up the North Platte, and up the Sweetwater to South Pass. The Pass was the key to the Continental

Divide, and the Platte was the broad avenue thereto, made to order for ox- or mule-drawn covered wagons.

Beyond South Pass there were mountains and deserts, and all manner of obstacles, but routes were found—principally via the Snake and Humboldt rivers—to reach the Coast. The tortuous Pacific slope is beyond the scope of this study; and it would take a separate volume to deal with the Wyoming section of the trail from Fort Laramie to Fort Bridger, via South Pass. This work is dedicated to a study of the trunkline of the Great Migration across the central High Plains, up the Platte and the North Platte, from Fort Kearny to Fort Laramie.

The route from Fort Kearny to Fort Laramie was the superhighway of westward expansion. There were many "jumping-off places" for emigrants along the Missouri River from Independence to Omaha, but all of these strands converged at Fort Kearny to become one great migratory, military, and communications route. Fort Kearny was the official end of the prairie lands and the gateway to the Great Plains, with its endless level horizon and strange treelessness; Fort Laramie, with Laramie Peak looming to the westward, marked the transition from the Great Plains to the Rocky Mountains. Beyond Fort Laramie there was the divergent Bozeman Trail to Montana, and beyond South Pass the divergences and cut-offs multiplied.

Between Fort Kearny and Fort Laramie there were only two divergences that are noteworthy; both pertain to the late period of the trail. Until 1859 all travel on the south bank of the Platte crossed the south fork of the river west of its junction with the north fork. The trail then moved northwest up the "peninsula" between the south and north forks of the river and through Ash Hollow before reaching the valley of the North Platte. It then continued up the south bank to Fort Laramie. The discovery of gold in Colorado led to the Pike's Peak Trail southwestward up the South Platte and another connecting trail northward to the North Platte via Court House Rock, for which Julesburg, Colorado, became the new junction point.

"Platte" is the French word for flat, and it is an honest translation by French explorers of "Nebraska," the Omaha Indian name for this broad, shallow, braided river, over 1,000 miles long from its mouth to the sources of the North Platte and over 800 miles long to its junction with the Sweetwater.

"Platte River Road" is an authentic historical term, used by many travelers. It is the most logical term to cover all continental trails up the Platte, from 1830, when Smith, Jackson, and Sublette took the first wagons up its length, to 1866, when the Union Pacific Railroad reached Fort Kearny.

In the popular mind "Oregon Trail" is synonymous with covered wagons, but the historical Oregon Trail ran only from Independence to the Willamette valley, primarily for five years beginning in 1843. It scarcely seems appropriate to talk about California-bound gold-seekers on the Oregon Trail. During the big Gold Rush it was called, logically enough, the California Trail or the California Road; and on the statistical basis of destination alone, California Road would win. But California Road won't do for those who went to Oregon, Colorado, Montana, or Utah. A classic example of the confusion here is Francis Parkman's best-selling book originally published in 1848 as *The Oregon Trail*, which was hastily converted in the 1850 edition to *The Oregon and California Trail* (and has since been reconverted to its original title).

In historical times it was also commonplace to name the Platte route for the point of origin. Thus there is frequent reference to the Independence Road, the St. Joe (St. Joseph) Road, and the Fort Leavenworth Road; at other times we find reference to the Overland Stage Road, the Pony Express route, the Government Road, the Fort Laramie Road, or the Denver Road.

Historians today are in the habit of referring to the trail north of the Platte as the Mormon Trail, since the Mormons, or Latter Day Saints, primarily used that route. But again we find that today's terminology bears little resemblance to the contemporary fact. This trail was actually blazed by fur traders in the 1830s. Thousands of non-Mormons, or "Gentiles," used this north route during the California and Montana gold rushes, and they probably outnumbered the Mormons in 1849 and most years thereafter. There was a distinctive Mormon trail from Nauvoo, Illinois, to Council Bluffs, but west of the Missouri River the Mormons had a road monopoly only briefly. Thus, in contemporary usage there really was no distinct Mormon Trail from Council Bluffs to Fort Laramie. It was, instead, the Council Bluffs Road or, optionally after 1854, the Omaha Road. If a traveler was more oriented to

destination, he would call it the Salt Lake Road or even the Virginia
City (Montana) Road.

Contemporary map-makers, both government surveyors and
guidebook publishers, were equally confusing; one is apt to find
on these old parchments anything from Oregon Trail, to Nebraska
City–Denver Stage Line, to Omaha–Fort Kearny Military Road.
The only way to give intelligent consideration to the phenomenon
of the Great Migration is to recognize that there was *one* major
route, from Fort Kearny to Fort Laramie, which may logically be
called the Great Platte River Road. (Other contemporary terms
will be used in context, but all relate to this trunkline.)

There were five major approaches to Fort Kearny from the
Missouri River. First was the route from the Kansas City area,
(Independence Road) branching off the Santa Fe Trail at Gardner,
Kansas. This crossed the Kaw River in the vicinity of Topeka, went
northwest along the Vermillion to the Big Blue crossing south of
Marysville, Kansas, then followed the Little Blue, reaching the Platte
valley just east of Fort Kearny. The next two were the roads from
St. Joe and Fort Leavenworth, which were separate roads only as
far as Horton, Kansas, where they came together and then went
on to join the Independence Road at Marysville. The fourth route
was from the first Fort Kearny (later Nebraska City) on the Missouri
River, to the second Fort Kearny, where it joined the combined
Independence–St. Joe road.

The fifth and northernmost approach to Fort Kearny was north
of the Platte, in the vicinity of Omaha. The earliest use of this
route was by Indians, fur trappers, and explorers, beginning first at
Sarpy's Trading Post (later Bellevue) just south of Omaha, then
later at Fort Atkinson (Fort Calhoun), a few miles north of the
present city limits. Mormons, fleeing from persecution in Illinois
and determined to find a haven in the Far West, founded Winter
Quarters in 1846 (present Florence in north Omaha); and in 1847,
on the Iowa side, they founded an emigrant station named Kanesville, which became Council Bluffs (erroneously transposing Lewis
and Clark's Council Bluffs in Nebraska, at the Fort Atkinson site).
From Winter Quarters to Salt Lake the Mormons followed in the
tracks of American Fur Company traders. Later this route was
heavily used by non-Mormons rushing for California and Montana
gold.

Those who started in the Council Bluffs–Omaha area, being on the north side of the Platte, were apt to stay there until they came to Fort Laramie, where they first crossed under the mistaken impression that the north side was thereafter impassable. After 1852 many stayed on the north side after leaving Fort Laramie, thus being well ahead of the "south-siders" who had to cross to the north side sooner or later via one of the Upper Platte ferries. Most Council Bluffs travelers noted when they were opposite Fort Kearny, but few felt that a visit there was worth the ordeal of crossing. So to the "north-siders" Fort Kearny was a milestone rather than a stopping point.

Today Interstate 80 follows much of the Platte River from Omaha to Cheyenne. It is a divided highway to accommodate two-way traffic with maximum safety. In historical times the Great Platte River Road was a divided highway likewise, except that the Platte River itself formed the median, and the traffic was mainly one way (westward) on all lanes. This parallel is not too strained, for in historical times the Platte was not obscured by dense vegetation, and emigrants on the Council Bluffs and California roads could occasionally glimpse one another's twinkling campfires or even sunlit wagon tops across the wide Platte, crawling along the bank like two columns of white ants. In some recorded instances, when the Platte was drier than usual, some emigrants would even cross over from their respective "rest areas" to swap information and provisions.

Today one can drive a car west from Omaha at seventy-five miles an hour, perhaps 600 miles in one day, and reach California in three days. By heroic effort, and under optimum conditions, the covered wagon emigrant might make as much as forty miles in one day; but he would do remarkably well to average fifteen or twenty miles a day, and reach California in four and a half months. His means of locomotion were crude and many things slowed him down, but one of the advantages he had was the comparative ease of travel on the Great Platte River Road. The Platte valley is a great natural migration corridor, a fact appreciated by modern highway engineers as well as the California Argonauts, who had no paving, no bridges, in fact no road at all in the modern sense.

The Platte River valley was largely barren of timber and was scarred by buffalo tracks, but it had three cardinal virtues, all recognized by Gen. William T. Sherman on an inspection of forts in 1866: it was dry, it was level, and it went in exactly the right direction. When mountain man James Clyman traversed the Platte in 1824 he was starving, pursued by Indians, and in no condition to take notes. Twenty years later, however, as he guided a wagon train to Oregon, he observed that this was "as firm a road as any in the Union or even in the world." This sentiment was echoed by Dabney T. Carr, who affirmed: "In travelling up the south side of the Platte River we found one of the best natural roads, of the distance of 400 miles, that is to be found on the face of the earth."

The Pacific Wagon Road surveyors of 1857, and the Corps of Topographical Engineers at various times, made sporadic and half-hearted efforts to ease hill gradients and facilitate river crossings. The emigrants themselves would sometimes pause to cut back a creek bank or build a crude bridge, but no one really stopped to do a job of engineering. It is accurate to say, therefore, that for all practical purposes the Platte River Road was in an untouched state of nature. Yet Fitz Hugh Ludlow, traveling by stagecoach in 1863, found it "compact and smooth as the finest gravel roads of the east. The entire route astonished me with its excellence." One might suppose that this was the result of years of heavy travel; yet, according to James Squire, the road had been just as good in 1849: "The first section of the road [St. Joe to Fort Laramie] is over a vast tract of prairie . . . and is the best you ever saw. This marl and clay packs, and is equal to the plank road east of your city. There are a few bad places in crossing streams or deep ravines, but not more difficult than you would find in the States upon improved streets."

In 1850 Henry Coke described the road from Scott's Bluffs to Fort Laramie as "broad as any turnpike in England." In 1858 Dr. C. M. Clark found that "the road had an average width of thirty feet of well-beaten track, and was as smooth and hard as a brick yard pave." He reaffirms Carr's judgment: "It is undoubtedly the best natural road in the world." Maj. Osborne Cross, with the U.S. Army in 1849, was no mean prophet when he penned in his report: "It is in the power of the Government to make it one of the best public highways in the western country."

The Platte River Road and its approaches is traceable on maps, using government surveys as well as emigrant journals. The trails can be followed today by automobile, approximately, by staying on established roads, whether federal, state, or county, even though this often involves zigzagging along section lines. Sometimes it may be necessary to follow ranch, farm, or canal roads, parking the car and hiking through brush or cropland (with owner's permission) for short distances. East of Fort Laramie the trails are much obscured by cultivation and road construction. In some locations they can still be charted by aerial photography, though invisible on the ground. In pasture land and along minor road rights-of-way there is sometimes clear evidence to be seen on the ground, aside from the abundance of helpful stone and granite markers and memorials.

CHRONOLOGY OF THE GREAT PLATTE RIVER ROAD

A chronology of Platte River travel from the fur trade through the covered wagon migrations will serve as a frame of reference for the following chapters:

1804—Lewis and Clark explore the mouth of the Platte River.

1812—Robert Stuart and six others in the employ of John Jacob Astor, returning from Fort Astoria on the mouth of the Columbia River, discover South Pass. Reaching Court House Rock in mid-winter, they retrace their steps to spend a miserable three months near the present Nebraska-Wyoming line. In the spring of 1813 they reach the Missouri, becoming the first white men to traverse the Great Platte River Road. On their downriver journey they identify and name Grand Island.

1819—The U.S. Army establishes Cantonment Missouri north of present Omaha. This is relocated next year, on the original Council Bluff's of Lewis and Clark, as Fort Atkinson.

1820—Lt. Stephen H. Long leads an exploring expedition up the Platte and South Platte rivers, making observations and sketches. Long reports "the Great American Desert" uninhabitable.

1823—Fur trappers in the employ of William H. Ashley of St. Louis, Missouri, encounter hostile Arikara Indians on the Upper Missouri and turn overland to the headwaters of the Green and Platte rivers, where they rediscover South Pass.

1824—Thomas Fitzpatrick and James Clyman cache their beaver on the Sweetwater River, are attacked by Indians, get separated, and hike down the Platte to Fort Atkinson, nearly dying of starvation. Later that same year William Ashley leads an expedition up the Platte from Fort Atkinson to explore the mountains.

1825—Ashley's caravan travels up the Platte from Chouteau's Landing (Kansas City) to the trappers' rendezvous at Great Salt

Lake, taking along a mounted cannon, the first wheeled vehicle to follow this trail.

1828—Hiram Scott, caravan leader for Ashley, dies near the great bluff in western Nebraska which bears his name.

1830—Smith-Jackson-Sublette partnership leads a caravan from St. Louis to the Wind River rendezvous, the first wagon train up the Platte—"a caravan of ten wagons, drawn by four mules each, and two dearborns, drawn by one mule each, eighty-one men in the company, all mounted on mules." The partners report to John Eaton, Secretary of War, on the feasibility of the Great Platte River Road. Also, the first contingent of the American Fur Company travels up the north side of the Platte, from Sarpy's Post (Bellevue), as recorded by Warren Ferris.

1832—Capt. Benjamin Bonneville leads trappers from Fort Osage up the Platte to cross the Continental Divide for the first time with wagons. Nathaniel Wyeth's first trading expedition, out of Independence, contributes four notable diaries of Platte River travel: those of Wyeth himself; his brother John; John Ball, who became the first Oregon settler; and John Townsend, naturalist, the first scientific observer up the Platte.

1833—Charles Larpenteur, another literate mountain man, reports a caravan journey to the Green River rendezvous.

1834—William Anderson tells of the establishment of Fort William (the first Fort Laramie) by Robert Campbell and William Sublette. Nathaniel Wyeth tells of the establishment of Fort Hall on Snake River. He is accompanied by Jason Lee, a Methodist preacher, the first missionary to Oregon.

1835—Presbyterian missionaries Samuel Parker and Marcus Whitman hurry up the Missouri from Liberty to Bellevue to join Lucien Fontenelle and others of the American Fur Company going to the Green River rendezvous and to Oregon.

1836—Narcissa Whitman and Elizabeth Spalding, missionary wives, are the first white women up the Platte, catching up with a company of traders under Thomas Fitzpatrick in the vicinity of Pawnee villages west of Bellevue.

1837—North Platte valley landmarks and Fort Laramie are sketched for the first time by A. J. Miller, artist accompanying Sir William Drummond Stewart in William Sublette's trading caravan to the Green River rendezvous.

1838—Fur trader Andrew Drips is accompanied by John

Augustus Sutter, who established a ranch on the Sacramento River which became the scene of James Marshall's discovery of gold ten years later.

1939—Remarkable journals are contributed by Asahel Munger, missionary to Oregon, and by the German physician Wislizenus from St. Louis and Chouteau's Landing, traveling with fur traders for his health.

1840—The last American Fur Company caravan to rendezvous in the Rockies is accompanied by Joel Walker, the first avowed Oregon emigrant, and Father Pierre Jean DeSmet, famous Catholic missionary, explorer, and historian.

1841—The Bidwell-Bartleson party, the first emigrant party, leaves Kansas River (Westport Landing) for Oregon, led by Thomas Fitzpatrick and accompanied by Catholic priest Pierre DeSmet and Nicholas Point and Methodist preacher Joseph Williams, who describes the building of adobe-walled Fort John (the second Fort Laramie). Bidwell, the first emigrant diarist (except for John Ball), describes the death of William Shotwell, the first emigrant casualty from accidental gunfire. Rufus B. Sage, accompanying fur traders from Westport to Fort Platte (rival of Fort John), leaves one of the richest journals of the period.

1842—Oregon Train from Independence is led by Dr. Elijah White and by Lansford Hastings, noted for the fatal misinformation he included in his later guidebook. More trustworthy journalists of the party are Medorem Crawford and Asa Lovejoy. In the same year Lt. John C. Fremont leaves Chouteau's Landing on his first exploring expedition, reaching Fort Laramie and the Wind River Mountains. Among his twenty-one voyageurs are Kit Carson and Lucien Maxwell. Fremont's narrative and map, prepared in coopereration with cartographer Charles Preuss, becomes the first reasonably accurate emigrant guidebook for the Great Platte River Road.

1843—The first large migration to Oregon, from Independence, consisting of some 1,000 people, is led by Marcus Whitman, anxious to wrest Oregon from Great Britain by packing the ballot boxes. This is a family affair, including 130 women and 610 children. Joel Hembree, run over by a wagon, sets the pattern for another common casualty of the Oregon Trail. Peter Burnett, Jesse Applegate, Overton Johnson, and James Nesmith are among the earliest of hundreds who kept diaries. Theodore Talbot records Fremont's second expedition.

1844—Four Oregon trains leave from Bellevue, St. Joe, Westport, and Independence. Among the more memorable diarists are John Minto, Pierson Reading, William Newby, William Case, and James Clyman, the old mountain man who had nearly starved to death on the Platte twenty years earlier.

1845—Over 5,000 people flock to Oregon, the most noteworthy recorders being Joel Palmer and Samuel Hancock. Most trains are from Independence, but Sarah Cummins' and Jesse Harritt's parties leave St. Joseph, and Sarah Helmick's follows the north bank. The Jacob Snyder party to California is an exception. This is also the year of the first U.S. military expedition up the Platte. Guided by Fitzpatrick, Col. S. W. Kearny leads four companies of Dragoons to an Indian powwow at Fort Laramie. This march is brilliantly recorded by Capt. (later Lt. Col.) Philip St. George Cooke and Lt. J. Henry Carleton.

1846—Oregon Territory is acquired by compromise, and California and the Southwest are involved in the war with Mexico. The relatively light emigration from Independence to Oregon and California, made notorious by the fate of the Donner party in the Sierra Nevadas, is fully recorded by J. M. Shively, Heinrich Lienhard, Nicholas Carriger, J. Quinn Thornton, Edwin Bryant, and the famous traveling historian, Francis Parkman. St. Joseph departees include Joseph Aram, Anson Cone, and Polly Purcell. This year the Mormons are ousted from Nauvoo, Illinois, fleeing across Iowa to Winter Quarters (Omaha), and the first Fort Kearny is founded at Table Creek on the Missouri.

1847—This year belongs to Brigham Young and his Mormon Pioneers, who follow the faint trappers' trail along the north bank to Fort Laramie and thence to the Great Salt Lake. Among the notable journals of this undertaking are those of William Clayton, Lorenzo Young, and George Albert Smith. Mormons who remained behind recrossed the Missouri River and started Kanesville (Council Bluffs). Non-Mormons who went west this year, mainly to Oregon, include Andrew Goodyear and Chester Ingersoll via Independence, and Elizabeth Geer, Loren Hastings, Hugh Cosgrove, and Isaac Pettijohn via St. Joseph.

1848—There is a mass exodus of Mormons from the Omaha area, and the new Fort Kearny is founded at the head of Grand Island.

On the south bank it is an emigration off year, the lull before the storm. Riley Root and James D. Miller record journeys from St. Joseph to Oregon. Bruce Cornwall traces a new pattern of overland travel from St. Joseph to Council Bluffs, there joining 500 Oregonians. He reports 4,000 Mormons on the move. Mormon journalists include Howard Egan, John Doyle Lee (of Mountain Meadows Massacre fame), Hosea Stout, John Pulsipher, and O. B. Huntington. News of James Marshall's gold discovery at Sutter's Mill electrifies the country.

1849—The mass migration to California begins. Most easterners prefer to take their chances on clipper ships out of Boston, New York, and Charleston harbors. There are overland companies from Massachusetts, New York, Virginia, and Washington, D.C., but the bulk of the landlubber Argonauts hail from Missouri, Iowa, Wisconsin, Illinois, and the Upper Mississippi valley generally. This is a good wet year for grass on the plains, but it raises the specter of Asian cholera and the often fatal penalties resulting from inexperience and optimism. Primary jumping-off places are Independence, St. Joseph, old Fort Kearny, and Council Bluffs, with St. Joseph being statistically out in front. Available data, gleaned from emigrant journals, newspaper accounts, and reports of the official Fort Kearny and Fort Laramie registers, indicate something like 30,000 Argonauts for 1849. Of 145 Forty-Niner journals accounted for (the largest number of any migration year), there are fifty-eight kept by diarists starting from St. Joseph, thirty-eight from Independence-Westport, fifteen from Council Bluffs, and ten from old Fort Kearny. (The remaining diarists jumped off from Fort Leavenworth or from points unknown.)

The Gold Rush in its early stages was largely a male affair, and this is reflected in the journals. Among the more informative publications are those of Alonzo Delano, Vincent Geiger, Wakeman Bryarly, David Leeper, Lell H. Woolley, Isaac Wistar, Joseph Sedgley, Israel Hale, D. J. Staples, Chas. A. Kirkpatrick, R. C. Shaw, Kimball Webster, Niles Searls, William Kelly, Lucius Fairchild, James Pritchard, David Dewolf, J. G. Bruff, E. B. Farnham, Peter Decker, and Charles E. Boyle. Noteworthy manuscript journals include those of Joshua Breyfogle, Col. James Tate, Henry Shombre, Thomas Eastin, Daniel Gelwicks, Amos Bachelder, Charles Parke, David Cosad, Elijah P. Howell, and Tipton Lindley. Military observers out of Fort Leavenworth are represented by Maj. Osborne

Cross, Capt. Howard Stansbury, and Capt. William Gunnison.

Fort Laramie is purchased this year by the U.S. Army from the American Fur Company, the Mounted Riflemen under Capt. Sanderson move in, and new military construction is started under Lt. Daniel P. Woodbury.

1850—Although "Forty-Niners" has since become synonymous with the California Gold Rush, the year 1850 is the banner year statistically, with something like fifty-five thousand hopefuls hitting the gold-dust trail. Through the publication of numerous guidebooks, like those of Joseph Ware, John Steele, Hosea B. Horn, Franklin Street, and Andrew Child, and the dissemination of 1849 experiences through letters and newspapers, the mid-century emigrants are better prepared. Again, however, fate deals with them harshly. This year the Asiatic cholera is rampant and, as if to scold men for their greed, nature now withholds the rains. The prairies are parched, and oxen also die by the thousands.

The percentage of diary-keepers takes a sharp drop, less than 100 being accounted for. But if these diaries are an accurate gauge, Council Bluffs and St. Joseph (with about thirty-five recorders each) take a commanding lead as jumping-off places among Missouri River towns. About ten writers leave Independence-Westport, and the same number depart from old Fort Kearny.

Noteworthy among published journals are those of Franklin Langworthy, Reuben Knox, James Bennett, Henry Coke, Carlisle Abbott, John Wood, William Kilgore, Leander Loomis, Madison B. Moorman, Margaret Frink, Cyrus Loveland, and Orange Gaylord. Among exceptional manuscript journals are those of Silas Newcomb, Byron McKinstry, Solomon Gorgas, W. McBride, W. Montgomery, Henry Bloom, M. Littleton, N. A. Cagwin, Henry A. Stine, and James W. Evans.

1851—Largely as the result of the calamities that befell the 1850 migration, the curve this year takes a nose dive, with only about 10,000 emigrants or one-fifth the number of the preceding year. A further evidence of disillusionment with California is the fact that many emigrants this year and next switch their objective to Oregon. Among the small scattering of published journalists this year are Rev. Robert Robe, Rev. C. H. Crawford, William Lobenstine, and Heinrich Mollhausen. Also of value are the Daniel Bacon and J. L. Johnson manuscripts. Sgt. Percival G. Lowe of the Dragoons appears for the first time with his valuable reminiscences. The Fort

Laramie treaty council, held near Scott's Bluffs, is an important event for the Plains tribes.

1852—The California Gold Rush is revived on a scale of 50,000 overland travelers, making this the second biggest year of traffic on the Great Platte River Road. Something like eighty journals have turned up, with approximately half reflecting departures from Council Bluffs; the north side route would maintain this lead henceforward. St. Joseph remains the dominant river town in the Missouri-Kansas area, with thirty-three entries as compared with thirteen for the Kansas City area. A few continue to use old Fort Kearny as a base. Some of the choicest published journals are those of Jay Green, William Byers, E. S. Carter, Lucy R. Cooke, David Cartwright, Thomas Turnbull, Lodisa Frizzell, Mr. and Mrs. Benjamin Ferris, Gilbert Cole, Cornelia Sharp, Hosea Stout, and William Variel. Among useful manuscripts are those of William Rowe, Caroline Richardson, William Hampton, Jared Fox, John Lewis, and Samuel Chadwick.

1853—Travel this year continues at a brisk pace, but with a much lower head count (perhaps twenty thousand). The Council Bluffs Road is used by the majority of some forty writers, reflecting heavy travel from Iowa, Wisconsin, and Illinois and improved steamboat passenger service from the lower river. As in 1852, a surprisingly large number of diarists head for Oregon rather than California. Missouri stations are well represented, but old Fort Kearny declines in importance. Significant printed journals include those of Dr. Thomas Flint, Celinda Hines, Amelia Knight, Henry Allyn, Basil Longsworth, Washington Bailey, James Linforth, Harriet Ward, Stephen Forsdick, Rebecca Ketcham, and Count Cipriani. Among unpublished gems are the writings of J. R. Bradway, Abraham Hite, Isaiah Bryant, and Calvin West.

1854—The passage of the bill creating Nebraska Territory is quickly followed by the founding of Omaha, opposite Council Bluffs, and of Nebraska City, at the site of old Fort Kearny. Another portentous event is the annihilation of Lt. Grattan's command near Fort Laramie, inaugurating two decades of intermittent Plains warfare. The migration is relatively light, perhaps on the order of 10,000. It is a poor year for diaries, only a few being accounted for. Those of Edwin Bird, Sarah Sutton, Joseph Francl, and Scott Ebey are worthy of mention.

1855—This is the year of the white man's revenge, the Harney

Expedition against the Sioux, and the second swing of the pendulum of Indian warfare. With stepped-up military activity, Fort Leavenworth becomes increasingly prominent, and freighting activity from Leavenworth, Atchison, and Westport becomes a major industry. Capt. John S. Todd of the Harney Expedition well represents the military aspect, while William Chandless is the earliest among a very limited number of literate bullwhackers. Emigrants are scarce this year, with hostilities on the trail and the California mines petering out. Among the handful of journalists are William Keil, Lydia Waters, and William Chambers.

1856—Migration continues at a low ebb, and journals are scarce. Still, those of Caleb Green, Helen Carpenter, Emily Horton, Jo Hamelin, and William Pleasants are among the best of any year. Moses Sydenham, with his recollections, is a good representative of the freighting fraternity.

1857—The Cheyenne Indians and the Mormons become troublesome, and army activity increases. The best accounts are those of Capt. Jesse A. Gove, Pvt. Cornelius Conway of the Utah expedition, and Sgt. Lowe of the Dragoons. This year Lt. Bryan explores a new route up Lodgepole Creek and Bridger Pass, anticipating the Union Pacific Railroad, and the Pacific Wagon Road Surveys get underway under Lander and Magraw. The journals of the surveyors add much to our knowledge of the Platte trails.

1858—The tempo along the Great Platte River Road accelerates with the heavy freighting of military supplies to Fort Laramie and Utah and the discovery of gold at Cherry Creek, touching off the Pike's Peak Gold Rush. Nebraska City begins its career as the steamboat landing and principal depot of the new traffic to Colorado. Late in the year fortified ranches, serving travelers with crude lodgings and provisions, begin to spring up along the Platte, frequently in the vicinity of U.S. mail stations. There is a rash of new Colorado guidebooks, and there are several notable civilian observers, like freighters George Beehrer and Thaddeus Kenderdine, gold-seekers Anselm Barker and Martin Patterson, and news reporter Kirk Anderson. An expedition of the Topographical Engineers to the mountains is recorded by Wm. P. Seville and William Lee. The first photographs along the Great Platte River Road are taken by C. C. Mills, a member of this expedition.

1859—Although the extent of travel in the late 1850s is guesswork, this seems to have been a well-traveled year along the Platte, but one with no distinct migration pattern. People leave all major points along the Missouri for Colorado, though some traffic continues to Utah, California, and Oregon. Atchison, Kansas, and Nebraska City are now the primary depots for the great freighting concern of Russell, Majors and Waddell. Plattsmouth and Brownville (Nebraska) turn up as new points of embarkation, as witnessed by the respective journals of H. M. Chillson and William A. Maxwell. Other journals of interest include those of J. A. Wilkinson, Martha Missouri Moore, Harlow Thompson, Romanzo Kingman, Thomas Cramer, and Charles Tuttle. Capt. Randolph Marcy publishes his fine trail guidebook, and Horace Greeley makes his famous journey on the Leavenworth and Pike's Peak Express stagecoach to Denver and Fort Laramie.

1860—While the nation is poised on the brink of civil war, migration continues briskly up the Platte to all western points of the compass. There is a silver strike in Nevada, and the famed Pony Express from St. Joseph to Placerville, California, is launched by Russell, Majors and Waddell. Two distinguished travelers up the Platte, observing the pageantry of Pony riders, overland stages and mail stations, are Samuel Clemens (Mark Twain), bound for the silver mines, and Richard Burton, English globe-trotter and lecturer, bound for Salt Lake City to gather material on the Mormons. Capt. Albert Tracy leaves an illuminating account of a journey in reverse, from Salt Lake City to Atchison. Typical emigrant observers include Dr. C. M. Clark, Wm. Hedges, Wm. Earnshaw, James Lowry, Mary Jane Guill, and Lavinia Porter. (One young emigrant writer, E. E. Ayer, would later benefit historians by collecting hundreds of other journals and donating them to the Newberry Library in Chicago.)

1861—The impact of the Civil War is immediately felt in the Far West by the disruption of garrisons, the defection of southerners, and the withdrawal of regulars for front line duty. Volunteer troops take over guard functions. The momentous news of Lincoln's election and the firing on Fort Sumter is conveyed in record time by the Pony Express thundering up the Platte. The famed "Pony" goes into bankruptcy and out of existence when Edward Creighton's Pacific Telegraph is completed. Light emigrant travel is represented by Ira Butterfield, Marie Nash, and John Bonner. Oscar Collister tells of his adventures as a telegraph operator on the Upper Platte.

Fitz Hugh Ludlow describes a ride on the mail wagon from Atchison to Denver.

1862—Gold is discovered on Grasshopper Creek and in Alder Gulch, giving birth to Bannack, Virginia City, and the Montana gold boom. Sioux Indians in Minnesota run amuck and by chain reaction rekindle warfare on the Plains. (These events do not affect Platte River travel until the following year.) Overland journalists this year, mainly out of Omaha, are represented by Randall Hewitt, Charles Teeter, Ada Millington, Wm. Smedley, Hamilton Scott, William Brackett, and Mr. and Mrs. Burlingame.

1863—Montana travelers have their choice of a steamboat ride all the way up the Missouri or a covered wagon ride up the Platte to connect with the Bozeman Trail beyond Fort Laramie. Col. Samuel Word is among the first to reach the mines by this land route. An Englishman named Maurice O'Connor Morris makes a memorable trip to Denver and leaves a vivid account of Platte ranches. California travelers are represented by T. J. Redman, Louise Sweetland, and Wm. Fulkerth. Ben Arnold and Jno. J. Pattison leave a record of soldiering along the Oregon Trail.

1864—The Sioux Indian uprising and the military reaction along the Platte River valley are brilliantly recorded by Capt. Eugene Ware. Ranches along the Little Blue are ravaged. Fort Cottonwood (Fort McPherson) and Fort Mitchell at Scott's Bluffs are conspicuous among new army outposts scattered along the Platte this year. Civilian travelers include James Roberts and A. J. Dickson (to the Idaho mines), Mary Warner, George Harter, Philura Vanderburgh, and John S. Collins (later a sutler at Fort Laramie). Except for military and freighting traffic out of Fort Leavenworth, the bulk of travelers during the 1860s funnel through Omaha and Nebraska City. Steamboat passage up the Missouri to these points saves over 200 miles of overland travel, thus reducing the strategic value of St. Joseph and Kansas City. The civilian emigration this year is one of the heaviest of the war years. William Larkin, out of Omaha, says, "it is one continuous string of wagons all the time."

1865—This is a year of more bloodshed on the Plains, including attacks at Plum Creek, Julesburg, Mud Springs, Horse Creek, and Platte Bridge (Casper, Wyoming). In this final year of the Civil War, volunteer troops such as the Seventh Iowa and Eleventh Ohio cavalries, which performed so valiantly in guarding the Great Platte River Road, are gradually replaced by U.S. Army regulars, veterans of the Civil War. The experience of soldiering during this hectic year along the Platte is revealed by Geo. Holliday and Jake Pennock. Among civilians who go west and live to tell of their adventures are three unrelated young men named Young. Charles and Frank both travel, by coincidence, from Atchison to Denver; Will Young is hired by Seth Ward at Nebraska City to clerk at Fort Laramie. Dennis Ferrell freights on the Plains. The confused state of affairs this year is illustrated by the Sarah Herndon party, which leaves Plattsmouth intending to go to California, but gets talked into going to Montana instead.

1866—This is a climactic year on the Plains. An effort to achieve a peace treaty with the Sioux at Fort Laramie comes to naught. The Eighteenth U.S. Regiment of Infantry, led by Col. Henry Carrington and guided by Jim Bridger, marches out of Fort Kearny to relieve volunteer troops as far west as Fort Bridger. Carrington leads several companies up the Bozeman Trail to build Forts Reno, Phil Kearny, and C. F. Smith. Sioux and Cheyenne under Red Cloud carry on guerrilla warfare, climaxed by the December massacre of Capt. Fetterman and eighty men.

Gen. Sherman recommends the abandonment of Fort Kearny as the construction of the Union Pacific Railroad advances westward, hastening the demise of both stagecoach and covered wagon as transcontinental conveyances.

There are stray references to overland wagon journeys in 1867–1868, and the "wedding of the rails" does not occur until 1869. Nevertheless, 1866 is the last significant year of civilian travel by wagon up the Platte River. Of some seventy overland journalists of the 1860s noted, there are at least thirteen who, in 1866, give a final burst of glory to the literature of the Great Platte River Road. Military affairs are portrayed poignantly by Pvt. William Murphy, wagon-hand Finn Burnett, and the wives of three officers attached to the Eighteenth Infantry—Margaret Carrington, Frances C. Carrington (at that time Frances Grummond), and Elizabeth Burt.

The business of wagon train freighting in its heyday is described in detail by Perry Burgess, James F. Meline, John Bratt, Thomas Creigh, and William H. Jackson. (Jackson, whose work is preserved at Scotts Bluff National Monument, has immortalized scenes along the Platte River in water color sketches.) Julius Birge, George W. Fox, and Sarah Wisner are three travelers who help to write the epilogue.

II

The Great Migration

TRAVELERS ON THE Great Platte River Road can be broken down into three principal categories. First were the soldiers who occupied the military posts and marched and galloped up and down the Platte on government business. Second were the non-emigrants, that is, civilians who made a living in the wilderness, such as trappers and traders in the early years, and teamsters, laundresses, and telegraphers in later years (mainly serving the military). Also classified as non-emigrants were the general run of stage passengers as well as stage drivers, Pony Express riders, station-keepers, and mail contractors. The non-emigrant class also included a few objective observers, both foreign and domestic. Among them were Englishmen like Sir William Stewart (1837), William Kelly (1849), and Sir Richard Burton (1860); the German Heinrich Mollhausen (1851); and American writers such as Francis Parkman (1846) and Mark Twain (1861).

Emigrants, of course, comprised the third group, the one with which we are mainly concerned. A bona fide emigrant, for the purposes of this study, was anyone, American or foreign, whose principal object was to cross the continent to improve his fortune. Never mind if he expected to return east; if his object was to acquire gold nuggets in California or Montana, silver in Nevada or Colorado, a farm in Oregon, or salvation in Utah, he was an emigrant. Our principal concern is with this class of traveler, whose lasting symbol is the ox- or mule-drawn, white, canvas-covered wagon.

As we have seen from the preceding chronology, emigrant traffic along the Platte was a spasmodic trickle until 1843–1848, when it swelled modestly with Oregon and Utah emigrants. Traffic reached epic proportions in 1849 and the early 1850s, dwindled in the middle fifties, zoomed briefly with the Colorado Gold Rush, dropped off during the early Civil War years, then crested again in the mid sixties. It could be said that the pre-settlement history of the Platte River Road covers the period 1812 to 1869, or from its discovery by Robert Stuart's party to the completion of the Union Pacific, the first transcontinental railroad; but here we are primarily concerned with the covered wagon migrations which spanned a quarter century, from 1841 to 1866.

In the early Gold Rush years, emigrant registers (referred to by eyewitnesses, but unfortunately no longer in existence) were kept at Fort Kearny and Fort Laramie. Newspapers at the border towns and at Salt Lake City also provide some hints as to travel statistics, as do scattered military reports in the National Archives; and occasionally a traveler himself will testify to hearsay migration estimates. Evidence of the travel count in the late 1850s and the 1860s is particularly skimpy, yet the journals and newspapers of those years do indicate moderate to heavy travel. Ezra Meeker, pioneer of 1852, estimated over 300,000 emigrants from 1843 to 1859 or half a million from 1843 to 1869, but this latter figure seems excessive. Calculating all migrating travelers along the main Platte from 1841 to 1866, regardless of origin or destination (but not counting troop movements, stage lines, or commercial traffic), we come up with a more defensible total estimate of some 350,000, almost half of whom migrated in the five-year period between 1849 and 1853.

The annual figures in the following table are necessarily based on general impressions as well as meager documentable statistics:

Year	Estimate	Year	Estimate	Year	Estimate
1841	100	1850	55,000	1859	30,000
1842	200	1851	10,000	1860	15,000
1843	1,000	1852	50,000	1861	5,000
1844	2,000	1853	20,000	1862	5,000
1845	5,000	1854	10,000	1863	10,000
1846	1,000	1855	5,000	1864	20,000
1847	2,000	1856	5,000	1865	25,000
1848	4,000	1857	5,000	1866	25,000
1849	30,000	1858	10,000		
				TOTAL	350,000

RECORDS OF THE MIGRATION

What are the sources of information about this historical phenomenon? Newspaper accounts, military records, and a few diaries of soldiers, foreign observers, and other non-emigrants do much to illuminate the scene. But 90 per cent of the story is revealed by the emigrants themselves in the form of diaries kept en route, letters sent home or to the home town editor, and later recollections. Over 700 Platte River travelers have left such personal testaments, and the heaviest percentage of these are emigrant journals or diaries written on the Trail. Letters, written only infrequently, tend to lump the experiences of many weeks together; and recollections are of limited value, since the passage of time obscures memory. But most diaries have an immediacy and a vividness which brings the Great Migration alive.

Dividing 350,000 by 700 provides a ratio of one written eyewitness account for every 500 travelers over the study period. However, there is a wide divergence in this ratio from one year to the next. The year 1849, one of the big years by numbers but by no means the biggest year, has yielded to date nearly 150 diaries, a ratio of one to 200 travelers. The banner years 1850 and 1852 do have a ratio of one to 500, but in late years the ratio drops off sharply. No ready explanation is at hand, only the surmise that the California Rush produced more writers in its early climax years because of its novelty and excitement. Or it may be that the ratio of diary-keepers was just as high in later years, say in the 1860s, but their diaries were apt to be discarded by descendants for some inscrutable reason.

The average well-stocked public library may have one or two dozen published overland journals. Where did the 700 come from? For the most part these journals were passed down by the authors to succeeding generations until someone recognized their historical value and sold or donated them to a publisher, museum, library, school, or historical society. Many have been acknowledged as documents of vital interest to scholars or the general public, and so have ultimately appeared in print. Scarcely half of the total have been published, and most of those published are now out of print and scarce. Many published recently are in limited editions which do not reach most public libraries. The largest number of emigrant records—manuscripts, rare books, or limited editions—may be found only in state historical society libraries or in a few major foundation or university libraries which specialize in the trans-Mississippi field (and are identified in the Preface). A few remain in private ownership, but copies have been furnished for this study. The appended bibliography certainly does not exhaust the field. Every year a new diary or two turns up from some obscure hiding place, and these tend to gravitate toward book dealers or historians interested in such esoteric literature. (For example, three such Gold Rush diaries—those of Alexander Ramsay, Joseph Rhodes, and Elijah Farnham—brought to the writer's attention by descendants, have been edited by him for publication.)

Some journals long published, like those of Parkman, Stansbury, Burton, Thornton, Langworthy, Wistar, Mrs. Ferris, and Edwin Bryant, are frontier classics, while more recent discoveries, like those of Bruff, Pritchard, Moorman, and Geiger-Bryarly, are approaching that status. Others long out of print, like Cartwright, Hewitt, Frizzell, Flint, Holliday, and Sedgley, and still others more recent, like Berrien, Ketcham, and Knox, are almost unknown, but offer a wealth of detail. The journals of Peter Decker and Elisha Perkins were available only in manuscript form for study by the author, but have since been edited and published, so the scholarly work continues. However, there remain hundreds of unpublished journals, many of which are historically valuable. Those of Bachelder, Breyfogle, Bird, Gelwicks, J. L. Johnson, Eastin, Wilkinson, J. Evans, W. McBride, and Helen Carpenter are only a few of these hidden jewels.

While most emigrant companies, of course, had no journalists of record, a surprisingly large number produced two or more. Most remarkable is the fact that two companies of 1849 have furnished five recorders each. One of these was the company from Jerseyville, Illinois, headed by a Dr. Knapp, with J. E. Brown, Charles Kirkpatrick, Henry Page, Joseph Hackney, and Henry Tappan. The other was the Granite State Company of New Englanders, represented by the journals of Amos Bachelder, Joseph Stuart, Kimball Webster, R. C. Shaw, and Charles Gray. Next in order of productivity would be the Charles Town (Virginia) Company, offering the journals of Vincent Geiger, Wakeman Bryarly, Benjamin Hoffman, and Edward McIlhany, while an unidentified company, of which Dr. Israil Lord was a leader, was represented by M. L. Wisner and Epaphroditus Wells. J. E. Arrmstrong and Edwin Banks of the

Buckeye Rovers have been rejoined in publication recently. Dale Morgan, editor of the Pritchard journal, has also called attention to the association of Dr. Boyle with Peter Decker, Charles Gould with David Staples, and J. G. Bruff with Dr. Austin.

Combinations of letter-writing Forty-Niners from the same communities (and for the most part traveling in company) have been brought together in collections such as *Letters from Home: The Story of Ann Arbor's Forty-Niners*, edited by Russell Bidlack. Interrelated diaries of 1850 include those of Mary Jane Hayden with John Steele of the Wisconsin Blues, Seth Lewelling with Franklin Street, and William Montgomery with Dr. Reuben Knox.

While it is true that there were relatively few female Forty-Niners, at least three of these left a record: Mrs. Caples, Catherine Haun, and Sallie Hester, plus the reminiscences of Belle Redman Somers. For the entire period there are over sixty female witnesses out of an approximate 700 total. This is a fair literary showing, since men heavily outnumbered women on the trail. Some of the distaff diaries, notably those of Helen Carpenter, Rebecca Ketcham, Lucy Cooke, Sarah Herndon, Cecelia Adams, Amelia Knight, Lavinia Porter, Ada Millington, Mrs. Ferris, Mrs. Frink, and Martha Missouri Moore, are equal to the best in historical importance.

To judge from the evidence given, almost all of the female writers were in their youth at the time of passage. Lucy Cooke traveled with a baby. Algeline Ashley, Martha Moore, and Sarah Helmick were on their honeymoons, and Agnes Stewart was married en route. Most were unmarried but marriageable, age sixteen and upward, and the diaries of Martha Chambers, Juliette Fish, and Harriet Ward reflect their wide-eyed romantic innocence. Many of the girl travelers were children, ranging from Polly Purcell, age three, and Belle Redman Somers, age six, to Elizabeth Keegan and Sallie Hester, age twelve, and Philura Vanderburgh, thirteen. Except for Sallie, their experiences appear only in recollections.

The difficulties of keeping a record under trail conditions may well be imagined. James Abbey apologized to his diary for his "inklings" as "I write seated upon a bucket, with a board on my knees, a candle in a lantern, wind blowing, and extremely cold." Randell Hewitt apologized for "notes written on a cracker box, by the feeble light of a sputtering candle," while Israel Hale complained, "wind shakes wagon so much I cannot write." Elizabeth Geer confided, "I could write a great deal more if I had the opportunity," being able to get to her diary only at night, "when my babe and all hands are asleep."

A correspondent of the *Missouri Statesman* wrote from Chimney Rock: "You can hardly conceive the difficulty of preparing letters, for in the first place we have just as much labor to do as keeps us constantly busy, and in the next place a fellow must tuck himself up on the ground in the open air, with his legs crossed like a tailor, and write in his lap." In 1850 Henry Stine wrote to his mother from Fort Laramie, "'sitting on a wagon tongue, my Port Folio on my lap," and explained why he didn't write often—forever on the move, a hundred things to be done in camp, and "We are rather tired when we stop and do not feel much like writing." William Montgomery was unable to find time to jot down anything until he found himself "recuperating from his legs being run over." John Wood, another emigrant of 1850, exclaimed, "The task of keeping my journal is now almost intolerable, and I sometimes almost conclude to give it up."

All original journals are documents of value, but there is a wide range in their usefulness. Opposed to the highly legible, literate, and observant are those which suffer from too much brevity or illegibility. Chapman's journal of 1849 is but a fragmentary scribble. Like many others, H. D. Barton leaves only meager notes, without future historians in mind: "April 30, Started from California in the afternoon—went 10 miles—fine day. . . . May 3 Nothing remarkable—drove about 20 miles." Yet another Forty-Niner, John Benson, has an entry for every one of his 142 days on the road, but usually in this unhelpful style: "Glorious day—22 cases of cholera."

David Pease and Randall Fuller are difficult in an opposite way. They write profusely, but in a crowded script without punctuation or paragraphing, which makes reading interesting but difficult. The Mary C. Fish, Franklin Starr, and Scott Ebey journals give great promise to judge from snatches; but, because of fading ink or yellowing paper (no fault of theirs), they are only semi-legible. Washington Bailey and Elisha Perkins, while exceptional writers, write in so crabbed and jiggly a fashion that a magnifying glass is essential to read their manuscripts.

Foreign language imposes another barrier. The Italian Cipriani and Germans like Lienhard have been happily translated. The translator of Hagelstein had difficulty coping not only with obsolete

German, but also a thinly penciled script, without punctuation, and soaked by flood waters.

Presumably to conserve paper, at least two Trail writers, Reuben Knox and William Swain, adopted a remarkable calligraphy, writing not only in tiny script, but crisscross, that is with vertical lines crossing over the horizontal.

At the opposite pole from the faded, the abbreviated, and the enigmatic are the essayists and lyricists who somehow found time to write extended, colorful, and sometimes learned passages. Of particular note among the former are Dr. Tompkins and Charles Darwin, who ramble around freely with discourses on Indians, fur traders, prairie dogs, and other Trail phenomena. Some romanticize, like Walter Pigman: "Tonight I am on watch and as I write by my fire all is silent but the bark of the wolf, the croak of the wild goose, or the shrill yell of the Indian." Peter Decker almost sings: "The golden beams of the sun kissed the undulating plains and lighted a clear and beautiful sky. The heavy drops of dew hung like pearls in the wild oats. . . ." Marie Nash, "seated on the grass writing on the side of the Platte river and listening to its gurgling," has a melancholy air: "O there is so much in the world that is beautiful. O I have seen plainly the works of the Almighty. . . . Farewell sweet May, we love this as the day of thy death."

The importance of the Lewis and Clark exploration journals has not been impaired by erratic spelling; neither do the quaint variations found in many emigrant journals detract from their historical value. We are intrigued, in fact, to learn that William Newby had trouble "crawsing the Caw River . . . the bote sunck with one family, tho all waws save. . . . The Caw Indians tollerably theavish. . . ." and after a bad "knight," says Newby, "we went 5 miles for brec forst." We know what David Pease means when he crosses the "Meessouria river," but we have to look twice when Leander Loomis says he saw "cauntites" (quantities) of buffalo, and when Castleman looked around the "prearia" for "fewell." David Staples, on the other hand, says his company formed a "caralle" on the "prara," while Alexander Love avows he "crossed the Beautifullest pararie eye ever beheld." This by no means exhausts the different ways to spell "prairie." Indeed, James Mason, with his "bufflow" on the pariare . . . paria . . . parie," is careful to spell it differently each time!

Emigrants could mail their letters from post offices at Fort

Kearny, Fort Laramie, or Salt Lake City. Otherwise they might have them precariously entrusted to turnabout emigrants or to fur traders or Mormons bound for the settlements, who sometimes charged 25¢ or 50¢ a letter. A few emigrants mention sending mail with an enterprising outfit identified as Blodgett's Express (Fox, 1852). There was also a mail rider from Salt Lake, an operation of government contractors Hockaday and Liggett, and later the mail wagons and stagecoaches of the California Overland and Pike's Peak Express Company and the Overland Mail Company, but these fast vehicles would not normally stop to benefit the ordinary pilgrim.

Not all emigrant writings were confined to paper. Thinking to contact friends or relatives behind them, many wrote messages on rocks, trees, buffalo skulls and shoulder blades, or "the blessed bones of cattle." On the Lower Blue, in fact, Francis Sawyer found a human skull in use as a bulletin board. George Waggoner refers to this means of communication as the "prairie telegraph." This term was also used, however, to refer to rumors flying among the wagon trains.

Among non-emigrants, there are several who nevertheless observed or traveled in company with the emigrants, and who have left a rich historical legacy. Among the more notable groups of these writers are (1) U.S. Army officers, including Lt. J. Henry Carleton, Capt. Howard Stansbury, and Maj. Osborne Cross; (2) enlisted men, such as Percival G. Lowe, George Holliday, Lewis B. Hull, and Ben Arnold; (3) army officers' wives, like Margaret Carrington and Elizabeth Burt; (4) fur traders and trappers, like Charles Larpenteur, James Clyman, and Warren Ferris; (5) ox-team freighters, like William H. Jackson, Thaddeus Kenderdine, and Thomas Creigh; (6) domestic newspaper correspondents, such as Matthew Field of the New Orleans *Picayune* and numerous writers for the St. Louis *Missouri Republican* and other newspapers of that city (some of them believed to be army officers using *noms de plume*); (7) civilians whose motives were primarily scientific and scholarly, such as John Townsend, Francis Parkman, Rufus B. Sage, and Dr. Wislizenus; and (8) quite a star-studded list of foreign observers, including Heinrich Mollhausen, Maurice O. Morris, William Kelly, and Richard Burton.

THE CALIFORNIA GOLD RUSH

Precious metals in Colorado, Nevada, and Montana became magnets to emigrants, but the Great Migration was inspired first and foremost by the discovery of gold in central California. This was the big breakthrough of westward expansion. It was a stampede, a hysteria, caused by an illusion. California was seen through a golden haze. It was not just a far country; it was the new Eldorado, the land of Ophir. The electric atmosphere, created by sensational reports initially received through home town newspapers, was further supercharged by dramatic reports sent home by early arrivals, such as Peter Burnett: "The gold is positively inexhaustible. One hundred million dollars will be taken out in two years." Bennett C. Clark heard of a notice in the San Francisco *Californian* giving "a wonderful account of the gold mines," suggesting wealth of such magnitude that "gold is nothing more thought of than dirt." Joseph H. Johnson quotes Lilburn Boggs to this effect: "There are no poor in California and need not be, that the poorest can count there gold by the thousands." Intelligence reports received along the trail kept hope aflame: Near Fort Kearny, E. Wells reports, "A company of Mormons passed here. . . . One of them told . . . that they had all the gold that they wanted, and that the stories told about the richness of the mines were true to the letter." Franklin Langworthy, in 1850, met one man from Michigan "returning with $75,000."

After 1849, letters and rumors from California which expressed disillusionment heavily outnumbered the optimistic reports. There was gold, but it was beyond the reach of most in significant amounts. Kirkpatrick acknowledged: "We are all bound on the fool's errand to California." There were hardshps unimaginable. "Do not, for God's sake," exclaimed J. E. Squire, "ever start, or let your friends start, on this route. It is attended with inconceivable hardships and difficulties, and it is far preferable to go around the Cape, or even to go by way of China." But the Argonauts were in no mood to be "confused with the facts." Unlike Ulysses, they were bound to no mast, and they hearkened to the siren call. The pandemonium of the emigration at St. Joe in 1850 caused McBride to exclaim: "Whom the Gods have determined to destroy they first make mad!"

Writing to the *Missouri Republican* from Fort Kearny in 1849, the correspondent "Pawnee" was shaken by the spectacle: "Since my last [dispatch] the army of gold-diggers has received mighty powerful reinforcements. It now numbers 10,000 men." One year later, at Fort Laramie, the correspondent "Cheyenne" asks, "What has broken loose in the States? About every five minutes a wagon rolls in from the frontier. . . . This California gold must be turning the nation crazy. All honest and industrious pursuits appear to be abandoned for the precious occupation gold digging which at best, is nothing more than a grand lottery where the blanks far outnumber the prizes."

The Great Migration represented "almost every town and county in the United States," but Octavius Howe reminds us that there were also companies from foreign countries, including France, Germany, Japan, and Australia, not to mention "Cherokee Indians and Methodists."

Tumultuous scenes painted by William H. Jackson in 1866 are but an echo of Franklin Langworthy's 1850 journal: "At a general view the trains [west of Scott's Bluffs] have the appearance of a vast army, moving in two columns through a boundless Plain." "In the year that we crossed," writes Ezra Meeker of his 1852 journey from Council Bluffs, "this army made an unbroken column fully 500 miles long." Alonzo Delano likens it to the passage of Napoleon's army, and calls it "the greatest crowd of adventurers since the invasion of Rome by the Goths, such a deluge of mortals had not been witnessed, as was now pouring from the states . . . for the gold shores of California." The sentiment is echoed by Solomon Gorgas, resting his sore and blistered feet at Chimney Rock: "This certainly is a spectacle the world since its creation has never witnessed."

At a point west of Marysville, Kansas, where the Independence and St. Joe roads came together, the congestion reached epic proportions, as described by Mrs. Frink: "It was a grand spectacle when we came, for the first time, in view of the vast emigration, slowly winding its way westward over the broad plain. The country was so level we could see the long trains of white-topped wagons for many miles. Finally, when the two roads came together, and the army which had crossed the Missouri River at St. Joseph joined our army . . . it appeared to me that none of the population had been left behind. It seemed to me that I had never seen so many human beings before in all my life."

ORGANIZATION

There were stray individuals and maverick outfits, but the majority organized themselves into companies for mutual advancement and protection. At Independence and St. Joe in 1849, it seems almost everyone was bonded together one way or another. At Council Bluffs in 1852, according to Ezra Meeker, at least half of the departing trains were officially under a company banner. They might organize at their home town, at a jumping-off place, or somewhere along the trail, but sooner or later they organized. And sooner or later (with few exceptions), the organizations disintegrated under grim trail conditions.

The companies, particularly in the heyday of the Gold Rush, often bore impressive titles, like the Boston and Newton Joint Stock Association (Staples), the Iron City Telegraph Company (Johnson); Dubuque Emigrating Society (Cooke); the Rough and Ready Company (L. A. Norton); Grand Mustang Company, Mutual Protection Company, and the Social Band of Liberty (*Frontier Guardian*); Wild Rovers (D. A. Shaw); Springfield Rangers (Gatton); Peoria Pioneers (Wells); or Wisconsin Blues (Hayden). Others were content to be identified simply by their geographical origins, such as the Jerseyville Company, or by their leaders, such as Col. Jarrott's Company (Berrien) or the Hardinbrooke Train (Herndon).

The highly organized Mormons set themselves into units of Tens, Fifties, and Hundreds. Oregon-bound travelers of the mid-forties had some sizable trains of 100 or more wagons, which strung out a mile or more and which proved to be most unmanageable. Jesse Applegate's 1843 train of sixty wagons was broken for convenience "into fifteen divisions or platoons of four wagons each," but this plan proved unfeasible after a few weeks' experience. Among California-bound emigrants all sizes of trains were found, from two- or three-wagon outfits to Elijah Howell's "17 wagons, 57 men, 2 ladies," Franklin Langworthy's Western Enterprise Company with "40 wagons, 140 men and 4 women," and Capt. Ankrim's Pittsburgh Company of 271 men, mentioned by Wm. Johnston. J. M. Shively suggests "not less than twenty but not more than fifty wagons" as manageable. Joseph Ware advises not more than fifty men (not wagons), but Langworthy says at least fifty men, as "smaller companies are subject to pillage" by unfriendly natives. Discounting small random groups that were not really "organized," starting trains of about fifteen to twenty-five wagons appear to be average, managed by from fifty to one hundred men, or an average of four men attached to each wagon as a team, or mess; Thomas Eastin's company divided into messes of five, each with one wagon and ten mules. Sometimes there were six men or more to a wagon (R. C. Shaw), but this was crowding. Simeon Switzler advised, "Avoid a large mess; let it not exceed four men of known even temper." These figures apply to emigrant trains of 1849 and the fifties. A different formula, involving more wagons and fewer men, would apply to the large freighting outfits of the late period.

The most thoroughly organized (but not always the most cohesive) were those companies which originated in the home town, like J. G. Bruff's Washington City and California Mining Association, made up of government clerks and other city dwellers, and McIlhany's company from Charles Town, Jefferson County, Virginia, consisting mainly of "farmers, mechanics and lawyers." There was a lot of catch-as-catch-can organizing and reorganizing at the Missouri River towns. Theodore Potter's train of nine wagons, organized at St. Joe in 1852, represented nine different states. Some individuals, like Elisha Lewis of the "Millwaukie Company," were voted in by already established outfits. (Geiger tells of one applicant whom the voters rejected.) Many who disdained the formalities at the start changed their minds out on the road. Thus, R. C. Shaw's outfit was organized in a hurry after horses were stolen at the Kansas Crossing. John Bonner's company did not bother to organize until reaching Loup Fork—after some brushes with the Pawnee.

The Virginia company was a sample of a joint stock company, each charter member contributing $300 to the enterprise (McIlhany, Hoffman). Riley Senter's company required each to purchase a minimum of four $50 shares. Many groups were not stock companies but entrepeneur projects, with one man owning the outfit and making arrangements with others to hire on. There was a great variety of terms. Delano contracted with two men to work their way west, with no exchange of funds. Wm. Knight and other boys "paid $20 in advance for our grub." John Dalton and fifty others paid their captain $50 each, and he furnished "everything necessary for the trip." Dabney Carr says he hired his passage, paying the proprietor $100, "the regular price being $200." Isaac Harvey, a proprietor himself, advertised for "12 mechanics to go to California and work, and give me ½ of the net proceeds for 12 months." Niles

Searls and L. H. Woolley were passengers on the ill-fated Pioneer Line of Turner and Allen in 1849, which seems to have been a unique kind of tour group with each of the 150 passengers paying for the privilege of crossing the continent. Rambunctious mules, Platte River hurricanes, and the cholera combined to make this project a grim fiasco; but then, most of the various contractual arrangements soured in some degree before the promised land was reached.

As with any good American organization, there was usually a document of some kind, which might be called a constitution, code, resolution, or bylaws. There was a great deal of language about officers, camping and marching regulations, taboos on gambling and spirituous liquors (except for medicine), penalties for infractions, and certain "social security" provisions, such as taking care of the sick or bereaved and disposition of the shares of a deceased person (Senter). Effort was made to forestall turnarounds by providing for the forfeiture of "all belongings except clothing" by anyone who got too homesick. Except for the joint stock companies, these agreements had no legal force except what suasion the membership could bring to bear on the recalcitrant or discouraged traveler. They were pieces of paper—no more.

The best organization was one with a minimum of official routine, led by one strong, fair-minded leader; but the tendency was to over-organize. James Tate, in a company of fifty-eight men, found himself elected "President, possessing military powers, and President of the Judicial Board," with vice presidents, lieutenants, "sargents," and a "legislative body." B. R. Biddle reports the appointment of a "general superintendent," who had an "advisory board." The leader was most often a "captain." To be effective, the wagon train leader, whatever called—president, general, captain, wagonmaster—had to keep a firm eye on the whole situation day and night even though delegating specific duties such as guarding, hunting, and cooking. A few companies stayed under one management clear to Sacramento, but frequent changes were more common, either by orderly rotation provided for in the "constitution" or by the more familiar process of disobedience and peaceful rebellion.

The messes themselves required some mutual understanding, organized or not, particularly in the matter of who would cook. This thankless job was also wisely passed around, otherwise there was a danger that the "permanent cook" would tell the complainers to assume the mess duties if they didn't fancy his brand of cooking. Delos Ashley says that in a wagon train it was folly to give too many special assignments and best to let each man be "a Proteus in occupations."

One form of over-organization adopted by some companies was to transform themselves into units resembling those of the U.S. Army. Several outfits marched out of their home towns as if going to war, complete with martial music and uniforms designed for the occasion. The seventy-three men of Joseph Stuart's Granite State Company were all "uniformed in gray suits, holstered and saddle-bagged, ½ Spanish saddles upon our horses, with rifles and double-barrelled shot-guns." Langworthy says his company had military training and target practice. Writes Bryan Dennis at Council Bluffs: "Myer drilled the company. Marched through the camp a few times. Inspected the arms. Find all in good order and fully equipped. Dismissed us until we cross the Missouri . . . determined to go forward or die in the attempt." This note of brave soldierly determination is echoed by Charles Tuttle, who reports, "Our life is a regular military one. We now move as if in hourly expectation of attack." Others took their military duties less seriously. While doing her washing out on the Platte, Lucy Cooke wrote, "Our men amused themselves by marching in a procession headed by a drum and fife, each one with a gun or other weapon." They visited other camps, intrigued the Indians, and "scared off the horses." The Mormons had a brass band at Council Bluffs for a while, which did wonders for the flagging morale of the "Saints." A bugle was an adjunct of many well-regulated trains, used mainly for reveille and to sound the alarm in case of Indians or stampede. A patriotic gesture, with military overtones, was the common use of the American flag, hoisted at camp or, occasionally, by wagons on the march (Bruff, Pettijohn).

Experience showed that long trains were unwieldy, with a high number of malcontents. J. L. Johnson considered it "foolish to be caught in a large train of 50 to 100 men, for 15 . . . are considered all-sufficient, and most have split into smaller parties." McBride thought that three or four wagons were ideal.

After a few days on the "shake-down cruise," the elaborate organizations were subject to severe strains, and the process of disintegration began. The Oregon companies, with strong family bonds, held together better than the Californians, who were united only in their lust for gold; but even the Oregonians suffered from division, the most notable example being Jesse Applegate's famous "cow column," which fell to the rear in 1843. The 1844 migration split into four main companies. In 1845 Capt. Carleton of the Dragoons observed the spirit of revolt by Oregonians against "a martinet who insisted that even the cattle must march in cadenced step."

Big trains were reduced to the speed of their slowest members; impatience became epidemic, and constitutions and bylaws notwithstanding, the process of dividing and subdividing started before the Little Blue was reached and was in full swing along the Platte. According to Hoffman, the Charles Town train of 1849 held together to Sacramento, despite much quarreling and the death of five, but this was a rare exception. As McIlhany says, "All were finally sorted out by speed."

After the much-feared Indian attacks failed to materialize, the recitals of company disintegration in the journals became monotonous. Wellman Packard wrote, "The large trains are daily breaking up." Isaac Foster regretted that his company broke into three sections "after much altercation," but reflected that the seventeen wagons in his unit seemed to be an ideal number. Elisha Lewis reported: "The company we have been connected with divided, and every mess turned loose on their own hoock." Lucy Cooke sadly reported that the brave new Dubuque Emigrating Company "soon fell apart. We have only a small party with us now, for each company, when they have travelled a few weeks, fancy some plan of theirs is the best." Catherine Haun's train, 120 strong at Council Bluffs, was reduced at Sacramento to "not more than a dozen."

The Jared Fox train kept subdividing until "we were left with horses, and our little wagon and our traps." Some of the floating population attempted to form new combinations, but the "division fever" was unquenchable. Dr. Boyle attempted to stem the tide by threatening to shoot the dividers, but this was just a bluff. Of course there was a limit to the splitting-off process, since one man was indivisible; but often this limit was reached. J. Evans observed a two-man outfit split up. Gilbert Cole recorded the ultimate example of disintegration—two quarrelsome partners sawed their wagon in half and flipped for the front end! Not all wagon trains were atomized completely, of course; but as trains progressed westward the tendency was to string out more and more until individual wagons were pretty much on their own. At Fort Laramie, says Albert Thurber, the division process reached its peak. Here many wagons were reduced to carts, and many others were discarded in favor of pack-mules. During the sixties, when the Indians more frequently molested emigrants, orders were issued at Fort Kearny to combine wagons into large, well-armed trains, but even this military dictum could not be enforced. The American tradition of self-reliance and rugged individualism was never displayed more dramatically than westward along the Great Platte River Road.

OUTFITS

The most important element in the success of a trip to Oregon or California, next to self-reliance, was the "outfit"—not the train to which a person might be attached (which was a temporary affair at best), but the unit of rolling stock which conveyed families, goods and chattels, across the continent. In most cases this boiled down to a particular covered wagon and its means of locomotion. This meant animal muscle-power, and the available animals were horses, mules, and oxen. The comparative uses of these three "makes and models" were debated as furiously in 1849 as we dispute today the comparative virtues of automobiles. During the Great Migration oxen were most numerous, from all accounts perhaps a good 60 per cent, with horses and mules about equally dividing the remaining 40 per cent.

According to some, horses were mainly for stagecoaches, Pony Express riders, and the U.S. Army, which could provide stations where they could be rested and fed grain. They were noble beasts, and a well-heeled company would have a string of them for hunters and outriders; but they were not practical to pull the ordinary emigrant wagon across the wilds of the West. In that age a good horse was expensive, about $200 for one of medium quality, and his upkeep was also demanding. Unless feed was carried, he was useless (Scharman). A horse could not forage well on the dry grass of the Plains, the insects pestered him, and the tepid waters of the Platte gave him distemper. Horses were used, to be sure, but they succeeded mainly in well-to-do outfits which could haul grain. If horses were to be used, J. M. Shively advised in 1846: "Swap your horses for Indian horses, and be not too particular, for the shabbiest Shawnee pony . . . will answer your purpose better than the finest horse you can take from the stables." He also advocated that "you take with you plenty of horse-shoes and nails, a hammer and clinches, to keep your animals shod." As one last bit of advice, he added, "If any of your animals give out, leave them, for your time is more valuable than all your horses."

Mules were tough and durable. They could survive on Plains grasses and a certain amount of alkali water, but they were much given to mayhem. The most prized mules were bred in Missouri, but many emigrants preferred smaller "Spanish" or Mexican mules. B. C. Clark found that young mules were not suitable and recommended that they be five years old or older. McCoy says that their cost at Independence in 1849 was in the range of $50 to $90; the *Missouri Republican* reported that choice quality brought up to $125. Simeon Switzler asserts that the best outfit of all was a stout wagon designed for one horse, but drawn by four good aged mules with two for spares. Sgt. Lowe of the Dragoons extols mule vitality. If they became crowbait before the trip was over, it occurred only because they were grossly overloaded, starved, or abused.

There is quite a body of literature on the temperament of mules. McGlashan "found reports of kicking and stubborn propensity exaggerated," but this might be related to the fact that his mule purchases had been "driven only a week [before] from Texas, and were reduced to skeletons." Wilkinson and Redman both relate that their mules were tractable enough to pull along steadily, even while the drivers were asleep, but it's possible that these mules were debilitated. The normal experience with mules was heartrending, particularly when readying them for a life of useful endeavor. The only mules the emigrants could buy seemed to be unbroken ones. McIlhany says it took him a month to "get acquainted" with mules purchased at St. Joe. Here also John Clark was invited to select his mules from "a large corroll full of stock, many of them young and unbroken. We had to . . . risk our lives in roping them. After being kicked across the pen some half dozen times & run over as often, we at last succeeded in leading them out. . . . It was laughable . . . to see the wild devils run with all hands hanging on to the ropes to keep them in check." Those attempting to ride these animals found them incorrigible. "Many valiant riders," writes R. C. Shaw, "found themselves in very undignified positions." Vincent Geiger speaks of one man being thrown "Hell, west & Crooked." Some of the beasts were never thoroughly subdued until they became food for coyotes. Niles Searls paints an appalling picture of the feat of taming and harnessing 150 mules of the Turner & Allen train at Independence. Mrs. Ferris observed that contrary mules could sometimes be brought to heel by twisting their ears, and it seemed to reassure them if they had a bell-horse for company. Joseph Berrien records the use of a nose stick: "The loop of the rope is to be placed around the upper lip of the animal and by the aid of the stick twisted tight. . . . no matter how vicious and stubborn, they are easily conquered. . . . I was perfectly astonished at the power of this instrument."

The efficacy of Berrien's nose stick seems to have escaped the packers, that is, those who traveled not by wagon but by mule pack-train, walking alongside. (One of the better-known pack trains was that of Edwin Bryant, veteran of the slow 1843 migration to Oregon, who in 1849 reached California in record time.) Dr. Wislizenus' journey of 1839 began "under evil auspices" when he had to pack his mule, and he describes the process: "The baggage is divided in two equal parts, each part firmly bound up, and hung by loops on either side of the yoke-shaped pack saddle. The whole is further fastened by the so-called lash rope of stout buffalo leather, which is first wound round the barrel of the animal, and then in diamond-shaped turns . . . around the pack. My baggage weighed 150 to 200 pounds, a quite ordinary load for a mule. . . . At first packing causes novices much trouble. . . . Here the towering pack leans to one side; there it topples under the animal's belly. At one time the beast stands stock still with its swaying load; at another it rushes madly off, kicking till it is free of the burden." Kimball Webster's experience was similar: "A wild unbroken mule is the most desperate animal that I have ever seen. We tried in vain to break our mules by putting large sacks of sand on their backs and leading them about. . . . It took as many men to pack a mule as could stand around it, and we were obliged to choke many of them before we could get the saddle upon their backs. They would kick, bite and strike with their forefeet, making it very dangerous to go about them."

Oxen were the number one draft animal of the Great Migration. In 1849 Isaac Foster passed ninety-six teams opposite Fort Kearny, "all oxen but two." Thissell claimed that 80 per cent of the wagons in 1850 were hauled by these creatures. The oxen had it all over mules and horses, according to their admirers. "M. M.," writing

to the *Missouri Republican*, states: "ox-teams are allowed by all,
or nearly so, to be the surest teams." George Harker wrote to the
St. Louis *Reveille*: "From what I have already seen I am fully
convinced that oxen are preferable to mules." Both were speaking
from experience gained in the 1849 crossing. In 1843 Peter Burnett
credited the ox with superior hardihood and greater adaptability
to the prairie grasses. John McCoy said oxen were slower and
required fifteen more days on the road than mules, but there was
less danger of their running away, and "the Indians will not steal
them as they care nothing for an ox, but they will steal a mule
whenever they can catch him." By the time he reached Fort Kearny
with his oxen, Charles Maltby reported, "We are constantly passing
mule teams that left St. Joe earlier."

Oxen being plentiful were inexpensive, from $50 to $65 per
head at Independence and Weston in 1849, according to the correspondent "California." James Pratt was able to buy twenty yoke
at $40 per yoke, which he acknowledged to be "cheaper than any-
one else has purchased this spring." Chester Ingersoll credited
"Northern Illinois cattle" with being faster than the Missouri
variety. "Oxen should not be less than five years old nor more
than seven," writes M. M. "In no case will four year old steers
hold out. . . . Your yokes should be of the lightest material. The
bond must not be too tight, if they are, your steer will be found
to swell up as tight as a drum head." James Linforth urged that
starting be delayed on a wet morning, as "dampness is bad for
necks of oxen." Breaking oxen, much less an ordeal than breaking
mules, was accomplished by yoking younger oxen between the two
leaders and the two wheelers.

Ox hooves wore down to the quick, usually by the time Fort
Laramie was reached, and this required attention. Blacksmithing
could be accomplished at Fort Kearny, Fort Laramie, or Robidoux's
trading post at Scott's Bluffs. If shoeing was done by the owner,
according to Lydia Waters, a shallow ravine or trench was dug
and somehow the animal was turned upside down into it to get
at his hooves safely. When cloven iron shoes were lacking, the
emigrant resorted to nailing on sole-leather or smearing the hooves
with tar or grease and then fastening on boots of buffalo hide.
Burnett and Delano speak of cattle being lamed by the "foolish
rivalry" of drivers racing for position. Cramer refers to "the disease

called 'Foot Evil' which is caused by travelling in the mud too much."

Every family had great affection for their oxen, which were greeted with names like Rouser (Ivins), Old Bailey (Brooks), Brindle and Bright (Inez Parker), and Old Smut and Snarley (Carpenter); and when, in the extremity of the journey, oxen died of thirst or exhaustion, the owner's grief was as much for the loss of a valued friend as for being marooned in the wilderness. The joy of the Belle Somers family knew no bounds when "the late lamented Snider," an ox, reappeared in the desert, having survived only because he stumbled upon a waterhole.

Oxen were the main reliance of the freighting contractors. William H. Jackson, Thaddeus Kenderdine, Charles Young, and others provide vivid pictures of their indispensable role in provisioning the army posts and the western cities before the advent of the railroad: the long serpentine wagon trains, the daily circus of yoking up, and the cracking of whips. Under great burden and merciless lashing by the teamsters, oxen perished by the thousands. Approaching Scott's Bluffs in 1858 Kirk Anderson exclaimed, "There ought to be a Heaven for all ox that perish under the yoke, where they could roam in the fields of sweet clover and timothy. . . . It is astonishing what a number of these animals have fallen under the yoke this season, the road is literally lined with them . . . the traveler could find his way with no other compass or guide than his nose alone." Virginia Ivins kept a camphor bottle handy to combat the smell of dead cattle.

Ezra Meeker, who crossed in 1852, said oxen were always patient and usually quite obedient; but when heated and thirsty, they became headstrong and reckless and would sometimes stampede blindly for a river or a waterhole. Nothing could stop them until they had collapsed or had gotten bogged down in the mud. He pointed out the surviving oxen had great economic value to pioneers in clearing forests or breaking prairie sod after reaching their destination. Writing in 1915, he expressed sorrow that "the oxen have all but passed away, their great work accomplished. It was only with the help of the patient oxen that [the emigrants] were able to push the boundary of the nation across the continent."

The high mortality rate of draft animals frequently resulted in some strange combinations. When oxen faltered, dairy cows and saddle horses were put to harness, and an assortment of bulls, cows, and horses was not uncommon (Geer, H. Kingman, Cutting).

Recommendations for an ideal wagon load varied from 1,600 to 2,500 pounds (Delano, E. Lewis, J. Ware). The best chance of success, of course, depended upon having a light load in a light-weight but sturdy wagon, drawn by enough animals to make the going comfortable. Conversely, difficulties arose from overloads, inferior wagons, inadequate pulling power, or any combination thereof. Scharman suggests as ideal a wagon capable of supporting 6,000 pounds, but loaded only with 2,000 pounds, and pulled by four yoke of oxen or six mules. While up to twelve yoke of oxen (twenty-four animals) might be required to pull the biggest of the freight wagons, from two to four yoke were par for an emigrant wagon.

Although Ezra Meeker said his outfit was "boat shape," the classic prairie schooner of the emigrant did not resemble the big-wheeled, boat-curved Conestoga wagon of the freighting outfits. It was smaller and lighter, usually with a straight bed; but, said Shively, its construction had to be of the best seasoned materials or it would fall apart. Oak, hickory, maple, and other hardwoods were, of course, prime lumber. Ingersoll described wagons sold at Independence in 1847 as "of the Ohio form," with wide tracks and boxes two feet high and eleven feet long. He thought northern Illinois wagons the best, however. M. M. recommended a "light two horse wagon," which presumably would come out about the same as Switzler's "heavy one-horse wagon."

The wagon bows were usually hooped to a height of about five feet from the wagon bed (Ingersoll), but sometimes, as with the Helen Carpenter rig of 1856, the bows were square, providing extra head room. Shively advocated that the bed be lined with "wooden boxes of half or three quarter inch pine boards. . . . in these place your provisions. . . . close by hinges . . . and on them is a comfortable place for women and children to ride through the day and sleep at night." Mrs. Frink and Helen Carpenter both describe a double-deck arrangement, with supplies and provisions on the floor and bedding above, but most wagons were single-decked and calked for ferrying across rivers. The McIlhany train included two wagons with improvised beds of sheet-iron to serve as boats. The famous wagon cover, frequently described as double thickness, seems to have consisted variously of heavy rainproof canvas

(Pleasants), "linen, well oiled or painted" (Shively), white drilling (Carpenter), white muslin (Thissell), sailcloth (Senter), and oilcloth (Aram). Names or mottoes like "Kaliforny" (Smedley), "Prairie Flower" (Thissell), and the immortal "Pikes Peak or Bust" were frequently daubed on this material.

Since tongues, spokes, and axles were subject to breakage, spare parts were carried whenever possible, slung under the wagon bed. Grease buckets, water barrels (or india rubber bags), whips or goads, heavy rope, and chains completed the running gear accessories. If grease was not applied liberally to wheel bearings, a "hotbox" developed (Porter). When store-bought grease was exhausted, boiled buffalo or wolf grease served.

A minimum of 100 feet of heavy rope was recommended by Ingersoll to aid in man-handling or double-teaming wagons through mud, across creeks and ravines, and in braking downhill. There were no wheel brakes worthy of mention, and on steep declines catastrophe was averted only by the use of chain locks, log-dragging, or improvised windlasses.

As wagons began to deteriorate from overload and other factors, much ingenuity was required to stay on the trail. Wagon rims often became dislodged from jolting or from the dryness of the atmosphere and had to be reset by soaking the wheel in water and wedging with buffalo hide. When spare parts were no longer available to repair wagon or wheel fractures, the only choices were to seek out and shape suitable timber, if any, to cannibalize abandoned wagons, or to take the drastic step of reducing basic equipment. This might involve shortening the wagon bed or cutting it in half and making carts, the latter expedient often necessary in the event of wheel failure. When Mrs. Burlingame's wagon sprained an axletree, she wrote: "It was decided to metamorphose our vehicle" and, after throwing out cooking utensils, washtubs, and flatirons, radical surgery was performed on the wagon bed. "Thus trimmed and reefed," she continued, "our ship sailed on over the prairies." Fort Laramie was a favorite spot to make this adjustment. Sometimes all gear was abandoned there, and the wagon train became a pack train (Coke, Thurber, W. Kelly).

Intermingled with the westering cavalcade of the Great Migration was the shuttle-weave of stagecoaches, freighting trains, mail wagons, fur trade caravans, U.S. Army troops, supply trains, and dispatch riders. There were also occasionally large numbers of cattle (Loveland, Chillson) and sheep (Flint, I. Butterfield), herded westward to Utah or California markets, and sometimes a horse herd from California to Missouri. As to emigrant outfits, there were some strange contraptions among the orthodox covered wagons and the infrequent packers. Not uncommon on the north side, or Council Bluffs Road were the Mormon handcart expeditions. Organized by the Mormon church in the 1850s to provide the passage of impoverished recruits from England, these strange processions involved the actual pushing and pulling of crude loaded carts by human beings, all the way from Council Bluffs to Salt Lake City, and resulted in great hardship and suffering. In contrast, Mary Warner, Isaac Pettijohn, and Wm. Chamberlain describe some affluent emigrants traveling up the California Road in horse-drawn carriages. Searls and Woolley, who were passengers, and others who were observers, tell of the motley assemblage of buggies and other vehicles used by the Pioneer Line in 1849. Dr. C. M. Clark describes a "wind wagon" powered by sails which headed for Pikes Peak in 1859, and William H. Jackson describes a "steam wagon" out of Nebraska City which was a glorious fiasco. Perhaps the strangest spectacle in all the procession was the funeral cortege, led by William Keil, that went all the way from Missouri to Oregon with a casket in which were embalmed the mortal remains of his son Willie.

Honorable mention, at least, should go to the small army of men and women who walked, not rode, across the entire continent. Most of those who accompanied wagons were able to climb aboard occasionally or ride horseback. If they mainly walked, they still had the benefit of wagon camps, although that did not reduce their bunions. Seth Lewelling complains, "My feet ware verry sore but my faith being strong I endured the pain without flinching." In 1851 Quincy Brooks thought he had hit upon a good plan: "Mr. C—— and I purchased a horse in partnership. Soon after he started, however, Mr. C——'s feet became sore by walking. . . . I let him have the horse, and was compelled to take it on foot to Green River." Margaret Frink speaks of a "fellow passenger" getting peeved about something and "deciding to walk," strapping blankets and provisions on his back to do the remaining 1,500 miles on his own.

But there were a considerable number who started out on foot from scratch. The packers were of this number, of course, keeping company with their string of horses or mules. But while pack-train members at least had each other for mutual aid and comfort, there were many individuals all by themselves, with or without animals. In 1849 Wm. Johnston spied "two men alone and on foot, their tent an umbrella, packs with thirty days supplies." In 1850 Hagelstein and McBride were among several who observed numbers of men on foot with heavy packs on their backs. Among other oddities, Mc-Bride observed "one man with a small cow harnessed to a home-made cart," and also, "near Fort Kearny, a poor footman [who] borrowed fire from us to make his coffee. He laid upon the cold earth, without blanket or overcoat. . . . he seemed to be a man of good ordinary sense." On the Little Blue, James Evans observed "six Dutchmen walking to California and driving cows packed." He offered a sardonic comment on their chances for success: "What fine sport the Prairie Wolves will have in picking Dutchmen's bones this season!"

Henry Kingman mentioned a California-bound "cart pushed and pulled by four men." Lucy Cooke ran into "five men who draw a truck. . . . [Next day] Poor fellows, it had broken down, and they have now taken pieces of it for poles, and thus slung their provisions and carry on their shoulders. . . . I should like to know how far they get in this fashion." Several observers of 1850 mention a colorful "man with a wheelbarrow," who became something of a celebrity among the trains.

Johnston's hikers of 1849 "passed all trains" along the Little Blue, and McBride points out that "these men possess great advantages over the teams as long as their provisions last, and they soon outstripped us." But the odds against survival of these "foot-men" were much higher than for the covered wagon emigrants. They were essentially shelterless, often cold or hungry, and in case of accident or disease they were in mortal danger. No hiker, to our knowledge, kept a journal, or even came up later with reminiscences. These rugged individuals just disappeared into the unknown.

PROVISIONS

Details of provisioning, diet, and menu are not among the most glamorous of the Great Migration, but they were of vital importance to the emigrant, whose exertions required at least as many calories as a farmhand at harvest time. The food supply was the heaviest and most essential part of a covered wagon cargo. A delicate balance had to be achieved, for pulling too great a quantity of foodstuffs would wear down the animals, while not enough in the way of groceries could result in starvation. Although some wild game and fish, roots, and berries might supplement the diet, it was risky to rely too much on success in hunting or foraging on the semi-arid and thinly covered High Plains. There were no stores or even any respectable trading posts on the route (until reaching Fort Laramie) prior to June, 1849. The army quartermasters at Fort Kearny and Fort Laramie were authorized to sell grain and provisions in emergencies, but these were normally in short supply even for the military. In 1849–1850 Robidoux's post at Scott's Bluffs and the two army post sutlers had meager supplies at extortionate prices. Charles Lotts and Wm. Chamberlain mention California-bound traders encamped near the South Platte crossing who sold groceries to distressed emigrants, but these were fly-by-night outfits. With the Colorado Gold Rush of 1859 and thereafter, ranches and trading posts sprang up along the Platte to serve the traveler, but during the earlier California Gold Rush, emigrants were pretty much on their own all the way and liable to arrive at the mines in scarecrow condition.

Thus, the inventory of provisions assembled at St. Joe or Council Bluffs was of crucial importance. Lansford Hastings, one of the earliest guidebook writers, advocated that each emigrant be supplied with 200 pounds of flour, 150 pounds of bacon, 10 pounds of coffee, 20 pounds of sugar, and 10 pounds of salt. The basic kitchenware was a cooking kettle, fry pan, coffee pot, tin plates, cups, knives, and forks. Stoves were advantageous, the smaller the better; yet cooking was possible with a trenched campfire, hence stoves of every description were among heavy items most commonly abandoned.

The bread-bacon-coffee formula was the staple emigrant diet. More extended and refined checklists, such as those given by Joel Palmer, Basil Longsworth, Romanzo Kingman, Mary Jane Hayden, and Carlisle Abbott, included these additional items: chipped beef, rice, tea, dried beans, dried fruit, saleratus (baking soda), vinegar, cheese, cream of tartar, pickles, ginger, and mustard. Although every pioneer woman knew how to bake bread at home, it was difficult to knead the dough and bake the bread in Dutch ovens or reflector ovens under prairie conditions, what with having to contend with stingy buffalo chip fires, flying ashes, dust, gravel, and insects. A welcome alternative to frequently burned, soggy, or stale "home-baked bread" was cornmeal, also known as Indian meal or pinola. Also, it was possible to stock a variety of manufactured wheat products, identified variously as pilot bread (C. M. Tuttle), sea biscuit, ship's biscuit (Senter), and hardbread or hardtack (Hayden).

One does not think of the Oregon Trail as a place to bake pies, but there are a surprising number of references to the creation of this delicacy, using raisins, dried apples, and peaches. At Fort Laramie, Caroline Richardson baked enough pies and cakes for a week. A Dr. Stone in the J. E. Brown train was a master at baking pies, "a very great luxury to us on the Plains." After two months on a steady diet of coffee, bacon, and bread, Julius Birge was the beneficiary of a peach pie donated by a motherly emigrant. It was one of the highlights of his whole trip.

Although the science of dietetics was then only dimly understood, there were various suggestions to ward off scurvy, dysentery, and other ailments obviously related to improper or inadequate food. Abigail Duniway advises, "for health's sake, leave hogs' lard and bacon at home, and provide fruit instead." She recommended dried beef, venison, and well-smoked ham, for they are "salt meats and will keep." Bacon was among items most frequently thrown overboard, but Frizzell and Horton caution that bacon should be hoarded, not only for food, but also as an antidote fed to oxen who sickened from drinking alkali water. H. Kingman recommended dark brown sugar over white, and green coffee over roasted. F. S. Dean found that "a little airing" would do much to combat deterioration of meal, flour, and hams from heat, dampness, worms, and maggots.

The canning of foodstuffs in pre–Civil War days was still in the experimental stage; besides, canned goods were heavy and therefore seldom used. Delicacies such as oysters, occasionally mentioned by Mrs. Ferris and others, were, of course, canned.

A few pioneers carried eggs or butter normally packed in barrels of flour or meal. Some of the resourceful brought milk cows along, which apparently managed to supply milk at least until arrival in the alkali regions of Wyoming. Whole families stayed healthy by means of such traveling dairies, and soups made from hot milk restored to health many who had been stricken with disease (John

Wood). Helen Carpenter says their milk was carried in covered cans swung from the wagon bows; soon it would be churned. Live chickens in portable coops were taken along by Capt. Andrew S. Burt's family en route to Fort Bridger. W. Sullivan's chicken coop was fastened to the tail gate, and each evening the chickens were "turned loose to forage on grass-hoppers, bugs and worms." But most emigrants got along with the minimum, often putting up with "beans like gravel" (Birge). Sometimes when stormy weather prevented campfires, they settled for "cold coffee and a crust of bread" (Haun). On one dreary occasion Wm. Chamberlain made a meal of "bread soaked with a little whiskey."

Charles M. Tuttle describes the daily menu of a typical emigrant: "for breakfast, coffee, bacon, dry or pilot bread; for dinner, coffee, cold beans, bacon or buffalo meat; for supper, tea, boiled rice, and dried beef or codfish." With this Spartan fare, he says, "Our appetites are good, our digestive organs strong, our sleep sweet."

In the pristine days of the Trail, perhaps 1830 to 1849, when game was more abundant and a case-hardened old fur trapper might be guiding the train, there was considerable living off the land, with feasts of buffalo and antelope steak. Small buffalo herds along the Trail were common enough through the fifties and sixties, and emigrants on horseback frequently gave chase and once in a while shot a buffalo. Usually, however, the kill was too far distant from the train to permit bringing in more than token slabs of the prized meat, preferably ribs, tongue, or hump. Charles Larpenteur, a trapper who lived almost exclusively on buffalo in the thirties, found most of it "tougher than whalebone," although fat cows were somewhat better than bulls. In 1860 Lavinia Porter found that dried buffalo meat didn't taste so bad, but it was unchewable: "The longer you chewed the larger it grew." T. J. Redman pronounced the dark red meat "good if young and fat," and jerked or dried buffalo meat fairly good if one had time to give it a good boiling. The process of jerking, according to Washington Bailey, was simply a matter of cutting the meat into strips to be dried either by heating over a slow fire, or by exposure to the summer sun, Indian fashion. G. W. Thissell says that better results were achieved by first dipping the strips in brine. E. Goughnor found that meat cut in ribbons and draped from wagon bows would be converted into something edible by simple exposure to the dry climate, without benefit of direct fire or sunlight. Helen Carpenter's "jerky" was hung on the outside: "Tonight the wagons are decorated with slices of meat dangling from strings, fastened to ropes that reach from front to back, along the side of the wagon, looking very much like coarse red fringe." However, she feared that this delicacy would suffer somewhat from accumulated dust and dirt.

Antelope meat was scarce except for parties led by seasoned plainsmen, for the fleet animal (more properly classified as a pronghorn) was rarely within gunshot. Opinions varied widely as to the virtues of antelope meat, but it enjoyed a better reputation than that of the bigger, clumsier buffalo. To Daniel Bacon, it tasted like veal. Franklin Starr reckoned, "It was well ahead of anything I ever ate." Other Plains creatures which occasionally turned up in emigrant stew included sage hen, rabbit, badger (McBride), prairie dog (Longsworth, Dunlap), rattlesnake (Lowe), and eagle (Wyeth). The last four named were eaten experimentally and pronounced unpalatable.

Domestic oxen, horses, and mules were eaten in dire emergencies, but these occurred more commonly farther west in the mountains and deserts; and by that time the livestock would be lean and stringy. Gelwicks reports that one alternative to dying of thirst was to drink the urine of mules, which "tastes like coffee;" at any rate, it would not be much worse than the radiator water resorted to by an autoist trapped in the desert today.

Easterners did not understand the Indians' many uses of Plains vegetation, but in season they enjoyed gooseberries, chokecherries, and serviceberries which abounded on the Platte (Flint). Inez Parker's mother was ahead of her day when she "gathered fresh greens for our delectation as well as to prevent a scurvy." Fish abounded in the Blue, the Loup, and the Elkhorn. Dr. Flint and others report successful fishing in the Platte, but references to fishing are infrequent. Either the emigrants were not equipped to catch them, or they were too busy moving during the day and too tired at night to bother.

It would be inappropriate to omit reference to one more item in the emigrants' bill of fare—whiskey. This was brought along in casks or barrels, and it was an important item. Furniture, mattresses, stoves, anvils, or even fine linen and silver might be discarded, but never whiskey. Not all trains carried this commodity, of course, but a high percentage of the journalists mention its use. The fur-trade caravans of an earlier day packed it along in quantity

as a trade item or for Indians or trappers at their mountain rendezvous, where it was used in very convivial fashion. The emigrants
used it on very special occasions, as on the Fourth of July or to
celebrate a birthday or arrival at a milestone like Fort Laramie, but
their original intention was that it be purely medicinal, to combat
colds and cholera, or to restore flagging energy and spirits after
moments of crisis, such as punishing hailstorms or dangerous river
crossings.

Addison Crane mentions another use: "Most emigrants take five
to ten gallons of whiskey to a wagon under the notion that by
mixing it with the bad water it becomes in some mysterious way
healthy and purified." Cagwin says that molasses was used as an
extender, and the resultant combination was known as "skull-
varnish." Whiskey by the drink or by the bottle (Chamberlain paid
50¢ a quart in 1849) could be bought from itinerant peddlers, from
the sutlers at Fort Kearny or Fort Laramie, at trading posts such as
Robidoux's at Scott's Bluffs in 1849–1850, or at ranches along the
main Platte in stagecoach and freighting days. It is to the credit of
the main body of emigrants that they largely stuck to their resolve
to restrict the use of the precious whiskey to medicinal or restorative
purposes, and when they celebrated, they did so with decorum.
Instances of conspicuous intoxication seem largely to be found at
the border towns or among the freighting fraternity. Among emigrants there was a large number of teetotalers who wouldn't touch
the stuff even when they were half drowned or dying from disease
(McIlhany).

Abandonment

One of the dismal aspects of the Great Migration was lack of
skillful preparation, which resulted in overloading, a failing particularly devastating in the early years of the Gold Rush. Its most
common result was the abandonment of worldly possessions, strewn
along the Platte River Road. Almost every greenhorn had an
overload which, coupled with draggy sand and mud, hills, jolting
buffalo tracks, and creek crossings, rapidly exhausted the irreplace-
able mules and oxen and threatened breakdown in the wilderness.
The standard solution was to heave things overboard just as you
would from a sinking balloon. This jettisoning process began in a
mild way a few miles out of Independence or St. Joe. It began in a

serious way at Fort Kearny and continued to its climax at Fort
Laramie.

Everything taken at the outset was deemed indispensable. The
definition of indispensability was rapidly revised in the interest of
survival and priorities established on the scales of size, weight, and
immediate usefulness. The journals suggest the variety of items
abandoned:

> stacks of bacon a half a ton in place, piles of hard bread, and stacks
> of flour, lead and powder.—Isaac Foster, 1849

> beans and other unnecessary things.—Castleman, 1849

> bacon, salt, iron nails, boxes, barrels, wagon bodies . . . clothes,
> tobacco, trunks . . . mattresses, quilts, beef, bacon, rice, augurs, hand-
> saws, planes, shoes, hats, thread, spools, soap, scythes . . . a splendid
> set of blacksmith tools.—Dr. T., 1849

> chains, ropes, saddles, crow-bars, and a complete outfit for a saw-
> mill . . . mining augur, sheet iron, gold-washers . . . we discard our
> tents and sleep in the open air.—R. C. Shaw, 1849

> rocking chairs, mirrors, wash-stands, and corner what-nots.—Haun, 1849

> We passed eleven wagons that had been broken up, the spokes of the
> wheels taken to make pack-saddles, and the rest burned or otherwise
> destroyed. The road has been strewn with articles . . . thrown away.
> Bar-iron and steel, large blacksmith's anvils and bellows, crow-bars,
> drills, augurs, gold-washers, chisels, axes, lead, trunks, spades, ploughs,
> large grindstones, baking-ovens, cooking-stoves without number, kegs,
> barrels, harness, clothing, bacon, and beans. . . . The carcasses of eight
> oxen, lying in one heap by the roadside this morning, explained a
> part of the trouble.—Stansbury, 1849

> Like the march of armies, each train has left sad memorials of its
> passage . . . bones of oxen and mules, broken fragments of wagons,
> cast off implements of agriculture. . . .—Mrs. Ferris, 1852

Dr. Ormsby observed, "None of the emigrants know how to fit
out for their journey. They are all split upon the same rock."
Isaac Foster points out the irony of the fact that possessiveness
compelled most emigrants to cling to their burdens until they wore
out their teams; *then*, in desperation, they threw their things away.

A few, such as Bennett Clark, were able to sell some of their
surplus early in the journey, but such was the glut that soon it
couldn't be given away and was thrown out. A few underweight

emigrants scavanged the pickings. Emily Horton says she "hailed with delight" chairs and a fine sheet iron cook stove. For the most part discards went begging. "Don't bother to bring cooking stoves," Israel Hale advises, "I could pick one up anywhere." Those charitably inclined penned notes offering their goods freely to whoever followed. In 1852 Lodisa Frizzell and Thomas Turnbull both encountered a cow with a label imploring someone to adopt her. Ezra Meeker speaks of hundreds of wagons left and hundreds of tons of property, often with a posted sign, "Help Yourself." It was his recollection that people "seemed to vie with each other in giving away their property." Some, however, elected to destroy the goods they couldn't use themselves. Says Martha Morgan in 1849, "Wagons were cut up, burnt and destroyed." Dow Stephens reports that bacon was "piled up like cordwood," saturated with turpentine, and set afire.

Equipment of well-organized companies with experienced guides was slimmed down to start with, or resolutions were passed enroute to reduce the poundage per person. David Staples says that after a few days on the trail his captain limited members to 100 pounds each, including arms and ammunition. At Fort Kearny, Henry Shombre's company cut back the quota to seventy pounds per man. If the typical wagon leaving St. Joe carried 2,500 pounds and had a complement of eight men, this would leave an unrealistic cargo of over 300 pounds per man, much of which would be jettisoned. The lesson was clear to all who heeded. Proclaimed Forty-Niner G. C. Pearson: "To lighten up at the outset was our salvation."

TRAVELING

The exodus each year from jumping-off places on the Missouri River began on the approximate date when it was agreed that grass would be sufficiently green on the plains to support the animals. It was all very well to get a head start and beat the crowd, but if animals weakened from malnutrition an outfit would find itself stalled while the "tidal wave" swept by. Dalliance in getting an outfit together permitted the crest of the wave to roll ahead; the nice green grass would be eaten off and the waterholes fouled. Everyone laid bets on the magic date, and when it was suddenly revealed by rumor, or "prairie telegraph," everybody tried to take off at once. For this reason, there were traffic jams, not only at the ferries of the Missouri River towns, but also at the Blue and the Little Blue, the Elkhorn and the Loup. The wave held a definable crest all the way to Fort Kearny. Thereafter it flattened out for a few weeks as the variables of speed and degree of preparation came into play.

A drouth could delay departures alarmingly, increasing prospects of getting snowbound in California's mountains in the autumn; but a rainy season could slow things down, too, as wagons mired in the mud before they were well started. Since Council Bluffs was 200 miles north of Independence, with a correspondingly late spring, departures from there might be a bit delayed. But give or take a week or two, a good standard target date for departure from any of the jump-offs was April 15, for arrival at (or opposite) Fort Kearny, May 15, at Fort Laramie, June 15, and at South Pass, July 4.

Arrival at a destination in Oregon or California by September 1 was hoped for, but October 1, well ahead of snow in the Sierra Nevadas, was considered satisfactory. An ideal passage would be four months, or 120 days, April 15 to August 15. Computing an average distance from the Missouri River to California at 2,000 miles, this meant an average of fifteen miles a day. Much more than fifteen miles could be traveled on a good day, but there were bad days when little or no progress would be made, and there were Sundays, when some felt it would violate God's law to turn a wheel. Thus, four and a half months, from April 15 to September 1, was more nearly par for the course, while painful trips of up to six months' duration have been noted. If it took longer than this, travelers feared they might share the dreadful fate of the Donner party, trapped in the snow in 1846. Most of the really late comers spent a miserable time wintering at Fort Laramie or Salt Lake City.

In 1846 J. M. Shively claimed that an experienced crew of packers would go from Independence to Oregon in seventy or eighty days, though proof of this kind of speed is lacking. Wagon trains, of course, were another matter. Charles A. Tuttle of the 1849 Kingsville, Ohio, Company claimed to have reached California from Independence in 114 days, traveling one day fifty-three incredible miles. Single days of forty miles or more were rarely achieved. Mark Manlove indicates, "We traveled 33⅓ miles a day, 200 a week, and rested on Sunday." This was pretty fair traveling, but he was referring only to the mainline Platte River Road, not the entire trip. In 1850 Lemuel McKeeby's train traveled the 500 miles from

Council Bluffs to Fort Laramie in twenty-two days including two days' rest, an average of 22.2 miles per day, with daily distances varying from fifteen to thirty-six miles. In 1852 Jared Fox completed the same course in twenty-one days without any days off, an average of twenty-four miles per day. On thirteen days he went distances of twenty-five to thirty-seven miles. But these are exceptional cases. The daily average for most trains on the Platte River Road as far as Fort Laramie was fifteen to twenty miles with no rest stops, and the daily average dropped west of Fort Laramie because of tougher terrain.

James Blood figured an average daily run of twenty miles or ten hours, from 6 A.M. to 5 P.M. with one hour's rest at noon. This would indicate a traveling speed of two miles per hour, but Blood does not take into account the briefer stops of about ten minutes each hour mentioned by Catherine Haun, or the unscheduled dead stops caused by accidents, disease, and stream crossings. According to James Pritchard, by actual day-long measured timing with a watch and a surveyor's chain, the cruising speed of an ox-drawn covered wagon "on firm roads averaged 3 miles per hour; when the roads were heavy, from $2\frac{1}{2}$ to $2\frac{3}{4}$ miles per hour."

While many of the daily mileage figures which appear in the journals are guesswork, these guesses were by men who traveled by wagon enough to estimate distance accurately. There was always a guidebook of some kind, like Ware's or Horn's, or a well-known early journal, like Fremont's or Bryant's, to check against the streams and the landmarks, and some wagons were equipped with a simple odometer or "viameter," which gave fairly accurate mileage by counting the revolutions of a wheel of known circumference. Such an instrument is often mentioned (Clayton, Goldsmith, Gibbs, and Bruff). Its use is implied in the Isaac Pettijohn journal: "travelled $18\frac{1}{2}$ measured miles and 4 unmeasured."

Within a wagon train there was some semblance of order imposed by the wagonmaster. Because there was a certain amount of prestige in being in the lead, and because all who followed ate progressively more dust, every well-regulated train had a democratic system whereby the lead position was rotated among members. Delos Ashley's wagons were designated by number, and at the end of each day the leader fell to the rear. In Lydia Waters' train the lead changed several times each day.

The big problem on the road, however, was not the formalities within a train. It was how to stay in position and keep pace with the hundreds of other wagons of all shapes and sizes which crowded the road at the crest of the migration wave. On the open prairie there was room for two or more columns to relieve the pressure, but through much of eastern Kansas and Nebraska—that is, along the tributary approaches to Fort Kearny—topography simply dictated using a single file, and the result could be frustrating. Coming up the Little Blue, Forty-Niner McIlhany counted up to 300 wagons in a string, and "once in line you stayed in line all day," with no chance of passing anyone and the certainty of falling far behind if you stopped for breath.

Where some open country permitted passing, says William Rowe, there was great rivalry between trains to keep ahead of each other, much foolish flailing of bullwhips, loud quarrels, and jockeying for position, as if the object were a Roman chariot race rather than a trek to California. On the Council Bluffs Road, Amelia Knight writes, "When we started this morning there were two large droves of cattle and about 50 wagons ahead of us, and we either had to stay poking behind them in the dust or hurry up and drive past them." Although he was threatened with pistols, her husband elected to take a bypass and, says Amelia, "We left some swearing men behind us." Later in the day, she continues, "While we were eating we saw them coming. All hands jumped for their teams, saying they had earned the road too dearly to let them pass again." Similarly, Gilbert Cole had a complaint about the behavior of fellow emigrants on the south side of the Platte: "There were frequent quarrels among the drivers of cattle and horse teams; the former being largely in the majority and having the road, many of them seemed to take delight in keeping the horse teams out of the road, and crowding them into narrow places. These little pleasantries were indulged in generally by the people from Missouri, as many of them seemed to think their State covers the entire distance to California."

There was not much night driving; the way was hazardous, and covered wagons were not equipped with headlights. Cole, however, says, "Sometimes we would move on in the night" in order to get around some of the more obstreperous trains. He also indicated that ox-teams were started earlier and driven later at night than horse and mule teams, probably to make up for a slower pace. Emily Horton found that those who did not rest their teams enough, wearing them down, would soon pay the penalty. Her well-rested train would often pass the passers, and "thus we often saw the same people twice or more."

The essential midday halt was called a "nooning," even though, as the result of getting away early, it might happen to be at 10 A.M. "When we stopped at noon," says Stephen Forsdick, "'the cattle were not unyoked, but were unhitched and allowed to graze. We never corralled at noon, but stopped with the wagons strung out."

The first order of business at the end of the march was the formation of a corral. This wagon-ring, designed to provide maximum security against Indians, desperadoes, and wild animals, was an inviolate institution, and if there were three or more wagons a corral was formed. As long as the larger companies with long wagon trains managed to hold together as an organization corralling was quite a ceremony, presided over by the wagonmaster. The lead wagon went into the designated position, and there was a certain routine whereby the other wagons took positions, either by following the leader or by alternating left and right. The corral formation was normally circular or oblong in shape, with the tongue of one wagon chained to the rear wheel of its neighbor to form a fence (Herndon, Forsdick). There might be one or two openings for the passage of livestock, which could be closed with a wagon tongue.

Three other kinds of corrals are mentioned. A semicircle would suffice if the train was small or if things seemed to be fairly peaceful (Waters). Theodore Potter says that his train always camped in the form of the letter "U". "Still another kind," says Forsdick, "was made by driving the wagons close together [in a circle] with the tongues on the inside. This corral was only used when a train was attacked when on the move" (This rarely happened except in later dime novels and television programs).

CAMPING

The virtues of a campfire—to dry wet clothes, fend off the chill, and, most important, to cook a hot supper—are beyond debate. Along wooded streams fuel was no problem, but trees thinned out rapidly and then became nonexistent. The Platte River bottoms today seem choked with timber; a hundred years ago frequent prairie fires kept trees from maturing along the Platte. How, then, did the pilgrims thaw themselves out and fry their bacon? By wading or swimming the river, green willows and stunted cottonwoods were found in the bogs or on the islands (Burnett, L. Sawyer). A hike of several miles into the sandhills produced cedar shrubs (J. Evans). Driftwood from last year's flood or an abandoned wagon bed were finds, and farther west grew the gnarly wild sage (Kilgore). Dry prairie grass in sufficient supply would make a feeble flame, and Rev. Hinds found his supply of alcohol a fine fuel in an emergency. But for the most part along the Platte a camp fire developed from the ubiquitous dried droppings of the buffalo, sometimes called dung or manure, but more commonly called "buffalo chips."

The reaction of easterners, particularly the ladies, was predictable. At first exposure they found the chips nauseous, but they rapidly learned to accept, then welcome, this aromatic fuel of the Plains. The stuff would not burn when wet, of course, but when perfectly dry, W. McBride found it resembled rotten wood, making a clear, hot fire. Since it burned rapidly, it took two or three bushels of chips to heat a meal (Bowen, Geer), and Cramer found that the chief objection to its use, therefore, was "the vast amount of ashes which it deposits." Often an unusual concentration of chips would dictate the selection of a camp (J. H. Clark); more often, a camper had to cover a lot of territory, as Lavinia Porter says, to get a supply. Persons detailed to collect these malodorous specimens used sacks or aprons, or any handy container, and often the spirit of competition enlivened the proceedings.

Matches, carried in sealed containers, were highly prized; these were conserved by borrowing a burning brand from a neighbor. In the absence of a camp stove, the best bet for a fireplace on the Plains was to dig a shallow slit trench two or three feet long, in line with prevailing winds and just wide enough to accommodate a camp kettle (Frink, Cartwright). A refinement of this scheme, reported by R. C. Shaw, was to create a natural oven by "selecting a spot a short distance from the steep river bank," digging a hole about twelve inches deep for a fire, and providing an air tunnel by forcing a ramrod horizontally from the river bank for the required draft.

Farther west the waterless or alkaline desert would be a grave peril to the Great Migration, but water was not a primary problem from the Missouri River to South Pass. The Kansas River and its tributaries offered a generous water supply. While the Platte

River drained a vast territory, the water problem along its length
was one of quality, not quantity. Spring water was, of course,
preferred, but good springs were scarce. In 1846 J. M. Shively
could identify only two good springs—at Scott's Bluffs and Willow
Spring—between the headwaters of the Blue and the Sweetwater,
the entire Platte route. He missed Fremont Springs and Ash Hollow,
but he was more right than wrong. Good springs were infrequent.
The only reliable daily source was the Platte River itself.

Platte River water was obtained in two ways: by scooping it
up out of the main stream or its backwaters, or by digging a hole
two to four feet deep in sandy soil near river level. The latter
method was used by many, and while there was more exertion,
according to Addison Crane, by this method "most excellent cold
pure water can be obtained anywhere. It leaches through the sand
from the river and is perfectly filtered." Most emigrants disagreed,
however; well water was more apt to be warm, dirty, and often
alive with tiny creatures. After trial and error, several (Bennett,
Lyon, Richey) affirmed that "river water is safer." Hence, the
majority drank water straight out of the Platte. If river water was
deemed safer than well water, it still held few charms for the
fastidious. John Wyeth warned that a Platte River cocktail "is
warm and muddy, causing diarrhoea." Celinda Hines observed that
this water "partakes of the same laxative properties of the Missouri
and Mississippi." Getting his out of a slue or backwater, John
Dalton called it "nasty, filthy stuff." D. A. Shaw proclaimed it
"useable only if filtered and strained" with a cloth, since this is
not a river at all, but "simply moving sand." Randall Hewitt came
up with another formula for dealing with "the mud of a river
intent on wearing away half a continent." He recommended putting
a handful of meal in the bucket, and "a few moments time is
sufficient to precipitate the silt and render the water very palatable."

Some of the women recommended boiling, not to kill bacteria,
which they had never heard of, but to immobilize the wiggle-tails.
Tompkins was ahead of his day in believing the "secret of boiling
water [was] to evaporate its deleterious properties." Drinking
untreated shallow well water and Platte River water was doubtless
a factor in the high mortality rate.

A good camp was any location with wood and water, preferably
out in the open to avoid skulking Indians. Some people preferred to
stay away from the river bottoms, where the mosquitoes could be a

plague (Flint, Webster) and where a rise in the river could swamp a camp (Potter). Often there was little choice, and camp turned out to be wherever the emigrants halted from sheer exhaustion, without benefit of any amenities.

Practice varied as to the disposition of people and livestock in relation to the corral. One would suppose the emigrants, with or without tents, would sleep inside the corral for maximum security and livestock would graze outside, under guard but ready to enter the corral at a moment's notice. Potter says that in his case, "All tents were inside the enclosure." But more often it seems to have been the other way around. W. McBride agrees with Forsdick: "The tents were always pitched and the fires built outside the circle of wagons. This was done so that, in case of an attack by Indians, we could get behind the wagons and the firelight would show us the attacking party."

As a rule the cattle were grazed outside while there was still daylight, then driven into the corral for the night and the "gate" closed (Herndon, Forsdick). If the camp happened to be near a green Platte River island, the cattle were sometimes driven there with reasonable assurance that they wouldn't drift away. The normal place for horses and mules seems to have been outside the corral. They might be free to graze unfettered in the neighborhood under the watchful eye of night herders, but more often the stock was hobbled or picketed to reduce the chances of the dreaded stampede.

In a strange land, as J. M. Shively emphasizes, "A night watch is necessary, Indians or not." Guards took turns on guard duty, though they hated it. Wm. Earnshaw lamented that one night on guard duty seemed as long as "living one thousand years." The larger trains had well-organized guard systems, as witness McGlashan: "The Company has to have sentinels stationed four at a time, who are to admit none within the lines without a countersign. The watch is to be relieved every three hours." Wrangling over guard duty in his train was settled by requiring the guards to serve in alphabetical order. Tipton Lindsey agreed that a guard was needed but felt that the dangers were exaggerated and the procedure was "run into the ground" by drafting everybody, big or little, old or young, all loaded with knives, hatchets, pistols, and guns, to confront a nameless enemy. The Stephen White party came to the conclusion that guard duty was a waste of time. He writes, "After a

week or two we quit it, lay down and slept as soundly as if there
were no Indians nearer than a thousand miles of us, especially after
a Company of U.S. Calvary passed near us."

There are documented instances of prowling Indians stampeding the herds. Much more often, however, the nervous guard fired
in panic at rustling grass, causing a great commotion in camp and
sometimes triggering the very stampede he was enjoined to prevent.
Wolves and coyotes skulking around the herd were a real problem,
but firing at them was against the rules, according to Joseph Buffum.
The wisdom of this regulation was demonstrated by incidents in
the Cole and McCoy trains, wherein guards fired at these phantom
creatures and precipitated bedlam. McCoy's man was soundly
jeered "for confusing the yelp of a wolf with an Indian war cry."
A featherbrained employee in Lewis B. Dougherty's train raised
havoc by a prank in which he pretended to be an Indian and drew
the fire of the guard. It is small wonder that guard duty was not
among the cherished memories of the Great Migration.

There is occasional reference by emigrant ladies to mattresses
and featherbeds (F. Sawyer), but for the most part sleeping arrangements were elementary. The women and children might sleep on
packing boxes in the wagons, but most likely a bed was a blanket,
a piece of canvas, an india rubber cloth, or a buffalo robe on the
ground. Tents were luxuries often blown away by prairie gales or
thrown away as excess baggage. Most emigrants sooner or later
slept on Mother Earth with a canopy of blue sky or bright stars.
(If it rained, they might crawl under the wagon, or in the wagon
if there was room.) The experience took some getting used to.
Says Niles Searls, just out of Independence, "We rose this morning
from our bed upon the ground with sensations similar to that I
imagine must pervade the frame of the inebriate after a week's
spree." However, no sleeping pills were needed to pull the emigrant through. With fatigue for his pillow, the ground soon
became soft enough.

III

Elephants of the Platte

ELEPHANTS ONCE ROAMED the Platte River Valley—mammoths and mastodons, that is, which flourished during the Ice Age as recently as 20,000 years ago. To read the diaries of the Gold Rush, one might suppose that elephants flourished also in 1849, but the emigrants weren't talking about woolly mammoths or genuine circus-type elephants. They were talking about one particular elephant, *the* Elephant, an imaginary beast of fearsome dimensions which, according to Niles Searls, was "but another name for going to California." But it was more than that. It was the popular symbol of the Great Adventure, all the wonder and the glory and the shivering thrill of the plunge into the ocean of prairie and plains, and the brave assault upon mountains and deserts that were gigantic barriers to California gold. It was the poetic imagery of all the deadly perils that threatened a westering emigrant. Thus, on his first day out of St. Joe in 1852, John Clark wrote, "All hands early up anxious to see the path that leads to the Elephant." In 1849 James D. Lyon, ten miles east of Fort Laramie, was defiant: "We are told that the Elephant is in waiting, ready to receive us. . . . if he shows fight or attempts to stop us on our progress to the golden land, we shall attack him with sword and spear."

No one has quite nailed down the origin of this mythical figure, often more vivid in imagination than the real three-dimensional rattler or buffalo. This creature seldom appeared except on the fringes of danger, and then it was only a fleeting glimpse. During

61

a cattle stampede, says Martha Morgan, "I think I saw the tracks of the big elephant." Excited about his first buffalo chase, David Staples "went out to get a nearer view of the elephant." This phantom appeared most often during violent storms. James Abbey felt "a brush of the elephant's tail," while Niles Searls "had a peep at his proboscis." In a particularly vicious hailstorm, writes Walter Pigman, "The boys concluded the elephant was somewhere in the neighborhood."

C. G. Hinman entitles his odyssey *A Pretty Fair View of the Elephant*. Despairing after a long succession of stampedes and deaths by cholera, Joseph Wood exclaimed, "Now methinks I see the elephant with unclouded eyes!" Of turnarounds—that is, emigrants who gave up and went back home—it was said that "they had seen enough of the elephant." Of one who turned back after having gone 700 miles, Francis Sawyer said, "He had seen the Elephant and eaten its ears."

The joys and sorrows, the hazards and heartaches of the covered wagon emigrants were enough to populate a whole continent full of elephants.

EMIGRANT SOCIETY

The Oregon migrations of the mid-forties were family affairs, running at least 50 per cent to women and children. In contrast, the great California migrations of 1849 and 1850 were composed largely of bachelors and absentee husbands. Catherine Haun's family train was quite exceptional. Most wagon trains of record were exclusively male. Charles Kirkpatrick noted one woman in company with fifty-two men, a female average of 2 per cent which was close to the overall average. Figures reported in the Fort Laramie register for 1850 bear this out: as of May 31, totals of 8,352 men, 68 women, 39 children (Frush); as of June 18, totals of 30,964 men, 439 women, 508 children (McBride). In 1852 there was a marked increase in the number of family trains. By this time women had rebelled against the idea of languishing back home while their husbands went on their great adventure. That year, for example, Rachael Rose noted ten women in one company. In the Theodore Potter train of thirty-five persons, four were unattached bloomer-clad young ladies from New Orleans and Memphis. "They were members of Southern hunting clubs and were taking the land route to California for the purpose of hunting large game." Fortunately, this disconcerting trend toward female equality on the Platte was heavily counterbalanced by old-fashioned romance.

Most young gold-seekers elected to spare their sweethearts the rigors of the trail and contented themselves with impassioned letters; but Lucy Cooke speaks admiringly of one chaperoned couple en route whose engagement "stood the strain" of crossing the continent until they could be married in California. The scarcity of girls in the wilderness made what romance there was more piquant. Thus, J. P. Hamelin in camp at old Fort Kearny noted: "Steamboat *Eliza Stewart* arrived after supper, loaded with Californians, among whom were a number of fine-looking Mormon girls. Fell in love with several."

There are numerous instances of marriage vows exchanged at the jumping-off places or along the trail. Perhaps the first trailside wedding of record was that reported by John Bidwell in 1841, where the Independence Road intersected the Platte: "This evening a new family was created! Isaac Helsey was married to Miss Williams. . . . the ceremony was performed by the Rev. [Joseph] Williams." In 1846 J. Q. Thornton reported that Rev. J. A. Cornwall married two couples at the South Platte crossing. In '47 Loren Hastings scribbled near St. Joe, "Wedding in camp this night, and a very tall spree." In '53 Mrs. Rea spoke glowingly of a young man in a bachelor company at Council Bluffs: "Changing his mind at going without his sweetheart he left the company, hurried back to Sangamon County, won her consent to immediate marriage, bundled his bride into a wagon, and caught up with his train."

In 1862 Jane Tourtillot wrote, "a young couple came to our camp to get a minister," were duly hitched, and for this special occasion assigned a tent of their very own. They fared better than the usual newlyweds, who were "shivarreed" by the company, entering into a conspiracy against their privacy, a fleeting thing at best under covered wagon conditions. Perhaps the most touching romance of all was that of Stephen Forsdick, who in 1853 eloped with a girl from a Mormon train, was married and found sanctuary at Fort Laramie, where he obtained employment with the post sutler.

There was a high incidence of childbirth on the trail, and these kinds of entries are frequent: Longsworth in '53 reports, "Daughter born today in Mr. Mason's family;" and Hamilton Scott in '62,

"Jim Bailey's wife brought a newcomer into camp last night which caused us to lay by today." For reasons unexplained, the birthrate shot up in '64, according to William Larkin. "Mother," he wrote, "this is a great country for babies. Almost every train has had one and almost every one you meet expects to have one. It beats all!"

It was not uncommon for emigrant mothers to name their trailside babies for the nearest natural feature. Daniel Bacon recorded the advent of little "River Blue Hurlbut," while Phoebe Judson proclaimed the birth of her own son, Charles La Bonte Judson (both babies being named for streams).

Tragedy often stalked new arrivals. Louisa Sweetland's son, born in Council Bluffs, traversed the continent, only to die on arrival in California. Margaret Inman recalls of her trip by ox-train: "I carried a little motherless babe five hundred miles, whose mother had died, and when we would camp I would go from camp to camp in search of some good, kind motherly women to let it nurse, and no one ever refused when I presented it to them." J. H. Clark witnessed the burial of parents beyond Scott's Bluffs: "The children will now journey on with strangers." Abigail Duniway reports orphans of Capt. Gray's company "adopted by the Bald Hill Train of Wisconsin." Any number of witnesses report husbands dying and leaving their wives with young children to care for. William Frush found one distraught woman with nine fatherless children. At Ash Hollow Phoebe Judson found "a mother buried here, leaving five helpless little children, the youngest six weeks old. (See Chapter IX.)

Not only cholera but nerve-wracking hardships of the trail often tore families apart. Martha Morgan was horrified when "old Z—— and his wife had a tremendous fight," and vowed to separate (rather difficult to do in a covered wagon). At Fort Laramie, J. Evans records instances of a husband's abandoning his family, a wife's abandoning her husband, and "a boy found by soldiers." Elisha Brooks says his mother took six children to California to join their father in the gold mines and was deserted by her teamster, leaving her to carry through on her own. Apparently she made it, but the strains of the journey, including Indians and cholera, drove some women insane. Mrs. Geer pitied an "emigrant woman gone berserk," while Kilgore had to restrain a German woman who "begged to join her husband" who had drowned in the Kansas River. Indians, who treated their squaws as property, often coveted emigrant women and children, preferably blondes. Their offers to swap horses for a white woman were uniformly and indignantly refused, and cases of actual kidnaping from wagon trains along the Platte (as distinct from ranches and stations) are not recorded. However, all this helped to reduce some emigrant women to nervous collapse.

While there were these harrowing cases, more typical were the thousands of women who rode the wagons to Oregon and California with nerves and scalps intact. Inez Parker remembered neither romance nor danger, but "the wild wind in the wagons, the long slow marches, smoky campfires, and monotonous meals." Perhaps the biggest problem that Mary Warner faced was insomnia, caused by the restless horse herd, chomping, snorting, and whinnying through the night to the accompaniment of coyotes' howling.

A few fortunate ladies, such as Mrs. Ferris and Mrs. Sawyer, started their journeys in style, with comfortable berths in a well-appointed wagon or carriage. At the old Fort Kearny crossing Mrs. Sawyer wrote: "I have been in bed in my carriage all day, for it is very disagreeable out. The wind commenced blowing at a high rate last night and it has continued to blow a perfect gale. . . . Mr. Sawyer got up in the night and pulled the carriage, with me in it, out into the prairie, for fear that timber would fall on us. The men do all the cooking in bad weather, though I never have to do anything but make up the bread." But Mrs. Sawyer was an unusual case; Elizabeth Geer, for example, managed a family of eight children. In their usual custom, most men took their women for granted as a useful part of a covered wagon outfit, to drive the oxen, gather buffalo chips, and boil the coffee. A few were critical. In a rather superior vein, J. M. Shively averred, "Women and wives and daughters are of little help. Attacking grizzlie bears and savage Indians are all out of their line." Fine praise for the ladies by an emigrant male is difficult to find, but accounts of deeds of endurance and quiet heroism by women speak eloquently for themselves in the emigrant journals.

The Great Migration required youthful vigor for its fulfillment; over 95 per cent of the emigrants were probably ages sixteen to fifty. Men and women over seventy were a rarity, but there were enough of these to counterbalance the newborn and give poignancy to the scene. A certain fame has accrued to Grandma Keyes of the 1846 migration, who knew she wouldn't survive but came along anyhow, and was respectfully buried at Alcove Springs. Less well-known is the "little old lady" mentioned by Harlow Thompson in '59 who brought along a metallic coffin which didn't have to be used until she reached Fort Laramie. Gelwicks counted several stalwart old Kentuckians among the Forty-Niners. Kirkpatrick included an "old grayhead" in his company, and on the Little Blue he observed an outfit consisting of an old couple with their grandchildren, the parents presumably dead of cholera.

In eastern American society class lines were well defined. On the emigrant trail the principal distinction was one of property, and a man's social status was judged by the size and quality of his outfit. Even this distinction was blurred under the rigors of trail conditions; there has probably never been a truer democracy than existed along the Oregon and California Trail, where every man prided himself on self-reliance, yet depended upon a cohesion of sorts with his fellows to survive. Exceptions to this blending process may be noted briefly. There was some discrimination against Mormons, ex-Confederates and Confederate sympathizers, and "crackers," the illiterate and impoverished folks from southern Missouri, Arkansas, and Tennessee who turned up for the Gold Rush. At the other end of the scale, Mrs. Ferris speaks of a "horse aristocracy," implying that those who drove fine teams lorded it over those with oxen and mules, but this phenomenon was not widespread.

The propertied Missourians and southerners who took the Platte route did turn up occasionally with slaves, and the status of Negroes at the jumping-off places and along the trail must be interpreted in the light of conditions that prevailed prior to the Emancipation Proclamation. At St. Joe, Wm. Knight saw a Negro boy sold at auction for $700. John Dalton refers to a "Darkey" runaway at Papin's Ferry who asked permission to join his company. Castleman lists "Churchill's slaves" among his company, while Theodore Potter refers to his "two colored servants." Free Negro emigrants (frequently victims of cholera) are mentioned also by J. E. Brown, Montgomery, Thurber, and others. These people did their share, and more, of trail labor, and Isaac Pettijohn pointed out that all emigrants had the same color at the end of the day—that of the universal brown dust.

EMIGRANT STYLES

There was, of course, no standard emigrant costume, but prevailing styles may be noted. John Wyeth, an early bird along the trail (1832), wore "coarse woolen jacket, a striped cotton shirt, cowhide boots." In 1843 W. C. Kennerly's party of sportsmen to the Rockies wore "flannel shirts, corduroy trousers, heavy boots and spurs." In 1846 J. M. Shively advised: "Let each man and lad be provided with five or six hickory shirts, one or two pair of buckskin pantaloons, a buckskin coat or hunting shirt, two very wide brimmed hats wide enough to keep the mouth from the sun. For the want of such hat thousands suffer nearly all the way to Oregon, with their lips ulcerated, caused by sunburn. Take enough coarse shoes or boots to last you through—three or four pair a piece will be sufficient."

When the Forty-Niners exploded on the scene, some strange specimens turned up. At St. Joe, Dr. Lord exclaimed, "Imagine to yourself a biped five feet four inches high, with big whiskers, red mustachios, steeple-crowned hat, buckskin-coat, done up with hedge-hog quills, belt, pistol, hatchet, bullet pouch, bowie knife 20 inches long, red shirt . . . and five-inch spurs. . . . it seems to me that the boys take pains to make themselves ridiculous."

Dandified military or buckaroo-type outfits, complete with wicked-looking cutlery and firearms, were plentiful enough. But most of the men, who were unpretentious young fellows from farms and villages, wore plainer, utilitarian garb. They might make a concession to vanity with a loud red flannel shirt (Ferris, Cooke) or "a pair of boots with a half moon and some stars" (Lowe), but most wore drab hickory or butternut shirts, stout homespun pants or jeans, and wool hats. These wool hats were rather shapeless; cowboy-style Stetsons did not figure in the Gold Rush. Delos Ashley's wardrobe consisted of "one strong winter suit, with a change of drawers, shirts and sox." As the emigrant trudged westward he had a real problem keeping himself in shoe leather. Sometimes Indian moccasins proved to be a happy alternative to going barefoot (Porter).

Gentleman adventurers like Fitz Hugh Ludlow might turn up with a "broad slouch hat of finest felt . . . blue flannel all-weather shirt, stout pantaloons of gray cheviot, tucked in knee boots . . .

and light loose linen sack over all." Gelwicks mentioned an over-coat, but for protection against the elements it was more the custom to wrap oneself in a wool or india rubber blanket, like a Spanish serape. Outer coats of india rubber or gum are mentioned also (Gould, Longsworth), but these early style raincoats did not prove impervious to the drenching prairie rains (McCoy).

Insight into feminine apparel is given by Lavinia Porter: "I started out with two blue cloth travel dresses with an array of white collars and cuffs, scorning advice about homespun and linsey woolsey. . . . These were soon discarded. . . . Fortunately I had with me some short wash dresses which I immediately donned, tied my much betrimmed straw hat up in the wagon, put on a big shaker sun-bonnet and my heavy buckskin gloves, and looked the ideal emigrant woman." Lavinia discarded her old worn-out hoop skirt, which was immediately appropriated and worn with pride by a huge Indian brave.

Swimsuits were quite unheard of during the Great Migration, but Lucy Cooke confides that when she went bathing in the Platte River she wore "a flannel gown for a bathing suit." Such modesty was not emulated by Randall Hewitt and his companions, who bathed in "a secure little cove" opposite Chimney Rock. "Our suits," explained Hewitt, "were bare skin."

Many of the girls, like Mrs. Porter, left St. Joe or Council Bluffs in their Sunday best. Near Chimney Rock, Sarah Herndon says she dug down in her trunks for finery to make social calls on her sister campers. But these fashionable garments, if worn, were soon reduced to tatters and, if stored, were likely to be thrown out as excess baggage.

The big fashion note of the California Gold Rush was ladies' bloomers, a kind of Turkish pantaloon popularized by an early advocate of women's rights, Amelia Bloomer, who in the sixties, according to Randall Hewitt, was herself a resident of Council Bluffs. Mary Warner rejected this garment, saying she was brave enough to cross the Plains but not brave enough to wear bloomers! John Bonner was repelled by what he saw in Council Bluffs and condemned all Bloomer girls as "ugly women in breetches." But outlandish as they appeared, they were immensely more practical than the long skirts and dresses that collected dust and mud and were quickly torn to ribbons on the trail (H. Thompson). The prevalence of bloomers among emigrant women is attested to by

Marie Nash, Lucy Cooke, Theodore Potter, and by Ezra Meeker, who has the last word on Great Plains apparel:

> Of the fortitude of the women one cannot say too much. Embarrassed at the start by the follies of fashion, they soon rose to the occasion and cast false modesty aside. Long dresses were quickly discarded and the bloomer donned. Could we but have had the camera trained on one of those typical camps, what a picture there would be. Elderly matrons dressed almost like little girls of today. The younger women were rather shy in accepting the inevitable but finally fell into the procession, and we soon had a community of women wearing bloomers. Some of them went barefoot, partly from choice and in some cases from necessity.
>
> The same could be said of the men, as shoe leather began to grind out from the sand and dry heat. Of all the fantastic costumes, it is safe to say the like was never seen before. The scene beggars description. Patches became visible upon the clothing of preachers as well as laymen; the situation brooked no respect of persons. The grandmother's cap was soon displaced by a handkerchief or perhaps a bit of cloth. Grandfather's high crowned hat disappeared as if by magic. Hatless and bootless men became a common sight. Bonnetless women were to be seen on all sides. They wore what they had left or could get, without question as to the fitness of things. Rich dresses were worn by some ladies because they had no others; the gentlemen drew upon their wardrobes until scarcely a fine unsoiled suit was left.

Whatever their garments, a few weeks on the trail altered appearances drastically. Delano refers to the Great Migration as "the great unwashed and unshaved." "Old Boone" reports to his editor from ninety miles west of St. Joe that "we can present a fine array of whiskers and tanned faces." Apparently some emigrants took the trouble to shave, at least in the early stages, but according to J. L. Johnson: "Most do not shave, and present a savage appearance." By the time he reached the Platte, Dr. McCollum said his hands had the color of brown mud and were "rougher than a hemlock board."

What about hygiene on the Oregon Trail? Since in most cases it was primitive back home, it must have been more so along the Platte, with the Plains grass and the murky river water serving most purposes. Marie Nash washed her feet in Plum Creek at noon and bathed in the Platte by moonlight, but other examples of forthright cleanliness are hard to find. Henry Coke claims he bathed once a week, but concedes that "not one man in 20,000 washes his face once a month," explaining that "as to appearances, they are no object here." The Hollywood concept of clean-shaven, square-jawed young men and fragrant young ladies with cheeks abloom does not seem to square with the facts.

EMIGRANT CHARACTER

Emigrants generally were of good character, with strong moral convictions and a firm faith in God. It took resolution of high quality to take the wilderness plunge in the first place, and it took more of the same to see it through. Although some diaries, like newspapers today, are apt to focus more on the unpleasant and the sensational, there is ample evidence of the high caliber of the majority.

Dr. E. A. Tompkins gives a rundown on the character of his fellow travelers, making out all but himself to be fools or villains; but when he donned a halo and magnified others' faults, he distorted human nature. The real heroes of the migration were its fine leaders, most unknown and unsung, but of the quality of Peter Burnett in 1843; or Pritchard, Dr. Lord, or J. G. Bruff in 1849; or Dr. Knox in 1850. James Evans summed it up properly: "Safety consists not in numbers but in a few of the right kind of men," who could meet a crisis with calm courage. With all the opportunities for cowardice, cheating, and averting the gaze from human suffering, Katherine Dunlap saw "many instances of manly generosity." McIlhany asserted, "When the emigrants found a man who had lost his property, they would help him out." Howe said that company organizers made every effort to "select men of good character," and that altogether the group he was writing about (Massachusetts) "represented the best and the manliest in the Bay State." Many instances are noted of charity toward unfortunate strangers, such as comforting or taking aboard the widows and orphans, the injured, and the destitute (Hambly, Cutting, Snodgrass). Although cholera frequently caused panic, there were many heroes during the plague. In 1852 Theodore Potter's train volunteered to bury six members of one family and to rescue the only surviving child.

Rev. Joseph Williams, Charles Kirkpatrick, and Mrs. Ferris deplored the vulgarity and profanity to which they were exposed, but wrestling with oxen and mules, warding off hailstones, and crossing rivers without benefit of bridges would wilt the spirit of a saint. Profanity was probably a well-nigh universal release from pent-up frustrations and cannot be viewed as an index of the essential strength of character required for trail survival. The moral quality of the later emigrants seems to have slipped a notch or two, becoming "more mixed," according to Packard, while Catherine Haun speaks of certain "undesirables." Whatever the year, the devil came out of hiding after the first few weeks of trial by tribulation. It must be assumed that most defects of character which were exposed were those which anyone might be guilty of under similar circumstances.

The simple exhaustion of travel over a wilderness road was a factor. Fatigue might induce sleep instantly, as it did in Delano: "A hyena might have tugged at my toes without awaking me." Or it might just leave everyone, as Goldsmith reports, "too tired for anything but smoking and talking," while some, like Dow Stephens, were content to sit still and nurse their tortured feet, or their rheumatism. But the same exhaustion and quivering nerves could lead to bickering and quarreling. Jacob Snyder says, "Quarrels in camp are a frequent occurrence. Here men display their true character." John McCoy says, "Friction is unavoidable and grumblers can easily find material for complaint." Dr. Tompkins found opportunity for "a thousand frivolous collisions with his fellows." Delano puts it this way: "A mean streak will come out on the Plains." N. A. Cagwin cautions a man when he "gives vent to his spleen" or "fans the spirit of discord."

Some days were worse than others. Wm. Lampton finds everyone in his train peeved at one another because of a late start. Martha Moore, on the other hand, says that her outfit "got into camp late. . . . Everybody mad as usual." The next day, she confesses: "Laid over to wash. I don't believe I was ever so tired in all my life. I am so sore all over I can scarcely move."

Sometimes the quarrels got beyond words. Fist fights were frequent. Wrote Henry Shombre: "Had a fight in the evening . . . had a court-martial . . . the sentence was an admonition by Captain W—— and punishment for the next offense." At the Kansas River, Wm. G. Johnston noted: "Fist fight came off this evening between two members of Captain Kirkuff's mess. [The man who] provoked the quarrel . . . was rewarded with rings around his eyes bearing a strong resemblance to ebony goggles." L. A. Norton had to regain his prestige at Shell Creek by thrashing a man who had badgered him along the trail. James Evans on the Little Blue came upon evidence of "a company that got into a fight among themselves. . . . burnt fragments of wagons, stoves, axes, etc., with a great quantity of harness cut to pieces; and with a quantity of torn shirts, coats, hats, etc. all besmeared by blood."

William Clayton of the Mormon Pioneers speaks of one mean fellow who stole grub. But human weakness could take more sinister forms, as in the abandonment of fellow human beings. Several instances are noted. Joseph Ware, the guidebook writer, was abandoned to die east of Fort Laramie. Kilgore reports a cholera sufferer abandoned by a company which also fenced off some precious grass "selling at $300 a ton." Staples and others mention several mortally sick and injured left by their companions with the Fort Laramie post surgeon (which was better than leaving them alone on the trail, of course). J. L. Johnson describes the drowning of two men in the Kansas River, while their companions trudged on, not looking back, pretending not to hear their calls for help. J. H. Clark notes that men "get very hard on the Plains" and are "callous to burials."

Exhaustion and hardship, cholera and accident all took their toll. But it would be a distortion to emphasize this seamy aspect of the Great Migration. Many found the experience, at least in its early stages, a challenge. Says Cagwin: "We begin to think Jourdon a long and hard road to travel but we murmur not. We have enlisted heart and hand for the whole campaign. Our nearves and muscles fully braced for anything that may rise up or seem to oppose our onward march." Writing from Chimney Rock, Old Boone lists a peck of troubles, including a cold northwester, no wood, whiskey dwindling, and a division of the company. "Yet, in general," he reports, "we were a jolly crowd and laughed heartily at each other's experiences, and cheered our lowering spirits by bright prospects ahead." Lodisa Frizzell's party had some fun when her husband shot an abandoned sheep and claimed it was antelope meat. She was glad for "something to joke and laugh about . . . for it is seldom you meet with anything for merriment, on this journey."

The biggest ally of morale was good health, and those who were not ruined by overloads or overtaken by cholera were apt to discover new horizons within themselves. Observed Benjamin Ferris: "In a well-regulated train, the pleasant excitements far outbalance all the inconveniences. There is a freedom and elasticity of mind . . . all the buoyancy of a boy liberated from the school-room." There are several other testimonials:

> My health has improved. . . . I can now stand four times the work I could two months since.—RILEY SENTER

> I do not feel any ill effects from exposure, for I have never experienced better health than when out on the prairies.—JOHN McCOY

> I like this way of living and it agrees with me. I am very much sun burnt but am getting as fair and rosy-cheeked as a country girl. . . . we are all in good health I never enjoyed better health than I have had since I have been on the Plains.—BOLIVAR KREPPS

> I have now been out 47 days and nites, sleeping with no covering but blankets, and the sky above me for a shelter, living most of the time on buffalo meat. . . . I never enjoyed better health than I do now.—ANDREW GOODYEAR

The full spectrum of human emotions could be found along the Platte River Road. On the one extreme there was grief and agony of spirit; on the other, the exhilaration of high animal spirits. This expressed itself most vividly in the ability the emigrants frequently showed in entertaining themselves or celebrating despite the fatigues of the day. Often a campsite was cleared for dancing (Thompson, Frizzell) with violin, tambourine, and flute among available instruments (Geer, H. Kingman). Wilkinson describes a minstrel show near Fort Kearny, featuring two fiddlers. Bryan Dennis describes a songfest which ended with a dance: "The Linn Ct. Co. camped close by. They gave us a splendid serenade. . . . After the singing the men felt like walking twenty miles and concluded to have a French Four with Cotillion, formed a ring and chose their partners. . . . the way the prairie grass suffered was a sight."

The Fourth of July found most emigrants somewhere between Chimney Rock and South Pass. Wherever they were, they joyously gave the day over to a patriotic celebration, or a "grand blow-out," as Goldsmith phrased it. This took various forms—oratory, marching, firing rifles, breaking out hoarded delicacies for a feast, and, of course, the proud display of the stars and stripes. If there was any whiskey left after the rigors of river crossings, it was apt to be requisitioned in the name of George Washington and toasts drunk to all the patriotic patron saints. (Dr. Flint was a killjoy; invoking future emergencies, he refused to permit his men to open a cask of medicinal spirits.) A typical Fourth of July was that of Simon Doyle: "We had a barbecue, tapped a keg of good old brandy, and all hands got gentlemanly tite." The men in Virginia Ivin's party climaxed their observances by rolling a wagon off the top of a high cliff.

EMIGRANT RELIGION

Religion played a large role in the Great Migration, for the majority of pilgrims were devout churchgoers. The local minister prayed over departing gold-seekers, and sometimes his zeal inspired him to join them. Dozens of preachers of the gospel hit the trail, though whether to keep watch over their wandering flock or to better their own fortunes, none can say. Of the New England companies, Howe says they marched to their church in a body: "No regiment in Cromwell's Ironsides ever went to battle with Bibles or more religious instruction than the California companies of 1849." Beset by cholera out on the hostile Plains, John Wood proclaims, "Religion is all that sustains us," and he is convinced that this is true, he says, even though "I know no more about the great Naniboujou than a hog knows about metaphysics."

A man could take his religion or leave it alone six days a week, but it was on the seventh day that he had to declare himself. Whether to observe the Sabbath or not was a perennial issue among the emigrants, and few were neutral on this burning topic. "'Keeping the Sabbath" meant having religious observances and keeping worldly activities to a minimum. Translated into trail terms, this meant that the wagon train should be halted for the day with sermons, prayers, and meditations the only legitimate activities. Such observances were built into company constitutions, and, although the regulation was one of the most violated, some devout companies did achieve the ideal, including those of Goldsmith, Cagwin, Bloemker, and Inez Parker. The Mormons, of course, were models in this regard; but it must be confessed that the majority of travelers, overwhelmingly Protestant in their faith, were not quite equal to living the Biblical tenets.

The great difficulty was that the spiritual goal was so often out-weighed by considerations that were not merely practical but necessary to survival. While no one disagreed that periodic rest was needed by men and teams, it didn't always work out that Sunday was the right day. True, Ware's guidebook piously exhorted, "Never travel on the Sabbath, and you will get to California 20 days sooner," and with the gift of hindsight Delano proclaims, "Were I to make the trip again, I would take care to stop every 7th day, if not for scruples of conscience, certainly for dictates of humanity." But often there were plain facts which argued for exceptions to the rule. Thus, Pigman, on the Little Blue: "Sunday, intended to lay by, but grass of no account so go 18 miles." The Phoebe Judson party normally rested on Sunday, but were prevented from doing so by alkali water west of Ash Hollow. The principal prod, of course, was the time limit, the need to cross the Sierra Nevadas before snow fell. Many captains insisted on moving when travel conditions were right, Sunday or not, since they were held up all too often on weekdays by storms. The Sabbath, like overloading, was a rock on which many companies split asunder.

The bylaws of the Wisconsin Blues read: "We will observe the Sabbath Day by laying in camp when circumstances permit." But the devout quarreled with the practical over these "circumstances." Elisha Lewis roundly condemned his leader for transgressing "the laws of God and our constitution" by moving on Sunday. Rev. Hinds deplored "'that he could not get a majority of his company to enforce the Sabbathe." L. Sawyer's party voted each week on the matter and usually decided to rest that day except when absolutely necessary to travel. "The General" boasted, "While I commanded, we would not travel that day," but he was voted out of office for his obstinacy. Martha Moore exclaimed, "This is Sunday but we observe no Sabbath here. May the heavenly Father remember his erring children in mercy!" Decker said he "remonstrated with the Captain against travelling on the Sabbath but to no purpose. . . . No Sabbath is observed on the Plains!"

Decker was wrong. The Sabbath was observed widely on the Plains, but in most cases not with the rigidity expected by those who took the Bible literally. A very practical approach to the matter was taken by the Haun party of 1849. "When the camping was desirable enough to warrant it we did not travel on Sabbath. Although we were generally busy mending wagons, harness, yokes, shoeing animals etc., and the women washed clothes, boiled a big mess of beans, or perhaps mended clothes . . . all felt somewhat refreshed on Monday AM. . . . If we had devotional services the minister pro tem stood in the center of the corral while we all kept busy on with our work. There was no disrespect intended."

Religion was important to Lucy Cooke, who in 1852 attended all the church meetings she could find, including one on the site of present downtown Omaha: "It being Sunday, preaching was announced at 4 O'clock. The majority of us, about 80, attended. The serman by a Mr. Shafer, was a rather poor effort, but the novelty of our surroundings, I guess, absorbed all our effort. . . . Indians seen skulking in the bushes." And again, "Today we laid by, Pa having resolved not to travel on Sunday unless compelled." It is significant, however, that while the Cooke train stopped every Sunday, by the time they reached Fort Laramie they had overtaken other Omaha trains "which had not observed the Sabbath." Who was to say that the spiritual and the practical had to be separated?

Most emigrants took the liberal view that stopping on Sunday was necessary for purposes of recuperation, but whether there was a sermon or whether time was spent in more worldly pursuits was optional. Loud, however, were the denunciations by those who took the Fundamentalist view. George Short observed his colleagues shoeing horses, hunting, and "doing the washing." He protested, "It is not necessary to do so. . . . May God have Mercy on their souls." Delos Ashley also railed at those "irreligious scamps" who did not attend services but spent the day "washing kerchiefs, shooting at marks and scribbling." The thunderous voice of conscience sounds much more convincing when the moralists condemn such practices as gambling, drinking, and merrymaking in general. And it seems that the Emily Horton train had a better grasp of theological niceties. She said, "We would lay by a day every 8 or 10 days, where it was favorable," thus resting according to the dictates of geography rather than the Old Testament. On Sundays God could be served with a prayer as the emigrants traveled westward.

EMIGRANT CRIME

From television shows one gains the impression that lawlessness was rampant during the Great Migration. Impressed by the scenes that he beheld at St. Joe in 1849, C. G. Hinman took this jaundiced view: "A large majority of the Californians are desperate fellows and they practice most all kinds of crime." Actually, while violence flourished in the hectic atmosphere of the border towns, the incidence of crime along the Platte was low, much lower for the floating population of some 350,000 over a period of some twenty years than in many American cities of comparable population today in one year. The usual human weaknesses aside, emigrants were subjected to extremes which tested to the limit their endurance and fortitude. Under the circumstances, the vast majority behaved admirably. There were no civil laws, no marshals or sheriffs to protect those who crossed the Plains, and the degree of protection offered by the military was severely limited. The only effective law was the inward sense as well as the outward form of justice habitually observed by the emigrants. Under trail circumstances this informal justice was sometimes brutal, sometimes fickle, but its unseen presence doubtless served as a powerful deterrent.

There are few documented cases of theft and felony. A sprinkling of desperados among a vast migration would be expected, with predictable results. "Buckskin Mose" reported the discovery of horse thieves who were expelled from his train. The appropriation of stray livestock in all innocence would be difficult to distinguish from genuine theft. That there were actual thieves abroad appears from the report of correspondent W. R. R.: "There is a tribe of white Indians upon these plains at this time that are more dangerous than Pawnees. They carry on horse and mule stealing pretty extensively and even oxen do not escape their attention. One of these gentlemen who had been caught was undergoing trial yesterday evening."

Louisa Sweetland reported the armed robbery of emigrants by other white men. Robbery was sometimes accompanied by murder. Francis Sawyer's party of 1852 found a man's still-warm body in a ravine. He had been murdered for his money, and the slayer had disappeared. Richard Hickman and others noted on the Little Blue the grave of a murdered man: "'All his clothes were burnt with the exception of his shirt. . . It had quite a number of holes in it, where he had been shot and stabbed, and it was all covered with blood." James Evans reported the fate of a boy orphaned by his father's drowning in the Kaw River and left with two renegade Dutchmen: "'There is no doubt in the world [they] killed the boy last night and threw him in the river for the sake of getting the wagon and team!"

Contrary to the impression left by novelists and scenario writers, sex crimes were not commonplace in covered wagon days. Although the relative scarcity of women on the Trail might seem to contribute to such crimes, this is not borne out by available evidence. Alonzo Delano speaks of one emigrant whose wife received a "gross insult" while he was out rounding up cattle. David Staples reports that Fort Laramie deserters "robbed an emigrant of $200 and ravaged his wife," but these are isolated cases. Two authentic examples of a California Trail "triangle" have been found, the first reported in 1849 by Dr. Ormsby at the headwaters of the Platte, where a jealous husband "got a notion in his head that the familiarity that existed between Mr. L. and his wife was greater than the nature of the case warranted," made accusations, and was shot for his trouble. The offending third party was "arrested" by neighboring emigrants, barely escaped a flogging, and was abandoned on the trail without arms or equipment. The second case appears in the 1854 journal of a German emigrant, H. Hoth, who deplored the fact that his "wife's old love affair with . . . the tailor seems to have started all over again." In camp at Chimney Rock, he confided, "'Late at night I again had a quarrel with my wife on account of the tailor, and I beat him so his eyes were blackened and his right arm lamed." As nearly as can be determined from the difficult German script, this affair seems to have terminated without further violence.

While it was no crime for young people to fall in love on the Oregon Trail, as elsewhere, this activity could result in serious trouble to judge from a Kansas grave marker observed by Littleton in 1850: "Wm. Wilkerson, 19, killed by a man for making too free with his daughter." In 1852 Addison Crane's party came upon a corpse mutilated with knife and buckshot wounds. While providing a decent burial, they speculated on the motive. The most common motive of covered wagon murders was not robbery but unleashed antagonisms, small personal matters greatly magnified. These clashes often led to open combat, with fatal results. A classic case is described by John Steele:

> Two men who prepared their outfit in company at Independence, had frequent quarrels in regard to their traveling and camping arrangements. Going into camp near Chimney Rock, the quarrel was renewed. . . . in the heat of passion, they drew out their hunting knives and closed in mortal combat. In a few minutes one fell and almost instantly died; the other, fainting from loss of blood, was carried in the shade

of a tent where, within an hour, he too expired; and with the grim irony of fate, at sunset they were laid side by side in the same grave.

When there was a survivor of one of these lethal duels, it was a tossup whether he would get off scot-free or suffer a penalty. In 1852 Cole witnessed the deliberate murder of a wagon-owner by a man he had befriended. In this case the murderer was surrounded by friends, and there was no prosecution. Sometimes the murderers would be punished lightly, simply by being expelled from the train, with or without equipment. However, if their deed was known along the trail they would be ostracized. At Fort Laramie Dr. Ormsby received a petition from such a man to join his train, but he was rejected. "The murderer doubtless thought he had got ahead of the report, but I happened to get wind of it—charged him with murder—he owned it, mounted his horse and put forward."

A grim, little-known facet of the migration was the drumhead trial and execution of murderers. It is questionable whether these extralegal proceedings should be classified as lynchings or an extension of Anglo-Saxon justice. At least twelve occurrences of this kind are noted. In 1850 near Court House Rock, Joseph Rhodes observed: "Today one mess had a fracus. One man stabbed another and it it thought he will die before Monday. Monday he is to be tried. It is thought that they will hang or shoot him if the man dies."

We don't know how this affair came out, but we do know that several prompt executions did take place. Francis Sawyer reports thus on one man who bludgeoned a mess-mate and "was hung to a tree by the indignant emigrants," apparently in this case with no semblance of a trial. But a trial of sorts was the usual thing. The speed of these transactions is suggested by Gould: "Young shot Scott dead. The company had a trial and found him guilty. They gave him a choice to be hung or shot. He preferred being shot, and was forthwith." Inquiring about two graves near Fort Laramie, John Dalton was informed that "Tate had killed Miller while his brother and Miller were fighting, stabbing him with a knife and cutting his throat," whereupon Tate was then strung up by his company. Further on were two more fresh graves "where Horace Dolly had killed Charles Botsford yesterday by shooting, and for which the company killed said Dolly today, by hanging. Said Dolly had a wife and two children."

The ruthlessness of these reprisals was blood-chilling. At Council Bluffs a Missouri teenager, who was suspected and tried for an ax-murder, received a unanimous verdict of guilty. Writes Henry Allyn: "He was delivered up to the emigrants, to take him to California or execute him on the spot. A resolution was offered to keep him till 10 AM Monday, in order to make his peace with God. . . . The resolution was lost and two hours was given him and he was hung on the limb of a basswood tree."

If trees were lacking, Yankee ingenuity supplied a solution. J. C. Moreland reports the fate of another prisoner of a covered wagon court near Green River: "'The next morning, just as the sun was breaking over the plains, two wagon tongues were run up in the air and fastened together, and from them he was hanged, and then buried by the side of the road." While impromptu justice or vigilante action of this sort may have been warranted in some cases, it is not evident that guilt was always established or that punishment was always deserved. Sometimes mob action of this sort, with a veneer of legality, created further injustice. Ezra Meeker tells of a man, accused of robbery and murder, who was hanged on the Sweetwater in 1852, leaving a wife and four little children. Although some protested the action, "the council would not be swerved from its resolution," but thoughtfully agreed "to insure the safety of the family by providing a driver to finish the journey."

Many consciences were disturbed by these summary proceedings, yet if "justice" was not done on a voluntary basis by fellow travelers, the only alternative was to turn the culprit over to the military. Actually the U.S. Army on the frontier had no defined civil jurisdiction; its primary mission was to protect the emigrants from the Indians rather than the emigrants from each other. No doubt officers on their own initiative occasionally attempted to adjudicate quarrels among transient civilians, and they probably took some trouble-makers into protective custody to sober them up after a drunken spree or, in cases of felony or murder, to deliver the culprit to civilian authorities in a border town.

Exceptions to the above appear in at least two instances where Fort Kearny officers were reported to have conducted civilian trials. The first, reported by Delano in 1849, was the case of the aggrieved husband whose wife received the "gross insult" noted earlier: "In a country where there was no law . . . he determined to protect his own honor, and raising his rifle, shot the scoundrel down. His companions took him back to the Fort (with his consent), where an investigation into the circumstances was made, and he was honorably acquitted." The second case is cited by Frank Young in 1865, when an ax-murderer on the Little Blue was brought in and turned over to the Fort Kearny commander; Young heard that "the accused chose death by shooting." There was probably substance to both cases, but if it is a fact that these civilian trials were actually held by the military, they were both unusual and illegal. Certain other instances more accurately reflect the awkward emigrant-military jurisdictional relationship. D. A. Shaw reports a shooting near Lone Tree, opposite Ash Hollow, which resulted in a trial; but the decision in this case was made "that the prisoner be taken to Fort Laramie and delivered up to the military authorities to be sent home for trial. . . . The prisoner made his escape before reaching Fort Leavenworth." In 1849 Eastin reports "a most painful and shocking affair," in which one man dangerously wounded another, "but it is doubtful if the military at Fort Laramie have civil jurisdiction. It was thought better to cut him loose where the deed was done. He now has to work out his own solution." In 1858 Wm. Lee reported a fight at Ash Hollow, with similar results:

> Shortly after coming to camp two of our men Potter and Tuckett had an altercation and T——t attempting to strike P——r with a spade he [Potter] stabbed him with his bowie knive inflicting severe wounds one being just below the apex of the heart. Tuckett is in a very precarious condition and is not expected to live until morning.
>
> July 21 . . . Poor Tuckett died last night. . . . Potter, after being tried by a drumhead courtmartial, was discharged from the train and started 188 miles from the nearest settlement (Fort Kearney) with his blankets strapped on his back.

In at least one case, cited by McBride, a thief was taken all the way to California to be turned over to a civil court (although no California court would have had legal jurisdiction over a crime committed in unorganized territory.)

DISEASE AND DEATH

While the journey up the Platte River Road may have been a joy and tonic for some, far too often it was an ordeal in which, after running the gauntlet of hardships, there arose the sinister threat of disease and death. No valid mortality tables, of course, are available. Writing from the perspective of 1866, Sarah Wisner calculated that from 1842 to 1859 there were 30,000 who died on the Plains, while during the peak Gold Rush years, graves between Fort Kearny and the head of the Platte River averaged one to every 200 feet. A more conservative figure is 20,000 for the entire 2,000 miles of California Trail, or an average of ten graves to each mile. Again assuming a grand total migration of 350,000 this averages one death for every seventeen persons who started.

Observing "scenes of desolation" along the Little Blue in 1850, Dr. Tompkins suggested that there were five contributing factors: (1) the high saline and alkaline content of the water; (2) eating fish; (3) the poor preparation of camp food, "often a perfect mass of indigestible filth too crude even for the stomach of an ostrich;" (4) chilly night watches and sleeping on cold, wet ground; and (5) the constant hard and exhausting toil. Although he presumably had little knowledge of germs and viruses, Tompkins probably touched on the main factors which made emigrants vulnerable to disease. Impure chemical water got most of the blame from other writers. As early as 1846 J. Q. Thornton said he was "unwell since coming upon the waters of the Nebraska, owing to mixed salts, glauber salts, alum and magnesia." Among other villains most often accused were boiled beans, rancid bacon, buffalo meat eaten after a chase, the lack of fruits and vegetables, and the all-pervasive, lung-choking dust.

Vaccination against disease was not unknown, but it was little practiced. (The only actual instance discovered is that of Lucy Cooke in 1852, whose two children were vaccinated on the steamer en route to St. Joe; one was "taken nicely," the other's arm was "terribly inflamed.") The normal precaution was to take along a medicine chest with an assortment of trusted home remedies for everything from baldness to the bubonic plague. Elizabeth Geer's inventory included "a box of physicing pills, a box of castor oil, a quart of best rum, and a vial of peppermint essence." The latter ingredient, combined with a glass of brandy, would, according to John King, cure most ills. Catherine Haun's portable apothecary shop included quinine for malaria, hartshorn for snakebite, citric acid for scurvy and blueness, and opium and whiskey for almost everything else. Laudanum, morphine, calomel, and tincture of camphor were other potent drugs frequently resorted to. Among name brands mentioned are Ayer's Pain Killer (Thissell), Dover's Powders (Lampton), and Jayne's Caminative Balsam (Snodgrass).

A popular belief was that tuberculosis, then called "consumption," would be overcome by outdoor exercise, and what better exercise than walking across the continent? An afflicted man in John Minto's train in 1844 started to Oregon "'to secure the life-preserving qualities of the country air," but soon died from "continuing dampness." On the other hand, William Case and Catherine Haun are among those who claim to have been so afflicted and so cured. The gamut of contagious diseases associated with childhood are indicated as causes of adult death on the Trail: whooping cough (Waters), measles (Short) or vareloid (Hickman), mumps (Vanderburgh), and smallpox (Kilgore). Other serious conditions often reported are "pneumonia or lung fever" (McBride) and malaria, identified also as "fever and ague" (Lowe). The common cold or its symptoms were much in evidence, but the most common among non-fatal afflictions were internal disorders variously identified as "derangements of liver or kidney" (Langworthy), "bilious complaints" (J. Ware), "inflammation of the bowels" (Biddle), "summer complaint" (Geer), "the ailment incidental to travel on the Plains" (McCoy), or just plain dysentery or diarrhea (spelled, of course, at least fifteen different ways). The most common symptom of this complaint is ruefully reported by David Staples: "Have been busy attending to the wants of nature," and he kept score on the number of side-trips he made from his train. Philura Vanderburgh's father had a standard remedy for this condition: "Fill saucer with brandy, sugar and mutton tallow."

Among miscellaneous sicknesses reported are "congestion of the brain" (Searls), delirium tremens (Anon.), hydrophobia (Hedges), bloody flux (Snodgrass), intestinal inertia (Cipriani), inflammatory rheumatism (Bradway), vertigo (Reading), and mountain fever (J. Stewart), the last possibly a western variant of dysentery. The agony of toothache, sometimes relieved by opium or amateur extractions, was another frequent phenomenon of the prairies.

All of these complaints and illnesses of the Great Migration pale into insignificance, however, beside the great killer Asiatic cholera. Variously spelled in diaries colory (E. Lewis), chollery (Stine), or coleramer (Shombre), this virulent plague raged intermittently along the Platte River Road and its approaches during the climax years of the California Gold Rush. It was carried by rats on ships

from Asiatic ports to New Orleans, thence by river steamer to St.
Louis and up the Missouri River to emigrant jump-off towns. Niles
Searls expressed the opinion that "the Gold Rush caused more
bereaved than the late Mexican War." Most of the fatalities were
from cholera, and most of these occurred between the Missouri
River and Fort Laramie. The following two scenes were typical:

> We pitched our tents but soon found we were in a distressed crowd.
> Many Oregon families. One woman & two men lay dead on the grass
> & some more ready to die of cholra, measels & small pocks. A few men
> were digging graves, others tending the sick. Women & children crying,
> some hunting medicine & none to be found scarcely; those that had
> were loathe to spare. With heartfelt sorrow we looked around for some
> time until I felt unwell myself. Ordered the teams got up & move
> forward one mile so as to be out of hearing of crying & suffer-
> ing.—JOHN CLARK, 1852, east of Big Blue Crossing

> We found that Amos Hinshaw was dying. He has the cholera morbus
> and measles set and took him right off. We feel that we have lost a
> friend who we highly prized. He died on Sunday at about 11 o'clock
> A.M. May 30, 1852. At about 4 P.M. same day we buried him about
> 12 or 13 miles East of Ft. Kearney on a little eminence in Platte
> River Bottom. . . . The epitaph on the walnut board at the head of
> his grave is "A Hinshaw of Clinton Co, Ohio, Died May 30, 1852,
> aged 32 years."—J. D. RANDALL

Forty-Niners were the first to feel what William Pleasants calls
"the sharpness of the monster's sting." The casualties on steamboats, and at Independence and St. Joe, were fearful, but the disease,
which Charles Kirkpatrick calls "the ruthless destroyer," followed
the emigrants out on the Plains. "The road from Independence to
Fort Laramie is a graveyard," McCollum wrote, and he put the
number of burials at 1,500 to 2,000, which would be an overall
mortality rate of 6 per cent. But some large trains lost two-thirds
of their number (Foster), and several instances are found of children
orphaned or entire families wiped out, their wagons abandoned
like ships without rudders (Goldsmith).

The fearful scourge was repeated in 1850. Langworthy places
the number of cholera victims that year at "more than 1,000," while
Ezra Meeker conjectures 5,000. Accepting a figure of 2,500 an
average of four graves to a mile between St. Joe and Fort Laramie
gives credence to the assertion of Abraham Sortore that along the
Platte he was "scarcely out of sight of grave diggers." Reaching

Fort Laramie in mid-June, Micajah Littleton counted over 130 graves (mostly fresh, but a few from 1849) between that point and Ash Hollow; but, since he was at the midpoint of the migration wave, there would be many more dug that season. Carlisle Abbott has it that in 1850 the cholera "struck like a cyclone on both sides of the Platte," but Rev. Hinds and Franklin Langworthy emphasize that while cholera raged along the south side of the Platte, the north side was relatively immune. Thissell reports south-side emigrants crossing the Platte at Ash Hollow to escape the epidemic.

In 1851 casualties were light; on his journey Daniel Bacon found but one fresh grave and "little sickness on the Plains this year." But in 1852 the Asiatic cholera was loose again. J. H. Clark "passed camps every day waiting for someone to die." West of Ash Hollow he found three men returning who were the only ones left out of a party of seventeen. Again the scourge seemed to be worse on the south side, but this soon changed. Jared Fox on the Council Bluffs Road observed: "Plenty of teams, miles of them, on the other side in sight, and many crossing and some drowning in the attempt. . . . The cholera is raging on the south side of the Platte at a dreadful rate and all were hustling over to try to escape it . . . but now they are falling on this side." Ezra Meeker, also on the north side, found it healthful on that side until opposite Fort Kearny, and here "the epidemic struck our moving column where the throngs from the south side of the Platte began crossing." From that point on, says Meeker, it looked like a battlefield: "The dead lay sometimes in rows of fifties or more. . . . Crowds of people were continually hurrying past us in their desperate haste to escape the dreadful epidemic." This impression of disaster is echoed by Richard Hickman, opposite Court House Rock: "We done some good travelling, for we were in the midst of sickness, pain and death, and thought if we could manage to out travel the bulk of immigration we would not be so much exposed to the cholera, measles and smallpox, which is scattered along the road." Cholera persisted through the fifties, but it had passed the peak by 1853.

Several curious facts emerge about the Destroyer of the Great Migration. Children were orphaned, but children themselves seemed to be relatively immune to the California Trail variety of cholera. Kimball Webster noted that emigrants from Missouri, the state most heavily represented, suffered the highest casualties. There is little pattern to the geographical distribution of cases from the

river to Fort Laramie, except for their prevalence on the south side
prior to 1852. "Beyond Fort Laramie," says Lowe, "the sickness
abates," and many attributed this to the drier air and higher altitude. Carlisle Abbott noted that in 1850 a blizzard seemed to
check the disease. To George Hearst, "it seemed that the cholera
was worse while it was raining," while Dr. Caldwell (who later
himself died on the trail) thought that cholera was greater *after* a
spell of wet weather. Although some who contracted the disease
lingered for many days, it usually struck suddenly, and often the
victim was dead within hours, usually after "great agony" (Chapman). Diarrhea was such a common forerunner of cholera (Benson)
that many emigrants speak of death by cholera or diarrhea as if
they were synonymous (Ebey, Crane). Sore throat, vomiting, and
bowel discharge seemed to be the most common symptoms. Efforts
to stamp out the plague were sometimes made by burning clothes or
wagons of the deceased (R. C. Shaw, Duniway). Not all cases were
necessarily fatal. John Scott and Wm. Pleasants indicate high recovery rates of the afflicted in their trains. An illuminating account
of cholera symptoms and treatment is given by Dr. Lord of New
York:

> The cholera is a rapidly fatal disease, when suffered to run its
> course unrestrained, & more easily controlled then most diseases when
> met in time. . . . It commences with diarrhoea in every case. A single
> dose of laudanum, with pepper, camphor, musk, ammonia, pepper-
> mint or other stimulants usually effect a cure in a few minutes. If
> pain in the bowels was present, another dose was required. If cramp
> in the calves of the legs had supervened, a larger dose was given. If
> skin had become cold, and covered with sweat (which did not happen
> unless the disease had run several hours or days) the doses were fre-
> quently repeated until warmth was restored. The medicines were
> aided by friction, mustard plasters, and other external applications.
> If to all these symptoms vomiting was added, there was no more to
> be done. Vomiting was the worst symptom, and every case proved
> fatal where vomiting, purging, cramp and cold sweating skin were
> present. . . .

An impressively large number of medical men joined the Gold
Rush and so were present to help combat the plague. Many large
trains made a point of having a doctor or surgeon along, and many,
like Dr. Lord, themselves kept journals. (Among the more notable
are those of Drs. Knox, Flint, Crane, Dalton, Pleasants, and Brad-

way.) Most doctors performed heroically, some succumbing to the disease themselves. In keeping with their Hippocratic oath, most doctors were available to assist victims in other trains (Sawyer) and probably, like the physicians commended by John Benson, "declined payment," but Wm. Frush reports a Dr. Brown who was all business and charged $2 to treat cholera. In an age when medical ethics were ill-defined, it is not surprising to find at least two traveling doctors who advertised their services. Francis Sawyer noted signs posted at intervals for a "J. Morely, Physician and Surgeon." Helen Carpenter was indignant at a Dr. J. Nobles, who daubed his name in red paint on several grave markers.

While families might grieve, the attitude of emigrants generally toward their fallen associates underwent gradual change as they moved westward. If death occurred during the first few weeks out, as along the Blue River, there might be full-dress funeral services, as Henry Shombre, for example, reports of a dead companion: "He was placed in the coffin and conveyed by the herse followed by some 40 of his friends and neighbors," and after the burial there were "a few appropriate remarks and a prayor." J. G. Bruff and James Tate also report funeral ceremonies with processions and the fanfare of trumpets; but as the migration moved out along the Platte, and emigrants began to die in wholesale lots, the "spirit of gloom" gave way to a sense of panic with the realization that "Sierra snows were waiting" (E. Brooks), and burials and funeral services were performed perfunctorily, sometimes with indecent haste. Sometimes a company would encamp waiting for a stricken member to die; more often he would be carried along in a wagon, suffering with every jolt, "gradually yielding to the embrace of the monster" (Scarls). When death seemed imminent, some trains left "watchers" to wait for the end and provide burial; others simply abandoned hopeless cases along the roadside. Carlisle Abbott and Lucy Cooke cite cases of men digging graves within sight of a dying companion, while Elisha Brooks makes the horrible accusation that "some were buried before life was extinct." Helen Carpenter, herself a highly sensitive person, suggests that there was a numbing process of dehumanization in which emigrants along the Platte were "robbed of all sentiment." She noted one party using the exposed skull of a white man for target practice.

While isolated graves were the rule, there would be "many places with 12 to 15 graves in a row" (Webster), and Ezra Meeker

once counted 57 at one campground. Such clusters of graves—
virtual cemeteries—would most likely be at points of concentration
such as the crossings of the Big Blue and the South Platte and the
mouth of Ash Hollow. Montgomery, McIlhany, and Carpenter call
attention to well-worn side-paths that led to emigrant graves,
indicating that they were frequently visited by their contemporaries.
Bruff, Littleton, William Hampton, and John Clark of Virginia
are noteworthy among diarists of 1849–1852 who made it their
business not only to count the number of graves observed each day,
but to jot down inscriptions on headboards and tombstones. These
were usually limited to names and dates, but they often gave additional information on the cause of death and place of origin.

With the decimation of emigrants by cholera and similar mala-
dies, coupled with the high rate of accidental deaths, the trail to
California took on the resemblance of an elongated cemetery.
While one writer was exaggerating when he said that he "could
walk on emigrant graves for 300 miles," graves did become the
highway markers of the Great Platte River Road.

Ida McPherren says emigrants "had a horror of being buried
without a coffin," but this dismal piece of furniture was too cumber-
some to take along "just in case." While still within reach of
timber, along creeks in eastern Kansas, crude coffins could be constructed. Out on the Plains a "rude box" might be made by pirating
from tail gates or packing boxes, but this source was soon gone,
and the departed was fortunate if he was wrapped in so much as a
blanket. Another of Shombre's friends who died on the Little Blue
"was buried in his common cloaths, and placed upon a bed of
green bushes." What with the big hurry, and a shortage of spades
along the Platte, the deceased was likely to be buried not only
without coffin and without ceremony, but in sand so shallow that it
could scarcely be called a grave. Hasty burials would also result
in the settling of the loose soil, with a resultant pit instead of a
mound. Thissell reports one further example of Californian trail-
craft: six corpses buried in a common grave.

The gruesome results were predictable. The graves were
promptly invaded by wild animals. Succeeding emigrants were
greeted, not only with scattered bones, buttons, and bits of clothing,
but hands, feet, and various other parts of the human anatomy in
varying stages of decomposition, with "prairie wolves howling over
their loathsome repast" (Chamberlain). On one occasion, reports

David Cartwright, "While we were in the midst of a funeral service the coyotes were on a knoll about 60 rods from us, fighting and howling so dismally it was difficult to hear the preacher. They were doubtless in scent of the corpse, and in angry waiting for a chance to tear it to pieces." Horrified by the desecration and havoc wrought by wild animals, the emigrants experimented with methods of protecting the mortal remains, covering and lining the grave where possible with rocks (W. Bailey), stone slabs (Cartwright), or timbers. That these precautions were of little avail is evident in the journals of Walter Pigman and Emily Horton, who found that the ravenous prairie creatures were adept at tearing all graves apart or digging tunnels slantwise and underneath a grave if the improvised coffin proved unyielding. In 1853 Agnes Stewart philosophized about desecrated emigrant graves: "It seems a dreadful fate, but what is the difference? I would as soon not be buried at all as to be dug out of my own grave!"

In addition to the frequently inscribed headboard or headstone, there are occasional references to other grave markers such as elk horns, crude wooden crosses, and iron rims from wagon wheels. However, graves were not always marked. Polly Purcell recalled that Indians robbed emigrant graves. To forestall this practice, efforts were made to conceal graves by driving back and forth over them, in some cases going so far as to replace sod, prickly pear, and other vegetation. When this succeeded, the deceased was preserved, of course, but his last resting place was forever lost to posterity unless later plowed up by Kansas or Nebraska farmers or highway construction crews. In 1849 and later, Ellenbecker points out, Indians had a healthy respect for epidemics and left the graves to the mournful coyote.

In 1849 Capt. Stansbury found one marked grave which, "instead of containing the mortal remains of a human being, had been a safe receptacle for divers casks of brandy." J. G. Bruff understood also that "the emigrants had many semblances of graves, which were actually caches of goods." He describes one such "quondam grave" which "some cute chaps had opened up and emptied."

With some graves too shallow, some destroyed by animals, some deliberately concealed, and some faked, it is a wonder that any identifiable emigrant graves survive, but some do. Examples of these mute memorials are noted in later chapters.

ACCIDENTS

The Great Platte River Road was fraught with perils, but not all were the kind that the emigrants anticipated. Indians and wild animals there were aplenty, but as it often turned out, if left alone they were unobstrusive. The great dangers were disease and accident, with death always waiting. Except for sanitary precautions, which were then little known or understood, disease was perhaps unavoidable. But accidents were a built-in, do-it-yourself hazard. The safety record of the Great Migration was terrible.

Trail accidents could be classified, in descending order of magnitude, as shootings, drownings, crushing by wagon wheels, and injuries resulting from handling domestic animals. These were the four big causes of maimings and killings. All other discoverable causes combined, such as sharp instruments, falling objects, rattlesnakes, buffalo hunts, hail, and lightning, did not equal one of these four major causes.

The emigrants were walking arsenals, armed to the teeth with rifles, shotguns, and revolvers, supposedly used to hunt buffalo and defend themselves from Indians. More often what they managed to do was blast, wound, or annihilate themselves instead, and in alarming numbers. Firearms did not have the safety features that exist today. Shively warned, "Keep your gun in good order, but never have caps in them unless you are going to shoot; when you come in from the hunt be sure to take your cap off before you put your gun in the wagon. . . . flint locks are always dangerous, and should never be taken along." Many emigrants were strangers to their deadly weapons, and all underwent the fatigue which impairs judgment. A random sampling of the journals turns up at least fifty recorded cases of mutilation or death from accidental shootings.

Sometimes a man carelessly shot someone else, but more often himself. Sometimes he escaped with minor injury. One man bloodied his nose from a recoil (Earnshaw). While charging buffalo, another lacerated his thumb when it caught in the hammer of his revolver (Guill). In another case the bullet from a revolver was deflected by a rib (Staples). One man was blinded by a burst gun (Reading), another was disabled by a bullet in the shoulder (Tate), and several managed to cripple themselves in the foot or leg (Delano, Gould) and were compelled to complete the agonizing journey in a jolting springless wagon. Others were still less fortunate:

> Mr. S——in attempting to draw the gun out of the wagon accidentally cocked it and it went off, lodging the contents in Mr. Twiddie's knee.—EASTIN, 1849

> We found . . . Lafayette Dwitty, rolling in agony, and his clothes on fire. . . . Fears are entertained that amputation will be necessary, when we reach Fort Laramie. . . .—J. E. BROWN, 1849

> A man shot foolishly holding a target.—SEDGLEY, 1849

> Smith Dunlap of Chicago, shot accidentally while hunting cattle. . . . leaving wife and six small children.—ELIZABETH GEER, 1847

> A prankster in a buffalo robe crept up on the camp, alarmed the guard, and was almost killed.—BREYFOGLE, 1849

> Death of Nicholas Boisemus from the accidental discharge of his gun. . . . He uttered but a single, unintelligible exclamation.—GELWICKS, 1849

> An emigrant died near Scott's Bluffs. . . . his jaw was shot away when a loaded pistol fired from his breast pocket.—McBRIDE, 1850

> A young Jermin shot himself accidentally. . . . the ball passed through his breast and lodged against his shoulder blade. The poor fellow fell, rolled and hollowed. Bled like a hog. He lived but a few hours.—JOHN WOOD, 1850

"Shot himself accidentally" was the monotonous refrain on emigrant grave markers and the primary cause of accidental death. A close second were the drownings at the river crossings, the result of wagons or ferries tipping over, of some tired teamster getting snarled in harness, or of a fatigued hiker perishing in the cold water. Drownings were routine on the Kansas, the Blue, the South Platte, and the Laramie.

The big emigrant wagons were efficient when rolling forward with a load, but clumsy and inefficient when it was necessary to stop. From a variety of causes an impressive number of men, women, and children got caught in or fell under their monstrous wheels and (with some amazing exceptions) were mutilated or killed. Joel Hembree was the first to die in this manner on the Oregon Trail; his tragic death was followed by several dozen others. Children, falling out or thrown out of wagons by lurching teams, were the chief victims. If the load was light or the ground was soft or sandy, they might escape with bruises or broken bones (Langworthy, A. J. Ashley, Jewett, P. V. Crawford, Zilhart), but crushing and mangling by these giant rollers was the more common result. Reuben Miller records: "'Smith's child injured by team getting alarmed at a yoke of bulls, and the wheels of the wagon pressing its head." Gilbert Cole reports a little girl who died instantly under the wheels when her father whipped the team forward at a crossing. In 1846 Nicholas Carriger was horrified when "a boy fell under two wheels run over one leg and the other foot and ancle nearly cutting the leg off, breaking the bone." The child lingered a few days while the wound became gangrenous, then died while his leg was being amputated with crude instruments.

Fatigue and carelessness probably accounted for the wheel-crushing of adults. Women were frequently injured. Dr. Ormsby heard this report: "A woman had her head run over . . . but by some fortunate depression in the ground, she escaped with her life." One man's coattails caught in the spokes; he spent several weeks recuperating (Ferguson). Another got "entangled in the whiffletrees," but escaped with severe bruises (Buffum). Montgomery "had the misfortune to fall under a forewheel. . . . altho it did not fracture any bones it obliged me to ride in the wagon for about two weeks." At Fort Laramie in '49 Dr. Ormsby found three men in tents dying. One's wife hysterically explained: "Why sir, a wagon ran over his head; we thought he was dead, but he seems to be some better." As to the others, "the same wagon had run over both. One had been severely cut through the groin . . . lacerating everything to the arteries," and the wound was now crawling with maggots. "'The other had the wheel run square over his back, producing a partial paralysis of the lower extremities." All had been left to their fate by their companions.

Except for a broken bone or two suffered by overzealous buffalo hunters and a rare instance of rabies from wolf-bite (Larpenteur), emigrants found that the wild animals which abounded in the Plains were relatively harmless. The dangerous animals were the friendly beasts of burden. Not only did they rotate the wheels that crushed people, but when temperamental they committed mayhem on careless teamsters. Kicking mules fractured bones (Stine, Littleton) and lacerated scalps (Bradway). A man was crushed by a rolling horse (Mowry); a small boy tangled in a horse rope was dragged to his death (Angell). Commonplace were plunging horses, runaway teams, and stampeding herds that broke bones and caused dislocations and concussions (Dewolf, Lampton, Pettijohn).

Deaths from lightning are reported by Lydia Waters and Dr. Flint; no deaths, but serious injuries from hail are noted by Goldsmith and others. Rattlesnakes, curiously, seemed most often to attack Mormons, to judge from Clayton (1847) and Bermingham (1856). While there were no recorded deaths from this cause, Catherine Haun reports "an amputated ankle." Remarkably few cases are recorded of tenderfoot injuries from knives and axes. Woodward managed to gash his foot at Fort Laramie, while Keller reports a man from St. Joe who disabled himself with a hatchet "while pursuing a squirrel up a tree." Stephen Gage was "taken with a lame breast from hard lifting at the wheel," Gould sprained his back in a wrestling match, and Athearn suffered a cut scalp from a collapsing tent pole, while the captain of Mary Hayden's train "died from drinking alcohol." Generally speaking, however, one who could swim and had a healthy respect for firearms and wagon wheels had an excellent chance for survival—if he didn't get the cholera!

ROUGH WEATHER

Not least among hardships along the Platte and its approaches which none escaped were cold, dust, mud, and insects. The weather in April or May could be uncomfortably cold, and the meager supply of clothes and blankets which trainmasters allowed was sometimes inadequate. The J. Evans party was "chilled by a Nor'wester." Geo. Keller almost succumbed to snow and cold at California Crossing and had to be revived by a liberal intake of cognac. Caught in a snowstorm at the forks of the Platte, the Ferguson party "had to burn three wagons" to keep from freezing.

When the weather moderated, it was insect time, particularly along the river bottoms; and in an age when insect repellent was unknown, there were endless complaints on this score. On the Platte, Kimball Webster found "mosquitoes more plentiful here than I have ever seen before. I would judge there are more than 40 bushels of these pests to the acre." Opposite Chimney Rock, Louise Rahm wrote, "muskitoes almost eat me up. The children look like they had the measles." In the same locality, Nathaniel

Wyeth complained, "My face like a plum pudding. The skin is entirely off one of my ears." Seeking to avoid the mosquitos by the river, he found the "ghnats" on the bluffs equally troublesome. This latter species were the "buffalo gnats" which at times swarmed in great clouds. Geo. Holliday describes an attack on his company of soldiers by the "black galinippers." "Before we were aware of their presence," wrote Cornelius Cole, "these silent little fellows devoted their whole attention to us, as shown by our livid and swollen faces." Hewitt and Smedley contrived to make cheesecloth veils to protect themselves from the onslaught.

Mud and dust were twin evils. In low places during the rainy season the teams and heavy wagons would often bog down, requiring heroic exertion to free them, sometimes by "double-teaming," sometimes by all hands literally putting shoulders to the wheel. The reverse of the picture was the dry dust-cloud created by the passage of endless wagon trains.

Ezra Meeker writes: "The dust was intolerable. In calm weather it would rise so thick at times that the lead team of oxen could not be seen from the wagon. Like a London fog, it seemed thick enough to cut. Then again, the steady flow of wind . . . would hurl the dust and sand like fine hail, sometimes with force enough to sting the face and hands." Under these conditions, eye irritation and redness was a common condition. There were instances of temporary blindness resulting from exposure to dust. In 1866 James Meline observed the use of goggles—both green and blue— among stagecoach passengers, but no such refinement was available to the emigrants.

While road conditions were often annoying, weather was a terrible adversary. In the spring the Platte valley is often ravaged by violent storms, with results that can be disastrous even to modern communities. A covered wagon encampment suffered in greater degree. Amelia Knight's experience on the Council Bluffs Road was typical:

> May 17 we have a dreadful storm of rain and hail last night and very sharp lightning. It killed two oxen. . . . We had just encamped in a large flat prairie, when the storm commenced in all its fury and in two minutes after the cattle were taken from the wagons every brute was gone out of sight. . . . all gone before the storm like so many wild beasts. . . . The wind was so high I thought it would tear the wagons to pieces. Nothing but the stoutest covers could stand it.

The rain beat into the wagons so that everything was wet, in less than 2 hours the water was a foot deep all over our camp grounds. As we could have no tents pitched, all had to crowd into the wagons and sleep in wet beds, with their wet clothes on, without supper.

The swiftness with which these storms can develop can best be described by those who felt their wrath: "When a small black cloud appeared," says John Carr, "it was time to look out," for in a moment there opened up "the whole artillery of the heavens." And Daniel Gelwicks observed, "It is somewhat astonishing the little time it takes to get up a furious thunderstorm in the Platte Valley." It seemed to Charles Tuttle that most Platte River storms occurred at night, lending nightmarish terror to the scene.

The awful sublimity of the warring elements moved several witnesses to flights of rhetoric. Exclaimed Delano, "King Lear in the height of his madness would have been troubled to have got his mouth open to vent his spleen on such a night . . . a worse night than on which Tam O'Shanter outran the witches." In 1849 there seems to have been a succession of the thunderstorms for which the Platte is famous. Of one of these Thomas Eastin wrote, "The lightning flashed incessantly, making the rain far around appear like so many rich jewels, and the loud thunder roared terrifically, making the earth tremble under its power and rendering the scene one of the most majestic I ever beheld." In 1851 Daniel Bacon wrote his mother, "You may think it rains in Indiana but if you want to see it storm come to the Platte." In 1854 Edwin Bird encountered a storm which seemed to be "one constant blaze of lightning and roar of thunder. . . . Enough of the article was manufactured for home consumption and to spair to batter down the walls of Sebastopol." In 1859 Wm. Knight speaks of "the merciless fury of the worst storm which ever visited these plains," during which "hailstones came near knocking the daylights out of me." In 1866 stage passenger Gurdon Lester wrote, "The Platte bottoms look like one vast sea of water" as the result of storms which "rained and hailed as it does in no other place in the United States."

According to an article in the Smithsonian Annual Report for 1960, the biggest hailstones on record occurred at the city of North Platte in 1959. Hail insurance comes high in Nebraska today, indicating the emigrants were probably not exaggerating when they reported their encounters with what Julius Birge calls "the big ice bullets on the Platte." The size and velocity of hailstones may be gauged from the metaphors used in the journals: quail eggs (Pig-man), "larger than a turkey egg" (Bidwell), hens' eggs (Gage), musketballs (Townsend), hickory nuts (Searls), lemons (C. W. Smith), and apples (Flint). Louise Rahm's hail, "big as one's fist," knocked two men down, gashing their heads. E. S. Ingalls suffered cut lips and cheeks. In Niles Searls' train "Captain Turner was struck on the finger by a hailstone which dislocated the joint. Delos Ashley was "pelted to soreness." Kirkpatrick, out for a stroll, saw the storm coming but could not get back to the shelter of the wagon; so, he says, "We had to bow our heads and take it." In a real bruiser, wagon covers as well as tents were ripped and shredded, and crawling under a wagon bed was the only hope—unless the stock had stampeded and run off with that shelter. The casualties of one storm witnessed by Elias Draper were a stunned man and a woman with a miscarriage. Of a vicious hailstorm on the South Platte, James Lyon wrote: "All the wagon-covers looked as if they had been used during the Mexican War as a breastwork, or had received a shower of brickbats: and the men one would have thought had received a shower of Indian arrows, to have seen the blood stream-ing from their heads . . . but none of them had any fracture of the skull."

The ones in worst shape in the event of storm and hail were the hikers and packers, with no shelter at all. On one occasion the Goldsmith party, assailed by stones asserted to be five inches in diameter, managed to protect their heads with camp kettles and pack saddles, but injured their hands. For the most part, however, these vulnerable travelers could only agree with Wislizenus that "all we could oppose to the elements was our equanimity."

The wind that frequently howled across the Plains was itself a menace. "The wind blew so hard I could not get out of the wagon for fear of being blown away," complained Martha Moore. "The wind so rocked the wagons that in vain I wooed the goddess Sleep." But the wind that accompanied a Platte valley storm could be downright ruinous. This caprice of the wind was experienced by William Knight: "A sudden gust wrenched my felt hat from my head and the next instant a blinding flash revealed it more than 100 feet in the air. I never saw it again." If there was time to batten down the hatches, it might be done as J. Carr reports: tie the mules to the wheels, and lash the wagons down to picket pins. Or one might follow Abbott's recommendation: place wagons in

the form of a V, pointed west, and stake down every horse inside
the V. But if the gale was of sufficient force, precautions were
futile; tents were blown down and wagon covers were ripped away
(Kirkpatrick, Webster). Jared Fox exclaimed that the hurricane
"nearly turned our wagons wrong side out." East of Fort Laramie,
F. S. Dean saw two wagons blown upside down. When McGlashan's
wagons were upset amid flying sand and gravel, he philosophically
observed that "such hurricanes are not uncommon in this part of
the continent."

If the wind was not too violent, and if in the proper direction,
it could be a help in moving the heavy wagons along, according to
Katherine Dunlap. But the prevailing winds blew from the west,
and as a rule they had to be bucked. Sometimes, like a sailing
vessel in danger, wagons were purposely turned around to ride
out the storm. Thus, after losing two vehicles to a "whirlwind"
Niles Searls' party found that "our only course was to turn our
teams to leeward and scud before the gale."

Tornados were witnessed by at least two parties of emigrants. In
1841 on the "Big Platte" John Bidwell reports: "Dark clouds
rushed in wild confusion around and above us, soon with amazement we saw a lofty water spout, towering like a huge Column to
support the arch of the sky." In 1849 the Col. Jarrott train arrived
at the summit of California Hill, near present Brule, Nebraska, and
Berrien was "gratified with a magnificent spectacle. A tornado was
whirling across the prairie and though there was but little on which
to exert its fury still the commotion of the clouds and the immense
masses of vapour whirling around with inconceivable rapidity . . .
while the roaring of the wind could be distinctly heard at 2 miles
distance, furnishing a sight seldom witnessed. . . . After the tornado
had passed clouds of Grasshoppers fell from the sky. . . . The Cloud
presented the appearance of a long funnel the small end down-
wards as black as ink. . . . fortunate for us was it that it did not pass
near or over our waggons which had it so occur'd would have been
scattered to the four winds of Heaven."

Thunder and lightning, hail, hurricane, or tornado were more
spectacular, but the most demoralizing and all-pervading enemy
was rain. True, it made the essential grass grow, but one could
get miserably wet and come close to drowning in it. William Lee
awoke not to the pitter-patter of raindrops but to the surge of a
"young river" through his tent, soaking his blankets; and the young

tenderfoot learned in a hurry about digging a ditch around the tent to divert groundwater. But a ditch six feet deep would scarcely keep out some Platte River cloudbursts. Washington Bailey's camp was visited by a "waterspout" and was soon under two feet of water. Henry Coke was twice driven from his bed to seek refuge in the wagon, perching with a fellow sufferer "back to back on top of our luggage," and was astonished to note that the rain came in such torrents that it "ran over our ankles even though on a hill." Storm-bound at Fort Kearny, Meline explained his dilemma: "You can't lie down without being drowned or stand up without being struck by lightning." The non-waterproof tents of that day, complained Amos Bachelder, were "but spider's webs before these storms." If the tents and wagon covers blew away, the soaking would be thorough. Wrote Dalton: "The wind came whistling & knocking our tent into a cocked hat, tearing up the pins & letting the cloth right down upon us. . . . in a few moments where we lay the water was over shoe mouth deep; & there we poor monomaniacal gold hunters had to take it for three long hours." Carlisle Abbott found one exposed cholera victim in a wagon bed, "just as wet as if he had been pulled out of the river." Martha Moore found it difficult to be philosophical under these circumstances, concluding that a tent-dweller should have "a more amphibious nature."

Lightning could produce eerie effects. Wrote Hewitt, "Every-thing which stood upright seemed to be an illuminated pillar of fire of electric flame, even the mules's ears." Lightning sometimes stunned and killed animals and men. Archer Walters tells of lightning in the middle of a handcart brigade which "struck a brother and he fell to rise no more." Dr. Flint and Lydia Waters reported grave inscriptions which indicated lightning as the cause of death. But the biggest hazard of lightning was the scare it threw into oxen and mules, making it the chief villain in the dreaded stampede. Indians, buffalo, a tumbleweed, anything could cause this phenomenon, but lightning was almost guaranteed to generate the panic which could become a disaster.

STAMPEDE

Whatever their other differences, all three draft animals—oxen, mules, and horses—could become panicky and stampede. Oxen were the flightiest, but the others could "blow" any time. Birge tells of a flight of mules on Lodgepole Creek, while Snodgrass tells of horses rampaging along the Platte. A typical stampede caused by an electrical storm is described by G. W. Thissell: "The cattle swayed from side to side, bellowing and goring each other. All hands were called out on guard. With one wild and mad rush, 250 head of oxen went crashing over the wagons, trampling one man . . . to death, and wounding several others." Because of this hazard, James Linforth explained that it is best to tie animals up outside a corral. Sometimes stampedes occurred while animals were still in harness, causing great havoc. Martha Morgan reported the death of a woman from this cause. John Wood witnessed the furious rush of 200 cattle attached to wagons; in this case disaster was averted by the drivers' permitting the animals to run themselves to exhaustion, with no wheels lost. Later he saw a herd stampede out of camp in a storm: "Away they went like quarter horses," the guards chasing them while lightning fitfully illuminated the scene. Langworthy likened the sound of stampeding cattle in the distance to the rumbling of an earthquake.

Buffalo stampeded like runaway freight trains, sometimes causing havoc among camps and animals, particularly in the 1840s; but documented instances of this are rare. (See Chapter VIII.) More common are cases where grazing cattle mingled with wandering buffalo. When owners attempted to retrieve their animals, the buffalo would stampede in panic, the cattle along with them. This happened to Samuel Hancock's train in 1845.

Following the stampeding or drifting of a herd came the grueling process of rounding up the critters one by one. They were often scattered a distance of up to twenty miles away, and their recovery might take days; often the stock was not recovered at all. Most emigrants were honest, and if a strange cow turned up in their neighborhood they would hold it to turn over to the anxious owner. Sometimes, of course, greed prevailed, and the lost animal was appropriated on a "finder's keepers" basis which could result in a quarrel. When there were disasters such as the great storm of 1849, with a wholesale stampede and intermingling of herds, the ensuing ownership snarls were king-size. Cipriani gleefully notes that after one such mix-up in 1853 he wound up with more animals than he lost. More often emigrants sadly record a deficiency in their inventory of the animals necessary to take them to the Pacific. At best this might require the shifting of loads and the abandonment of wagons. At worst it was a calamity which would leave the party stranded in the wilderness, thrown on the mercy of more fortunate travelers or the military, or compelled to return.

TURNAROUNDS

Among those who "jumped off" there were two groups who never made it to their destination—those who died and those who turned back. While we can honor those who struggled through and shed a tear for those who succumbed, it would be an injustice to condemn the turnarounds as cowards, especially when viewing the Great Migration from today's comfortable vantage point. In view of the reports of hardships and suffering, and the cold truth about California gold, it seems that these second-thinkers should almost be commended for their good judgment. But alas, it was not careful reflection that put men "on the back track," but careless preparation or plain bad luck, or a combination thereof.

It was not unheard of for Oregon emigrants of the 1840s to reverse their field. In 1846 near the forks of the Platte, Joel Palmer met families who were compelled to return because of stock lost or stolen. In 1849, despite the Gold Rush hysteria, there is evidence of many returnees, usually from some point not more than 200 miles from St. Joe or Independence. Eastin and Krepps both mention the return of several disgruntled parties, but these were clearly a negligible minority. In 1850, however, the proportion of early turnarounds was much higher, apparently the result of drouth and poor grass, perhaps coupled with the cholera scare. On the Little Blue, McBride met returning emigrants daily, alarmed at the scantiness of grass and supplies and "the immense multitude of emigrants en route. Seth Lewelling met a train of 300 out of provisions, returning to St. Joe. One St. Louis correspondent commented on the number of "long sour faces, on the retrograde march." "W. R. R." for the *Missouri Statesman*, reported also from the Little Blue: "We meet more or less returning Californians every day. They all exhibit woeful physiognomies and have many wonderful tales to tell us of the elephant ahead. These backsliders are very useful to the emigrants as they supply the place of a mail and can always tell how far ahead to wood and water." According to Dabney Carr, these were mainly victims of their own foolishness who made the error of leaving the states too early in a dry year:

"There was no grass and they were obliged to give their provisions to the animals to keep them alive. We met several going back who said that all their animals had died, and all they wanted was to get back alive. There is more suffering on this trip than one can well imagine, and how it is to end God only knows." John Wood pitied the poor souls who when "thoughts of their wives or lovers enter their noodle, they set up a howl, and strike a beeline for home."

Timidity may have been a factor with those who returned early, but it was grim circumstance which dictated the return of one group who reached a point west of Fort Kearny. Addison Crane wrote: "Yesterday a party of Irishmen were met on foot on the back-track. They had undertaken to pack through with mules, and a distance beyond Fort Kearny were set upon and robbed of everything by a party of Indians, and one of their number killed." In 1852 E. S. Carter found that a party turning around at Chimney Rock was a demoralized remnant of a large company which had been ravaged by cholera. At Ash Hollow, J. H. Clark met three returnees who had just buried four companions. In many cases the bereaved lost livestock as well as loved ones and would have perished themselves had they not relied upon the charity of the U.S. Army. Mrs. Frink met a squadron of Mounted Riflemen returning to Fort Leavenworth with a woman who had lost husband and child. Below Chimney Rock, Martha Morgan found a government train with several "unfortunate gold-diggers, a crazy man, and several crippled by stampedes."

Thoughts of returning haunt the pages of many journals. In her first day out, Catherine Haun was in the "Slough of Despond." Mrs. Burlingame found "the ladies wonderfully sick of their romantic journey," and Isaac Harvey "had the blues." Eastin "felt an over-powering sensation of sadness, and the tears started, but," he adds, "with an effort I dashed away these women's feelings and once more turned my horse's head in the direction of the land of promise."

Sometimes only a challenge to manhood prevented a panic retreat, as witness Joseph Rhodes: "The Captain and some of the boys are out of heart now and wanted to go home, but did not for we laughed at them so."

The McIlhany train of 1849 came up with a remarkably astute idea: When they were only a few days out of St. Joe, beset by cholera and storms, "some suggested we go no further and start a colony." This idea was just about ten years ahead of its time; most of the Californians went through, confounding C. G. Hinman's prophecy that "about ⅓ of those who start to go through will back out."

It was in 1859 that turning around became truly fashionable, and eastbound traffic reached epidemic proportions. This was the result of reaction from an oversold Pike's Peak Gold Rush, or, as Dr. C. M. Clark observed, "The scales are beginning to fall from their eyes. The road [to Colorado] is not paved with golden sands but common dirt." J. A. Wilkinson encountered hundreds streaming down the Platte, quarreling over their route, displaying patches on their buckskins and "specimens of the Brass gold dust the mines are salted with." So also with Wm. Knight, himself headed for California in '59: "The great army of humbugged Pike's Peakers had commenced their return. Their visages were long and wrathy and their replies were short and sour. That day we passed 250 wagons of hoaxed gold-seekers."

IV

The Jumping-off Places

THE GREAT PLATTE RIVER ROAD began at new Fort Kearny at the head of Grand Island, where five major travel routes sprouting from a 200-mile arc of the Missouri River were fused together into one grand trunkline. However, an understanding of these branches, or feeder lines, is necessary to an understanding of the main route; and these branches are meaningful only in terms of their beginnings, the Missouri River border towns, commonly referred to as the "jumping-off places." In the mid-nineteenth century an overland trip from the states to the Pacific Ocean, over vast treeless plains, the awesome Rocky Mountains, and scorching deserts, must have seemed roughly equivalent to today's venture into outer space.

The crucial role of the river towns has been obscured by the historical emphasis on Oregon, California, Utah, Colorado, and Montana—destinations which were not always as glamorous as advertised, but which seemed so to the emigrants with their "westward vision." Furthermore, since covered wagon days, most river towns have grown into sprawling modern communities, with little trace left of their historic beginnings.

Lewis and Clark suggested that the mouth of Platte River would be a good place for a fort, and in the late fifties the town of Plattsmouth did materialize there; however, the Great Migration route up the Platte did not begin at its mouth at all, but at five major points now roughly equivalent to the modern communities of Kansas City, Weston-Leavenworth, St. Joseph (St. Joe), Nebraska

103

City, and Council Bluffs–Omaha. There were also several minor crossings along the center of the arc, between St. Joe and Nebraska City. A few general observations about the jumping-off points collectively will be helpful before examining them individually.

The complex of sites around Kansas City were on the west side of the Missouri River to begin with, and wagon trains had the immense advantage of starting off on dry land. Weston, St. Joe, Council Bluffs, and the old Fort Kearny Ferry (not the fort itself) were rallying and recruiting points on the east side, the departure from which first required the dangerous crossing of the Missouri by flimsy rafts or ferries at the mercy of its brown turbulence. At one stage or another all of the five main ports were reached by precarious St. Louis steamboats. Indeed, the Kansas City and Weston jump-offs were normally approached by steamer, and overland travel to them from the east was the exception. Quite the reverse was true of the other three, which were mainly the objectives of wagon trains fanning out from points throughout the Upper Mississippi valley.

The relative importance of the five major jump-offs may be roughly charted through the incidence of diaries written by emigrants starting from each terminal (indicated in the chronology, Chapter I). Evaluated also is the internal data reflected in such diaries, in contemporary newspapers, and in controls such as the fort registers. The first westward trips up the Platte River, exploring expeditions of Stephen Long in 1820 and William Ashley in 1824, were along the north bank. During the 1830s there were fur company caravans up both sides of the Platte, from Bellevue and from the Kansas City area. The latter was the main starting point for the covered wagon migration to Oregon. The year 1846, which saw the creation of the army post at Table Creek and the Mormon arrival at Council Bluffs, was the last year in which Kansas City served as the number one funnel for the Platte River Road. The year 1847 was a Council Bluffs year, with the pioneer Mormon trek to Salt Lake City.

During the California Gold Rush the evidence digested from journals and other sources shows the following: In 1849 St. Joe was first, Kansas City second, and Council Bluffs third, but with sizable participation also by Weston and old Fort Kearny; in 1850 Kansas City shows a marked decline, while St. Joe and Council Bluffs seem tied for first position; by 1852 Council Bluffs was clearly in the lead.

When Omaha and Nebraska City materialized as river ports in

1854, with the creation of Nebraska Territory, eastern Nebraska's lopsided dominance of Platte River traffic was expanded. During the late 1850s lower fares and technical improvements in steamboat transportation to Nebraska points, combined with a saving of 200 miles of land transportation, led to a sharp decline of covered wagon traffic out of St. Joe and Kansas City. Military, freighting, and stage line travel from Fort Leavenworth and Atchison increased, of course, during this period, but the pre-railroad covered wagon emigration shifted to, and stayed in, Nebraska Territory. The Pike's Peak Gold Rush was largely a Nebraska City–Denver affair. The bulk of Montana gold-seekers overland were of Omaha origin, as were those who traveled in the sixties on their own to Utah, California, or Oregon before the completion of the Union Pacific.

Thus the wheel came full circle. Council Bluffs was the jump-off for Stephen H. Long and William H. Ashley, who in the 1820s initiated western travel up the Great Platte River Road; Council Bluffs–Omaha and Nebraska City were the primary points of embarkation on the prairie sea for the seventeen years prior to the advent of transcontinental train travel. If the Missouri cities are remembered most vividly as the starting points for Oregon and California during the climax years, the Nebraska towns should be remembered as the first and the last of the jumping-off places, and over the decades they launched the greatest number of those who followed the Great Platte River Road.

Kansas City

The complex of sites around Kansas City is the best known, partly because this area was the principal jump-off for the Oregon migration, partly because it was in the business of outfitting explorers, fur traders, and emigrants longer than any of its rivals. Kansas City was important because of a simple accident of geography. It was located at the point where the Missouri River, after its westward course through the state of Missouri, makes a sharp bend northward to Nebraska; hence the seemingly logical point to get out of a boat and pursue westward objectives overland.

Greater Kansas City today, approaching a population of one million, has all but obliterated the evidence of its origins. Within this metropolitan area, complete with skyscrapers, elaborate traffic-ways, and jet planes overhead, there were once four focal points of covered wagon concentration. The earliest of these was Fort Osage, a government post established in 1808 at a point recommended by William Clark several miles downstream from present Kansas City and now restored as a Jackson County park. It figured in the opening of the Santa Fe Trail. In 1832 Capt. B. L. E. Bonneville made up his three-year trading expedition at the settlement which succeeded Fort Osage.

Next came the Chouteau brothers of St. Louis, licensed to trade with Indians "near the mouth of the Kaw" or Kansas River. Their long-vanished trading posts of the 1820s, their precise locations somewhat conjectural, were the spiritual predecessors of the 1839 river port variously called Chouteau's Landing, Kanzas, Kansasmouth, Kanzasville, or Westport Landing. It was this strategic spot which became "the city of Kansas" in 1853, now the river edge of the towering downtown business district of Kansas City, Missouri. Early travelers, such as American Fur Company caravans, Matthew Field with Andrew Sublette's train in 1843, and Fremont's expeditions of 1842–1843, used this point of departure.

Independence became the third and most important point of overland departure. Independence today is a separate city, a metropolis of western Jackson County. However, for all visible purposes it is a suburb of Kansas City with the principal connecting artery, Truman Road, named for its most distinguished citizen. A modern shopping center surrounding a splendid brick courthouse, built on the site of the 1849 courthouse, now dominates the square which once echoed to the braying of mules, the bellowing of oxen, and the blasphemies of their drivers. The only tangible links with the past are a protected "emigrant spring," a log cabin dubiously represented as the original 1827 courthouse, and the restored Jackson County Jail and Marshal's House, of 1859 vintage.

Independence was established in 1827 to succeed old Franklin and Arrow Rock farther downriver as the main depot of the burgeoning Santa Fe trade. In 1830 it was the springboard for the historic Smith-Jackson-Sublette caravan of carts and wagons from St. Louis to the Wind River rendezvous in the Rocky Mountains, the first bona fide "wagon train" up the Great Platte River Road. In 1832 John Townsend of Wyeth's expedition thought the location "on a high point of land overlooking the surrounding country" very beautiful, but the town itself "very indifferent," with a scattering of "low and mean" houses composed of logs and clay and "a few stores, taverns and tippling houses." He noted that the Mormons had recently been ejected from Independence and taken refuge in Liberty, a town upriver and a few miles north which came to play a minor role as an outfitting point.

At the height of the Oregon migration in 1846, J. Quinn Thornton described Independence as "a great Babel of African slaves, indolent dark-skinned Spaniards, profane and dust-laden bull-whackers going to and from Santa Fe with their immense wagons, and emigrant families bound for the Pacific, all cheerful and intent on their embarkation upon the great prairie wilderness."

Inevitably, Pacific-bound gold-seekers with the California fever swarmed over Independence like a plague of locusts. There were no gold mines in Missouri, but a jumping-off place in 1849 was as good as a gold mine for merchants and livestock traders, who accumulated enormous profits. David Staples says, "'Independence grew up in one night like Jonah's gourd." The town had been a bustling little frontier community serving Santa Fe traders and Oregonians; it now became a bedlam in the center of a vast ring of encampments, with emigrants busily assembling their gear and provisions and breaking in oxen and mules while they waited for green grass on the prairie. Few Forty-Niners arrived cross-country; the bulk of the migration came by steamboat from St. Louis, some bringing their outfits with them, others making their purchases at this famous outfitting point.

Since Independence was a few miles inland, it was served by various steamboat landings rearranged annually by Missouri River floods. In 1849 there were two: old Independence Landing, and a new excrescence of shacks by the glorified name of Wayne City. According to James Pratt, the latter was the best place of debarkation, being only three miles from town, "although owing to a curve of the river it is 15 miles further up." D. Jagger refers to this as the Independence Upper Landing. Immediately upon arrival there his party went through a standard procedure, reconstructing wagons which had been dismantled for the steam voyage, struggling up the steep bluffs, and locating a camp on the outskirts of town.

Arriving in March, Wm. Johnston had several weeks to take in the sights, noting among other refinements "a daguerrotype gallery, with its frightful array of portraits." A month later the emigrants had arrived in force, and "noise and confusion reigned supreme. Traders, trappers and emigrants filled the streets and stores. All were in a hurry, jostling one another, and impatient to get through with their business. . . . Mules and oxen strove for the right of way. 'Whoa' and 'haw' resounded on every side; while the loud cracking of ox goads, squeaking of wheels and rattling of chains, mingled with the oaths of teamsters, produced a din indescribable."

James Pratt of the Wolverine Rangers noted that there were two public houses, Independence House and Noland House, crammed to capacity with emigrants paying $5 per week for board and lodging, while other emigrants boarded at private homes; but the bulk were obliged to camp out with their wagons. Among other facilities were "two gambling houses open day and night" and a "little 7 x 9 post office" which was "'crowded when open. It takes a long time to get waited on, so great is the rush. The mail comes only tri-weekly, and by land at that, which takes 4½ days from St. Louis."

Despite the crowds, Pratt observed that "most of the emigrants move further up the river" to Weston and St. Joseph. Although 1850 yielded an overall migration nearly double that of 1849, the number using Independence dwindled. Among those who did jump off here was Henry Stine, who found it now "a splendid little town" with "some handsome houses and hotels, all kinds of stores. . . . Californians can get an outfit cheaper here than in St. Louis . . . plenty of mules and horses here at reasonable prices, but boarding $1. per day." He noted that Independence was now linked to Wayne City by a primitive kind of railroad. Dr. Tompkins admired Independence, "laid out like the square of a checkerboard. In the center of the city is a beautiful Park in the midst of which is a Brick Court House, with a conical roof."

The Asiatic cholera brought along by steamboat passengers from St. Louis was particularly deadly around Independence, and graves multiplied. This, coupled with the rivalry of neighboring Westport and the advantages of going farther upriver by steamer, led to the decline of Independence in the fifties as a significant jump-off.

From Independence the original Santa Fe Trail headed southwest over Blue Ridge to intersect the boundary between the United States proper and Indian territory (now the Missouri-Kansas line) at a neighborhood called Little Santa Fe, or Fitzhugh's Grove, near present 103rd Street and State Line in Kansas City.

The town of Westport was on the uplands between Turkey Creek and Brush Creek, a few miles south of Westport Landing and just inside the state line. Now largely obliterated by Kansas City, it once occupied the equivalent of about 40 city blocks. Westport survives today only in token form as a two-block restoration area along Westport Road. Among the few genuine structures surviving from covered wagon days are the homes of Col. Jack Harris and the Rev. Nathan Scarritt, and Westport Inn. The latter was built sometime between 1848 and 1854 by merchants W. G. and W. W. Ewing, and later owned by the grandson of Daniel Boone. Three other structures, once in the old Westport countryside, and now within quality residential areas, are the home of the freighting tycoon Alexander Majors at 91st and State Line, the West 55th Street home of William Bent and Seth E. Ward, both fur trade notables, and the Wornall home at 61st Terrace and Wornall Road.

In 1831 Isaac McCoy and Johnston Lykins set up a Baptist Mission to the Shawnee and Wyandot Indians, displaced from Ohio by President Jackson, in Indian Territory (now Kansas), west of the Missouri line. In 1833 John Calvin McCoy, Isaac's son, set up a trading post for the Indians two miles east of the Mission, and this was the beginning of the Westport settlement. Later a trail was hacked through the timber of the Missouri River, and the boat landing evolved there; meanwhile Westport began to tap the lucrative overland Santa Fe trade. After 1846 the Westport Trail became the main emigration route westward, superseding the original route along Blue Ridge; present Westport Road is that section of the trail which took covered wagon traffic through town.

In 1839 Dr. Wislizenus found the border village, by his reckoning six miles from Chouteau's Landing, to consist of twenty to forty houses. At that date he described Westport as "the usual rendezvous for travelers to the Rocky Mountains as is Independence to Santa Fe," referring, of course, to the fur traders and early missionaries.

One of Westport's most illustrious visitors was young Francis Parkman, who recorded events of 1846 in his classic *Oregon Trail*. His party landed at Kansas, "about 500 miles from the mouth of the Missouri" and set out in a wagon for Westport to buy mules and horses for their journey. After a drive along "a miserable road" through rough timbered country (which would be a north-south meander through present Kansas City), he arrived to find Westport "full of Indians, whose little shaggy ponies were tied by dozens along the houses and fences. Sacs and Foxes, with shaved heads and painted faces, Shawanoes and Delawares, fluttering in calico frocks and turbans, Wyandots dressed like white men, and a few wretched Kanza wrapped in old blankets, were strolling about the streets, or lounging in and out of the shops and houses." Westport was not yet as large or bustling as Independence, which Parkman also visited and where he observed "an incessant hammering and banging from a dozen blacksmith's sheds, and emigrant throngs, including a multitude of healthy children's faces peeping out from under the covers of the wagons . . . here and there a buxom damsel seated on horseback, holding over her sunburnt face an old umbrella or parasol," and men among their oxen, "zealously discussing the doctrine of regeneration."

During the Gold Rush, Westport played a considerable role, but apparently it never quite supplanted Independence. Joseph Buffum indicates that Kanzas, or Westport Landing, was devastated by cholera in 1849, so landings here were discouraged. That year Henry Shombre stopped en route from Independence, finding a population of 500 with "5 stores, 2 doctors, 1 church, 1 school, and 2 smiths." He attended church but saw much drinking, culminating in a "shameful riot." In 1853 Phoebe Judson reported that the emigrant rendezvous was at "West Port. . . . Here we found a comfortable boarding place, where all the work was performed by slaves." That same year Rebecca Ketcham of William Gray's party records that they took lodgings in Westport while preparing for Oregon.

Westport and Westport Landing, like Independence, after 1849 yielded to upriver towns as primary jumping-off places for the Platte. But while Independence retains its identity to this day, its arch rivals survive only as historical footnotes.

WESTON–FORT LEAVENWORTH

Since the Platte River 200 miles north of Kansas City was the road to Oregon and California, and since the Missouri River above Kansas City kept veering westward even as it pointed north, it dawned on a rapidly increasing number of emigrants that the best way to shorten the laborious overland trip was to go as far upriver as possible by steamboat. These belching paddle-wheeled monsters, carrying hundreds of passengers and their equipment, went by a variety of colorful names, like *Belle Creole* (Sedgley), *Meteor* (Bruff),

John Hancock (Boyle), *Grand Turk* (Pearson), *Highland Mary* (Hamelin), and *Sacramento* (Johnston). Often their boilers exploded, killing and maiming scores of people, as the *Saluda* did near Lexington (Richardson), or they came to grief on a rock ledge or sandbar, like the *Pontiac* near Weston (Dalton). But eggshells and firetraps though they were, from 1849 on, the Missouri was alive with this snorting traffic which transported cargo to a series of east-bank border towns as far north as Council Bluffs. The first of these upriver towns was Weston, across the river and four miles above Fort Leavenworth.

Fort Leavenworth was founded in 1827, fronting the Kansas wilderness some thirty miles north of Westport Landing. At first this was strictly a military affair, to impress the Sac, Fox, Missouri, and Potawatomi Indians. Fur traders, often with cargos of illicit whiskey, gave the place a wide berth, and citizen emigrants were at first not even thought of . When Oregon migration focused attention on the Platte River Road, army engineers pioneered a patrol line northwestward from the fort which joined the St. Joe Road to the Platte. In 1849 a substantial number of gold-seekers started off on the Leavenworth Road, looking upon this as a shrewd way to avoid congestion at Independence and St. Joe. The fort itself was off limits to the emigrants, so it was rarely described by them. From aboard a steamer in 1852, John Clark of Virginia thought it "a dull looking place on the Indian side. Garrison on the hill a short distance from the river."

Weston, Missouri, was founded in 1837 by Joseph Moore, an ex-Dragoon from Fort Leavenworth, and was prospering three years later as a tobacco market and as the river port on the east shore serving Fort Leavenworth. An influx of emigrants from central Europe, building picturesquely on the steep hillsides, gave this town the nickname of "Little Switzerland." During the Gold Rush as many as eight steamboats would be docked here at one time.

It was at Weston early in 1841 that Antoine Robidoux lectured on the attractions of distant California, whereupon John Bidwell tells us that he organized the first covered wagon expedition to that magic land. Weston was a stopping point in 1843–1844 for Peter Burnett, John Minto, and other emigrants en route to Oregon. In the latter year Minto watched Sac and Fox Indians, in town for their annuities, "performing their war dances in front of the few business houses" and "planting slobbery kisses" on all donors to their whiskey fund. Although Forty-Niner journals tied in with this river port are scarce, it must have been a major crossing that year, for the correspondent "California" puts it in the same category with Independence and St. Joe as places "crowded to their utmost capacity," where newcomers were obliged, "for want of other lodgings, to accommodate themselves in uncovered wagons and uncovered outhouses." In 1850 C. W. Smith regarded Weston as "as good a starting place as any" and found several hundred wagons here, waiting to be floated laboriously by "common flatboats propelled by oars." This same year J. S. Shepherd traveled via Weston and Leavenworth on a "new road made by Uncle Sam's men this spring." In 1853 Calvin West reported thousands of emigrants in town and on both sides of the river.

Outfitting and supplying both soldiers and emigrants brought Weston's population in 1858 to more than 5,000. For a few years it rivaled Independence and St. Joe in population, but it rapidly shrank when it was stranded by the railroad boom of the 1860's, together with the shift of the Missouri River channel to the west bank.

Today Weston is a relaxed community, largely ignored by tourists and historians alike, but distinguished for its tobacco auctions, its 1856 whiskey distillery founded by David Holladay (brother of famed Ben), and a number of well-preserved homes that go all the way back to the Gold Rush. Typical of these is the Sebus home, a brick dwelling complete with slave quarters that was built by Weston's own Capt. Charles Murphy, a Pied Piper who led a contingent of Forty-Niners to California and then disappeared.

St. Joseph

Joseph Robidoux, who established a trading post at the Blacksnake Hills about 1825, was a man of vision. He anticipated not only an influx of settlers, but also the need for a trail to the west which would join the Blue River and the Platte. Blacksnake Hills had it all over Independence, being substantially closer to the Platte River; two extra days by steamer would save two weeks by ox-team. So when, in 1843, the canny French-Canadian laid out the city named for his patron saint, little time elapsed before Yankee traders arrived, bought lots, and started the metropolis of north-western Missouri. (Legally it was St. Joseph, but in everyday parlance it was usually St. Joe.)

In 1844 Oregon emigrant John Minto found here "a mere village of two or three stores and one hotel," which Robert Morrison still referred to as "Rubadeau's Landing." Four years later Riley Root pictured the "new town on the Missouri river . . . with about 1800 inhabitants, which five years ago was a field of hemp. . . . Among its inhabitants are 15 lawyers, 11 doctors, 2 silversmiths and 2 gunsmiths."

It was in 1849, of course, that St. Joe was rocked by explosions of human vitality, and the trail to the Big Blue Crossing—the St. Joe Road—became the royal road to California riches. Delos Ashley and Georg Hagelstein echoed the general sentiment when they wrote that St. Joe was the best starting point and the emporium of most California-bound travelers. "California," correspondent of the *Missouri Republican*, reported, "From what I have been able to ascertain, there appears to be a greater number of emigrants rendezvousing at this point than at Independence." George Gibbs confirms this, describing "the great trail from St. Joe" as the most traveled of all routes.

E. Wells was impressed by St. Joe as a place that "has been built in five years." "The Missourie River here," he explained, "is $\frac{1}{4}$ mile wide and the other side is out of the United States, it being Indian Territory." Most Argonauts were impressed with two things: the town had a certain picturesqueness, and it was now being inundated with humanity. Joseph Merrill, arriving by steamboat, reported: "This town like most of the western ones is built on a high bluff; it contains more brick buildings than any I have noticed." J. Hamelin thought it "the prettiest townsite on the river." James Tate found it "beautifully situated. . . . It reminds me of an ornamental garden laid out with much care." Dr. Boyle climbed up on the courthouse cupola to admire the panoramic view and observed, "there are but few women to be seen here, nothing but men, mules and tents. The town is six years old and contains 1500 to 1800 inhabitants." Charles Kirkpatrick guessed there were 2,000 inhabitants, but "emigrants to California make it a very crowded city . . . men of every description and character, a race of thieves, liars and murderers." He reported two ferryboats running day and night; it was here at the ferries that one could observe "selfishness in all its native deformity."

The primitive ferries were flat-bottomed scows with big sweeps and couldn't begin to cope with the throngs. "'Old Boone" reported the ferry "overrun and some four or five days behind." Charles G. Hinman observed: "We are about the 20th team from the Ferry; yesterday morning the 70th. We crowd up as fast as we can. 300 teams waiting to get over." Tate said that each boat could cross only about thirty-five teams per day; "sometimes there is great contention." This was surely an understatement; with the great surge of impatient wagoneers waiting at the ferry, lined up for a mile or more jostling for position, and whiskey flowing freely in the taverns, there were many heated arguments, occasional fist-fights, and a few brutal beatings and killings. The situation was improved a bit in 1850 with the advent of a steam ferryboat, described by James Bennett. N. A. Cagwin was grateful to "cross the Rubicon in the Indian territory," but in passing through six miles of bottomland, he found "every rod of the way being occupied by tents, wagons, etc. What a rush for the great Eldorado!"

In 1850 John Wood found the town of 3,000 again swamped with 10,000 emigrants and plagued with "Gambling Hells." It seemed that he was never out of hearing of quarreling and wrangling, and the streets were terrorized by drunken men brandishing knives. Although Stephen White "saw no disorderly conduct," he found that "to reach the P. O. was no little trouble. Men formed in long lines to reach the P. O. window." In 1852 the pageantry was repeated, writes John H. Clark: "We unloaded our goods this morning and encamped on the great plain that stretches southward from the city of Saint Joe. . . . I had lived in this world a good while and thought I had seen great crowds and so I had, of men, but not of wagons. The river was to be crossed and such a crowd of wagons rammed, jammed and locked together I never saw and I do not think the world ever saw the like before. It seemed as if the salvation of every man depended on his getting his wagon over first." John Clark of Virginia estimated that the vast array of wagons, tents, and animals resembled "the grand encampment of 1812." Theodore Potter wrote that in 1852 "the number of teams waiting to be ferried . . . was so great that four steam ferry boats were kept busy transporting them. Our train . . . took its place . . . at least half a mile from the ferry . . . and it was not until the afternoon of the next day that we were landed on the west bank of the raging Missouri." In 1853 Agnes Stewart was critical of the drinking habits of the population: "Every man I meet looks like an ale cask himself." She blamed liquor for the drowning of four men when one of the famous ferryboats upset.

The St. Joe scene was enlivened also by the natives. Wrote John Clark: "Early this morning a caravan of some two hundred Potawatami indians made this their crosing point on their way to the buffalo range. On coming down the street the scent, or wild odor from the band and dirty looking bagage, bundels of skins & so forth made every horse & mule in their way brake and leave for the commons below."

St. Joe continued to serve emigrants during the fifties, but was overshadowed by Council Bluffs. In 1859 the Hannibal and St. Joseph Railroad arrived, and in 1860 the fleet Pony Express began its meteoric career here. After the Civil War, St. Joe became a railroad and agricultural center.

While prosperous enough, St. Joe is no longer a boom town; its population of around 75,000 has remained fairly constant for several decades. The community is proud of the Pony Express, commemorating it by statues and monuments and the preservation of two ancient buildings—the Pony Express stable, and the grandiose Patee House—which were used by the entrepeneurs Russell, Majors, and Waddell. Unfortunately the civic memory of the much more significant Gold Rush is short. Its only discernible trace is the unmemorialized river bank at the foot of Jules and Frances streets, named for old Joe's relatives. Once jammed with emigrants waiting their turn for the makeshift ferryboats, the locale is now the setting of the Goetz brewery, an iron foundry, and other impedimenta of the twentieth century.

THE MIDDLE CROSSINGS

We have indicated five major crossings of the Missouri River— Kansas City, Weston-Leavenworth, St. Joe, Nebraska City, and Council Bluffs–Omaha. Because this is a neglected aspect of the Great Migration it is important to get a glimpse of the minor ones, which mainly occurred between St. Joe and Nebraska City. Charles G. Hinman says that in 1849 there were "12 crossing places." If we allow two widely separated crossings at Council Bluffs (Upper Mormon and Bellevue), and count all other major crossings as one each, that leaves six to be accounted for. The journals enable us to make tentative identification of these extinct jumping-off places.

It would be a mistake to suppose that these middle crossings were used only by those approaching overland from the east. On the contrary, it seems that they were used mainly by emigrants who first arrived at St. Joe and originally intended to cross there, but then changed their minds and decided to drive up the Missouri River bottoms and uplands to find a different crossing. This northward trail is clearly set forth by the correspondent "California" at St. Joe in 1849: "The roads in every direction, are lined with wagons of emigrant parties from the lower counties of Missouri and from Iowa, Wisconsin, Michigan and Illinois. The *majority* of these intend moving leisurely as far as [old] Fort Kearny and Council Bluffs, and *then* make a final start."

There were two primary reasons for this switch in plans. First was the terrible congestion at the dismally inadequate St. Joe ferry; second was the increasing recognition of the fact that the higher you crossed, the closer you were to the Platte River Road. Mormon agents who had a business interest in the Council Bluffs Road may have been at work in St. Joe and elsewhere, and some St. Joe emigrants (such as Basil Longsworth and Martha Morgan) did drive all the way up to Council Bluffs before crossing; but most of those on this northward land route finally crossed at old Fort Kearny (Nebraska City) or some point below there. Often as not there was no fixed, preconceived plan; crossing might be made on an impromptu basis, wherever rumor suggested or a crowd gathered. These appear to be the six middle crossings:

1. "The Upper Ferry," five miles above St. Joe. G. C. Pearson says this was used heavily in 1849: "The motive power of the scow-shaped, flat-bottomed boat was the strong current of the river . . . using a large hawser fastened to a tree on the bank upstream . . . and block and tackle playing freely on the rope attached to both ends of the boat. Five dollars per wagon was paid for ferrying four wagons, and the cattle swam across." This ferry was also used by Alexander Ramsay's Indiana Company and Col. Jarrott's train, as described by Joseph Berrien.

2. "Mr. Duncan's Place, three miles north of Camden Point," referred to by E. S. Carter in 1852. This could have been the same as the Upper Ferry. It is also referred to by Solomon Gorgas and Jay Green.

3. Savannah Point, Savannah Landing, and Caples Landing were all names for a popular crossing about twelve miles above St. Joe. The present town of Savannah existed in 1849 also, but this crossing was west thereof, near the bottomland town of Amazonia. Among numerous references to this crossing are the journals of Hite, Hale, G. Cole, Tinker, and Pettijohn.

4. "Thompson and Haymon's Ferry" is mentioned by Nicholas Carriger in 1846, location unknown, but possibly the same as the "Oregon Crossing" referred to by B. W. Evans in 1849, or the Nodaway Landing used by Stephen White in 1850. This would have been west of the present town of Oregon, Missouri.

5. "Harney's Landing," used by the Alonzo Delano party of 1849. This is described as thirty miles below Fort Kearny, which would put it in the vicinity of present Craig, Missouri.

6. Brownville, Nebraska, came into being in 1854 as a steamboat landing, roughly equidistant between St. Joe and Omaha. Wm. Maxwell indicates it also served as an emigrant ferry crossing in 1857.

OLD FORT KEARNY—NEBRASKA CITY

In 1835 Rev. Samuel Parker and other missionaries apparently drove north up the east side from Liberty, Missouri, to cross at Bellevue, so a north road of some sort existed for some time. Although the army relied mainly on steamboats to reach old Fort Kearny, the existence of a land route along the river to that point is also suggested by Lewis Dougherty, whose father was the post sutler. In 1849 a sizable number drove from St. Joe to old Fort Kearny, doubtless using a well-worn road. This passage, of course, entailed the difficult crossing of the Nodaway, Nishnabotna, and Tarkio rivers, the first two being equipped with ferries.

Connecting the Iowa side to old Fort Kearny was a precarious ferry run by John Boulware (sometimes spelled Bullard or Bowler), who was reputedly in business from 1846 to 1864. Among emigrants of 1849–1852 who made the north overland journey from St. Joe to use this ferry were Bruff, Lindsey, Wells, McGlashan, Wilkins, Doyle, F. Sawyer, Richardson, Frink, Trowbridge, and Wilson. (Randall Hewitt followed the same route as late as 1862.) There was, of course, another way to go north, and that was by steamboat. Hamelin, Montgomery, and Ira Butterfield were among those who reached old Fort Kearny–Nebraska City by this easier but more expensive method.

The U.S. Army created the Nebraska City crossing, just as it created the Leavenworth crossing, by the establishment of a military post on the west bank; but in the former case there was never an opposite town equivalent to Weston. In 1846 Col. Stephen Watts Kearny and his Dragoons were transported to the mouth of Table Creek and there erected a crude fort, named Fort Kearny (the first or old Fort Kearny, of course, not to be confused with the second, more permanent, and better-known Fort Kearny at Grand Island on the Platte, some 180 miles west). Table Creek had the virtue of being the point on the Missouri which was closest to the point where the Independence–St. Joe Road reached the Platte; the army supposed that this was the logical place to station troops to protect the Oregon migration and at the same time be supplied by steamboat.

The first Fort Kearny did not get beyond the blockhouse and log cabin stage before it was replaced, in 1848, by the second Fort Kearny. Two things contributed to this. First, there was the war with Mexico, which skeletonized the Table Creek garrison. Second, there was the superior logic of the fact that the heavy traffic was from the Independence and St. Joe areas, up the Blue and the Little Blue, and the place for a fort was where the covered wagons were, at the point of their convergence with the Platte, not some hypothetical point on the Missouri River. Even so, the existence of abandoned old Fort Kearny was magnet enough, somehow, to bring a respectable number of emigrants up the river to use this as a jump-off.

Emigrant journals throw some light on ill-fated old Fort Kearny. O. B. Huntington, a Mormon, visited the site in 1848, arriving by steamer from St. Louis, and found "70 of our boys at work for Uncle Sam, teaming." Presumably this activity related to the transfer of equipment and goods to the new Fort Kearny.

If the U.S. Army had any ground-plans or building inventories of old Fort Kearny they seem to have disappeared. The best surviving evidence of the physical appearance of this abortive Missouri River post is the well-known 1849 sketch in the collections of the Wisconsin Historical Society, herein reproduced. Long a mysterious "unknown," the artist has just recently been identified by John Frances McDermott in his book *Artist on the Overland Trail* as

James F. Wilkins, a professional illustrator who traveled to California to capture scenes for a moving "circular panorama" planned for public exhibition. Three unpublished 1849 diaries are also illuminating:

> Crossed over the ferry at Fort Kerny this afternoon. . . . Fort Kerny is quite a place. Lots of log houses and an eight square Blockhouse in the Center. There is a Sargent there to protect the U.S. Govt. property. The parade grounds are beautiful. No one is allowed to camp on it.—Dr. Charles Parke

> . . . brought up on Missouri River opposite Ft. Kerny that once was. . . . by hard squeezing we got over the river today, every fellow swearing it was his turn but we beat them. . . . Ft. Kerny that once was is beautifully situated on a fine slope of prairies as beautiful as ever laid out of doors, ½ miles from the river. . . . it is only a small Blockhouse with soldiers quarters.—Simon Doyle

> April 19 . . . reached Fort Kearny or Table Creek. . . . This site . . . handsomer . . . than Jefferson Barracks or Leavenworth, though entirely destitute of good buildings. . . .
> April 20 . . . our mess went into quarters and such quarters were perhaps never before seen. . . . Slept on my camp-bed of blankets in a house without a roof, door or windows, but as I expect to soon sleep in one large as all out-doors thought I had better be getting myself initiated. . . .
> April 25 . . . a company of 60 Californians from St. Louis, who have been in camp here since our arrival, started today on their long journey.
> April 28 . . . a company of Californians from Ohio crossed the river and encamped near us. . . .
> April 29 . . . At sundown the *St. Joseph* [steamboat] arrived. . . .
> May 4 . . . Steamboat *Mandan* up. . .
> May 6 . . . Plenty of troops have arrived here in the last few days.
> —J. P. Hamelin

These entries indicate that though the establishment was technically abandoned, it continued to be a focal point of military as well as emigrant debarkation. Doyle's entry suggests that those using the Fort Kearny ferry in 1849 were in such numbers that there was stiff competition for priority in crossing.

In 1850 John McGlashan was among those who traveled the land route north from St. Joe to this point, "by which means we could make some 40 miles of westing before entering Indian country." Opposite the fort he found a large number of emigrants waiting to be ferried over and signing a register. Dr. Reuben Knox camped here after ferrying, "trying to get regulated and break the mules." He wrote to his wife, "I have retired to an old shell of a blacksmith's shop, once used by the Army." He was fortunate to receive mail here by steamboat. Wm. Montgomery arrived by boat: "At this point we left the boat for land carriage. . . . we encamped at the old fort on the hill in log huts without doors or windows, where each one does his own cooking for a few days." Rev. Henry T. Davis, who eleven years later was a resident minister of Nebraska City, first arrived at the site in May, 1850, being among those who drove up the east side from St. Joe:

> Old Fort Kearney stood right where Nebraska City now stands. Here we crossed the Big Muddy in an old dilapidated ferry-boat. . . . We pitched our tent on the western slope of "Kearney Hill" . . . now a part of Nebraska City. Table Creek winds along the foot of Kearney Hill. Just across this creek, and a few hundred yards to the northwest, stood Old Fort Kearney. . . . The garrison here consisted of a block-house, made of logs, with port-holes for cannon and muskets, and two rows of barracks in the shape of an angle. . . . In 1850 . . . the Government property was in the care of H. P. Downs.
>
> When Nebraska City was founded and platted in 1854, the old block-house stood on Main Street, near the center of the city. Here it remained until 1886, when it was removed.

In 1852, according to Francis Sawyer, the old Fort Kearny ferry was still a livewire concern:

> May 1 . . . We arrived within one mile of Old Fort Kearny this evening, and Mr. Sawyer went to the ferry to register his name. To our discomfiture we learned that there were a great many before us waiting to cross, and it will probably be several days before our turn will come. . . .
>
> May 18 . . . the wind is blowing very hard today and the waves are rolling so high in the river that the ferry cannot run. Up to this time 906 wagons have crossed the river this year.
>
> May 19 . . . the old Fort is on the opposite side of the river, but there is not much left of it to be seen. The ferryman has a log cabin here and keeps some groceries and whiskey to sell at high prices.

The Kansas-Nebraska Act of 1854 created territories out of the Indian lands and put Fort Kearny, so to speak, back in business; Nebraska City rose phoenix-like from the figurative ashes of the army post. Founded by land speculators, Nebraska City benefited from the sharp increase in Missouri River steamboat traffic and burgeoning demands of the U.S. Army for provisioning by freight contract. With the Utah War of 1857 and the Colorado Gold Rush of 1859, Nebraska City took on boom proportions. In the spring months of the late fifties and the sixties its streets were alive with sweating humanity and the crack of bullwhips and revolvers, a prelude to the outflow of ox-drawn freighters and gold-seekers. The raucous growth of this border town may be traced through the journals of J. A. Wilkinson and Romazno Kingman in 1859, James Lowry and Wm. Hedges in 1860, Ira Butterfield in 1861, and Ada Millington in 1862. Vivid pictures of Nebraska City in its violent heyday, 1866, embellish the accounts of bullwhackers William H. Jackson, Julius Birge, and John Bratt.

Nebraska City today is a solidly respectable county seat with a conventional town square and courthouse, stately frame houses, and gigantic elm trees. Its hesitant beginnings as an army post are suggested only by a 1938 blockhouse replica, now at Fifth and Central, some distance from the original site. Its rambunctious career as the premier outfitter for the Pike's Peak and Virginia City gold rushes is suggested only faintly by a few venerable brick buildings, onetime warehouses and saloons, which survive from the sixties. A large white house at 14th and Third Avenue is believed to be the one-time home of Alexander Majors of the great freighting firm of Russell, Majors & Waddell.

COUNCIL BLUFFS–OMAHA

The Greater Omaha area, the northernmost of the Missouri River jumping-off places, embraces portions of Douglas, Washington, and Sarpy counties in Nebraska and Pottawattamie County in Iowa. Omaha proper, with a population now approaching one-half million, was not in existence until 1854, but Bellevue, now at Omaha's southern edge, old Florence at its northern city limits, Fort Atkinson a few miles farther north, and Council Bluffs on the Iowa side date from the beginnings of river travel up the Missouri.

Bellevue, at the mouth of Papio, or Papillion, Creek and now global headquarters for the Strategic Air Command, was the site of a trading post as early as 1810 and of a famous Presbyterian mission to the Omaha Indians in the 1830s. This was actually the earliest continuous settlement in Nebraska. Cabanne's Post and Manuel Lisa's Post, north of Omaha, were also in the early fur-trade competition, but they were short-lived.

Council Bluffs is the name given by Lewis and Clark to the site of their Indian parley in 1804 some twenty miles north of Omaha on the Nebraska side, near present Fort Calhoun. In 1819 Fort Atkinson was established at this same original Council Bluffs, but among fur traders this gradually became a generalized name for the entire district. In the fullness of time it became relocated on the Iowa side, opposite present Omaha. Although Council Bluffs, Iowa, has come to be associated with the Mormon exodus from Illinois-Iowa to Utah, its career as a frontier community started well before and continued well after the passage of Brigham Young. In 1837 Company C of the First Regiment of Dragoons, under Capt. D. B. Moore, came up from Fort Leavenworth and erected a block-house on the bluff to protect the Potawatomi from alleged enemies. In 1838 Father Pierre J. DeSmet arrived here to assist in setting up a mission among these Indians. With the permission of Col. Kearny, the Jesuits converted the blockhouse into a chapel, and the three log cabins of a half-breed trader became their dwellings. The blockhouse-mission was within the area now bounded by Broadway, Voorhis, Union, and State streets in Council Bluffs' downtown area.

In 1841 the Council Bluffs Mission was closed, given up as hopeless because of Sioux hostilities and the scourge of alcohol among the Potawatomi. Less than five years later, early in 1846, the advance guard of Mormon refugees from Illinois straggled down Indian Creek and Mosquito Creek into the Missouri River bottom below the old Jesuit mission and knocked together the first log cabins, which they dubbed Millersville or Miller's Hollow. By June several thousand of the Saints were encamped here. Anxious to get beyond the reach of unsympathetic Gentiles by circumventing the law against settling on Indian lands, Brigham Young made a deal with the Omaha to protect them against the Pawnee and promptly ferried his sizable flock across the Missouri. He erected a log and dugout village where his people died like flies during the following winter, but which, in 1847, became the base for his triumphant pioneer journey to the Great Salt Lake. This so-called Winter Quarters, sacred in Mormon history, later became the townsite of Florence, now annexed to Omaha.

The Mormon occupation of Winter Quarters was illegal, for

settlers were forbidden on Indian lands. Brigham Young was induced by Thomas H. Harvey, Superintendent of Indian Affairs, to evacuate this site, and "old Colonel Miller," resident agent of the Potawatomi, was given the job of seeing to it that the Mormons complied. In May, 1848, O. B. Huntington heard Brigham Young deliver a sermon in which he roundly cursed the United States in general and Miller in particular, "for his meanness and abuse." Nevertheless, the 1848 season was devoted to the evacuation of Winter Quarters. In May and June, according to James Little's account, Young and his Apostles led 2,500 people and nearly 1,000 wagons to the new Zion in Utah. The remainder, mainly the poor who had no outfits, were shuttled back across the Missouri and downstream once more to Miller's Hollow, where they populated a town which they called Kanesville in honor of Thomas Leper Kane, a Gentile friend.

The Mormons never intended to remain here. Kanesville was but a station on the Mormon migration route, and it was ably managed by three of the Twelve Apostles, Orson L. Hyde, George A. Smith, and Ezra Taft Benson. In February, 1849, Hyde began publication of the *Frontier Guardian*, which kept up morale and gave news of the migration. This year some 1,500 Mormons were launched toward Salt Lake, but the California Gold Rush came hard on their heels, and the road north of the Platte, which had begun to look like a privately-owned Mormon trail to Salt Lake, now became the Council Bluffs Road, the north lane of the Great Platte River Road.

There are no dependable estimates of the number of California emigrants leaving from Kanesville. The figure of 5,000 for 1849 seems reasonably conservative, to judge from general impressions and the excess of figures in the Fort Laramie register over the Fort Kearny register. (At Fort Laramie the Council Bluffs travelers crossed to the south side of the Platte.) There may have been 3,000 more Saints in 1850 and 1851, and their numbers in 1852 probably reached 7,500; but, at the same time, the number of Californians swelled to an estimated 20,000 in 1850; 10,000 in 1851; and 25,000 in 1852. (In 1850 Upton Swingley estimated 10,000 emigrants camped along the Missouri River here at one time.)

In 1849 George Jewett found Kanesville, which is often spelled Cainsville or Canesville, a "scrubby town of 80 to 100 log cabins," situated "3 miles from the river in a deep hollow." Randall Fuller found "one tavarn, one church and two groseries," in addition to the collection of "very small" houses. In 1850 William Kilgore found 350 houses, "principally of logs" at Kanesville, or "what is known as Council Blufs." Bryan Dennis found these strung along the hollow four or five miles and observed also that "Cainsville should be properly called the Bluffs." Fancher Stimson placed the "business section" in 1850 on Indian Creek, at the corner now occupied by the First Methodist Church. John Steele distinguished between Kanesville at the foot of the bluffs and Kanesville Landing on the river.

At the time, Kanesville did not seem like a very permanent settlement. In the peak Gold Rush year all the Gentiles seemed bent on getting to California, while the Mormon inhabitants, according to Riley Senter, were "all anxious to get off to the mountains." Fuller thought that the Mormons were "the poorest of all people that I ever saw." Relations between Mormons and Gentiles were on the whole peaceful, notwithstanding Dennis' observation that in trade "the Mormons shaved the Californians and the Californians shaved each other." Jewett mentions an incident in which the Mormons broke up a Gentile dance on the Sabbath; on the other hand, Reuben Miller says that Mormon trains were willing to accept Gentiles as "passengers," and vice versa, provided everyone avoided arguments over religion and just stuck to the business of getting across the Plains.

For many years the principal crossing of the Mormons was not due west of Kanesville, but about ten miles north at the original Mormon ferry, sometimes referred to as Upper Ferry. In 1849, according to Catherine Haun, there was a simple rope ferry with a flatboat big enough for two wagons. (The stock was usually obliged to swim.) On the west bank, of course, the emigrants were greeted by the rather dismal spectacle of abandoned Winter Quarters, or Camp of Israel, which Fuller describes as "250 loges houses, covered with poles and dirt, and handsomely laid out in streets." Martha Morgan came up with a count of "700 to 800 hovels deserted." In April, 1850, Kilgore witnessed the destruction of the ghost town:

> 29th [April] . . . We went up the river 12 miles to the Ferry. . . . This evening . . . crossed with the team, we went out a half mile to a Camp that we expected to joine. It [was] dark by this time & the wind blew a perfect herricane, whirled the tents topsie tervy and the

fire Came in flames & Sparks filling the whole heavens. This Came
from an old Mormontown that was on fire. It had been built of
Cottonwood logs that had Stood long enough to get thoroughly Dry.
. . . The town contained about Six hundred houses and nearly all on
fire. This was Called winterquarters.

John Steele agrees with 600. He and Abraham Sortore both
describe the unsightly ruins and "relics of old fireplaces."

The *Frontier Guardian* for February 20, 1850, ran an advertise-
ment plugging the virtues of "The Old Original Mormon Crossing
at Kanesville, Council Bluffs, Missouri River," as the "Nearest, Best
and Healthiest Route to the Salt Lake and California." But the
Mormon Crossing, operated by Mormons, had stiff competition
from a second ferry in the Council Bluffs area. Crossing about six
miles south of Kanesville, opposite the trading post and mission of
Bellevue, this southern ferry was probably pioneered by fur traders
who long antedated the Mormons. Usually identified as the Lower
Ferry, this was at a river bend called Trader's Point by Langworthy
and Trading Point by the *Frontier Guardian*. On the Iowa side in
1850, according to Steele, was "a village of low log houses" called
St. Frances. The *Guardian* for July 10, 1850, attempts to explain
the confusion about geographic names: "Kanesville Landing is at
Council Point about four miles above Trading Point or St.
Francis. . . . the name of the post office at Trading Point, formerly
called Nebraska Post Office, has recently been altered to Council
Bluffs Post Office." According to Jerome Dutton, Kanesville was
also a post office.

The Mormon exodus was stepped up in 1852. On May 21
Kanesville was still "filled with Mormons," says Charles Stevens,
"but the largest part of them are going to Salt Lake this spring"
and "about one third of the Houses in town are for sale." Henry
Bradley fixed the population at 1,000 or 1,500. Rev. John McAllister thought it "not a very desirable place to live," being crowded
into a ravine with one street. From this focal point he calculated
it was "8 miles to the lower ferry, 3 to the middle and 12 to the
upper." This is the first evidence of the opening of the middle
ferry, which would coincide roughly with the present bridge crossing to downtown Omaha.

At this western limit of civilization William Rowe observed
emigrants from Michigan, Indiana, Kentucky, Minnesota, and
Missouri and Arkansas, the last two indicating the popularity of

the northern route, even for those living much closer to Independence or St. Joe. No census was taken of the 1852 influx, but its immensity is suggested by the statement of L. A. Norton that it took up to six weeks for an emigrant to wait in line for a turn at the ferry. Mary Ackley reports a register of those wanting to be ferried, and her party twiddled its thumbs for three weeks. Ezra Meeker describes the spectacle at the Lower Ferry as resembling "a big white flatiron" with several hundred wagons closely interlocked, waiting for a crossing. The ferry operator here had two small keelboats (Hall) or scows, which, according to E. W. Conyers, would each accommodate two wagons at $4 per wagon. This price dropped upon the arrival of the steamboats *Robert Campbell* and *El Paso*, which made themselves available to emigrants at the extortionate rate of $10 to $20 per wagon (Richey).

In 1853 the Mormons made their final official exodus from Iowa, and in one great spasm over 3,000 of the faithful migrated to Salt Lake, abandoning Kanesville. The empty houses and barns were soon appropriated by Gentiles who decided to linger before going to California; and from this time on the name Kanesville rapidly gave way to Council Bluffs, although it would remain a few more years.

Council Bluffs still failed to impress anyone with its scenic qualities. "About all there was in Council Bluffs," says Stephen Forsdick, "was up in the hollow and did not amount to much." Henry Allyn says "the city of Cain" was "wedged in a hole" and complained that he "came very near upsetting in the main and only street, on account of gullies." To George Belshaw it was "only a little Burg between two high bluffs," but it was crammed to capacity with emigrants' teams and wagons, while the river bottom was one vast camp. No figures are available on the '53 migration, but it seems to have been on the scale of its predecessors. With the Mormons departed and no civil authority yet in evidence, there were many scenes of lawlessness. Velina Williams described an Indian orgy, inspired by Kanesville firewater. Allyn observed a knife fight in town and, along with Belshaw, witnessed a lynching. Harriet Ward was spared this scene but held her ears against "such profanity I never dreamed existed."

The Lower Ferry, which John Smith calls Sarpy's, and which Forsdick calls Lone Tree Ferry, was cheap (at $1.50 per boat load) but apparently a poor risk. Washington Bailey scorns it as a "home-made fur boat, an old ark, calked with buffalo tallow," and it took the Forsdick party ten days to ferry thirty-three wagons with the contraption. The Middle Ferry was much more expensive, but here for the first time the Missouri River was crossed in style, in a specially designed "steamboat ferry." Allyn calls this boat the *Hindo* and paid $10 per wagon, while Belshaw describes its capacity as eleven wagons and 100 head of cattle. Notwithstanding this premium toll, the Middle, or Council Bluffs, Ferry was the most in demand. Virginia Ivins' party drove "across the wide flat to the Missouri River." Here they found 500 wagons and thousands of cattle, and "We are told we must wait our turn, which probably would not come for several days." Mr. Ivins "was in no mood for waiting, so watching his opportunity he rushed in while some slower person was getting ready and before night we were on the Nebraska side and made our camp where the city of Omaha now stands."

A similar craft, the *Patrick Henry*, was in operation at the Upper Ferry. Dinwiddie describes it as commodious and a bargain at $5 per wagon. Late arrivals found the steam ferries gone and had to cross the hard way. Belshaw says the steamers went upriver to "get furs."

In 1854 the Middle Ferry apparently became the principal one. Scott Ebey found the cost of passage still $10 per wagon and crowds still causing long delays. This year Nebraska Territory was created, and settlement on the west bank was legalized. The earliest discovered diary reference to Omaha appears on May 1, in the reminiscences of Manfred Nott: "Just across on the west side a little town had been started a short time before."

In 1855 James Enos says he camped "where Omaha now stands," finding "a trading post and a few Pawnee Indians." However, Lydia Waters crossed by steam ferryboat to find a town platted for two miles, a few houses, and one brick building, the post office. (It is possible that Enos confused Omaha with Bellevue.)

The name Kanesville died hard. Although Ebey in '54 refers to "Bluff City, formerly Kanesville," the earlier name is still used in '55 by Lydia Waters and D. White. Lydia found the place crawling with Indians, who in turn crawled with lice and cleaned themselves with animal entrails. White says that on the west bank he was entertained by dancing Omaha Indians.

The earliest emigrant reference to Florence, the settlement which bloomed on the ashes of Winter Quarters, is to be found in the 1856 journal of Archer Walters, an English Mormon. In 1858 Martin Patterson, bound for the Colorado gold fields, figured Omaha at 3,000 inhabitants. In 1859 David Anderson put the figure at around 1,500, including dogs and Omaha Indians, but this is challenged by Charles Cummings, who figured 6,000 "inhabitance" and recognized that "Omahaw is a flourishing little city. It stands right opposite Council Bluffs on the Missouria River. It is the Capital of Nebraska. The Capital building is built on a hill a little out of town. I think for the chance Omahaw has, she is far ahead of council bluffs city."

In 1860 Mary Jane Guill thought Council Bluffs "a very pretty town." She crossed the murky Missouri in a boat called "the old *Nebraska*, well loaded, all Californians. Pass through the city of Omaha about as large as the bluff city. The State house was a nice building. Here we see Indians all around us. . . . From Omaha is the military road out to the forts." Randall Hewitt arrived on the scene in 1862, overland via Glenwood. He crossed the river by steam ferry for $3.50 and was impressed with what he saw:

> Omaha was the capital of Nebraska Territory and the legislative hall was a spacious structure for the period, situated on a sightly eminence overlooking a vast area of undulating country. The view from Capitol Hill was truly magnificent. . . .
>
> From Capitol Hill also countless tents and white-covered emigrant wagons were in view, covering the whole country around the city like the tented hosts on the plains of Jerico. Numerous trains of pilgrims, all like ourselves, bound for the new Eldorado, could be seen wending their way over the hills to the west, and passing beyond one's vision.

With the increase of steamboat traffic to Montana and the Upper Missouri in the mid-sixties, coupled with dense overland traffic, Omaha was in a boom stage. Construction on the Union Pacific Railroad began here in 1864, presaging the end of overland wagon traffic. George Harter worked on the first grade out of Omaha in order to earn the cost of an outfit to California. Philura Vanderburgh recalled a double-decker ferryboat in operation this year, which she considered big enough to hold "300 wagons and hundreds of loose cattle." The emigrant flood through Omaha is described by A. J. Dickson:

On the following morning, June 6, we drove up on the ferry and carried across to Omaha. At the wharf a boat load of goods from St. Louis was being unloaded. Bales of dry-goods, hundred-pound sacks of sugar and "State" flour, bags of cured meats, coffee and dried fruits, cases of lard and molasses, casks of butter and salt-fish and various other staples were dumped unceremoniously upon the landing and promptly hauled away.

We picked our way along the deeply rutted main street through a tangle of traffic, reaching the business section more by the grace of God than by our skill in driving. Here were stores and warehouses combined. . . .

Sounds of hilarity issued from the numerous saloons and dance halls, where strapping bull-whackers and muleskinners, during a care-free hour, were being adroitly relieved of their surplus cash through the agency of velvet-handed card experts or the age-old trinity, wine, women and song. Variously-clad papooses pressed grimy faces against tempting show windows, scurrying to cover whenever some lusty reveler came striding uncertainly along the sidewalk. Here and there a soldier mingled with the crowd. Horses, mules, cattle, dogs, the rumbling of wagons, the shouting of drivers—all contributed to the general confusion. . . .

Once clear of the jam we pulled out to where the City hall now stands, followed the military road northwest, about five miles, and camped for the night on the Papillion.

THE COUNCIL BLUFFS ROAD

The emigrant road north of the Platte River from the Council Bluffs–Omaha area to Fort Laramie was an integral part of the Great Platte River Road. It was the north half of the "Interstate highway" of the Great Migration, with the river itself forming a broad, watery median. Although modern scholars and writers are fond of tagging this north route the Mormon Trail, there was not much contemporary use of this term. It was sometimes referred to simply as the Northern Route, but most of the time during the early covered wagon migration period it was most widely known as the Council Bluffs Road. In later years it became the Omaha-Denver Road or the Omaha–Fort Kearny Military Road. In the sixties it also became the route of the Western Stage Company lines to Fort Kearny, and the wilderness of the emigrants was soon "thickly settled with thrifty farmers." In 1861 the Council Bluffs *Daily Telegraph* listed over fifty ranches catering to travelers.

Since there were three principal Missouri River crossings in the Council Bluffs vicinity, it follows that there were three principal trails which had to merge somewhere before there could be a main north road. This point was in the vicinity of present Fremont, Nebraska, where there was a Mormon marker called the Liberty Pole.

All trace of early trails has vanished under the spreading Omaha metropolis. They can be indicated only in a general way from the notes and maps of General Land Office Surveys of the 1850s and 1860s. The terrain between the Elkhorn and the Missouri is typical broken Missouri River benchland. Modern land leveling and grading has ironed out the worst of the wrinkles, but Omaha is still a city of topographical ups and downs. The emigrants, who could scarcely have imagined today's paving and traffic lights, had to traverse the area in its primitive state. They followed ridges where possible, so that their routes were more nearly level, but of course devious. Before reaching the Platte the principal concerns were the crossings of the Papillion and the Elkhorn (usually called the Horn), which here shares with the Platte a common flood plain.

From the North, or Mormon, Ferry at the Winter Quarters site there were two options, one trail going north to the vicinity of the original Council Bluffs (present Fort Calhoun) to get around the headwaters of the Papillion, then veering westward. The second way from Winter Quarters was up the bluffs and then southwestward over the upland. From the Middle, or Omaha, Ferry there was one primary road through the present downtown area. In the vicinity of the present Douglas County Courthouse it went northwestward to a point beyond Central High School, where there was a divergence, the main emigrant road swinging westward to the vicinity of Boys Town and then northwestward. The later military road via Fort Omaha veered to the northwest to join the Lower Mormon Road in the vicinity of the Benson shopping center.

The Trader's Point–Bellevue Ferry led to the Bellevue trading post and mission and the Mormon settlement called Mormon Hollow. From this neighborhood there were three routes westward. One very circuitously followed the north bank of the Platte River. A second went up Papillion Creek as far as the town of Papillion, then went west via present Millard to join the Bellevue–Platte Valley Road on the Elkhorn bottoms. A third Bellevue route went northwest to join the Omaha Road at Boys Town.

While the Lower Bellevue Road went north up the Elkhorn, the recombined Omaha Military–Lower Mormon–Upper Bellevue Road went west through present Irvington, and the north Mormon Road meandered west along the Washington-Douglas county line to the north of present Bennington. These two main routes then united to cross the Elkhorn in the vicinity of Rawhide Creek, a few miles north of present Waterloo. In the spring the Elkhorn was a wide and rambunctious stream, and its crossing was the first real challenge of the Council Bluffs Road. Because of the frequently disastrous results of attempts to ford and swim this river, the normal mode of crossing was the calking of wagons or the construction of rafts for floating. Upsets were commonplace. In 1850 Kanesville businessmen remedied this situation somewhat by providing "one large and substantial boat capable of crossing a wagon and team every five minutes" (*Frontier Guardian*). Although there were several efforts to construct a crude pole and plank bridge, there is no evidence of any permanent structure until the 1860s.

Indians of many tribes were to be seen occasionally in Council Bluffs and later in Omaha, but they were first seen in quantity and in all their bizarre trappings at the Elkhorn and beyond. At camp or along the trail they appeared singly, in family groups, and in whole village brigades, often materializing out of nowhere, lending local color to the landscape, but making themselves a great nuisance by importuning tributes of sugar, coffee, and whiskey.

The several roads along the Platte bottom followed the general line of the present Omaha-Fremont highway and the Union Pacific Railroad. They did not fuse into one road until reaching Liberty Pole, or Fremont, the main exception being that a wet-weather alternate hugged the edge of the Platte River bluffs, passing Fremont several miles to the north. Since the weather during the migration season was frequently sopping wet, this bypass road saw much service. There is simply no way to determine the number or percentage of those who followed the several routes approaching Fremont. However, it is estimated that over 100,000 covered wagon emigrants used the Northern, or Council Bluffs, Road prior to 1867; of this number, perhaps half used the two Mormon Road branches from the Upper Ferry, while most of the remaining half used the emigrant road via downtown Omaha, since the Middle, or Omaha, Ferry was the principal one during the late period of heavy use,

1858–1866. Numerically, the Bellevue roads were not a primary factor.

From Liberty Pole–Fremont to Fort Laramie the Council Bluffs Road followed the north bank of the main Platte, and its monotonous scenic and vegetative characteristics were pretty much identical with the situation on the south bank, the side of the Nebraska City Road and the main Oregon-California Trail. The principal exceptions to this were a few short sandhill detours in central and western Nebraska, and the fording of the Loup River. In 1858, upon military recommendation, a dependable ferry was installed at the mouth of the Loup, right at present Columbus, so that the journey along the main Platte was uninterrupted. Prior to that year, however, the emigrants deemed it necessary to continue up the Loup many miles before crossing.

Passing an 1846 Pawnee village southwest of Columbus, the original route as pioneered by Brigham Young in 1847 continued up the north bank of the Loup to Beaver Creek. Here in 1857 the town of Genoa was founded, a ferry established, and a new road pioneered south to reach the Platte near Clarks. However, in the earlier climax years the emigrants followed the Mormon lead southwestward along the Loup past the mouth of Cedar Creek, where the pre–1846 Pawnee town was destroyed by the Sioux. The place selected by the Mormon Pioneers and most others to ford the Loup was just above Cedar Creek and about three miles downstream from Fullerton.

Because of the softness of the banks, and the quicksand in the river, the Loup always posed a problem. Once across, the emigrants kept along the south bank of the Loup for several miles, and then turned due south over the dry divide to Wood River, striking the Platte about ten miles upstream from Central City.

There was another crossing of the Loup farther upriver, about four miles north of Palmer in Merrick County. It passed the Skidi Pawnee village, then traversed Howard and Hall counties south and southwesterly to strike the Platte near Alda, about ten miles west of the modern city of Grand Island.

From the general vicinity of Central City and Grand Island, the combined trails from the Loup went west along the main Platte, substantially the same route as the present U.S. Highway 30 and the Union Pacific Railroad. (This would also parallel the route of Interstate 80 between Grand Island and North Platte.) Covered wagon trains, variously filled with potential citizens of Utah, California, Oregon, and Montana-Idaho, traversed the sites of Central City, Grand Island, Shelton, Gibbon, Kearney, Elm Creek, Lexington, Cozad, and Gothenburg before these communities were conceived. (They would not have crossed the site of modern North Platte, since that is between the two forks.) Along the North Platte River they would have joined U.S. Highway 26 opposite Ash Hollow and then proceeded through the future streets of Lewellen, Oshkosh, Lisco, Northport, Bayard, Scottsbluff, Mitchell, and Morrill (Nebraska), and Torrington (Wyoming) on their way to the Fort Laramie crossing.

Having gotten over the Loup, travelers via the Council Bluffs Road "had it made" as far as stream crossings were concerned; there were none of consequence until they finally crossed the North Platte itself. They did have some unpleasant swamp and sandhill crossings, but these were too routine to deserve detailing. Their experiences with storms, buffalo, Indians, and French traders paralleled those of their south-side contemporaries. They suffered less from cholera, but had to content themselves with viewing from a distance the famous south-side landmarks of Ash Hollow, the Court House, the Chimney, and Scott's Bluffs. Only two landmarks, or rather groups of landmarks, deserve mention.

Between Oshkosh and Broadwater in western Nebraska were the Ancient Bluff Ruins, scarcely equal in grandeur or distinction to the Chimney or Scott's Bluffs, but still a curious set of formations which the north-siders could brag about on their own. Here they camped for a spell, did their chores, prayed, were threatened by rattlesnakes, and clambered about to get the great panoramic view westward and the first glimpse of the amazing Chimney Rock, about forty miles away, a shimmering needle on the horizon.

There were many famous Lone Trees along the emigrant trails. There was one west of Kansas City and another along the Blue River. The Council Bluffs Road had three such rarities. The first was on the Omaha side of the Missouri and gave its name to Lone Tree Ferry, apparently a variant of the Lower Ferry. The second Lone Tree was at Central City and was acknowledged to be the last bit of timber along the Platte (not counting the scraggly willow and cottonwoods on the islands) for a distance of 200 miles. The third Lone Tree was directly opposite Cedar Grove, about two miles downstream from Ash Hollow. Like all Lone Trees, it was gradually hacked at and dismembered even as it was being admired, and by 1866 it was only a memory. The three Lone Trees serve mainly to remind us that the Great Plains belt was so monotonously devoid of timber that any stray specimen was a marvel and that the Great Migration was sorely handicapped by the lack of wood for fires and wagon repairs. This is a point we tend to overlook with the relative profusion today of shelterbelts, ranch groves, and streamside timber.

Of some 700 overland accounts noted, approximately 150 pertain to journals along the Council Bluffs Road. This does not include many Mormon journals known to exist but unlisted, and in any event the number is not a true index of the proportionate number of emigrants who followed the north bank, over one-fourth of the total. References by California Road emigrants to those on the Council Bluffs Road are abundant:

> All day wagons winding along the opposite shore.—C. W. SMITH, 1850

> Campfires on the north side seem as numerous as on the south side.—W. McBRIDE, 1850

> It looks like the heaviest portion of the emigration on the north side of the Platte.—PHOEBE JUDSON, 1853

> Most of the emigration is on the north side of the river.—ADA MILLINGTON, 1862

The classic Mormon account was that of William Clayton, official scribe of the 1847 Pioneers. Appleton Harmon also made an exceptional record. Hosea Stout, O. B. Huntington, and John Pulsipher are illuminating for 1848. Later Mormon journals of note include those of James Linforth, Leander Loomis, and Twiss Bermingham. Of the non-Mormon journals, the following may be considered as exemplary for details of the Council Bluffs Road:

> 1849: Martha Morgan, Catherine Haun, and Riley Senter.
> 1850: Franklin Langworthy, William Kilgore, Fancher Stimson, John Steele, G. W. Thissell, Henry Bloom, Henry J. Coke, and Byron McKinstry.
> 1852: James Akin, E. W. Conyers, Henry Bradley, Addison Crane, Ezra Meeker, Jared Fox, and Thomas Turnbull.
> 1853: Thomas Flint, Amelia Knight, J. B. Bradway, Stephen Forsdick, and Henry Allyn.

1854–1859: Lydia Waters, Charles Cummings, Charles M. Tuttle, Taylor Snow, and Martin Patterson.

1860–1866: James Roberts, Mary Warner, Lavinia Porter, Louise Rahm, George Fox, A. J. Dickson, George Harter, William Larkin, and Jane Tourtillot.

V

Approaches to the Nebraska Seacoast

THE INDEPENDENCE ROAD

THAT SECTION OF THE Oregon-California Trail commonly known in emigrant days as the Independence Road was first used by trading expeditions out of the Kansas City area in the 1830s. It followed the established Santa Fe Trail southwestward for some forty miles, then broke off to head northwestward for the Platte River. Eastern Kansas is tall-grass prairie country. While trees are plentiful today, they were scarce in 1849 as the result of frequent prairie fires. The lack of wood and the numerous stream crossings were the biggest problems faced by the emigrants. Once the streams were crossed, the idea was to get on high ground between drainages. Modern roads make it possible to approximate this route today, but it is a disappointing effort since intensive cultivation, highway construction, and timber growth have practically obliterated the evidence; there is, however, the usual quota of helpful granite markers.

The original Santa Fe–Oregon–California Trail dropped southwestward from Independence along Blue Ridge via present Raytown to the old Red Bridge crossing of the Blue River (Missouri), and intersected the boundary between the United States and unorganized Indian territory (now the Missouri-Kansas line) between present 103rd and 120th streets and State Line Road in Kansas City. This was called simply The Line, denoting separation between white settlement and Indian wilderness. On the Missouri side of

The Line were Fitzhugh's Mill and Little Santa Fe, where wagon trains would camp to recruit and reorganize. In 1849 William Kelly says there was also a tavern called the House of Refuge, which straddled The Line where lawbreakers were safe from the Jackson County sheriff. Henry Shombre says he visited a "dogery" on The Line near Westport to have one last spree before jumping off.

The Westport Trail likewise went southwesterly, intersecting The Line about sixty city blocks north of the Independence Road. At The Line it split, one branch going to McCoy's 1831 Baptist mission, the other going past the 1839 Shawnee Methodist mission. (Three brick buildings still exist in Johnson County, as a Kansas state park). The branches rejoined near present Milburn, Kansas, and proceeded past Lenexa to Olathe. Near these missions were the flourishing farms of the civilized Shawnee and Delaware Indians, dressed in turbans and fringed buckskins, who often assisted the white men as hunters and guides. Beyond was Indian Creek, a rendezvous point, and then the open prairie, which undulated, wrote William Kelly, "like the huge lazy swell of the Atlantic in a calm." The verdure of spring, spangled with flowers, gave zest to the adventure. It is "the finest prairie ever beheld," wrote I. M. Hixson. "Were the country only timbered it would be the garden spot of the world."

The prairie road itself, ever winding to take advantage of contours, led Richard Hickman to exclaim, "A more crooked road never marked this green footstool!" Wm. Johnston reported the surface of the Santa Fe Road (often spelled Santafee) hard and smooth, but Joseph Ware cautioned, "You cannot, on the average, make more than 15 miles per day," because of many stream crossings. Steep muddy banks had to be cut down with spades. Wagons were frequently lowered and hoisted with ropes and chains, and double-teaming—all stout shoulders to the wheel—often was a necessity. Thomas Eastin complained that the guidebooks failed to mention the ordeal of fording prairie streams.

The second principal campsite, about forty miles out, was at the head of Cedar Creek south of Olathe, a place caled Sapling Grove, Round Grove, or Elm Grove in early days, but in 1849 called Lone Elm because of a single tree which had escaped the campers' axe. And it was "fast being hacked away by the travellers, for firewood," wrote James Pratt. In 1852 Gilbert Cole reported that there was "no Lone Tree to be found."

The main junction of the Westport and Independence roads was in the vicinity of Gardner, Kansas (now on the Santa Fe Railroad), just before the Independence Road (Oregon Trail) veered from the parent Santa Fe Trail. This was east of the crossings of Bull Creek and Cow Creek, where lived a Shawnee named Rogers whose sons were all named for Presidents (Talbot) and who became the beneficiary of gifts from emigrants who already realized that they were overloaded (Johnston). In 1839, when he turned here for Fort Laramie, Dr. Wislizenus had found the Trail so indistinct that "our leader at times lost it." Now it was fast becoming a boulevard. "Our crowd is so large," wrote James Pratt in 1849, "it seems like a village wherever we stop."

Up to this point the trains had been veering in the wrong direction, toward Santa Fe, but they did this to stay on the divide between the Kansas and Osage river drainages, avoiding any serious stream crossings. Now it was necessary to move north, with the fording of Bull Creek and Captain Creek first on the agenda. Skirting an eminence called Coon Point, or Observation Bluff (southeast of Eudora), where they often clambered to get the grand view, the emigrants entered Douglas County, Kansas, crossing the headwaters of the Wakarusa. Here they left the Shawnee provinces and entered the territory of the Kaw, or Kanzas, Indians. In 1843 Theodore Talbot represented this latter tribe as colorful, with shaved heads and roaches, or feathered scalp locks, and heads and bodies daubed with vermilion in "rings, streaks and stripes." Their mud-daubed stick houses were circular, thirty to forty feet in diameter, and resembled giant inverted pots or "a collection of giant molehills." In 1850 Dr. Tompkins calls them "degraded beings, lazy, filthy, thievish." They frequently accosted the emigrants with greasy documents, signed by Indian agents, attesting to their honesty, which Tompkins calls "lying papers."

The trail went due west in Douglas County past the Blue Mound (mentioned by John C. Fremont), crossing Spring and Coal creeks, then turned abruptly north to cross the Wakarusa River, touch the present university town of Lawrence, and then resume the westward drive to Big Springs, or Coon Hollow (Palmer), just east of the Shawnee County line. From Lawrence westward to St. Marys the Independence Road paralleled the Kaw River.

The Wakarusa Crossing, sixty miles from the settlements, was the most vexing thus far, emphasizing the strain on men and equipment and leading Micajah Littleton to complain, "We shall break down all our wagons!" According to Thomas Eastin, Wakarusa meant black corn. It was spelled every imaginable way, including Wakerusia (B. C. Clark), Walka Rocha (Reading), Wakseruthia (Love), and Wahanissi (Pratt). Pratt found here also another Shawnee who was making a fortune by trading oxen and pulling wagons out of the mud.

From Big Springs there was another trail split, the south branch keeping well below Topeka to reach the earliest Methodist mission settlement of Union, or Unionville (1835), and cross the Kaw (Kansas River) below modern Rossville. Union was ten miles west of Topeka or 110 miles out of Independence. A north branch hugging the Kaw went later through Tecumseh and crossed the Kaw at Pappan's (or Papin's) Ferry (1842), near the present bridge in the Kansas state capital of Topeka. There was a third or intermediate Kaw ferry of late vintage called Smith's Ferry (1853), about three miles west of Topeka.

Regardless of which Kaw ferry was used, everyone first had to cross Shunganunga Creek (subject to another wide variety of spellings, such as McCoy's Shawankunk). Union was at the junction of Otter (or Blacksmith) and Mission creeks. Here also was the U.S. Agency for the Potawatomi, who preferred hunting and fighting to the art of agriculture, but whom Dr. Tompkins conceded to be at least "half civilized," in contrast to the Kansas beggars and the Pawnee savages. These braves, too, wore roaches and sometimes turned up in outlandish costumes, ranging from silk hats and parasols, calico and castoff army uniforms, to near nakedness. William Kelly refers to their "grotesque dandyism."

James Pratt said this "Indiantown had seven stores and 80 houses of logs rudely but well constructed." Sgt. Lowe thought it the only civilized place west of the settlements. James Evans said it had the appearance of a French village and that civilized Shawnee seemed to run the place, keeping shops and beer houses. Near Union they also owned the ferry, consisting of two little scows.

The Lower Ferry at Topeka was run by Joseph and Louis Papin, according to Matthew Field in 1843, and their outfit consisted of a platform floating on three dugout canoes propelled by poles. This same kind of a rig at the "Cansas Ferry" was in operation in 1849, according to Wm. Johnston, who describes the operation: "By means of a rope, one end of which was coiled around a tree, the wagons were let down the steep banks of the river, and placed in the boat. Two wagons and 12 mules were taken over at a time, the boat being propelled by poles. A Frenchman and his two sons, half-breed Kaws, own and work the ferry. Their charge is $4. for each wagon, 25¢ for a mule, and 10¢ each man. Double teams are required to haul the wagons up the northern bank, and through the deep sands extending ¼ mile back from the river." Some emigrants, like Wm. Pleasants, rebelled at the rates and rigged up their own rafts. Upsets and drownings were a frequent occurrence at the Kaw crossings, for this major stream, described by D. Jagger as 600 feet wide, was often in an angry mood.

At Smith's Ferry there was a Baptist mission to the Potawatomi from 1848 to 1859. A limestone building of the mission survives as a dairy barn, but all trace of Union has vanished.

The emigrants continued along the north bank of the Kaw through slow bottomland, often stumpy and mud-bound. Opposite Papin's was Soldier Creek, according to J. Q. Thornton named for an incident in which Dragoons from Fort Leavenworth overtook whiskey smugglers and "knocked in the heads of the barrels." About seventeen miles west, above Rossville, was Cross Creek, which seems to be synonymous with Eastin's Turkey Creek and Hixson's Mill Creek. Here the odorous but canny Potawatomi had a toll bridge and a horse-powered sawmill; making a fast buck was one of the white man's accomplishments they imitated quickly. Littleton's company of the 1850 migration objected to an increase of the toll from 10¢ to 50¢ and built a bridge of their own.

A few miles west of Cross Creek was the log and bark village of St. Marys and an L-shaped log building which was a Catholic mission. This was twenty miles above "the Frenchman's Ferry," or 120 miles from the settlements. Richard Hickman describes it as a log building with a bell in its cupola. Although the log structures have vanished, St. Marys is still in operation as a Catholic school.

About ten miles farther west the Independence Road started a big swing northward, making the difficult crossing of the Little, or Red, Vermillion, intersecting the Fort Riley–Fort Leavenworth Road, crossing Rock Creek, and then following grassy uplands to present Westmoreland, seat of Pottawatomie County. It proceeded northwestward from here across the Marshall County line past present Bigelow to the tough crossing of the Black, or Big, Vermillion. Both Vermillions were steep-banked, requiring heavy spading and

The north side lane, known as the Council Bluffs Road, approaching Ancient Bluff Ruins near Broadwater, Nebraska.

—Photo by Merrill J. Mattes

Deep trough near the summit of California Hill, en route to Ash Hollow from the Upper Ford near Brule, Nebraska.

—Photo by Merrill J. Mattes

Westport Landing (now Kansas City, Missouri), which rivalled Independence as one of the earliest jumping-off places.

—"The United States Illustrated,"
Kansas State Historical Society

St. Joe as it was universally called (St. Joseph, Missouri), the main jumping-off place in 1849 and 1850.

—from an old print,
St. Joseph Historical Society

Council Bluffs, Iowa (formerly Kanesville) in the early 1850's. Oil painting by George Simons.

Omaha, Capital of Nebraska Territory, in the middle 1850's, from the November 6, 1958 issue of Frank Leslie's Illustrated Newspaper.

Old Fort Kearny abandoned, 1849. Sketch by James F. Wilkins, 1849.

—Wisconsin Historical Society

Pawnee village, south side of the Platte, 1856, en route Nebraska City to New Fort Kearny. Sketch by George Simons, sketchbook for N. P. Dodge.

—Collections, Council Bluffs Public Library

New Fort Kearny, 1849. The forlorn character of this post in this climactic year is conveyed in this sketch by James F. Wilkins. Structure on the left, being shingled, is the frame hospital. Large building in center foreground is the sod storehouse erected in 1848.

—Wisconsin Historical Society

Fort Kearny, circa 1863, by an unidentified artist. On the reverse side of a miniature photocopy a soldier (also unidentified) wrote: "Where I stay is in the building to the left of the flag staff. The Post Office I have marked "P.O."

—Nebraska Game and Parks Commission

After leaving Fort Kearny the emigrants began the monotonous trek up the Big Platte, with its endless waves of sand hills. Sketch by William H. Jackson, 1932, based on notebook sketches of 1866.

—Oregon Trail Museum
Scotts Bluff National Monument

The Platte Valley was frequented by enormous buffalo herds, which sometimes stampeded and endangered the wagon trains. Sketch by William H. Jackson, 1932, based on field sketches of 1866.

—Oregon Trail Museum,
Scotts Bluff National Monument

Oregon emigrants fording one of the smaller prairie streams. In this case the wagon beds are getting only slightly damp.

Emigrant family fording the Platte. Lashing logs to the wagon beds helped, but sizeable logs were scarce.

Despite the deep impression made on emigrants by Ash Hollow, with its hor-rendous hill and sylvan glades, emigrant sketches of this locality are rare. One of the very few identified is this on-the-spot rendering in his journal by Forty-Niner D. Jagger.

—California Historical Society

No emigrant ever had the opportunity to get this magnificent airplane view of the precipitous hill (today called Windlass Hill) dreaded by all emigrants. Note the deep trough of the Oregon-California Trail following along the crest, and the radiating scars on the hillside.

—Nebraska Game and Parks Commission

rope work. Eastin says his party couldn't cross the Black Vermillion until they had built a raft with connecting timbers as a temporary bridge.

At the first Vermillion the emigrants entered territory technically claimed by the Pawnee and extending all the way up the distant Platte River to its forks. Actually, the Pawnee were kept busy defending their western claims against the Sioux and Cheyenne, and likewise, during 1849–1850, against the various Kansas tribes. Reports of Indian-emigrant battles and massacres appear in Sedgley's, Jagger's, and C. W. Smith's accounts, but these seem to be rumors. For the most part the emigrants were exposed to nothing worse than thievery, but they were sometimes the horrified witnesses to tribal warfare, usually the Pawnee against everyone else.

Most of these scenes occurred between the Kaw ferries and the Black Vermillion. In 1842 Peter Burnett witnessed the triumphal return of allied Kanzas and Osages, daubed in red paint and laden with Pawnee scalps, complete with ears. The next year Pierson Reading observed another such gruesome cavalcade, this time with other hacked-off portions of Pawnee warriors. In 1850 Micajah Littleton was startled to see a band of Potawatomi "come flying across the road," either in pursuit of Pawnees or being chased by them, he couldn't be sure. Dr. Tompkins said that full-scale warfare had indeed broken out, and he provides vivid descriptions of war dances, feasts, and genuine Indian-style campaigning: ambush, charge and counter charge, unearthly yells and screams, the pursuit of the vanquished, and the unhappy fate of Pawnee prisoners. He credits the Potawatomi with skill in firearms, which they learned from white traders. He expresses little sympathy for the Pawnee, "the most perfect savages," who were armed only with the bow and arrow and went about clothed in smelly buffalo hides "tied with a string."

Delos Ashley has it that "Weston Road" came in above the Black Vermillion, although the main road from Weston and Leavenworth tied in with the St. Joe Road. The main Independence Road went northwestward from Bigelow to reach famous Alcove Springs and make the original crossing of Blue River, called Independence Crossing, a good 200 miles from Independence Courthouse. There was another Big Blue Crossing at Marysville, about eight miles north, on the St. Joe Road.

Alcove Springs, just above the crossing, is preserved today as a local park, and the timber in the neighborhood is so thick it is hard to imagine emigrant wagons getting through this country to the Big Blue. George McKinstry says it was named by Edwin Bryant, his fellow traveler in 1846. One can still see the famous rock ledge over which once played "a beautiful cascade of water." McKinstry himself carved the name "Alcove Spring," which is still legible here. One of the most notable Oregon Trail graves is that of Mrs. Sarah Keyes of the same wagon train, who "died May 29, 1846. Age 70." Hixson found another grave, that of "John Fuller, 20, accidentally shot April 28, 1849." Wm. Johnston found a note in a notched stick written by Capt. Paul, another early bird Forty-Niner from Pittsburgh, explaining that Fuller had accidentally shot himself: "The mode was the usual one . . . the muzzle was toward him and went off by itself."

The Big Blue (called Blue Earth River by Elizabeth Geer and J. Q. Thornton) was second only to the Kaw in difficulty of crossing. Samuel Hancock says the Oregon emigration of 1845 was held up here three weeks by flooding. The 1846 expedition, having buried Grandma Keyes, addressed itself to crossing the Big Blue, says Thornton, "by the construction of large canoes, to be used, when lashed together, as a sort of raft. . . . Two large cottonwood trees . . . were felled. . . . It was intended to unite them by means of cross timbers, so as to admit the wheels of the wagon . . . then to attach lines to both ends of this 'Big Blue Rover' . . . and by pulling backward and forward, convey over all our wagons and goods." In 1850 Dr. Tompkins found the Big Blue "12 rods wide and so deep that floats or rafts are indispensable for crossing. . . . Several persons are drowned at this crossing every year. . . . Such horrid noises caused by the braying of the asses, lowing of oxen, screaming of women and children with the fiendish cursing and swearing shouted in all languages by furious madmen was enough to becraze the greatest stoic in all Christendom."

THE ST. JOE ROAD

The St. Joe Road was rivaled only by the Council Bluffs Road as a prime feeder line to the Platte River, and during the period 1849–1852 this could with propriety have been dubbed "Gold Rush Alley," so dense were the emigrant throngs. The main emigrant road meandered west about 150 miles, back and forth across present U.S. 36 from St. Joseph to Marysville, Kansas (which route is not to be confused with the later Pony Express route, joining the Fort Leavenworth Road, farther south). From the bottomlands opposite St. Joe the route climbed upland near Wathena, went north of Troy to reach Highland (the Indian mission), thence westerly via Hiawatha and Sabetha to a line about eight miles north of Seneca, not far from the Nebraska line, then southwestward to Marysville and the Big Blue. (Except for the Indian mission near Highland none of the towns mentioned then existed west of St. Joe.)

There were numerous stream crossings, the principal ones mentioned being Mosquito and Wolf creeks and the Big and Little Nemahas, at the approximate distances of twenty, twenty-five, ninety, and one hundred miles, respectively. Between the Wolf and the Nemaha the object was to stay on the divide between the Missouri and Kansas river drainages. This resulted in some pretty tortuous windings. Charles Kirkpatrick observed, "In order to keep a good grade the road sometimes forms a complete letter S," so that sometimes the cavalcade seemed to be doubling back on itself.

Water was normally plentiful, but wood was much scarcer than today. Henry Page asserted there was "no timber, except on the immediate banks of creeks, and then only where the banks were very steep and broken." He continued, "It is [a] curious sight to come upon a creek & for miles & miles not find ten trees on its banks, the grass growing down to the water's edge."

From the Missouri bluff line to Wolf Creek, as James Bennett observed, the country is very much broken, with frequent gullies and limestone outcrops. West of Wolf Creek the terrain gradually converts to smooth and undulating hills. The emigrants debated whether "the great American Plains" properly began at the river bluffs or at the Indian mission near Wolf Creek. The heavy rains made rough going in the bottomlands and creek crossings, but for the most part, Lucius Fairchild asserted, "the roads are splendid, as hard as plank," while Henry Page considered the St. Joe Road better "than I have ever found in Illinois." Solomon Gorgas rated the St. Joe Road, covering the 300 miles to Fort Kearny, as "exceedingly good, with the exception of crossings the first fifty miles."

In peak years the timbered Missouri River bottoms were dense with noisy emigrant camps and assembling trains. These bottoms were either six miles or two miles across, depending on whether the main ferry in St. Joe was crossed or the Upper Ferry four miles above; either way, most emigrants embarking on their great adventure struggled up the bluffs via the head of Clear Creek near present Wathena. The view westward from the top of the bluffs made a deep impression. To Wm. Chamberlain the vast landswells "resembled the blue ocean." Abigail Duniway thought the prairie in springtime "a sight for angels to admire." John Clark was a bit more specific: "On our arrival I held for a moment taking a general view of the wonderful & baren looking desert of the West . . . long ridges, dry knobs, deep gullies, few flowers, and short grass; now & then a stunted grove or lonely oak."

In 1852 Theodore Potter calculated there were 10,000 emigrants camped on the edge of this prairie waiting for the rains to stop. Then, he reported, "The morning of the eighth of May brought us good weather and the entire body . . . formed a great procession." He noted a startling phenomenon: "Previous to this time there had been but one trail over which the wagons could pass. But 10,000 people starting from the same locality on the same day made it necessary for more trails, which were very easily made on the open prairie. . . . During the first day's march there were at least twelve roads for twelve teams abreast."

The first difficult crossing was at Mosquito Creek, which John Clark called Indian Run and Vincent Geiger called Spider Creek, a mean little crevasse which often required a combination of brush fill and roping to put the wagons across. It was also the first occurrence of a phenomenon which often startled the traveler—isolated trees bearing platforms of Indian dead. Dr. Boyle "went to examine an Indian grave on a tree top that is a trough made from a log," with "knife and other accoutrements of the deceased to fit him for his entrance into the Indian paradise." Geiger was told this crude coffin contained the four-year-old remains of a chief of the Iowa tribe, and he helped himself to "a bead from the box." As they advanced over the Plains and trees became even scarcer, the emigrants would find many scaffold, or platform, burials, with the body placed on four upright poles and the desecration of these heathen biers would become routine.

At St. Joe and in the west bottoms the emigrants had been pestered by "dirty looking redskins" (John Clark) looking for handouts. These were the more shiftless members of the Kickapoo, Sac, and Fox tribes who had been settled on the west bank of the Missouri River in the early 1840s. West of Mosquito Creek these tribesmen had more clothing and fewer lice, and their begging assumed more sophisticated forms, of which Lucius Fairchild's experience was typical: "We met two Indians one a Sack and the other a Fox both chiefs with a paper from the Indian Agent saying that the Indians complained of the emigrants burning their timber and requested all to pay them something so we gave them a half dollar which satisfied them." In 1852 several indignant travelers mentioned the levying of tribute at the rate of 25¢ per team just to cross the reservation. "The tariff," wrote Jay Green, "I did refuse to pay as I thought it a skeem of speculation got up by the Indian Agent."

The real payoff, however, was at Wolf Creek, five miles beyond the Mosquito, described by Lorenzo Sawyer as "a rocky gorge 20 feet deep and 40 feet across." Here the agency Indians in 1849 built a rickety pole bridge and, although W. McBride complained about their making "a snug little fortune," it would seem that they were just as entitled as the Kansas Potawatomi to a toll for their pains. This was normally "two bits," an expression in the English language the Indians were able to master, but on occasion a particularly smooth operator would try to extract $5 per wagon (Sawyer, Potter). This much-maligned bridge did save a lot of back-breaking rope work, but several emigrant parties rebelled and made a crossing of their own "after a great deal of hard labor" (Burrall, Gelwicks). Theodore Potter "joined others to build a new bridge," but "it was said that there were four such bridges built in two days over that narrow stream." As soon as the emigrants had passed, the Indians lost no time in demolishing these rival structures. Several diarists refer to a village of Indian lodges made of woven brush (Page), with "both sexes selling moccasins and lariats" (Woodward). Those coming in from the Savannah Ferry joined the St. Joe Road near this point (Sawyer).

In 1837 on Mission Creek, a few miles west of Wolf Creek, the Presbyterians built a mission to the Iowas (Sac and Fox), and this also became a government station known as the Greater Nemaha Sub-Agency. In 1846 a three-story stone and brick building of thirty-two rooms replaced the original log structure as Indian school and boardinghouse; two miles east and a little north of Highland a substantial part of the original building still stands, being preserved by the State of Kansas. Much space was devoted in emigrant journals to the mission and agency, the only signs of civilization between St. Joe and Fort Kearny (until the birth of Marysville in the late fifties).

In 1844 John Minto visited the early log "barrack-like buildings of the Iowas to purchase some of their dried corn." Washington Gilliam of the same Oregon train said that agency Indians stole several herds of cattle, but that "the Agent made restitution out of the annuities." In 1848 Riley Root visited the "Ioway and Sack Mission Boarding School" and was shown around the new structure by Rev. S. M. Ervin. To the Forty-Niners this was a memorable landmark. There are many descriptions of the impressive layout, which, in addition to the big brick school, included log houses, stores, shops, a "horsemill" for grinding grain, and about 100 acres fenced and under cultivation to wheat and corn. Thomas Woodward says that in 1850 there was an emigrant register at the mission.

The Californians who camped all over the premises were unfair in their judgment of the Indians, who were described variously by such phrases as "repugnant to labor" (Biddle) and "the nastiest Indians I ever saw" (Hackney). Watson thought these "remnants of Sacks, Foxes and Ioways . . . too fond of hunting and painting their faces." Gelwicks bought corn at the "Government mission" for 75¢ a bushel and enjoyed the pageantry of Indian horseracing, red blankets, and shrill war whoops, but pronounced them "a dirty, squalid, miserable looking set of beings, meanly clad and foolishly disfigured." N. A. Cagwin thought them "fine looking Indians," but mercenary, eager to obtain gratuities from the whites by challenging them to footraces and placing bets on their marksmanship with bow and arrow.

West of Wolf Creek and Mission Creek the emigrants came upon unbounded prairie which Jacob Bartholomew thought "beautiful beyond description." It abounded in wild turkey gobblers (J. L. Johnson), prairie hens and plover (Cagwin), outsize turtles (Geiger), and a profusion of "elkhorns of immense size" (Gelwicks). Elk and deer, wolves and antelope were now getting scarce, however, because of the emigrant traffic. There was an occasional prairie fire, throwing aloft pillars of white smoke by day and a fiery red glow at night, or the black evidence of recent fires which sometimes, Dr. Thomasson complained, left "ashes and dust blowed all over our vitules." Another annoyance was what Gelwicks calls "a shower of bugs," which darkened the sky and "fell like hail," frightening the livestock. Capt. Stansbury called them black beetles and said "They could be heard all night, pattering against the tents like large drops of rain in a heavy shower." Much more serious was the cholera epidemic—described in Chapter III—which assumed alarming proportions on the St. Joe Road and left it dotted with graves.

The main stream east of Big Blue was the Big Nemaha, and almost as disturbing as the problem of its crossing was the problem of how to spell it. Was it Nimahaw (Harritt), Minneyhaw (Starr), Neiman (Andrews), Miniho (Woodward), Miniwa (Bartholomew), Mine Craw (Frush), or Minehaugh (McBride)? According to D. B. Andrews, it had the most timber of any stream encountered to date. At the emigrant crossing, between Seneca and the Nebraska line, it was described by Biddle as "a very beautiful stream with rocky bottom and timber on its margin," and he found every tree decorated with "bits of paper with emigrant news," a kind of prairie bulletin board. It was also deeply U-shaped; during the peak years there were no enterprising Indians with bridges here, so ropes and chains had to be resorted to. According to Lorenzo Sawyer, the Nemaha was the boundary between the Iowa and the Pawnee by the Fort Leavenworth Treaty of 1836. However, most emigrants thought of the Big Blue as the boundary. The forty miles between the Nemaha and Big Blue seems to have been an Indian no-man's-land.

It was at the Big Blue, about ten days out of St. Joe, that the emigrants felt the first flick of the Elephant's tail. Here was a chance to repair and to reorganize, but here also, where the St. Joe and Fort Leavenworth caravans converged, rode three sinister Horsemen—death by epidemic, death by drowning, and violence at the hands of the Pawnee. At low water the Blue was fordable, but in the emigrant season it was more often on the rampage, and the blockaded trains accumulated into a sizable city of tents and wagons, "like the descent of locusts in Egypt" (Berrien), without a trace of sanitation. Cholera and other ailments such as measles and smallpox felled the emigrants like a giant scythe, and both banks of the Blue became a cemetery. Uncounted deaths resulted also from accidental drownings; but the Pawnee menace at this point was over-advertised. Joshua Breyfogle wrote that after crossing the Blue, "We are now in the enemie's country," and all hands assumed a military posture. At this point, wrote Stephen Gage, "We are now in the Pawnee Nation, a hard people who prey on emigrants," and he claimed that they indulged in extortion, running off emigrant stock, then demanding payment for its return. Bartholomew heard of "three men killed by Indians" at this point. On the other hand, the Pawnees that James Bennett encountered here appeared quite friendly, and "one party came in bearing a white flag." The Pawnee would not be a serious problem until later, and then they would prove to be a nuisance, rather than a terror.

Vincent Geiger put in an early appearance on May 20, 1849, and found the Big Blue "a stream of beautiful, clear water . . . very palatable to a thirsty man . . . 40 rods wide, deep enough to touch the wagon beds, but not swift and rough." A few days later, when Benjamin Gatton arrived, he found it sixty yards wide, but still fordable. Later Elisha Lewis found it in flood stage and traffic backed up for three miles. At high water the emigrants had to re-sort to crossing by calking their wagons or constructing crude rafts. In 1850 James Bennett's party manufactured a large canoe, "capable of carrying a thousand pounds with perfect safety," to transport the goods, and the empty wagons were floated over. Several of his party were "completely immersed in water" during their ordeal, but sur-vived. Wm. Frush paid $1 to swim his horse alongside a raft, plus 30¢ to get himself and baggage ferried in a leather bottom boat. In 1851 the Quincy Brooks party made a platform of planks over two dugout canoes lashed together, and Sgt. Lowe of the Dragoons im-provised a ferry with rope and wagon beds. The Big Blue was a challenge to Yankee ingenuity.

In 1852 a white man named Marshall squatted on the east bank and went into the ferry business on a permanent basis. Snodgrass paid him $3 per wagon. J. D. Randall found him "fixing for a store and stopping place for the mail." John Clark said the ferryman had "a little trading post on the bank that sells awful dear. Sugar, coffee & bread, 50¢ the pound. Whiskey six bits the pint, or 50 the drink. . . . Many are drunk & some fighting. It was near sundown before we cross the ferry & camp at the edge of the Pawnee plains. A short distance from the crossing is the graveyard & good spring to fill your cans."

In 1850 W. McBride thought there was here "sufficient timber to sustain a small settlement." The ferryman of 1852 was still in busi-ness in '54 with a "trading house east side . . . whiskey $4. a gallon" (Anon.). This establishment was evidently the beginning of the "small settlement" of Marysville, first identified by Capt. Todd in 1855 (and called Palmetto City by Cornelius Conway in 1857). In 1858 Marysville was a metropolis boasting twenty log houses, a news-paper, and villainous whiskey (Lee). Sgt. Lowe reported that the infant settlement was invaded by 2,500 Pawnee this year, but they were just passing through—in flight from attacking Sioux. In 1859 Thomas Cramer found the Marysville ferry doing a land office business with the Pike's Peakers, who were going in both directions. Under the influence of whiskey and angered by the toll, some attempted to seize the boat. Several men were killed in the ensuing gunfight. Marysville became the seat of a county named for the enterprising Mr. Marshall, its first settler; it was also a station on the Pony Express.

THE FORT LEAVENWORTH ROAD AND THE PONY EXPRESS ROUTE

As the principal U.S. Army base on the Missouri River, Fort Leavenworth was destined to supply a sizable percentage of the traffic on the Great Platte River Road. This was augmented in the late fifties by stage lines and heavy freight traffic out of nearby Atchison and in 1860–1861 by the Pony Express out of St. Joe, which followed a route quite at variance with the emigrant road, and which tied in with the Fort Leavenworth Road.

The Fort Leavenworth–Fort Laramie Military Road angled northwestward from the fort to a point called Eight Mile House, where the connecting road to Fort Riley and Santa Fe broke off. It then followed the divide between the Missouri and Kansas River drainages, paralleling Stranger Creek to the west as far as present Lancaster. The Atchison Road came in at Chain Pump, about six miles east of Lancaster. Continuing northwestward, the military road crossed the headwaters of Delaware, or Grasshopper, Creek to a point west of present Horton, thence to the crossing of the Nemaha at present Seneca. To get around the Black Vermillion, the Leavenworth Road arched northward, reaching a line north of present U.S. 36 then dropping southwestward to join the regular emigrant road from St. Joe west of Marysville. Emigrant journals are replete with accounts of military outfits merging with the covered wagon caravans, beginning with the expedition of Kearny's Dragoons in 1845 and continuing through the buildup of western forts during Gold Rush years and the innumerable expeditions to supply these posts and conduct the Indian campaigns.

Capt. Randolph Marcy's *Guide* suggests distances of twenty-seven miles from Fort Leavenworth to the Atchison Junction, seventy miles to the junction with the Pony Express route, and 125 miles to Marysville. There is an extensive literature on the Fort

Leavenworth Road. Military personnel are well represented by Lt. Gunnison, Capt. Todd, Capt. Gove, and Capt. Stansbury, Maj. Cross, and enlisted men Gibbs, Seville, and Holliday. Civilian travelers included Richard Burton, Fitz Hugh Ludlow, J. Hamelin, George Suckley, James Meline, and Thaddeus Kenderdine.

The Pony Express route out of St. Joe went due west of Wathena to Troy, then swung several miles to the south of the emigrant road (and south also of present U.S. 36) to join the military road at Kinnekuk Station, near present Horton. Emigrants of the sixties out of St. Joe (including Lavinia Porter, Marie Nash, and Samuel Word) apparently followed the Pony route and the "Gold Rush Alley" was abandoned. Known Pony Express and stage stations, about fifteen miles apart, are identified as follows:

> *Troy Station,* in the existing town of the same name.
> *Lewis Station,* at the head of Independence Creek, southeast corner of Doniphan County.
> *Kinnekuk Station,* one and a half miles southeast of present Horton. This was also the site of the old Kickapoo Indian Agency, beginning in 1857.
> *Goteschall, or Kickapoo, Station,* on Big Grasshopper Creek, twelve miles east of Horton and the setting of a Kickapoo Indian mission.
> *Granada Station,* on Lockman's Creek, just inside the Nemaha County line, which was an alternative to
> *Log Chain Station,* at the head of Lockman Creek. A log cabin surviving is represented as an original structure.
> *Seneca Station,* at the present town on the Nemaha. The original two-story brick structure has been moved three blocks from its original location.
> *Ash Point Station,* on the Black Vermillion two miles northeast of Axtell on the Nemaha-Marshall county line.
> *Guittard's Station,* on the west fork of Black Vermillion, north of Beattie.
> *Marysville Station.* At 108 South Eighth Street the original Pony Express Station still stands, disguised as a modern cold storage plant. Beyond this point the Pony Express route fairly coincided with the Oregon Trail until the South Platte crossings.

The Independence–St. Joe Road

The main approach to the Great Platte River Road was along the Little Blue River, which had everything the emigrants needed—

wood, water, and a valley going in the right direction. The Independence and St. Joe roads merged west of Big Blue Crossing and followed the general northwest course of the Little Blue valley for 120 miles to its ultimate headwaters on Thirty-two Mile Creek, then traversed a barren divide twenty miles to reach the Platte about eight miles east of Fort Kearny. This was the grand entrance to the fabled Coast of Nebraska, the true beginning of the Great Platte mainline and the classic Oregon and California Trails.

Taking an airplane view of the route from the Big Blue to the Platte in relationship to present communities and political boundaries, the convergence of trails is seen at a point two miles north of U.S. 36 on the Marshall-Washington county line, roughly ten miles from Marysville and four miles from Hanover. After crossing the Cottonwood, the Trail goes sharply northwest, staying on the uplands parallel to the Little Blue for some ten miles to intersect the Nebraska boundary in the southwest corner of Gage County. From a point five miles east of Steele City in Jefferson County, it turns almost due northwest, paralleling the Little Blue at a distance of about three miles, crosses Rock Creek (which also appears as Wyeth's Creek or Turkey Creek), then goes to a point four miles north of Fairbury, where it intersects State Highway 15. Here the Trail veers due westward across the Little Sandy (sometimes called Walnut Creek) and the Big Sandy to the point of intersection with the Jefferson-Thayer county line, then pursues an upland course midway between the Little Blue and the Sandy. Northwest of Hebron the Trail re-enters the Little Blue valley, staying with its uniformly northwest course all the way across Nuckolls, Clay, and Adams counties to the hydrographic divide near present Kenesaw, thence continuing northwestward to the Platte valley at a point just west of the Adams-Kearney county line.

During the California Gold Rush this route was strictly primitive; there was no significant settlement or habitation of any kind until 1859. In that year events dictated the need for stations to serve freighters, stagecoach passengers, and Pony Express riders. Since these stations were roughly synonymous with the famed ranches of the Little Blue, described by travelers in 1860–1863 and devastated by the Sioux in 1864, it is appropriate to identify them (bearing in mind that they did not exist during the prime migration years).

Cottonwood Station, one and a half miles northeast of Hanover, overlooking Cottonwood Creek. This onetime Hollenberg Ranch is a Kansas state park. The original building still stands.

Rock House Station, about three miles northeast of Steele City, at the junction of a late-period shortcut from Atchison called Oketo Cutoff.

Rock Creek Station, six miles southeast of Fairbury. There were rival ranches and a toll bridge here as early as 1859. The locale is famous as the setting of the Wild Bill Hickok–McCanles affair and for a nearby sandstone formation that once bore the inscriptions of Fremont, Carson, and other traders, explorers, and emigrants.

Virginia City Station, four miles north of Fairbury. It or a nearby station also bore the name of Lone Tree, for a solitary but majestic oak that once stood here.

Big Sandy Station, about three miles east of Alexandria.

Thompson's Station, or Millersville, about seven miles northeast of Hebron.

Kiowa Station, about ten miles northwest of Hebron.

Oak Grove Station, or Comstock's in the northeast corner of Nuckolls County. In this neighborhood was the famous Narrows or Black Pool and the Roper, Emory, and Eubank ranches, scenes of the 1864 massacre. *Little Blue Station* was four miles northwest of Oak Grove.

Liberty Farm, just north of Deweese in Clay County. The road from Fort Riley to Fort Kearny entered here.

Spring Ranch, earlier Weston & Roper's Store and later Pawnee Ranch. A second Lone Tree Station is also identified nearby.

Thirty-two Mile Creek, six miles southwest of Hastings, also known as the Dinner Station or Elm Creek Station. A "government well" and some famous bacteria-laden water holes or buffalo wallows were in this neighborhood.

Sand Hill, later Summit Station, one and a half miles south of Kenesaw. The next station, called variously Valley, Hook, Dogtown, or Junction, is referred to in Chapter VII.

The valley of the Little Blue today is much more densely wooded than in emigrant days, and it is now occupied by farms and small communities. Because of the general cultivation and road construction, all trace of the California Road has vanished, except for its occasional appearance as grassy troughs at the edge of creeks and draws and somber reminders such as the 1849 George Winslow grave on a hillside east of Fairbury. Even so, much of the "feel" of covered wagon days on this route remains because of the pastoral

and generally unspoiled character of the terrain along the Blue and
its small tributaries, as well as along the ridges, between which the
Trail alternated. One can feel a rapport with diarists such as
James Pritchard, who wrote of the Little Blue: "The seenary was
so enviting that it induced [us] to take a stroll down that way. . . .
We found beautiful Spots and romantic Situations. The current
was very Swift and rapid, yet the water rippled over its gravelly bed
as clear as chrystle," and he and his companion then "deliberately
undressed and pitched into the transparent Stream to take a bathe
. . . regardless of any danger from Indians who doubtless were then
learking in the brush . . . but were held at bay by the appearance
of our Ky. Rifles."

Bolivar Krepps thought this "the most beautiful country I ever
saw since I left the States," and he referred to the stream, fringed
with oak, willow, and cottonwoods, as well as the uplands, which
seemed "one vast rolling meadow." To James Meline the prairie
here was "like the sea, with the same boundless sweep to the eye. . . .
A distant wagon is a sail, and wrecks strew its strands." To Littleton these plains presented "the great arch of the universe . . . boundless as eternity," and he was delighted that the immensity of blue
and green was spangled with "wild roses, morning glories and a
large yellow flower resemling the Hollihawk." Joel Palmer rejoiced
in "the pea vine that grows wild in great abundance," and others
reveled in catches of the turtles and catfish which abounded in the
streams. Edwin Bryant observed: "The country appears to be the
most desirable, in an agricultural point of view, of any which I have
yet seen. It possesses such natural wealth and beauties, that at some
future day it will be the Eden of America." Geo. Holliday of the
Volunteers also thought the Little Blue "the Garden Spot of the
World" and optimistically noted that many of his companions resolved to make their future homes in Nebraska.

In 1850 there was less enthusiasm because of drouth conditions.
The Sandy and other tributaries went dry, and to Thomas Woodward the country appeared broken and barren: "The eyes ache with
looking for timber and water." He refers to the uplands as Dry
Prairie Ridge and was moved to exclaim, "Taken all in all the
Plains is nearly as Bad as the Lybian Desart." The last leg across
the divide to the Platte was always the most arduous, because of the
sharp ascending gradient, the sandy soil hugging the wheels, and
the total lack of wood and water. But on the achievement of this

climax, the emigrant was rewarded by the vast panorama of the Platte—road to a golden future.

Benjamin Watson and G. A. Smith were impressed by the "surpassing beauty and richness of the soil" and predicted settlement here, but Meline noted the gradual transition from "rich black loam" to "sand and clay, bearing only aloe, prickly pear, and saxifrage and presenting an occasional ugly alkaline crust." Thomas Eastin saw that after the Sandy crossings the soil substratum was black gravel or sand. He wrote, "The wagons have worn through the soil and the sand and gravel come to the surface and forms a firm road." He did not think, however, that the land was adapted to cultivation for "when ploughed up the sand would come to the surface and the soil wholly disappear." Capt. Gove had the notion that, though the soil was good, "there was no timber at all, which almost disqualifies it as a farming region."

During peak Gold Rush years the Little Blue was still alive with game. In 1850 Thomasson noted "turkeys, deer, antelope, wolves . . . and buflows." That same year Wellman Packard reported a "mass attack" of buffalo on his train, but the firing of the emigrants' guns turned the herd, and it swept by "like a rolling cloud" or "sawlogs over rapids." Buffalo were still in abundance in 1860, according to Lavinia Porter, whose camp was "almost over-run;" but after that date the huge animals seem to have forsaken the Little Blue. The antelope, said Thomasson, was "the cunenist animal I ever saw." Rufus Sage and others tell of many vain efforts to approach and kill these fleet and shifty broken-field runners. (The sophisticated plainsman would explain that it was easy; wear a red bandanna on the head or wave one from a stick from a place of ambush, and the transfixed antelope, approaching from curiosity, would become an easy target.) Pritchard glimpsed "a large Mountain Woolf," which "made his Debut and brought one of those hideous howls that will startle one from the profoundest sleep—and make him think that one of the Fiends of the infurnal regions was standing before him." Other creatures mentioned were plover and doves (Porter) and "rattlesnakes as thick as a child's arm" (Hagelstein).

The Little Blue had a telegraph style of its own. Wrote G. A. Smith, "Thousands of names are written on trees by emigrants." Benjamin Gatton found not only trees "skinned and written upon, giving names of individuals and companies," but "all trees near the road covered with cards, some of paper and some of boards." B. R. Biddle was constantly passing by notices written on paper, elk horn, and boards, "so that we are appraised of all going on ahead of us." Gatton said that these informal "postoffices, as they are called, we found at all the crossings."

Another phenomenon, not confined to the Little Blue but occurring here more than in any other section, was that of the eastbound fur caravans from the vicinity of Fort Laramie bound for St. Louis. Almost every year, beginning in 1841 with John Bidwell, emigrant trains would encounter one or more bands of swarthy mountaineers, "strangers to razors," accompanying their wagons piled high with the greasy hides of buffalo and "white wolves." Their outfits were masterpieces of ingenuity, usually carts made from broken and abandoned emigrant wagons and "oxen abandoned or traded" (Lowe). The principal outfits encountered in 1849 were those of "Mr. Robidoux," who had a trading post at Scott's Bluffs, and "Mr. Pappin," who represented the rival American Fur Company. Daniel Gelwicks of the Jarrott train described "Robidoux of St. Joseph" as a former schoolmate of Col. Jarrott, who cheerfully exchanged buffalo meat for bacon, provided travel data, and "obligingly took letters." "Papin of St. Louis" was another acquaintance, "a young Frenchman, affable, intelligent, energetic and benevolent." (We will have occasion to meet both of these Frenchmen later in their western Nebraska strongholds.) In 1852 John Clark of Virginia found the mountaineers not unfriendly, but "hard-looking men of every hue . . . smoked from years around camp-fires." At the head of the Little Blue, he met "Robidoux's train of 18 wagons from the mountains—the drivers were greedy and filthy looking with six or eight span of poor mules or oxen to each wagon that was filled with robes & furs at least eight & ten feet above the beds. The wild odor or smell from the train [caused our stock to leave] the road in spite of drivers until the black and greasy crowd was far past."

Other identified mountain traders encountered at various points along the trail from time to time included "Beauvais and Bisonet" (Lowe, '57), Pallardie (Johnston, '49), Tom Fallon of the H. B. C. Company (Cornwall, '48), Kit Carson (Ingalls, '50), Jim Bridger (Nott, '54), and Andrew Sublette and Joseph Walker (Gilliam, '44). While some of the French-Canadian hired hands looked mean and grubby and spoke indifferent English, their leaders were often men of substance, perhaps bearded and colorfully garbed in buckskins, but palpably successful in a very dangerous business. Some of the St. Louisans traveled in style. In 1849 Capt. Gunnison described a trader named Misonet (Bisonet?) going to Fort Laramie. "He looks quite aristocratic in a buggy, and having been west some twenty times knows how to manage matters."

When the mountain beaver trade declined after 1840, the traffic in Plains buffalo hides took its place, but this could not absorb all the experienced hands. Many mountain men obtained employment as guides to the missionaries and emigrants, particularly during the late thirties and the forties. After 1849 the trails to Oregon and California were fairly well defined, and a guide seemed a superfluity. Even so, several of the big trains of 1849 and 1850 employed such pilots. Among guides mentioned were Tom Fitzpatrick (Gray, '36), Capt. Thing (Howe, '49), Joe Meek (Purcell, '46), James Headspeth (Johnson, '49), Old Bill Williams (Rhodes, '50), Black Harris (Collins, '44), Stephen Meek (Helmick, '45), "Roubedou" (Aram, '46), and "Gaspero" ("The General," '50). In the early fifties Tom Fitzpatrick was often seen also, coming and going in his capacity as Indian agent for the Sioux and Cheyenne of the Upper Platte.

Equally colorful, but definitely undependable where not downright dangerous, were the Pawnee, whose territory extended from the Big Blue Crossing to the forks of the Platte. The Kanzas, the Potawatomi, and the Sac and Fox were semi-civilized, at least to the point that there was some semblance of legality to their extraction of funds from the emigrants. The Pawnee were warriors and buffalo hunters who roamed their vast domain looking for trouble. They found plenty of it in the form of Sioux and Cheyenne to the west; and emigrants who had found themselves in the thick of tribal warfare on the Kansas River might have the experience repeated along the Little Blue and the Platte. There were a few reliable reports of fighting between Pawnee and white emigrants. In '49 Capt. Stansbury confirmed that "a fight had taken place on the north side of the Platte between [Pawnee] and emigrants, in which the former were defeated." For the most part, however, the rumors of battles and massacres were untrue, and the Pawnee merely threatened and blustered, demanding tribute of some kind for crossing their lands, although they would not be above robbing and sometimes murdering stragglers.

The Pawnee could behave admirably on occasion. In '43 the Burnett train to Oregon had a powwow with a band returning from a successful buffalo hunt, who shared their dried meat. Two years later, however, Samuel Hancock's cattle were stampeded and shot full of arrows. In '46 J. M. Shively urged, "Keep watch all the way, particularly the Pawnee country, from the crossing of the Blue to the crossing of the Platt." In '49 the Pawnee seemed to haunt the Little Blue valley, causing many alarms and excursions. Delano reported a straggler robbed and stripped of his clothes. Another traveler "saw the emigrants burying a man whom the indians had speared." Edwin Banks reported the murder of a man who had wandered from the road, the wounding of "the pilot of the U.S. infantry" and the pursuit of "two hunters of a Virginia train." Occasional grave markers named Indians as the cause of death. Probably untrue was a rumor reported by Banks that "22 men [were] killed, 16 wagons burned by Indians a few miles ahead."

William Kelly's train was approached by about twenty-five Indians who "discharged a few arrows at close range . . . but they can be easily dodged." A few rifle shots aimed at the presumed chief put an end to the episode. Eastin's train was braced for trouble, but "when we met the Pawnee," he wrote, "they were all smiles and very courteous and polite, shaking hands . . . and begging very earnestly for bread and tobacco." Later these same emigrants shouldered their rifles and "buckled their armor" when they saw several hundred Indians filing over a nearby bridge, but these proved to be Sioux on the trail of the Pawnee. The Hixson party of fifty-four men ran into these Sioux, whom Hixson estimated to number 1,000; there was some premature gunfire by the nervous whites, but no damage was done, and the Sioux were placated by "presents of provisions" and resumed their relentless pursuit of the foe. Cheyenne Indians armed with steel-tipped lances, encountered by Wm. Pleasants in 1856, were also indifferent to emigrants in their implacable search for Pawnees. Gifts of sugar and flour would normally placate most Indians who blocked the path of the emigrants.

In later Indian wars it was the Sioux and not the Pawnee who were the white man's foe, but somehow the Sioux enjoyed a better reputation among emigrants. J. M. Shively wrote in '46 that, unlike the Pawnee, "the Sioux will not likely molest you in any way." Israel Hale asserted that "Pawnee will kill a man for his horses, but not the Sioux." Mrs. Ferris understood the Pawnee so be "the most dreaded of any on the route." W. G. Johnston branded them "a cunning cut-throat race of villains, with an endless propensity for stealing." Woodward asserted that "a more savage, snakeish, thieving pack of scoundrels it is impossible to imagine" and that the Pawnee could be depended upon to rustle cattle, employing simulated wolf howls and the sounds of wild turkey on their stealthy approach. Few travelers shared Carlisle Abbott's recognition of the fact that the Great Migration was scattering the buffalo herds which kept the Indians alive; their actions were motivated by starvation rather than by criminal intent.

It was the Sioux and Cheyenne, not the Pawnee, who ravaged the ranches and stations of the Little Blue and the Platte in 1863–1864, burning, killing, raping, and kidnaping; the detailed history of these raids is beyond our scope, although they cast a pall of horror over the history of the Little Blue. After the massacre of Sioux at Ash Hollow in 1854 and of the Cheyenne at Sand Creek, Colorado, ten years later, the Indian mood of vengeance is understandable, even if their methods were barbaric. While on the Little Blue in 1863, Louisa Sweetland makes a contemporary emigrant observation which suggests that the guilt was about evenly distributed: "[We] pass a station where Indians had burned three men to a crisp . . . pass stage loaded with soldiers. They had an Indian at the back of the stage and were dragging him to death. . . . he had several scalps on his belt."

One of the more graphic accounts of the violent summer of 1864 along the Little Blue was reported to the Omaha *Nebraskan* by Lt. Porter of Fort Kearny, who quotes frightened stage passengers:

> The particulars of the troubles I give you as related to me by the passengers of the overland coach from Atchinson which arrived about 1 O'clock this morning [August 14].
>
> H. C. Solomon of Denver . . . says that the first we heard of Indians was when we arrived at Kiowa Station, 75 miles east of Kearny, where two men had just been killed. We left Kiowa about 6 P.M. Sunday, and on arriving at Oak Grove Ranch, 7 miles, found two more men killed named Butler and Kelley. . . .
>
> On arriving at Little Blue Station, we found that place abandoned.
>
> About 4 miles after leaving Oak Grove, we found the bodies of two young men killed and stripped of all their clothing.
>
> We next came to Hubank's [Eubank's] Ranche and it was deserted and about 200 yards off we found the body of young woman, stripped of all her clothing. She was scalped and had been horribly abused and then mutilated—she appeared to be about 17 years of age.

On the opposite bank of the Little Blue we found the body of Mr. Hubank—the others killed were his two sons and daughter.

A young woman . . . who was on a visit at Hubank's was carried away captive—and also a child of Hubank's. . . .

We collected all the stage and other stock and proceeded to Pawnee Ranche Station. . . . Just before we arrived [here] a man was killed by the Indians in sight of the place—we found his body and buried it. . . . A few miles on the way a messenger overtook us and desired our return, stating that the buildings at Liberty Farm were in flames and it was thought that they would attack Pawnee. . . .

Three miles east of 32 Mile Creek we found a mule train of 6 wagons that had been attacked and all men killed and stock driven off—the goods were lying around in every direction. . . .

We came safely through to Kearny and did not see any Indians, but heard of them as having been at Hook's. In all we saw 17 that had been killed between here and Kiowa Station.

Two facets of Blue River geography relating to the Pawnee deserve mention here. Among the several branches of the Pawnee was one called the "Republican," because when they were visited at their village near present Red Cloud by early Spaniards, followed by Zebulon Pike in 1806, it seemed to these explorers that the Pawnee had a republican form of government. The river on which the Pawnee village of Pike's visit was located thus came to be called the Republican. This joins the Smoky Hill near present Junction City, Kansas, to form the Kaw (Kansas) River, and the Big Blue flows into the Kaw a few miles below at Manhattan. Some early mapmakers got things mixed up and had the Big Blue as a branch of the Republican. As early as 1841 Rufus Sage recognized the error, but many emigrants compounded the original error by identifying the Little Blue as "the Republican Fork of Blue River."

The Little Blue was intersected by the so-called Pawnee Trail, or Great Pawnee Trail, which ran southwestward and connected their Platte River villages with buffalo grounds of the Kansas and the Arkansas. Niles Searls in 1849 said, "The route taken by them in visiting Comanche country" was "a broad trail resembling in some respects several wagon roads in close proximity." W. McBride says it "consists of eight deeply beaten paths sufficiently wide for pack animals to walk abreast." (Neither recognized these as travois marks.) There is some confusion as to its exact location. Nathaniel Wyeth in 1832 places it "10 miles west of Big Blue" and in 1849

Charles Kirkpatrick seems to place it in the same neighborhood, above Cottonwood Creek. However, Rufus Sage in 1841 and Medorem Crawford in 1842, as well as Searls and McBride, clearly place the intersection near the summit of the divide between the Platte and the Little Blue. For example, Sage wrote, "About sunrise we crossed the regular Pawnee trail, and at 10 o'clock reached the Platte river."

While the Little Blue has scenic charm and a wealth of Indian history relating to emigrants, Indians, and stage stations, there are two places of primary concern to the story of the Great Platte River Road. One is at the beginning, the other at the end of this route. One is the celebrated junction of the Independence and St. Joe roads; the other is the long-awaited Coast of Nebraska.

Aerial photographs might identify the junction west of Marysville, but on the ground it is lost in cornfields. (It was probably not just one place anyhow; like the turn-off of the Independence Road from the Santa Fe Trail, it probably shifted within a radius of a mile or more.) Yet few places in western history can quite match this point for sheer dramatic impact. Almost all emigrants, from one point or the other, were impressed by the spectacle of the merging columns:

> By noone today we came to where the St. Joseph road and Indipendance road came togeather. It was allarming to see the long strings of wagons that were on the road. I counted just passing before us as we came into the St. Jo. road 90 Ox teams in one string. And as far as the Eye could reach forward and back the road was just lined with them. It would appear from the sight befor us that the Nation was disgorgeing its self and sending off its whole inhabitance.—JAMES PRITCHARD, 1849

> Today we passed the intersection of the Independence road. . . . The multitude that is going is wonderful. It seems as if the whole world was going to market.—EDWIN BANKS, 1849

> [We] came to the St. Joseph Road. . . . much more traveled than the one from Independence. At this point 100 wagons in sight, trains from Missouri and Illinois and Kentucky.—HIXSON, 1849

> At the junction the numbers doubled. . . . they will probably double again from the Council Bluffs Road. . . . it did seem that when they all would all come together they would be like a swarm of locusts. . . . often more than 700 wagons in view.—W. McBRIDE, 1850

[We] came to where the Independence and St. Joseph Roads intersect. Five hundred waggons with 2,000 men at one view could be seen today.—JAMES EVANS, 1850

THE COAST OF NEBRASKA

The Platte River dominates Nebraska geography, and its dominant characteristic is its flatness. "Nebraska" is the approximate Omaha Indian equivalent for "flat water," and the French word "Platte" is synonymous. The earliest explorers and emigrants sometimes used "Nebraska" to refer to the river and not the territory. Thus, "Coast of Nebraska" and "Coast of the Platte" were interchangeable. It is not known who invented the term, but it was used by the explorers John C. Fremont and Howard Stansbury and appears in occasional emigrant journals (D. Jagger) and in late-period travelogs (James F. Meline). It was not widely used, but it expresses beautifully the impact upon the emigrants of this strange river which made possible a road which would take them to the Continental Divide and California. The term is particularly poetic in its imagery, for the vast shimmering flatness of the Platte valley, at the edge of sand dunes, did have a remarkable resemblance to the seashore of the Atlantic Ocean. It was prophetic that this first exposure to the Platte produced an eerie, unearthly (or at least unfamiliar) atmosphere that created an aura for the remaining journey.

From the summit point, the hydrographic divide between the Blue and the Platte, the strangeness first made itself felt. Although the wagons were now going downhill, it still seemed to some, Delano, for example, as if they were struggling upward because the vast expanse of horizon seemed tilted the wrong way and the sandy soil tugged at the wheels. In a dry year like 1850 the sand drifted and wagon wheels sank into it; J. Scheller paid $5 to get pulled free.

The line of descent to the Platte is marked by sandy hummocks. No one would think of calling these mountains today, but to Meline the rough line of sandhills "at least looked like a mountain" when contrasted with the "smooth, ocean-like verge of the prairie," and he noted that their summits "mark the line of demarcation between the table-land and the Platte." Niles Searls described them as "a long range of blue points above the level surface of the plains," and the descent was by a scarcely perceptible incline "through the towering points which overlook the valley for many miles." These "sloping and clay hills," wrote W. McBride, "were destitute of vegetation."

On a vivid sunshiny or soft hazy day this small belt of desert further prepared the emigrant for wonders to come by the seeming magic of deceptive distances and mirage. To Mrs. Ferris, "A half dozen crows will look like men . . . a battered stove-pipe becomes a skulking Pawnee." To McBride, a dozen men walking ahead looked "like great giants 14 or 15 feet high" while "horses look double their natural life." Mrs. Frizzell saw not only men fifteen feet high, but also "beautiful streams, bordered with trees, small lakes and islands . . . and once or twice we saw what appeared to be large and stately buildings." Jay Green saw "a lake at a great distance" and above it "air rising like columns of smoke."

As the emigrants passed over the last line of sand dunes into the bottom, they obtained their first panoramic view of the river Platte. Frank Young's view of the great valley was a continuation of the mirage effect: "We see the long thin line of . . . timber [on the island] . . . [and] a broad hazy line which furnishes a sort of quivering background to the trees and on certain parts of which by a palpable mirage, the trees are raised above the horizon and stand out in relief." Tompkins proclaims, "The land stretches out in a wide plain like the surface of a vast lake," but this time he is not talking about a mirage but about the actual appearance of the broad Platte valley, level as a table top. McBride's view of the "broad yellow Nebraska" with glorious sunset and transparent atmosphere was "a combination worthy of a painter's pencil." The "coastal effect" was perhaps expressed best by James Evans:

> From the sandhills, it had the appearance of a great inland sea. It looked wider than the Mississippi and showed to much better advantage, there being no timber on the banks to check the scope of the human eye. Grand Island which lays just opposite in the middle of the river is one hundred miles long, and has some cottonwood trees upon it. There is no tree timber here growing upon the margin of the river, not even a willow switch. There are, however, some timber and brush growing upon the various small islands in the river which can be obtained by wading rapid sloughs two or three hundred yards across. My first impression on beholding Platte River was, that as it looked so wide and so muddy, and rolled along within three feet of the top of the bank with such majesty that it was unusually swollen and perfectly impassable. Judge my surprise when I learned that it was

only three or four feet deep. . . . The water is exceedingly muddy, or I should say sandy; and what adds greatly to the singular appearance of this river, the water is so completely filled with glittering particles of micah or isingglass that its shining waves look to be rich with floating gold. . . . the plains are so low and level that if Platte River could rise five feet it would cover a country at least ten miles wide!

When Richard Hickman beheld the Platte at flood, it seemed at first to him, too, that it was so huge "it had the appearance of being navigable for the largest sized steamboats." Rufus Sage saw it at normal flow, but recognized: "Its waters are very shallow, and are scattered over their broad bed in almost innumerable channels, nearly obscured by the naked sand-bars that bechequer its entire course through the grand prairie." His statistics are about as accurate as anyone's: "The valley of the Platte is six or seven miles wide, and the river itself between one and two miles from bank to bank."

The Platte resembled no river any of the emigrants had ever seen before, contradicting their idea of a "normal" stream. It was miles wide and inches deep; thanks to Indian-set prairie fires and grazing buffalo, no timber grew on its banks; and it seemed to flow almost higher than the surrounding country. This phenomenon of an inverted river was noted by Alonzo Delano, who was rather mystified that the "Platte seemed to flow through higher ground than the tributaries of the Kansas; and that should a canal be cut from the Platte it would descend to the Blue, through a series of locks." Exclaimed Martha Missouri Moore: "The river is a perfect curiosity, it is so very different from any of our streams that it is hard to realize that a river should be running so near the top of the ground without any timber, and no bank at all."

Equally remarkable was the gelatinous character of the water itself. Not many thought, like Evans, that it looked like gold, but several agreed that the dominant shade was yellow, from the high sand content. Cornelius Conway called the Platte "a moving mass of pure sand." Pritchard noted: "The bed of the river is composed of sand, and this is all the time shifting its possition and fresh deposits are constantly being made. . . . The banks . . . are low and at this time (the river being high) do not rise more than 18 inches or two feet above the surface of the water. . . . I judge that the bottom is rarely if ever inundated. . . . Such is the breadth of the channel that an immense quantity of water would be required to raise it above its banks." He was entirely correct in his contradiction of Hickman: "The stream is beyond the possibility of ever being made navigable."

The grass in the bottoms was excellent except for patches on alkali soil. Cagwin called it "the best grass of the entire trip." Conway suggests that this was the result of "land subject to great overflow and irrigation." This made a prime camping ground and a logical place to pause before the advance upon Fort Kearny. Here is the famous lonely grave of Susan Hail, who died in 1852. Here also is the evidence of another vital junction point: the road from old Fort Kearny—later Nebraska City—joined the Independence–St. Joe Road to become the main Platte River Road to California.

THE NEBRASKA CITY (OLD FORT KEARNY) ROAD

The most underrated and least understood approach to the Platte was that from old Fort Kearny at Table Creek, which became Nebraska City in 1854. Approximately fifty overland journals have been accounted for which describe this route (or routes) to new Fort Kearny. These journals mirror the fact that hundreds of emigrants of the 1849–1852 California period came this way, while thousands traveled the route during 1858–1866 to Colorado. In addition, this was a major route for Russell, Majors and Waddell and other freighting outfits which served the military posts, Denver, and Salt Lake.

California journals of exceptional value for the Fort Kearny Road include those of Bruff, Wilkins, Parke, Lindsey, Hamelin, Doyle, and Elijah Howell in 1849; Knox, Wood, Montgomery, and McGlashan in 1850; Robe and Cranstone in 1851; and Caroline Richardson and Francis Sawyer in 1852. In the late fifties travelers on this route included Wilkinson, Maxwell, Barker, Chillson, Crandall, and Romanzo Kingman. During the sixties useful emigrant journals include those of Millington, Fulkerth, Ira Butterfield, Herndon, and Cutting. Among literate freighters out of Nebraska City or Plattsmouth were Lowry, Burgess, Creigh, and W. H. Jackson.

Irene Paden's description of this route is as follows:

> It kept well up on the divide between the watersheds of the Little Nemaha and Salt Creek, and it crossed no large stream until the Big Blue was reached—high up toward its source. This was readily forded

immediately above its confluence with the West Fork. The wagons then remained for a day's journey on the northern bank of West Fork and encountered Beaver Creek, which flows into it from the north. This they forded almost at the junction, and proceeded along its south bank. Near the old Millspaw ranch they finally left the headwaters of the little stream behind them and picked up the course of an uncertain sloughlike creek, which provided them with water for the stock until they reached the Platte.

This would follow a line roughly from Nebraska City to Avoca, to Lincoln, to Milford, then south of York and Aurora to the Platte. This would be an almost direct route of not much more than 160 miles between the two Fort Kearnys. This seemingly logical course appears on the Harvey map as the "Great Central Route" with the notation, "worked and opened 1861. Every stream bridged." This may well have been the primary route in 1861 and thereafter. However, earlier journals suggest two entirely different routes, substantially longer but calculated to get the wagons onto the broad Platte River bottoms as soon as possible. Without adequate maps, emigrants did not fully appreciate the fact that the Platte made a northward curve between its mouth and Grand Island, which took them quite a few miles out of the way; but they wouldn't have cared anyway, since the main idea was to get on the Platte River.

The clues to the actual route of the early Fort Kearny, or Nebraska City, Road are furnished not only by identifiable topographic features but by the existence of two earth-lodge villages of the Grand Pawnee Indians which have been archeologically identified by Dr. Waldo Wedel. These are the so-called Clarks site, on the right bank of the Platte about ten miles downstream from Central City, and the Linwood site, also on the right bank near the town of the same name, about six miles southeast of Schuyler. The Clarks site, abandoned about 1845, and the Linwood site, occupied thereafter (both referred to by many journalists and neither of which would be touched by the Paden route) serve as fixed reference points. These, coupled with a check of mileages given, particularly on the route of travel along the Platte, help to make tentative reconstruction of a route that time and extensive civilizing by plow and road grader have almost obliterated.

The route that impinged on the eastern Pawnee village, the Linwood site, would have followed the divide between the Nemaha and the Weeping Water, crossing the latter stream in the vicinity of

Elmwood and crossing the Salt Creek between Greenwood and Ashland on U.S. 6 (affording a distant glimpse of the Platte), then heading almost due north to touch the Platte at Linwood (the inhabited Pawnee village). After crossing Skull Creek here (which appears sometimes as Shell Creek), the emigrants could follow the Platte with ease, since no significant streams tributary to the Platte were left to cross. After Skull Creek, all of the streams immediately south of the Platte drain away from it, toward Kansas. Knox, Butterfield, and Cutting are fairly specific about this route.

An alternate route, which conforms to other journals such as those of Barker and Richardson and which missed the occupied site at Linwood but touched the abandoned Clarks site, would be roughly westward from Nebraska City to Avoca, to Lincoln, across the heads of Salt and Oak creeks, thence northwestward from Lincoln to Seward, then north along the east side of the Big Blue to Ulysses, where the Blue turns west. At Prairie Creek would be the ideal opportunity to go directly northwest via Osceola to the Platte, striking it a few miles downstream from the abandoned earth-lodge village.

According to War Department records, in 1847 Lt. Woodbury calculated 197 miles between the two Fort Kearnys, although in 1849 he gave Charles Darwin a log via the Weeping Water, the Saline, Oak Grove, and "Pawnee Village" which came to 227 miles. The thirty mile discrepancy suggests that the U.S. Army was experimenting with alternate routes, but the earliest government supply trains as well as the majority of California-bound emigrants who started from the ferry or steamboat landing at Table Creek (old Fort Kearny) apparently followed the oxbow curve along the Platte, via present Linwood. In 1860 Ira Butterfield's log approximated the 200 miles of this curve. But in 1861 and thereafter, the routing of most emigrants and freighters from Nebraska City was apparently over the more direct route westward, while traffic along the oxbow was largely from new Plattsmouth via present Ashland. On the Harvey map these alternate routes are designated as "Great Central Route" and the "Old California Trail," respectively. Later, Sitgreaves simply labels them as "Nebraska City Road" and "Plattsmouth Road," and shows them coming together at Junction Station (Valley City), a few miles east of new Fort Kearny.

VI

Fort Kearny and the Forty-Niners

JUST AS IN ANCIENT TIMES all roads led to Rome, so on the frontier of the Great American Desert all roads led to Fort Kearny on the Platte. Here at the head of fabled Grand Island all of the trails radiating from the Missouri River border towns converged to form the main line of the Great Platte River Road. Historic Fort Kearny today is only a memory hovering over a small wooded state park two miles south and six miles east of the modern city of Kearney, which perpetuates a time-honored misspelling.

Lt. Daniel P. Woodbury of the Army Engineers, the founding father of Fort Kearny, tried to call it Fort Childs after one of his Mexican War heroes, and Fort Childs it was for a few months. (It comes out in some journals as Fort Chiles and Fort Charles.) Then the War Department instructed him to call it Fort Kearny instead, thereby atoning in some degree for its tactical error in putting the first Fort Kearny in the wrong place (at Table Creek on the Missouri River). To minimize the confusion of two Fort Kearnys, there was official reference for a while to "New Fort Kearny" or "the fort at Grand Island" or "Fort Kearny on the Platte." This was particularly necessary, since, as we have seen, the army continued for a while to use old Fort Kearny as a shipping point; and any number of emigrants of 1849 and the 1850s continued to cross the Missouri here. Some emigrant journals clearly refer to both Fort Kearnys, but others are quite vague as to which one they are talking about, so historians have been plagued by this confusion for the past 100 years.

Some Trail travelers compound the confusion by their own distinctive spelling. While the understandable misspelling "Kearney" has become almost standard, to the point where it is perpetuated by modern Kearney, Nebraska, it is disconcerting to note such freewheeling variations in the literature as Kerney, Korney, Carny, and Carne!

The idea behind Fort Kearny had its genesis in the 1844 report of the Secretary of War, recommending the construction of a chain of military posts from the Missouri to the Rockies to protect the Oregon migration. An act of Congress in 1846 authorized such posts and the creation of an Oregon Battalion, the Regiment of Mounted Volunteers. This led to the encampment at Table Creek, which soon proved to be a gross error in geographic judgment, and, on June 1, 1847, the War Department directed that an alternate military station be established "near Grand Island where the road to California encounters the Platte River." In compliance with army orders, Lt. Woodbury left old Fort Kearny on September 23, 1847, escorted by five officers and seventy-eight men under Capt. Andrew Sublette. Pioneering what would become the Nebraska City Road, on October 2 Woodbury arrived at the foot of Grand Island, where he began his reconnaissance for a new fort. The site he selected was, by his calculations, "two or three miles from the head of the group of islands called Grand Island," just seventeen miles above the intersecting Independence Road and 197 miles from old Fort Kearny. Returning to Table Creek on October 23, the enthusiastic explorer cited these advantages: a slight elevation two-thirds of a mile from the nearest bayou of the Platte, a guarantee against flooding; nearby, the heaviest timber of the Grand Island group; natural hay bottoms; and a strategic location for keeping the peace between the warring Pawnee and Sioux.

Before Christmas, 1847, young Woodbury was in Washington, D. C. on orders of Battalion Commander L. E. Powell to get things organized for the new post. In a series of communiques to Gen. Totten, Chief Engineer, he requested an appropriation of $15,000 for materials and labor, advocated the employment of Mormon farmers from Council Bluffs to supply the post, and urged the transfer from old Fort Kearny of a large stockpile of lumber and millwork. Although he failed to attain all of these objectives, Woodbury secured marching orders and clearance to construct a fort.

This construction was to be "from scratch," using local materials and "volunteer" soldier labor.

On March 12, 1848, Col. Powell and his indefatigable engineering aide marched out of ill-starred old Fort Kearny at Table Creek with an advance guard. By May 1 Table Creek was abandoned, and by June all officers and men of the Missouri Volunteers had arrived at the "Head of Grand Island" to erect the "1st military station on the route to Oregon." (This was promptly but prematurely christened Fort Childs, in honor of Col. Thomas Childs, who led the assault on Monterrey.) The first order of business, the construction of a post, began at once, with a detail of 175 men erecting temporary sod shelters, manufacturing bricks and adobes, and cutting and sawing timber for later permanent structures.

The new fort had been envisioned in 1844 by the army explorer John C. Fremont; it was also foreseen by Oregon emigrant J. Quinn Thornton, who camped by Grand Island on June 8, 1846. "This island," wrote Thornton, "is about fifty-two miles long. . . . It is well wooded, and has a fertile soil; and the annual rise of the stream does not overflow it. There are many circumstances which unite to make this a suitable point for the establishment of a military post in the lower Nebraska, if it be, indeed, an object with our government to keep open a communication with the future Pacific States." Two years later, almost to the day, Thornton was echoed in Lt. Woodbury's first dispatch to Gen. Totten: "Forty emigrant wagons passed a few hours ago on the way to California and the roads clearly show that many hundreds had passed before our arrival."

There was nothing in the trickle of 1848 to foreshadow the torrential emigration of 1849, and in the paltry few journals of 1848 there is no reference to the construction of Fort Childs. The main excitement afforded the troops that summer was an Indian uprising, which turned out to be a false alarm. Riley Root, who passed this way in May, had commented: "Those Indians located at Grand Island, called the Pawnee tribe, are at present a feeble race, liable to be driven about by the Sioux at all times. The day before we arrived at Grand Island a band of Sioux rangers discovered some Pawnees on the banks of the Platt, drying and preparing buffalo meat for their winter's stock of provisions. They entered their camp and drove them away so suddenly, that in their wild flight they were obliged to throw away robes and other property, which was strewn along the road 15 or 20 miles distance." The persecution of the Pawnee by their fellow aborigines is further disclosed in a St. Louis dispatch of June 20: "Recently a party of Iowa and Sauk took 17 Pawnee scalps. . . . On the 7th the Sioux burnt a Pawnee village while the inhabitants were away hunting." The Pawnee, therefore, were hardly in a position to wage war against the United States. On August 22 the *Missouri Republican* correspondent "Nebraska" told of the fiasco "of our last Indian war, in which the chivalry of Missouri, yclepted the Oregon Battalion, was arrayed on one side, and the squaws, pappooses, and decrepit warriors of the Pawnee nation, on the other." In brief, two officers had paused at the Pawnee village to interview the principal chief. Through a misinterpretation of the chief's sign language, which included the gesture of throatcutting, the officers spread the alarm, and Col. Powell led 250 stalwarts complete with twelve-pounders to deal with the "hostiles." It soon developed "that what appeared to our two Lieutenants as war against the whites to the knife, was the enacting of a nice little episode in a private family," in which a young squaw was slain by her husband, who in turn was dispatched by his father-in-law. "After showing the Pawnees what we would have done had they given us half a chance, we quietly shouldered our firelocks and trudged off again for Fort Childs," bringing in tow the reprobate father-in-law, "not for what he has done lately, but for the misdeeds of his past life," the correspondent concludes.

In a more dignified vein, shortly after this martial exercise Capt. Stewart Van Vliet of the Quartermaster Department negotiated with the Pawnee to extinguish their title to Grand Island (thus supplementing a treaty of 1833 whereby the tribe ceded to the United States all lands claimed by them lying to the south of the Platte). In consideration for this real estate, the Pawnee tribe received the princely sum of $2,000 in goods and merchandise, including desperately needed blankets and guns.

Since it was now clear that the Pawnee posed no serious threat, and since the term of their enlistment was expiring, the Volunteers chafed to return home. In September units were gradually dispatched by Col. Powell via old Fort Kearny to Fort Leavenworth. The colonel himself departed in early October, leaving behind Lt. Lefauvre and some eighteen privates. The state of affairs at Fort Childs on October 6, 1848, was described by "Nebraska," evidently himself one of these leftovers: "No fears may be entertained for those who remain behind, for they will be able to defend themselves against all comers, as each man is armed with a fine brass 12 pounder, and some 500 rounds of fixed ammunition. . . . The Pawnees, numbering some 1200 shirtless warriors, armed with bows and arrows, can doubtless be kept off. . . . The Sioux and Pawnees are still actively employed in taking each other's scalps. . . . The Sioux are the best warriors but the Pawnees are decidedly the best thieves. Everything they rub against appears to stick to them as if attracted by a powerful magnet. . . . The entire Pawnee nation has just swept over us on its way to the hunting grounds on the Blue, and scarcely a single light movable article is left behind. A second such a visit would ruin us."

On October 28 the skeleton garrison was grateful to be relieved by Companies I and G of the new Regiment of Mounted Riflemen. Commanding these regulars, and thus the second post commander at Fort Childs, was Capt. Charles F. Ruff. Aside from a record of gallantry in combat, Ruff was distinguished by his association with the family of old John Dougherty of Liberty, Missouri, once of the glorious company of Rocky Mountain fur traders and now a merchant of substance with the commission of first sutler at Fort Childs. Dougherty's daughter Annie, Ruff's devoted wife, was the first white woman to inhabit the mud walls of new Fort Kearny. In fact, she arrived on the premises with the troops and her baby daughter Margaret before there were any buildings to inhabit; her first abode there was probably an army tent. Dougherty's son Lewis, and thus Ruff's brother-in-law, appeared on the scene in December to help his father set up shop.

Before his departure for Fort Leavenworth, "Nebraska" groused like any good taxpayer: "The Battalion has now been in the service one year, and can show two buildings nearly half completed, one is a sod stable, and the other a store-house. As these buildings have only cost the United States $200,000 [*sic*] each in their incomplete state, it is difficult to say what sum Uncle Sam will have to shell out to finish them." Soon after his arrival, more substantial complaints to his superiors were voiced by Capt. Ruff, whose troops were compelled to face a severe winter with grossly inadequate food, clothing, and shelter. Since his horses faced starvation, most were driven back to Fort Leavenworth. On December 7, 1848, Lt. Woodbury was able to report in a more hopeful vein: "During the past month the adobe store house was finished. One building 20 x 50 feet and another 20 x 35 feet put up, two sod buildings 48 x 38 feet finished, and two temporary stables for 48 horses each erected. The officers and men are in tolerable quarters. I have now employed 20 men getting out timber, five more will commence next month. I am now under orders for St. Louis, where I have to obtain the additional supplies in part, the mechanics necessary for the operations of next year." The year 1848 was ushered out by the December 30 order of R. Jones, Adjutant-General, Washington, D. C., officially designating the new fort at Grand Island as Fort Kearny.

A few medical "firsts" for Fort Kearny may be noted by way of celebrating its first New Year. The first doctor on the premises was Surgeon Joseph Walker of the Oregon Battalion, who retired from the scene in October, 1848. The fort was doctorless until early spring (another legitimate complaint by Ruff), when Dr. Fullwood joined the command. He had been scheduled to arrive in December, 1848, but his escort was thwarted by an ice jam in the Missouri River at old Fort Kearny. He wasn't much help, however, when he did arrive, because he promptly fell ill and was confined to his bed with a mysterious malady. On April 18, 1849, without benefit of a doctor, a Mrs. Denman gave birth to a baby girl, the first child of record born on the premises. Meanwhile, on April 19, Capt. Ruff reported twenty-six men on the sick list, mainly with scurvy. "One man died with it on the 5th inst.," wrote Ruff, "and two others are daily looked for." Thus began the Fort Kearny cemetery, but its size increased alarmingly as the deadly cholera marched westward with the emigrants.

Beginning in January, 1849, with the greatest gold rush in history about to funnel up the Platte River, the U.S. Army made hasty plans for the reinforcement of Fort Kearny and the construction of new posts on the Oregon Trail at the Laramie and Bear rivers (which would soon materialize as Fort Laramie, Wyoming, and Fort Hall, Snake River, Idaho). The instrument of peaceful conquest, the police force of the Gold Rush, was the Regiment of Mounted Riflemen, of which Capt. Ruff's two companies were the advance guard, and the Sixth U.S. Regiment of Infantry. On May 10, 1849, the Mounted Riflemen left Fort Leavenworth for their several destinations on the Oregon route. On May 25 Maj. Sanderson arrived at Fort Kearny with two companies of Mounted Riflemen and one company of the Sixth Infantry, continuing the next day toward Fort Laramie. On May 28 and 29 Lt. Davis and Lt. Bootes with two companies of the Sixth Infantry reported for duty at Fort Kearny.

Commanding these units was Capt. Benjamin L. E. Bonneville, who at this time relieved Capt. Ruff of the Fort Kearny command. This third post commander was indeed the same Capt. Bonneville whose adventures as a mountain trader in the 1830s were immortalized by Washington Irving. On May 31 Col. Loring arrived with the rest of the Mounted Riflemen and the Quartermaster, Maj. Osborne Cross. By June 2 all of the Riflemen, including Capt. Ruff's company and his beloved Annie, were en route to Fort Laramie and points west, adding Army pageantry to the stream of westward migration.

On June 2 the peripatetic Woodbury faithfully reported to Totten: "On the 21st of last month I arrived at this post, bringing with me tools and building materials for this station and the one to be established at Laramie. . . . Immediately upon my arrival I commenced the erection of a hospital. . . . The buildings which I hope may be erected here this season are the hospital, two double blocks of officers' quarters, and one block of soldiers' quarters. The post is at present very poorly prepared to give the emigrants the assistance which very many have required, even at this point so near the beginning of their journey."

Woodbury had a point, all right. If there were a motto for Fort Kearny in 1849 it might have been: "Too much, too early." This little collection of sod houses on the Platte, this prairie outpost invested with the majesty of the U.S. Government, would grow and flourish like the green bay tree for two decades, but in the perspective of history its biggest year was its very first year of immaturity, that is to say, 1849. It is one of history's ironies that when the greatest gold rush in the history of the world first descended upon it, Fort Kearny was an infant of a post, despite Woodbury's heroic exertions, ill-supplied with manpower and provisions, and with only a few pathetic structures to remind the homesick Argonauts of the civilization they had abandoned.

Luckily, it wasn't a whole year of travail, it was only about forty-five days, from early May until mid-June. But during this period the Gold Rush of 1849 swept by like a tornado, spinning Fort Kearny around in its vortex. Thanks to the letter-writers, diary-keepers, and official head-counters at the fort, the course of this phenomenon can be fairly well charted.

Of the 30,000 (plus or minus) people who swarmed up the Platte River valley in 1849, some 5,000 followed the north bank out of

Council Bluffs; and few of these—if any—crossed the river to Fort Kearny this year, even to have a look. On the other hand, every one of the 25,000 who followed the south bank passed alongside the fort as witnesses. The Great Platte River Road came right up to the fort, passing its north side (somewhat closer to the river than the state road which now pasess Fort Kearney State park on the south). Of these 25,000, over 100, or an average of one out of 250, kept daily journals. In addition to these "Californians" there were several soldiers and newspaper correspondents (whose pseudonyms probably concealed literary officers of the garrison) who help to illuminate the Fort Kearny scene in this portentous year.

Assuming that the incidence of diaries roughly indexes the flow of migration, a Fort Kearny Gold Rush graph or "fever chart" can be constructed. It shows that May 8 and June 22 were the substantial bracketing dates of the migration. (There were some woebegone stragglers as late as July 11.) However, over fifty of these journals report during the period of May 18 to June 2, indicating that well over half the migration crested within a span of fifteen days. The sharp peak of the migration wave seems to have occurred during the three day period of May 22–24, when no less than twenty-four record-keeping Forty-Niners were concentrated at Fort Kearny.

The first emigrant to pass the fort showed up, alone and nameless, on May 6, 1849, two days ahead of our hypothetical chart. Writing on May 18, the correspondent "Pawnee" noted that "the first specimen [of gold-diggers] with a large pick-axe over his shoulder, a long rifle in his hand, and two revolvers and a bowie knife stuck in his belt, made his appearance here a week ago last Sunday. He only had time to ask for a drink of buttermilk, a piece of gingerbread and how 'fur' it was to 'Californy,' then hallooing to his long-legged slab-sided cattle drawing a diminutive yellow-top Yankee wagon, he disappeared on the trail toward the gold 'diggins'."

Joshua D. Breyfogle of Delaware, Ohio, who left St. Joseph on April 25, is the first identified emigrant at Fort Kearny, arriving on Tuesday, May 8. His triumphant entry into Jericho deserves notice: "Started this morning ½ past seven traveling over a splendid road and through the broad and beautiful valley of the Platte. . . . We arrived at Fort Kearny after noon. Here we had an opportunity of sending letters to our friends. The officers are going to send a mail to the States in the morning and kindly offered to transmit any letters we wished to send."

William Kelly, who left Independence on April 16, was close behind Breyfogle. He too arrived on the eighth, but not until "early in the evening." Here, reported Kelly (an Englishman writing for an audience), "The States have stationed a garrison of soldiers in a string of log huts, for the protection of the emigrants; and a most unsoldierly-looking lot they were: unshaven, unshorn, with patched uniforms and lounging gait. Both men and officers were ill off for some necessaries, such as flour and sugar; the privates being more particular in their inquiries after whiskey, for which they offered one dollar the half-pint; but we had none to sell them even at that tempting price."

Third in the Fort Kearny sweepstakes, on May 9, came the company of Col. Jarrott of Belleville, Illinois, efficiently equipped with everything, including two fine diarists. As they approached the fort, said Joseph Berrien, they met "2 Draggoons who had just left with the mail," which furnished an opportunity to send letters home. Daniel Gelwicks observed, "Fort Childs, on a bend of the river, and built of unburnt mud bricks, presented but a sorry appearance. . . . The fort has much the appearance of a hacienda in Mexico. Carpenters and blacksmiths were busily engaged in getting out timbers and making hinges, etc. for a new and tasteful fort, which it is the intention of the Government to erect the coming summer. We bought 500 lbs of flour at the fort, and several other articles that we needed from the sutler. It will ultimately be a beautiful spot, but it is not so now. . . ."

Three days later, David Cosad reached "Fort Carney," finding some eighty men stationed there: "This fort is built of dobes or mud dried in the sun, one foot by two in length and from three to six inches thick. Some timber or poles inside to keep it up and it is covered in the same way and the fence about the fort is built of turf also." (There was no stockade wall around Fort Kearny; Cosad's "fence" was probably the garden wall.) Cosad was also an eyewitness to a hair-raising episode in the Sioux-Pawnee feud: The day before reaching the fort his small three-wagon outfit was threatened by a Sioux war party in pursuit of Pawnee, "of which they killed three and took one prisoner and stripped him stark naked according to their custom." Here the story takes on a special poignancy, since the prisoner turned out to be "a small boy," whose mother had somehow escaped while the massacre was in progress. On May 13, in camp twelve miles west of the fort, the Cosad party was overtaken again by the blood-stained Sioux (with a small boy prisoner), who threatened them again. "We took our guns," David said simply, "and made a mark and would not let them come over it." Then came a very dramatic moment. "We saw 45 horsemen a comming from the Fort in pursuit of them. The soldiers were armed with a short rifle, a pair of pistols and a heavy sword, and had good horses. They cantered along two and two and looked verry hansome." Apparently the Sioux were impressed too, except that, according to Dr. Boyle of Columbus, Ohio, who reached Fort Kearny on May 14, the culprits were not Sioux, but Cheyenne.

The Boyle version: "We here learned that the Cheyennes we had met were but part of a war party consisting of about 1100 men who were out on an expedition into the Pawnee country. That the day we saw them they had taken several scalps and one prisoner, a Pawnee boy about 12 years old, who was released by the troops of the fort with but little difficulty. I saw the little fellow at the fort with the interpreter attached to the station." Boyle described this interpreter as a Negro, born in St. Louis but raised among the Indians. "He spoke English, French, and several Indian languages, and had been in Paris." This man is not identified, but his presence here indicates that members of his race participated also in the pageantry of the Great Platte River Road.

Peter Decker, a companion of Boyle's, has bequeathed one of the most vivid pictures of Fort Kearny at this time:

> Fort Childs came in sight unexpectedly at 9 O'c Houses to us are a novelty and remind one of civilization Fort consists of 6 or 8 buildings . . . one story high. Some with windows. Others kind of grated holes. Roofs of ground or sod. Others of brush and grass. On one of former is a garden, vegetables growing as if on "terra firma." Several spots of several acres each for cultivation are enclosed with a mud fence 3 to 4 feet high and a ditch around. . . . Lots of timber, shingles, etc., are preparing to build more permanently. A home power saw is at work. This fort or mud town is now a miserable looking place externally. The houses are comfortable. Thick walls, warm in winter and cool in summer. Roofs hard to make water-proof. Ceiling of muslin. Some ground floors and a few board. . . . Brevet Captain Walker now in command [?] is as all the officers and men here, accommodating and gentlemanly. Had a wheel of wagon repaired at Blacksmith shop. Called at House of a Mormon family in company with Canfield and took supper and a good civilized supper it was.

Seemed strange to eat at table. . . . This Mormon family lost their stock last year on their way to "the brethern" at Salt Lake, and stopped here, and expect to go on next year. . . . A daughter of the family, who attended at table, is well dressed, tidy and ladylike and withal pretty. . . . Bought beans and corn meal of emigrants overloaded and whiskey at $150 [$1.50?] per gallon at house of Mormon family who got it of Commissary 100 percent higher than at Columbus retail. Buffalo robes bought of Indians for pint or quart whisky. . . . Officers have fine lot of grey hounds. Have fun after wolves. . . . Colored interpreter for station raised among Otoe Indians.

On May 15, one week behind the leaders, William Johnston of Pittsburgh, Pennsylvania, pulled into view: "The fort buildings consisted of ten cabins built of adobes comprising the barracks for men and officers, besides three large pounds in which were gathered the cavalry horses and cattle. The sutler's store was well stocked with goods. We laid in . . . some syrup . . . and a tin coffee pot, as the one in use had developed sieve-like qualities. A number of our men tarried to write letters. . . . Some also obtained a meal which gave them much satisfaction, and these provoked considerable envy by telling of a young maid who waited on them, such sights being rare of late."

The earliest available box-score on passing emigrants was given on May 17 by "M. M. G.," who, like most Kearny correspondents, served the St. Louis *Missouri Republican*: "A good many of the adventurers and navigators have arrived at this point, on their way to the happy land. About three hundred wagons have passed; the foremost train about ten days ago."

On May 18 the tide began to swell. On the nineteenth another *Republican* observer stated: "Yesterday 180 wagons passed here making in all 656, a cart load of letters started for the frontier this morning, and I presume many mothers, wives and sweethearts will soon be made happy." Out of about 180 wagons one might expect to find about 1,000 men; and, if the formula of one emigrant writer for every 250 men holds true, there should be four or five emigrant writers on the eighteenth; and, amazingly enough, there are: Pease, Milner, Love, Pritchard, and one anonymous. Pritchard, otherwise one of the most articulate Forty-Niners, had little to say about "Fort Kerny." John Milner of Georgia wrote to his sister from "Fort Childs, 300 miles in the Indian Country. . . . there are thousands of men going along the road in fact it looks like the wagons hauling cotton to Macon just after a rise in the staple. I believe there are wagons stretched in sight of one another for 500 miles."

On May 21 the *Republican* observer counted 214 wagons, for a total to date of 1,203, "not including the military train of 50 wagons, the advance guard of the Rifles, under Major Simonson, destined for Bear River." On this date the fairly accurate prediction is made that "5000 wagons, 20,000 to 25,000 men and 50,000 animals, will cross the plains this season."

Next day, May 22, the passage of another 200 wagons and 1,000 or more men may be estimated on the strength of five more identified diarists. Benjamin Watson of Illinois commented only on "200 soldiers of the Rifle Regiment, bound for Oregon." Joseph Merrill, an eighteen-year-old from Massachusetts, complained that he had to camp a mile east of the fort: "We are not allowed too near the fort, as Uncle Sam fears the emigrants' animals will steal his grazing." He was not impressed: "The fort is a dull dreary looking place. At the store the traveller can pay a big price for poor goods. The fort is built of mud; I noticed a few sticks of timber lying about, but do not see where they could have been taken from."

On May 23 the emigrant tide was approaching its peak. No wagon count is available for that date, but the advent of at least six diarists of record betokened a new rise in the graph to a probable 300 wagons and some 1,200 men. Tipton Lindsey came via old Fort Kearny and thus carefully refers to "New Fort Kearny" here. He found the post office, store, and bakery "strange things in a wilderness." The most articulate of the May 23 arrivals was our old friend Delano. He found the fort "nothing but a cluster of low, one-story buildings . . . but preparations were making to erect a horse-power sawmill, as well as to enclose the barracks with a wall." This wall never materialized.

The biggest single day in Fort Kearny's Gold Rush history was undoubtedly May 24, when, to judge from the index of a record twelve journalists, there may have been a tidal wave of 500 to 600 wagons and 2,000 to 2,500 emigrants.

Sallie Hester, the first girl emigrant diarist of record to pass Fort Kearny, did so on this epic date, but betrayed her sex by being very uncommunicative about the fort. Joseph Buffum mentioned "Captain Rop, who commands here." Charles Gray observed that the fort was built of mud and logs, "and looks as if a good rain would wash it away." In a more optimistic vein, an unidentified member of the Newark (New Jersey) Overland Company reported some real progress on the construction front: "a saw-mill driven by 12 mules" and "several frame buildings in process of erection." Charles Maltby, one of a large train of Springfield, Illinois, emigrants, wrote in a May 24 letter from the fort that near here they met "a company of traders from the Rocky Mountains. We hear [from them] nothing to discourage us, and hope to reach California in September." Benjamin Gatton, another Springfield citizen, also advised his home town editor of a "circular sawmill" and other signs of preparations to build extensively. He reports flour at $2.50 and bacon at $1 per hundredweight, cheap because of large quantities of these commodities thrown overboard.

Israel Hale of the May 24 brigade described Fort Kearny as "a number of rudely constructed huts built of the sods or turfs of the prairie, laid up after the manner of laying bricks. . . . Some of them had glass windows and very decent looking doors. . . . They have two fields fenced in with the same kind of material."

According to Joseph Hackney, the weather on May 24 was most foul: "This has been one of the worst days that we have experianced since we left St. Joseph it commenced raining soon after we left camp and rained all day we passed fort childs at noon it is situated opposite the head of grand island thear is nothing hear now but a few mud huts but theay are a going to build a regular fort thear is two company of regulars stationed hear we took the wrong road at the fort and had to go through a number of swamps."

Another member of the Jerseyville, Illinois, train of fifteen wagons under the leadership of Capt. Knapp was Charles Kirkpatrick (whose diary is misdated to May 25). He deplored the "few drunken soldiers" and roads muddy from the all-day rain. To make matters worse, in camp that night, "while we were picketing our cattle the flood gates of Heaven seemed to have been opened." Henry Page, also of the Jerseyville company, wrote to his wife Mary during the noon halt: "We find from the record kept at the fort, that 1980 teams [perhaps 8,000 people,] had passed the fort up to last night. Thus we are in advance of the great rush of emigrants."

May 25, oddly enough, is mentioned by no diarist, but it is not concluded from this that the Gold Rush had ground to a sudden halt! Nineteen journals are scattered through the seven-day period May 26 to June 2, from which it is concluded that the emigration was tapering off, but not sharply. This is indeed borne out by the

data supplied by the correspondent "Pawnee." As of May 26 "the
army of gold diggers" totaled 2,527 wagons, or roughly 10,000 men.
On May 28 (represented by five journals) he reported the very respectable number of 460 wagons; on May 29, a total of 381 wagons;
on May 31, 194; and on June 2, a total of 470 "in the last two days."
Total wagon count past Fort Kearny as of June 2, exclusive of government vehicles, was 4,403, with an assumed tally of some 17,000
people, or a gain of 7,000 during this one-week period. If the 25,000
stands as a legitimate total passing Fort Kearny (on the south side of
the Platte) for the season, then by June 2, marking the exit of the
Mounted Riflemen, the emigration was more than two-thirds over.

A sampling of emigrant entries during this crowded week is instructive. On May 26 Sterling Clark disposed of his books: "Gave
some to Capt. McLane and some to Major Rough, U.S. Army." In
a letter of May 27 from "Fort Childs, Pawnee Territory," Epaphroditus Wells of the Peoria Pioneers reassured his wife that no new
cases of "cholrae" had developed. He calculated (incorrectly) that
his company was about in the middle of the migration, "the foremost ox-team being about 100 miles ahead of us, and some mule
teams more than 300."

On May 28 three emigrants reported dealings at the sutler's
store. John Benson described this emporium as "built of sod walls,
roof covered with poles, brush and sod. Dirt floor, very muddy,"
but he was glad to buy flour, bacon, and dried beef at bargain-
basement prices. (They were a drug on the market, since these same
articles were being thrown away by most emigrants.) Elijah Farnham of Ohio wrote, "Tried to sell some of our ammunition here
but could sell nothing but a small portion of our lead at half what
it cost in St. Louis. Powder we could get nothing for." Vincent
Geiger of the Charles Town (Virginia) company had better luck:
"Drove up to the Fort, and succeeded in selling some flour, bacon,
etc." A great deal of food that the sutler wouldn't buy was abandoned forthwith, since the individual weight allowance now (by
company regulations) "is 100 lbs of flour and 50 lbs bacon to a
man." However, it appears that this weight-reducing program was
nullified to some extent for, at the same time, the company "got 15
gallons of whiskey at the fort."

The sod buildings "look comfortable," continues Geiger, "reminding me of a Mexican rancho." (Another Mexican War veteran,
obviously.) But most travelers agreed in principle with Dr. Caldwell

that Fort Kearny was "a hard looking place." Hamelin found it "situated on a low bottom, which must prove very disagreeable in wet weather and would be considered first rate foundation in our country for the ague. . . . The only recommendation it has is the illustrious name it bears." Echoed Charles Parke: "Fort Kearny is a poor looking place." However, in contrast to the acid commentary of some of his predecessors, Parke compliments "the troops here, preparing to go to Oregon. They are a fine looking set of men, especially the officers."

One of the most illuminating descriptions of Fort Kearny in 1849 was that of George Gibbs, a Mounted Rifleman:

> May 28. . . . about four o'clock reached what is called Fort Kearny. Here we were most hospitably received by the officers, and for the first time in a month sat down under a roof and watched the smoke of fire on a hearthstone. . . .

> May 29. . . . The situation is on the low flat bottom, about a third of a mile from the Patte river, near the head of Grand Island, and fifteen from where the trail enters the valley. A more unfortunate one in some respects could hardly have been chosen. Entirely unprotected by trees or high ground, its climate is excessively severe in winter and in the spring the plain is rendered a marsh by the heavy rains. Water can be obtained anywhere by digging to the depth of four or five feet. It is cold and palatable at first, but has a taste of sulphur after standing in the holes for some time. No wood is to be had except the soft cottonwood found on the islands of the Platte, which is brought up with difficulty and not fit for building when obtained. The original design was to form an inclosure of pickets, inclosing the building and an area of about four acres, with blockhouses on the diagonal corners containing each four guns. The number of these is however reduced to two each. The pickets and blockhouses are expected to be built of cottonwood, and the whole is to keep in awe a broken tribe of Pawnees, fast disappearing under their wars with the Sioux and whose nearest village is now 125 miles distant. The establishment, including the expenses of the Missouri battalion, cannot have cost less than half a million dollars. The turf buildings are already so dilapidated as to be almost uninhabitable in wet weather. Were any substantial aid contemplated to the migrants by retaining this post there might be wisdom in so doing, but so far as keeping the Indians in awe is concerned, a moving camp of dragoons during the summer would be far more serviceable.

> It is due the officers stationed here, and more particularly to

Captain Van Vliet, the quartermaster, to say that every attention and kindness which they can personally afford the emigrants has been cheerfully rendered. The scene at the office during the time we have stopped here has been most amusing. Men are coming in at every moment bringing letters from the states, dispatched from here twice a month by a government express, making thousands of inquiries on every conceivable subject, offering to sell or to buy everything under the sun, and asking for every sort of assistance and information. . . .

The condition of the emigrants already forbodes the disasters that await them. . . . Government, I learn today, has with wise liberality directed that the commissary shall hold a surplus of provisions for the relief of emigrants broken down and returning to the states.

The number of wagons which have passed here up to tonight amounts to nearly four thousand. Allowing four persons to a team, which is less than the average, at least 16,000 men have already reached this point and probably half as many more are on their way. This does not include [trains] moving on the north side of the river from Council Bluffs. [These are] composed principally of Mormons, who may amount in all to 10,000. . . .

June 1. The regiment moved a couple of miles to fresh grass, as we had to await the arrival of the beef cattle, and encamped fronting and about a mile distant from the Platte, with a swale of water on the left and front. We found near the road two or three emigrants, who had concluded to abandon their journey and SETTLE. They had pitched their tent for a permanent location, plowed several acres of ground, and were about to put in a crop.

June 2. The first squadron marched at noon, the others following.

Two emigrant writers and one soldier close the book on the month of May. Henry Shombre managed to sell some flour at $1 per sack. He may very well have invested the proceeds in the sut- ler's whiskey; at any rate he thought he counted "some 40 turf houses [double the number usually reported] some look very neet. . . . saw some ladies in a house   went to see them   they were very sociable." Newspaperman George Harker's account of May 31 "Near Fort Kearny" appeared in the St. Louis *Weekly Reveille*:

Since I wrote my last letter, we have been travelling on by slow stages over very good roads, most of the time in company with the Government train, which has been swelled to over 300 wagons by over- taking another division. The animals in this train seem to be in poor order, especially the mules. I conversed with several wagon masters and one or two officers, and am led to believe that only a very small portion of this train will reach Oregon. The soldiers and teamsters will desert on or before their arrival at South Pass; and strike for the gold diggings of California; and most of the officers will no doubt throw up their commissions, and follow suit [This prediction would come true only in part, as it related to enlisted men]. . . .

If I recollect rightly, in a letter written from Independence, I gave it as my opinion that a less number of persons would start for California from the different starting points on the Missouri river than was at first anticipated; but since then I have seen and heard enough to warrant me in saying that not less than 8,000 wagons, and 25,000 persons have left those points. Already 4,000 wagons passed Fort Kearny according to a memorandum kept by the Quartermaster, and most of the ox trains are still behind, so that my estimate cannot be far from the mark. . . .

Fort Kearny is altogether a different sort of place from what I had expected to find it. . . . Not a stick of timber can be seen on this side of the river, and the timber on Grand Island opposite is very sparse. There are about twenty occupied houses at the Fort, all constructed of mud cut in oblong blocks from the prairie, and roofed with poles and mud. There is a store, blacksmith shop, horse saw mill, and a boarding house kept by a Mormon. The soldiers' tents are scattered around with less regularity than in any ordinary encampment. We saw a few pieces of cannon, but no fortifications. A fine frame house is in process of being built, which is probably destined for the commander's quarters. Major Ruff, who has been in command, was succeeded a few days since by Col. Bonneville.

Maj. Cross, in stiff official tones, has this May 31 entry:

We left our encampment at five O'clock this morning for the fort, the distance being about ten miles over a sandy road, and reached it at ten o'clock simultaneously with the rifle regiment. . . .

The site for this post is not a very pleasing one, having nothing to recommend it in the way of beauty. . . .

What few buildings were inhabited, I observed, were made of sward, cut in the form of adobes. The hospital was the only building which was being erected. These buildings were under the direction of an officer of the engineer corps, who for want of proper materials, was unable to progress very rapidly with them. . . .

In the partial cultivation of the soil it has been discovered not to be productive. Gardens have been started, but to little purpose except that the experiment had partly convinced them that it was only labor lost. Still, I am of the opinion when time has been allowed

to find out its qualities better, that not only vegetables may be raised
in abundance, but grain of every description. . . .

While at Fort Kearny I had occasion to converse frequently with
Colonel Bonneville [who] had been many years ago among the Indians
in the Rocky Mountains and had obtained while there much valuable
information which he freely imparted to me. I found it, in more than
one instance before reaching the Columbia River, of great importance.

The June 1 and 2 departure of the Mounted Riflemen under
Col. Loring and their first encampment above the fort were noted
by Elijah Howell and John Scott, who counted some 200 wagons
and 800 Dragoons in the procession.

Arriving here on June 1, Lucius Fairchild "stoped 2 days to air
our provisions and arrang our wagons." He went over to take a
look at the fort, finding "Col. Bonewell" in command of the mud
houses. (Another emigrant speaks of "Major Bowenville.") Fairchild's Wisconsin company left the fort on June 3, and on the following day "3 trains of Mounted Riflemen bound for Oregon
passed." Thus they witnessed the departure of the last section of
this regiment. Likewise, on June 3 an unidentified letter-writer
from Hoxbury, Massachusetts, reported "more clothing on the
ground at Fort Kearny than would fill the largest store in Boston."
Wm. E. Chamberlain from Iowa, having equipment problems, says
he went to the fort, "exchanging tents with Lieutenant Woodbury."

On June 4, P. F. Castleman observed the "Casells of sods" here,
there being "no plank used except the doors and window shutters
which are brought from the Missouri River." He also noted the
rather sorry state of the agricultural project: "Two miles west of
the fort we past some two or three men who were engaged in planting corn   the preraria had been broken and they were breaking a
small hole in the sod droping a few grains of corn there and covering it slightly   left it to the mercy of animals of the plains as they
had no fence around it   nor any way of making one only by diching
which would cost more labour than there crop would be worth."

Chamberlain and Castleman were both impressed with the emigrant crowds of 1849, the latter noting "a no. of waggons on the
road which looked like they were all of the same company as they
were extended for some five or six miles on the road in a perfect
block." But the tide was beginning to ebb. On June 6 "Pawnee"
reported that emigrant wagons were rapidly diminishing in number,
with a cumulative tally of 4,804 to that date. The tally through

June 7 was 4,862, reflecting only 58 wagons on that day in contrast to the average 250 to 300 a day that had held during the preceding three weeks.

The decline in the emigration curve is confirmed by M. L. Wisner, who wrote from the fort on June 6, "We are about 10 days behind the crowd." Unaware of the official count, he too conservatively estimates 5,000 wagons to date, including 1,000 up the north side, and averaging only three men to a team. Thus, "if the savages are disposed to be ugly, they will have to contend with 15,000 riflemen, well armed, and the most of these good marksmen." He deplores the fact that the soldiers "have no one to preach to them on the Sabbath; probably do not want any one." Dr. Israel Lord, physician to the Wisner company, had some penetrating observations on the value of Fort Kearny accommodations and the state of its farming operations:

> At the fort, as it is misnamed (for there is neither wall nor picket, nor fortification of any kind) they get very good water only three feet below the surface. The grass is all fed very short, and but for having some blacksmithing done, we should have left early. By the way, if we had no blacksmith we should have to wait a day or two. The government shop was at our service, gratis. The officers and soldiers very polite, gentlemanly, and accommodating. . . . The place is built of turf with two or three exceptions. It was commenced last fall, and the buildings look well considering the material. Some of them are shaved down so true and smooth as to look really well. The largest are perhaps 25 or 30 feet wide, and 70 or 80 long—and there may be 20 in all. One frame building is now nearly completed, and a great number more will be erected this season. They have a steam saw mill in operation, and are making large quantities of brick. The soldiers have extra wages, if they choose to work, which most do. There are a great many tents pitched about. . . . They have a store filled with goods, and they were just receiving a large supply by land from the Missouri.
>
> Vegetation is backward. The gardens have been planted three or four times, and the seed has mostly rotted. Potatoes were two inches high, and peas in full bloom, five inches. Rope sells for 4s. a pound, salt 10 cents, 4 quart pans 50 cts., cheapest suspenders 4 to 6 shillings, etc. The weather has been so cold till the last three days as to require overcoats in the middle of the day.

On June 8 Niles Searls mentioned finding at the fort "several enclosures . . . made this spring and sowed with grain." However, he found "no settlers here except a family of Mormons who keep a boarding house and with whom a large number of our men made an excellent supper of bread, milk, fresh butter, doughnuts and all the little et ceteras so acceptable to those precluded from them for nearly a month." After partaking of a hearty breakfast at the Mormon house on June 9, said Searls, "We again took leave of civilized society. Near the fort I saw a man planting corn in the open plain." This serves to locate the military's cornfield west of the fort.

Searls was a passenger on Capt. Turner's Pioneer Line, with its 120 passengers at $200 a head, which had left Independence on May 11. This outfit was making dismally poor time—thirty days to go some 300 miles—resulting from wagons too heavily loaded and carriages with six passengers drawn only by two small mules. A few days after the Kearny stop, Searls related, the fat was in the fire: "All sorts of abuse has been awarded to Captain Turner some blaming him for not going faster, others for travelling at all during the continuance of the present bad state of the roads. Our baggage train has been heavily laden and the unprecedented rainy weather has rendered our progress slow and toilsome. Captain Turner resolved to lighten up by destroying everything not essential to our comfort. Liquors to a large amount were turned out, and extra articles of various kinds broken up."

A vivid description of the fort was given by a Kentuckian, Thomas Eastin, the only journalist of record present on June 9. He made the mistake of identifying the post corral as "the fort":

> I had never seen a Fort before and confess I had a good deal of curiosity to see this one. As soon, therefore, as we had encamped, in company with one or two others of our party, I started to pay it a visit. I was greatly disappointed with its appearance. It is a low square block, constructed with turf from the prairie. It is about 200 feet square and ten feet high and its walls are about 3 feet thick. It is on the banks of the Platte. It is true there is no commanding position from which this defense could be canonaded, even with guns of the heaviest calibre, but it does seem to be an exceedingly unmilitary position. With a half dozen 24 pounder, it might be blown to attoms in a few moments.
>
> All the out buildings [actually the main fort] are constructed of the same material except the hospital, which is a frame. There is a trading store, blacksmith and mechanics shop here, also an upholsterer

and a tailor. It is a nasty dirty looking hole and the very air breathes of pestilence. . . .

I had a long conversation with Col. Bonneville, the commanding officer of this post. He informed me thier were 5,000 waggons ahead of us, averaging about 4 souls to each. But he said we were in plenty time and had no excuse to be discouraged and advised us by all means not to abondon the usual travelled rout. . . . It was determined to remain here the balance of the day, to give all who desired an opportunity of writing to their friends and sweethearts.

"Pawnee" reports a total of 5,092 wagons by sundown of the ninth. This gain of 230 for the two-day period June 8 and 9 seems to represent the last measurable upsurge of emigration past Fort Kearny. From June 10 on there was a rapid falling off. "Pawnee" estimated not more than a thousand wagons to come, which, at the four to one ratio, would fill in the 25,000 generally accounted for on the south side of the Platte. Emigrant journals decline sharply in number and proportion, although some of the late comers are among the most vivid reporters of Fort Kearny in 1849.

On June 13 Joseph Sedgley, representing the Sagamore and California Mining and Trading Company of Lynn, Massachusetts, found 140 soldiers here under "Colonel Doniphan," meaning Bonneville. He apparently was as confused as Eastin in speaking about "the fort *and* buildings made of mud," as if there actually were a walled fort. He found "four emigrants here, who have been accidentally shot, and another has had his arm amputated in consequence of the bite of a rattlesnake." According to David Dewolf of Ohio, who paused on June 14, these disabled Argonauts would not yet have the benefit of the new hospital, for "there is a building now in process for a hospital which will be a good building *when finished.*" He found "in and about the fort about 20 huts, built of the turf or sod of the prairie which they spad up in blocks about three feet square and lay them up on coarses with the grass side down. . . . They make quite a novel appearance."

Writing on June 14 from his "Camp No. 13" near Fort Kearny, William Swain reported "some 120 troops cituated here all busily engaged in building the fort." He asked his brother to give his love to his wife Sabrina "and tell her I am determined to have my share of the Rocks if possible." He was anxious to get the letter in the mail, "as the mail leaves here every 2 weeks for Independence."

Yet another June 14 diarist, Elisha Perkins, indicated that the fort was still a lively place:

> It seemed as tho some vast army was encamped before it, so great a multitude was there of wagons, tents, etc. of California emigrants. . . . There must have been 200 wagons with their mules and oxen scattered on the plain. . . . The scene was a very animated and exciting one. . . . From the fort came the sound of the merry drum and fife and the hum of many voices, and I felt my spirits quite elated at the approach of an inhabited and civilized community again. . . . Found the establishment tho quite extensive to be in a primitive state as to buildings etc. With one exception the buildings were all made of blocks of turf. . . . The sutler's store . . . was built in the same style as the others and had a ground floor. Around were ranged his shelves with a pretty good stock of all sorts of notions, cigars, sardines and some fine extras for officers' use. . . . Well might he say as he did to me, that if he had had on hand all the articles California enquired for he could have made more money than by going to the Gold Region itself. . . . I had some conversation with Maj. Chilton the commandant [actually at this time second in command]. Very pleasant man. I found him out shooting at a mark with one of his Colt's revolvers.

On the sixteenth Charles Gould and David Staples, both of the Boston and Newton Joint Stock Association, referred also to the frame hospital under construction. Both patronized the popular Mormon boardinghouse. The proprietor elicited praise from these emigrants: "It was equal to any diner in Boston to us." According to Staples this establishment served as boardinghouse for the officers. The Boston company laid over on Sunday, the seventeenth. Staples wrote, "We stop here to keep Sunday. . . . This evening we had a prayer meeting   prayers were made by Mr. Crist and Sweetser and hymns sung." To Gould, patriotism rather than religion was the keynote: "We are not forgetful of this day, so sacred to Americans, especially to New Englanders." (June 17 is the anniversary of the Battle of Bunker Hill.)

J. Goldsborough Bruff, captain of the Washington (D.C.) and California Mining Company, hove into view likewise on the seventeenth:

> Cloudy, with strong breeze from S.E. Temp. 52 occasional showers. I visited the Fort after breakfast, and was most kindly received by Col. Bonneville, Lieuts. Boots & Davis &c– This place is as yet merely

the site of an intended fort; it has some adobe embankments, quarters
—&c. of adobe and frame, and a number of tents and sheds. Is on
the bank of the Platte, where Grand Island makes a narrow branch
of the river between it and the shore. They had, somehow, at the Fort
got a rumor of my death, by Cholera, and knew no better till my
card was handed the commandant by the 2 men I sent ahead.

Officers,—Col. Bonneville, cmdt; Major Chilton (with family);
Capt. Van Vliet, Drags Q.M.; Lieuts Ths. Davis, Levi Boots, Ogle,
Donaldson, Inft.; Dr. Hammond U.S.A.

Had to send a cart several miles, to the hills, for cedar wood fuel.
Water we obtained from a slew. . . . Held a meeting of the Company,
and equalized the private baggage—disgarded a great deal of superfluous weight—Sold a wagon to the Sutler for $30—and the Ambulance
to the Officers for $50—a perfectly useless article, except to encourage
lazy men to ride—Forge, anvil, bellows, some lead & iron, we sold to
a Mormon family here for $32.

On the seventeenth Joseph Stuart camped one and a half miles
below the fort. The tribulations of the Boston Pack Company are
reflected in his journal:

June 18—Were busy all day repairing saddles and overhauling packs.
The clothing of each man was limited to 50 pounds and weighed.
Some of these loudest in denunciating our lightening process had to
dispose of extra clothing and take mess baggage. . . .

June 19—Went to the fort to sell a gun bought of Mr. Moore and
got some sugar for the mess. Our Company bought some flour from
the Government stores at $2. a hundred pounds. Lt. Stansbury's train
camped a half-mile below us.

This visitor was Capt. Howard Stansbury of the Corps of Engineers, en route to make the first official survey of the Great Salt
Lake. In his journal Stansbury reported:

We travelled up the Platte fifteen miles, and encamped within two
miles of Fort Kearny, on the bank of the river, for the sake of water
and grass. Wood for cooking could be procured only by wading the
river, and bringing it from the opposite side on the shoulders of the
men. After encamping, rode up to the fort, and called upon the commanding officer, Colonel Bonneville, whose adventures among the
Rocky Mountains are so well known to the world. He received us very
courteously, offering us every facility in his power in furtherance of
our progress. We remained at this post until the afternoon of the
21st, to recruit the mules, get many of them shod, and to procure

such necessary supplies as could be obtained. The post at present consists of a number of long low buildings, constructed principally of adobe, or sun-dried bricks, with nearly flat roofs; a large hospital-tent; two or three workkshops, enclosed by canvas walls; store houses constructed in the same manner; one or two adobe stables, with roofs of brush; and tents for the accommodation of the officers and men. There were stationed here two companies of infantry and one of dragoons. I was told that the hailstorms had been very frequent this season and quite destructive, cutting down the weeds and stripping the trees of their foliage.

One of the last emigrants of record to pause here was a German, H. B. Scharman, on June 22. His contribution to our history is fairly anticlimactic: "I went to the commander of the fort and asked him for some fresh bread to satisfy my wife's longing. In the most accommodating and courteous way he supplied me with an order on the quartermaster's department, which I obtained fifteen pounds of fresh bread very cheaply." However, he gets credit as one of the few prophets among the Forty-Niners who could envision central Nebraska as a place of settlement: "The site is on an immense plateau thickly covered with grass which could serve as a dwelling-place for an almost unlimited number of human beings, since the cultivation of this land and the raising of cattle would amply recompense them all within a few years."

The epitaph of the Forty-Niners at "Fort Kearny, Indian Territory," was written on June 23 by "Pawnee" in the August 5 issue of the *Missouri Republican*:

DEAR SIRS: The great California caravan has at length swept by this point, and the prairies are beginning to resume their wonted state of quiet and loneliness. Occasionally, however, a solitary wagon may be seen hurrying on like buffalo on the outskirts of a band, but all the organized, as well as disorganized companies have cut loose from civilization, and are pushing towards the Pacific. Five thousand five hundred and sixteen wagons up to the present time, have passed here, on this bank of the river, while, on the other, from the best information that can be obtained, about six hundred have gone along. These two roads unite at the base of the mountains, and the whole emigration will then roll along over the same road. At a moderate calculation, there are 20,000 persons and 60,000 animals now upon the road between this point and Fort Hall. This is below the actual number, as the numerous trains of pack mules are thrown in. The question naturally suggests itself, can this vast crowd succeed in crossing the mountains in safety? It cannot. The leading trains will doubtless succeed, but those behind, will find the grass gone, and their heavy teams must then fail.

Many are but scantily supplied with provisions, and any little detention, which will throw men behind their time, will bring famine upon them. There is one thing, however, in favor of the emigration, which will be of vast advantage. The grass is better this season than it has been for years. The heavy rains, although they have made the roads bad, have made most ample amends in pushing forward an unusual amount of growing grass. Had some of the sawmill, blacksmith shops, gold diggers, grind-stones and gold workers been left at home and lighter wagons provided, a large number would have made much better progress than they are now making.

Much sickness has prevailed against the emigrants, and many have died. The different roads leading to the frontiers are lined with graves.

VII

Fort Kearny, Gateway to the Great Plains

IN LESS THAN TWO MONTHS in the year 1849, Fort Kearny, outpost of the U.S. Army on the prairie, became the epicenter of an American revolution on wheels. Although no year would excel 1849 for feverish excitement, the period 1850–1866 was climactic in American frontier history, with gold rushes, Indian wars, the Pony Express, and the Pacific Telegraph and Overland Stage Lines crowding in on each other's heels. Through all this Fort Kearny played a primary role.

Unlike Fort Laramie, the second principal military bastion on the Great Platte River Road, Fort Kearny was rendered obsolete in 1869 with the completion of the Union Pacific Railroad on the opposite bank of the Platte, though the death sentence was not carried out until 1871. But longevity was never the measure of greatness. For two decades, from covered wagon to stagecoach days, Fort Kearny's star burned brightly in the West. It was the sentinel of all the trails which converged on the fabled Platte River valley. It was the official gateway to the Great Plains.

Several contemporaries have offered convincing testimony of Fort Kearny's value. One of these, Dr. C. M. Clark, commented in 1860 en route to Pike's Peak:

> Fort Kearny is considered by the emigrant as the great intermediate point between the Missouri River and Denver City. It is the place he looks forward to after "starting out," for there he expects to get news from home.

192

On reaching this point, the emigrant feels that he has reached an oasis; he sees once more the evidence of civilization and refinement, the neat and comfortable tenements of the officers, the offices and stores, all remind him of home, and as he looks aloft at the masthead, where the stars and stripes are proudly waving to the breeze, he fully realizes he is still protected, still inhabits *America.*

In 1865 Frank C. Young wrote:

Fort Kearney is today without doubt the most important point in all this vast country north of the Arkansas, and between the Missouri River and the Rocky Mountains. It is the general military headquarters, and not only exercises autocratic sway over other and smaller posts which dot the Plains at intervals of a hundred miles or less along the Platte, but it practically has under its care the safety from Indian attack of at least a thousand miles of highway. . . .

The Fort's location may be said to be the real beginning of the great overland thoroughfare. It is true there is here the continuation of . . . roads starting westward from the River at various points. . . . it is not until these one by one become merged that the highway can in reality be called the great Oregon Trail, as Parkman calls it—and the last of these junctions is the one we have just made, a few miles east of Kearney. It is at Kearney, also, that you really begin to enter upon the true "Plains."

And in 1866 young bullwhacker William H. Jackson summarized the psychological impact of Fort Kearny:

At last we have reached the first point or place of any importance on our route. We have thought and spoken of Kearney as if it was our destination, and nothing beyond it, but now we regard it as a starting point. Here all routes converge and again diverge.

Fort Kearny was the true beginning of the Great Platte River Road, for it was here that various trail strands joined to become one grand highway for the westward migrations. Although the actual physical convergence of the St. Joe–Leavenworth–Independence Road and the Nebraska City–Plattsmouth Road occurred a few miles east, Fort Kearny was recognized as the port of call of the Nebraska Coast, the end of the shakedown cruise across the prairie and the beginning of the voyage across the perilous ocean of the Great Plains, a place to pause and reflect, to recuperate, to reorganize, to get your bearings. For the fainthearted it was a good opportunity to change their minds, make a 180-degree turn, and go back where they came from before they became committed to California and later, somewhere out in the Great American Desert, reached the point of no return. Finally, it was across from Fort Kearny that the Council Bluffs Road became part of the primitive superhighway which was the Great Platte River Road.

Fort Kearny was usually identified as "at the head of Grand Island," although some sticklers for accuracy, such as Littleton, place it "a few miles below the head," and Frink has it "four miles from the head." Grand Island today means the Nebraska town of that name. But the historical Grand Island was a genuine island, claimed as the largest, or at least the longest, river island in the world—just how long is a moot point. Fremont judged it to be fifty-two miles. Journal estimates range from sixteen miles (Cagwin) to one hundred miles (J. Evans), although figures of forty or fifty are more common. Susan Cranstone has it fifty miles long and five miles wide, but this width, at least, seems grossly exaggerated. However long it was, at most it could only have been a band splitting the Platte into two main channels. No topographic maps were made in emigrant days, so no determination can be made as to its historical length or breadth. Whatever is left of Grand Island today has been fragmented by new channeling.

Fort Kearny and the head of Grand Island were nearly synonymous in terms of general location. They were both reckoned at midpoint between St. Joe (the number one jumping-off point on the Missouri River) and Fort Laramie, a distance of some 600 miles plus. As to the merits of the fort's location, many elements were considered other than the equidistance from the Missouri River to Fort Laramie, the relative proximity of the 100th meridian (the theoretical dividing line between prairie and plains), or the quantity of timber on Grand Island. As we have seen, Lt. Woodbury figured it was on a "slight elevation," which would, of course, be helpful from a drainage standpoint. If a military engineer said it was elevated in 1848, perhaps it was, but today the "elevation" of the Fort Kearny site above the surrounding terrain, if it exists, is so slight as to be negligible. Capt. Gove in 1858 wrote of it as "on a slight elevation" and Col. Word in 1863 called it "an elevated portion of the Platte Bottom," but most travelers described the site as dead level, whether open prairie or river bottoms. Capt. Todd in 1855 recalled it was "a low level plain," while J. L. Johnson in 1851 spoke of "the garrison in the open plains . . . site rather low." In

October, 1850, Capt. Stansbury, returning from Great Salt Lake, described it as "in the level plains, three quarters of a mile from Platte River."

While the general topography today is unchanged, the rank growth of timber along the river and the groves on farmsteads might not permit Fort Kearny to be seen today as much as one mile away, even if it were fully restored. In historical times there was little timber on the mainland to hinder visibility. Also, the California Road approached Fort Kearny on a gradient of some six to eight feet to the mile. Thus it is not too surprising to learn that on a clear day the fort was visible to approaching travelers for a considerable distance. In 1852 Gage wrote, "Fort Karney was in sight miles before reaching it." That same year John Clark claimed that the fort could be seen at a distance of fifteen to twenty miles, "with the ade of the glass from the bluff." In 1866 Birge reported that the flag was visible at a distance of ten miles. Perhaps the most graphic impression of the Fort Kearny approach from the east is given by Capt. Seville in 1858:

> We reached the long-looked-for Fort Kearney. . . . Our course lay along the valley, and the Fort was in sight throughout the march. It first consisted only of a chimney and a flag-pole, but every mile added something to it. A large house we found was attached to the chimney, and a flag to the pole, and at last the place grew into several extensive buildings, flanked about by adobe houses.

Opinions differed widely on the aesthetic qualities of the fort. Col. Word spoke glowingly of its "beautiful location," and Thomasson thought it a "butiful situation." Such favorable impressions were probably influenced by emotions similar to those of McGlashan, who was "happy to see some signs of civilization," and Lobenstine: "The resemblance of this place to the civilized world awoke in us a great feeling of happiness." After several weeks of slogging across the wild prairies with no habitation in sight save a Winnebago hut or a Pawnee earthlodge, travelers were understandably pleased to see a genuine outpost of their own culture, however unprepossessing. Thus, J. H. Clark thought Fort Kearny, at a distance at least, had the appearance of a comfortable old farm "in a sea of verdure," while Helen Carpenter likened the surrounding country to her familiar "Grand Prairie of Illinois." On his first visit there Moses Sydenham looked upon the fort as "an oasis in the desert."

However, not everyone was charmed. In 1850 Wolcott thought it "an isolated, desert-looking spot," while Littleton condemned it as a sickly place, rendered malarial by marshes and "musquetoes by the bushel." In 1857, even after there were many improvements, Capt. Gove regarded the post as "desolate, indeed the most forbidding place I ever saw."

Many travelers, disappointed at finding no grand fortification here but only a random collection of buildings, freely use such words as drab, squalid, and homely. Such critical observers failed to take into account three vitally important facts. First, Fort Kearny was not established as a tourist attraction but as a functional military post. Second, with the scarcity of materials and labor, construction of any kind here required great ingenuity and heroic effort. Third, the importance of Fort Kearny was to be found, not in its architectural style, but in its role as way station, sentinel post, supply depot, and message center for travelers on the Great Platte River Road. Fort Kearny might not have won any beauty contests, but it was the most vital link between the Missouri River and Fort Laramie, and therein lay its unique importance.

Today the modern road which passes Fort Kearny State Park adjoins the southern perimeter of the old parade ground. Thus, it requires an effort of the imagination to put the California Road in its proper location, to the *north* of the old fort, between it and the river. Most journals fail to specify this; a few, however, mention that the fort was "to the left of" the trail (heading westward). Due to cultivation, no clear evidence of the trail here survives today, but all doubt is dispelled by the itinerary of the Magraw engineering party of 1857, which used the Fort Kearny flagpole as their zero point. According to their field notes, "Road lies to the right of fort and about 50 yards from it." This is borne out in the Sitgreaves map of the 1860s.

The road which passed Fort Kearny, like most of the road along the main Platte, was a broad, well-defined, beaten track from which all vegetation had been erased, somewhat sandy and dust-laden during most of the year, but during wet weather a veritable bog. It was "the hardest kind of wheeling," complained Gage, in which wagons would sink to their axles, requiring a dozen yoke of oxen to extricate them.

One thing about the Fort Kearny "road system" that is little understood today is the river crossings. True, the great majority of travelers, north or south, were happy to stay on their respective sides and cross the Platte River only when they had to, which was normally much farther west; but there were three classes of people who chose to cross the river at Fort Kearny, even if they were in the minority and even though this could be a very distressing, if not fatal, experience. These were: (1) emigrants on the south side who, through fear of cholera, elected to cross to the north side; (2) emigrants on the north side who, though they liked it where they were, wanted to make a side trip to the south side to transact business at the Fort Kearny Post Office; and (3) travelers on the later stage line from Omaha to Fort Kearny, who had no choice.

There was no such thing as a good place to cross the Platte; but some places were worse than others, and travelers tried to avoid them. The fine art of crossing the Platte without drowning or dying of exposure will be explored in the next chapter, dealing with the main South Platte crossings; here are considered only briefly the Fort Kearny crossing locations and the pattern of their use.

First is mentioned the proximity of the parallel routes and the fact that they were sometimes within sight of each other. In 1849 there were no river crossings here of record, and it may be more than coincidence that in the spring of 1849 Grand Island was still timbered in this area. However, by the end of 1849 the soldiers had harvested the timber closest to the fort, so that by 1850 there was really nothing to interfere with vision except the distance between banks, then estimated at two to three miles. Thus, in 1850 Jacob Bartholomew, while having a Saturday bath in the Platte near the fort, "saw teams on the other side." That same year, as he approached Fort Kearny from St. Joe, W. McBride wrote: "A great many camp-fires were seen . . . on the other side of the river. . . . [They] seemed as numerous as they are on our side." From the north bank in 1853 Henry Allyn saw many wagons and "droves of cattle" on the St. Joe Road, and he also saw the Fort Kearny buildings. That the Grand Island timber may have experienced a regrowth and thus again obscured vision is suggested by the fact that in 1862 one emigrant on the Council Bluffs Road was able to see the Fort Kearny flag, but nothing else. He was also able to hear "the night and morning guns." In 1864 Dickson, also on the north side, says he couldn't see Fort Kearny at all for the trees.

Although there must have been earlier instances (as, for example, Fort Kearny soldiers gathering wood or hunting buffalo or Indians), the first crossing of record, north or south, was in 1850, when Mormons of the Kilgore party "waid across to send letters." In 1851 J. L. Johnson mentioned a crossing fifteen miles above the fort. In 1852, crossing south to north became common to judge from the evidence of at least ten journals, and this was simply because cholera raged along the south bank, while the north bank was supposedly free of the plague. David Cartwright, J. H. Clark, and Caroline Richardson are among those who mentioned a crossing "just above" Fort Kearny which offered no difficulty. Isaac Foster and Abigail Duniway speak of a crossing eight miles west, while R. Hickman and Potter crossed fifteen miles west of the fort. Lodisa Frizzell gives a detailed account of an adventurous crossing at this latter point, about four miles east of Elm Creek, which would coincide with the 1851 crossing point mentioned by Johnson. Her account makes it clear that in 1852 emigrants were deserting the California or St. Joe road near Fort Kearny in large numbers.

In 1860 the Lowry party, for reasons not given, crossed the Platte south to north at Fort Kearny, finding it two miles wide and encountering ten channels. But after 1852 most emigrant crossings of record were north to south, side trips from the Council Bluffs Road to visit Fort Kearny. On July 4, 1853, the Washington Bailey party realized they were opposite Fort Kearny when they heard a cannon firing to celebrate the holiday, and they sent a boy over on foot for news of friends. Since he had no problems it may be safely assumed that the river was quite low at this time. (It was in May or June, during the usual migration peak, that the river normally crested.) In 1859, two of the Martin Patterson company undertook to make the crossing on horseback, and one nearly drowned in the vain attempt. In 1860 Edward Ayer had a similar experience: "I volunteered to go across the river to get the mail for the train, if they would let me ride one of the horses. I got into a deep hole, and came nearly drowned."

In 1862 William Smedley, evidently determined to get his mail at all costs, decided to tackle the Platte in a different way. He forded with a large wagon drawn by six yoke of oxen and as insurance against drowning cased his wagon with a "waterproof sheet iron bed," which in a crisis would become a boat. Despite all this effort, Smedley found no mail. Like James Roberts in 1864, he had "nothing for his pains but a view of the town."

In November, 1862, Charles Teeter tackled the Platte at Fort

Kearny in the hardest way imaginable. Hauling a load of merchandise from Omaha to Denver, he found the Platte full of slush ice and visibility near zero from snow. Although the river was not more than two and a half feet deep, his team nearly foundered. Teeter waded alongside to whip the oxen along, resting on the chain of islands. After two hours of freezing struggle, he walked into the fort a human icicle, but with load intact. "Strange to tell," says Teeter, "I took no cold, nor suffered any inconvenience from this experience."

It is not possible to pinpoint one standard crossing of the "Omaha and Fort Kearny Military and Stage Road." As reported by Olga Sharp Steele, early General Land Office maps show "the Military Road" crossing downstream from the fort. The "Platte River Ford at Fort Kearny" on Col. Carrington's map of 1866 is shown directly north of the fort proper; this seems to have been the case also in 1859, according to David Anderson: "At a point opposite the fort the Platte River was three miles wide, containing numerous small islands and many deep and treacherous channels; yet this was the only really safe fording place between Julesburg and the Missouri River." The Sitgreaves map of Fort Kearny environs shows the Omaha Road approaching the Platte directly opposite the fort, but then it swerves upstream about a mile before crossing. In 1866 stage passenger Gurdon P. Lester says he "landed 3 miles above Kearney Station," or about three and a half miles above the fort. This was also the route used by Randall Hewitt in 1862. He was not a regular stage passenger, but, feeling the universal urge to visit the post office, he paid $3 to the driver for the privilege of crossing a part of the river. Why he didn't ride all the way across he fails to explain. According to his account, the stage crossing was about four miles above, or west of, the fort, which would bring it in west of Dobytown and not far from the highway bridge south of present Kearney, Nebraska:

> Reached the ranch   a station opposite Fort Kearny   at 12 A.M. and was obliged to wait the . . . stage, which did not appear until 3 P.M. The crossing we found to be four miles above. Here the river is nearly 3 miles wide, and runs in 3 channels, 2 of which we forded by stage. The third, nearly 1¾ miles wide, is shallow, with an occasional deep channel, and a very rapid current. This we crossed in a miscellaneous combination of sticks and lumber, miscalled a boat. . . . On the south side we procured passage down to the Fort, 4 miles,

in the mail wagon. On reaching the post office, with feelings running
high with anticipation, we found nothing to repay us for our pains. . . .
This was a severe blow and a bitter disappointment. We had travelled
12 weary miles, crossed in fact three rivers, tramped through a jungle.
. . . nothing could now be done but to retrace our steps as quickly as
our physical condition would allow. . . .

This is our experience crossing Platte River; the meanest of rivers—
broad, shallow, fishless, snakeful, quicksand bars and muddy water—
the stage rumbles over the bottom like on a bed of rock; yet haste
must be made to effect a crossing, else you disappear beneath its turbid
waters, and your doom is certain.

FORT KEARNY AND THE MIGRATION FROM 1850

Having considered some of the general aspects of Fort Kearny,
including its approaches, now considered, in turn, will be three
primary phases of its history: first, its relationship to emigrants
and other civilian visitors; second, the physical evolution of Fort
Kearny and its two satellite communities, Valley City and Kearney
City; and third, a brief summary of its military involvements,
including the identification of some commanders and garrison
units. In conclusion, post-military events leading to the present
situation of old Fort Kearny as a historic shrine will be discussed.

No visitor statistics at Fort Kearny from 1850 are available, but
of course these would approximate the totals of all migration years
up the Platte, minus the totals up the north bank, or Council
Bluffs Road. Occasional glimpses of figures are given in emigrant
journals; these, in turn, were gleaned from the Fort Kearny emigrant register. This official record book, or set of books, is not to
be found anywhere and presumably has long since vanished. What
a pity, since this record would have given not only the statistics,
but the names and places of origin of almost all who followed the
California Road, at least until 1853, which is the last year for which
there are definite figures. Already examined in detail are the 1849
data. A brief sampling of journals during the following few years
is illustrative.

Perhaps the most illuminating entry of 1850 is that of Rev.
Henry Davis, who revealed the recording procedure: "The Commander ordered every emigrant to pass into one of the offices where
a clerk registered each name, his former residence and destination."
Davis failed to mention what is self-evident from other journals:

that the registry also provided differential data on men and women, adults and children, wagons, and types of animals used.

The earliest entry of 1850 is that of McGlashan, who on May 3 noted 300 wagons to date. On May 11 the commander told Wolcott that 5,000 emigrants were ahead of him; also, that ox teams were just beginning to show up. (This latter, highly significant, entry confirms the generally accepted principle that horse and mule teams got a head start from the border towns because they could feed on transported grains until the grass came up.) On May 19 Shepherd reported 2,300 wagons ahead. As of May 21 a St. Louis newspaper reported 2,754 wagons averaging four and a half men to a wagon, or some 12,000 men to "76 ladies," giving a startling Gold Rush ratio of one woman to 150 men.

In a Fort Kearny letter of June 1, Reuben Knox wrote, "About 30,000 have passed already this side of the river, and probably one fourth as many on the north side. While resting here yesterday probably 1,000 wagons passed and very likely as many will pass today as there is a continual stream ever in sight." Considering that the peak day in 1849 yielded some 500 wagons, Knox's estimate for one day in 1850 seems exaggerated, but his total figure does not conflict with the evidence. It is generally accepted among Trail historians that, on the basis of data available at St. Joe, Fort Laramie, and Salt Lake City, in 1850 there were over 50,000 travelers to California via Fort Kearny.

J. L. Johnson is the only emigrant of 1851 who kept score. Officers told him that as of the date of his visit, May 26, there were 3,176 wagons; 16,880 men, women, and children; 31,780 cattle, horses, and mules. "This statement was near correct as the Commanding Officer had each day kept a subordinate at the road keeping tally. . . . We considered ourselves in the forefront of the emigration so you may judge the number behind. All those from Kanesville or Council Bluff passing up on the north side of the Platte he had no account of."

The same routine appears in the 1852 journals of Snodgrass, Hampton, and C. Richardson. Writing on June 5, Mary Baily said, "We went into the register office and looked over the names of those who had been before us, some 20,000 men and 4,000 women." This sudden change in the sex ratio, with women now outnumbered by only 5 to 1, suggests that the social patterns of the migrations were now undergoing a drastic change.

Register data for 1853 comes largely from two young Oregon-bound ladies. "The Captain informed Pa," Celinda Hines noted on June 4, "that there had passed here 85,000 head of cattle, and 8,000 men" and that most of these were going to Oregon. On June 11, said Rebecca Ketcham, "We drove up to the fort to report ourselves. Mr. Gray wrote on a piece of paper the number of animals he had, the number and names of the persons, and sent it in to the officers. He says if a company does so they are more likely to have assistance from this fort if they get into difficulty."

The absence of figures after 1853 suggests that the army thereafter dropped the registry idea. It seems unlikely that such a practice would have gone unnoticed by the many that followed.

Emigrants were in competition with the military for the meager grass and wood supplies. Grass, of course, was a very scarce item; emigrants frequently did without, while the army had to graze its animals in an ever-widening arc from the fort. In 1850 Reuben Knox noted: "There is not a tree on this side for twenty miles that I know of, and but here and there a scattering on the other side." In 1856 Helen Carpenter's brothers waded in the Platte up to their chins to get a few skimpy green willows. But, except in desperate cases, it was not worth the trouble to wade the Platte, so the emigrants at this point normally settled for what buffalo chips they could scrounge or ate their meals cold. Timber here was actually nonexistent except on the island (or islands), and this was rapidly stripped by the soldiers, who had to keep alive all winter somehow.

It was customary for the War Department to set aside a military reservation of 100 square miles; here, in addition to the usual rectangular block ten miles square, the reservation was extended in a strip downstream for an additional four miles to include more Grand Island timber. Although the boundary was neither fenced nor posted, emigrants camping in the vicinity were often politely informed they were on the reservation and could not camp thereon. The fort was located, not in the center of the rectangle, but at a point two miles from its western boundary, or eight miles from the eastern line. Consequently, the largest camping area was just beyond the western line. The military was not often so fussy about camping to the east, and covered wagon camps would sometimes be strung out in that direction for miles. When he came within six miles of the fort the evening of May 26, 1850, James

Evans estimated no less than 2,000 campers within view. "Wagons and tents all looking so white and neat are scattered over the plain everywhere."

The regulations as to the location of campsites at Fort Kearny were pretty elastic. In 1850 Bennett says he was not allowed to encamp within one mile of the fort, the grass being reserved for public animals. In 1852 Richard Hickman tried to camp just a half mile beyond the fort, but had to move: "After remaining there for some time the Captain sent us a message to leave within thirty minutes or be cannonaded. We chose the former." This sounds like drastic treatment, but 1852 must have been one of the rougher years for Fort Kearny campers; Gilbert Cole said that when he came to the east line of the reservation he was instructed to stop there "or go clear through." He decided to camp right there, since he would otherwise have had to go several miles farther through rain and darkness.

In 1853 Celinda Hines wrote that her party was forbidden to camp within three miles of the fort and had to settle for "no wood and nothing but rain water standing in puddles on the prairie." In 1856 Helen Carpenter said nothing about military restrictions: "Camped a mile from town and half a mile from the river." Far from being challenged, she noted that the only man in sight in a uniform was one lone soldier on guard, who paced back and forth "entirely oblivious to our presence, not deigning to glance at the very best looking women of our party." In 1859, however, Wilkinson said, "We were not allowed to camp near the Fort. . . . camped four miles out."

In 1863 the ban was still in effect, for Cutting reported in that year a sign posted in the sutler's store which read: "No camping allowed 5 miles east, or 2 miles west of this Post." At this time, it seems, the army was also cantankerous about civilians wandering around the premises: "While passing Fort Kearny, Tobey rode into the centre of the place and among the barracks. While crossing the parade ground he was halted by a soldier and told he must go to the guardhouse for crossing the parade ground. He demurred, was taken before the Lieutenant Colonel and, after an explanation, was let off." As late as 1866 Julius Birge was told "that two miles in each direction from the Fort extends the Government reservation, and that a notice had been posted on the wayside forbidding the drivers of teams across the property." On reaching "these sacred precincts" Birge daringly rode through on horseback.

Except for the few instances of complaint noted, the emigrants seemed willing to abide by camping regulations in view of the vital services rendered. Aside from protection from Indians, which was an intangible benefit as long as no Indians were in sight, the most appreciated service was provisioning.

No one ordered an emigrant to California—this was his own idea—but if he started in that direction he was supposed to have enough imagination and prudence to provide himself with the necessities. But through inexperience, bullheadedness, or act of God, many citizens reached the fort, only one-sixth of the way west, destitute. The commanding officer was authorized by the War Department to assist these hardship cases by selling supplies from the government warehouse upon requisition. If the degree of desperation precluded payment, the officer could relinquish limited supplies anyhow in exchange for a promissory note, which, in most cases, was worthless. (Shepherd, lacking cash, said he traded dried peaches and loaf sugar for 175 pounds of flour.)

In the early years the post commissary itself was sometimes sorely lacking in resources. In 1850 Dabney Carr noted the plight of "premature emigrants" who jumped the gun at St. Joe and lost a gamble on early grass. The fort had no grain to spare.

The most important items to be obtained from the commissary were grain (when available), bacon, pickled pork, and flour, the price of which fluctuated wildly from $4.50 per hundredweight (Pigman) to $30 per hundredweight (J. Evans). In 1853 Cipriani negotiated here for 1,000 pounds of flour and 600 pounds of horse biscuit. When he reached Ash Hollow, he found the flour crawling with worms, but no other adverse comment on the quality of Fort Kearny staples is noted.

The post garden was a sorry affair, seldom able to supplement the vitamin-deficient diet of the garrison, much less that of transients, so fresh vegetables were rarely to be had. An order issued early in 1854 directed that "farm culture be discontinued." A much more dependable local source of vitamins was buffalo meat, brought in in quantity by professional hunters, particularly in the 1850s, when the herds still roamed in the neighborhood. Lewis Dougherty described buffalo hunts by fort personnel, which offered a prime diversion from monotony. In 1850 William Montgomery was told that a herd of 15,000 buffalo had frequented the fort area the previous winter, so the post larders must have been filled with meat; but this commodity was not available to emigrants at Fort Kearny. They had to hunt their own buffalo.

After the post quartermaster, the most important suppliers of goods and services were the post blacksmith and the post sutler. As the result of inferior materials or accident much of the wagon gear, especially wheels, reached the fort in a weakened condition, and animals needed to be re-shod. In 1852 Snodgrass said he "had some repairing done," but J. H. Clark found the blacksmith shop on a do-it-yourself basis. Apparently the blacksmith was frequently missing, as the Celinda Hines party in 1853 "found the blacksmith shop, but no smith." Mary Bailey's father paid $1 per pound for horseshoe nails, a fact which suggests that if he sold enough nails, the smith wouldn't have to work!

Addison Crane was well treated here: "They are very kind to emigrants, as an instance of which I may mention that a blacksmith shop has been opened for their accommodation where they may mend their numerous breaks free of charge. Procured here a good meal of bread, fresh butter and milk, and ate so much that it gave me a violent headache and made me quite sick all night. . . . There is a Suttler's store where many articles can be had at enourmous prices."

The post sutler, being a businessman and not a philanthropist, was frequently the cause of complaints about "prices extragavantly high" (Dalton). There are a few fleeting glimpses of the kinds of merchandise available in this sod emporium. In October, 1850, Capt. Stansbury noted that "the sutler's store will supply travellers with groceries, cloths, and many useful articles." In 1854 Edwin Bird said he "procured several little luxuries, such as lotion, syrup and soap." In 1856 Helen Carpenter reported the purchase of a can of peaches and one of blackberries, and some cheese: "The latter should have been mustered out long ago, it is too old to be in the service, one mere taste took the skin off the end of my tongue."

In 1851 J. L. Johnson said he had at the fort "a touch of the beaver," meaning that he had a drink of whiskey. In 1852 Hampton said he "partook of some good ale." These stray references are among the few which suggest the dual function of the sutler's store as a tavern patronized by the emigrants and other citizens; this shop was off limits to enlisted men. In 1866 James Meline mentioned the purchase at Fort Kearny of corn at $1.50 per bushel; whiskey, $10 a gallon; and "great quantities of canned meats, fruits and vegetables." Since the commissary did not issue whiskey except to military personnel for morale or medical purposes, Meline must have made these purchases at the sutler's store.

The Fort Kearny post office, which apparently was operated by, or in conjunction with, the post sutler, was another favorite haunt for emigrants, as we have seen. As the result of the vagaries of the mail service, particularly in early years, most inquiring emigrants came away disappointed; only a few would emerge triumphant with missives from loved ones. Thousands of letters, scribbled on packing boxes by candlelight, were mailed at Fort Kearny; only a dozen or so have survived (e.g., Knox, King).

The occasional heroic efforts of "north-siders" to reach Fort Kearny for their mail have been noted, this being their only chance to communicate with home until Fort Laramie was reached. Very typical is the entry in Cagwin's journal: "We made a tarry here to mail letters." Shepherd, posting his mail, noted that it "leaves on the 21st for the States." J. L. Johnson said, "deposited a letter for the monthly mail." These entries are reflections of the fact that contract mail was carried only on a monthly schedule (Indians and blizzards willing) from 1850 to 1858. The military had its own courier service as occasion required, which, of course, did not serve civilians. Lucky emigrants might find returning travelers or traders who would be willing to carry their mail to St. Joe or Council Bluffs, usually for a consideration. Beginning in 1859 with the advent of stage service, and in 1860 with the Pony Express, mail moved more frequently.

The arrival of personal mail was also a big thing for the military. In 1858 Kirk Anderson described a scene as he arrived with the mail wagon: "We arrived at Fort Kearny yesterday, where we left the mail, which was instantly surrounded by a crowd of officers, anxiously looking for letters and papers."

Aside from the failure to receive letters, only one complaint about the Fort Kearny postal service has been encountered. Dr. C. M. Clark comments:

> I will state that the P.M. is not as courteous and obliging as he might be; but perhaps the dignity of his position and the rules of office

do not permit him to be gentlemanly to what he considers to be the poor, plebian gold hunters. On making inquiry for letters, ten to one, if you are not eyed with a suspicious look and then referred to the list of "advertised", pasted on the walls. If you expect papers, it is needless to ask for them, for he is the proprietor of a news depot, and considers them as his perquisites.

The man in charge of the post office was Moses Sydenham. He freighted across the Plains in 1856 and returned to Fort Kearny in the autumn of that year, becoming a clerk in the employ of the sutler and "taking charge also of the post office affairs of the Fort, by my appointment as postmaster, which post I filled for not less than 15 years," or until abandonment of the fort. He must have been the same individual Clark complained of, for Frank Root says that Sydenham "was at the time proprietor of a small book, stationery and news depot, in connection with the post office." Perhaps Mr. Sydenham had an off day when Clark visited, for he is well spoken of by others, including Margaret Carrington, who in 1866 speaks of "the genial Sydenham."

Clark also mentions a post hospital, "in part for the benefit of the emigrants." However, in 1855, in a letter from "Camp near Fort Kearny, Indian Territory," John King said there was a man stricken with cholera whom the post surgeon would not allow on the premises. If this is true, it is an isolated instance of callousness on the part of fort personnel. Although records are meager, kindness seems to have been the general policy. In contrast to King, G. A. Smith in 1852 wrote: "Concluded to lay over and visit the Fort. Had fine supper there. Closed the scene by dancing a cotillion with the soldiers in the Fort." Celinda Hines and family, though forced to camp at a distance, sampled Fort Kearny hospitality: "The sergeant invited us to his house where we were pleasantly entertained." Cole, the same one who was held up at the reservation line, said the next morning: "We hitched up and drove into the fort where we were kindly treated by the commanding officer. . . . He tendered us a large room with tables, pen and ink, paper and envelope paper."

J. L. Johnson reported that "the officers were gentlemen, giving satisfactory answers to all." Crane said that he called on "Captain Horton" and "found him much a gentleman. He was from Phildelphia and with his family had resided here two years." This was Capt. Henry W. Wharton, Sixth U.S. Infantry, who was the post commander from 1851 to 1857 and seems to have been a favorite. Bradway in 1853 describes him as "a very gentlemanly fellow."

The post commander at Fort Kearny didn't make a practice, of course, of entertaining every emigrant who came along, but when he and his wife did entertain civilian visitors, it was a memorable event. Mrs. Benjamin Ferris, whose husband was bound for Utah as Territorial Governor in 1852, recalled:

> Captain Wharton introduced himself . . . and extended an invitation to come directly into dinner, in a way which precluded all possibility of a refusal. . . . At the entrance we were met by Mrs. Wharton . . . and we were ushered into a prettily furnished parlor. I was completely bewildered. . . . I had never dreamed there was anything civilized about the fort—I had only thought of officers living in a very rude, boisterous sort of way—but here we were in the very midst of refinements. . . . They seemed absolutely grateful for our coming. . . . everything is neat and orderly about them. There is a well cultivated vegetable and flower garden; and adjacent to it, an immense field of corn—and everything wears the appearance of the establishment of a wealthy farmer.

Two visitors of 1853 gave an adverse impression of the commanding officer, though it is uncertain if they specifically referred to the esteemed Wharton or a subaltern. Thus, Count Cipriani wrote: "I found most of the troops stretched out in the shade . . . drinking and yelling louder than Neapolitans. . . . I asked to see the commanding officer. He turned out to be the most dishevelled of the lot." William Gray of the Oregon mission was quoted by Rebecca Ketcham to the effect that the fort is in miserable condition and "everything looks as though it were going to destruction as fast as possible." For this reason, he concluded, "Everything around here looks as though the commanding officer liked strong drink better than anything else." Both of these observations, by the snobbish count and the notoriously malicious Dr. Gray, may be regarded as defamatory and unwarranted.

EVOLUTION OF FORT KEARNY

Although it was the scene of momentous events associated with the covered wagon migrations and the Indian wars, Fort Kearny was never a large post on the scale of Fort Leavenworth and Fort Laramie. It was primarily a recruiting and jumping-off point rather than a central military station. Its garrison rarely exceeded 200 men, and normally there were less than half that number to answer the roll call. The civilian population residing at the post—mechanics, teamsters, quartermaster employees, telegraphers, laundresses, soldiers' families—probably fluctuated between 100 and 200. When a military expedition was being organized, the population might swell to 1,000 or more, but then most of these transient troops would be sheltered in tents. Physically, Fort Kearny was on a small scale.

Whereas its historic twin, Fort Laramie, has been well preserved, often represented pictorially, and amply recorded in official records, Fort Kearny has suffered comparative eclipse. All traces of the original fort have vanished except for archeological evidence. Ground plans and military records in the National Archives are skimpy and erratic. Of contemporary pictures only a few photographs and sketches have been found. Our grasp of the events of the year 1849 is happily aided by a sketch of the fort by James F. Wilkins. Two scratchy photographs credited to C. C. Mills survive from an 1858 military survey party (Seville, W. Lee). William H. Jackson made a pencil sketch in 1866, and later several water color versions. A few other sketches by unidentified soldiers and emigrants have turned up, but no other pictorial records remain. All the more valuable, therefore, are the many written impressions of the fort left by civilian travelers on the Great Platte River Road.

The beginning of post construction under Lt. Woodbury, 1848–1849, has been mentioned. Because of the immense cost of transporting finished lumber, millwork, shingles, hardware, and other needed items, the earliest buildings were primarily of sod with native timber supports and earthen roofs, though there were some experiments with pebbled adobe, burned brick, and rammed earth. Late in 1849 a beginning was made on a few more substantial and more presentable structure of frame. By the spring of 1850 the principal buildings in evidence were a large adobe storehouse with a lead roof, numerous temporary sod structures to house officers and men, and two frame buildings—a hospital and a double two-story officers' quarters. These were roughly grouped around a basic square, which became the parade ground.

From earliest days there was a flagpole within this square, exact height unknown, but of sufficient height to make the national flag the first thing visible from a distance. One can only speculate where the post engineer got a tree tall enough for this pole; possibly he

had to splice together two of the largest trees to be found, and these
might even have been hauled from the Missouri River, for there was
no tall timber in the whole Fort Kearny region.

By the end of 1850, with construction continuing, the parade
ground boasted a frame guardhouse and the beginnings of two more
large buildings—a crude two-story soldiers' barracks and the quarters
of the post commander, in a style which might be called "frontier
Cape Cod." On May 30 of this year Wolcott referred to "any number of turf huts" and "4 good frame buildings in process of erection." Among the random assortment of outbuildings were stables,
corrals, and the sutler's store, all squat buildings of sod with roofs
of poles, brush, and tamped earth supported by Grand Island
timber.

An early ground plan shows that Woodbury contemplated a protective fence or stockade around the entire fort, complete with
blockhouses, but this was never built, partly because of the lack of
lumber, partly because the Indians never really posed a serious
threat to the fort itself. (The later Fort Mitchel was on a much
smaller scale.) The absence of fortification at this "fort" was a disappointment to emigrants. Henry Stine, for example, observed in
1850 that the fort "is nothing but a few houses." He found it "built
mostly of turf cut into square pieces of about 2 feet and piled up
like bricks. . . . The roofs of the houses are covered first with logs
and poles and then sodded. . . . There are 3 pretty good frame
houses for officers. The rest of the buildings look like piles of mud."
McBride thought that with "no walls, palisades or ramparts around
the houses," the place "looks more like a trading post." Of the sod
structures he comments: "They make warm and dry but dark habi-
tations." A third observer on the 1850 scene is Dr. Tompkins:

> No fortification but a rude garrison for the fragments of three com-
> panies of soldiers. One of the companies are the remains of an old
> company of mounted men, a kind of dragoons. Their habitations con-
> sist of a kind of sod brick or sods cut into the shape of bricks and
> heaped up after the form of a wall. . . . The floor is of solid earth.
> The quarters of the officers are a little more aristocratic, being a fine
> two-story frame building. The object of this garrison is said to overawe
> the Indians of this region.

In 1851 J. L. Johnson found "some four or five frame buildings,
with several singular looking outhouses or irish built hovels com-

posed of sod, some quite lengthy, 7 or 8 feet high, covered with grass and weeds." It did not occur to him that people lived in these "dark and gloomy" heaps; he speculated that these were "no doubt first intended to burrow some wonderful beast of the forest."

William Lobenstine was impressed by the "five frame houses, two for the use of commanding officers, the rest for soldiers, all built in good style." He discovered also "a church for the service of the Lord which is frequented by soldiers, civilized Indians and passing emigrants." Only one other reference can be found to a Fort Kearny church (see below), and its location and style of architecture are unknown.

There were several 1852 observers. Caroline Richardson thought Fort Kearny "quite a settlement, assuming a military appearance." She did not understand sod construction, thinking that "most of the houses are built of wood and plastered with mud outside." Dalton spoke of "some half dozen very good buildings" and a well 8 to 10 feet deep, the principal water supply.

A third frame officers' quarters was apparently added in 1852. Isaac Foster said: [Of these] three fine buildings . . . one was for the Captain, another for the teacher and doctor, and one for the inferior officers." Lodisa Frizzell wrote of "2 or 3 good frame buildings here. Saw some children playing on the porch of one of them." She noted: "The barracks and magazines are mostly of turf; the place is not inclosed & presents no striking appearance, but we liked to look at a house as it had been some time since we had seen one." Mrs. Ferris left a vivid impression of the place:

> My lofty ideas of a fort were doomed to be sadly disappointed. I had a confused notion of massive granite walls and frowning battlements, surmounted with cannon ready to belch forth their thunder; and surrounded with bastions and parapets, with grim visaged men . . . pacing to and fro with guns. . . . As we rode up I could not help the conviction that we had mistaken a trading post for this fortress—but it was Fort Kearny and nothing else.
>
> The principal building was a two-storied dwelling with a stoop in front—in fact it appeared on the outside like . . . a comfortable farmhouse. In the vicinity was a low, mud building which might easily be mistaken for an ice-house, but was, in reality, the magazine.

In 1853 Celinda Hines referred to six wooden buildings, four large ones and two small ones (which would be one soldiers' barracks, three officers' quarters, the hospital, and the guardhouse).

Most of the barracks, she noticed, were still "made of mud [and] there is a store where they sell about the same things as in Kansas." Rebecca Ketcham spoke of "3 quite large wooden buildings" and "one long, low one built of unburnt bricks," which would be the large adobe warehouse. "The stables are also of unburnt brick with thatched roofs. There is a piece of ground near the buildings enclosed with a rail fence, or what was a rail fence once. It is now nearly torn down. Taking the whole affair together, it is most miserable. Everything looks as though it were going to destruction as fast as possible."

This same year Count Cipriani described the fort as "only a large square structure boasting two rusty and neglected four-inch cannon in the court." By this statement the romantic Italian conjures up an erroneous impression of a medieval castle. In 1854 another observer spoke of "a few gun carriages and a sentinel." There are several other references to this artillery exhibited on the parade ground.

We have a competent witness in 1855, the year of the Sioux Expedition, in the person of Capt. Todd, who would one day become post sutler at Fort Randall, Dakota Territory:

> I have had no opportunity of looking more closely at Kearney, but surely the exterior view is most uninviting. It is situated on a low level plain about 2 miles from the Platte & the same distance from the Sandhills & is an open work. Comg officers quarters & hospital on one side, a block of officers quarters on the right calculated for four and with the most miserable arrangements either for comfort or convenience being upstairs and down stairs for each two. On the third side is one block of Company quarters & on the fourth a guard house and sod store rooms. The quarters for the laundresses are built of adobes and sod, so are the stables. Take it altogether it is the most undesirable place I have ever seen in the army.

The most attractive buildings at this post, the officers' quarters, were on the south and west sides of the parade ground. This fact was noted by Helen Carpenter in 1856, who described them "on two sides of a square plot, presumably where the soldiers drill." It was Moses Sydenham's recollection that landscaping was beginning to appear this same year, for he says that upon his arrival he observed "a double row of cottonwood and ash trees lining the driveway around the parade ground."

Post records indicate that there were sundry additions in 1855 and 1856. These included more stables, an adjutant's office, laundresses' quarters, a bakery, and a powder magazine. The most important addition, however, was a second frame soldiers' barracks. By 1858 the original famous adobe warehouse was in a state of collapse; this led to two new quartermaster buildings. A third frame soldiers' barracks was added also about this time, superimposed on the site of the adobe warehouse. Construction activity in 1858 seems confirmed by the journal of William Lee, for in the spring he describes this as "a very mean place," while on returning in the autumn he found things "very much improved."

Other 1858 observers contribute to our understanding of Fort Kearny's appearance at this time. Kirk Anderson, journalist en route to Utah, gave an interesting detail about the soddies: "The walls are thick, and the interior is lined with coarse canvas. They are comfortable but not impervious to snakes, which bore through and very frequently bivouac on the beds." Thaddeus Kenderdine, bullwhacker, agreed that the fort was "not a very prepossessing place, but after a journey of 300 miles through the wilderness, we welcomed the sight, as we also did the sound of the bugle that night, and the roll of drums and the shriek of fife the next morning."

When he had gone west with the Utah expedition in August, 1857, Capt. Gove had expressed abhorrence: "[Fort Kearny has] one of the most Godforsaken looks that you could well conceive." After his return the next year from Utah, which was even more Godforsaken, Gove was able to give a more objective and balanced picture in his anonymous role of correspondent for the New York *Herald*:

> The fort consists of 5 unpainted wooden houses, 2 or 3 stories high, and about 2 dozen long, low buildings. The houses are built around a large open square or parade ground, while the mud buildings extend in every direction out from the roads that run along the sides of this square. Trees have been set out along the borders of the parade ground, and they are the only bushes that can be seen in any direction except a few straggling ones on the banks of the Platte, several miles distant. Intermixed between these immature trees on the sides of the square are 16 blockhouse guns, 2 field pieces, 2 mountain howitzers, and 1 prairie piece. . . . On the west side of the parade ground stands the house of the commanding officer. It is a large, ill-shaped, unpainted wooden structure, 2 stories high, with piazzas extending across its entire front on both floors. Within, however, the building is much

more respectable, being commodeious, comfortable, well finished, and neatly furnished.

Directly opposite the commanding officers' house, on the other side of the square, is the soldier's barracks, . . . 2 stories high. The barracks has never been finished; it is now in bad order; it can accommodate very well 84 men. The other wooden buildings are the officers quarters the hospital and the sutler's. These deformed structures do not present a very inviting appearance to the eye, but they are charming palaces when compared to the hideous spectacle of 24 long, winding, broken-backed, falling down mud houses. Such infamous buildings are a disgrace to any fort. . . . They are inferior to wigwams. They could only be rivalled by the mud hovels of the Irish or dirty Asiatics. Yet it is in such buildings that the government stores are stored, or rather are placed to rot and be ruined.

Gove stated that $35,000 worth of government stores were condemned in 1856–1857 "on account of no protection being furnished by these mud piles," in spite of the fact that "since 1851 the U.S. Government has paid out $350,000 in their construction." As a result the new post commander, Capt. J. P. McCown, "is down on mud houses and intends to have good substantial wooden buildings erected in their place." Among the buildings which he erected, with the benefit of a new sawmill, was "a fine bakery" and "a new commissary store." Gove also made note of the extremely high winds that prevailed at Fort Kearny: "The flag-staff in the centre of the parade ground, like the mast in a ship, is secured by ropes from being blown away," and sometimes "men have been blown away from the fort." According to Gove, one man was blown away and lost, and "next spring his bones were found four miles distant."

In 1863 the Seventh Iowa Volunteer Cavalry made further improvements to the post, which included a log and earth magazine, new log quarters for laundresses, and a new hospital to replace the 1849 model. Another soldiers' barracks was apparently added also at the same time. The English traveler Morris was still not impressed, however, finding Fort Kearny "only a barrack for a small number of soldiers; the parade ground looked pretty neat, with a few field-pieces about, but the stables, as we passed, looked filthy and unkempt." He was pleased, though, to see here "the wooden spire of a tiny church"—the only other reference to a place of worship here besides that of Lobenstine in 1851.

Frank Root, stage driver, first saw the fort in '63 and recalled with emotion:

> It was a grand sight, after travelling 150 miles without seeing a settlement of more than two or three houses, to gaze upon the old post, uninviting as it was, and see the few scattered buildings, a nice growth of shade trees, the cavalrymen mounted on their steeds, the cannon planted within the hollow square, and the glorious stars and stripes proudly waving in the breeze above the garrison.

That the Fort Kearny plantings had begun to mature at this time is confirmed by Cutting, who noted "some fine looking buildings with shade trees in front of them." He noted also "three large Government stables" and many odd buildings, but "nary a fort." He described the post office and the sutler's store as separate buildings at this time, both "low sod houses" (which contradicts Gove's testimony that in 1858 there was a new sutler's store of frame). These were located to the northwest of the parade ground area, quite handy to the California Road.

The last wave of construction at Fort Kearny occurred in 1864, being prompted by the Sioux raids on the nearby settlements along the Little Blue and at Julesburg. Dr. Roger Grange, formerly of the Nebraska State Historical Society, has described the circumstances:

> These attacks prompted the construction of a series of fortifications at key locations around the Fort Kearny building area. Capt. Lee P. Gillette of the 1st Cavalry Nebraska Veterans Volunteers was post commander at the time and indicates in his reports that the work was done during the month of November, 1864. The fortifications are shown on the 1864 plans of the post. West Fort or Fort Livingston was to the northwest some distance away from the parade ground near the sutler's store. Fort Gillette was associated with a corral on the north side of the parade ground. East Fort or Fort Mitchel was a short distance to the southeast of the parade ground and connected to a long rifle pit or trench which protected the south side of the parade ground. These fortifications were never used as Fort Kearny was not attacked by Indians.

No photographs or artist's sketches are available to show the appearance of Fort Kearny from the California Road, but its effect, even with the new frontier-style stockades, must not have been overpowering, for in 1865 Frank Young says that he pushed on to his camp westward "without fairly realizing that we passed the Fort or came through its grounds on the way. . . . It strikes us as very odd to be told that this rather large enclosed space on the plain, in the shape of a parallelogram, whose lines are marked partly by adobe houses and huts . . . and partly by a log stockade—that this is the fort itself. . . . [However] the sight of Old Glory flying from the top of a tall flagstaff in the centre of the enclosure is singularly cheering and welcome amid the desolation of this vast plain."

Sarah Herndon, also of 1865, was impressed by the trees, making it "quite a pretty place, away out here in the wilderness, but there is no stockade, or place of defence, with mounted cannon." This last observation is a puzzle. It is difficult to see how she could have missed the new Fort Mitchel stockade, even though she says she "rode through Fort Kearny [while] the wagons kept the road ½ mile north." This omission is equally puzzling in the case of Meline, who visited here in 1866 and declares that "of the fort there is no longer any vestige, pickets or blockhouses having long since disappeared." One would have supposed that the 1864 stockade works, which measured roughly 250 feet square, would not have gone unobserved. If Frank Young hadn't mentioned it, and if it weren't for the archival and archeological evidence, one would almost suppose that it had never gotten off the drawing boards.

The last clear description of Fort Kearny at its zenith is to be found in the account of Julius Birge, June 18, 1866:

> There was really no fort at Fort Kearny. There was a small plaza or park, bordered by cottonwood trees, in the center of which stood the flagstaff. . . . near by were mounted 2 or 3 small brass cannon; around the plaza were built the barracks and officers quarters. . . . A soldier was pacing back and forth before the open door of the magazine, and another was performing a similar duty in front of the guardhouse, from which came the notes of a familiar melody sung by the recreants within, who were making the best of their confinement. The only semblance of a fortification was an adobe wall [?] facing the bluffs.

THE FORT KEARNY SUBURBS

Beginning in 1858 there were two famous—or infamous—appendages of Fort Kearny, primitive communities which supplied vital needs for civilians and soldiers alike. Eight miles to the east, just off the reservation line, was Valley City, or Dogtown. Just beyond the west reservation line, two miles away and therefore a much bigger and livelier place, was Kearney City, or Dobytown. These places were intimately related to the frontier transportation industry which revolved around Fort Kearny.

Monthly mail between Independence, Missouri, and Salt Lake City, Utah, began in the summer of 1850. In 1858 mail service went on a weekly basis, and with this began the systematic transportation of passengers, first by mail wagon, later by the famous Concord stagecoaches. To facilitate this service, the company built stage stations at intervals of ten or twelve miles. This was the actual beginning of Valley City and Kearney City. The former was related to a "swing station" where horses were changed; the latter evolved from a "home station" where drivers were changed and meals offered the passengers. The original Fort Kearny Station was a group of buildings one and a half miles west of the fort, consisting of an office, storehouse, barn, stable, and eatery. According to Frank Root these were constructed mainly of cedar logs hauled from distant wooded ravines. Kearney City sprang up simultaneously about one-half mile farther westward to accommodate stage passengers and employers, emigrants, freighters, and soldiers with goods and services banned within the military reservation.

In 1862 stages were operated two or three times weekly; by 1865 they were on a daily basis. The principal line, from Atchison, Kansas, to Denver and Salt Lake, operated by Ben Holladay, followed the old emigrant road to Fort Kearny. Beginning in 1863 it was joined here by the Western Stage Company, originating in Omaha. This latter followed the old Council Bluffs Road and then crossed the Platte above Fort Kearny.

The Pony Express of 1860–1861, operated by Russell, Majors & Waddell, of freighting fame, shared most of its stations with the Holladay company along the main Platte; accordingly, there were Pony Express stations at Valley City and in the Fort Kearny vicinity. Contrary to a widespread impression, the Pony Riders did not gallop up to Moses Sydenham's sod post office near the Fort Kearny parade ground; they kept right on going to the log station west of the fort, and mail by stage or Pony Express was carried back to the fort from there.

When the Pony Express went out of business in October, 1861, Fort Kearny became a key point on the new Pacific Telegraph line. This line was from Omaha to San Francisco; hence it followed the

Council Bluffs Road and crossed the river at Fort Kearny, the telegraph crossing being noted by Ada Millington and other travelers. Because the telegraph was of such vital importance to the military, the Fort Kearny telegraph station was right at the fort; by special arrangement it was first housed in the sod post office building by courtesy of Moses Sydenham, then later moved to the old post hospital structure in the southwest corner of the parade ground. The first operator was a Mr. Ellsworth, well remembered by both Frank Root and Sydenham. He handled messages for relay by the Pony Express from November, 1860, when the telegraph reached the fort, until October, 1861, when the transcontinental line was completed. Referring to the officers at Fort Kearny who suddenly had to "choose up sides," Sydenham recalled:

> I can see some of those men in memory now as they sat silent and thoughtful in the private room of my post office, listening to the reading of the telegrams just fresh from the stilus of Mr. Ellsworth. . . . as he wrote sheet by sheet from the ticking telegraph before us for Fort Kearny and the Pony Express, to convey to Denver, Salt Lake and San Francisco the momentous and alarming news of the firing on Fort Sumter.

Because of its emigrant traffic, freighting trains, military expeditions, Pony Express, telegraph, and stagecoaches, Fort Kearny and its satellite communities from 1860 to 1866 was a hub of western frontier transportation. There are no eyewitness accounts of the Pony Express run through here. There are several impressions, however, of overland staging, when the heavy Concord stages arrived daily, bursting with mail and passengers, all coming from or going to Omaha, Atchison, Denver, San Francisco, and intermediate points. The scene was frequently enlivened by squabbles among passengers for seats at this major junction point. When Holladay took over the rival Western line from Omaha, things became more orderly.

Of Valley City very little is known, except that it served routinely as the first station east of the fort and was often referred to as Dogtown. Frank Young implied that Dogtown, with "its half dozen wretched shacks above ground," got its name from a vast prairie dog city here. In 1860 Richard Burton erroneously called this place "Kearny Station," where he was served "vile bread and viler coffee" for 75¢. Morris called it "Sobiski, or Junction, from the fact of the converging roads from St. Joe, Nebraska City and Omaha meeting at this point." This supports evidence that there was an Omaha crossing here at one time.

Ada Millington in 1862 spoke of "about a dozen houses, a sort of trading post" where her "Pa" sold a cow for $14. Frank Root said that in 1863 the station keeper was M. H. Hook, who also kept a post office. He described Valley City as consisting of three buildings, a "stage stable, Gregory & Graham's Store, and the home of M. H. Hook." This tiny place does not seem to fit Ben Arnold's 1862 reference to it as "a tough pioneer settlement." On the contrary, it was rather genteel, if one may believe the experience of Sarah Herndon, an 1865 visitor:

> We came through a little town—Valley City. There is a very pretty attractive looking house near the road. . . . Our inclination to enter that pretty home was irresistible, so we dismounted, took off our habits, hitched our ponies, and knocked at the door. A very pleasant lady opened the door and gave us a hearty welcome. . . .
>
> The gentleman of the house is postmaster, and has his office in the room across the hall from the parlor. While we were there the coach arrived, and the mail was brought in.

The postmaster found the mail "a mass of pulp . . . because they send such old leaky mail-bags on this route." Miss Herndon helped Mr. Hook and his wife dry out the mail in the hopes of salvaging something for claimants.

In 1859 David Anderson, en route from Denver to Omaha, stopped at "the old Boyd Ranch, eleven miles east of the fort. . . . Here James E. Boyd operated a small trading post and ranch, carrying on a large traffic with the officers and soldiers of the fort." Despite the discrepancy in mileage (Hook's was supposedly eight miles from the fort), it is possible that the Boyd and Hook places may have been the same, but with two successive proprietors.

Kearney City, or Dobytown, two miles west, had a wicked reputation that seems well deserved, but it is a mistake to think of it only as a den of iniquity dealing exclusively in sin. It was a legally established frontier community which provided facilities that the times required. According to Andreas' *History of Nebraska*, this place was initially called Central City, being founded by "an adventurous company from St. Joseph." It had become Kearney City, however, by 1859, and in 1860 the Nebraska Territorial Legislature

designated it as "the seat of justice" of newly-organized Kearney
County. Among the original county commissioners were Moses Sydenham and Mr. Hook, mentioned above. In 1859 David Anderson
figured the population at 300. His characterization is typical: "a
great rendezvous for outlaws and gamblers, who practice their ne-
farious arts on the unsophisticated pilgrims." Dr. C. M. Clark stated
that it was "inhabited by as scurvy a set of bipeds as ever demoralized a community . . . who have squatted along the line of travel
for the purpose of genteel robbery." Yet even in 1859 the image of
"nothing but" saloons and gambling dens is not an accurate one.
Martha Moore describes no orgies here, only that she "purchased a
dress at Kearny City, paid 20¢ a yard." Dr. Clark himself specified
only groceries and a blacksmith shop and was fascinated mainly by
the uniform architecture:

> This town is composed of a few mud houses. . . . constructed of blocks
> of sod . . . laid up tier after tier, to form the walls, which have the
> thickness of two feet. . . . a ridge pole is erected, and then a series of
> small poles are laid across to support a layer of sod, which constitutes
> the roof. These houses are very comfortable, being cool in the summer
> and warm in winter, besides being very durable, lasting twenty years
> or more—their cost is from three to four hundred dollars. The outside
> surface . . . is coated over with . . . lime.

In 1861 Butterfield spoke of "Kearney village," and the following year Hewitt, going to check on his mail, paused at "dobey town"
near the Western Stage Company's station. "Here," says Hewitt,
"congregated the worshippers of Bacchus and the Dealers of cards."
In 1863 Morris noted that "Dobee Town" did a land office business
with travelers. His only purchase, however, was "a sheet of vile
note-paper, for which I paid three cents." He was informed that
wood was so scarce here that a cord of green cottonwood brought
$12 to $14. Dobytown comes alive in the 1863 recollections of Ben
Arnold of the Eleventh Ohio Cavalry:

> There were no streets, and people built their houses wherever
> preference or caprice dictated. The townspeople were mostly frontiers-
> men who settled there for the sole purpose of . . . preying upon those
> who travelled the Oregon Trail. The population consisted chiefly of
> men; about two dozen permanent inhabitants, mostly gamblers and
> saloon-keepers, some loafers . . . and a few women of well-known
> reputation. When immigrants put their herds out to graze these fellows
> would sneak them away at night and run them off a few miles around

a bend of the river, reporting that the Indians had taken them. . . . In a conveniently short time a suitable reward was offered, the vagrant would go out and bring in the stock, deliver it to the owner, and get from the latter a liberal reward in cash and gratitude.

Since emigrants could not camp on the reservation, the vicinity of Dobytown swarmed with campers of every description. Among the types observed here by Arnold were "refugees from the border states . . . many Northerners in sympathy with the South escaping the draft . . . Missourians from Pike County, Hoosiers from Posey County and Arkansawyers from Izard County . . . disappointed miners from Colorado . . . freighters returning empty to Missouri River . . . mule skinners, many of them Mexicans, scouts in buckskin suits and broad-brimmed hats, bushy-whiskered hunters . . . men of royal blood looking for adventure." It seemed to Arnold that the men all wore whiskers, which, combined with sunburn, dust, and travel stain, made them "all look like tough customers." There were women and children, too, who emerged every morning, practically all barefooted, with baskets in which to pick up buffalo chips. Ben Arnold vividly described some of the primary facilities of Dobytown:

> Doby Town had a sod grocery store where one could buy tobacco, gunpowder, flour, sugar and coffee. Baking powder was an unknown article. Bread was made exclusively of sour dough and soda, the dough being kept from meal to meal. There were no canned vegetables, no condensed milk. Coffee was necessarily black. The only canned goods that I had ever seen at that date were oysters and sardines. The only ready-to-eat groceries to be found . . . were ginger snaps, crackers and sardines. Beer was not used, as it was too heavy to haul that long distance. . . .
>
> In the season of heavy traffic Fort Kearney and Doby Town had guides and scouts open to hire. . . .
>
> At Doby Town was located the stage barn for the daily stage line running from Omaha. . . While I was standing one day at the stage barn, the stage with a four mule hitch swung into view, surmounted by the driver and the express messenger. The coach was equipped for 10 passengers inside, and a boot for baggage was hung on the hind end gate with the outer end suspended by chains from the top of the coach. The roof of the coach was floored solid and surmounted by a railing, so that mail sacks and, if necessary, passengers could be carried on top. . . .

The saloon . . . in which I spent most of the evening consisted of
a long narrow room with a bar made of rough boards extending the
entire length of one side . . . some square pine tables covered with
woolen blankets used for card tables. Some gambling was going on
night and day, but at night . . . the tables were always full. . . .
languages used were Mexican, French, English and . . . profanity.
Occasionally some exultant winner would express his delight by firing
his pistol through the roof or into the sod walls . . . and a little loose
dirt would trickle down. The air was heavy with the blue smoke
from the guns and the lighter tobacco smoke; and the fumes of both,
mixed with the stench of the liquors slopped over the bar by unsteady
drinkers, made a combination of foul smells unknown outside a whiskey
dive.

Two years later, when the military tempo was stepped up, Frank
Young found that Kearney City was "mainly composed of boarding-
houses and quarters for the officers stationed at the Fort." Looking
for a change from the monotonous salt pork diet on the road,
Young investigated the possibilities of a square meal in one of the
"boarding-houses." In his rough trail garb he was refused admission
by the "mistress of the house," behind whom he caught a glimpse
of "a confused jumble of gold braid and tassels and blue coats and
gilt buttons." Much abashed by this "gorgeous display of commissioned majesty," he retired "in deep humiliation" and settled for a
loaf of bread bought from a little "dobe bakeshop."

There is little doubt that the principal commodity sold here was
whiskey of a dubious type identified by one victim as "popskull."
Gen. William T. Sherman called it "tanglefoot" and noted that its
effects were so damaging that freight train captains sometimes tried
to avoid camping nearby for fear of losing some of their help. Birge
says that one enterprising merchant sold a bottled concoction known
as "Hostetter's Bitters," the consumption of which would begin a
"season of Saturnalia" among revelers. When George Holliday
marched through here with his cavalry unit, a small riot took place
in this "dirt vilage" when the thirsty soldiers rebelled against the
price of whiskey at 25¢ a glass.

The Union Pacific Railroad tracks reached a point opposite Fort
Kearny in 1866. As construction pushed westward boisterous railroad camps suddenly erupted on the Plains. While some of these
later vanished, others evolved rather rapidly into a chain of settlements that have become modern communities along this railroad,

such as Fremont, Grand Island, Gothenburg, Cozad, Julesburg, Sidney, Cheyenne, and, of course, Kearney. The details of the transition of settlement from old Kearney City, or Dobytown, to the new Kearney, north of the Platte, are obscure. Certainly by 1869, when the railroad was completed and fully operating from Omaha to California, the main transportation route, and therefore the interest of the citizens, was on the north side of the river. While Fort Kearny lingered on, however feebly, it is supposed that certain elements of Dobytown lingered also, to administer to soldier needs. However, since Fort Kearny itself was finally phased out in 1871, this is doubtless the definitive date of Dobytown's demise.

In 1866 James Meline provided insight into another aspect of Kearney City, namely its introduction to journalism. He described the Kearney *Herald*, with its "advertisements of ranches" and listings of wagon train arrivals and departures. One item told of emigrant trains moving west at the rate of 80 wagons and 160 people per day, not counting freighting outfits. The function of Dobytown Flats as a wagon train assembly point is considered in a review of Fort Kearny's military role.

OUTLINE OF MILITARY HISTORY

Fort Kearny was never attacked by Indians, never besieged, and no battle of size was fought within a radius of 100 miles. Its garrison seemed pitifully small in contrast to the emigrant hordes and to the savage Sioux and Pawnee bands who prowled up and down the Platte on each others' trail. Nevertheless, the Fort Kearny soldiers proved equal to their role as guardians of the trail, made innumerable patrols, kept Indians pacified, and provided emigrants with supplies, advice, and the moral support so desperately needed on their 2,000-mile pilgrimage. Furthermore, this was the assembly point for numerous military expeditions, which, beginning at Fort Leavenworth, here rallied forces for invasion of hostile territory. Fort Kearny was not really a fort. It was sentinel post, launching platform, and gateway to the hostile Great Plains.

Although lack of quarters during the winter of 1849–1850 prompted the adjutant-general to authorize the removal of one company to Fort Leavenworth, it appears that Maj. Chilton elected to keep his entire command at the post, huddled in the gloomy sod shelters. In the spring of 1850 the fort roster listed 14 officers and

135 men, comprising one dragoon and two infantry companies. This tallies with McGlashan's description on May 3 of "two companies of infantry, and some dragoons" and McBride's estimate on May 16 of "200 soldiers here, and many other hands and retainers in the service of the fort."

The 1850 migration was relatively undisturbed by Pawnee marauders. Sgt. Lowe mentioned a skirmish with Pawnee horse thieves two miles away, but nothing else. Keller got the impression that the Pawnee were lying low through fear of Cheyenne vengeance of the year before, as well as the ravages of cholera among them. According to Lewis Dougherty, the Indians were not looking for trouble, being preoccupied with survival. He recalls:

> Every year the Pawnee Indians would pass the Fort on their way to buffaloes for their summer hunt. There were so many that a whole day would pass and still they would be tramping to camp. . . . They had many contrivances to move their belongings. Travi [travois] was most generally used.

In Fort Kearny annals, 1851 was notable as the year that Capt. Henry Wharton, Sixth U.S. Infantry, became post commander; and he served until 1859, with distinction. Things were quiescent along the Trail in 1851, but "Pawnee prisnors" in the compound, mentioned by J. L. Johnson, suggest there were continuing tribal infractions. The Pawnee became more unruly in 1852, molesting emigrants with more arrogance, particularly along the Little Blue. Cartwright said that they were no longer begging; they exacted tribute. For this reason he was somewhat annoyed to find that at Fort Kearny these Indians were being issued barrels of flour and pork.

Several 1852 diarists (i.e., Hampton, Dalton) note a garrison strength of sixty to seventy-five this season. This fits in with the testimony of Richard Hickman, who reported that "most of the soldiers are out after Pawnees," including artillery units. Crane noted that "a detachment of soldiers were absent on a crusade against some Indians who had robbed a pack train." He also heard rumors of Sioux and Cheyenne war parties 100 miles above the fort, but "Captain Horton" assured him there was little danger in that direction. Far from being a serious threat at this time, the Sioux seemed friendly, happily filling in the vacuum left by the unwel-

come Pawnee. Just below the fort Lodisa Frizzell's party received
a Sioux delegation:

> Several indians of the Sioux tribe came to our tent. The best looking
> indians I ever saw, they were tall, strongly made, firm features, light
> copper color, cleanly in appearance, quite well dressed in red blankets,
> and highly ornamented, with bows and arrows in their hands. We
> gave them some crackers and coffee, with which they seemed very much
> pleased. They signified that they wished to trade.

No hostile action of great moment is noted in 1853 or 1854. The
relative peace and quiet may help to explain Cipriani's observation
of "two rusty and neglected . . . cannons in the court" and "garrison
composed of 50 infantrymen and 20 cavalry." In 1854 the Murphy
party reported an encounter with Cheyenne east of the fort, and
"the captain ordered out a dozen men after them." The soldiers
failed to chastise the offenders, who were pounced upon by Pawnee
west of the fort, and several Cheyenne were slain. Much more significant to Fort Kearny was the Grattan affair east of Fort Laramie,
the repercussions of which would result in a sharp buildup of military activity—not just routine patrols against the feckless Pawnee,
but full-scale war against the Sioux and Cheyenne to the west.

In May, 1854, when Edwin Bird migrated through here, things
were quiet: "Went down to see the fort to knight. . . . At present it
contains 50 soldiers and 15 cannon." The next day he returned to
watch the soldiers drill and to have a look at the famous buffalo
calf which seemed to be the fort mascot. A year later, however, this
pastoral scene would be changed. The prize eyewitness account of
events associated with the 1855 Sioux Expedition is that of Capt.
John S. Todd. The captain arrived at Fort Kearny on June 13 and
was first engaged in escorting the Salt Lake mail to O'Fallon's Bluffs
and return. The Plains that summer were alive with buffalo, and
Todd and his fellow officers had much sport with these "monsters of
the plains," noting their "curious gyrations" when riddled with
musket balls. On July 3, Todd told of the arrival of a large party
of Cheyenne:

> [They] were on a war party against the Pawnees. These Indians of
> the plains are larger and more robust than those nearer the whites
> & more under their influence. . . . They professed a great deal of
> friendship with the whites as usual with all of them when begging but
> the scamps did not fail to levy black mail from the trains both above

and below the Post. Each was mounted and armed, mostly with bows and arrows, and the lance, while behind him he led his war horse. He is only used in battle or the chase, and cannot be bought. Their toilet is most elaborately finished, when a Streamer, dangling from the scalp-lock and ornamented with large silver plates, sweeps the ground after them. These plates are eighteen in number and beaten out of Mexicon dollars.

Four Dragoon companies under Col. Cooke arrived to patrol the road to Fort Laramie. During July the Indians seemed to be pacific, and the bored Todd predicted that "there will be no campaign this fall." On July 30, however, Maj. Woods arrived from Fort Riley to report there would be an immediate expedition against the Sioux, and on the following day "an express arrived from General Harney directing Major Cady with four companies at this post to hold himself in readiness to take the field." On August 1 Gen. Harney himself arrived with artillery and mounted infantry. On August 24 the Sioux Expedition of some 500 men left Fort Kearny to "punish the Sioux for their various depredations committed for years against our people." On September 3 they would have a fatal rendezvous with the Sioux near Ash Hollow. (See Chapter X.)

Thoroughly subdued, the Sioux and their confederate Cheyenne were not to be seen at Fort Kearny in 1856 (except for Spotted Tail and other prisoners en route to Fort Leavenworth), but in that year, says Helen Carpenter, "Pawnees are in evidence everywhere," much emboldened by the defeat of the Sioux. She was intrigued by these aborigines:

> They have no clothing but are wrapped in very unsanitary looking blankets, and are adept in the management of them, without pins or string, the blankets are kept in place, and there is no undue exposure of the person. . . . We are told that they have just returned from a buffalo hunt and horse stealing expedition, and are here at the Fort for the express purpose of disposing of their dried meat to the emigrants.

When Moses Sydenham arrived on the premises in October, two companies of infantry and two dragoon companies comprised the garrison. The redoubtable Capt. Wharton was still in charge in June, 1857, when Fort Kearny became involved in the Cheyenne expedition commanded by Col. E. V. Sumner. Two exceptional figures on this campaign were Lt. J. E. B. Stuart, quartermaster (who would later become a famous Confederate commander), and Sgt. Percival Lowe, unofficial scribe. At Fort Kearny, Sumner's command was joined by two troops of the Second Dragoons, leaving the garrison once more depleted.

The year 1857 was also rife with alarms and excursions incident to the military campaign directed to quell the insurgent Mormons in the short-lived Mormon War. This involved the launching of the most elaborate military expedition to date, under Col. Albert S. Johnston. Among the advance guard to Utah, following the departure of Sumner, was Capt. Gove of the Tenth U.S. Infantry. Arriving here on August 7, the captain noted that "there are now at Kearny 100 soldiers . . . and about 100 other persons" under Capt. J. P. McCown.

Yet another highlight of 1857 was the advent of the Fort Kearney, South Pass and Honey Lake Wagon Road Company. This was a project authorized by Congress to survey the Great Platte River Road and its extensions to the Pacific. Fort Kearny was selected as the starting point for the first scientific measurement of this road. The journal kept by M. N. Long reveals that the engineering party under Col. Magraw encamped on July 30 just a half mile east of Fort Kearny. Just below this point the surveyors had passed a Pawnee village of 150 lodges, these Indians having just returned from their grand summer hunt; the party was pestered by squaws who sought to sell buffalo meat in exchange for sugar, tobacco, or "two bits," this being the extent of their English. The Pawnee effort to sell directly to the consumer was hampered by the fact that on top of the raw buffalo meat brought in on horseback "were seated their naked riders."

Returning from a visit to the fort on August 3, Col. Magraw brought the unsettling news of Indians in the other direction:

> A cattle train some 25 miles in advance of us, belonging to Messrs. Russell and Waddell, had been attacked by the Cheyenne Indians— one man killed and one man wounded. . . . A party of fifteen soldiers were dispatched from the fort to recover as much of the property as possible and to bury the dead man.

The ugly temper of the Cheyenne was understandable, and clarification is given by Sgt. Lowe, who encountered the Tenth Infantry, as well as the Magraw party, while in camp at the Upper Ford of the South Platte:

Captain Dixon . . . and Captain Clark . . . crossed the river en route to Utah. They bring news that Colonel Sumner had a fight with the Cheyennes on the 29th of July. Large body of Indians formed in battle array, and the cavalry charged with drawn sabers. Twelve Indians were left on the field and many wounded; cavalry lost two men killed, and Lieutenant Stuart and eight men wounded. Captain Foote . . . of Sixth Infantry bringing the wounded to Fort Kearney. The fight is said to have taken place on Solomon's Fork of the Kaw River.

Some of the Cheyenne fled north. Four of them were taken prisoner by Lt. Lowe's squadron near the South Platte Crossing and escorted to the Fort Kearny guardhouse.

Freighting across the Plains became big business with accelerated military campaigns of 1857 and 1858, and one of the biggest was the contracting firm of Russell, Majors and Waddell. Thaddeus Kenderdine, a bullwhacker, arrived at Fort Kearny in August, 1858, and throws some light on that activity: "When within a mile the train was stopped, and orders given for each man to overhaul his load, and put the flour which was in any way damaged by rain in the bottom, so as the load would pass governmental inspection. We were forced to become parties to this fraud."

In August of that same year Sgt. Lowe was again en route from Leavenworth to Utah with a quartermaster train. On August 12, some distance below the fort, he casually notes: "2500 Pawnees, men, women and children, passed east, running from the Sioux, with whom they had a battle. Some losses on both sides; Sioux got most of the Pawnee horses." Another development this year was an outbreak of malarial sickness, particularly among the employees of the army quartermaster, as well as the contractors' trains. Lowe's entry of August 15 describes his arrival: "After prescribing for the sick men I rode to the fort, presented letters to Colonel [Charles] May, commanding officer. . . . called on Dr. Summers and explained the sickness in trains. He said that he never saw as much malaria and fever and ague as there was in the trains from the East."

As reported by "Artificer" Wm. P. Seville, Company A of the U.S. Engineers was making a round trip from West Point, New York, to Utah in 1858 with the object of developing a new road from the Platte River to the Green River, which would be more direct than that via the North Platte. This would be the route up the Lodgepole to Cheyenne Pass, explored by Capt. Bryan in 1857, which would become the Overland or Union Pacific route. On the outbound journey Company A reached Fort Kearny on May 26, and Seville noted in cryptic fashion: "Inhabitants: Infantry and washer-women. Goods for sale: buffalo skins and whiskey. Game: buffalo and wolves. Products: prairie grass and cacti. Water very poor." The return visit was on September 18: "We encamped in the rear of the fort, where the water is most convenient. . . . Darkness brought with it a fiddler from the Fort . . . who sang all the Negro songs in the catalogue."

In 1859 Wilkinson noted that "the soldiers put up lots of hay and have a vegetable garden." Military functions this year appear to be routine. On May 15, 1860, a Pike's Peaker named Hedges gives us a glimpse of "the commanding officer out riding with a fine rosy-looking lady who was also a good horsewoman. I was told it was the famous Captain May and his wife." On August 10 Richard Burton arrived there in the mailwagon, which halted only a few moments. Thus, he had no time to call on Capt. Alfred Sully, the new post commander. Burton's driver was worried about vengeful Cheyenne because: "Captain Sturgis, of the 1st Cavalry, U.S., had just attacked, near the Republican Fork of Kansas River, a little south of the fort, with six companies [about 350 men] and a few Delawares, a considerable body of the enemy, Comanches, Kiowas and Cheyennes, who had apparently forgotten the severe lesson administered to them by Colonel . . . Sumner . . . in 1857, and killed 25, with only two or three of his own men wounded."

At the outbreak of the Civil War in April, 1861, the Fort Kearny commander was Capt. Charles H. Tyler, a Virginian and a secessionist. He promptly resigned and soon became a colonel in the Confederate Army. On May 25 Ira Butterfield visited the fort and learned that Tyler had made an effort to subvert the garrison. "He had ordered the guns spiked but the man were loyal and would not allow him to complete the work."

In June all regular troops were withdrawn to aid in putting down the Southern rebellion, and for the duration they were replaced by volunteer regiments, mainly from Iowa and the eastern settlements of Nebraska and Kansas Territories. According to the post returns, all heavy ordnance was likewise transferred to Fort Leavenworth, leaving the post without heavy armament.

In May, 1862, Ada Millington found here two companies of "Kansas Home Guards." Mrs. Burlingame, arriving on June 1, identified the commander as Capt. Thompson, who, with his "esteemed lady," dispensed lavish hospitality.

Despite heavy emigration and military and freighting traffic past the fort to Denver, Salt Lake City, and the new Virginia City (Montana) mines, the period 1861–1863 was relatively peaceful. In 1863 Morris, the English traveler, "heard of a battle between Sioux and Pawnee, in which the latter had the best of it," but of this there is no clear record. Ludlow mentioned that "the Sioux robbed a stray Colorado soldier near the fort, pulled out his beard and left him naked on the prairie." This seems to be an isolated incident.

In October, 1863, the Seventh Iowa Volunteer Cavalry passed through Fort Kearny en route to the Upper Platte. "I was told," says Capt. Eugene Ware, "that Fort Kearney marked the western line of the rights of the Pawnee Indians. . . . There was also said to be a buffer territory, and that the western Indians were now allowed to come east within forty miles of Fort Kearney; so that there was a strip north and south of forty miles wide upon which no Indians by right could go. But it was only a talking point. As a matter of fact, the Indians went where they pleased."

Indian troubles were brewing, but apparently they did not disturb Maj. John S. Wood, Seventh Iowa, who was detached to take command of Fort Kearny. He preferred hunting buffalo to hunting Indians, and for this purpose made good use at the post of a pack of greyhounds "which seemed to be sort of community property." Ware said that the hounds were left at the post in 1854 by the British traveler Sir George Gore, who was on a grand hunt, and their descendants were now post property.

The Seventh Iowa drew all the necessary implements and hardware to build a new post at Cottonwood Canyon, 100 miles farther west—"all the necessary paraphernalia to start housekeeping in the wild country." The inventory of provisions did not mention a surreptitious barrel of whiskey which Ware had "boxed up as hardware" to provide for emergency use. This was released by the post quartermaster, who showed Ware a storeroom "almost as large as a small house," stacked to the ceiling with whiskey barrels, which were "carefully handled and only used for issue to fatigue parties." Thus, it appears that the construction of Post Cottonwood was destined to get off to a rousing start.

In the summer of 1864 occurred the Sioux outbreak, with wholesale destruction of ranches and stage stations and butchery of their inhabitants, particularly along the Little Blue to the east and to Julesburg and beyond in the west. (See Chapter V.) Fort Kearny soldiers were kept in constant movement during the hostilities, but never managed to catch up with the raiders. Almost every station for a radius of over 150 miles was molested, and the survivors fled to Fort Kearny for sanctuary. Undermanned though it was because of outbound patrols, Fort Kearny was never attacked. The hostiles shunned the place like the plague, not because it was fortified (its defensive works were negligible), but because they had an aversion to frontal attack on men who were well-armed and in sizable numbers. Their preference was for lonely road ranches, women, children, and stragglers—any occasion when they had an overwhelming advantage.

The army was aware of the weakness of its defenses; the 1864 hostilities prompted the construction of fortified stockades on the perimeter of Fort Kearny, as previously noted. But these structures were for psychological effect upon the garrison and citizens who fled thence from all points of the compass. It is doubtful whether the Sioux would have attacked Fort Kearny even if the post engineer had not gone to the trouble of raising stockades.

In 1864 Indian hostilities erupted for a period of about six weeks, with dire consequences described by Lyle Mantor:

> Commerce on the plains came to a standstill. The overland mail, which had been running on a daily schedule, regularly for more than three years, stopped. The flow of emigrants across the plains ceased entirely and hundreds of wagons loaded with all kinds of freight were forced to corral at the most convenient point and remain motionless for weeks. . . . Troops were sent out from Fort Kearny by Colonel William Baumer, the commanding officer, to guard the trail from further attack. Additional posts were temporarily established at Junction Station, forty miles east of the fort, and at Millallas Station, fifty miles west. Troops were sent from Fort Kearny to garrison each of these stations.

In October the raids had subsided sufficiently to permit limited resumption of stage and freight traffic past the fort. In January, 1865, however, the Sioux and Cheyenne, enraged by the massacre of Indians by Col. Chivington's Colorado Volunteers at Sand Creek, attacked Julesburg and again raided along the Platte, paralyzing communications. Frank Root made a daring stagecoach ride from Atchison to Denver in February with a heavy load of accumulated

mail. Except for Fort Kearny itself, he found the stations along the
Platte abandoned or in ruins, with many fresh graves. It was a
scene of desolation. In this same month, however, Gen. Grenville
M. Dodge, commanding the "Department of Missouri, Fort Leavenworth," ordered out additional military units to give full protection
to the Overland Stage Company. Soldiers were quartered at several
rebuilt stations along the Platte, and commerce was slowly revived.

A primary function of Fort Kearny and its satellite posts during
this period of stress was to provide armed escort for the stagecoaches. George Holliday was a witness of this brief but exciting
pageantry:

> Those who have not seen an overland stage on the road from the
> Missouri River to the Pacific slope, cannot form an idea of the speed
> with which they travel. Stations are from 10 to 30 miles apart. These
> stations are the most desolate looking places that the eye of man ever
> looked upon. The stables . . . contain from 12 to 20 head of excellent,
> well fed, but hard worked horses. Beyond Fort Kearney all stations are
> guarded by soldiers, generally a detachment of infantry and cavalry.
> The coach is always accompanied by from four to 20 cavalry guards, as
> the danger may require. . . .
>
> See, away yonder in the distance, a cloud of dust is visible. Now
> it clears away and nothing can be seen. But it is enough; the men of
> the ranche understand it, and in an instant all is business about the
> stable, and soldiers' quarters, which are under one dirt roof. Six
> match horses are harnessed and rushed out in front. Then a squad of
> cavalry, mounted upon ponies, take their places near the road, a keg
> of fresh water is placed in readiness, and everything is ready. . . .
> Look! there they come, just yonder over the butte, 15 miles per hour,
> on, on, not slacking their speed for any obstacle, up and down, at a
> fearful gallop, now they dash down the road leaving a dense cloud of
> dust behind them, and in an instant the rubber is applied and the
> panting, foaming horses come to a stand-still.
>
> The mounted guard, covered with dust, straggle in close order be-
> hind. The driver, who is the most important man on the plains (in his
> judgment) has cast his lines to either side and the horses are quickly
> removed, fresh ones take their places and in two minutes the old stage
> moves rapidly away, and soon is lost to sight like a ship on the sea.
>
> There is no time to be lost, for this stage must run 700 miles in
> seven days.

Although Indian attacks on stagecoaches have long been a staple
of Western fiction, authentic instances of such attacks are rare. One

of these is given by Samuel Bowles, who reports an incident that occurred east of Fort Kearny in May, 1865:

> Today's news shows that some of the Indians had broken through or run around the military lines. They commenced by ambushing a party of some 12 to 20 soldiers, mostly converted rebels, on their way up from Leavenworth to Fort Kearny, but without arms. Two of these they killed outright, and most of the rest they wounded so savagely that they will probably die. The next day they assaulted the incoming stage, which had some six or eight passengers . . . circling around and around the vehicle on well-mounted horses, and shooting their arrows fast and sharp . . . at horses and passengers. The horses were whipped up, the men on the coach had two rifles and kept them in play, and thus the Indians were held at bay until the protection of a station and a train was secured, when the attacking party, finding themselves baffled, retired. They numbered about 25 in all.

During these troubled times Fort Kearny saw the zenith of its floating population, for emigrants and freighters were held up here for indefinite periods until military escort could be provided or the civilian trains were in sufficient strength to proceed. Dobytown was the focal point of these vast assemblages. In 1865 Frank Young's outfit was told that it could not start west from here "without permission of the authorities," who stipulated that before proceeding there would be "no less than 100 wagons or a like number of armed men." Since only twenty wagons were in sight, it looked like a long wait; but soon a messenger came from the fort to announce that "a small Government train will start within an hour with supplies for Fort McPherson." Young joyfully reports, "We soon find ourselves making part of a caravan of 28 wagons and 35 men, escorted by a troop of 16 cavalrymen. We are quite impressed with a sense of our importance as we see these blue uniforms of Uncle Sam in the saddle."

During the 1866 season Meline again reported "an officer to register trains to resist Indians." He indicated that the regulation applied more to emigrants than to freighting outfits, but this is contradicted by William H. Jackson, who found that

> There is a regulation in force that no train of less than thirty wagons will be allowed to pass the post. . . . During the last few days we have heard any quantity of rumors of Indians threatening to clean off the whole road in less than 20 days. Several men have been killed between Kearny and Nebraska City. We consider ourselves fully

competent to make our way through. Most of the boys have Colt's Revolvers and then the train has a number of carbines & muskets.

The pageantry of the scene at Dobytown Flats was most vividly described by Julius Birge in June, 1866:

> Soon we observed a long mule train approaching from the east beyond Kearney. It halted for a few moments, and like a huge serpent it slowly circled round the reservation; and by orders from the guards its wagons were finally corralled. . . .
>
> As was the custom with all large outfits, the train, although moving in an unbroken line, consisted of two divisions. On being ordered to corral, the head wagon of the first division made a sharp detour to the right . . . and vice versa . . . making a great circle or enclosure in which all mules were unharnessed. . . . The immense wagons of this train were of the type known as Espenschied, a kind largely used by the Government. . . .
>
> There also rolled around the Kearney reservation closely in the wake of the big train, a small outfit consisting of half a dozen wagons with horse teams. . . . There was therefore now camped upon the arid plain beyond Dobytown a sufficient number of armed men and wagons to meet the requirements of the War Department. . . . It was with remarked celerity that the long-eared animals were harnessed to their respective wagons, and the command to roll out was given by the captain. Accompanied by the vehement shouts of the drivers and the cracking of their whips, the train of 40 wagons gradually uncoiled itself, stretching slowly out into the road, and in a solid line of perhaps two-thirds of a mile in length trekked westward in a cloud of dust. . . . The time for our own departure soon arrived, and all who remained of the campers . . . were ordered to move on.

It appears that all of this elaborate effort to require wagon trains to consolidate at Fort Kearny was misguided, for, wrote Birge:

> The orders of the War Department did not provide that after leaving any post a train should thereafter continue as a consolidated organization. To avoid unnecessary dust, and for other reasons, it was therefore mutually agreed among the parties composing our train that we should separate at our convenience.

The most important military event of 1866 was the use of Fort Kearny as the staging area for the Eighteenth U.S. Regiment of Infantry, which was to relieve volunteer regiments at various western posts in the new Department of the Platte and to construct and man new posts along the Bozeman Trail to Montana, northwestward from Fort Laramie. By May 15 the entire Third Battalion and companies of the First and Second Battalions out of Fort Leavenworth had assembled here under Col. Henry Carrington, a force 2,000 strong. Most were raw recruits, but the whole outfit was held together by an elite corps of regulars, shaped and hardened in the crucible of Civil War battlefields. The wagon train, drawn by 226 mule teams, was heavily laden with equipment and provisions to establish the new military posts. Several officers were accompanied by their wives; at least two of them—Margaret Carrington and Elizabeth Burt—have left vivid recollections. The pageantry of this last notable occasion at Fort Kearny is portrayed by Mattes in *Indians, Infants and Infantry*:

> May 19 dawned "bright and promising, notwithstanding such a cloud of dust as only the plains can supply." Bugle calls set the regiment on the march, led by Colonel Carrington riding on the black Kentucky charger that had carried him through many Civil War campaigns. He was accompanied by Captains Phisterer and Brown, Major Horton and the illustrious "Major" James Bridger, chief guide of the expedition, and his assistant, H. Williams. Then came one of the newly mounted companies, followed by the marching infantry and the serpentine wagon train. The remaining "cavalry" brought up the rear, while the ambulances carrying the officers' families rode freely alongside the column.
>
> The coppery sun glared down. The mass of men and animals created a small choking dust cloud of its own. No man knew what dangers lay ahead but morale was excellent as the companies swung smartly away from Fort Kearney and Dobytown. The strains of martial music by the regimental band, thirty strong, kept steps and spirits high as the 18th Regiment of Infantry marched westward to bolster Federal sovereignty in the long-neglected Great Plains and the Rockies.

Fort Kearny Memories

According to Thomas Creigh, the post commander on June 5, 1866, was Brig. Gen. Henry W. Wessells, Eighteenth U.S. Infantry. The general exodus westward under Col. Carrington left him with only a handful of soldiers, and this was symbolic. The departure of the regiment was the last military event of significance in Fort Kearny history. Inspector-General Babcock, who arrived here just before Carrington's departure, reported to his superior: "The transitory state of affairs at Fort Kearney prevented the neat appearance that would otherwise characterize the post," and, in view of the pending railroad, he recommended that it be dispensed with forth-with. Fort Kearny's effectiveness as the gateway to the Plains ended with the advent of the Union Pacific Railroad, which followed the north bank, leaving the post stranded. The situation in 1866 is emphasized by Gen. William T. Sherman's report of August 21:

> On Saturday, August 17, General Dodge gave us a special train and accompanied us to the end of the Pacific Railroad, the whole finished distance, 190 miles. The road lies in the flat prairie bottom of the Platte, and we found the construction trains laying rails within about five miles of Fort Kearny, where our ambulances awaited us. The railroad lies on the north side . . . and about four and a half miles will lie between the fort and its depot. . . . We had to cross the Platte, as mean a river as exists on earth, with its moving, shifting sands, and I feel a little lost as to what to say or do about Fort Kearny. It is no longer of any military use. . . . At Kearny the buildings are fast rotting down, and two of the largest were in such danger of tumbling that General Wessells had to pull them down. I will probably use it to shelter some horses this winter, and next year let it go to the prairie dogs.

The process of liquidation was not quite as prompt as Gen. Sherman anticipated. For a time Fort Kearny was found useful as a proving ground for several models of the new breech-loading rifles introduced after the war. Here also, according to post returns, the relative merits of the ammunition manufactured by the Ordnance Department and by private firms were tested. But after 1866 there were no significant events, and by 1870 the garrison had dwindled to fifty men. Early in 1871 the War Department ordered the aban-donment of Fort Kearny as a military post and the removal of its garrison to the new Omaha Barracks.

The abandoned Fort Kearny Military Reservation of some 65,000 acres was first occupied by squatters, some of whom probably made their own headquarters in the empty parade ground struc-tures. Within a few years, however, these buildings either rotted away from neglect or were dismantled for salvage. In 1876 an Act of Congress transferred the land to the U.S. Department of the In-terior for disposition by settlement under the provisions of the Homestead Act of 1863. The quarter section which included the parade ground was filed on and patented by William O. Dungan, a Civil War veteran. In 1922 citizens of the Kearney, Nebraska, area organized a Fort Kearny Memorial Association. They were successful in raising funds to purchase forty acres, which were deeded to the State of Nebraska. In 1929 the Nebraska Legislature created Fort Kearny State Park, which is now managed by the Game and Parks Commission.

Unfortunately, the park includes only some 50 per cent of the original fort building complex. It does include the parade ground proper and all known building sites east, north, and south thereof except the cavalry stables near the river. A county road on the west boundary of the park has obliterated all trace of the commanding officer's quarters, adjutant's and quartermaster's offices, and the original post hospital. All other building sites to the west, including the new hospital, surgeon's quarters, bakery, warehouses, laundresses' quarters, shops, post office, and sutler's store have vanished under the farmer's plow.

The site of the officers' quarters south of the parade ground was identified in 1948. During the summers of 1960 and 1961 the Nebraska State Historical Society conducted archeological excavations within the park to verify the structural evidence of archival ground plans and obtain data and artifacts useful to future park development and interpretation. At this time there was limited testing and substantiation of the following structures: the blacksmith-carpenter shop, the guardhouse, the 1859 soldiers' barracks (superimposed on the 1849 adobe warehouse), the 1859 quartermaster and commissary warehouses, and the 1864 fortified stockade called Fort Mitchel (which was also superimposed on an early military sod structure).

Until recently, all physical evidence of Fort Kearny had so far disintegrated that a visitor, even if he were a military historian, had a hard time visualizing the historical scene. There were faint traces of foundation stones, pits, and mounds (most notably the 1864 stockade outline), but this place had become so forested with hackberry and cottonwood that it looked like a pleasant little place for picnicking and birdwatching, but nothing else. Now the Game and Parks Commission is developing the historical aspects of the park, including a museum and the reconstruction of a few of the historic structures. Although it is not in the visible future, a fully restored Fort Kearny eventually is not inconceivable. Such a *third* Fort Kearny would be a historical shrine to remind Americans that there once stood here a rough-hewn military post that marked the junction of all major trails, the true beginning of the Great Platte River Road, the gateway to the Great Plains.

VIII

The Great Platte River Valley

America's Valley of the Nile

OPPRESSED BY THE TREELESS infinity of the Great Plains, Lt. Long of the Topographical Engineers could see no civilized future for them in 1820. He called them the Great American Desert, as if the billowing grassy expanse actually bore some resemblance to the sandy wastes of the sun-baked Sahara. In 1832 George Catlin thought that the Plains were habitable, but only by Indians, for whom most of these lands should be made a vast "national park" or reservation. In 1849 Amos Bachelder was oppressed by "vast naked plains, and barren hills, grand in their loneliness and solitude," and he complained, "The sun . . . scorches us like a hot iron on these sandy roads." He agreed: "This country now seems suitable only for the residence of the wild, wandering savage." In 1846 J. Quinn Thornton thought "the Nebraska" held little promise except as a highway to the Pacific, for "no part of the valley through which it flows affords timber to sustain settlement."

The much advertised Platte sandhills are not true sand dunes, but loose, sandy soil. However, the desert concept is not altogether incongruous, for on dry, windy days the soil does swirl and drift. Thus, Sarah Cummins fancied herself in the "wild regions of Africa," and she exclaimed, "Had we but camels . . . we would have had the semblance complete." Peter Burnett compared the "level sandy plain" of the Platte with that of the Nile, while James Evans

238

spoke in awed tones of "sand on the move, a world of desert." Such was the effect of the strange, seemingly barren landscape on Charles Ferguson that he swore: "If the Government would offer me a patent of all the land from Fort Kearny to Fort Laramie I would not accept it."

Not all travelers believed the Platte valley to be worthless. W. McBride considered it rich in soil, and "Nothing but the absence of timber could prevent this from being a beautiful farming country." Cornelius Conway was also somewhat of a prophet when he wrote: "God has blessed us with a season and a climate that leaves this vast expanse open to the husbandman." At Fort Sedgwick in 1866, James Meline reported: "The surgeon at this post insists that the entire Platte Valley is susceptible of as high a state of culture and fertility as that of the Nile. For the sake of . . . the future State of Nebraska I sincerely hope he may be right." Forty-Niner E. D. Perkins predicted that this valley "one day will be the garden of the world, so rich and fertile." The Platte valley was not without its charm for many other observers. Martha Moore wrote, "The scenery along this river is very beautiful. It is true there are no Alpine heights to strike with awe the beholder but one perfect scene of rural loveliness." Rev. Williams was hypnotized by the level plains, which offered "such a scenery of beauty as is seldom witnessed." Frank Young exclaimed, "Who shall describe the beauty of a fine morning on the Plains? Grant them to be as desolate and dreary as they are, yet there is an exhiliration in the air at sunrise that is beyond description." Wm. Lobenstine thought the Platte valley sublime and that emigrants buried there could take satisfaction in having finished their course in "Nature's Garden." Lorenzo Sawyer thought the Platte "a rich and beautiful country," and he found the panoramic views from the highest knolls quite spectacular. Recommending this locale to "persons of wealth and leisure," he declared, "The exercise, the exciting sports of the chase, and the pure air of that region, would do more to restore health, or the waning beauties of city belles, than a dozen seasons dancing at [Saratoga] Springs." Although few could go along with the more extravagant descriptions (Tompkins refers to "a continuing scene of matchless beauty"), many easterners were intrigued by the strange sights. First among these, of course, was the vast river itself, a continuing source of amazement.

Such a river, with the rough dimension of "a mile wide and an

inch deep," was unheard of. Julius Birge complained that it could
not be ferried for lack of water and it could not be bridged for
lack of timber. George Gibbs condemned it as "bad to ford, destitute of fish, too dirty to bathe in and too thick to drink." Although
it drained "one-fourth of a continent," Gibbs continued, "an
Indian canoe cannot float upon its broad waters." Maj. Cross was
"impressed with its total uselessness and insignificance." To James
Evans, "The Platte River . . . counterfeits the majesty of the Mississippi and even surpasses it in width, but it is a . . . complete
burlesque of all the rivers in the world." Declared a St. Louis
correspondent with Gen. Harney in 1855: "In truth this Platte
River is a humbug. It is about dry, and a person can cross it dry
shod."

Capt. Gove found that the Platte varied in width from 700 yards
to two miles, although George Gibbs asserted there was a width at
one point of seven miles. D. Jagger agreed with Gove that the rate
of fall from Fort Laramie to the mouth was about six feet to a mile,
making a current that was not exceptionally swift but inexorably
powerful. John Bidwell was not entirely correct in asserting that
the big Platte never overflowed, but normally, even in flood, it
stayed well within its low embankment. Even so, to the amazed
traveler, the river seemed to be virtually on the same level as the
valley flood. From a hilltop, Peter Decker noted a common illusion:
The Platte looked like a streak of silver flowing *above* the plain.

At the point of intersection of the Platte by the St. Joe–Independence Road, in the vicinity of the Grand Island, the Platte in
flood was apt to be one enormous channel. Capt. Stansbury here
noted that its appearance was precisely that of the Mississippi, a
muddy white expanse with the current "constantly boiling and
eddying in restless turbulence." Forty-Niner G. Pearson, observing
"a setting sun reflected in an ocean of rolling, turbid yellow water,"
was seized with the idea that "this must be the parent stream instead
of a tributary of the Missouri." To Amos Bachelder, the river at
this place resembled an inland sea, bounded only by the horizon.
It is significant that there is no record of emigrant crossings of the
Platte below historic Grand Island.

Above Grand Island and Fort Kearny, the Platte assumed its
classic character, braided with islands and studded with sandbars
that became exposed river bed in low water. Forced to drink from
the river or its seepage, the emigrants had much comment on its

sandy character. Thus, Cramer: "To one who has seen this stream
it is easy to understand where the old Missouri gets its bad complexion." McBride observed, "The bed of the stream is a mass of
rolling quicksand." When he tested the sedimentation in a cup,
he noted that the bottom fourth in the receptacle turned to mud.
James Evans described the Platte as "a wide sheet of water only 3 or
4 feet deep, running over a vast level bed of sand and micah . . .
continually changing into short offsets like the shingled roof of
a house."

The depth of the river was not just an academic point, for sooner
or later the emigrant knew that he would have to cross it; also, the
islands offered the only wood supply around. In full flood the
Platte was not to be trifled with, for one had to contend with
both quicksand and relentless current. And there were hidden
hazards, as Tompkins testifies: "The river . . . varies in depth so
much that one undertaking to cross it . . . in shallow water at one
instant may the next plunge into a depth of 10 or 15 feet." But
for much of the season the river could be forded without grave
danger. Breyfogle waded across "without wetting his waist," while
Bachelder reported, "It may be forded in many places by rolling
up the pantaloons above the knees."

The Platte had a peculiar fascination. Says Waters Curtis: "[It
is] one of the most splendid rivers I ever saw to look at . . . winding
its course through entire prairie." Here was a river without trees
on its banks because frequent prairie fires took out the seedlings.
But these fires could not ravage the islands, so timber—mainly
willow, cottonwood, and poplar—grew there freely. "The beauty of
the Platte," asserted Charles Kirkpatrick, "consists in the number
and variety of its islands." Its appearance was not so much that of
the dense, tangled timber belt of today, but more that of little
islands, singly and in clusters, in a watery expanse. E. D. Perkins
counted "nearly 30" from one vantage point. The number of
islands, picturesquely grouped, reminded James Meline vividly of
the Thousand Islands of the St. Lawrence. To Gilbert Cole,
"Nothing is more beautiful than the Platte Islands of Nebraska."
They seemed to him like emeralds scattered by "the maker of the
universe."

At the edges of the Platte valley, which averages five to seven
miles in width, are the celebrated Nebraska sandhills. From Fort
Kearny westward they grow gradually in elevation, reaching their

greatest height on the south side below the forks. Motorists today are not likely to get very excited about these "potato hills," as James Evans called them, but many emigrants were almost as impressed as an astronaut is today on a lunar landscape. Often they made side trips to enjoy what Eastin called "sand-hill exploration," and then jotted it all down:

Sand-hills tower up in majesty.—JAMES MASON, 1850

Fanciful shaped cones and ridges which I can compare with nothing else in form than huge drifted snow heaps.—ALONZO DELANO, 1849

For the last 15 miles our route rises rapidly, and the hills approach the river denuded even of the scant herbage with which they are clothed near Fort Kearny, arid and broken into separate and rugged peaks and elevations, like some gigantic ocean breaker dashing its immense volume into a hundred different waves.—JAMES MELINE, 1866

Thus we have the portrait of a wide barren valley bisected by a wide river of gold and silver hue, dotted with green islands and edged by brown serrated sandhills. To fill in the missing part of the painting, we summon four eyewitnesses who clambered up a hill to get the grand panoramic view:

The only thing the eye can detect is one continuous plane . . . occasionally dotted by emigrant wagons and cattle.—DR. T., 1849

White tops remind one of sailing vessels that I had often seen on Lake Erie, beating against a light head wind.—PHOEBE JUDSON, 1853

A sinuous line with vari-colored wagon covers resembling a great serpent wriggling up the valley.—WM. THOMPSON

Nothing could be discerned that was the product of human agency save the distant trail near the river, along which our train was lazily creeping, like a wounded anaconda.—JULIUS BIRGE, 1866

From Fort Kearny to the lower ford of South Fork, which Ingersoll reckoned a distance of 120 miles, the Great Platte River Road was one of the finest natural roads in the world, and under ideal conditions it elicited just praise. In 1845 Jacob Snyder proclaimed it "thus far as good as any in the United States, not excepting any," while in 1850 Dr. Thomasson judged it to be "as prity a rode as I ever saw. . . . it is level and smooth as a plank floor."

In 1858 Thaddeus Kenderdine figured the road was about a mile from the river, "which we were unable to approach nearer on account of numerous sloos." However, the main emigrant road in 1849 did not attempt to follow the meanders of the Platte but kept a fairly straight course up the valley, except for detours such as the one at O'Fallon's Bluffs, thus being sometimes close to the river, sometimes one or two miles distant. While one has difficulty today in locating the road except with the aid of General Land Office Survey maps, it was glaringly visible years ago. George Gibbs in 1849 found that the passage of thousands upon thousands of emigrant teams, trampling the grass, made a broad white band stretching to the horizon. In 1853 Rebecca Ketcham wrote:

> I am very much surprised to find such a well-beaten road. It is as broad as 8 or 10 common roads in the States, and with a very little work could be made one of the most beautiful roads in the world. . . .
>
> Where the prairie is rolling the pitches are very steep in some places, and often there are mud holes at the bottom. . . . It would be very easy and not very expensive to bridge the streams, fill up these mud holes, and that would be nearly all that is necessary. . . . Over the level prairie the road is not as smooth. The water does not run off so soon after rain, and it is very much cut up by cattle going over it.

Thus the Great Road was broad as a boulevard but not always as smooth and comfortable. In the rainy season the bottoms might flood, and the roads could become a muddy bog, miring wagons down to the axles. Wet, heavy road conditions were usually accompanied by a plague of mosquitos and buffalo gnats which chafed the cattle, while excessive exposure to mud and dampness made them footsore and lame. Delano and Cramer advise that the cure for this condition was a liberal application of hot grease and tar to the hooves. On the other hand, if it were exceptionally dry, the wagoneers had to cope with great clouds of dust and on windy days had to face into a sandblast, sometimes getting coated white in the vicinity of saltpeter and saleratus beds.

A road hazard unique to the main Platte was the buffalo, sometimes the animal himself, but always his tracks, regular grooves resulting from single-file formations, which Joel Palmer says measured almost exactly fifteen inches in width and four inches deep, "worn into the soil as smoothly as if cut with a spade." These buffalo trails ran from the river to the sandhills, at right angles to the line of emigrant traffic. Sarah Cummins complained that they "were as regular as any set of ploughed furrows, so we rode on a constant rocking motion." Likewise with Washington Bailey: "We see buffalo trails every day where they go to the river to drink. It makes the road rough." The Wm. Pleasants train was compelled to "detour to avoid eroded Buffalo trails." Broken axles frequently resulted from the washboard effect.

The novelty of traveling along the Big Platte was heightened by the phenomenon of the mirage, which took even stranger forms than those seen on "the Nebraska Seacoast":

> Saw the mirage and a beautiful sight it was. The wagons ahead of us were reflected in the air and looked like moving spectres.—CHARLES KIRKPATRICK, 1849

> At one time we were gladdened by the sight of a large lake with bluffs and headlands . . . and with vessels sailing majestically on its calm bosom; but sad to relate, on nearer approach, the lake turned into a low fog, the headlands dwindled into the old monotonous chain of sand-bluffs, and the vessels metamorphosed into three or four rusty looking ox-wagons.—WM. SEVILLE, 1858

> Optical illusions are common here. This forenoon I noticed that the bluffs on our left, as far ahead as we could see, appeared higher than they really were, and as though they were in a thick fog, and their tops appearing above it.—AMOS BACHELDER, 1849

The endless shimmering valley had a hypnotic effect upon the emigrants, described succinctly by Peter Burnett: "The monotony of the Platte makes one drowsy." Wrote Rebecca Ketcham: "We are all afflicted with drowsiness, partly in consequence of having so little time to sleep, partly owing to the climate. It is dreadful. . . . While riding along in the carriage, it is with the greatest effort we can keep awake. . . . This morning every soul in the carriage was asleep at once, and the horses going along as they pleased." A related phenomenon, a kind of emotional anesthesia, is described by James Evans: "A company of pack mules overtook me. My mule kept up with them for some distance, but I never so much as turned my head to look at them . . . for such is the unsocial habit of nearly everybody after they have long been on this monotonous and stupefying trip."

Grass was the indispensable fuel of the animals, without which getting to Oregon and California was impossible. Under normal circumstances the Platte bottoms were carpeted with grass from Fort Kearny to the South Platte crossings, though this commodity was in distressingly short supply as wagons progressed up the North Platte. Lampton found "The grass up this bottom is very fine indeed," and Tate proclaimed, "The grass is very nourishing and stock are very fond of it." Inevitably during the peak years the trailside grass was badly beaten and grazed to the roots. Wrote Ketcham: "Sometimes we swing more than a mile from the road to camp in order to get good grass for the animals."

The real menace to the precious grass, aside from drouth, was the disastrous prairie fire. Noting the absence of timber except on the islands, Capt. Stansbury theorized that

> The almost total absence of this feature in the landscape . . . must be attributed, in part at least, to fires which periodically sweep over the country in autumn, destroying everything before them. . . . On our return . . . the country, for more than 300 miles, had been completely devastated by these conflagrations, insomuch that our animals came near perishing for want of herbiage. The north side of the river does not appear to suffer so much from this cause; which may, in part, arise from the direction of the prevailing winds.

According to John Wyeth it was the Indian custom to set fires to the high grass once or twice a year to start the game. James Clyman calculated that most prairie fires were caused by lightning or "electric fluid," but there is ample evidence that white travelers did their share of the mischief. Frank Young reported a fire started deliberately by ox-teamsters in a playful mood, while on one occasion stage hands started one at night "for illumination." Walter Pigman blamed "Denison's train ahead of us" for burning the grass at every camping, implying that it was with malice aforethought, and he muttered darkly about reprisals. The year 1850 seems to have been particularly disastrous, because the old 1849 grass crop was heavy. J. M. Stewart and "The General" also blamed advance trains for carelessness with camp fires. Wm. Seville, with an army engineering unit, reported fires caused by "some careless individual lighting his pipe and the prairie at the same time." He continued, "We were turned out by the long roll [of drums] to do battle . . . with the devouring element; our weapons were gunny-sacks and blankets." Once the blaze started, few bothered to combat it; if fanned by high winds, it could become a holocaust, scorching the entire countryside.

The spectacle of a prairie fire was awesome. In 1862 Randall Hewitt on the Council Bluffs Road described a great fire on the south side which "sent up dense clouds of smoke all day and at night the southern sky was made lurid by the flames which shot upwards in sheets miles in extent." Daniel Gelwicks reported a similiar spectacle in 1849:

> The sight was magnificent and grand beyond description. The fire came rushing, roaring and crackling on its wild, mad, impetuous, irresistible fury and with the velocity of a locomotive. The high winds, the light flames, and the dark and gloomy appearance of the clouds presented an awful and majestic spectacle. On, on the flames rushed like "the red waves of hell," leaving in their wake a dark and dreary solitude.

Kilgore, McGlashan, and "The General" report seeing the carcasses of thousands of buffalo, wolves, antelope, and other wildlife which perished in the "fiery tornadoes." J. M. Stewart noted buffalo still alive, singed and blinded, which ran berserk, colliding with emigrant wagons. Despite Stansbury's observation, much of the reported destruction of grass was on the north side, where in 1850 Stewart's train traveled for ten days "through a territory burned over."

NAVIGATION OF THE PLATTE

In 1850 and thereafter, fur traders from posts on the North Platte always transported their smelly cargoes of peltries and robes to Westport Landing by carts or wagons. Emigrants would encounter these apparitions along the way, usually along the Little Blue or the Platte, and several travelers have described the swarthy crews and their ill assortment of reconverted, creaking emigrant wagons, castoff animals, and greasy hides piled high as a hay load, resembling at a distance marching elephants (Decker, Johnston, Gage). Prior to 1850 the traders, wearied of the long overland haul, sometimes tried to float their furs down the Platte, hoping that the June rise would neutralize the sandbars. The history of the navigation of the Platte is colorful but brief.

To the emigrants it was perfectly clear that the Platte was unfit for commerce. When Cornelius Cole plunged bravely into the Platte to swim to an island, he almost cracked his skull on the shallow bottom. Discovering he could hike through the water with ease, he noted that it barely came halfway to his knees. This scarcely seemed like a navigable stream. He discovered the hard way what other Forty-Niners readily observed. Benjamin Watson thought the Platte "of no value to commerce on account of its shallowness." This is echoed in 1850 by McBride, who thought it "unfit for any kind of navigation, not excepting pirogues and canoes," while McGlashan asserts that it is certainly "not navigable for a barge." Pigman described the Platte as "a singular stream two miles wide which could be waded at nearly every point, and never could be made navigable."

Fur traders in boats were not an entire novelty to the gold-seekers, particularly those crossing the Missouri River at Council Bluffs. In 1849 O. J. Hall mentions fur traders with keelboats tied up at Kanesville Landing. The next year Langworthy found here "two mackinaws from the Yellowstone." But these and other Argonauts would have been startled a few years earlier to see the boat traffic on the fickle tributary Platte. It wasn't heavy, and it often came to grief; but the fur traders get credit for a noble experiment.

The first recorded effort to negotiate the Platte was in 1813, when Robert Stuart and his companions from Fort Astoria, relieved of their horses by Indians, hollowed out a cottonwood log at their winter camp near the Wyoming-Nebraska line and attempted to float down. After repeated groundings they gave up until they reached Grand Island. Here they fashioned another canoe, which did manage to float them back to civilization. When Fort Laramie was built about twenty years later, the fur captains again attempted to put the Platte to work when it was swollen with melting snow from the Rockies.

Crude rafts and hollowed-out cottonwoods were not suitable for commercial loads. The fur traders first attempted a modification of the circular Indian bullboat. This was an ingenious contrivance, resembling an enormous oval basket up to twenty-five feet in length. The framework was composed of long and pliable poles from green aspen or willow. This was covered with dressed buffalo hides sewn together and then soaked. The shrinkage produced a tight covering, the seams of which were made water-tight by a mixture of buffalo fat and ashes. This resulted in a craft of extreme buoyancy which could transport up to three tons without displacing more than ten inches of water. The bullboat could be quickly and easily manufactured, but it would as easily be wrecked by snags and hidden bars in shallow water, and in deeper water it would readily capsize.

After several disasters with this crude craft, the fur men switched to the use of flatboats, or mackinaws, made of crude lumber, similar to but smaller than those favored on the Missouri. These were flat-bottomed affairs on the principal of a barge, elliptical in shape, up to thirty feet long, and with sides up to five feet high. They were propelled by a crew of oarsmen guided by a helmsman in the stern, and probably also had a crewman at the prow to take soundings and assist in avoiding or climbing over sandbars.

In 1836 Oregon-bound missionaries were treated to the spectacle of a bullboat flotilla near Scott's Bluffs, apparently having no problems (Gray). In 1841 John Bidwell and Rev. Joseph Williams on the Platte describe their encounter with six flat-bottomed boats coming down from Fort Laramie, loaded with robes and skins and manned by a piratical crew of bearded, dirty, and ragged mountain men.

Rufus Sage reports that in 1842 he was a passenger in one of two boats leaving Fort Laramie, each laden with some sixty packs of robes and each manned by five or six men. Alternately floating and rowing, the men were successful until they reached Scott's Bluffs, where they were grounded for two weeks until the river rose again. Thereafter they were able to make but a few miles each day, and only with great hardship, by repeatedly unloading and reloading and carrying their boats by main force over sandbars and exhausting themselves in seeking a nonexistent main channel. The boats finally had to be abandoned before reaching the forks, and the cargo cached. Kennerly in 1843 and John Minto in 1844 describe encounters with flatboats or bateaux. Minto spotted a fleet in the vicinity of the future Fort Kearny; if they made it this far it is assumed they made it all the way, but data on completed voyages are scarce.

In 1845 emigrants Snyder and Palmer and Lt. Carleton of Kearny's Dragoons encountered voyagers from Fort Platte stranded near Prudhomme Prairie, between Ash Hollow and Court House Rock. "Each boat," they informed Carleton, "is laden with one thousand buffalo robes, which they will have to haul back to the fort, transport by land to Independence, or guard until the next rise of the water." According to Snyder, the fur was unloaded and men sent to the fort for wagons. Those left at the scene of the wreck, writes Palmer, "were a jolly set of fellows." Francis Parkman in 1846 mentioned a group of eleven boats rowed by Mexicans that ran aground fifty times a day. The *Missouri Republican* for July 8 indicates that eight of the mackinaw boats seen by Parkman reached Fort Leavenworth, where the cargo was transferred to a steamer. This outfit of Pierre Chouteau, Jr. & Co. was under the guidance of P. D. Papin.

The fur trade voyages were still in evidence in 1849. Speaking of the Platte west of Fort Kearny, Elisha Perkins wrote:

> The only things made by man that float on its waters are the Indians canoe & the Makinaw boats of the Am. Fur Company of which latter we have seen a number. They are barges some 40 or 50 feet in length roughly & slightly put together loaded with furs which are piled up in the middle 10 feet high & covered with tarpaulins leaving a space at each end for oarsmen & cooking operations. In this trim they are manned by some of the hardy Employees of the Company & sent to St. Louis where the Cargoes are disposed of & the boats knocked to pieces for wood.

Since 1849 was an unusually wet year on the Plains it may be assumed that optimum conditions prevailed for floating on the Platte. After this year evidence of fur trade navigation is lacking, a fact probably related to the American Fur Company's sale of Fort Laramie to the government.

In his promotional book *Kanzas and Nebraska*, Edward Hale states that the steamboat *El Paso* ascended the North Platte above Fort Laramie in 1853, but Hale was entirely mistaken when he wrote this, as a steamboat would have been in trouble before it ever reached the mouth of the Elkhorn River. More credible is Thomas Cramer's report of an incident of 1859 near Plum Creek: "Today at noon five skiffs built at Denver City . . . passed us, each having two or three men in it. . . . On this current I suppose they would make about fifty miles a day." This is the last Platte River voyage on record.

WILDLIFE OF THE PLATTE

In season the Platte valley teemed with wildlife; overland journal data on the subject would fill several volumes. Dr. Wislizenus and J. G. Bruff have painted vivid word pictures of the abundance and variety of game, running the gamut from the lordly buffalo to the comical prairie dog, the soaring buzzard to the earthbound snipe. Montgomery, observing in 1850, starts his list with "pidgeons, plover, crows, and marsh quails," while in 1859 naturalist George Suckley listed over fifty specimens. W. McBride was impressed with wild geese, "white hawks with dolphin-like tails," and "droves of large snipes running over the ground devouring snails, with dismal and unwelcome screaming." As a stage passenger, Ludlow was entertained by "prairie hens, tame as barnyard fowl, running ahead of the horses."

Wild horse herds (of Spanish origin) were described by Townsend in 1832 and Burnett and Reading in 1843. Deer, abundant in the Missouri River bottoms and in the mountains, are seldom mentioned on the plains. Isaiah Bryant and Bennett Clark claim to have sighted elk east of Fort Kearny. In 1849 Eastin spotted a black bear near the forks of the Platte; however, as Sarah Wisner explains, it was more likely to be along the North Platte, from Ash Hollow to the Sweetwater, that one would find "grizzly, cinnamon and black bear disputing the right of way." Sometimes emigrant reports were not scientifically exact, as in the case of Dr. Thomasson, who said, "some of the boys caut a young varmint this evening. . . . some said it was a badger and some said it was a grisly bare. . . . it has every appearance of a bare." We are equally puzzled by Peter Burnett's "rare carnivorous animal, much like a hyena," and George McCowen's reference to "a snake with a head at both ends"! Much more indigenous to the scene were badgers, skunks (Gould), lizards (Thornton, Ingalls), and jackrabbits, which Charles Parke said were invisible until they suddenly burst from underfoot as if shot out of a cannon. But these were curiosities. There were five species of animals which dominated the wildlife scene along the Platte. In ascending order of importance, these were the prairie dog, the coyote, the wolf, the antelope, and the buffalo.

Joel Palmer found dog towns along the Platte in extent from 100 to 500 acres. Others report prairie dog villages covering dozens of square miles, containing more inhabitants, according to James Bowen, than New York City. R. C. Shaw said, "The Plains were completely honeycombed" with these colonies. Langworthy calls them "doggeries," but in size they more resembled large cities, and in acknowledgment of this fact emigrants often wrote that they would camp in prairie dog "suburbs." This curious rodent, which could be seen scrambling around or perched motionless on the heaped and rounded edge of his hole, was called "dog" because of the high-pitched barking noise he made when danger approached. If several were barking, it sounded like a frenzied conversation. Lodisa Frizzell thought he resembled "both squirrel and puppy." Joel Palmer described him as "something larger than a common sized gray squirrel, of a dun color; the head resembles that of a bull-dog." Martha Morgan acknowledged that he "resembled a dog, but partook more of the nature of a rabbit." Lorenzo Sawyer figured him "as large as a wharf rat, but the color of a red squirrel but not quite as bright."

The prairie dog hole was a menace to the galloping buffalo hunter, threatening to break the horse's leg and the rider's neck. The colonies also had a special fascination for emigrants who understood that these were the common abode of prairie dogs, rattlesnakes, and owls, living in subterranean harmony. That this may have been fact rather than folklore is suggested by Capt. Stansbury:

> When shot, they fall back into their holes, where they are generally guarded by a rattlesnake. . . . Several were shot by us . . . but when the hand was about to be thrust into the hole to draw them out, the ominous rattle of this dreaded reptile would be instantly heard. . . . A white burrowing owl also is frequently found taking up his abode in the same domicile. . . . I have never personally seen the owl thus housed, but have been assured.

The biggest nuisance on the Plains was the wolf, the two primary species of which most emigrants lumped together: the true wolf, or lobo, otherwise called gray wolf, white wolf, or buffalo wolf, a variant of the nearly extinct western timber wolf (*canus lupus*), "larger than a Newfoundland dog" (Bachelder) and with "teeth as large as shears" (Staples); and the smaller, still existent coyote, or kiota (*canus latrans*), more frequently referred to as the prairie wolf, being somewhat the size of a collie dog. Stephens refers to "large, long-legged Buffalo Rangers," and others considered the black wolf a special breed, but all were simply color or size variants of the two basic species described. They were "traveling musicians" who serenaded all night with unearthly yowling. Pleasants calls the coyote "the rooster of the plains, for he invariably howls at the dawn of day . . . one grand chorus of yells, snapping of teeth, and mournful howls." Starr credits wolves also for howling around the camp every night in hordes: "Each wolf makes as much noise as five dogs, and probably 500 howl at once."

Both coyote and wolf haunted the fringes of the buffalo herds, picking off stragglers and pouncing on the young and infirm. Still ravenous, they would kill sheep and calves and hamstring horses and oxen (Flint, Zilhart, Meline). There are several instances of wolves, emboldened by starvation, giving chase to stray, unarmed emigrants. Pettijohn reports that a fellow emigrant, searching for a cow, stumbled upon a wolf pack which "set up a howl and made at him, chasing him back to camp." Bartholomew became so enraged by one arrogant specimen that he "took after it with sword and revolver, emptying all barrels;" then the tables were turned and he was chased back to his wagon. These predatory creatures were so stealthy that they could seldom be killed, even though they would brazenly gallop alongside the train. Brady's father attempted to sneak up on one pursuer, but each time he leveled his gun, the wolf would vanish to turn up on the next knoll. Sometimes, in hungry desperation, wolves came in close enough at night to make a target by firelight (Cartwright, Staples). However, they were so numerous and ammunition was so precious, it was best to let them go their phantom way, but keep the stock well guarded. With the advent of the Platte road ranches, strychnine was used freely; Burgess and others saw dead wolves stacked up like cordwood.

While they hated the wolf, emigrants were uniform in their admiration for the fleet and graceful antelope, more scientifically known as the pronghorn, which "The General" called "the American gazelle, of all animals the most beautiful and innocent." They were second only to the buffalo in numbers. Still common in Wyoming and western Nebraska, in emigrant days the antelope abounded along the Little Blue and the Platte. George Jewett thought the creature a cross between a sheep and a deer. They ran in herds of up to thirty in number. Wrote W. McBride: "They came to us like the wind, till within 60 or 80 rods, stop and examine us for a few minutes, then away they would go and come up upon the other side of us . . . in full lope, like prairie hens on the wing." It was rare that a hunter could kill an antelope by rifleshot at long range. Explains Charles Tuttle, "Due to their fleetness they are not taken." Dr. Townsend was greatly distressed at the "murder" of one of the sloe-eyed creatures; Marie Nash secretly exulted because the hunters of her train had no luck.

Today the distant antelope is shot with more powerful and accurate firearms; then it could be killed only by trickery, taking advantage of its fatal inquisitiveness. The standard procedure was to tie a bandanna or other piece of red cloth on a stick or ramrod, wave it from a place of concealment, and when the animal circled nearer, fire away. Parke, Word, and Holliday describe successful hunting by this means. Capt. Albert Tracy reported that antelope abounded near Mud Springs, and the station-keeper kept himself well supplied with meat by the simple expedient of enticing the unwary antelope right up to the porthole of his stage station by the display of his red flannel drawers.

Unless it was the mythical California Trail Elephant, bringing his assortment of miseries, no animal along the Great Platte River Road created more excitement than the lord of the Plains, the big, lumbering, shaggy-maned buffalo. If he was nowhere to be seen, says Dr. Wislizenus, all hands kept scanning the horizon expectantly, like shipwrecked sailors searching for an island. When he first appeared, whether in solitary majesty or in a modest family-size group, the effect on travelers was electric, and there was a general rush for weapons, to sally forth and engage the monster in thrilling combat. When his numbers multiplied by the tens of thousands and became an enormous herd, blackening the earth and making it tremble with his passage, the emigrants were transfixed and overawed, for nothing they had read or dreamed of had prepared them for the spectacle.

It was not until the 1880s that the buffalo came near being exterminated by professional hide-hunters. During the peak migration years the buffalo population, still in climax phase, was in the tens of millions, and the Platte River, including its two forks, was a primary habitat. Not only did the Platte traverse the most extensive grassland in the world; it supplied the millions of gallons of water consumed daily by these huge grass-eaters. The Platte was not an obstacle to these beasts; they crossed and recrossed it as often as they pleased, and the Platte bottoms offered the most succulent grazing. Thus, the emigrant passage up the valley brought about a strange confrontation.

In historical times buffalo were first seen on the Little Blue, but by 1852 they were to be found mainly west of Fort Kearny (B. Ferris). As early as 1834, according to Jason Lee, the forks of the Platte were considered the true center of the buffalo range. Certainly the confluence was a focal point of their congregation in the early forties, to judge from Bidwell and Capt. Fremont. In 1850 Fancher Stimson stated that the greatest number were to be found between Grand Island and Scott's Bluffs. Much depended on the vagaries of the season. In the spring of 1860 Dr. Clark saw few during his passage to Denver, "but in September, when we returned, we saw vast herds."

That the bison were reaching the point of overpopulation is suggested by the observations of Bidwell, Pettijohn, and Pearson as to the great numbers of buffalo skeletons and carcasses found in the ravines and scattered about the bottoms, presumably those gaunted and unable to withstand the rigors of winter. But more positive evidence is to be found in the numerous accounts of buffalo herds so vast as to stagger the imagination:

> We saw them in frightful droves, as far as the eye could reach, appearing at a distance as if the ground itself was moving like the sea. Such large armies of them have no fear of man. They will travel over him and make nothing of him.—JOHN WYETH, 1832

> Buffalo abounds along the Platte River in such vast numbers that it is impossible for mortal man to number them. . . . Sometimes our way seemed entirely blockaded with them but as we approached they would open to the right & left so we could pass thro. Thousands of them sometimes would run towards the river, plunge down the bank into the water, tumbel over each pile up, but all would come out right on the other side of the River & continue the race. Sometimes we would see the Plain black with them for ten miles in width . . . [north side].—JOHN PULSIPHER, 1848

> The buffalo resemble forests of cedar, and present a low, black, and undefined appearance, but occasionaly shifting to and fro like the dark shadows of a cloud. . . . the road appeared like a well-stocked cattle yard, covered with manure.—J. McBRIDE, 1850

> Buffalo extended the whole length of our afternoon's travel, not in hundreds but in solid phalanx . . . thick as sheep in a pasture. . . . I estimated two million. . . . [north side].—WM. KILGORE, 1850

> I am perfectly safe in saying I have seen in one herd many millions. . . . When the buffalo stampede, it is like the continuous roll of distant thunder.—HENRY DAVIS, 1850

> As we were entering the buffalo country every one was on the alert to catch a view of that celebrated animal. . . . finally the huge

animals, in very deed, burst upon our vision. Since then we have seen thousands upon thousands. . . . They first appeared in small scattered squads and gave the impression of cattle grazing in their pastures.—Mrs. Ferris, 1852

We saw one black, living, moving mass spread out far and wide over the bottom. Yes, all the buffalo from the four quarters of the globe seemed to be congregated there.—Charles Teeter, 1862

Some noted that the buffalo were not always in an amorphous mass, but would present certain patterns. Theodore Potter observed that, while on the march, these "monarchs of the Plains" moved in squadrons or companies of 100 to 300, each led by the most powerful bull. Washington Bailey thought that buffalo droves tended to assume a V-shape, with leaders "at point." Amos Bachelder noticed a different arrangement: "upward of 80 of the noble fellows marching in a single file in Indian fashion across the Plains." Cornelius Cole observed "groups of paths, forty or fifty in number, about three feet apart, perfectly parallel with each other. . . . These armies of brutes, in their migrating movements, marched in solid phalanx . . . like Roman legions. . . . For ought we could see these groups of paths may have extended all the way from Texas to the border of Canada." These deeply cut parallel columns resulted in the axle-breaking furrows noted above. According to Capt. Gove, these tracks tended to converge at the most fordable point, with a corresponding point on the opposite bank.

Occasional traffic snarls along the mainline Platte were caused not by wagons running into wagons, since there was ample room for extra lanes, but by wagon trains bumping into buffalo herds, or vice versa.

The whole country . . . presented a mass of buffaloes on a stampede, coming towards us. . . . we immediately went to work preparing ourselves as best we could, by driving the wagons around in a circle, to make a fortification . . . against the approach of these formidable travellers of the Plains. Several of our company more daring than the others took a position on an eminence and keeping an incessant firing of guns and pistols, succeeded in a a diversion of their route, to within two hundred yards of us. . . . It was estimated that this army of buffaloes was at least two hours in passing. . . . immediately following them were immense gangs of wolves, making the most hideous noise.—Samuel Hancock, 1845

In 1845 part of a train of emigrants was run over by buffaloes and badly wrecked. Several members were crippled. Mrs. Markham of Portland, Oregon, was badly hurt at this time, having several ribs broken.—MARY JANE HAYDEN, 1850

Our company was much alarmed last night by a herd of buffalo rushing by our encampment. . . . As the vast herd was coming up they sounded like distant rumbling thunder and grew louder and louder till they passed. . . . This morning whilst engaged in harnessing the horses a herd a buffalo were seen coming under full speed. All save the teamsters rushed for their arms. . . . as they drew closer they espied us and sheared very slightly to one side. . . . As these huge creatures came booming along, their beards, being pendant from their jaws and almost sweeping the ground, their long naked but tufted tails sticking straight out behind, their great brawny necks and shoulders covered with long flowing hair and mane . . . with their eyes rolling and fiery, they looked like a most noble and formidable enemy. —W. McBRIDE, 1850

We suddenly came upon an immense herd of these monsters of the Plains. They started to run in three mighty streams, two of which went directly through the gaps of our trains. As they thundered past in blind fear, shaking the very ground beneath their feet, it seemed to me as though everything must be dashed to pieces. I thought I could then realize something of the terrific . . . charge of cavalry.— MRS. FERRIS, 1852

One morning a large herd was seen on the other [south] side of the Platte River in full sweep toward our camp. . . . Into the river they plunged, forced on by the mass in the rear, churning the water into foam and heading straight for us as the only landing place in the vicinity. We all turned out and by shouting, gesticulating and firing into the herd we succeeded in sheering them off a little to one side and escaped with only the destruction of a tent or two and some shattered nerves.—ELISHA BROOKS, 1852

Suddenly there was a sound like an approaching storm. Almost instantly every animal in the corral was on its feet. The alarm was given and all hands turned out. . . . The roar we heard was like that of a heavy railroad train passing at no great distance. . . .

In the darkness . . . we could see first the forms of the leaders, and then such dense masses that we could not distinguish one buffalo from the other. . . . When daylight came, the few stragglers yet to be seen fell under the . . . rifle.—EZRA MEEKER, 1852

Sometimes lone bulls would make a suicidal attack on a camp, usually as the result of being maddened by hunters (Kirkpatrick, Gelwicks). Peter Burnett's camp bore the brunt of an attack by seven old bulls "charging across the river." Livestock which could be stampeded by a butterfly were understandably nervous in the presence of charging buffalo, and there were frequent runaways of horses and oxen on these occasions (McKeeby, Beehrer). Oxen particularly seemed to have an affinity for the buffalo, and if they became intermingled, sorting them out could be a problem of appalling magnitude (J. Williams). Dr. C. M. Clark's train was not charged or stampeded, but was surrounded and immobilized for several hours by a buffalo swarm which simply grazed on and on contentedly; the emigrants wisely decided not to make a fuss about it. L. Sawyer's train also found itself surrounded by a peaceful herd, but was able to quietly thread its way out of the maze.

Although most specimens weighed out at 800 to 1,200 pounds, king bulls might weigh up to 2,000 pounds, and the immense size of these creatures astounded the emigrants. G. A. Smith described them as "larger than oxen and have a savage appearance." Jagger described his specimen as "a noble looking object. . . with his high humped shoulders and long mane and noble eye. . . . to me [he] looked more like an African lion than any other animal I ever saw."

An emigrant buffalo hunt was seldom an organized affair. Whether they spotted one lone animal or a sizable herd, the excited pilgrims were apt to take off in full cry. The results were unpredictable, but always it was something to record for posterity. Skillful riders dashing into a herd Indian style occasionally brought down a trophy, but most buffalo shooting was without sporting style:

Today [at the Forks] we saw . . . not buffalo by the dozen but by the thousand if not tens of thousands. . . . the buoys had a great frolic after them. . . . they outrun all our horses. . . . we got two or three amongst hands.—ISAAC PETTIJOHN, 1847

We rode up quite close to where a few were rolling in the dirt . . . [shooting one] . . . at every shot he would wheel and charge us, and more than once he came near ripping the side of a horse with his sharp, curving black horns. . . . The pursued animal finally stopped running and stood at bay, madly pawing the ground . . . his bloodshot eyes full of rage and defiance. . . . taking running shots at his side . . . he was finally dispatched.—WM. PLEASANTS, 1849

One stray herd came running into the midst of our cattle, so that our huntsmen took aim and brought down one of them, but unhappily they also killed one of our best cows.—H. B. SCHARMAN, 1849

I discovered a tremendous bull about 100 yards off running directly towards me. I had powder and ball but unfortunately no cap, and as the gentleman appeared to be running right at me, I concluded to back out and let him pass. He ran within twenty feet of me. I cursed myself a thousand times for not having saved my fire for this fine looking fellow. . . .

The main body of the buffalo bore down upon the ox train and the women shrieked and the children squalled, the oxen became alarmed and one wagon was broken. . . .

Our party met a large bull which had become separated from his companions and was closely pursued by a number of our men. . . . on foot I ran up and fired one shot into him just as he sank upon his hind legs. Several other shots were fired at him and he fell dead pierced by more than fifty bullets. He died a glorious death, often whirling upon his pursuers and putting them to flight.—THOMAS EASTIN, 1849

Today I got on chace of a large buffalo, but to escape from us he plunged into the River where it was over a mile wide and was soon across it. He was then headed by some emigrants on the other side, and here he came back again; the water was deep enough to strike his breast where it was one continual roll of foam. We were ready for him on this side again; but before he reached the shore he perceived us and turned toward the other side again. Finding that he would be as hard to capture as a steam ferry-boat I left and tried to overtake the train.—JAMES EVANS, 1850

Buffalo have a clumsy sort of canter, yet they are not slow as it takes a good horse to overtake them. . . . gun broken by a friend who said he had a hand-to-hand encounter.—C. W. SMITH, 1850

This morning we have an exciting time. Three buffalo ran into our camp. All rushed for their guns but not until 20 balls had entered his hide did one buffalo come to the ground. In 20 minutes his hide was off and his carcass in the wagons.—G. W. THISSELL, 1850

Killed a buffalo today. . . . we saw 12. . . . our company took after them. . . . we broke his leg the first shot with a revolver then shot him through the lites. . . . I jumpt off my horse and gave him a death shot in the brain. . . . fine sport was this for all the boys. . . . we had a fine mess of beef.—GEORGE BELSHAW, 1853

It took a lot of ammunition to drop a buffalo because most

emigrants didn't understand how the animal was built. C. W. Smith fired twelve balls at his quarry which "rebounded from his head as from solid rock." J. M. Stewart pronounced, "These old fellows are hard to kill," after sending eighteen balls into his target before it dropped. "The endurance of buffalo is amazing," noted Goldsmith. "They will fight as long as a spark of life is left." While his victim "glared wickedly," he fired seventeen bullets into him. As Pleasants explained, "It is a waste of ammunition to shoot a buffalo in the face. The front of the skull, naturally of great thickness, is rendered impervious by a long-standing accumulation of sand and dirt several inches thick matted in the woolly front." Cartwright advised that the correct point of aim should be close to the forelegs and one-third up the body.

It wasn't always necessary to give chase to get a buffalo, though that method was doubtless the most exhilarating. When a stampeding herd swept by their camp, McBride's party just stood and fired into the plunging ranks. He philosophized: "As these noble looking but persecuted monsters of the plains came up, I felt a deep sympathy for them. It seemed like they were running the gauntlet." If the wind was blowing from the herd toward the hunter, they wouldn't get the human scent, making it possible sometimes to stand still or lie prone and shoot buffalo one at a time, in leisurely fashion (the method of the later professional hunters). Langworthy encountered a herd of 5,000 and was amazed that the buffalo "will not run when fired upon . . . standing like cattle in a pasture." When Theodore Potter's train was held up for a slow-passing herd, some careless fellows started shooting away. In this case, instead of panicking, the buffalo moved slowly and ponderously on: "If we shot one down, that would not stop the herd."

Buffalo hunting by horseback might have its moments of elation, but it also had its hazards, aside from bone-breaking falls and trampling by plunging animals. Hunters often got lost. Mary Ackley's men hoisted a lantern on a high pole, as a beacon to guide back overdue hunters.

There was much criticism of buffalo hunting on grounds of wastefulness, but the most serious complaint was the damage to horseflesh. McBride asserted: "I thought too much of my good mare to ride her at full speed in wanton sport after these animals." McGlashan intoned: "I would here caution anyone crossing the plains to avoid charging buffalo with horses which they expect to carry them to the Pacific." Chambers says flatly: "Buffalo hunting damages horses and wastes precious time." Even more pointed was the criticism by some conservation-minded emigrants about the cruelty of the sport and the depletion of the herds. With everyone banging away, Carlisle Abbott deplored the "flagrant waste of buffalo by emigrants while the Indians starve." Rather illogically, he blamed the government for permitting this "Turkish savagery." Dr. C. M. Clark condemned "the wholesale murder of these noble creatures merely for pastime."

Indians of the Platte

At one time the Pawnee claimed the Platte up to the forks, but by 1849 the Sioux had gained the upper hand in this territory, and any Indian met west of Fort Kearny was likely to be Sioux or Cheyenne. One of the most colorful spectacles of the Platte River pageant was that of a war party, bristling with shields, lances, and old flintlocks, on its way to pillage the Pawnee (Bachelder, McGlashan, Cutting). Emigrant trains were not seriously molested by the Sioux along the main Platte. Stragglers and stray hunters were sometimes robbed and maltreated (Palmer, Ingersoll, Delano), and the natives were not above sneaking up on a camp and making off with the livestock. Reports Pettijohn: "One of the guards shot at an Indian last knight. . . . He was crawling up to steal a horse, pulling grass as he came so that the guard would take him for a calf. . . . He left in so great a hurry that he left his moccasins." Julius Birge's train was threatened with general plunder by a large Sioux band which circled the train, but their bluff was called by rich profanity and the raising of rifles. Usually the tribesmen were guilty of little more than begging, which they did with great dignity and veiled hints of reprisals for the stingy. During the peak migration years to Oregon and California there are almost no certified instances of a Sioux or Cheyenne armed attack upon a wagon train between Fort Kearny and Fort Laramie. The presence of troops at these posts was a deterrent, of course, but during this period these tribes had no real quarrel with the emigrants. They had not yet fully comprehended the fact that the migration was the prelude to their downfall.

During the mid-sixties, when the Sioux and Cheyenne rampaged up and down the Little Blue and the Platte destroying stage sta-

tions, they attacked any white man. The general desolation left
by the marauders in 1864–1865 is vividly described by Eugene Ware
and Frank Root. Julius Birge tells of the Sioux terrorizing Baker's
Ranch (vicinity of Sutherland), while John Bratt saw Midway
Ranch (opposite Gothenburg) in flames after an Indian attack; and,
he writes: "We began to meet east-bound coaches that had been
savagely attacked by Indians. Sometimes one or more horses had
been killed and one passed us in which there was a dead passenger."
But even through this unpleasantness, directed mainly at freighters
and stage operators, the general run of emigrants themselves went
unscathed.

In the journals there are few horrendous accounts of Indian
violence; but there is quite a body of literature on the pageantry of
Indians peacefully met en route:

> a short time before stopping for the evening we saw on the other
> side an encampment of Sioux. . . . A deputation, consisting of the
> old chief and about 80 of his party, came over to see us. This old
> savage had tried to make himself look as respectable as possible and
> had given . . . vermillion to his grey locks. . . . His only article of dress
> was a green frock coat that reached to his ankles. On his shoulders
> were an old pair of epaulets. . . . his cap was made of grizzly bear
> skin. . . . a medal suspended from his neck, made in 1809 with the
> likeness of President Madison. . . . this was the celebrated Bull Tail.
> . . . he left after getting a little whiskey which he coolly put into the
> tripe of a buffalo which he had killed that day.—CAPT. HOWARD
> STANSBURY, 1849

> On a tree on an island, the body of a defunct Indian . . .—WM.
> JOHNSTON, 1849

> At Plum Creek . . . we were honored with a visit from about a dozen
> Indians this morning, while we were partaking of our breakfast. They
> are of the Chien tribe. . . . Some had their heads adorned with skulls
> and brass rings about 2 inches in diameter.—CAROLINE RICHARDSON,
> 1852

> Here [just above the Forks] we were visited by the distinguished war
> chief of the Ogalalla Sioux, Red Plume, fine large and well formed
> man of the true eagle-beaked and warlike contour of face . . . but
> no Neapolitan lazarone could be a more inveterate or skillful beggar.
> . . . He was so much pleased with Molly's liberality to him that he
> proposed to swap me a squaw for her.—THOMAS CRAMER, 1859

> Indians with travois pass. . . . They consider themselves superior

to palefaces, trudging along like squaws. . . . Their taste evinced in
the matter of dress is peculiar. . . . Many are seen wearing fancy
colored shirts, gaudy vests, and old felt hats; and one . . . had an
umbrella which he carried spread above his head. . . . They all wear
trinkets such as coils of brass wire and bands of silver on their arms
and fingers, together with a long string of circular pieces of silver,
graduated in size, and attached to a leather strip, which is . . . suspended from the black hair like a queue. . . . Their clubs, lances and
bows are often thickly studded with brass nails. . . . Many wear looking
glasses . . . around their necks.

The old squaws are very solvenly in appearance, wearing a loose
tunic . . . which is daubed with grease and dirt; their faces corrugated
with wrinkles, and their hair hanging disheveled, the abode of creeping
things. . . . The only method used for their eradication is picking
them out with the fingers and eating them—DR. C. M. CLARK, 1860

I thought the Indians very ugly. They were of a dull copper color,
or of wet clay and had rather long black straight hair. They are very
friendly and want to shake hands with us, and say "how, how." . . .

[At Cottonwood Springs] 25 wigwams . . . three or four Indian
graves . . . [At a funeral ceremony, the Indians were] uttering loud
cries and laments. The graves were made of four upright posts driven
into the ground and about half way from the top were boards fixed
across and the body laid on . . . high enough to be out of reach of
wolves.—ADA MILLINGTON, 1862

Upon the island was an Indian village. . . . Cluttered rather closely
upon the island, and standing out clearly in the bright sunlight, were
seventy white circular lodges . . . a scene of animation, in which
warriors, squaws and children confusedly intermingled like a legion of
busy red ants in a city of ant hills, each forming a moving dot of
bright color. . . .

[We] had the temerity to visit the camp . . . ponies switching flies.
. . . lodges of white buffalo skins. . . . the larger tents were 25 feet
high, generally with 30 poles supporting each. . . . Around the lodges
were scores of squaws, many of them at that hour half reclining in
the doors of their tents, in costumes quite decollette.—JULIUS BIRGE,
1866

PRINCIPAL FEATURES OF THE MAIN PLATTE, FORT KEARNY TO
ASH HOLLOW CROSSING, BEFORE 1859

The news from Pike's Peak in 1858 precipitated plans for
ranches along the Platte to accommodate the new wave of gold-

seekers. There is evidence of a start on such establishments, as well as new mail stations to Salt Lake, late that year. However, as far as overland travelers were concerned, it was not until 1859 that there was any semblance of serious settlement along the Platte except Fort Kearny itself and two ramshackle trading posts of uncertain vintage, Morrow's post at the forks and Beauvais' post at California, or Ash Hollow, Crossing. Prior to that date the valley was largely an unspoiled wilderness, with the Council Bluffs Road on the north side and the Oregon Trail, later the California Road, following the south side of the river to the various crossings of the South Platte and thence over the peninsula between the forks to Ash Hollow on the North Platte. The most notable features of this earlier period are the following:

Plum Creek, 35 miles above Fort Kearny. This was the first wood and water supply of consequence after Kearny (Frush, Richardson, Nash), though by the sixties both articles seemed to be in short supply (Birge, Millington). In 1854, according to Cramer, the pillage of the U.S. mail at this crossing by the Brule Sioux was one of the reasons for Harney's expedition of the following year. There was much debate over the name, some claiming that it abounded in wild plums (Teeter), others that "no plums have ever been known to grow on its treeless margin" (Birge).

Brady's Island, the lower end of which is in the vicinity of the present town of Brady, is mentioned by Munger in 1839 and Fremont in 1842. Franklin Starr says that it was "named after a man who was murdered there some years ago by one of his comrades. . . . His grave is on one of the ravines which we crossed." Wislizenus understood there were two burials here: "Came to a burial place where two Americans are interred. One, while drunk, shot the other, then himself. This incident happened several years ago; a simple stake marks the spot." According to Rufus Sage, writing in 1841, the murder occurred "some eight years ago" and involved a feud between two boatmen on a downstream voyage with furs.

Fremont Springs, approximately opposite Hershey, Nebraska. Lowe puts this "at the head of a big slough that parallels the South Platte 20 miles." Lavinia Porter thought that here was "the finest water between the Rocky Mountains and the Missouri River. . . . We felt like falling down and worshipping this fountain." Ada Millington counted "sparkling springs five in number . . . discovered several years ago by General Fremont."

O'Fallon's Bluff, opposite and west of Sutherland. Emigrant Starr places this seventeen miles above Brady's Island and says it was named after a man who made a fortune selling liquor to the Indians at this place. Meline thought it was named after a hunter killed there by Cheyennes. Birge understood that this unfortunate was Benjamin O'Fallon of St. Louis. According to Thomas Twiss, Indian agent, a party of thirteen Cheyennes attacked Almon Babbit and two companions near this point, killing all three. Babbit, a citizen of Council Bluffs, was traveling to Salt Lake City in 1856 to assume duties as Secretary of Utah. Frank Young later observed that this bluff "seems to be as much an object of dread to these Plainsmen as the doubling of the Hatteras Cape is to the sailormen." Since the bluff came nearly to the river, most travelers avoided any threat of Indian ambush here by taking a trail which detoured southward over the bluff, described in the Council Bluffs *Daily Telegraph* as "a precipitous sand ridge." This would have put them along the edge of today's Sutherland Reservoir.

The Forks of the Platte (or, more accurately, the confluence of the North and South forks) were reckoned to be about 110 miles from Fort Kearny or 450 miles from Independence. While it is clear enough today when viewing the city of North Platte and vicinity from an airplane, the exact location of the confluence was a puzzle to most emigrants. In 1849 Joe Hamelin explained that because of wet bottoms the road was several miles from the river at this point, while Pvt. Gibbs explained: "The division takes place a little below our camp . . . but the forks separate so gradually, and the main stream is so filled with islands, that the exact point is not easily noticed." Charles Gould says he "passed the division without knowing it," while L. Sawyer engaged in "debate as to where the forks are." Lacking visual confirmation, the emigrants knew they were on the South Platte by a slight shift of the course southwestward and the appearance of the peninsula bluffs on the north side (Sutherland to Paxton).

Three Crossings of the South Platte (prior to 1859). The object was to reach the North Platte via Ash Hollow. The first question was where to cross the South Platte. Travelers could cross almost anywhere they determined to do so (Joseph Ware, Thomas Woodward); however, three main crossings over a spread of forty-five miles are clearly identifiable from the mileage figures given in various journals. Several emigrants specifically refer to their choice of three crossings (Tate, Richardson, Tompkins). In his guidebook W. Wadsworth says there are "three fords, all bad if the river be high, and all good, if low."

These were commonly known as the Lower, Middle, and Upper crossings (or fords). Their respective locations would be roughly (1) a few miles west of the city of North Platte, in the vicinity of Fremont Springs, opposite Hershey; (22) a few miles east of Ogallala; and (3) a few miles west of Brule, Nebraska.

The one most heavily used was the Upper Crossing, otherwise known variously as Kearny's Ford (from the 1845 expedition), Beauvais' Crossing (from the nearby trading post), Laramie Crossing, Ash Hollow Crossing, or California Crossing. After 1859, with a new California Crossing at Julesburg, this became the Old California Crossing. (The terms Lower California Crossing and Upper California Crossing used by some latter-day historians to differentiate between the Ash Hollow Crossing and the Julesburg Crossing are nowhere to be found in emigrant journals and have resulted only in confusion. Frank Root seems to have invented this usage in his reminiscences.)

The Lower Ford near the forks was a close second in importance in terms of emigrant use prior to 1859; it was earlier used by fur caravans to and from Fort Laramie. It is described by the explorer John C. Fremont and was popular with Oregon emigrants of the mid-forties (Palmer). The Middle Ford was first used by Capt. Bonneville in 1832. It was not used much after that until the Gold Rush, when it was sometimes referred to as "the new ford."

Those using the Lower and Middle fords could go directly over the peninsula between the two forks, from two to nine miles, respectively, and then follow up the south side of the North Platte, where the old trail is now partially inundated by the reservoir called Lake McConaughy. Because of the bluffs which jutted into the North Platte, they had to alternate between the bottoms and the uplands, finally reaching Cedar Grove opposite the Lone Tree, and then up one more incline to enter Ash Hollow from the east at its midpoint. Among those crossing directly over from the Lower Ford were Sedgley, Bidwell, Wadsworth, Thomasson, Snyder, Hale, Lampton, Edwin Bryant, Sage, Thornton, Gould, Frink, J. H. Clark, Staples, and E. Howell. The other option for those using the Lower Ford was to proceed along the north side of the South Platte to the Middle Ford, then cross over. This option was exercised by Fremont, Lotts, Gelwicks, Wislizenus, Dewolf, Parke, Athearn, Minto, Andrews, and Frush, among others.

Those using the Middle Ford and going diagonally to the North Platte from there are represented by Bruff, Delano, Dalton, Lindsey, Lobenstine, Riley Root, Bartholomew, Berrien, Ingalls, Elisha Lewis, and Lewelling. Others who crossed at the Middle Ford but stayed on the north side of the South Platte to the Upper Crossing included C. Richardson, McCoy, Bennett Clark, Caldwell, Tinker, Hines, Benson, and Ketcham.

Emigrants crossing at the Upper Ford climbed up California Hill, also called Ash Hollow Hill (not to be confused with so-called Windlass Hill on which they descended into Ash Hollow), where deep gouges remain today from the passage of the multitudes of emigrants. From the summit of California Hill it was about eighteen miles in a northwesterly direction to the head of Ash Hollow. There is a long roster of those employing this fairly standard route. Among those affording useful descriptions are Parkman, Lowe, Bennett, McBride, Tompkins, the Wyeths, McGlashan, Shepherd, Gaylord, Harritt, Carleton, Cooke, Wilkinson, Kenderdine, Bradway, Cagwin, Littleton, Starr, and J. M. Stewart.

No imaginative prose by modern writers can better convey the sobering experience of crossing the South Platte than that of the emigrants themselves:

> At length he encamped, caused the bodies of the wagons to be dislodged from the wheels, covered them with buffalo hides, besmeared with a compound of tallow and ashes, thus forming rude boats. In these they ferried their effects across the stream, which was 600 yards wide, with a swift and strong current. Three men were in each boat, to manage it; others waded across, pushing the barks before them. . . . A march of nine miles took them over high rolling prairies to the north fork.—CAPT. BONNEVILLE, 1832

> Hunted buffalo and killed 2. . . . We wonted thare hides for to make bots to craws the river. . . . I will heare remark that I waded and swam in the river 7 times.—WM. NEWBY, 1843

> The Platte . . . was so deep and broad it could not be forded. . . . The wagons were caulked water-tight and raised and lashed to the tops of the standards, and cattle were swum over, men swimming alongside.—INEZ PARKER, 1848

The only way a passage could be made was to double team, and then keep in constant motion, for on stopping the wagon would sink in the sand, and in time disappear entirely. One wagon, to which was hitched unruly or frightened cattle, began to sink, and was only drawn out by hastily hitching on an additional force of well-trained cattle.— ALONZO DELANO, 1849

As we neared the spot where we designed to cross we observed at least 400 waggons on the bank and at least 3,000 oxen. . . . The shouting and hallooing combined with the bawling of cattle made a confusion of stunning sounds. . . .

The water was high and consequently we found it quite impossible to ford the river without swimming our horses as we rode them. . . . Ox teams . . . were thrown into confusion, some would become unyoked or get the chains over their backs instead of between them, and some would turn their heads in the wrong direction. The waggons would swing about in deep water. . . . Often they would be submerged, and their contents greatly injured, or they would upset and thus destroy all they contained, or float away to parts hitherto unexplored.— DR. TOMPKINS, 1850

A place was discovered . . . where by raising our wagon beds a foot on the bolsters we would be enabled to cross. . . . The river is over a mile wide . . . with a current outrunning the Missouri . . . and its course over an uneven bottom, boiling and eddying until it is completely mixed with sand. . . . Into this flood, fearful and dangerous to look at, our wagons commenced plunging one after another, the first dive completely immersing the axletrees and nearly sweeping the drivers off their feet. . . . On reaching the opposite shore the drivers found the legs of their pantaloons literally cut to pieces by the sand and force of the water.—JAMES BENNETT, 1850.

What an unfavorable morning for fording Platte River . . . cloudy and chilling, . . . river a mile and a half across, very muddy, and somewhat rough, for the wind was blowing upstream. After a waggon has started in, if the team should stop it would sink deeper and deeper in the sands. . . . The water came up into the waggon beds a few inches. The bottom of the river is composed of innnumerable pitches and offsets of about six inches, which caused the mules to walk with a kind of limping gait.—JAMES EVANS, 1850

The Pawnee . . . told us never to attempt to go straight across a stream, but to strike a current, and follow it up or down until we struck another, and follow it up or down, and so on until we reached the opposite bank. . . . The river was . . . over half a mile wide, but the course of the different currents we had to follow up and down made the journey from side to side nearly two miles. This had to be done with four and six horses, and a man to each wheel. . . . Sometimes the wagons would be left standing so long the water would wash the crust away from the wheels and down they would go, and we would have to unload and carry everything to a sand bar, then take the wheels off and float the box down, put the vehicle together again, load up, and make another start. . . . Every man of us was in the water from morning till night, and must have traveled in the three days of crossing, ten miles in the water.—CHARLES D. FERGUSON, 1850

From a guide-book we had with us, we learned that the proper way to cross the streams was to take a diagonal course,—first down the stream, then up again. Accordingly, after diving into the water, we turned down at an angle of forty-five degrees till we reached the middle of the river; then, turning up stream at the same angle, we arrived safely at the northern bank, nearly opposite our point of entrance.— MARGARET FRINK, 1850

More excitement, more fun, more bad whiskey drank at this place [the Lower Ford] than any other point from St. Joe to the Pacific. . . . safely across, the Capt. passed around the "big jug."—JOHN H. CLARK, 1852

We were obliged to double teams, making eight yoke of oxen to each wagon. The beds of the wagons were raised a number of inches by putting blocks under them. . . . We plunged into the river, taking a diagonal course. It required three quarters of an hour to reach the opposite shore. . . . We found the river so deep in places that, although our wagon box was propped nearly to the top of the stakes, the water rushed through it like a mill race, soaking the bottoms of my skirts and deluging our goods.—PHOEBE JUDSON, 1853

Where we went down into the water, the river bank was steep and about four feet high, so on our first entrance into the stream, the wagon came so near standing on end, that view of the team was cut off for a few seconds. . . . When the wagon was righted, there was little to reassure us. The water runs very swiftly, and that together with the sand washing from under the wheels, or the wheels settling down into the quicksand, caused a shaking trembling sensation that was truly terrifying. . . .

Each team and wagon cut down into sand which was at once washed away, leaving an entirely different footing for the one . . . after.—HELEN CARPENTER, 1856

We begin preparations for crossing by making a temporary platform across the top of our wagon boxes to get our provisions above water. . . . We put 6 yoke of cattle on a wagon and with 2 men with a long Rope ahead of the leaders and men on each Side of the wagon with poles to keep it from upsetting when going into holes. Some times the leaders are in Swimming water but the Rope takes them along. . . . The channel is changing all the time and the Indians make something acting as guides. We got over all right—changed our clothes, took a turn at the jug just for Spiritual consolation.—J. A. WILKINSON, 1859

As the river was rising at the rate of six inches in twenty-four hours, they considered it dangerous to delay and they proceeded to dig away the bank to make a road. . . . All being ready, the ladies sitting upon the boxes inside the wagon, holding the children, the Burlingame outfit plunged in. The front wheels went down with a crash, the water poured into the wagon bed in torrents and the horses were almost submerged. . . . the wagon [became] so deeply imbedded in quicksand that four horses could not move it. . . . a number of gentlemen rode into the river to render assistance. They jumped from their horses in the midst of the roaring current, put their shoulders to the wheels . . . and, raising them out of the sand, enabled the horses to move on. . . . By the aid of our heroic and daring friends, and our good, stout steads we were at length rescued from a watery grave.—MRS. BURLINGAME, 1862

Mules are great cowards in water, they prefer drowning to swimming. . . . I and three others brought seven wagons across, making 14 times that we crossed the river that day. . . . We usually rode on the back of our steers on the return trip. . . . The skin of my neck, arms and body was badly sunburned, blistered and irritated. Had my flesh been seared by a hot iron I could not have suffered more.—JOHN BRATT, 1866

STATIONS, POSTS, AND RANCHES, FORT KEARNY TO JULESBURG, 1859–1866

This study is concerned primarily with the covered wagon emigration up the Platte and not the development of overland transportation, communication, and settlement. However, there would be a very large gap in the history of the Great Platte River Road if there were not a bird's-eye view, at least, of the famous road ranches, stage stations, and military sub-posts along the 200-mile mainline stretch from Fort Kearny to Julesburg on the South Platte. It was the report of Colorado gold in 1858 and the Pike's.

Peak Rush of 1859–1860, together with increasing military urgencies on the Plains and the demands for transcontinental services, that transformed the Platte valley from a wilderness of buffalo and nomadic tribesmen to a thin line of settlement, with facilities for emigrants and freighters as well as stage lines and telegraph. Often snapped by Indian depredations, this line nevertheless was the first extension of civilization, however rough and tentative, west of Fort Kearny.

Prior to 1859 scattered references are found to fly-by-night trading establishments along the Platte and the North Platte, usually in portable tents or tipis operated by squaw men. Robidoux's several posts in the Scott's Bluffs vicinity and Beauvais' post at Old California Crossing were the only ones that had the semblance of permanent structures. It was not until 1859, however, that civilians began to settle along the Platte in quantity, in fortified adobe or cedar-log structures. If these were initiated by overland stage or Pony Express operators, they were called stations. If they were launched privately, as hostelries or groceries and saloons, they were called ranches, in the singular sometimes spelled "ranche." If the army built or occupied an outpost to protect telegraph facilities (or, later, Union Pacific Railroad construction), it would be designated a military post, even though the facilities might be meager. Occasionally one outfit had a complex of buildings that served any two or all three purposes. A few observers have illuminating comments on these primitive facilities:

> The country is fast settling up, the inhabitants build themselves sod houses and manage to live on nothing.—MARTHA M. MOORE, 1859

> Why these buildings are called ranches is more than I can say. The proprietors do not cultivate the soil, nor do they raise stock, they have merely squatted along this line of travel, for purposes best known to themselves. . . . Some are of the adobe species, while others are constructed of rough logs and poles, and sometimes we meet with one built of square cedar posts. . . . The proprietors are generally rude specimens of humanity . . . many of them dress in garments made from elk and deer skins . . . their hair has been suffered to grow, giving them a ferocious look . . . many of them have squaw wives, who inhabit a lodge erected nearby.—C. M. CLARK, 1860

> There are no towns or proper farms in Nebraska. . . . things take on a California or New Mexico tinge, and a house is now a ranch,

generally a log building roofed with earth and grass, and an adjacent enclosure . . . with an air of half dwelling, half castle.—FITZ HUGH LUDLOW, 1863

A ranche is not a dwelling, nor a farm-house, nor a store, nor a tavern, but all of these, and more. It is connected with a large corral, and capable of standing an Indian siege. You can procure entertainment at them . . . and they keep for sale liquors, canned fruit, knives, playing-cards, saddlery and goggles. . . .

These ranches are seen at a distance of from four to six miles on these dead levels, and loom up like a Fortress Monroe or Castle St. Angelo. A stable or house with its square openings for light and air resembles, at a short distance, a brown stone fort, with embrasures. The dwelling is sometimes adobe, but more frequently . . . log . . . and a corral of pickets or adobe constitute the prairie castle.

Strictly speaking, [the adobe] is not adobe . . . being simply prairie sod, cut in blocks. They are laid, grass down, in walls three feet thick, and make the coolest house in summer, and warmest in winter, known in this region. . . . it is impossible to fire it, and arrows can do no damage.—JAMES MELINE, 1866

Ranches provide alike for man and beast. . . . A large yard is surrounded by a stockade paling, with stabling, feed-troughs, and hay-ricks, with here and there loop-holes for the rifle. In places of imminent peril from Indian attacks . . . the wall of the upper stories and every angle of house or stable has its outlets for firing upon an approaching foe. The log or adobe house is often small; but like an eastern omnibus or street car, is unlimited in accommodations for all who seek shelter.—M. CARRINGTON, 1866

The following checklist of Platte River stations, posts, and ranches does not pretend to be all-inclusive. Neither is it necessarily of certified accuracy, since there is much confusion among sources as to exact distances and exact identities (sometimes complicated by shifting ownership and changing locations). In most cases cultivation, road construction, or flooding have obliterated all physical trace. The number given is the approximate mileage west from Fort Kearny, with the principal controls used being Coast and Geodetic Survey maps and a U.S. Army report on ranches of 1866 (abbreviated USA 66). Other principal sources (and their abbreviations if any, for reference purposes) are the Postmaster General's order modifying its contract with the Overland Mail Company, 1861 (PG 61); Root and Connelley, *Overland Stage to California,* relating to a trip of 1863 (R & C); O. Allen's *Guide Book*, identifying U.S. mail stations in 1859; and several travelers: for 1860, Burton, Tracy, and C. M. Clark; for 1861, Ira Butterfield and the Council Bluffs *Daily Telegraph* (CDT); for 1862, Millington; for 1863, Morris; for 1864, Col. Sitgreaves and Capt. Eugene Ware; for 1865, Frank Young and Maj. O'Brien; for 1866, Bratt, Birge, and Meline.

2 miles from Fort Kearny (MFK): Kearny City, or Adobe Town (Dobytown), 200 inhabitants (USA 66).

10 MFK: Keeler's Ranch, 1859 (David Anderson); Eight Mile Point (CDT, 1861); Townsend's Ranch, adobe house (USA 66).

12 MFK: A mail contract and Pony Express station earlier called Platt's (PG 61) or Platte (R & C); five years later O'Brien called it Craig's Stage Station, noting log stables. At this twelve and a half mile point, about five miles southwest of present Kearney, the emigrant road closely paralleled the river (Young).

14 MFK: McClain's and Russell's Ranche (USA 66). Despite the discrepancy, this could also be the site of Burton's Seventeen Mile Station in 1860. It is at the mouth of an unnamed draw which in early emigrant days boasted a few trees.

22 MFK: About six miles southeast of Elm Creek, this place had a bewildering variety of names. As a Pony Express station it was called Garden (PG 61). C. M. Clark named it Shakespear's, while CDT lists Sydenham's Ranche, and the Harvey map of 1862 calls it Biddleman's Ranch. Strangely enough (since it is a reversal of the nomenclature given for 12 MFK), USA 66 calls this place "Platte Stage Station, log construction." In 1865 Frank Young found it a smoking ruin.

35 MFK: All sources, of course, agree on the name and location of Plum Creek Station, about ten miles southeast of present Lexington. William Lee found a "new trading post" here in 1859. This was probably the Pony Express station erected by Russell, Majors & Waddell. Sitgreaves shows the plan and environs of "Post of Plum Creek" about 1864. USA 66 identifies it as "'stage station, telegraph office and military post" of substantial log construction and describes a Thomas Ranch near by of adobe and frame. R & C says Plum Creek, being in the heart of the buffalo region, was famed for its buffalo steaks. Howard Cutting in 1863 speaks of Plum Creek Station as a large and quite comfortable place. Here he "met the mail coach, four mules and five passengers going east."

In 1865 Frank Young passed several wrecked and burned ranche-houses before reaching Plum Creek, and here found "quite a large garrison of soldiers," since Plum Creek "for some reason is considered especially liable to Indian attack. It was here the savages opened the ball in last summer's raid on the Platte, and their work is commemorated in the big mound just one mile east of the station." This cemetery, containing the remains of eleven men murdered by Indians on August 8, 1864, is well preserved today.

41 MFK: Freeman's Ranch, destroyed (USA 66). This was Daniel Freeman (not the one of homestead fame) according to CDT, 1861.

51 MFK: Allen calls this Willow Bend. In 1860 this was a mail and Pony Express station called Willow Island. USA 66 names it "Willow Island, or Mullally's Ranche, Stage Station and Military Post," with adobe house and stables, and frame store. Pat Mullally is identified by Morris as the ranche proprietor in 1863; that same year Ben Arnold calls this Spread Eagle Station. The Sitgreaves plan calls it "Post of Millilas." The site is about eight miles southeast of Cozad. The original log cabin on the site was moved by the American Legion to Cozad for the use of Boy Scouts. A plaque was dedicated in 1938.

60 MFK: C. M. Clark has a Smithe's Ranche here in 1860. On this approximate site also (USA 66) was Miller and Penneston's Ranche and Stage Station, adobe house, and log store. This is referred to also by Young. Morris names it Miller's Ranch and, "like most about here, bore as its emblem a pair of stag or elk horns fastened over the door." The site would be due south of present Willow Island. John Bratt lists it among stations in 1866 "abandoned or burned to the ground."

65 MFK: Midway was a mail and Pony Express station (Allen, PG 61), and in 1863, according to R & C, it was a home station on the stage line and "one of the best eating places on the Platte." He says it was so named because it was about halfway between Atchison and Denver. In 1866 John Bratt found the station burning from an Indian raid. Three miles south of Gothenburg, an ancient log structure still stands on Harry Williams' Lower 96 Ranch, being carefully preserved by the owner as a surviving Pony Express station. If it is an actual Pony Express facility of 1860–1861, it somehow had to withstand the fire witnessed by Bratt. (O'Brien confuses the issue by placing Midway Sation sixty miles from Fort Kearny.)

70 MFK: Dan Smith's Ranche, Stage Station, and Military Post, log construction (USA 66). This is identified also by O'Brien, Morris, Young, and Carrington. Near Smith's, Dr. Allen encountered a Pony Express rider. He writes, "We have frequently seen this express on the road, the pony on the full run and wet with perspiration." Among other Pony Express witnesses is Mark Twain, who describes a rider streaking past his stagecoach, "swinging away like the belated fragment of a storm!"

80 MFK: About eight miles due west of Gothenburg was Gilman's, a Pony Express and stage station uniformly identified by all sources. M. O. Morris said, "There is a log stable and corrall" and here, for the first time, "Cedar supplants the cottonwood." Sitgreaves shows the plan and environs of Gilman's Station. USA 66 characterizes this as "Gillman's Ranche, Stage Station and Military Post." Of it Frank Young writes: "Gilman's used to be a favorite trading post with the Sioux Indians. . . . It is now a military station of some importance, the soldier's quarters occupying about a dozen log houses." It was near Gilman's that Young wrote poetically of the stagecoach:

> In the . . . splendor of the night . . . soon a distant rumbling breaks in . . . and approaches rapidly. . . . in a very few minutes the overland coach, with a dozen horses or mules on a steady gait, glides by on the road . . . with three or four shadowy figures on top . . . all in absolute silence except for the dull roll of wheels. . . . It disappears down in the western sky among the stars.

91 MFK: South of Brady there is a site of considerable mystery. It is not mentioned in the U.S. mail contract for the Pony Express or by R & C. There was a station in this neighborhood which was called Dan Trout's Station by O'Brien, Joe Bower's Ranche by Morris, and Boken Ranche by USA 66. The site is on Harry Williams' modern Upper 96 Ranch, Lincoln County, and a log blacksmith shop survives here; but in 1931 the main two-story log structure was dismantled, taken to Gothenburg, and there reassembled as a one-story tourist attraction and called a Pony Express station. According to local tradition, reflected in bronze tablets, it was called Machette's, and goes clear back to 1854 as a trading post. A "Guide to the Gold Mines" in the Council Bluffs *Daily Telegraph* for April 9, 1861, identifies "J. Machette's trading post" at Cottonwood Springs, in competition with McDonald's (see below), but that would be six miles west of this point. Gilman's and Cottonwood Station, both known Pony Express stations, are only sixteen miles apart, and normally there would not have been a Pony Express station in between. Accordingly, the identification of this mystery site as a Pony Express station is without any documentable proof. However, it seems probable that the log structures in question relate to some kind of an early road ranche with one of the assorted names given above.

94 MFK: Dr. Clark refers here to Fox Spring, while USA 66 identifies a Frost's Ranche, of cedar and adobe components.

97 MFK: Cottonwood Springs, or Cottonwood Station, on the east side of Cottonwood Creek. There is no debate about the location and identity of this famous Pony Express and overland stage station, also called McDonald's Station (Root) or McDonald and Clark's Ranche (CDT). Midway between Fort Kearny and Julesburg and blessed with an abundance of water and cedar wood, it became the logical place for later Fort Cottonwood (1864) and Fort McPherson (1866), about one-fourth mile west of the original station. The present Fort McPherson National Cemetery south of Maxwell is one mile northwest.

In 1860 Dr. Clark speaks of several ranches here and complains that the place was infested with thieves and robbers, preying on emigrants. That same season Richard Burton complained of "the foul tenement" where he spent the night. In 1863, however, Root says that Cottonwood was a home station and "Nearly everything about the premises appeared homelike."

> McDonald had a year or so before . . . built . . . a cedar-log store building. The main building was about twenty feet front and forty feet deep, and was two stories high. A wing 50 feet extended to the west. . . . Around it in the rear was a large and defensible corral. . . . In the stage station was a telegraph office. . . . There was also on the other side of the road a place where canned goods and liquors were sold.—EUGENE WARE, 1864

> By noon we reached Cottonwood Springs. Here we drive into a large corral, an extensive stockade of logs, on one corner of which, at the front, is the station house, and in the other corner, separated from it by the main gateway, are two or three log cabins. . . .
> A little way up the road is Fort McPherson, 100 miles west of Fort Kearny, and second only to it in military importance. Its log buildings

occupy a space fully 250 yards square, enclosed by the usual stockade, five or six feet high. . . . The same rule as to 100 wagons of 100 men [to be assembled before departure] is said to be enforced here.—FRANK YOUNG, 1865

[We] lay over at Fort Cottonwood, waiting for the minimum of 20 wagons and 30 armed men.—PERRY BURGGESS, 1866

On the evening of June 22 our national flag was seen in the west, streaming out from the staff at Fort McPherson. As we passed, we observed three small buildings made of cedar logs, also a quartermaster's building, and a small barracks of the same material. Three adobe barns were in the rear. . . The agreeable fragrance of cedar induced us . . . to purchase a small log to carry with us for fuel. . . . two companies of U.S. Volunteers and two companies of U.S. Cavalry were then stationed at the post.—JULIUS BIRGE, 1866

Since the history of Fort McPherson and its appurtenances has been extensively treated in a book of that name by Louis Holmes, more description here seems unwarranted.

99 MFK: Fitchie's Ranch, of cedar logs (USA 66), mentioned also by Young, Bratt, and Carrington.

100 MFK: Box Elder Stage Station and Telegraph Office, cedar construction (USA 66). It is a little difficult to determine what a stage station was doing just three miles up the road from Cottonwood, but there it was. A half mile south was Ronan's Ranche, and in the same neighborhood was Justus S. North's Ranche with a cedar-log house (USA 66).

101 MFK: Hindman's Ranche (USA 66). This man was a blacksmith, in the employ of McDonald (Ware).

108 MFK: Just below the confluence of the North and South forks was one of the most famous of all Platte ranches—Jack Morrow's Ranche, or Station, sometimes called Junction House. "Known as the half-way house between Omaha and Denver" (CDT), it was an exceptionally large and well-supplied hostelry and store with a very colorful proprietor. Margaret Carrington speaks glowingly of Morrow as "the prince of ranchmen and the King of good fellows."

One of the best stations on the road . . . building composed of square cedar timbers. On one side is the *old building* . . . constructed of rough logs; on the opposite side is a good corralle. . . . Jack Morrow . . . has been employed by the government to carry mail through to Fort

Laramie. . . . He is a small, slim personage, rather below the average stature, light complexion, long auburn hair . . . a very social man. . . . He has had several squaws. . . . By some it was thought he was connected with the organized band of thieves, for did any one mention that they had lost animals, he would offer to find them for a certain remuneration.—C. M. CLARK, 1860

Jack Morrow's ranche, said to be the finest on the whole route. . . . He is one of the characters of the Plains, famed as a scout, and happy in the possession of a squaw, or some other kind of influential Indian connection said to insure him against attack. He has a handsome and extensive log building, filled to the roof with a general stock of Plains staples . . . tier on tier of sardines, tomatoes and peaches . . . and stacks of log cabin bottles of Drake's Plantation Bitters. . . . these empty bottles blaze the trail. . . . Hard by Jack's prosperous-looking store we saw an Indian burial on poles.—FRANK YOUNG, 1865

We stayed on an hour or so trading at the Morrow ranch and I had the privilege of meeting that noted ranchman, who wore a diamond in his yellow and badly soiled shirt. There were several hundred Sioux Indians, squaws and papooses camped near the ranch. . . . This noted ranch had a hard name among emigrants on account of its record of Indian thefts. Scarcely a train passed it but that lost stock and when the owner would appeal to Morrow, that gentleman would be truly sympathetic and offer to sell him others at a big figure.—JOHN BRATT, 1866

113 MFK: Here, due south of present North Platte, was a Pony Express and stage station called Cold Springs by R & C and Cold Spring Ranche and Stage Station, of cedar and adobe, by USA 66.

120 MFK: About halfway between North Platte and Hershey, opposite Fremont's Slough, was Fremont Station (Clark), Bishop's Station (O'Brien), or Bishop's Ranch (USA 66). Bratt says it was later called Beers' Ranch.

128 MFK: Opposite Hershey and at the site of the Lower Crossing of the South Platte was Fremont Springs Pony Express and Stage Station, another home station (R & C). Clark calls it Buffalo Ranch, while Burton says, "The building is of a style peculiar to the south, especially Florida—two huts connected by a roofwork of thatched timber, which acts as the best and coolest of verandahs."

130 MFK: O'Fallon's Bluff Station (O'Brien), or Military Post (USA 66), east of the famous bluff itself, at the point where the upland detour began (Sitgreaves).

135 MFK: Opposite Sutherland and just below the famous bluff itself was Bob Williams' Ranche (Clark), also listed by Morris and USA 66. If the Indians infested this area as much as is claimed, it must have been an exciting place.

138 MFK: An equally exciting place, apparently right at O'Fallon's Bluff, was Moore's Ranche (CDT, 1861), or the O'Fallon Road Ranche (Bratt), the adobe walls of which were in ruins when the army made its 1866 report. Morris refers in 1863 to Baker's "very neat ranche." In 1866 Bratt speaks of "the well known Lou Baker road ranch and stage station, dreaded on account of its frequency of Indian attacks." Julius Birge, in the same year, goes into considerable detail about the Sioux insolence toward Baker and his family, and concludes, "Although his ranch for that day was spared by the band . . . it was twice attacked and destroyed by Indians within the ensuing 18 months."

140 MFK: Just west of O'Fallon's Bluff was a Pony Express station identified by PG 61 as Dansey's, but it was more accurately spelled "Dorsey" (CDT) or "D'Orsay" (Morris). Burton calls it Half Way House. O'Brien calls it Elkhorn Station and in USA 66 it appears as Elk Horn Stage Station, an affair of cedar.

155 MFK: There was a Pony Express and stage station here (a home station, according to R & C), about seven miles west of Paxton. In 1860 Clark names it Pike's Peak Station, but it seems generally to be known as Alkali Lake (R & C) or "Alkali Station, Telegraph Office and Military Post" (O'Brien and USA 66). Young and Meline both describe the place as surrounded by the white incrustation of alkali. All agree it was "a dreary, desolate location." Sitgreaves shows the post plan and environs.

160 MFK: Here were the adobe ruins of Omaha Ranch (USA 66). Somewhere in this same area was the Middle Crossing of the California Gold Rush.

165 MFK: Across the river from Ogallala was a routine Pony Express and stage station variously called Gills (PG 61), Sand Hill (R & C), and Sand Hill Stage Station (USA 66). Frank Young found it occupied by soldiers, and it looked "as comfortless as a Siberian picture in a story-book."

175 MFK: Opposite and less than a mile west of Brule is the identified site of the Pony Express and stage home station called Diamond Springs by everyone without argument. It was of cedar (USA 66).

178 MFK: This point, four miles west of Brule, was the famous pre-1859 Upper Crossing or Old California Crossing and the identified site of Beauvais' Ranche. M. O. Morris and Sarah Herndon call it the Star Ranche. Young describes it as "a famous old trading post. Beauvais is an old French trader who has been located here for the best part of a generation." He found here, in addition to cedar houses, one big "doby storehouse, with three or four small dobys alongside, and a barracks for a small garrison." This was called Beauvais Ranche Military Post (USA 66), or Beauvais Station by Sitgreaves, whose map of the environs shows the South Platte Ford less than one half mile west of Beauvais Station.

189 MFK: In Colorado, about two miles east of present Julesburg, was a Pony Station called Frontz in the U.S. Mail contract, Elbow Station by O'Brien, and South Platte Station by others (R & C, USA 66). Its marker designation as Butte Station seems to be in error.

195 MFK: Here was O'Brien's Butte Station of 1865, the same as Butt's Ranch, an adobe establishment listed by USA 66. Frank Young refers to Burt's Ranch.

205 MFK: Famous Julesburg deserves a book of its own; only the briefest account will serve here. The old original Julesburg and its 1865 replacement after a Sioux Indian raid are both on the south side of the South Platte, of course, and in no way to be confused with later Julesburg, a station on the Union Pacific Railroad, north side and several miles distant. The community was born in 1859 as the trading post of Jules Beni (who was later killed by Jack Slade) and a new station of the relocated Leavenworth and Pike's Peak Express. The location was determined by the necessity of establishing a new trail junction where the new northwestward connection to the North Platte River, Fort Laramie, and California split off from the new road down the South Platte to Denver. The route to Fort Laramie followed Lodgepole Creek and the future Union Pacific Railroad route to a point three miles east of Sidney, thence generally north past Mud Springs to Court House Rock.

Old Julesburg was sacked and destroyed by Sioux and Cheyenne Indians in February, 1865, and the populace retreated to nearby Fort Rankin, which later became Fort Sedgwick. A random sampling of visitors to Old Julesburg will serve:

> In its palmiest days, during overland and staging and freighting, old Julesburg had, all told, not to exceed a dozen buildings, including

station, telegraph office, store, blacksmith shop, warehouse, stable and a billiard saloon. At the latter place there was dispensed at all hours of the day and night the vilest of liquor at "two bits" a glass. . . . Being a sort of rendezvous for gamblers, for some time it was regarded as the toughest town between the Missouri River and the mountains.—ROOT and CONNELLEY, 1863

See the ruins of the first Julesburg, from the savage raid of February. The new Julesburg, hardly two months old, is a mile farther on, and embraces three or four lone adobes and a cemetery, large for so young and small a town.—FRANK YOUNG, 1865

At Fort Sedgwick this grand territorial highway branches. . . . Fort Sedgwick is the most important of the military posts on this route. . . . It is now a four company post, garrisoned by two companies of 5th U.S. Volunteers, one company of 18th Regulars, and one company 2nd U.S. Cavalry, all under Captain Neill. . . . It is the best ordered and disciplined fort we have seen since leaving Leavenworth. The position is commanding, being high, and yet very near the river.— JAMES MELINE, 1866

IX

Ash Hollow, Royal Road To the North Platte

ASH HOLLOW IS A PICTURESQUE wooded canyon in Garden County, Nebraska, three miles southeast of Lewellen. It is traversed south to north by U.S. Highway 26, which dives off the high tableland between the forks of the Platte River and plunges boldly down the canyon bottom to its debouchement in the valley of the North Platte. While it is in the Hollow for about three miles, the highway coincides with the Great Platte River Road, but it parts company with it at each end. Modern highway engineering, ironing rugged topography into gentle declines and curves, makes the automobile descent into the Hollow seem painless. Covered wagon emigrants entered Ash Hollow without benefit of engineering, taking nature as they found it, and so were compelled to take different approaches, made hair-raising and memorable by the most rugged terrain they had yet encountered. And while the highway now blithely leaps across the North Platte on a concrete bridge (and then follows the north bank via the old Council Bluffs Road), the historic trail to Oregon and California made an abrupt left-hand turn at the mouth of the Hollow and headed west up the south bank.

Statistically, by comparison with the Grand Canyon of Arizona, for example, Ash Hollow isn't much. Its measurements would be approximately four miles in total length, from about 1,000 feet wide between its gateway cliffs near the North Platte up to 2,000 feet rim to rim, and with an average depth of some 250 feet. But, as geography goes in Nebraska, Ash Hollow is in a class by itself.

It is the widest and deepest of draws or canyons converging on the Platte or any branch thereof. In a country otherwise devoid of noteworthy features, Ash Hollow, with its high white cliffs, flower beds, oasis-like patches of trees and shrubbery, and beneficent clear springs, is an outright marvel.

Historically, Ash Hollow was a notable milestone of the California Road. Here at long last was an abundant supply of firewood, and the most copious supply of pure water this side of the Missouri River. Here were often found peaceful encampments of Sioux Indians, noble-looking and colorful savages who did not belie the romantic notions of the easterners. Here also was a wealth of sinister campfire legend, inspired by many actual incidents of ambush and violence within the canyon walls; and, after 1855, the place became famous for the nearby clash between Gen. Harney and Chief Little Thunder, loosely called the Battle of Ash Hollow. Here the two principal trails from the South Platte joined, and through here funneled the great majority of Gold Rush emigrants. Finally, this site was the introduction to a section of the California Road that was notable for its scenic attractions—the famous series of North Platte landmarks from Castle Rock (seven miles west of Ash Hollow) to Court House Rock to Scott's Bluffs. This was indeed the royal road to the North Platte.

Ash Hollow is the name which predominates in the emigrant journals, but the following variants have been noted: Ash Halloe, Ash Hallows, Ashes Hollow, Ash-hallow, Ash holler, Cash Hollow, Quaking Asp Hollow, and Ash Bottom. A series of springs welling up in the sandy bottom created a sometime rivulet called Ash Creek in the emigrant guides. The other name which crops up here is Windlass Hill, the steep and terrifying declivity west of U.S. 26 at the head of the Hollow which was used by most emigrants who came across the Upper Ford of the South Platte near Brule. *The name Windlass Hill, however, is not to be found in emigrant journals or guides*; it seems to be a bit of folklore superimposed in later years. The fact is that during emigrant days the famous hill did not have any particular name; it was usually just "the steep hill," or "the perpendicular hill." But for convenience of discussion in this book, the later traditional name, Windlass Hill, will be used.

There is an Ash Hollow Hill referred to occasionally in journals, but it would be a mistake to interpret this as a synonym for

Windlass Hill. Ash Hollow Hill is but another name for California Hill, the rise to the tableland which emigrants had to negotiate just after crossing the Upper Ford of the South Platte. Like California Crossing and Ash Hollow Crossing, both terms synonomous with the early Upper Ford of the South Platte, Ash Hollow Hill referred to a general destination and not to the thing itself.

The two primary historical approaches to Ash Hollow were discussed in the previous chapter; their exact configuration with the topography of the Hollow is shown on the accompanying map. Briefly, however, the majority of emigrants entered at the Upper Ford and moved directly across the barren plateau to Windlass Hill and its roller-coaster descent into the southwest corner of the Hollow. A minority, having crossed the South Platte just above the forks, and then having followed the south side of the North Platte (approximately along present Lake McConaughy), entered the Hollow from the east and about a mile above its mouth. The latter descent, following an arduous climb up from Cedar Grove, was not nearly as horrendous as Windlass Hill. Some travelers approaching the North Platte ignored Ash Hollow and both entrances thereto, reaching the North Platte by other not clearly defined routes some distance west of the Hollow.

Topography aside, the great emigration of over a century ago left its imprint in two highly dramatic ways. Approaching the crest of Windlass Hill and then spilling abruptly down its face are the deep, trough-like remains of the California Road, some of the most spectacular evidence of heavy wagon traffic to be found along its 2,000-mile length. Only the passage of a mighty army could account for these great scars, which march to the brink of this awesome slope and then cascade over it. There is other trail evidence, of course, up from Cedar Grove and elsewhere, but Windlass Hill is the primary place to locate historic ruts.

Then there are the graves. There is documentary evidence of burials in the immediate vicinity of Ash Hollow, but only a pitifully few marked graves survive. The most noted of these, because of its reverent memorial treatment, is that of Rachel Pattison, who died June 19, 1849. Rachel's grave was the beginning of the Ash Hollow cemetery, developed by later settlers. It is on the west side of the canyon's mouth.

Emigrant graves, reminders of the ephemeral nature of human affairs, turn thoughts to the aborigines who found food and shelter in Ash Hollow over countless centuries. High on the eastern bluff, overlooking the North Platte, is a prehistoric shelter called Ash Hollow Cave, a place of impressive antiquity, with charred remains which date to around 8,000 B.C., so there was human habitation in Ash Hollow ages before the Gold Rush. However, California Trail travelers didn't know of this phenomenon. Who was the first white man known definitely to have seen and given written testimony of Ash Hollow? Various legends mention Verendrye, Villasur, the Mallet brothers, or Charlevoix, but actually the first was an American of Scottish ancestry, Robert Stuart, whom P. A. Rollins credits with no less than the "Discovery of the Oregon Trail," that is to say, the Great Platte River Road in reverse, from South Pass to the Missouri River.

In 1812 Stuart and six companions were exploring their way east from Fort Astoria at the mouth of Columbia River to the settlements. Having been relieved of horses and guns by Indians, these seven were compelled to spend the winter of 1812–1813 in a makeshift camp near present Torrington, Wyoming. Resuming their journey in early spring, on March 26 Stuart remarked on the crossing of "a creek thirty yards wide," identified as Blue Creek (scene of the Harney affair of 1855). His journal continues: "3 miles lower, another Branch joined the main stream from the south, it is thickly wooded a short distance from its mouth, but with what kinds we could not well distinguish. . . . For a considerable distance above but more particularly below its junction the River Bluffs are very near and sometimes constitute its banks. They are composed principally of a blue limestone and possess many cedars on which account we call the last mentioned Branch, Cedar Creek.—saw sixty Wild Horses." Thus Ash Hollow, and Ash Creek by another name, first appear in literature.

In the 1820s and 1830s trappers and trading caravans associated with William Ashley, the Smith-Jackson-Sublette partnership, and the American Fur Company variously used both sides of the Platte route. Since the early guides of the emigrant trains were these same trappers or mountain men, the conclusion seems inescapable that the road through Ash Hollow, with variant approaches, was blazed by them. Ashley's men hauled a small cannon all the way from St. Louis to the Great Salt Lake rendezvous in 1827, and the wheels of this gun carriage were, in all likelihood, the first ever to make the tortuous descent into Ash Hollow. In 1832, according to Washington Irving, Capt. Bonneville and his trading expedition followed the North Fork with their wagons (the first to reach the Continental Divide), apparently making the Cedar Grove entrance. Although Ash Hollow is not plainly identified, it seems the likely locale of "the wild and solitary pass" where they were "startled by the trail of four or five pedestrians, whom they supposed to be spies from some predatory camp of either Arickara or Crow Indians. This obliged them to redouble their vigilance at night."

Most of the Oregon-bound missionary groups of the 1834–1839 period followed the north bank from the Council Bluffs area. Jason Lee, with Nathaniel Wyeth's trading expedition of 1834, probably entered the Hollow; but Parker, Whitman, and Spalding, and the celebrated wives of the latter two, were with American Fur Company brigades north of the Platte. In 1837 William Gray of the Whitman mission, returning from Oregon, was attacked by Sioux in the Ash Hollow neighborhood. It is impossible to sort out the facts from Gray's obviously exaggerated account, so we must take it with a large grain of salt. His party consisted of himself, two other white men, one Snake Indian, one Iroquois (old Ignace of the Hudson's Bay Company), and three young Flatheads who were going to the United States

> to urge their claims for teachers to come among them. The party reached Ash Hollow, where they were attacked by about three hundred Sioux warriers, and, after fighting for three hours, killed some fifteen of them, when the Sioux, by means of a French trader among them, obtained a parley with Gray. . . . While the Frenchman was in conversation with Gray, the treacherous Sioux made a rush upon the . . . Indians belonging to the party, and killed them. . . . Gray had two horses killed under him and two balls passed through his hat, both inflicting slight wounds. . . . [At the parley] the party were feasted, and smoked the pipe of peace over the dead body of the chief's son; next day they were allowed to proceed with nine of their horses.

In 1838 Myra Eells and Mary Walker, missionary wives, entered the Hollow, probably the first white women to do so; but the record of their visit is mute except for a fleeting phrase in Mary's journal: "Scenery peculiar. Cedar wood for fuel."

In 1839, on the eve of the covered wagon migration to Oregon, there is evidence that the Ash Hollow route was in use but that the trail to the river had not yet been clearly defined. The German traveler Wislizenus, in the company of fur traders, reports that his party "camped near Ash Creek, which empties into the North Fork, but it was noon before we could find a passage for our carts." The missionary Asahel Munger writes, "Started across the prairies for the North Fork of the Platte, camped within 3 or 4 miles of it near the head of Ash Creek—had a heavy storm. Moved on toward the river but for want of a good place to descend the hill, or bluff, we travelled most of the forenoon on the high lands." Thus, it appears Munger failed to descend at all in the vicinity of Ash Hollow but pioneered an unknown route to the west.

The first emigrant train to reach the Hollow, the Bidwell-Bartleson party of 1841, entered it in a pall of gloom from a mournful accident that occurred on the morning of that same day, June 13. Writes Bidwell, "A young man by the name of Stockwell, while in the act of taking a gun out of the wagon, drew up the muzzle toward him in such a manner that it went off and shot him in the heart. He lived about an hour and died in the full possession of his senses. . . . He was buried in the most decent manner our circumstances admitted of after which a funeral service was preached by Mr. Williams. In the afternoon we passed on about 5 miles, making an inland circuit over the hills which approached boldly from the river and compelled us to leave its banks [at Cedar Grove]. We however reached it again by descending the dry channel of Ash Creek."

In June, 1843, Matthew Field, with the hunting expedition of William Sublette and Sir William Stewart, became ecstatic at the qualities of Ash Hollow spring: "No draught of ruby nectar, quaffed in the height of bacchanalian festivity, ever communicated one half the exhilaration of mind and soul that we obtained that evening."

In July, 1843, Charles Preuss, topographer for the first Fremont expedition, led a detail up the North Fork. In this vicinity he met "a large party of traders, and trappers, conducted by Mr. Bridger, a man well known in the history of the country," who warned against Sioux war parties. Preuss found the country wretchedly dry; in early September, however, when the entire expedition under Fremont returned east down the river at this point, late summer rains had made the valley "glorious with the autumnal splendor of innumerable flowers in full and brilliant bloom." It was not necessary to make the usual trip up the Hollow to circumvent the river bluffs for, writes Fremont,

The water in the Platte was extremely low; in many places the large expanse of sands, with some occasional stunted trees on the banks, gave it the air of the seacoast; the bed of the river being merely a succession of sand-bars, among which the channel was divided into rivulets a few inches deep. We crossed and recrossed with our carts repeatedly and at our pleasure; and whenever an obstruction barred our way, in the shape of precipitous bluffs that came down upon the river, we turned directly into it, and made our way along the sandy bed, with no greater inconvenience than the frequent quicksands, which greatly fatigued our animals.

Later that same month the Sublette-Stewart hunting party, returning from the Rockies, encamped for several days here, seeking shelter from drenching rains. W. C. Kennerly found the place abounding in cherries, black currants, and grapes, but "buffaloe scarce."

In October, 1843, Rufus Sage, in the company of fur traders bound for Fort Laramie, likewise camped at the mouth of Ash Creek. "As a whole," he writes, "the valley presents to the eye a pretty flower-garden, walled in by huge piles of argillaceous rock, and watered by murmuring streamlets whose banks are ornamented with shade trees and shrubbery." In contrast with this pastoral image, he notes, Ash Hollow was the scene of a fierce and bloody battle eight years before between those mortal enemies, the Pawnee and the Sioux, in the winter of 1835. The Pawnee, according to Sage, came out on the short end of this engagement, with sixty dead. "This disaster so completely disheartened the Pawnees, they immediately abandoned their station and moved down the river some four hundred miles—nor have they again ventured so high up, unless in strong war parties." Sage doubtless got his story from one of his fur trading companions but, he asserts, "The evidences of this cruel death-harvest were yet scattered over the prairie, whose bones and skulls looked sad, indeed. One of the latter was noticed near camp, with a huge wasp's nest occupying the vacuum once filled by the subtle organs of intellect."

Ash Hollow is not recorded in any writing about the Great Migration of 1843, and it may be supposed that it was bypassed in that year. The suspicion is strengthened by the report of emigrant John Minto of 1844: "As we took the decline toward the North Platte we passed trunks and big limbs of cedar trees, which would seem to have been buried as there was no green timber in sight. We chopped some of this and laid it into the wagons. . . . We struck the North Platte about twelve miles west of Ash Hollow, according to our guide, Black Harris."

In 1845, according to Carleton, writing in camp some miles west of the Hollow, there were then "two or three companies of emigrants still ahead of us, who . . . descended to this valley by a pass several miles above Ash Hollow, and in the afternoon we fell into their trace."

In 1846 Francis Parkman and party likewise detoured onto an unknown route to the west: "Passing behind the sandy ravines called 'Ash Hollow' we stopped for a short nooning at the side of a pool of rainwater; but soon resumed our journey, and some hours before sunset descended the ravines and gorges opening downward upon the Platte west of Ash Hollow." The entry in his original journal reads, "In the afternoon [we] descended from the sand hills by an abominable sandy trail to the North Fork."

Exploration of the terrain involved fails to disclose with any certainty the route (or routes) followed by Munger, Minto, Parkman, or the advance emigrant companies of 1845. Ash Hollow had its complications, but there was certainly no other route which could have made the valley descent much easier; and any other descent would miss the famous springs.

Among Dragoon officers who marched westward with Col. Kearny in 1845 were two whose journals are replete with romantic imagery. Ash Hollow summoned forth their pens, and Capt. Philip St. George Cooke wrote with Byronesque fervor of the "sun that rose with dazzling beauty upon the romantic glen" with its "crystal streamlet." But in this case the palm goes to Lt. J. Henry Carleton, whose journal also reflects the puzzlement which still attended the location of the proper Ash Hollow descent:

> After keeping our course for seventeen miles our progress became suddenly arrested. We all at once came to the edge of the high prairie, and from thence down to the valley of the North Fork, a distance of three miles, nothing but a chaotic mass of rocks, hills, precipices, and chasms could be seen; and through which it seemed as if it were impossible ever to proceed. We here found another large company of emigrants. They were halted and had been searching for a pass for sometime, but without success. We then turned off to the left, and having kept along for more than a mile just at the head of the deep gorges by which this "mauvaise terre" first begins, we also came to a

halt, and Mr. Fitzpatrick started off down one of them to see if he could not find a way by which we could descend to the river. In an hour or so he reported that we were then at the head of Ash Hollow— a celebrated defile with which he was well acquainted—and through which, with but little trouble, it was practicable to take the command. We were immediately put in motion again, and commenced following our guide through a perfect labyrinth of ravines. . . .

After proceeding in this way for a mile, and descending all the time —we came to a steep declivity, down which we were obliged to lower each wagon separately with ropes. By the time this was accomplished the sun was nearly set. . . .

We now found ourselves at the bottom of a gloomy defile but a few rods in breadth, and walled in by hills that rose perpendicularly hundreds of feet above us. It was so crooked and so abrupt in its turnings that as we proceeded along it was sometimes quite impossible to tell in what way we were ever to get out of it. . . . Through this defile there lay a wide, dry, and sandy bed of a wet-weather stream. Here and there, strewn along it, we passed a great many skeletons of buffaloes. . . . One more mile and we came to a beautiful grove of ash, and soon after a cool stream of water gushed out from the sand—the first drop we had seen since morning. . . . We had been so many days without seeing any trees that the reader can hardly imagine how grateful to us was the sight of those which we here so unexpectedly found. And the limpid water that flowed over the sand seemed to taste sweeter than any we had ever drank before.

The company of emigrants we left upon the high prairie had followed on after us. But their delay was so great in letting their wagons down the steep descent, that it was ten o'clock at night before they reached our first encampment. . . .

Ash Hollow has been the scene of many fights between the Pawnees and Sioux. In the winter time, several families of the latter tribe generally encamp in it. The men employ their time in killing buffaloes, and the women in dressing the skins into robes. We saw the remains of some of their temporary winter lodges which has been built of stick and straw—and also the scaffolds where they had hung their meat to dry. A new red blanket, cut by innumerable gashes, was found hanging up near this deserted village. Why it had been left there we could not tell; but afterwards ascertained that it is a custom with the Sioux whenever there comes up a heavy thunderstorm, to give as an offering the most valuable garment they may have, in order to appease the wrath of the Great Spirit.

This morning the immense tracks of a grizzly bear were discovered in the sand of Ash Creek. They were fresh, and some hopes were entertained that the animal might be discovered before we started—but he had probably seen us and secreted himself in the neighboring ravines. . . .

The traveller in coming down the North Fork would have no difficulty in finding Ash Hollow, as its entrance from the valley is over a half a mile wide—and has upon each side a high buttress of rock which resembles the ruins of some old fort. Between them is a grove, all in plain sight from the river—the only one that is seen for fifty or sixty miles, either above or below.

Jesse Harritt was among the emigrants mentioned above by Carleton, and Harritt's report is without embroidery: "Entered Ash Hollow, down which we travel five miles between large, projecting bluffs towering to a height of 200 feet, the summits which showed an aspect of chalk partly grown over with cedar and laurel, while the valley in places was thickly strewn with ash." In contrast, Joel Palmer, a more illustrious Oregon emigrant this season (1845), used the Cedar Grove entrance: "Our camp, last night, was in a cedar and ash grove, with a high frowning bluff overhanging us; but a wide bottom, with fine grass around us, and near at hand an excellent spring. Today five miles over the ridge brought us to Ash Hollow. Here the trail, which follows the east side of the South Fork of Platte, from where we crossed it, connects with this trail." The Palmer party is among the first of definite record to use the Lower Ford near the forks and the Lake McConaughy route to Ash Hollow.

In 1846 the first presage of civilization—a dwelling—appeared on this primitive scene. On June 13 Virgil K. Pringle, arriving at the mouth of Ash Creek, discovered "currants and chokecherries plenty, and a fine spring . . . and a cabin called Ash Grove Hotel. Inside at the bar we found the cards of all the companies that had preceded us, which was quite a treat." George McKinstry calls it "Ash Hollow Hotel . . . put up by some mackinaw boat men last winter as they were caught by the ice." The account of the structure is most clearly set forth by Edwin Bryant:

> We found near the mouth of "Ash Hollow" a small log cabin which had been erected last winter by some trappers, returning to the settlements who, on account of the snows, had been compelled to remain here until spring. This rude structure has, by the emigrants, been turned into a sort of general post-office. Numerous advertisements in manuscript are posted on its walls outside, descriptive of lost cattle,

horses, etc. etc., and inside, in a recess, there was a large number of letters deposited, addressed to persons on almost every quarter of this globe, with requests, that those who passed would convey them to the nearest post-office in the States. The place had something of the air of a crossroads settlement; and we lingered around it some time, reading the advertisements and overlooking the letters.

On May 28 of the year 1847, Isaac Pettijohn and company pulled up at the brink of Windlass Hill at midnight after a strenuous day of chasing stray cattle. They wisely decided to wait until daylight to make the descent. Even so, when they got to the bottom, nerves finally snapped, and the neat organization ratified at Independence, Missouri, simply disintegrated: "Our company divided into three divisions yesterday. The division caused some hard feelings."

But 1847, not a banner year for emigrants on the Oregon or California side of the river, was notable for the passage of the Mormon Pioneers up the north bank; and, as William Clayton makes clear, they did not fail to pay homage to the famous ravine:

On the opposite side of the river, the bluffs project near its banks. They are rocky and almost perpendicular, beautified for miles by groves of cedar. Opposite to where we are halted, we can see a ravine running up the blufls and at the foot, a flat bottom of fifteen acres. At the farther side of this bottom is a grove of trees not yet in leaf. Brother Brown thinks they are ash and that the place is what is called Ash Hollow and on Fremont's map, Ash Creek. We all felt anxious to ascertain the fact whether this is Ash Hollow or not, for if it is, the Oregon Trail strikes the river at this place, and if it can be ascertained that such is the fact, we then have a better privilege of testing Fremont's distances to Laramie. We have already discovered that his map is not altogether correct in several respects. . . . I suggested the propriety of some persons going over in the boat and Brother John Brown suggested it to President Young. The boat was soon hauled by the brethern to the river, and Orson Pratt, Amasa Lyman, Luke Johnson and John Brown started to row over, but the current was so exceedingly strong the oars had no effect. John Brown then jumped into the river which was about two and a half feet deep and dragged the boat over, the others assisting with oars. After some hard labor they arrived on the opposite shore and went to the hollow. They soon found the Oregon Trail and ascertained that this is Ash Hollow, Brother Brown having traveled on that road to near Laramie last season with the Mississippi company and knew the place perfectly well.

Orson Pratt, one of the 1847 oarsmen, mentions an 1846 grave and describes another notable landmark which was on the north bank and a short distance downstream from Ash Hollow—"Lone Tree":

> May 20 . . . This afternoon we travelled 7 ¾ miles and halted for noon directly opposite the place where the Oregon road strikes the North Fork. Four of us landed our boat and crossed over. . . . We found the grave of one of the Oregon emigrants buried last summer near the foot of the bluffs. . . . We soon recrossed the river which is here about ⅓ mile wide. . . . A short distance below our noon halt we passed a lonely cedar tree upon the north bank of the river, in the branches of which were deposited the remains of an Indian child. The grave, if it may be called such, was as solitary as the tree.

Only one noteworthy incident occurred in the Hollow in 1848, but it is memorable on two counts. It was in the dead of winter that ex-trapper Joseph L. Meek and Joseph Henry Brown, among others, headed east on a historic mission, to secure government aid in subduing the rebellious Cayuse Indians who had massacred Marcus and Narcissa Whitman. According to Brown, this mission had been warned by "old Pappelion" at Fort Laramie to travel only at night because of lurking Indians. And it was at night, therefore, that this group reached the Hollow. Here, to their surprise, they found the warm glow of a fireplace at "Rubedue's Fort, a trading post that was kept by a Frenchman by the name of LeBeau. We here traded for sugar, coffee and buffalo meat. Rested one day and started, reaching Little Platte [South Platte] next day." From this account we can only surmise that the Robidoux clan (whose headquarters next year would be at Scott's Bluffs) had meanwhile appropriated the log cabin of mysterious origin and were trading with the Indians for furs. But this operation would not survive the winter; at least this fly-by-night trading post is not mentioned by any of the journal-keeping Forty-Niners.

In 1849 the Ash Hollow theme changed from remote pastoral charm to mob scenes and frenzied excitement. The impact of the Forty-Niners on this wilderness Garden of Eden was predictable. There were heavy inroads on the wealth of grass and timber. But even greater was the impact of Ash Hollow on the Forty-Niners.

Joseph Ware apparently read Francis Parkman's *Oregon Trail*, and so was influenced to advise readers of his *Emigrant's Guide* as follows: "By descending the bluff 5 miles above Ash Hollow you avoid much heavy sand. The descent is good except in one place." Fortunately, few people paid any attention to Ware, and by 1849 there were two standard approaches: the Middle or Upper fords of the South Fork and Windlass Hill, or the Lower Ford and Cedar Grove, both going directly into Ash Hollow. An analysis of some sixty Forty-Niner journals shows eighteen arriving by way of Cedar Grove; so it may be inferred that those using Windlass Hill out-numbered others at a ratio of three to one.

Travelers entering through Cedar Grove were quite conscious of Ash Hollow's role as a junction point. Here, scribbled Dr. Cald-well, "the roads from the lower and upper crossings come together." Sheldon Young observed "the Upper Ford road coming in." And Vincent Geiger says he "struck Ash Hollow, where the main trail meets us."

The apprehension of those who followed "the main trail" and so had the experience of coming into Ash Hollow the hard way is reflected in the journals of many Forty-Niners. On May 21 one of the earliest arrivals, David Cosad, "travelled 18 miles over hills and sand and plains and went down an almost perpendicular bluff, and came to the North Fork." Similarly, on May 18 Breyfogle noted: "As we neared Ash Hollow the ground became quite broken and very wild. . . . Our road lay along a narrow ridge and in entering the Hollow we descended all most perpendicular Hill, and entered a beautiful Vale covered with fine grass and flowers of nearly every variety, . . . the sides lined with fine ash trees from which it takes its name." On May 20 Gelwicks calls it "a deep, dangerous, sandy, but wild and romantic pass." After reaching the foot of the hill he looked back: "It seemed perfectly impossible for wagons to come down it."

Since wagons of that era were not equipped with brakes, unless the crudest sort, one wonders what methods were employed to prevent the entire California migration from simply falling down-hill in a wild jumble of splintered wheels and broken bones—animal and human. Some accidents have been recorded, but no fatalities; it is apparent that some emigrants improvised braking devices; others trusted to Providence. Among the latter was the company of Bennett C. Clark: "The road was steeper than any we ever yet encountered. . . . Most of the wagons had descended the first step when Jno. Corum's team ran away & caused two other teams to do the same. One mule had a leg broken in the scrape & the tongue of one wagon was broken."

Maj. Cross, leading a supply train of the U.S. Army toward Fort Laramie, reported the simplest procedure for entering Ash Hollow: "We were compelled to let the wagons down into it with ropes." Pvt. Gibbs of the same expedition noted: "Gravel trails have been opened down this place, and ox-teams pass without much risk, but mule-teams require to be eased down with a rope." William Kelly described his experience with mules:

> As we advanced the ridge gradually rounded, leading to such a long and abrupt descent that we debated the propriety of detaching the bodies of the waggons from the wheels, and sliding them down; but as the driver of the lead one volunteered to essay a trial with rough double-locking and holding back with ropes, we tried the experiment, taking out all but the wheel-spans, which were left in merely to guide, and succeeded admirably until the last, in the descent of which the frayed rope parted, and the waggon slid, or more properly speaking, fell on top of the mules, upsetting and killing the one on the off-side and breaking the collar-bone of the teamster. . . the bows were all smashed, and the contents sent hopping down the steep [hill].

Lewis B. Dougherty, transporting supplies to the Fort Laramie post sutler, tells of another method:

> We reach the brink of a hill near one-third of a mile high which we have to descend to reach the level of the hollow. We detach all the oxen from the wagon except the wheel yoke, lock the two hind wheels with the lock chain attached to the body of the wagon, and wrap a log chain around the tire so it will cut into the ground. . . . Frequently the other five yokes of oxen are hitched with their heads to the wagon behind. They being unaccustomed to this treatment, pull back and help to slow down the wagon.
>
> Everything in the front of the wagons must be tied securely, or out comes the goods when the descent is begun. I cannot say at what angle we descend but it is so great that some go as far as to say "the road hangs a little past the perpendicular!" It must be seen for one to fully understand how steep is the hill.

Since almost everyone was going west, and almost nobody was going east, little thought has been given to methods of taking a wagon *up* Windlass Hill. Dougherty, who shuttled back and forth many times between Fort Laramie and the settlements, throws some light on that, too. "In ascending," he reports, "a zigzag route is taken which is unsafe with loads."

Just how does the "windlass" idea fit into this picture? No fixed contraption for lowering wagons is mentioned in any of several hundred researched emigrant journals during the period of our concern, 1830–1866. If there ever was a windlass, it had to be sometime after 1866—not during the migrations to Oregon and California but during the days of Nebraska cattlemen and home-steaders. Citing the hearsay testimony of old-timers, Mari Sandoz has described how an ingenious wagon boss, using ropes, chains, and an ash tree trunk, improvised a drum windlass to lower his wagons and that this device was used by freighters for several years. It is significant that she does not associate this legendary affair with the covered wagon emigrants.

Once down in the Hollow, emigrants found the road draggy, even though downhill to the river. Witness Charles Gray: "A road bad all day, sandy and heavy, particularly through a deep gorge in the bluff for two or three miles."

The terrors of the descent and the annoyances of sandy roads were soon forgotten in admiration of the bird's-eye view from Windlass Hill. Even while lowering his outfit gingerly down the infamous slope, Bennett Clark was able to appreciate the scenery of the heights, "the green hills for miles around presenting a picture varied in height and shade and rarely exceeded in beauty." On a fine June day, if one's mind was not too preoccupied with the mechanics of getting downhill, the prospect could be stunning. One emigrant considered it "the most sublime sight that I ever beheld since leaving the States." Stansbury exclaimed,

> A most magnificent view saluted the eye. Before and below us was the North Fork of the Nebraska river winding its way through broken hills and meadows, behind us the undulating prairie. On our right the gradual convergence of the two valleys, while immediately at our feet, the heads of Ash Creek, which fell off suddenly into deep precipitous chasms, on either side leaving only a high narrow ridge, or backbone which gradually descended, until, toward the western termination, it fell off suddenly into the bottom of the creek. Here we were obliged from the steepness of the road, to let the wagons down by ropes, *but the labors of a dozen men for a few days would make the descent easy and safe.*

Breyfogle found "a beautiful vale covered with fine grass and flowers of nearly every variety, the sides lined with fine ash trees from which it takes its name." E. B. Farnham considered this "the best looking place that we have seen for some time   it is cool shady looking place fragrant with different kinds of flowers of which roses and jasmine are the principel Grapes vines and currant bushes are plenteous." In his humble way Zirkle D. Robinson wrote: "The bluffs is very hansom here. the rocks on the hills is a splended sean."

William Kelly was more articulate than most but also given to overstatement for the benefit of his planned audience. After the jarring descent of the Hill he writes:

> Two more moderate descents brought us into a lovely wooded dell, so watered and sheltered that vegetation of every description appeared as if stimulated by a hot-house. The modest wild rose, forgetting its coyness in the leafy arbours, opened out its velvet bosom, adding its fragrant bouquet to that of the various scented flowers and shrubs that formed the underwood of the majestic ash-trees. . . . Cool streams, filtered through the adjoining hills, prattled about, until they merged their murmurs in a translucent pond, reposing in the centre of a verdant meadow . . . the bespangled carpet of which looked like the congenial area for the games and gambols of . . . fairyland.

But Kelly was not content simply to describe the scenery. There had to be a crashing climax:

> A gathering whirlwind . . . a small black cloud, that did not look bigger than a cannon-ball, came rushing and expanding through the sky with preternatural velocity. . . . The roar of the maddened elements burst upon us with appalling violence, projecting hail and irregular blocks of ice . . . that plumped through the exposed wagon covers as if they were wet paper, and made the animals wince and jump. . . . Several huge trees were uprooted near where we first halted, and limbs and branches whirled aloft like so many wisps.

Other Forty-Niners, with no eye whatever on posterity, confided their enthusiasm for Ash Hollow to their diaries. Sheldon Young called it "a great display of natural architecture"; Eastin, "a scene of exceeding beauty." Dr. T. described "Ash bottom" as a romantic place, surrounded by "mountains," alive with gooseberry and currant bushes, cherry trees, and every variety of wildflower, "a place where almost every emigrant rests a day or two."

Although gold was uppermost in their minds, few Forty-Niners gave any thought to the geology of Ash Hollow. One writer referred correctly to bluffs of limestone. Eastin speculated: "The stone here appears to have some sulphate of lime mixed in it, and the hills have a chalky appearance." Decker mentioned the volcano theory to account for what he calls "a dismal place." Gelwicks likewise supposed: "A violent irruption, must have rent the earth asunder, shattering the immense rocks into a thousand fragments, and left a dreary and desolate void here."

Gelwicks, inhaling "the delicious odor of wild cherry," noted that the Hollow derived its name from "a cluster of Ash Trees, stunted and gnarled, that encircled it," while Decker inventoried stunted ash, wild cherry, peas, grapes, and gooseberries. Dr. T. noted: "The ash trees are low not more than fifteen feet high and eighteen inches to three feet in diameter." Another writer refers to seven large cedar trees in the bottom as a conspicuous feature of the 1849 scene. David Dewolf encouraged stocking up on firewood and lumber for spare wagon parts, "as there will be no more wood for 75 miles." This prediction, frequently echoed, was substantially true, in the sense that the nearest place where there was timber in any abundance along the trail was at Scott's Bluffs. More accurately, however, trees and shrubs were available in some degree in ravines, on ridgetops, and in the river islands for anyone who had the time or inclination to scrounge for them.

Among Forty-Niners who followed the river road to the historic ravine was John Prichet, who writes: "We leave the river and pass up a very steep hill and along the side of a ravine, until we pass around the bluff that comes to the river and into Ash Hollow. . . . This is some of the most wild, rocky, rugged and barren scenery on this two or three miles that I have yet seen. It reminds me very much of Dr. Durham's description of some of the barren places in the Holy Land." Israel Hale ventures to suggest: "I think if they had named this place the Valley of Roses it would have been a more appropriate, for there were fifty rose bushes to one ash tree. . . . "We also passed a fine spring that boiled up in the middle of the valley and ran quite a distance before it sunk into the sand."

Kirkpatrick was one of the few Argonauts who was unable to appreciate the aesthetic qualities of Ash Hollow: "We came into Ash Hollow which is no doubt pretty but today we could hardly see on account of clouds of dust and a strong wind." Amos Steck just wasn't impressed: "June 9   Reached the celebrated Ash Hollow in the afternoon; it was nothing else than a bower very common in Pennsylvania." However, he concedes, "What I imagine has given celebrity to it is a most excellent spring about midway down, and it is really refreshing to drink of its pearly waters."

Despite spectacular entrances and the famous ash grove, the principal feature of the Hollow was its water supply. As we have seen, Ash Creek was not a true creek but a series of springs, culminating in an oasis near the mouth of the canyon. Searls explained that "a stream runs through its whole length at high water, but is now lost in the sand." Capt. Stansbury found: "The bed of the stream is entirely dry, but towards the mouth several springs of delightfully cold and refreshing water are found, altogether the best that has been met with since leaving the banks of the Missouri River." This tribute was seconded by Alexander Ramsay: "This was the first good wood and water for 400 miles back."

Most of the pilgrims, weary of drinking gritty and turbid water skimmed from the Platte, were simply grateful for the miracle of abundant pure water. Charles Tinker reported "a furstrate spring of cold water here, the only spring we have seen for 60 miles." Charles Parke was "disappointed at seeing so little timber" in Ash Hollow, but he admitted, "My disappointment was counterbalanced by the charming springs of pure cool sparkling water that gushed from the hillside." Only one Forty-Niner is recorded as finding fault with the celebrated spring. Jagger wrote: "Yesterday a man died suddenly after drinking of the water of the spring here and today several are complaining that it has made them very sick. I drank of it but felt no bad effects, but the general impression is that it is a poisonous fountain." There is nothing else in the record to support this statement. Tired and overheated emigrants imbibing too freely might readily incur the penalty of stomach cramps.

An added attraction at Ash Hollow during the migration of 1849 was an encampment of Sioux Indians, apparently the families and assorted relatives of French traders identified by Kirkpatrick as "two Frenchmen from St. Charles." The mobile village of seven lodges and some fifty Indians (Kirkpatrick's count) was at the mouth of the canyon, on the North Platte benchland. They are first noted in several journals among emigrants arriving on June 4, among them Charles Gray: "Passed an encampment of Sioux Indians. . . .

They were Frenchmen with Sioux wives, and some of their children were fair as our home productions. Several of our men bought of them leggings and moccasons made of deer and antelope skins. These Indians didn't look very Indian like." The Newark Company laid in a stock of "deerskin breeches," presumably as souvenirs rather than wearing apparel, since these Indian pants had no seats! Parke describes their lodges "of dressed buffalo skins stretched over about 20 poles and in the shape of an umbrella, but more point over the top. The fire is made in the center and a hole on the top fixed on two poles that they can move as occasion may require to keep the wind from blowing the smoke down the chimney. They are much to be preferred to our tents was it not for their weight." Delano observed that their lodges, of conical form, were well calculated to resist the action of the weather. Of the inhabitants he writes,

> Both men and women were better formed than any Indians I had ever seen. The men were tall, and graceful in their movements, and some of the squaws were quite pretty, and dressed in tanned buffalo skins, highly ornamented with beads, while many of the men wore barely a blanket around their waists, and one or two of them were quite naked. On our approach, one of the Indians, who was armed with an old sword, made us some kind of a speech, and invited us into his lodge, where he motioned us to be seated. . . . Almost the first request made to us was for whiskey, for which I verily believe they would have sold their children—showing conclusively that temperance societies were not yet well organized on the Platte. Of course we had no fire-water for them, and we left them lamentably sober, and encamped about a mile above them, where several came out to beg bread, whiskey and shirts.

That same evening Joseph Merrill visited the "wigwams covered with deerskin" and witnessed some kind of an altercation: "I entered the tent of the trader conversing with him for some time, when in came a Big John Indian quite drunk. He soon took offense at Mr. Frenchman who put him out; the next thing I knew, in came John's messenger through the side of the tent in the form of an arrow." The next day, according to Joseph Hackney, things were getting out of hand: "Thear is a camp of some Indians at the mouth of the hollow they wear all drunk when we passed them they offered Jarbo a fine pony for three gallons of whiskey."

Two days later the Sioux band appears to have sobered up.

When Israel Hale visited these same six lodges he found Indians "who appeared much more comfortably fixed than I expected to see them. They looked clean and were well dressed and had several good horses. I presume they were some of the better class." On June 8, Parke noted here "lotts of pretty little halfbreeds, whose father had been with the Indians 16 years, following trapping, etc." On this same day John Benson still counted "6 huts" and observed a number of "white wolves trained for dogs."

Within a few days this little Indian village had vanished, to judge from the absence of further references to it in subsequent journals. On July 5, about twenty-five miles above the Hollow, the explorer Stansbury encountered a village of Sioux consisting of ten lodges, accompanied by a trader named "Badeau" (possibly James Bordeaux of Fort Laramie fame). Having been driven from the South Fork by cholera, they had fled to the emigrant road in the hope of obtaining medical aid from the whites. We are free to speculate that this was the Ash Hollow community of a month before. There is no indication that the Ash Hollow band described by the emigrants was afflicted with cholera. But if it wasn't the group led by Badeau, might it have been remnants of the same doomed Indian group which Stansbury found on the north bank the day before, July 4, 1849?

> We observed yesterday, on the opposite side of the river, a number of Indian lodges, pitched on the bank, but the total absence of any living thing about them interested us from curiosity to cross the river, here nearly a mile wide, with a strong rapid current. I was afraid to risk any of the animals, so we decided to wade it. . . . After a very difficult and fatigueing journey we reached the opposite shore and proceeded to the lodges which had attracted our attention. There were 5 of them, pitched upon the open prairie, and in them we found the bodies of 9 Sioux, laid out upon the ground, wrapped in their robes of buffalo skins, with their saddles, spears, camp kettles, and all of their accoutrements piled up around them. Some lodges contained 3, others only 1 body, all of which were more or less in a state of decompisition. A short distance apart from these was one lodge which, though small, seemed of rather superior pretensions, and was evidently pitched with great care. It contained the body of a young Indian girl 16 or 17 years of age. . . . She was richly dressed in leggings of fine scarlet cloth, elaborately ornamented; a new pair of moccasins, beautifully embroidered with porcupine quills, was on her feet, and her body was wrapped in two superb buffalo robes. . . . She had

evidently been dead but a day or two. . . . I learned that they all died with cholera, and this young girl being considered past recovery had been arranged by her friends in the habiliments of the dead, enclosed in the lodge alive, and abandoned.

The somber fate of the Sioux band raises a question about cholera in 1849. At the Hollow there was an immense concentration of emigrants and westbound soldiers, with both major trails from the Platte funneling in here, and with all the inducements for lingering. Bennett Clark, for example, says that when he reached the Platte bottom he found it so narrow and so crowded with wagons as far as the eye could reach that he almost despaired of finding a camping place at all. "At last," he says, "we found room to stick ourselves between two Carols." One might expect that here cholera would reap a grim harvest of emigrants. Yet there is evidence of only two dead here from this or any other cause during the migration. One was Rachel Pattison, age eighteen, a bride of three months. Her train reached the Hollow on June 18 and paused for repairs. On the following day, according to Nathan Pattison, cholera struck her in its swift, terrible way: "Rachel taken sick in the morning, died that night." Rachel's grave has become a California Trail shrine. Joseph Green of the 1850 migration noted here the graves of "two who died last year." The second victim is unidentified.

There were at least two near fatalities, one accidental and one on purpose. Gould reports that a Mr. Crist was eating supper when he was accidentally shot by someone with a revolver. The bullet lodged near the backbone; but, apparently convinced that he would survive, his companions placed him in a wagon upon an "air bed" where he rode quite comfortably. On another occasion, according to John Brown, there was a quarrel between a Mr. Bush and a Kentuckian, the upshot of which was that the Kentuckian shot Bush in the ribs. The bullet somehow avoided damage to vital organs, but "at a meeting of the Company it was decided that the Kentuckian should be driven out of the Company. Accordingly, he left after night with two mules."

Some firearms were employed to better purpose, namely to hunt the big game which seemed to flourish in these parts. Deer, elk, grey wolf, "kiote," and buffalo were quarry, but buffalo, of course, were the prime target. Isaac Wistar, arriving on June 9, found that "nearly all sorts of game abound in the canons of the bluff,.

while the hunter's staff of life, buffalo, was grazing in all the open valley in innumerable multitudes. On the north side they absolutely crowded the bottom, down to the very river bank, and looked across at us with such lazy and provoking indifference that we were induced to try to cross the mile or more of river between us." This venture into the swollen North Platte proved ill-advised, for they were nearly drowned before scrambling back to camp. Others mention the profusion of buffalo bones in Ash Hollow. The Newark Company reported "thousands of freshly killed buffalo carcasses lined up on both sides of the road." A traveler on the Council Bluffs road estimated a herd of 10,000 animals congregated around Ash Hollow. Obviously, the canyon was a migration route for buffalo as well as gold-seekers.

The 1849 "tourist season" was pretty well over by July 3 when Stansbury reached this point: "The traces of the great tide of emigrants that had preceded us were plainly visible in the remains of camp fires, in blazed trees covered with innumerable names carved and written upon them; but more than all, in the total absence of herbage. It was only by driving our animals to a ravine some distance from camp, that a sufficiency for their subsistence could be obtained."

Although the Indians observed by the Forty-Niners were peacefully inclined, many emigrants, such as W. McBride, shuddered at the thought that here was an ideal spot for "Indian deviltries." Ash Hollow's reputation as a sinister place was reinforced by events there of September, 1849, reported by "Nebraska" in the *Missouri Republican*, in which the Pawnee rather than the Sioux were the offenders.

> Ft. Laramie (Ind. Terr.) Sept. 18, 1849—Those grand rascals of the Plains, the Pawnees, have again been imbruing their hands in the blood of the whites. Two men—Thomas and Picard—carrying the U.S. Mail from Fort Hall to Fort Leavenworth, were attacked by them a few days since, about half way between this post and Fort Kearny, and it is feared that both were killed. Lt. Donaldson, on his way to the post, found the dead body of Thomas, and the hat of Picard stained with blood. Before he reached the spot he met a war party of Pawnees, who evinced by their actions that they were the perpetrators of the deed. Thomas' body had several arrows in it. Lt. Donaldson had but two or three teamsters with him, and he could only give the body a hasty burial without searching very thoroughly for the other man.

The year 1850, the biggest Gold Rush year, brought forth another bumper crop of Ash Hollow enthusiasts. Of some forty journals examined, all but six reflect use of the Upper Ford and the Windlass Hill complex. Some of these add to the literature of inspiration. Dr. Shepherd wrote, "After travelling 15 miles over a barren plain, nearly destitute of vegetation, we came suddenly upon Ash Hollow, and a splendid scene presented itself. . . . I rather fancy we had a slight specimen of mountain travelling." The sense of wonder appears also in the journal of John Wood: ". . . descended a very steep and winding hill, which led us down into Ash Hollow . . . an old Indian battle ground. Along this hollow may be seen some of the most beautiful natural scenery. After having traveled hundreds of miles without seeing a tree it was almost enrapturing to behold the scene." Looking up from the bottom of the canyon, James Mason imagined that the rocks towered "to a great highet with small seeders standing on there rugged sides like so many Sentries."

James Abbey roped down the steep precipice but had no problems: "Removed steers but one yoke, locked the hind wheels, and went down snugly." The McBride party "had to remove the horses from the tongue, and then lashed long ropes to the hind axletree made the descent safely." However, Littleton condemned the Hollow as "a steep, bad and crooked place," and harked back to Francis Parkman's mysterious cutoff, suggesting "there might be a better place further to the left coming to North Platte by taking off some few miles." Another novelty noted by McBride was the profusion of birds, which "sang out and chirped to us we had not heard them for many long weary days." He also noted that "many of the famous stunted Ash trees were worn quite smooth under the lower branches. . . . This was done by the buffaloes rubbing against them."

On emerging from the marvelous ravine, wrote Dabney T. Carr, "The scene changes, the valley of the Platte spreads itself before you . . . the river rushing along with a velocity that is almost incredible in such a level country." The congestion at the campground was suggested by Cyrus Loveland: "Grass very, very poor while camps and cattle are all around us, thicker than the rings and specks on Jacob's cattle."

The prize Ash Hollow essay for 1850 was written by Madison Moorman:

June 18— . . . of all the road we have seen yet, this four miles
surpassed, in uneveness, and ruggedness. We had a decent of near a
mile, and no little portion of it at an angle of 45°. When down, on
either side towered lofty sand bluffs and isolated hills of gigantic
magnitude, not infrequently capped with a kind of soft, friable sand
stone in various forms and scarry shapes. One, I noticed, looked very
much like the statue of some heathen god, and to complete its resemblance some daring one had clambered up and placed upon its
head the overgrown horns of some fated ox. On the banks of the
little stream . . . grow ash, cedar, choke-cherry, gooseberries, currants,
raspberries and the greatest abundance of the most fragrant and lovely
wild roses the eyes ever beheld. Down near the mouth, a number of
springs of cold and crystal water gushed forth from under the high
and barren bluff, of which without ceremony, with common concent we
all partook most freely—the best & purest ever drank—"a beverage
prepared by God himself."—Our sick were all on the mend—and everyone appeared reanimated and in the highest flow of spirits—being
thus favored after so much detention and sickness and no good water
for the last 150 miles. To be thus surrounded and circumstanced, who
would, who could, with all the sincerity of the heart, refrain, from
giving praise to Him, who is so vigilant and faithful in his watch
over us. . . . This was an oasis of the desert.

Moorman's enchantment with the place was soon put to a severe
strain by "no grass for our hungry mules, and innumerable myriads
of blood-thirsty mosquitoes." On the banks of the Platte he found
good pasturage, but their camp was made miserable by a dark and
angry cloud that unleashed rain and hail, ruining their supper and
stampeding their stock onto an island.

The wholesale abandonment of goods to lighten wagons normally did not begin in earnest until emigrants arrived at Fort
Laramie, but this year there is evidence of such activity at Ash
Hollow. Margaret Frink said that her party salvaged some parts
here from abandoned wagons, and Keller (who calls it Cash Hollow)
reported that here a number of guns were broken and thrown
away, since "it is not supposed we would have trouble with Indians."

In 1850 the cholera extended west with more severity. There is
reference to a mortality increase at Ash Hollow, although only one
grave is identified today. This is the grave of Sanford Johnson of
Vermont, who died of smallpox on May 26 and is buried at the
cemetery in company with Rachel Pattison and the unknown emigrant of 1849. The anonymous writer to Greenville reports that on

June 17 Joseph McGirk died of cholera. He was buried with fitting tribute at sunrise, apparently on the divide between Ash Hollow and Cedar Grove. On June 29, which would be near the tail end of the 1850 migration, Littleton camped six or seven miles above the Hollow, having gone a commendable twenty-seven miles that day via the Upper Ford. He states that he passed sixteen graves that day, but these were scattered along the entire road and there is no way to judge which may have been within the Hollow. Oddly enough, Rachel Pattison's name is not among those identified by Littleton, even though her grave marker would have been among the most conspicuous.

Although parties on both sides of the river frequently noted each other's camps, Ash Hollow was not normally known as a crossing. This year, however, large numbers of emigrants on the south side crossed over to the Council Bluffs Road at Ash Hollow in an effort to flee the cholera. The Charles Ferguson party was one of these. Although the North road enjoyed the reputation of being cholera-free, this was not the case, apparently, in this vicinity in 1850. According to Thissell, deaths and hasty burials opposite Ash Hollow were commonplace, and "every man is panic-stricken."

Encampments of Sioux (often emerging as "Sues" or soe" in the journals) were again in abundant evidence in 1850. As early as May 13 Walter Pigman said that, right after descending the "very steep mountain," he found "two large towns of Indians [and] we camped between those two villages of red men. . . . Immediately upon getting into camp we were visited by some 300 Indians with Whirlwind at their head who presented us with his papers, stating that he was friendly. . . . We felt pretty safe here, notwithstanding if they had been hostile they could have cut us to pieces and destroyed every one of us without the least difficulty." Pigman described the chief as the largest man he ever saw, probably weighing about 250 pounds, who "often punished his own men for disturbing the whites."

Dr. Thomasson, on May 22, thought these were the finest looking Indians he had seen: "I was in thare wigwams. . . . thare was 36 wigwams in the village the interpreter has lived with them for 12 years and he has a Squaw and 2 childrin he sed if it was not for his childrin he would go to Calefornia." On that same day C. W. Smith found the Sioux here "very desirous to beg or buy provisions, particularly sugar, coffee and liquor. . . . Their dress is

simple and confined to adults, the children going naked, except
for a bit of cloth fastened about their loins. . . . The chief signified
that anything that we might lay out of our wagons would be
perfectly safe. . . . They look quite intelligent for Indians and
superior to what I had expected to see. Some of them are now
practicing with their bows and arrows for the amusement of the
emigrants." Smith did not fear for his safety: "Companies of emigrants have encamped all around us, at least 200 men could be
gathered in ten minutes."

On the north shore, says Loveland, was another Indian town.
"The Indians came to our camp this evening to sell us some
mockesons. They wanted one dollar a pair." Maj. Packard reported
also that these north-siders splashed across the river and swarmed
upon them:

> On the opposite side of the river was a Sioux village, and by the
> time we were fairly established in camp, a swarm of Indians—bucks,
> squaws and pappooses—were in our midst, and that to annoy. They
> were a job lot of all sorts and sizes, all of the regulation copper color.
> All were beggars, from the least to the greatest, and wanted everything
> they could carry away, but wanted corn the most—I suppose for seed.
> Here I held my first council with the "noble red man." The old
> chief, Mr. Sitting Bear, came over in due time—wading the river, like
> all the rest—and taking a deliberate view of the situation and the
> camp, stalked up to our tent, where I was standing alone on guard, and
> motioning me to enter, took precedence himself and lifting the flap,
> went in, and I followed. No doubt his rank (smell) entitled him to
> precedence. I cheerfully yielded the point aftering being shut up with
> him a few minutes, and though we had no serious disagreement in the
> matter in hand, the council was not altogether sweet. By signs and
> grunts Mr. Bear made me to understand that although he, a chief of
> the great Sioux nation, was a big good Indian, the lousy crowd outside
> would steal anything they could lay hands on and carry off. I thanked
> the fragrant old chappie, gave him some tobacco, and after telling me
> he would order them all across the river when the sun set, the council
> rose and one part of it gladly sought the open air.
> The old fellow now spread out his blanket for contributions, and
> got them in great variety, if not much value. Bestowing them about
> his august person, he then waded back to his tepee, the water being
> from knee to waist deep.

There are two 1850 references to a structure of some sort on the
North Platte bottoms. This seems strange, since the 1849 literature

is devoid of any references to a white man's structure or trading post except for the collapsible tents or tepees of the French traders. Yet on June 18 John Wood tells us that here, right at the mouth of Ash Hollow, he "camped near a French and Indian trading post of long standing," while Darby refers to "a building that sort of acts like a post office where letters are left for following and returning travellers." We can only conclude that they were talking about the same log cabin. Could it have been the same old deserted log cabin referred to by Edwin Bryant?

Beginning in 1851 with William Lobenstine's testimony, the first clear picture of an actual trading post comes into focus. He tells us that here "we met a kind of trading post where several articles for the remainder of the journey for a reasonable price can be got," and he fixes its location at the canyon mouth, "to the right of the creek about a mile from where you first strike it." Now it is crystal clear that Lobenstine entered Ash Hollow via Cedar Grove: "Two miles this side Ashes Hollow the road ascends a very steep hill. . . . After having got up to its highest point, the road gradually descends into the hollow which builds with the former a square angle." So the unidentified trading post of 1851 was a new structure in a new location, not at the canyon mouth like the 1846–1850 "post office" version, but half way up the hollow, between the canyon outlet and the Cedar Grove intersection, right near the famous spring.

In 1852 there are three references to some kind of an establishment, all presumably the same new structure described by Lobenstine, but each, confusingly, with a different name. Snodgrass reported "a small trading post in Ash Hollow," but Alvah Davis, traveling on the north side, said that he passed "Ash Hollow post office." Did he really mean the new trading post, or the old post office by reputation? Cecelia Adams, also on the Council Bluffs Road opposite, refers to "Ash Hollow Station, where a man stays alone." She clearly refers to the new place, for in 1853, through Count Leonetto Cipriani, a glimpse is given of its occupant:

> That evening we made camp in a small valley. Nearby was an attractive little cottage where a French naval deserter had been living for three years. Like all Frenchmen, he knew how to make life as comfortable as possible, embellishing his plot with flowers, fruit trees, and a vegetable garden. He earned his living by recuperating and fattening sick cattle acquired cheaply from passing covered wagon trains, then

selling them at an exorbitant profit a year later to other westbound caravans. In this way, he had accumulated a considerable fortune.

His hospitality was unbelievable. He insisted that we be his guests for supper. Having bought from us a barrel of flour, which he had been without for three months, he offered to make pancakes for us. But to his great surprise, when he opened the barrel, he noticed at once that the flour was spoiled! It was one of the barrels that the captain at Fort Kearney had sold to us. We checked all the other barrels and the cases of horse biscuits as well: all were spoiled! . . . As we could do nothing else, all of us cursed the captain roundly. . . .

The next day the Frenchman asked two favors of me. He wanted me to deposit for him in a San Francisco bank his savings, amounting to about forty thousand dollars, and to handle for him the sale of nearly a thousand head of cattle in California, for which he would share with me half the profit. Unwilling to assume so great a responsibility, I refused, but offered instead to buy horses and mules from him with what funds I still had.

There follows an account of a ride via "a narrow pass" to "an immense valley, completely enclosed by high rocky mountains." Here (says Cipriani) there were two remarkable caves, one "as large if not larger, than the Colosseum" and an "underground cavern with stalactites of every size and, further along, a pit one hundred metres deep, the crater of a still active volcano which ejected columns of smoke." Cipriani was indulging in flights of fancy, as such geologic features do not exist there. These romantic imaginings tend to cloud the Italian's statements about the remarkable "French naval deserter;" however, this is the only clue discovered to date. The Ash Hollow trader of 1851–1853 remains an enigma.

In 1854 Sarah Sutton found a trader here, "in the mouth" of the ravine, and once more in a trader's tent. This nameless operator was "buying up give-out things at five prices" and selling that chief commodity of the North Platte trade—whiskey—at $4 per gallon.

Mrs. Sutton makes another significant contribution: "There has been a good many Ash trees down in the valley but they are most all cut down to burn." However, she does note that cedar trees of substantial size are still to be seen on the adjoining islands. That same year Edwin Bird considered "ash holer" still a pleasant valley, although now its onetime famed "forest of ash trees, like every other place near the road, has been stript of its wood to make light & chearfull the camp of the emigrants."

The devastation of the Ash Hollow "forest" was probably hastened by the guidebook admonitions to lay in a supply of wood in view of the supposed absence of timber until one reached Scott's Bluffs. This prescription was echoed by Daniel Bacon: "Here you lay in wood for 86 miles unless you don't cross the North Platte. [In that event] then 60 miles at Scotts Bluffs."

Bacon took the unusual course of crossing the North Platte and taking the Council Bluffs road "32 miles from Ash Hollow . . . a circumstance I have never heard of before or since," illustrating that when someone took the notion they were apt to cross the North Platte (same as the South Platte) anyplace. However, it does appear from D. B. Andrews that 1852, like 1850, was a big year for crossing at Ash Hollow to the Council Bluffs Road: "Many teams ford North Fork and proceed up its Northern side."

The onslaught of cholera which continued through 1853 (probably influencing the flight to the Council Bluffs Road) is reflected in five journals, all of 1852 vintage except the 1853 story of Phoebe Judson. Caroline Richardson noted a grave on top of the rise from Cedar Grove and at the mouth of Ash Hollow "three old graves on the top of a knowl at the foot of a rock," one of which contained "A. K. Denison of Ohio, May 26, 1852." The old Ash Hollow cemetery was now filling up rapidly. J. H. Clark found here "four new made graves and three of older date, all side by side. Poor creatures. . . . Our camp keeps remarkably healthy, but we are expecting to be called upon to dig one another's grave at any time." William Hampton mentioned "8 graves" here, but Theodore Potter brings things to a climax:

> We passed through Ash Hollow, a narrow ravine leading down from the hills into the valley of the North Fork of Platte River, and in this valley, less than a mile long, we counted over sixty fresh made graves by the roadside. As we approached the river we saw numerous wagons halted as far from the road as they could get, each flying a red flag to indicate the presence of small pox. . . . For the next two days of our travel we saw these red flags flying from many wagons unhitched at the side of the road.

Phoebe Judson supports the conviction that Potter somewhat exaggerated the number of Ash Hollow graves, but she illuminates their tragedy:

> Coming down onto the river bottom, we passed a row of twenty graves. By the inscriptions on the rough head boards we learned that

they had died within a few days of each other of cholera. . . . It was my privilege in after years to become acquainted with a refined lady who had buried her husband here, and she, besides caring for her two little children, drove her team through to the coast. . . . A mother was also buried here, leaving five helpless children, the youngest six weeks old. The father brought the little family safely through, and they lived to become useful citizens of this country.

The Rebecca Ketcham diary of 1853 contains a strange echo of the Indian attack on the William Gray party sixteen years earlier:

Our night camp is on the brink of the river. After leaving Ash Hollow we came some three or four miles, with the river on our right and the bluffs on our left. We saw several camps on the other side of the river, and the smoke rising from their fires made them look from where we were like steamboats. Mr. Gray here pointed out to us the spot where he was attacked by a band of Sioux when going back to the states the first time. I can see that he has kept an anxious look out from the time of our first approach to the Hollow, it being a great resort of the Indians, and the best kind of a place for them to secrete themselves; but we have seen none.

Later in 1854, according to Henderson, contractor W. M. F. Magraw erected a U.S. mail station at Ash Hollow, for claims filed by Magraw with the government show that in April of the following year this mail station, including house and corrals worth $2,000, was destroyed by the Sioux.

On this ominous note is reached the year 1855, when Sioux encamped near Ash Hollow were attacked by U.S. soldiers, ushering in over twenty years of warfare on the Plains.

X

Little Thunder's Disaster

WHILE ASH HOLLOW WAS renowned among California-bound emigrants for its springs, its spectacular entrances, and its sylvan charm, it is best remembered today as a place of tragedy and terror. The "perpendicular," bone-shattering descent of Windlass Hill, the graves of cholera-stricken emigrants, and the tales of Indian ambush contribute to this, but Ash Hollow will be forever haunted because of its link with one of the catastrophes of the Indian frontier, the Battle of Ash Hollow, September 3, 1855. It is one of the ironies of history that this bloody engagement didn't occur in Ash Hollow at all, but six miles northwest, across the North Platte River in the valley of the Blue Water, now called Blue Creek.

Travelers speeding up and down U.S. Highway 26 today will scarcely notice that, at a point two miles west of Lewellen, Nebraska, they are crossing the mouth of Blue Creek; but those who recognize and are attracted by the historic name may be tempted to follow county and ranch roads that lead upstream to the site of the battle. Was it "Battle," or was it truly "the Harney Massacre," as some historians would have it? However interpreted, it was one of the most savage of all encounters between red and white men; and it was the first counter-swing of the fatal pendulum that symbolized the conflict on the High Plains. Blue Creek today is a crystal stream draining the sandhills, following a serpentine course through a pleasant green valley interspersed with rocky ledges and hillocks. Except for the signs and tokens of modern ranching, it is

311

the same stream that one hundred years ago was stained with the blood of the Brule Sioux—the folk of Spotted Tail and Little Thunder.

During the California Gold Rush of 1849–1854, the Sioux and other Plains tribes were peaceful, by and large. They were pesky beggars and thieves on occasion, but mainly honorable, aloof, and dignified. Considering the massive threat to their romantic way of life posed by the migration, with its attendant evils of whiskey, cholera, and the wasteful destruction of buffalo, it is somewhat puzzling that the Sioux stayed tolerant and law-abiding as long as they did. One explanation, given to Gen. Harney by one of their chiefs, is that, in their savage innocence, they assumed that the whites who passed up the Platte in such throngs were another tribe, however strange, which would soon disappear. It was beyond their conception at first that the emigrants were only a fraction of the millions who lived east of the Missouri River. When the menace to their way of life became more evident with the shrinking buffalo herds, the Sioux became wary—and angry. Their anger finally erupted in 1854 at a point eight miles east of Fort Laramie at the American Fur Company trading houses when a drunken interpreter, an inexperienced young army officer, and twenty-eight Fort Laramie soldiers were killed by a multitude of Sioux warriors awaiting the distribution of annuity goods. (See Chapter XVI.)

The Battle of Ash Hollow (or the Battle of Blue Water or "the Harney Massacre") in 1855 was the white man's reaction to the Grattan Massacre of 1854. These two bloody events, both due to tragic misunderstanding rather than deliberate malevolence, were probably inevitable in the historical scheme of things, and together they set the pattern of violence which would be climaxed two decades later at the Little Big Horn.

Newspaper editors, the military, and Indian agents were at first unanimous in urging retaliation for the Grattan affair, and Congress stirred itself to legislate extra funds for a massive expedition against the Sioux to dispel any illusions about American weakness. Gen. William S. Harney, iron-jawed veteran of the Mexican War with a well-deserved reputation for Puritanical severity, was hand-picked to lead the Sioux Expedition. Getting the message while on leave in Paris, he wasted little time in recrossing the Atlantic to assume the role of avenger. He paused briefly at U.S. Army Headquarters in New York City to compare notes with Lt. Gen. Winfield

Scott, and April 1, 1855, found him at St. Louis (Jefferson Barracks, Headquarters, Department of the West) getting things organized for an ambitious two-pronged conquest of the Northern Plains—one prong up the Missouri River to establish an anchor at the old fur company stronghold of Fort Pierre, the other prong up the Great Platte River Road to Fort Laramie—and then a giant pincers movement to squeeze the Sioux into submission.

As martial preparations went apace, there were misgivings. A. Cumming, Superintendent of Indian Affairs, wrote to Commissioner Manypenny, deploring the intent to "inflict chastisement" indiscriminately upon the Sioux and asking if it would not be better to single out the murderers and punish them selectively "before an expensive and inglorious war be commenced which must effectually cut off all emigration to Utah and the Pacific unless guarded by bayonets?" In a second letter to Manypenny, Cumming stated that he had conferred in New York with Capt. Garnett, formerly of Fort Laramie and now on recruiting duty, who expressed the conviction that the Grattan affair was not "the result of premeditation on the part of the Indians." But by now passions were inflamed, Indian pride and American patriotism were involved, and things had gone beyond peaceful solution.

By a number of depredations which followed the Grattan affair, making it seem less like a gory accident, hostile Sioux bands (by no means representing the majority) managed to fan editorial flames, feed Harney's ambition, and steel soldiers' spines. Tipping the scales against Little Thunder and his doomed band of Brules was the U.S. Army catalog of Indian sins:

> August 19, 1854—Grattan Massacre (Lt. John L. Grattan, Interpreter Augustus Lucian, 28 enlisted men—and Brave Bear, or Conquering Bear, or "the Bear," chief of the troublesome Brules).

> Sack of American Fur Company houses near Fort Laramie; murder of . . . the agent of Magraw and Reeside, Salt Lake City mail contractors; and theft of Company mules.

> September 15, 1854—Raid on mules at Independence Rock Station.

> November 13, 1854—At Horse Creek, murder of Caisson, Wheeler, and one other conducting government mail, and theft of mules, mail, and $20,000 in gold bullion (never recovered).

> November, 1854—Raid on mules at Fort Kearny.

February, 1855—Raid on mules at Fort Kearny.

April, 1855—Raid on horses and mules at Independence Rock; raids on John Richard's place at Platte Bridge and Ward & Guerriers west of Fort Laramie; destruction of hay, corrals, and Magraw-Reeside stations at Ash Hollow and Independence Rock.

As the Sioux Expedition shaped up, Superintendent Thomas Twiss of the Upper Platte Agency attempted to round up for safekeeping at Fort Laramie all Indians considered "friendly and peaceable." On August 20, 1855, he advised the Secretary of the Interior that he had accounted for four or five principal bands under his jurisdiction—Brule and Oglala Sioux as well as Arapahoe and Cheyenne. Of the mission Indians, Twiss wrote, "The Band which murdered the Mail party is called the Wasazahas [a branch of the southern Brules], and was the Bear's Band before his death [at the Grattan massacre]. I cannot ascertain where this band is, at present, hunting. I expect, however, that my Runners will soon bring news of them." Twiss concluded his report with the assertion: "The Sioux difficulties have been magnified by false and malicious reports. There is not, as I can find, within this Agency, a hostile Indian. On the contrary, all are friendly."

Although this cheerful note seems hardly to jibe with the record, Twiss was not insincere. In August, 1855, while Harney's army was rolling along from Fort Leavenworth to Fort Kearny, the Sioux seemed peaceful enough. No emigrant trains were molested. The Brules under Chief Stabber and Oglala bands under Man-Afraid-of-His-Horses and Big Partisan stayed close to Fort Laramie, fearful of their fate. Most of the southern Brules, together with renegade Oglalas, Minniconjous, and northern Cheyenne, were off on a gala buffalo hunt north of the Platte, taking time out to pursue a band of Omaha Indians on the Loup River and kill their leader, Logan Fontenelle. They didn't realize they had a war with the United States on their hands. And, as September approached, they went into camp on the Blue Water opposite Ash Hollow to dry out their buffalo meat. This scarcely seemed the action of Indians who were on the warpath against the whites. Yet this band under Little Thunder (successor to the Bear) harbored the mail-train murderers and the bulk of the Grattan Massacre participants, and by failing to come into Fort Laramie they were clearly violating the rules laid down by Indian Agent Twiss.

Little Thunder clearly knew of Harney's approach for he had been warned by Twiss; yet the posture of his encampment, with women and children exposed and housekeeping chores afoot, was certainly not one of defense. One can only conclude that these outlaw Indians were terribly naive, either thinking that Harney could not be serious about attacking, or else thinking that they could easily defeat any white force sent against them. They were soon to be dreadfully disillusioned.

On June 2, writing to "Head Quarters of the Army, New York" from "Head Quarters, Sioux Expedition, Saint Louis, Missouri," Harney listed his logistic problems and despaired of reaching Sioux country before winter set in. But, whatever the obstacles, Harney managed to surmount them. If he had waited to assemble an overland army of 1,200 effectives, as he had originally hoped for, Harney might not have reached the North Platte until 1856, and history might then have taken a different tack. But he was enough of a soldier not to wait helplessly around; he decided to reconnoiter up the Platte with an army half that size, asserting that "I shall not hesitate to attack any body of hostile Indians which I can overtake or chance to encounter." In his communique of August 3 from "camp near Fort Leavenworth," he outlined a grand plan to penetrate the Black Hills (of South Dakota) with converging columns from Fort Pierre, Fort Laramie, and "some point on the Platte between Ash Hollow and Fort Laramie," hoping by this maneuver to force the Indians to give battle. This scheme does not seem to be in harmony with his earlier idea of a "reconnoitre." Reporting on August 23 from "Camp near Fort Kearny," the general advised of his arrival at that point, much delayed by continuous heavy rains, but "I shall leave tomorrow in the direction of Fort Laramie with about 600 troops."

Gen. Harney's staff included Maj. Winship, assistant adjutant general; Cap. Van Vliet, quartermaster; Lt. Polk, aide-de-camp; Col. Andrews, paymaster; Lt. Balch, ordnance officer; and Dr. Ridgely, assistant surgeon (and the only medical officer with the command).

The mounted force, commanded by Col. Philip St. George Cooke (who had been up the Platte with Kearny's Dragoons in 1845), consisted of Co. I and Co. K, Second Dragoons, led respectively by Lt. Robertson and Capt. Steele; Light Co. G, Fourth Artillery, Capt. Howe; and Co. E, Tenth Infantry, Capt. Heth.

The infantry, composed of five companies of the Sixth, was commanded by Maj. Cady. Capt. Todd led Co. A; Maj. Woods, Co.

E; Lt. McCleary, Co. H; Capt. Wharton, Co. I; and Lt. Patterson, Co. K. Undoubtedly the saddest man on this expedition was Maj. Woods, who left Fort Kearny with the news that his family had just been wiped out by cholera at Fort Riley.

An unexpected and valuable reinforcement to the expedition, described by Harney on the twenty-third, was Lt. G. K. Warren of the Corps of Topographical Engineers:

> Lieut. Warren . . . his assistant Mr. Carrey, and an escort of six men of the country, arrived here last night direct from Fort Pierre, in a journey of fifteen days, and within a measured distance of 300 miles. The attempt was a bold and unauthorized one, but justified, I think, by the results. . . . This party was frequently on Indian trails, from one to three days old, and Lieut. Warren is of the opinion . . . that the Brules are now in the "Sand Buttes" on and South East of the Eau Qui Court [Niobrara River].

Capt. Todd's journal told of sportive buffalo-chasing along the Platte, "dreary fog and mist," and a crashing thunderstorm. On September 2 the expedition crossed the South Platte at the Upper Ford and, descending "the gorge of Ash Hollow," arrived at their riverside camp by 5 P.M. From the heights they could see the Brule camp. With a telescope Capt. Warren counted between twenty-six and thirty-three lodges, but a return train from Laramie which was passed at noon had reported that there were forty lodges under Little Thunder. (None of these observers took into account a smaller village of allied Sioux and Cheyenne above the Brule camp.) The guide, Joseph Tesson, placed the encampment on Blue Water Creek, six miles from Ash Hollow and six miles from the North Platte.

Warren asserted that "during the evening no Indians came in from the camp," and Gen. Harney mentioned no communication with the Brules that day; but Capt. Todd said that there was contact:

> As we descended the hollow we could distinctly see the camp of the Brules. These people sent word to Genl Harney that if he wanted peace he could have it, or if he wanted war that he could have that. The chief also sent word that he would come in and see him. The bearer of this message was Mr. Vasquez . . . an old mountain man and trader. He also informed us that some of the young men had amused themselves the morning before by kicking over the coffee cups of the teamsters attached to Russels train.

An unidentified correspondent for the *Missouri Republican,* with the expedition, clears up the point, saying that the "peace or war" challenge was a hearsay report by "the traders" of the eastbound train; and from this it must be assumed that the alleged messenger, Vasquez, was attached to the train and was not an authorized emissary of Little Thunder. The consternation of the Brules the next day when the troops advanced supports the conviction that, contrary to a widespread impression, before the day of the battle there was no communication between Harney and Little Thunder; in fact, all eyewitnesses agree that the Indians were caught, literally, asleep.

The hectic events of September 3 are reported officially by Harney, Cooke, Cady, and Warren. In addition there are illuminating private journal accounts by three officers, Cooke, Warren, and Todd, and at least one enlisted man, Eugene Bandel. There are also the reminiscences of Gen. Richard C. Drum, then an artillery officer. From these generally concurring versions a composite view of the action can be drawn.

There is reasonable conformity between the original Warren sketch-map and the terrain which may be observed today. The accompanying map of the Ash Hollow vicinity, reflecting Warren's data, makes elaborate topographic discussion unnecessary. Harney's camp of September 2 was along the North Platte bench just west of the Hollow. The mouth of the Blue Water is roughly three miles west of the Hollow, and Harney's camp after the battle was just east of this point. Although meandering in curlicue fashion, the tributary stream courses generally north to south for the distance of some 10 miles as depicted in Warren's map. The focal points of the action, moving northward from the North Platte, were the main Brule camp on the west side four miles from the river; the point of parley with Little Thunder, east side, five miles; the rough elevation which was the scene of the initial attack and of most noncombatant casualties, west side, six miles; the unsuspected Oglala village of eleven lodges, west side, and the opposite sand draw flight path, both about 7 miles; and the place of Col. Cooke's concealment, 8 miles. In the words of Lt. Warren,

> I present herewith a sketch of the "Blue Water Creek" . . . comprising the field of operation of the 3d inst. . . . The distances are all estimated and computed by magnetic bearings. All parts of the scene are included except about the last six miles of the pursuit by

the mounted force. Blue Water is about 20 feet wide and 2 to 3 feet deep flowing over a rocky or sandy bottom: the immediate banks are abrupt and 3 to 4 feet high requiring care when approached on horseback. It will be seen that the stream is tortuous and about every mile strikes against steep bluffs as it winds from side to side through its valley. This valley is about half a mile wide and contains several very miry sloughs. These things combined formed a serious obstacle to the pursuit.

Troops under Harney actually entering the fray numbered something like 500 (after deducting the wagon train escort and those fatigued by the forced march to this point.) The number of Indian lodges recorded by Warren was certified by Colin Campbell, guide and interpreter who had accompanied him from Fort Pierre. There were forty-one Brule lodges and eleven belonging to an assortment of Oglalas, Minniconjous, and Cheyenne. The total of fifty-two lodges sheltered some 250 Indians, according to George Hyde, which would be a somewhat lower population than the average usually estimated of seven or eight individuals per lodge. However many sleeping Indians there were, their fate was sealed by Harney's decision, made at the mouth of Ash Hollow:

> Having no doubt from information I had received from the people of the country I had previously met on the road, and from the guides accompanying me, of the real character and hostile intentions of the party in question, I at once commenced preparations for attacking it. I ordered Lieut. Col. P. St. Geo. Cooke, 2nd Dragoons, with companies "E" and "K" of the same regiment; Light Company "G" 4th Artillery, and company "E" 10th Infantry, all mounted, to move at 3 o'clock AM on the 3d instant; and to secure a position which would cut off the retreat of the Indians to the Sand Buttes, the reputed strong hold of the Brules. . . .
>
> At 4½ O'clock AM I left my camp with companies "A", "E", "H", "I", and "K", 6th Infantry, under the immediate command of Major A. Cady, of that regiment; and proceeded toward the principal village of the Brules with a view to attacking it openly in concert with the surprise contemplated through the cavalry.

Fatigued by the tough dry haul from the South Platte, the men listlessly ate a cold supper (There were no fires, lest the Indians be alarmed.) and then sprawled asleep. Although 3 A.M. was a fairly typical hour for reveille on the march, it came all too swiftly that night. Still, the mounted troopers, led by Cooke and guided by

Tesson, were tense with excitement as they splashed across the North Platte to their encounter with the Sioux.

Cooke's force was entirely successful in making a wide detour over the sandhills to the east, then circling soon after sunrise into a very favorable position behind a slight ridge and the bank of a dry affluent of the Blue Water half a mile above the upper village. This march of twelve miles was far longer than Cooke expected it to be. This was because the combined camp of the Sioux and their allies was much more extensive than Harney's scouts had reported. If it had not been for Tesson's scouting skills, Cooke might well have blundered into the camp prematurely. Cooke now held his cavalry in ready position and dismounted his irregulars, the mounted artillerymen under Howe, and the mounted infantry under Heth and arranged them in prone position to cover the valley escape route to the north. Here Cooke lay concealed in ambush for two hours, waiting for the signal to action, which was to be the fire of the infantry.

On schedule, Harney left camp at 4:30 A.M. with the five infantry companies under Cady, fording the North Platte and marching steadily up the east side of the Blue Water valley toward the Brule village "with a view to attacking it openly in concert with the surprise contemplated through the cavalry. But before reaching it the lodges were struck and their occupants commenced a rapid retreat up the valley in the direction from which I expected the mounted troops. They halted short of there, however, and a parley ensued between the chiefs and myself."

There is conflicting testimony at this point as to whose idea it was to have a parley and what took place there. From his Indian informants Hyde has it that Little Thunder asked for a conference as "an ancient stratagem" to enable the women and children to gain time in dismantling the camp. According to this version, Little Thunder, Spotted Tail, and Iron Shell rode out of the camp carrying a white flag. Harney showed willingness to talk, but, as an old Indian fighter, was not taken in by the trick and meanwhile kept his infantry advancing steadily. In panic (still according to Hyde) the chiefs broke off the talks and galloped back to camp, the infantry opening fire on their retreating figures.

What actually happened, according to the Todd and Warren journals and the Missouri news story, was quite different. The Indians did at first signal for a parley, but this was ignored by

Harney. As the Missourian expressed it, "as we had come for war and not for peace, we paid no attention to them." In his diary Warren wrote:

> Gen. Harney and his staff accompanied the Infantry. After crossing the river and advancing about a mile some Indians, mounted, were seen on the low round hills to our right, and having satisfied themselves set off at a gallop for their village. . . . As soon as we could see the Indian camp, we discovered that they were moving off up the valley of the stream, and by the time we came opposite it, they had struck nearly all their lodges and gone. The hindermost kept about a mile in advance. We did not go through the village, but left it about ½ mile to our left.
>
> Capt. Todd's Company formed the advance guard; I, having obtained permission from Gen. Harney, accompanied him.
>
> It soon became evident that we were not going to come up with the enemy, and Gen. Harney was very apprehensive that he would escape, especially from the fact that Maj. Winship, who had been to the right to reconnoiter, had reported that he believed the ground was too bad for the mounted men to reach their position.
>
> In order to gain time, and to learn something of the disposition of the Indians, Gen. Harney sent the interpreter Campbell forward for a talk, upon which the Chief Little Thunder came out to meet him, and said that he would come in if the troops were halted so as not to approach nearer his people. This being done, a halt took place on both sides, both sides being anxious spectators, but a few knowing its nature, and none its results.

Capt. Todd witnessed all of the preliminaries. As the retreating Indians moved off to the right, he changed the direction of his skirmishers, who, "obliquing to the right, rapidly approached them with every step." Campbell rode back and forth with messages, and finally both forces halted, the creek intervening.

> The General dismounted and advancing to the front of the skirmishers awaited the approach of the chief, who in a few minutes came down on horseback at full speed to meet him, and when within 30 or 40 feet stopped, and the "talk" began. This lasted over 30 minutes, probably nearly an hour. . . . The Genl reproached him with the murder of Lieut. Grattan and his party, the mail party in Nov. following, and generally, of the depredations committed upon the emigrants, the chief pleading that he could not control his young men, that he himself was friendly and finally that he did not want to fight. . . .

Once during the talk he desired to shake hands with the Genl. who refused the proferred courtesy. . . . The chief toward the close became quite uneasy, but the Genl. assured him that he had nothing to fear, as he would allow him to rejoin his people before he attacked. Finally he told him to go and tell his young men that a battle had to settle their differences and to come out and fight, and if he, himself, did not want to be hurt to get out of the way as quickly as possible. . . . When the chief had joined his people, the order to advance was given. . . . A few minutes after on being asked if I could reach them [with the new issue long-range rifles] . . . replying in the affirmative, the order was given to open. The words were scarcely out of his mouth before the rattle of the rifles of my company was heard, and the Sioux Campaign initiated in earnest.

The mounted force under Cooke was discovered before the end of the "talk," and Cooke knew that he was discovered but did not move until he heard the first fire of Todd's riflemen . Now in a very few minutes the Blue Water was a scene of carnage as the trap was closed. Most of the Indians, abandoning everything, at first took a defensive position on a hill pitted with "caves," or rather rock shelters, and here there was fearful slaughter of men, women, and children, victims of new long-range military rifles. Cut off by the cavalry to the north, the survivors fled through the only escape route, a sand draw to the east, but here many were cut down by infantry cross-fire and cavalry charges. Those who survived this gauntlet scattered through the sandhills, being pursued and slaughtered for a distance of six miles or more before the troops were recalled.

Indian casualties, according to Harney, were eighty-six killed, six wounded, about seventy women and children captured. "The casualties of my command amount to 4 killed, 4 severely wounded, 3 slightly wounded, and one missing, supposed to be killed or captured by the enemy."

This, in very broad outline, is the story of the Ash Hollow fight, or the Battle of Blue Water. Facets of this engagement and its aftermath are colorful and exciting from the conqueror's viewpoint, tragic and heartrending to the Indians and to at least two sympathetic observers.

Although the melodramatic qualities of the occasion probably escaped the Indians, the *Missouri Republican* correspondent never saw anything quite so exciting:

The conference was broken up and the Infantry were ordered to place their rifles at long range of from 600 to 1,000 yards, and advance rapidly. The Indians ran, of course, to the hills, and were in a fine position to repel an attack of Infantry when the Dragoons showed themselves, then . . . the fun commenced in reality. I never saw a more beautiful thing in my life. When the Infantry saw the Dragoons coming down in such beautiful style, they gave a yell, which resounded far and wide. The Indians threw away everything they had in the world. We suppose we killed about 70. You know they carry off their dead so rapidly that it is almost impossible to say with certainty as to the number killed.

The report of Maj. Cady is brief, since the infantry action was fully observed by the commanding general. The companies under Todd and McCleary "advanced with spirit diagonally across the valley and stream, and charged up the heights on the opposite side where they engaged the enemy. The two companies of Woods and Patterson, held in reserve by Harney, saw little action. This left me with but one company, 'I' under Wharton to proceed up the creek to meet the enemy in flank as they were retreating." This particular operation was not a success, for "the distance at which we were when we came in view was too great to allow for an effective fire even with the long range arms," and further pursuit by the infantry appeared useless.

Much more action appears in the Todd journal. Caught by the long-range rifle fire of the infantry, the Indians were swept off the heights and driven northward:

> About this time a warrior dashed out from the crowd and, approaching us, rode down the line at full speed parallel to it, and distant about 300 yards. Poor fellow! What hope of escape for him, what chance to come off scatheless from the Hundred Minnies levelled upon him, as furiously he dashed along this fiery gauntlet, his scalp lock and streamers trailing in the wind.

Under cover of this distraction the Indians dispersed, seeking cover among ravines and buttes, but all in vain. When the cavalry made its appearance directly in front of them, they veered to the east, attempting to escape by the only avenue left to them, the eastward ravine. Tood continues:

> As they passed, from a high commanding point . . . we poured a plunging fire upon them with our long range rifles, knocking them

out of their saddles, right and left. The party was large and compact and, as their people fell, others jumped from their horses and picking them up, replaced and carried them off. A few moments after, the cavalry came down, and our work ceased.

The infantry claimed twelve male Indians dead, ten or twelve women and children captured, and no soldier casualties. The mounted force claimed seventy-four Indians killed (sex and age not specified), five wounded, and forty-three women and children prisoners. Apparently most male Indians who didn't escape were killed. All twelve of the soldier casualties were under Cooke's command. These statistics clearly demonstrate that the cavalry saw most of the action. Col. Cooke, a man of no mean literary prowess, did the occasion full justice in his report.

After his presence was discovered by the Oglalas, Cooke was sorely tempted to kill two young naked warriors who rode up and down in front of him, daring him to fight. But pursuant to instructions he waited until "a volley was heard, and with exceeding alacrity and celerity my force was all in the saddle, and we galloped in a column of fours across the valley for the bluff on the enemy's rear," meanwhile sending Heth's company down the valley "to close that avenue of the enemy's anticipated retreat." Cooke sent Steele, Robertson, and Howe against the reverse side of the hilltop refuge, thus, he supposed, closing every avenue of retreat to the enemy.

> In the very short time that these dispositions were making, our fire was driving the enemy with much slaughter over the cliffs where they had ascended it; disappearing at first, they were soon apparent in full retreat, across the valley and up the long slope opposite, suffering a plunging fire from my company and the 6th Infantry, at from four to eight hundred yards. . . . Heth's company, too weak perhaps to have stemmed the current, could probably have prevented its outbreak, if he had chosen a more fortunate position, and in full view of the enemy.
>
> On the instant of the discovery, I galloped with Steele's company to the nearest practicable descent sounding "to horse" and "advance." . . . I sent Steele directly across to charge as foragers, & pursue the enemy to the death.

Steele's company formed the spearhead of the pursuit; other units were sent after the panicked Indians, and much of the cavalry was soon beyond earshot of the bugler's "recall," ordered by Gen. Harney, who was viewing the triumphant conclusion from a hilltop. Once the pursuit was set in motion it was not easily stopped, and there was danger in this:

> The indians flying in every direction in small parties over a rolling table land, with their far fresher ponies, could only be destroyed by an indefinite division of companies; throwing the men much from under the eye of any officer, until, finally from their better knowledge of the ground, the enemy could combine & cut off or intimidate these small parties.
>
> There was much slaughter in the pursuit, which extended from five to eight miles.

It was noon before all troops were returned and all but one accounted for. The missing man, Pvt. Marshall Ryder, was a member of Steele's rampaging Co. K, which alone had nine of the twelve casualties listed for the entire task force. It seems entirely probable that the unfortunate Ryder got too far ahead of his troop in the pursuit and was either killed outright or, more probably, tortured to death by the infuriated Sioux warriors.

Cooke scolded Heth for not doing a better job of blockading the escape route, a circumstance due in part to his mounted infantry getting entangled in a slough, and in part to being armed with awkward rifles rather than carbines. And Cooke thought that Howe might have been of more help in the pursuit if he had not been embarrassed by "impassable cliffs," the care of two men mortally wounded, some Indian women prisoners, and finally "want of practice as a mounted force." (These men were trained for artillery, not horsemanship.) But, for the most part, Cooke praised his men for a brilliant performance:

> Of my command, all the mounted infantry & nearly all the dragoons were lately recruited and unused to service; and the artillery company but lately mounted in part, & with a new arm. Under these circumstances they far exceeded my expectations; and in the night march, the surprise, in the action and the pursuit, and in all the fatigues of thirteen hours in the saddle, showed themselves good soldiers . . . and have won for themselves the gratitude of at least a portion of their countrymen, whose lives or property have been exposed to the necessary transit of this great central wilderness.

Cooke and Cady were in turn commended by Harney for "carrying out my instructions to them with signal alacrity, zeal and intelligence." Particularly commended for their performance "in closest contact with the enemy" were Todd, Steele, Robertson, and Heth. Bouquets went also to guides Tesson and Carrey, Lt. Warren for his map, and Dr. Ridgely, "indefatiguable in his attention to the suffering wounded, both of our troops and of the enemy."

The first and general reaction among military brass, President Franklin Pierce and his cabinet, and newspaper editors was that Harney was a hero: He had done a great thing out there on the Platte in giving the Indians their comcuppance after many atrocities. And this, precisely, was the first goal of the Sioux Expedition. After an interval in which there was time for stories of the affair to be somewhat embroidered, editors and churchmen quite understandably became exercised over the "Harney Massacre" of innocent savages, and particularly the inadvertent wounding of women and children. This sentiment led to the opprobious epithet of "Squaw Killer," which would haunt Harney's remaining days just as the term "Butcher" would be applied to Chivington for his treatment of the Cheyenne at Sand Creek, Colorado, nine years later. Historians of recent years have also passed harsh judgment on Harney; but, under the circumstances of Indian warfare, the accusation is unwarranted.

There is no question that adult male Indians (and older boys, as well) who evidently fought with great ferocity, were given no quarter. And it is a fact that women and children were killed and wounded; but, unlike Chivington's troops, the men of the Sioux Expedition did not deliberately slaughter the innocent. These pitiful casualties resulted from fire directed broadside at hostile armed Indians in the rock shelters and, to a lesser extent, in open flight, when distance or strangeness of dress or the camouflage of terrain sometimes prevented recognition of sex or age differences.

Col. Cooke asserts that "in the pursuit, women if recognized were generally passed by my men; but that in some cases certainly these women discharged arrows at them." Even so, after the feverish fighting, all the evidence is that captured women and children, wounded or otherwise, were treated with as much medical care and Christian charity as circumstances would allow. Gen. Drum recalled that after the first onslaught the Indians found defensive positions in a rotten limestone formation filled with little caves covered by underbrush, from which they directed their fire. Of his commanding officer, Drum wrote:

In passing round his line giving directions and encouraging his men in their exposed position he heard the piercing cry of a child, and at once sounded the signal to cease firing. . . . This was the first indication that the women and children were concealed in the caves and under our fire. All the male Indians had, by this time, been killed except two who, seeing the men bring their pieces to an order, jumped, raced, and thus got away. As it was, we killed 12 bucks and captured all the women and children in the caves, some of them being terribly wounded.

Corroborating this story, Warren wrote in his report:

I aided in bringing in the wounded women and children who were found near the place to which the Indians first fled. These had secreted themselves in holes in the rocks in which armed men also took shelter, and by firing on our men caused the destruction of the women and children, whom the soldiers were unable to distinguish in the confusion and smoke. Near one of these holes, 5 men, 7 women and 3 children were killed and several wounded.

Other reports make it clear that after the retreat Harney was prompt in detailing soldiers to recover the wounded. But the horror of the scene emerges most vividly in Warren's private journal:

At this time, the recall having sounded, I went with others in search of the wounded. The sight on top of the hill was heart-rendering, wounded women and children crying and moaning, horribly mangled by bullets, most of this had been occasioned by these creatures taking refuge in the holes in the rocks, and armed Indians sheltering themselves in the same places. These later fired upon our men, killing 2 men and wounding another of the artillery company. Our troops then fired in upon their retreat. Two Indians were killed in the hole, and two as they came out. Seven women were killed in the hole and 3 children, 2 of them in their mothers' arms. . . .

One young woman was wounded in the left shoulder, the ball going in above and coming out below her arm. I put her on my horse. Another handsome young squaw was wounded just below her left knee, the same bullet her baby in the right knee. . . . I had a litter made, and put her and the child on it. I found another girl about 12 years old laying with her head down in a ravine, and apparently dead. Observing her breath, I had a man take her in his arms. She was shot through both feet. I found a little boy shot thru the calves of his legs and thru his hams. I took him in my arms. He had enough strength left to hold me around the neck. . . .

With this piteous load we proceeded down the hill, and placing on the bank of the stream, I made a shelter to keep off the sun, and bathed their wounds in the stream. The same office was performed for those brought in wounded by the others in the morning, one little girl shot through the right breast, a boy in the thigh, another in his arm. A poor Ogallala woman was shot badly in the shoulder by a Dragoon after the fight was over. He saw her concealed in the grass and mistook her for a man. This woman and the one I brought down the hill on my horse were in some way left behind. All the others were brought to Dr. Ridgely, and from him and his assistant received all the attention that skill and humanity could bestow.

I did not get back to camp till the last of the command (10 PM). After getting to camp I aided to dress their wounds. I had endeavored to make a topographical sketch of the scene, but the cause of humanity prevented my doing much.

Other poignant experiences were recounted by Drum. In the tall grass he found "a little child naked, save for a scarf around its waist in which a little puppy was wrapped." The child was returned by a Dragoon sergeant to the North Platte camp, where the company tailor made her some garments out of Drum's hickory shirts. When visiting Spotted Tail at Fort Leavenworth the following year, Drum asserts that the grateful chief identified the daughter as his own, but said that she had died. However, Bordeau's daughter, Susan Bettelyoun, identifies this baby as Chief Iron Shell's boy, who grew up to become a noted warrior, Hollow Horn Bear.

In another episode, Drum recalled that there was one wounded squaw who turned out to be a white woman, evidently the same one whom Warren identifies as "a handsome young squaw" with leg wounds and a baby shot in the knees:

> In all my life I have never seen such grief as that of this poor woman. . . . One of the soldiers kindly went to her assistance and when the water he used on her removed the dirt, I found that she was undoubtedly a white woman. . . . the woman had evidently been captured in her childhood and grown up among the Indians; for in every respect she was a thorough hostile, except in the display of her grief at the loss of her child—for it is well known that the Indian is rarely demonstrative in sorrow.

Except for the return of the pursuit details, the military action was concluded by mid-morning, and Harney returned to his encampment by mid-afternoon to recuperate his exhausted men and animals. But the troopers who had the grim task of coming in with the dead and wounded in jouncing army wagons did not reach

camp until after dark (10 P.M., according to Warren). As Lt. Drum
of this rear guard groped toward the North Platte in the inky black-
ness and the wounded and bereaved mourned in a dismal chorus,
there was a sudden, violent lightning and thunder storm and a
severe drenching. It was an appropriate ending for a tragic day.

While deploring the harsh fate of the Indian families, it is
maudlin to accuse Harney of attacking an innocent camp. These
were hostiles, harboring Spotted Tail and other known murderers.
The captured articles alone established guilt beyond doubt. In his
official report Harney concluded:

> I enclose herewith several papers found in the baggage of the
> Indians some of which are curiosities, and others may serve to show
> their disposition to the whites. They are mostly taken, as their dates
> and marks will indicate, on the occasion of the massacre and plunder
> of the mail party, in November last. There are also, in the possession
> of officers and others, in camp, the scalps of two white females, and
> remnants of the clothing, etc. carried off by the Indians in the Grattan
> Massacre; all of which, in my judgement, sufficiently characterize the
> people I have had to deal with.

Todd mentioned that "one of the officers cut from the ornament of
one warrior three tresses of different colors, the scalps of white
women murdered on the plains." On one U.S. Post Office document
was an Indian pictograph of the mail party.

Among the known dead was Little Butte, a Cheyenne chief. But
among those who got away were Chief Little Thunder, the noted
warrior Iron Shell, and Red Leaf, Long Chin, and Spotted Tail, all
relatives of the Bear who died with Grattan, and all implicated in
the murder of the mail party. Spotted Tail carried away two pistol
bullets in his body and two saber cuts and lost a wife, child, and
most other female relatives. Two months later he, with Red Leaf
and Long Chin, would be forced to surrender to the soldiers at Fort
Laramie, fully expecting to be hanged, but eventually pardoned by
the government for diplomatic reasons after a winter's imprison-
ment at Fort Leavenworth. For all of its tragedy, the battle had an
extremely salutary effect on the Sioux attitude. Soon Harney would
journey to Fort Laramie and then across country to Fort Pierre on
the Missouri, traveling like an emperor, unopposed. So shocked was
the great Sioux nation by Little Thunder's disaster that these disorganized tribesmen, some 10,000 strong, remained relatively peaceful
for eight years, or until the uprising of the middle 1860s. The great

army of many thousands of warriors which had been envisioned by Adj. Gen. Cooper in his instructions to Harney of March 22 had simply melted away

Before leaving Ash Hollow, Harney had three chores to perform while bivouacked at the mouth of the Blue Water. First (to the anguish of future museum curators) he had the battlefield area systematically searched and all Indian equipment and provisions brought to a central point—tepees, robes, weapons, saddles, clothing, kettles and other accessories, and great quantities of buffalo meat. It was a veritable mountain of Indian loot, all that 250 Indians possessed, for in flight they were able to salvage almost nothing. He then had Quartermaster Van Vliet select those items which, in his judgment, might have military usefulness and could be carried, mainly robes and buffalo meat, which the troops later found to be so tough they used it as a substitute for chewing tobacco. Then he ordered that lamp kerosene be spilled over the remainder and destroyed in one awesome bonfire. The Indian ponies that survived the gunfire also became U.S. property by right of conquest.

Another awkward item was the disposition of prisoners, some of them in dying condition. After being patched up or operated upon to the best of Dr. Ridgely's ability, they were to be taken by wagons, when available, to Fort Kearny for safekeeping. Hyde pointed out that this was contrary to unfounded Indian tradition that the women were forced to march to Fort Laramie and in some cases were outraged by the troops. The ultimate fate of these victims is not known; it seems probable that several died from their severe wounds and that the survivors were eventually restored to their escapee husbands and fathers. The location of Indian burials consequent on this disaster has not been clearly determined.

The last item on Harney's cleanup agenda was the construction of Fort Grattan on the south bank of Ash Hollow, a few yards east of the present highway bridge. It does not appear that this was intended as anything but a temporary shelter and defensive work. Todd says that during the period September 4–8, "The Infantry have been very busy throwing up a small sod work, in which Captain Wharton with his Co. "I" and the wounded, prisoners and plunder, are to be left." Thus we may view Fort Grattan as a sort of convalescent station and military supply depot. It seems probable that, in view of the destruction of the Ash Hollow mail station the preceding spring, Fort Grattan was also designed to serve as a redoubt for passing supply trains and the government mail until a new mail station could be constructed the following year.

This fort, which was apparently abandoned before the spring of 1856 and possibly earlier, had no official standing as a military post and so is not listed in any official roster. When it was viewed by Grant Shumway about forty years after the battle, "the roof had been removed, and the sod walls with the square port holes were all that remained. It was about 20 feet north and south, and 40 east and west." In 1904 Robert Harvey found here "ridges and depressions" which were the only remains or evidences of the fortification. Today all but a trace of this work has been eroded away by the river. Indeed, as will be seen from emigrant accounts, the river had begun to eat it away as early as 1859.

By September, normally, any westbound emigrants would be far beyond Ash Hollow, and 1855 was a light year for emigrants anyhow (except for Mormons on the north side), so it is not surprising that the violent upheaval on the Blue Water went unobserved in emigrant journals. However, there is at least one witness of Harney's encampment, and there are several in the period 1856–1863 whose journals provide a kind of post-mortem.

One 1855 witness is William Chandless, a member of that rare species of literate teamsters, whose freight train "slid down one terribly steep hill" and entered Ash Hollow on September 6, three days after the battle. In the dusk, "the Hollow seemed the very perfection of a place for attack; it has an ill name with travelers, and the Sioux are known to be near and hostile." The Chandless train camped on the North Platte:

> On the opposite bank was camped General Harney's army of 700 or 800 men, and their fires were bright and thick as fire-flies. We heard they had fought a battle with the Indians the day before; this accounted for our seeing none at Ash Hollow, but as they were supposed to be still about, and only the more hostile, we were ordered to keep double guard, two messes a night, and well armed. Went out myself for the first time again, though very much exhausted with walking through the sand; did not care to have the weight of a revolver; the rest had their rusty old yagers.
>
> Sept. 7—A good many cattle missing; while they were being hunted up, a lot of soldiers came into our camp, some for provisions, of which they were very short, and others having crossed to build a fort at the mouth of Ash Hollow, that is, an earthwork high enough to protect

from arrows or bullets; it could be entirely commanded from the top of the Bluffs with Minnie rifles. Heard plenty about the fight, infantry and dragoons each making out they had borne the brunt of it.

In conversation with troops, Chandless was told that before the battle Harney made an inflammatory speech, larded with obscenities against the Indians, in order to key his men to the proper killing mood. "Northern newspapers," Chandless commented, "are apt to set down old Harney, who is a Southerner, as a truculent barbarian, but he is certainly popular with his army, and his policy is quite right. Shilly-shallying does not answer with the Indians." On his progress toward Salt Lake City, Chandless later found that "the news of this battle spread like wildfire over the prairies, and many tribes, even beyond the mountains, questioned us as to the rifles that killed at half a mile." When the Chandless train came opposite the mouth of Blue Water, he wrote:

> Landon, of our mess, crossed the water [North Platte] and made for the battlefield. A good many wolves and ravens were still at work, though most of the bodies had been already picked clean. L. started on his return with a large bag of buffalo meat that must have escaped notice previously, but when half-way to camp was fired at by a soldier, who took him for an Indian from his dusty face. . . . [Landon] also took the soldier for an Indian and, dropping the buffalo meat, ran for his life. The soldier had not time to reload, but ran too, each believing the other wanted to cut him off from camp; at last they came nearer and found out their mistake. The soldier was a good deal laughed at by his comrades, but L. lost his buffalo meat.

The Indian dead were carrion for crows and coyotes. Harney buried his dead on the south side of the river, evidently near his original encampment just west of Ash Hollow. According to the 1857 accounts of T. J. Ables and Capt. Gove, these graves were "immediately on the road" and "near the bluffs." At the Blue Water there had been four soldiers killed and accounted for, while four others were seriously wounded. Apparently one of these died in camp, for Helen Carpenter, in her 1856 journal, wrote:

> We passed the graves of five soldiers who were killed in September, 1855, in an action between the Sioux and the U.S. soldiers of Fort Kearny. Tomb stones made of cedar, brought from the bluff, hewn into shape, then painted white, with black lettering. This silent story brought to mind the song of Napoleon . . .

> "He sleeps his last sleep, he has fought his last battle,
> No sound can awake him to glory again."

Helen Carpenter dispelled the notion that Indians avoided Ash Hollow after 1855 out of superstition. Her party camped in the customary place at the mouth (the day before viewing the soldier graves):

> Before the teams could be unyoked, the camp was full of Sioux Indians. We were not accustomed to meeting Indians on such familiar terms, and were somewhat nervous to have so many standing about in the way of the camp arrangements for the night. Uncle Sam [the soldier escort?] kept charging us to keep on our guard, as "nobody knows what they may be up to." They are tall fine looking Indians— the women and men alike wear the hair in two long braids hanging down the back— from its sleek glossy appearance it shows the care it receives. The dress is the same as the Pawnees have, Government Makinaw three point blankets. They come with moccasins to trade for something to eat. . . . I got a pair for a quart of "soog" (sugar) they are very eager for sweetness of any description.

According to William Clark's account of 1857, not all Indians encountered in Ash Hollow after the battle were friendly. At the crossing of the Platte a trader eastbound with buffalo hides,

> told us the Indians had attacked the train. . . . At Ash Hollow there is a steep hill and, as the head teams were going down this hill, the Indians ran in and cut off the three hind wagons from the rest of the train and stampeded the cattle, upsetting two of the wagons. The third teamster got his gun and jumped behind the wagon, and succeeded in keeping the Indians off till the front teamster came up and drove them away, wounding several.

In '57, Capt. Gove of the Utah Expedition observed, "Just below us is a mud fort, Grattan, built by Harney's command, and one company was stationed there for some time; it is now abandoned." (It was evidently abandoned before the 1856 season, since no traveler of that year mentions it.) Echoes of the Blue Water appear also in the 1858 account of Thaddeus Kenderdine, another literate teamster. His train made the hazardous descent at midnight and camped at the bottom of Windlass Hill, all hands hungry and thirsty. Kenderdine managed to be both gloomy and inaccurate:

> Nothing could be more dreary than the region through which we passed. . . . It seemed as if some mighty volcano had once been at work here, blasting and desolating everything around in its upheavings.

Slowly our weak, hollow oxen drew the cumbrous wagons through the yielding sands, which arose and enveloped us in clouds. . . . At last we emerged from this valley of desolation, and moving about a mile up the river, we encamped near its shore. A rush was made for the river by both man and beast, and its warm, yellow waters soon quenched the thirst of all. [What about the famous Ash Hollow spring?]

Near the mouth of Ash Hollow we passed a mail station, near which was encamped a village of Cheyennes. The little naked children crowded around us as we passed by the lodges, whilst the old squaws, squatted around their domiciles, gazed quietly at us through their black, snaky eyes. . . . Near this spot a battle was fought a year before between the Cheyennes and the Americans under General Harney. The fortifications erected by the latter could still be seen on the flat extending between the bluff and the river. One of our men who had been an eye-witness of the fight gave us a graphic description of it.

It was a hard fought contest, but the skill of the Americans at last prevailed over the superior numbers of the enemy. The Cheyennes were entirely routed, with the loss of 200 of their number and all their tents and baggage, which were burned in a huge bonfire by the victors. The squaws were taken prisoner and distributed among our gallant soldiers, but were afterwards given up to their lawful owners. The severe castigation which the Cheyennes received here has humbled them greatly, and they are far less mischievous now than formerly. Old Harney is held in great detestation among them, and the mere mention of his name will bring a scowl on the face of a Cheyenne brave.

Another 1858 visitor was Kirk Anderson, bound for Utah. He recognized this as the "identical spot where Gen. Harney came in his Indian campaign, and on the opposite side of the river charged on the Sioux, and gave them the biggest thrashing they ever got."

The Ash Hollow fight and its consequences remained vivid to several later travelers who passed this way:

This is the place where General Harney killed so many Indians with the Soldiers. We met a lot of Sioux's today with their families moving. The wigwam poles some 20 feet long are lashed to the sides of the Ponies and Baskets are lashed to the poles behind the Pony where the Papooses are carried. This Hollow is the most dangerous place to be attacked by Indians that we have Seen on the whole Route. —J. A. WILKINSON, 1859

I was bitterly disappointed. . . . these Hollows have always been associated with dread in my mind, lurking savages, skulking cyotes and

deeds of crime that made my blood chill. I was surprised to find them
. . . a scene with which no one could connect a remembrance of the
murders said to have been committed here. After supper we visited
Mr. Carney's [sic] fortifications which were thrown up in haste to
protect them against the Sioux Indians. The river has caved in and
taken with it part of the wall while the rest are fast tumbling to
decay.—MARTHA MISSOURI MOORE, 1859

Here Gen. Harney had a battle with the Sioux in 1855. There are
still some vestiges of an earth work which he threw up to protect the
entrance to the gorge or Hollow. It is a wild and rugged place and
did seem to be in strict harmony with the character of the savage
warriors who here made a gallant attempt to stay the foot of the ruthless destiny which is treading out their race.—THOMAS CRAMER, 1859

Ash Hollow is such a sweet little spot. . . . It was here that the rude
children of nature had pitched their tents and were resting after a
long hunting excursion, when they were overtaken and surprised by
General Harney and his men, and an indiscriminate slaughter ensued.
Men, women and children were slain, with scarcely enough left to
carry the news to the next tribe.—MRS. BURLINGAME, 1862

We encamped for supper this evening near the scene of General
Harney's fight with the Indians in 1856 [sic]. He fought and routed
three or four thousand Indians with about 200 men. He lost but few
men and killed several Indians. It is known as the Ash Hollow fight.
We descended through this hollow to the river and near the mouth of
it the fight occurred. There are some sod fortifications to be seen on
the river that he built at that time. He, however, had to leave them
and cross the river with his artillery to fight.—SAMUEL WORD, 1863

    . . . a number of adobe or mud houses on an old Fort made out
of mud. . . . —T. J. REDMAN, 1863

Following the Indian destruction of the Ash Hollow mail station
in the spring of 1855 and the abandonment of the Fort Grattan
soddy by 1856, the first evidence found of a new establishment at
Ash Hollow is in 1858, when there again appears at the canyon
mouth a combination mail station and trading post. Kenderdine
refers to a mail station here that year, while Kirk Anderson speaks
of "a one-horse trading post," where he bought a box "said to contain sardines but which I think are Platte River suckers." That
these two activities were combined under one roof seems evident
from 1859 accounts. Taylor Snow, camping on the north side, referred to a "trading post on the south side of the Platte opposite

our camp. Post Office at the trading post." In his *Guidebook* Randolph Marcy advised, "Half a mile beyond [the spring] this road reached the river. Mail Station and a small grocery here." Allen's *Guide Book* identifies this as "U.S. Mail Station No. 21."

Any theory that this mail station–trading post occupied the remains of Fort Grattan is quickly dispelled, not only by preceding references to the ruinous condition of the fort, but also by the fact that both Allen and Kenderdine identify the two separate structures. The exact location of the 1858–1859 station–post office–trading post "at the mouth" is not known. Also not certain are the precise locations on which sat the Ash Grove Hotel of 1846, the early trading post near the spring, or the 1855 mail station. It is entirely possible that the 1855 and 1859 structures were the same with the old layout simply having undergone repairs, but this is also uncertain. There is no evidence, either, of the identity of the station-keeper or the trading post proprietor of 1859, but the station itself was probably built by mail contractor John M. Hockaday. Finally, we may assert that there is no evidence of a mail station or trading post here after 1859. This is not surprising, for beginning in 1860 the Ash Hollow route was largely abandoned in favor of a new one through Julesburg.

The virtual abandonment of the Ash Hollow route could not have been foreseen in 1857 when Congress authorized the development of a wagon road from Fort Kearny to Honey Lake, California. This involved surveying the best possible route, which might or might not coincide with the well-established California Trail, and making certain engineering improvements which were most needed. In thinking of improvements the surveyors naturally gave early thought to the horrendous hill at Ash Hollow, which, with the passage of countless thousands of wagon wheels and animal hooves, had gone from bad to worse to nearly impassable. Aside from its disconcerting "perpendicularity" (which, says Kirk Anderson, made it impossible for the driver on his box to see the ears of his lead mules), the old downhill routes were becoming powdery. "Besides being dreadfully steep," complained Helen Carpenter, "the road was badly cut up and the dust and sand so deep that the chuck holes could not be seen (but they were plainly felt)—and any way the air was so full of dust that much of the time the oxen were barely visible." The U.S. Army, of course, used this route all the time back and forth from Fort Laramie, but Ash Hollow was always a prob-

lem. Capt. Gove pictured the passage of the Utah Expedition in
August, 1857:

> When we arose the edge of the great basin the sight was wonderful
> to behold. As far as could be seen the bluffs, peaks and ravines pre-
> sented an awful spectacle. To have supposed that our immense train
> could by any possible means pass down through it to the river, which
> was visible through the main cut, was the farthest point from any
> reasonable conjecture. For 4½ miles we did wind down through
> these peaks and ravines, and as we wound round one another appeared
> in front just as insurmountable. . . . We at last came to the point of
> our descent; this is a steep fall of about ½ mile or less, perhaps,
> almost perpendicular. Here the whole command was halted and de-
> tailed to get the train over or down. Both the hind wheels of the
> wagons were locked, and a dozen men to each wagon holding back by
> means of ropes. In this way we got the entire train down without even
> a trace chain being broken.

So it is not surprising that Ash Hollow got certain special attention from William Magraw and Frederick Lander who conducted
the survey. In his field instructions Magraw, the dispossessed mail
contractor of 1855, singled out Ash Hollow as the one place between
Fort Kearny and Independence Rock which had priority for study.
When Lander reached Fort Laramie, he wrote to Magraw, explaining that he had examined Ash Hollow but the improvements
needed there were so extensive that any attempt to make an adequate road would preclude the expedition's arrival in California by
fall. Later in the year Magraw moved on to Ash Hollow, where he
"delayed for a time to make repairs." The exact nature of his repairs here remains unknown. Today there is evidence of some possible early excavation work near the summit of Windlass Hill
which just might represent the effort by Magraw to develop a more
moderate grade north of the main slope, but of this there is no
proof. It might represent instead efforts by homesteaders or road-
builders of the early settlement period of the 1880s. Another possibility is that Magraw's "repairs" were an effort to bypass Ash
Hollow altogether, in the manner of Francis Parkman in 1846. The
official papers of the survey, as well as the reminiscences of Sgt.
Lowe of the Dragoons, divulge the discovery of a way to avoid the
"perpendicular hill." This resulted from Lowe's personal exploration of 1857 while returning from Fort Laramie to Fort Leavenworth with a quartermaster train:

July 29 . . . Arrived at Ash Hollow at 10 o'clock and camped. . . . After lunch mounted my horse and with Billy Daniels for a companion went in search of a road out of Ash Hollow to avoid the one already in use, which is altogether impractical for us with our heavy loads— 3,500 lbs. in each wagon. . . . We found and staked out a route that could be travelled without much difficulty. . . . It took five hours of hard riding to find a route three miles through the bluffs. . . .

July 30—Off at 5, took the new route and at 8 o'clock all wagons were at the top of the hill in safety. . . .

August 11—[On the South Platte] I rode out and met Col. M. F. W. Magraw and his surveying party enroute to California with Tim Goodale, celebrated mountaineer and guide. . . .

August 13—Went with Colonel Magraw to Ash Hollow. He passed his train over my new route without difficulty, and named it "Lowe's Route avoiding Ash Hollow Hill."

It will be noted that this new method of descent to the North Platte did not avoid Ash Hollow (as Francis Parkman had done), but involved some way of entering it other than "the perpendicular hill" now known as Windlass Hill. The exact whereabouts of Lowe's route is not known, but it is suspected that it involved an approach on the east side of the Hollow (opposite Windlass Hill) to a point of intersection with the old 1849 route from Cedar Grove into the Hollow. Whatever its merits, and even though Lowe must be complimented on his ingenuity, it seems that later travelers from force of habit (or else from ignorance of Lowe's discovery), continued to use the older entrance. In any event, the Magraw-Lander highway construction program generally proved to be a fiasco, and the Ash Hollow declivity continued to be a menace to life, limb, and property. By this time the emigrant trains were tapering off, but there was a marked increase in the number of military trains and freighting caravans, particularly those of Russell, Majors and Waddell, as the result of an increased military tempo relating to the Mormon War, or Utah Rebellion, of 1857–1858. Thus the Ash Hollow route got an extraordinary workout with heavy wagons just before it was abandoned.

The event that finally put an end to Ash Hollow miseries was the discovery of gold in Colorado in 1858 and the rapid development thereafter of the Pike's Peak Road down the South Platte to Denver. Although this did not mean the abandonment of the North Platte road to Fort Laramie, South Pass, and Salt Lake City, it did make Julesburg a major junction point. Beginning in 1860, freighters, stagecoaches, and Pony Express riders reached the North Platte via Julesburg and Court House Rock, even though this was some twenty-five miles longer than the time-honored Ash Hollow route. They were doubtless happy to go a little farther and avoid the dubious blessings of California Hill, Windlass Hill, and the sandy drag up the North Platte River from the Hollow to Court House Rock.

Not that Ash Hollow was abandoned altogether. A few stray travelers of the 1860s used the old route, as previously noted. Samuel Word and T. J. Redman, quoted above, were the last emigrants of record. Ada Millington in 1862 is the last of her sex known to report an emigrant descent of Ash Hollow. Although her men double-locked the wagons, "that is, with the regular lock and with a log chain . . . we were all afraid to ride down, and got out and walked." But these people were exceptions; it is not known if they went through Ash Hollow by choice or were confused by out-of-date guidebooks. (An interesting footnote to Ash Hollow history is Capt. Eugene Ware's account of a wood-gathering expedition here in 1864, on detail from Julesburg Station. The strongly armed party was plagued by wolves and Indian alarms.)

Long ago consigned to the scrapbook of history and forgotten by all but a few Oregon-California Trail enthusiasts, Ash Hollow was recently given a new lease on life. In the Statehood Centennial year of 1967 it became Nebraska's newest state park. Thus, it is now assured that Ash Hollow, with its "perpendicular hill," its bubbling springs, its sylvan grove, its sometimes idyllic charm—and its special quality of terror inspired by many ambuscades and the nearby bloody clash between Harney and Little Thunder—will always be a unique living memorial to the Great Migration.

XI

Proceedings at the Court House

THANKS TO PUBLIC-SPIRITED citizens of the Bridgeport, Nebraska, area, Court House Rock, about six miles south of that town, can be reached today by auto. This makes it possible to clamber around and photograph from all angles one of the gigantic landmarks of the Great Platte River Road, a geological phenomenon which made a much more profound impression on plains-weary covered wagon emigrants than it does on more sophisticated travelers today.

Court House Rock—which was just plain "the Court House" to most emigrants—has three primary claims to distinction in Trail history: (1) it marked a crossroads, or junction point, of the trans-continental trail system, for here two major routes merged, the Oregon-California migration road through Ash Hollow and the later freighting and military road from Julesburg, thus fusing again into one trunk route the trails that had split off at the South Platte fords; (2) it was the dramatic introduction to a chain of picturesque bluffs along the North Platte which were considered among the scenic wonders of the West, on a larger scale of magnitude than Ash Hollow and its neighboring Castle Bluffs; (3) Court House Rock itself was a strange illusion, a magic trick that seemed to change shape and size on nearer approach and from different angles, leading to a bewildering variety of descriptions, often contradictory, and a confusing number of alternate names. Most common among these were the Solitary Tower, the Church, the Capitol, and the Castle.

339

Court House Rock stands near the center of a huge triangle formed by the convergence of trail routes here. The north side of this geometric figure is a double line, formed by the Council Bluffs Road north of the Platte and the main California Road south thereof, both heading in a general northwesterly direction from Ash Hollow toward Fort Laramie. The east side of the triangle is formed by the Julesburg Road going nearly due north from Mud Springs to join the California Road at a point about three miles southeast of Bridgeport. An early variation of this route was a track due northwestward from a point about five miles southeast of the Court House, which intercepted the California Road near Facus Springs, about six miles east of Chimney Rock. This branch came within one mile of the Court House and it was about four miles shorter than the above; it was abandoned, however, because it involved unnecessary pulling over sandhills.

The last leg of the triangle is the road that went directly from Mud Springs to Facus Springs, passing south and west of the Court House. While emigrants and freighting contractors preferred the more direct connection east and north of the landmark, this more southerly route was the preference of the Pony Express riders and the military. It was more direct and saved a few miles, although it involved a stiff climb to the plateau after crossing Pumpkin Creek. Margaret Carrington, in 1866, refers to this cutoff west of Mud Springs when she writes, "The old road and the telegraph route deflect to the right about six miles before reaching the Rock; but the present route saves nearly five miles of distance and is more readily made, although somewhat more rolling and sandy."

The Court House was involved with another trail system which roughly corresponded with the southernmost leg of the triangle. This was the Sidney-Deadwood Trail, which, beginning in 1876, crossed the North Platte River on the Camp Clarke bridge about half way between Bridgeport and Facus Springs. This episode of the Black Hills Gold Rush is, however, beyond the scope of this story.

The Court House sits on elevated ground like a massive fortress, dominating the countryside; its chameleon-like changes in appearance and its profound impact on the covered wagon observer will be examined below in detail. But two auxiliary features must be mentioned at the outset to clarify the topography involved. First there is that geological satellite, Jail Rock of today, standing immediately east of the Court House. Logically enough, this *was* called the Jail or Jail House by some emigrants (as Flint and Merrill), but never Jail Rock. It was called a few other things as well, such as "an out-building" (Gove), clerk's office (Wolcott), county building (Ingalls), a low country church (Shepherd), a pillar of the appearance of a lighthouse (Dinwiddie), a sentinel post (Sexton), a shot tower or magazine (J. H. Johnson), and even "the leaning Tower of Pisa" (Langworthy). Its separate identity is noted by Palmer and Stansbury (see below). And in some cases, though rarely, it becomes confused with the Tower, the Castle, or other synonym normally reserved for the Court House itself.

Most emigrants who mention the elevation now known as Jail Rock do so casually, without any effort to pin a label on it. One was Riley Root: "Near this Rock stands another, nearly equal in height, but inferior in size;" another, Peter Decker: "By its side 50 yards off stands a column or tower of the same material, separating it from the Church." The point to be borne in mind about Jail Rock is that for the most part it is not mentioned at all, perhaps only once in every ten references to the dominant Rock. As far as most travelers were concerned, the Court House was the great overwhelming attraction; hence Jail Rock does not figure prominently in this review.

The second topographic feature to bear in mind is the stream which runs around the south base of the Court House from the west, and at a point about three miles east joins a tributary and then turns northward to empty into the North Platte. This is a stream which impresses observant travelers today as it did a century ago for its pastoral charm and limpid clarity. But like the Court House it is plagued by a variety of names which continue to haunt modern writers and map-makers. For purposes of convenience, and to preserve the reader's sanity, it will be referred to here as Pumpkin Creek, since that name (or its variants "Punkin" or "Pumpkinseed") has been in use for over 100 years. (The earliest use of this name encountered is in the journal of H. D. Williams, in 1859.) According to Shumway, this name derives from the fact that the fur trader Manuel Lisa donated pumpkin seeds to the natives in a noble but predictably futile effort to convert those buffalo-hunters to agriculture. This story seems highly suspect, since there is no evidence that Lisa, a Missouri River man who died in 1819, ever came within 500 miles of this neighborhood; but this is the only explanation that has ever been offered, and there may be a grain of truth buried away there somewhere.

The tributary mentioned above (which also had to be crossed by travelers from Julesburg) is identified by Burton in 1860 as Omaha, or Little Punkin, Creek, so one might suppose that he would recognize the main stream as the Big Punkin. Instead, however, he calls it Lawrence Fork. This seems to be one of the very earliest names, probably an Anglicized version of the French Lorren, Loran, or Laurin, and probably named for a long-lost French Canadian trapper. "Gonneville" is another name that is given on early maps. Unless this name is a corruption of Bonneville (for the illustrious explorer who passed nearby in 1832), both Gonneville and Lawrence, or Lorren, were probably trappers in the same mysterious league with "Goshe" of Wyoming's Goshen Hole and Jacques LaRamee of Fort Laramie fame. These names were all perpetuated by mountain men who managed to survive their adventures of the 1820s and 1830s to become the emigrant guides of later decades.

One unverifiable bit of legend, again according to Shumway, is that Gonneville was killed by an Indian in 1830 near the point where Lorren's Fork joins Pumpkin Creek (possibly the junction west of the Court House). "The latter then became known as Gonneville Creek." This is apparently derived from Sage; if so, the correct date of Gonneville's demise was 1833.

Other names for this innocent stream which are found interchangeably in the journals include Dry Creek (Stansbury), Spring Creek (Lewis), Driftwood Creek (Wadsworth), Little Creek (Gaylord), Big Creek (Merrill), and Tower Creek (Geiger). It seems logical to suppose that, in actuality, Little Creek may have been tributary to Big Creek, or that Pumpkin may have been tributary to Lawrence (as Eugene Ware has it), or Lawrence tributary to Gonneville, or vice versa. But nobody seems to know for sure who was right historically. Hence, returning full circle, and by authority of the U.S. Geological Survey, it is Pumpkin Creek for the purpose of this book.

The really big thing about North Platte valley topography was the imposing range of hills to the south for some fifty miles between Court House Rock and Scott's Bluffs, which formed an unforgettable scenic corridor. Again, it is the viewpoint of the slow-paced emigrant of the wet and tree-covered flatlands, viewing the landmarks of the limitless high and dry plains. Those who have feasted on scenic spectacles in faraway places may regard these western Nebraska landmarks as somewhat prosaic or dull. To recapture the bright and unjaundiced vision of the Argonauts, one must heed Shakespeare's advice to view the world with the rapturous innocence of childhood. After all, the mystery and wonder of this world are centered, not in the physical dimensions of the landscape, but in our own roughly oval skulls!

When Pvt. Cornelius Conway of the Utah Expedition of 1857 wrote that, "between Forts Kearny and Laramie the magnificent scenery is unsurpassed, probably unequalled in the world," he was honestly impressed by what he saw. "From what is called Court House Rock," he continues, "by Chimney Rock, on to Scott's Bluffs there is an opacity in the mountains at once grand and sublime. Here indeed the mighty works of the Creator are recognized." The range of highlands and isolated bluffs west of the Court House he calls "a beautiful panorama of Pictured Rocks," far excelling in size and grandeur the famous bluffs of this name to be found along the Mississippi River.

Conway was not alone in referring to the North Platte valley bluffs as "mountains." Several easterners whose knowledge of mountains was limited to the Blue Ridge or the Missouri Ozarks speak of "coming down the mountain" at Ash Hollow. In the same vein John Carr in 1850 describes the scenery from the Court House westward as stupendous: "Mountains to the west are piled up against each other as far as the eye can reach." Carr's writing is in the form of reminiscences rather than a current journal. When he wrote this he had already crossed the Continental Divide, so it was not as though he had seen no real mountains, of the Rocky Mountain variety. In his mind's eye the great Platte valley landmarks would be remembered most vividly, perhaps because they were the first objects to loom against the western sky and fill him with awe. Another traveler impressed by the scenery in these parts was Eugene Ware, an army officer of 1864. Although on this occasion he was eastbound from Fort Laramie, he expresses most eloquently the impact of this valley of wonders upon the western traveler:

> The marching down along the Platte River was indescribably beautiful. The days were tranquil, and ahead of us there seemed to be old castles, ruined cities, and vast cathedrals strung along the route. . . .

We could see everything depicted in the outlines of these hills and bluffs that could be seen along the Rhine or amid the ruins of Europe. . . .

We halted at Punkin Creek, two miles from Court House Rock. I do not remember a march that was so thrilling. . . . Everything was absolutely wild. . . . The scenery was the handiwork of the Almighty, and a man as he rode along knew that he, the man, was master of the situation, and that the whole business belonged to the Almighty and to him. The men in the ranks enjoyed it as much as anyone. They thought they were leaving it for good, and they drank in the scenery and the situation as if it were champagne.

In the 1830s before it was ever identified as the Court House, this rock commanded attention as the first in a great chain of landmarks. In one of the earliest references to it, the naturalist Townsend, accompanying the fur trader Wyeth in 1832, remarked on this "dilapidated feudal castle" which stood guard at the east end of the range. In 1839 Wislizenus, also in the company of fur traders, remarked on this rock, "presenting the appearance of an old castle or citadel," which was the "first cliff in the first chain of reddish sandstone cliffs" which adorned the valley. In 1850 Dabney T. Carr also shows a grasp of the remarkable topography: "The rocky wall on the south now approaches the river so close as scarcely to admit of the passage of wagons, now recedes with a bold curve forming an amphitheatre . . . now broken as it were by some mighty convulsion of nature, forming those isolated mounds to which have been given the names of Court House, the Chimney and Scotts Bluffs." Several travelers identified these prominences as outposts of the Rocky Mountains; Berrien considered the Court House the greatest landmark of them all. He writes:

We turned our mules out to graze nearly opposite the Court House. This is a immense bluff which rises from the plain solitary and alone. . . . It is the first of a series of Bluffs very similar in character which skirt the valley for thirty miles, any one of which would be esteemed great curiosities were they not so completely eclipsed by the magnitude and imposing appearance of the first.

Having examined the unique role of the Court House as a trail junction monument and sentinel outpost of the famous series of valley landmarks, it is time to take a more careful look at the Court House itself. As previously noted, it was the center of a triangle formed by three major approaches, east, west, and south, each with a distinctive view of the Rock. There was actually a fourth major viewpoint also, directly from the north, which would be evident when travelers on the parallel California Road and Council Bluffs Road came abreast of the Rock. The essential point here is that the Court House was a tremendously impressive sight from all directions, its aspect continually changing as the traveler approached or as he circumnavigated the landmark.

According to Root and Connelley, there was a fifth viewpoint, which has been noted by no other contemporary and which the writer has been unable to confirm by observation. This was a fleeting glimpse of the Court House from the South Platte River Road to Julesburg: "There was one point, and one only," says old stage-driver Root, "on the stage road . . . between Alkali Lake and old Julesburg where, when the atmosphere was perfectly clear, we had a view of the somewhat noted Court House Rock, perhaps 50 to 75 miles to the northwest."

The usual approach was from the east, of course, up the trapper road from Bellevue which became the Council Bluffs Road or up the Oregon-California Road from Ash Hollow. The formation could first be discerned at a distance of nearly thirty miles, from the vicinity of Ancient Bluffs Ruins on the north or from Rush Creek on the south. From these vantage points, the Court House floated on the distant horizon and merged with the Jail as a monolith, which led to the early appellation of Solitary Tower (first used in 1845 by Joel Palmer).

As the easterner approached, he became more and more fascinated, to the point where he felt magnetically drawn to the Rock itself, even at the cost of a painful and time-consuming side trip on foot. The general appearance of the Rock on nearer approach was that of a huge public building. Parker and other early travelers thought it resembled a castle, but by the middle 1840s, with the advent of Oregon and California pilgrims, the Castle or Solitary Tower began to evolve into Court House Rock, or simply "the Court House." The general impression of a massive structure or ruin was the same, north or south, as one approached. From the north the Rock appeared on a slight elevation, with a gentle undulating plain between it and the Trail so that it seemed to float shimmering in the sunlit distance or to loom mysteriously when wreathed in fog. From the south its face presented a greater elevation, making it appear even more massive and more forbidding.

However, the trail from the south approached nearer, and the traveler could appreciate its romantic aspect and gigantic proportions without the necessity of the disillusioning side trip required from the other route.

Court House Rock, viewed from north or south, has an obvious resemblance to the familiar building in the city square back home, a vague building block with dome or cupola. This could be anybody's courthouse from Maine to Iowa, but Capt. Stansbury and others give particular credit to the famous old courthouse in St. Louis (constructed during the period 1839–1864 and now the headquarters for the Jefferson National Expansion Memorial), familiar to the traders or voyageurs who were first in the valley and thought they saw "a fancied resemblance to a well-known structure in their own city."

From the California Road, at a distance of about six miles, the Court House illusion is better than at close range, and several journalists comment on this. Capt. Gove refers to a sketch of the Court House (whereabouts now unknown) made by a fellow officer, Capt. Gardner, when "close to it. It is taken so near that the symmetry is injured very much. From the road it is very perfect."

We have seen that, when first viewed from the east, Court House Rock against the skyline, merged with its smaller companion Jail Rock, looked like a single formation, commonly referred to as Solitary Tower (Palmer) but occasionally as Solitary Rock (Richardson), Solitary Castle (Snyder), Lonely Tower (Cranstone), or Lone Tower (Cross). Once abreast of the Rock, however, the emigrant transformed the Tower into the Court House, with its attendant Jail noted far less frequently. Thus, Solitary Rock and Court House Rock, and their variants, are synonymous. Indeed, many emigrants freely interchange the terms. Thus one Forty-Niner speaks of "Solitary Tower alias Court House Rock," while Moorman in 1850 writes of "Lone Tower or Court House." Some diarists, unable to make up their minds, keep changing the name within their own pages. For example, in one paragraph Howell speaks of the Court House, the Church, and the Castle, all referring to the same thing, though a casual reader might suppose that he was describing three different places.

There are many other variants in the journals and guidebooks. Among the most common alternatives was the Church (Sedgley, Ware), with variations of Church Rock (Dr. T.) and Prairie Church

(Field). Other terms encountered, which by no means exhaust the list, are Court House Block (Conyers), Court House Bluff (Short), Court House Tower (Dalton), Nebraska Court House (Duniway), Castle Court House (Hoffman), Castle Palace (Hoffman), Castle Rock (Minto, Bradway), the Castle (Parker), McFarlan's Castle (Sage), the Capitol (Carleton), Capitol Rock (Fouts), Council Rock (Word), Convent Rock (Steele), Table Rock (Murphy), Devil's Tea Table (Field), Babel Tower (R. Root), and Tower of Babel (C. Richardson). Surprisingly, misspellings are quite infrequent, Wilson's "Cort House" and Green's "Coart House" being very much the exception.

Speaking of the Tower of Babel, naturally some confusion results from this bewildering assortment of names for one simple rock formation. The term "Capitol" is more commonly applied to Scott's Bluffs, but sometimes also to modern Castle Rock near Melbeta. "Castle" is more often reserved historically for Castle Bluffs by the sand road seven miles west of Ash Hollow.

The cause of confusion is furthered by one writer (Cagwin) referring to "The Chimney" when he doesn't mean Chimney Rock at all, but actually the small neighboring formation now known as Jail Rock. Others speak of the Church *and* Tower; the Court House *and* Church (Woodward); the Castle Rock *and* Lone Tower (Shombre); or Castle *and* Solitary Tower (Ingersoll). Forty-Niner Thomas Eastin says that as he approached the formation, the single "Solitary Tower becomes Tower Hill *and* Courthouse." In all these cases the writers confer separate identities upon the Court House and the Jail, but use names more frequently reserved for the Court House alone.

In most instances of landmark nomenclature in the journals, unless the name coincides with historically acceptable ones (such as Solitary Tower or Court House), identification can only be made by analysis of topography or mileages given. In some cases, of course, clear identification is possible in spite of the difference in names, as in the case of Philura Vanderburgh: "For days we travelled in sight of two great rocks across the Platte. . . . Table Rock we called one, and Court House Rock the other. Great piles of stone they were, like huge castles. It seemed we would never pass them."

The magical qualities of the Court House can best be appreciated by the comments of several travelers over a thirty-year period, from 1835 to 1866, representing a cross section of many traveling types, not only emigrants of varying background, but missionaries, soldiers, scientific explorers, and gentlemen adventurers.

While the first clear allusion to the formation known as the Court House appears in Townsend's journal, the first good description of it is given in 1835 by Samuel Parker, missionary to Oregon:

> We encamped to-day in the neighborhood of a great natural curiosity which, for the sake of a name, I shall call the old castle. It is situated up on the south side of the Platte, on a plain, some miles distant from any elevated land, and covers more than an acre of ground; and is more than fifty feet high. It has, at the distance of the width of the river, all the appearance of an old enormous building, somewhat dilapidated; but still you see the standing walls, the roof, the turrets, embrasures, the dome, and almost the very windows; and large guard-houses, standing some rods in front of the main building.

While his actual sketch of the Rock has not been found, the earliest known artist to attempt a sketch, Alfred J. Miller, has bequeathed to us this 1837 description, which includes the first known usage of the term "Court House"

> In its [Chimney Rock's] immediate neighborhood are formations not less singular, to which the Trappers have given names, indicative of their approach in form to different structures in civilized life; for instance;—the "Court House."

Rufus Sage, en route to Fort Laramie with traders in 1841, gives us this literate view:

> Oct. 24th. About noon we crossed Gonneville's creek, a large easterly affluent of the Platte. This stream also derives its name from a trapper, killed near it in an Indian fight, some eight years since.
>
> Upon the south bank of Gonnesville's creek, ten or twelve miles from the river, is a singular natural formation, known as the Court House, or McFarlan's Castle, on account of its fancied resemblance to such a structure. It rises in an abrupt quadrangular form, to a height of three or four hundred feet. . . . Occupying a perfectly level site in an open prairie, it stands as the proud palace of Solitude, amid her boundless domains.
>
> Its position commands a view of the country for forty miles around, and meets the eye of the traveller for several successive days, in journeying up the Platte. We have been in sight of it for three days, and even now seem no nearer than at first.

Here, for the first time, I remarked the deceptiveness of distances, on the high prairies and in regions adjacent to the mountains. Sometimes an object will appear as if within a mile, at most, which cannot be reached short of fifteen or twenty miles; then, again, objects will seem to be much further off than they really are.

I attribute this in part, to three several causes:—First, the variable state of the atmosphere, in regard to density. Second, the absence or plenitude of humid exhalations and effluviae in the air of different regions. Third, the peculiar locality of some places in regard to the reception of the sun's rays.

Joel Palmer was an Oregon-bound observer of 1845:

June 19. Five miles, today, brought us to Spring Creek; eleven miles further to another creek, the name of which I could not ascertain; there we encamped, opposite the Solitary Tower. This singular natural object is a stupendous pile of sand and clay, so cemented as to resemble stone, but which crumbles away at the slightest touch. I conceive it is about seven miles distant from the mouth of the creek; though it appears to be not more than three. The height of this tower is somewhere between six hundred and eight hundred feet from the level of the river. Viewed from the road, the beholder might easily imagine he was gazing upon some ancient structure of the old world. A nearer approach dispels the illusion, and it looks, as it is, rough and unseemly. It can be ascended, at its north side, by clambering up the rock; holes having been cut in its face for that purpose.

The second, or main bench, can be ascended with greater ease at an opening on the south side, where the water has washed out a crevice large enough to admit the body; so that pushing against the sides of the crevice one can force himself upward fifteen or twenty feet, which places the adventurer on the slope of the second bench. Passing around the eastern point of the tower, the ascent may be continued up its north face. A stream of water runs along the northeastern side, some twenty rods distant from the tower; and deep ravines are cut out by the washing of the water from the tower to the creek. Near by stands another pile of materials, similar to that composing the tower, but neither so large nor so high.

Also in 1845, with Col. Kearny's Dragoons, was Lt. Carleton, the cavalryman who reveled in North Platte scenery:

By four o'clock in the afternoon we passed another very considerable stream, called Laran's Creek. . . . About six miles to the southward of us, a large, natural structure, resembling the ruins of an old castle, rises abruptly from the plain. It is about three hundred feet in height, and some quarter of a mile in length. . . . Its outline, and general proportions are such, that it is difficult to look upon it and not believe that art had something to do with its construction. The voyageurs have called it the Courthouse; but it looks infinitely more like the Capitol. . . . There is something remarkable in these isolated towers. They are composed of precisely the same materials as the distant bluffs . . . yet why have they sustained themselves when the whole country round them has been dug out and carried off by the ages, until this great valley has been formed, whereon they stand in all their loneliness, like huge monuments . . . is a wonder. . . . If they were composed of more enduring substances than that part which has been gnawed off by the tooth of time . . . there could be a cause easily understoood why they remain—but such is not the case.

Edwin Bryant, California-bound in 1846, wrote glowingly of Court House Rock in a journal which was published before the Gold Rush and became in effect one of the better known guides. Later emigrants frequently allude to this passage:

The atmosphere this morning being clear, we saw distinctly the "Chimney Rock" at a probable distance of thirty-five or forty miles. Some ten or twelve miles this side of it we also saw an elevated rock, presenting an imposing and symmetrical architectural shape. At this distance its appearance was not unlike that of the capitol at Washington; representing, with great distinctness of outline, a main building, and wings surmounted by domes. This, I believe, has been named by emigrants the "Court-house."

As we approached this large rock, it assumed still more definitely the regular proportions of an artificial structure. At times its white walls and domes would appear in a perfect state of preservation; in other views they appeared partially ruinous, like some vast edifice neglected or deserted. . . . Desirous of examining this object more closely than could be done by an observation from the trail, accompanied by Mr. Lippincott, I left our party, turning our horses in a direction towards it. . . .

We continued our course towards the rock about three miles further, when its distance from us appeared to be still so great that we concluded we could not visit it and overtake our fellow-travellers before night. The rock appeared, from the nearest point where we saw it, to be from 300 to 500 feet in height, and about a mile in circumference. Its walls so nearly resemble masonry, and its shape an architectural design, that if seen in an inhabited country, it would be supposed some colossal edifice, deserted and partially in ruins.

The Court House did not go unnoticed, of course, by the Mormon Pioneers of 1847, among them William Clayton: "Opposite the camp on the south side of the river is a very large rock very much resembling a castle four stories high, but in a state of ruin. A little to the east stands a rock which looks like the fragment of a very thick wall." Byron McKinstry, a non-Mormon traveler on the Council Bluffs Road in 1850, remarks: "The large rock called the Court House on the other side of the river shows beautifully today and in some places the deception is complete as it looms up through the haze." Coming along two years later, also on the north side, John Kerns wrote: "Now in sight of Court House rock a solitary tower which is about ten miles south of here. It has the appearance of a court house or some public edifice from the road. On the main rock there is a small elevation resembling a cupola. There is a large rock on the side of the cort house which resembles a jail house."

During the California Gold Rush of 1849 the Court House came under the scrutiny of a host of Forty-Niners who followed the south bank. Typical is Joseph Merrill, who wrote:

About ten A.M. came in sight of the Court House. This great natural curiosity is a high mound of earth some 500 feet and in the distance resembles a building built after the Gothic style; near it is a similar one of smaller size which I shall style the Jail, as jails seem to be necessary appendages for court houses. This earth judging from all about it is a part of a high bluff, the vacuum about having been produced by some convulsion of the earth or the elements. Towards night we crossed a fine stream called Big Creek.

This P.M. Dr. McK. has been to the summit of the Court House and describes the view from the summit as most beautiful.

Another Forty-Niner who writes appreciatively is Elisha Perkins:

June 27. passed within about 3 or 4 miles of Courthouse Rock which presents a grand & imposing appearance. I should call it a castle as it is mainly round & looks as if it might be fortified. Its size must be immense though I had not time to go over to examine it. It rises abruptly out of the rolling country & stands entirely alone with the exception of a smaller square rock some hundred feet from it called "The Jail." It seems to be the vanguard of the Rocky Mts., as beyond it the rocks and irregular outline of bluffs & mountains increased in frequency with the distance. . . . this is the first large mass of rock we have seen. It is well worth a place in a sketch book of scenery.

A Forty-Niner who did visit the Rock was Peter Decker:

At noon stop 8 miles from the Court House or Church, its dome &
Chimney Rock in sight today very clear. . . . An "Italian sky" the
moon shown bright in day time. . . . Left camp at noon for the
Church or Court House over rough barren prairies, hills and vallies
found it a very hard walk. It seemed to recede into the distance until I
almost despaired reaching it finally reached it a huge mass of conglomerate or soft sand stone standing out in bold relief lonely and
singular looking with an almost perfect dome ascended it some
50 ft & had the folly like others to inscribe my name on it with
knife on this perishable rock or sand pile. By its side 50 yds off stands
a column or tower of same material with deep ravine separating it
from the Church. Good view from the Church.

The impressions of the government explorer Stansbury, who
passed here late in the 1849 season, are of particular interest:

Saturday, July 7 . . . This morning we caught a view of the celebrated "Chimney Rock" and also of the "Court-house," which latter
consisted of two bald elevations . . . to which the voyageurs, most of
whom are originally from St. Louis, had given this name, from a
fancied resemblance to a well-known structure in their own city.

In riding out from the road to visit this curious formation we
found the main bluff of the river to be about five miles distant. . . .
In our ride we crossed the dry sandy bed of a stream, about 250 feet
in width, which, in the rainy season, must discharge a large quantity
of water. It had little or no bank, and from the appearance of driftwood way out on the prairie, must overspread a large surface in the
spring. A mile and a half from this creek we came upon another,
called on the maps, "Dry Creek," but known among the mountain-
men as "Lawrence's Fork," from the fact that a man of that name had
been killed on it by the Sioux. The Court-house was but a few
hundred yards beyond this stream . . . I attempted to cross it, but the
bottom consisted of stiff marly mud, into which the feet of the
animals sank rapidly, and would with difficulty be withdrawn. Fearful
of miring them down, I gave up the attempt, and thus lost the
opportunity of examining this celebrated seat of justice more closely.

Two other illuminating accounts are provided by the great
migration of 1850:

We ascended it with some difficulty and no little danger to life and
limb—one place the ascent was about twenty feet perpendicular or
nearly so, we affected the ascent by means of rude foot and hand

holes put in the soft rock by means of knives. On reaching the summit the wind blew hard and chilly. The top of it is from 6 to 20 feet wide only, and on the south side of it was a perpendicular precipice of 300 Feet. I involuntarily shuddered as I looked over this dizzy height. The prospect was here indeed beautiful and picturesque, a large boundless slope or level plain, stretched away to the south, to the west arose a succession of cones, spires and all sorts of fantastic hills, among others in the distance towered up the far famed Chimney Rock like a huge shot tower, distant 20 miles. On the other side could be seen the winding trail of the emigrants road dotted here and there by groups of small white objects we knew to be wagons. . . .

Near the Court House but perfectly detached from it, stands a huge perpendicular square column inaccessible, but not quite so lofty as the Court House. This is called the Jail. . . .

Names so thick that all eligible locations for names were already occupied. I accordingly went without carving my name on this monument rock.—W. McBride

June 1 . . . away to the left loomed up to appear a most stately mansion, an old feudal castle with bastions, parapets, etc., entirely detached from any range of hills. . . . Surely nature casts up many a freak that geologists or naturalists can hardly explain. . . .

This being Sunday we laid by for the respite of man & beast—our camping ground is truly romantic. Apparently just over a rising swell of undulating Prairie stands out in bold relief one of nature's stately edifices, the Coart House or Church. . . . Though over 10 miles off, apparently it is not over three, so thought some of our Co., & others who started after breakfast as they thought of an hours stroll to view this, one of the Wonders of the valley of the Platte. . . . Tired and weary sometime after dark they returned fully satisfied that appearances indeed are very deceptive.

This handy work of nature is said to be over half a mile in circumference, and between 350 and 400 feet in height. An out tower near by of the same height and a limpid brook running at its base adds beauty to the scene.—N.A. Cagwin

W. Wadsworth, whose *National Wagon Road* was published in 1858 as a guidebook, makes this observation based on an actual journey in 1852:

This magnificent formation is situated upon the south border of the Platte river, about 250 miles west of Fort Kearny, and nearly eight miles to the south of the emigrant road, though it does not appear to be half that distance. It has doubtless derived its name from the peculiarity of its form as a national object, its colossal size, and remarkable isolation. Situated miles apart from any mountain range, this solitary rock, at a distance of six or eight miles, seems to rise up from the grassy plain, with sides nearly perpendicular, to the hight of nearly 400 feet, and above this a vast dome; the whole when viewed from a distance, and from two or more points along the emigrant road, presents an outline so perfectly regular and rounded, and the whole formation so completely resembling an edifice of vast dimension, as to appear more like a work of art than nature.

As you approach nearer than three miles, irregularities appear upon its surface which, with its sloping abutments, in ridges around its base, not distinctly visible from the road, mar somewhat, upon a closer view, the beauty of the formation. But as a conspicuous and noted object, seen by the traveller, as he passes along the great plains, that here border the Platte River, the "Solitary Tower", as one of Nature's own, will ever stand in the front rank for grandeur and magnificence.

Another kind of traveler was Thaddeus Kenderdine, bullwhacker extraordinary:

The next day, in the forenoon, we came in sight of the Court House Rock. This natural curiosity is situated about nine miles south of the road, but oweing to the dry and pure atmosphere of this region, it does not appear to be more than two or three. It is apparently about 300 yards long and 200 in height. It is composed of marl and earthy limestone, and is worn into its peculiar shape by the action of the elements on its soft constituents. Standing alone above the broad plain, its outlines rendered singularly regular by distance, it has an extremely majestic appearance, having much the look of an ancient feudal castle, and the sight of it formed a pleasing variation to the monotony of our journey.

A Mormon told me that while passing this rock one of his party was filled with curiosity to examine it closely, and under the impression that it was but a short distance from the road, he mounted his horse and rode towards it, thinking to regain his comrades in a short time. The plain seemed so level, and the Court House so near that he imagined that he was going on a nice little journey of pleasure, but he soon found himself mistaken. Deep ravines were continually obstructing his path, and worse than all, the object he was seeking seemed like the *ignus fatuus* to fly before him. . . . But . . . perseverance will accomplish anything, and he at least reaching this majestic landmark. . . . late in the night came up with his comrades, well wearied and hungered, if not satisfied with his side excursion.

Among the later covered wagon emigrants up the California Road from Ash Hollow was Edwin Bird, in 1859:

In front of us could be seen the selebrated far famed Court House Rock This afternoon . . . camped about four nearly opposite Court House Rock. It looks to be about two miles off but Mr. Parks says it is all of five miles. It is a pondrous mass of stone & in the distance looks very much like a large stone building black spots looking like doors & windows are plain to be seen I shoud like to visit it but the distance is a little too great two of the young men of the train firmly in the belief that it was not more than two miles started to make an evenings call at the ancient Hall of Justice Mr. F. says it is 600 feet high or one mile in circumference. . . .

The boys that went to the rock got back about 10 O'c fully satisfied that it was five miles off but thought they were well repaid for their trip.

One other traveler who cannot be ignored here is Richard Burton, English adventurer and connoisseur of exotic scenery, who approached the Court House in 1860 in a stagecoach via the Julesburg Road:

After a twelve miles' drive we fronted the Court-house, the remarkable portal of a new region, and this new region teeming with wonders will now extend about 100 miles. It is the *mauvaises terres*, or Bad lands, a tract about 60 miles wide and 150 long. . . .

The Court-house, which had lately suffered from heavy rain, resembled anything more than a court-house; that it did so in former days we may gather from the tales of many travellers, old Canadian voyageurs, who unanimously accounted it a fit place for Indian spooks, ghosts, and hobgoblins to meet in pow-wow, and to "count their coups" delivered in the flesh. The Court-house lies about eight miles from the river, and three from the road; in circumference it may be half a mile, in height 300 feet; it is, however, gradually degrading, and the rains and snows of not many years will lay it level with the ground. The material is a rough conglomerate of hard marl; the mass is apparently the flank or shoulder of a range forming the southern buttress of the Platte, and which, being composed of softer stuff, has gradually melted away, leaving this remnant to rise in solitary grandeur above the plain.

In books it is described as resembling a gigantic ruin, with a huge rotunda in front, windows in the sides, and remains of roofs and stages in its flanks: verily potent is the eye of imagination! To me it appeared in the shape of an irregular pyramid, whose courses were inclined at an ascendable angle of 35°, with a detached outwork composed of a perpendicular mass based upon a slope of 45°; in fact, it resembled the rugged earthworks of Sakkara. . . . According to the driver the summit is a plane upon which a wagon can turn. My military companion remarked that it would make a fine natural fortress against Indians, and perhaps, in the old days of romance and Colonel Bonneville, it has served as a refuge for the harried fur-hunter.

I saw it when set off by weather to advantage. A blazing sun rained fire upon its cream-coloured surface . . . and it stood boldy out against a purple-black nimbus which over-spread the southern skies, growling distant thunders, and flashing red threads of "chained lightning."

In 1865 Pvt. George Holliday was marching with U.S. Volunteers from Julesburg to Fort Laramie when he had a vision:

We had been riding along for hours in utter silence wondering if the desert would never end. Our canteens had long since been emptied and our ponies began to show signs of thirst and exhaustion, when just beyond us suddenly looms up like a vision, what appeared to be a gigantic house with a tall spire pointing far up into the clouds.

An exclamation of wonder burst from the whole command. Never were men more surprised. It was a diversion which served at once to relieve the monotony and help us forget our sufferings.

"We'll stop at the house tonight," said one of the boys.

"It can't be but a few miles away," said another.

"Boys," says Lieutenant Brazie, "That is Court House Rock, and it is thirty miles distant. We'll camp under the shadow of that rock tomorrow night, if the Indians don't head us off."

"Thirty miles away! It can't be possible," said several of the men, who would have bet on their carbines shooting into the very dome of the Great Sham Court House.

"Yes, its a big day's march for us," replies the Lieutenant who had been posting himself as to the scenes along the road.

Several men wanted to bet $50. and give their note payable "on or before next pay day," that he was mistaken on that point, but the Lieutenant already held their paper for all money due them from the United States, so no bets were taken. . . .

As the Lieutenant had said, we camped under this rock the first night after we left Willow Springs [Mud Springs]. As we approached we could see plainly the figures of several of our men who had gone on before and ascended to the very dome of the "Capital." Although they were many miles away, and did not look larger than a man's thumb, yet each one could be recognized, so clear was the atmosphere.

But while we were gazing upon the grand scene a curtain of mist spread over its crest and for a moment it was hid from our vision. Then it cleared away and we could plainly hear the shouts and see our boys waving their hats just under the passing clouds.

In the following year, 1866, the great Rock was visited by Julius Birge, who had a different experience:

For many miles we had observed the majestic outlines of the conspicuous landmark well known as Court House Rock. As our course finally approached within two miles of its cliffs, Ben and I determined to secure a view from its summit. That remarkable monument stands in solitary grandeur upon the barren plain; it has, however, a worthy associate not far away, another prominence known as the Jail; these high bluffs are appropriately named. From a distance Court House Rock has the appearance of some vast ancient ruin. The grandeur and beauty of its outlines and the majesty of its proportions have made it a notable landmark for all travelers who pass that way. We found its ascent comparatively easy, but the descent was somewhat difficult because of the projecting terraces which, though of hard material, were cracked, leaving projections that could not be depended upon for support. Although we might well have saved our energies for the hot tramp through the sands which lay before us, we obtained views of the "bad lands" to the west, which were very impressive.

It seemed as if in the Creation there had been a vast amount of crude material left over, which had been dumped into that waste, but the essential elements of life were wholly absent. As far as could be seen through the clear, hot, and quivering air of noonday everything was silent and dead. On reaching the trail Ben and I followed the track of our wagons in the white sand, which glowed like a furnace, and finally overtook our party, which was slowly dragging along with occasional pauses for rest.

From this cross section of observations one may discern certain patterns of comment that would be repeated and elaborated upon endlessly in trail literature. Chief among the usual notations or "proceedings at the Court House" were: (1) the Court House as number one in the chain of North Platte valley landmarks; (2) the solitary and lonely magnificence of the Court House or Solitary Tower; (3) the romantic imagery or many fanciful appearances conjured up by this apparition (more realistically, its impressive mass and dimensions); (5) the trickiness of the atmosphere in these latitudes, causing all kinds of deceptions as to distances and appearances; (6) the magnetic appeal of the Court House to

amateur mountain climbers; (7) the role of the Court House as
another register of the desert, similar to Independence Rock in
Wyoming, with countless carvings that have long since eroded away;
and (8) the awe-inspiring view from the summit, i.e. the dome
of the Court House or the highest battlement of the Tower.

Although it was actually only an erosional remnant of the chain
of bluffs that extended over forty miles up the valley (or an outpost of the Rocky Mountains if imagination is used), this connection
was not at first readily apparent from the trail, and many travelers
were impressed by the lonely splendor of the Court House, which
gave it an unreal quality. From far to the east this isolated knob
impressed itself on the wayfarers, by then wearied with sameness.
As they approached, the element of isolation and mystery was
enhanced, especially after the Solitary Tower fractured into the
Court House–Jail phenomenon. At the same time, the sojourner in
distant realms is anxious to see in the landscape the comfortable and
the familiar. Thus, the Lonely Tower becomes the old Court
House and vice versa. No other trail landmark resulted in such a
wavering between the strange and the familiar, between wonder and
recognition.

The term "Court House" was published for the first time in
Sage's account of 1841, but it appears not to have become the
principal designation until 1849. (Castles, Capitols, and Solitary
Towers dominate prior to this date.) The imagined resemblance to
the courthouse in St. Louis, mentioned by Stansbury, is echoed by
Searls in 1849, Gove in 1857, and others. The St. Louis structure
would have been familiar to many emigrants who funneled through
that city, as well as to earlier fur traders. Abbey in 1850 likened
it to the courthouse at Louisville (Kentucky, presumably). Lewis
Dougherty, whose father ran the sutlers' stores at Fort Kearny and
Fort Laramie, didn't specify the St. Louis courthouse, but explained
it this way:

> Twenty miles up you will see Court House rock resembling a Missouri
> court house so much as to deceive many on their first trip. Father
> was once passing with a colored lad driving his vehicle. He had
> heard of this rock, and when oposite, the boy called father's attention
> to the rock, saying, "Court must be in session, there are many horses
> hitched near the house." These were cedar shrubs growing at the
> front. This is not a rock but a hard, dry hill with little or no grass
> on it.

William Kelly took exception to the courthouse concept:

> Our next day's journey was through loose drifting sands that reached from the river edge to the bluffs, not presenting a single feature worthy of note or comment either in vegetable or animal life, with the exception of a huge isolated rock, about six miles from the river, called by the trappers Court House Rock, from its supposed resemblance to a large public building of that description; but there was nothing about it of that striking character to seduce me from my path so far aside to visit it.

But in the majority were those travelers who were sure the courthouse was there, plain for all to see:

> The Court House strongly resembled such a building, with wings; it rests imposingly on a bluff; the sides are near a cream color, with apparently, a black roof.—COOKE, 1845

> . . . a credit to its name. It was a huge affair and in its ragged irregular outline, seemed to impart to travelers a sense of protection and fair dealing.—COLE, 1849

> It bears some resemblance to a court house it is 200 feet high and stands out by itself on the open plain on the top is a mass or rock similar to the dome of a court hous.—HACKNEY, 1849

> . . . looks very like a court house with a foure corner roof.—THOMASSON, 1850

> The large rock called the Court House on the other side of the river shows beautifully today and in some places the deception is complete as it looms up through the haze.—McKINSTRY, 1850

> . . . looks like a large public building of stone.—BAILEY, 1852

> It very much resembles the Court House with the clerk's office. . . . it appears to be about the hight of the common court house. . . . It is a great natural curiosity.—RAMSEY, 1849

A capitol or statehouse may be considered a first cousin to a courthouse, presumably. At any rate several writers saw here nothing less than the nation's capitol, as for example, Conway: "As you approach these hills from the east, the first object that presents itself to your view is Court-House Rock, which is an exact counterpart of the Federal Capitol at Washington, standing out, isolated and alone, on the broad prairie." The likeness to the Washington, D.C., structure is echoed by Fairchild, Dewolf, and Buffum. Others, however, thought they saw the likenesses of their state capitols back home. "Like the State House in [Jefferson City] Missouri," says Rhodes. "Resembles the Capitol at Madison [Wisconsin]," says Harriet Ward. On the contrary, says R. Hickman, this rock, "one of the greatest natural curiosities I have seen since I left home, bears a striking resemblance to the state house in Springfield [Illinois]."

The church idea seems to have been mainly the responsibility of Joseph Ware, for his guidebook speaks of "Church or Court House," and we find several references which usually bracket these two similarities, as for example Decker (above), Hickman's "Church or Court House Bluff," and Hagelstein's "Church or City Hall." Margaret Frink writes in 1850, "We expect to reach in a few days some great natural curiosities. One is a large rock in shape like a court-house, or a church without a steeple!"

Many travelers, while acknowledging the Court House designation, felt that a better name could have been chosen. Rather than a hall of justice, thought Duniway, these were the "ruins of some colossal edifice which rises up as if to mock the plainer scenery around it." Benjamin Ferris felt it "a misnomer to give it so common a name." No mere courthouse would so rise from the plain in solitary grandeur. Rather, "from the distance it looks like an immense temple or castle reared to some heathen divinity, or by some feudal baron in ages gone by but is now in a state of decay." Jno. H. Clark, like these others of the 1852 migration, saw a lot more than a simple courthouse:

> Awoke this morning just as the sun was flooding [in] its golden light that Giant monument of the plains. . . .
>   is there anything more grand, more magnificent, more imposing . . . than that which you now behold? A solitary monument on the level plains, look at it and tell me if you are not enchanted with its beauty and its majesty? Scrutinize its huge but fair proportions and tell me if you have fault to find? . . . It is not a masterpiece of nature's architecture? Does it not look like some giant temple within whose walls have worshipped for thousands of years the "Children of the great West"?

Kirk Anderson, en route to Utah in 1858, thought that if this was a courthouse, it was the biggest one ever beheld:

> The huge proportions of the [Court House] stood out in bold relief against the horizon, and although we were many miles from it, we

had a good idea of its vast size. The name given to it is an inappropriate one, for in its native architecture and proportions it is very much like modern public edifices, except that it is not fluted, corinthianized and gingerbreaded, out of all taste, but its grooves and colonnades were carved out by the hand of the great architect and master-mechanic of creation himself.

Others, under the spell of a strange country, named the Court House and then began naming all kinds of other resemblances. Israel Hale's confused remark is typical: "We are encamped in full view of the rock called Court House or Church; it is distant about six miles and resembles a large castle in a dilapidated state." Eastin, another Forty-Niner, couldn't make up his mind either: "Sometimes it looked like the dome of the St. Charles at New Orleans. Sometimes the Center Dome of the Capitol at Washington, D.C., or a castle tower of the olden time." Then he thought he saw a "city of castles whose tops were covered with gold against the sun." Caroline Richardson in 1852 was even more uncertain of "this rather singular looking structure." To her it variously resembled a large cottage, a church or courthouse, the Tower of Babel, or simply a "strange looking mass of rocks rising to the height of 400 feet."

Probably reflecting their heavy indoctrination with classic Greek, Latin, and medieval history in the public schools of the period, many emigrants found all kinds of resemblances to fortifications and other features of antiquity. The identification of "castle" is most common in the earlier period, as with Parker, Townsend, and John Minto, who in 1844 felt that this Castle Rock was "too big for human use." A few other specimens from the romantic school of thought follow:

> . . . a ruined castle . . . with corner towers, a dome and a detached portion, as though the vestibule had been separated from the body of the edifice by decay. . . . As we encamped a thunderstorm broke over us, and the descending sun burst from the west through it horizontally . . . making the old "Church" glitter like burning silver, while a georgeous rainbow opened over it . . . and distant hills seemed like an original city with domes, towers and minarets. A gorgeous scene! The whole company paused in wonder at it.—FIELD, 1853

> Four or five miles from our nooning raises a bank of clay & rock having all the appearance of some old castle of circular shape the spire having been Blown down the main walls and dome roof in good

state of preservation and still showing the rubble rock of which the structure was formed.—CLYMAN, 1844

This curiosity is a single hill, shaped and bearing the appearance of a large castle with its turrets, battlements and wings; and at a distance of four miles, would deceive the most practiced eye were it not known that it is situated in a wilderness hundreds of miles from habitation. —SNYDER, 1845

It had the appearance of a vast edifice, with its roof fallen in, the great door-ways partially obstructed, some of the window spaces filled with rubbish, and many of the arches broken and fallen, while others seemed to remain as perfect as if they had really been built thousands of years ago, by a people who have perhaps gone down into the vortex of revolutions . . . leaving no trace of their existence, save these remains of architectural grandeur and magnificence, that now lift up their heads amid the surrounding desolation.—THORNTON, 1846

It but little resembles the dome of the Capitol at Washington [a dig at Bryant]. It represents somewhat an old fort, but struck me as resembling muchly the Bishop's Palace at Monterey, Mexico.—GEIGER and BRYARLY, 1849

. . . a remarkable resemblance to a stupendous edifice or rock castle, standing in lone majesty.—J. EVANS, 1850

I have seen a great many Natural curiosities Both in Europe and this country but none to exceed These for symmetry of shape and architectural Beauty It has the appearance of a cathedral in Ruins.—WOODWARD, 1850

. . . a great natural curiosity called the Church or Court House . . . ruins of an ancient European fortress of great magnitude.—GORGAS, 1850

Camped opposite Court House or Castle Rock . . . a rude massive building partly in ruins with one wing detached.—BRADWAY, 1853

. . . a large tower or castle in ruin. I thought were I only in Persia it would be easy to imagine this Babel's Tower, with the broad Euphrates at its base.—WILLIAMS, 1853

. . . a gigantic ruin, with rotunda, windows, cupola. . . . as we were never nearer than seven miles, there was plenty of room for imagination.—MRS. FERRIS, 1852

Earlier in the day we passed a detached rock quite as remarkable [as Chimney Rock] and far more picturesque and beautiful; a precipitous height, whose appearance was not unlike that which, from the description in Waverly, I had often imagined Stirling [Castle] would present, and which the Castle Hill, Edinburgh, looked at from the west, does; but this was more beetling, and seemed hardly to need the crown of battlement's one's eye fancied around its summit. I had been told many times there was no U. S. fortification nearer than Laramie, and yet I was deceived . . . for a couple of hours . . . as ever Eastern traveller was by mirage.—CHANDLESS, 1855

A few descriptions, though without classical allusions, manage to convey the sense of wonder. From the north bank Katherine Dunlap in 1864 observed the architectural features through her husband's spyglass and declared herself a "witness to the vastness and majesty of God's creation." Tompkins in 1850 expressed "utter astonishment" at this "very remarkable eminence," even though he realized it was only "hard clay mixed with pebbles." Pritchard, struggling for words, found that the Court House "presents to the Eye the appearance of an artificial Superstructure, with a round top, doams and Spires." Forty-Niner Johnston came up with something quite unique. The Court House, to him, resembled "an Inca Palace." To others it was simply an immense house (Dr. T.), or a large mansion house (Hoffman), or, to one highly original thinker, a "stolen mansion."

Helen Carpenter speaks of the "immense landmark," but failed to distinguish here anything more glamorous than "houses of sod." Shombre "went to see the castle" and conceded that "it looks like some ancient ruins standing to command the past," but upon closer examination was disillusioned to find that it was only composed of "sand with a crust of stone on the summit," nothing more than "a shapeless heap towering above the surrounding country." Two 1850 visitors were more severe in their judgment: Lampton and fellow Missourians "went up to the Courthouse Rock and found it nothing but a vast heap of sand blown up the height of about 300 feet above the level of the Plains," while Dennis (viewing things from the north side) complained that this rock "does not deserve the flattering encomiums given it by Bryant. This is a barren and desolate country." This is a far cry from Conway's "magnificient scenery unsurpassed, probably unequalled in the world." Again, truth lies not in the configurations of the visible world, but in the illusions of the mind's eye.

While most passersby indulged in fanciful imaginings of architectural forms and a small minority dismissed the Court House as a mere "heap of sand," there were some more practical-minded folks who attempted to describe it realistically, sometimes in geological terms, and estimate its dimensions. The actual height of Court House Rock today, by reckoning of the U.S. Geological Survey, is 4100 feet above sea level, or about 400 feet above the North Platte River. It is actually composed mainly of a soft sandstone called Brule Clay, of the Oligocene age, perhaps 40 million years old, with its upper sections described as Arikaree sandstone interspersed with fluted ledges or concretions of deposited lime, which harder material has contributed to the survival of the bluff, an erosional remnant of the High Plains of Pleistocene times. The emigrants had no way of knowing this, of course; nevertheless, many of them came close in their measurements as well as their geological theories.

Most travelers viewed the Rock from the California Road, thus beholding its north, or lowest, elevation. Those who approached from the south were able to see its south wall, which was its most impressive elevation. Some of the fluctuations in estimates result from the difference in height between the north and south walls. Contemporary estimates of height, in any event, range from 75 feet to 800 feet, with the majority putting it at 300 to 500 feet. Some of the more interesting calculations follow:

Babel Tower . . . is a precipitous bluff of clay, containing lime enough to give some degree of hardness to it. . . . It is 600 feet above the bed of the creek. . . . Near this stands another, nearly equal in height, but inferior in size.—RILEY ROOT, 1848

It was really about 200 feet high, although from the road it appeared only about fifty. . . . it stood upon a little ridge . . . was of circular form, with an elevation on the top much like a flattened dome. . . . Near it, on the east end, was another blunt point rock, not quite as high, which was not particularly remarkable. . . . Soft sand and clay, intermixed with lime, easily cut with a knife—probably of volcanic origin.—DELANO, 1849

. . . 500 feet long and 100 feet wide at the base & at the top from three to ten feet wide . . . on the north side it is about 300 feet high & on the south 500. . . . It is composed of stratum of soft sand stone & of hard sand stone.—DEWOLF, 1849

. . . rock of immense size . . . some 300 feet high by 100 square. At about 100 feet above the base, there is an offset in the wall, as though it had been drawn in to make it smaller. Some halfway from that to the summit there is yet another offset giving it a grand and imposing appearance. . . . It appears to be a composition or sement of gravel and dirt.—Dr. T., 1849

. . . crossed Spring Creek which is situated about 80 rods from said Tower . . . situated on high ground without any other bluffs near by the Elevation is between 6 and 800 ft abouve the leviel of the Platte.—ELISHA LEWIS, 1849

Tis said "distance lends enchantment to the view" just so in this case the distant architectural grandeur faded as we approached.

We found two large columns the east or smaller one being about 150 feet high & about 100 feet in diameter near the top and 150 at base, which was oval or egg-shaped it is composed of rock sand and clay just sufficient of the latter to cement the other together but as there was no way to reach its top I could not ascertain its composition exactly. . . .

The main Church or Tower is about 300 ft high & on the South side nearly perpendicular. On the north tis about 250 feet and length 300 x 100 feet.—PARKE, 1849

Passed a great curiosity a large mound or rock called the court house three stories high and looks like the work of an artist a large rock on the east side about 50 feet high.—COSAD, 1849

Among these fantastical formations are Court-House Bluffs and Chimney Rock—the former about 6 miles south of the road. It is 700 or 800 feet in length from east to west, and probably 300 or 400 wide and 250 feet high, and there are terraces worn around so that it resembles very well a Court-House. . . . I went to it and ascended to the top. . . . It is only from 2 to 8 feet wide on top, and some 200 or 300 long. It is composed of marl and sand, and so hard as to form a kind of rock, and is capped with a kind of lime-stone, which probably has preserved it from the action of the elements.—SQUIRES, 1849

. . . perpendicular escarpments of sandstone, 75 feet high standing as sentinels—THE GENERAL, 1850

this morning i had the curiosity of seeing the rock so i started for it but i found it 4 miles farther than i thought for it stands 300 feet high and the tip is small about 100 yds in circumference and about 100 feet high then it takes a swell of 300 yards in circumference then it takes an aburat [abrupt] slant till it gets over 1 mile round it i clim over 200 feet high and rote my name here i had like to fall down.—GRINDELL, 1850

. . . camp opposite Solitary Tower on Little Creek. . . . I went to
see the Tower through curiosity. It is . . . about 300 feet in length and
150 feet in width at its base. It is a rudely constructed mass of sand.
. . . I think that it once was connected to a high range of bluffs some
distance from it. It appears to have been washed through by some
great freshet, leaving a tower of about 250 or 300 feet high from the
level of the creek.

This tower is about 75 yards in length on the top and about one
rod in width. In places there is some sandstone. On the north side
of the tower a person can ascend to the top without much difficulty.
. . . It seems to be fast washing away. . . . A short distance to the
northeast of it stands another tower, not quite as high, but a great
deal smaller.—GAYLORD, 1850

We got a sight of the grate tower & grate it is this tower is about 6
hundred feete high & is composed of lime & sand something like
sement it is not a soled rock as many ones supposes but it is soft
so that it ma be cut with a knife. This is about a half mile in circumference & about half way up it is about 50 feet in diameter, and
from that down it is not so steep.—JOHN LEWIS, 1852

This is a remarkable eminence rising up in the midst of a low plain
of loose sand. . . . Its form is that of an irregular pyramid of successive
blocks. Its elevation is about 250 feet above the surrounding plain.
. . . Its composition is alternate layers of . . . sand and dark gray rock.
The top is one entire piece of exceedingly coarse gray rock of 18 or
20 inches in thickness. My impression . . . is that it is the remains
of a large bluff which has been swept away in some great overflow
or other mighty convulsion of the elements at a remote period.—
CRAMER, 1859

Sage in 1841 was the first to remark on those twin optical
phenomena of the High Plains, the abnormal clarity of the
atmosphere and the deceptiveness of distances. He offers three
plausible explanations relating to atmospheric conditions, but there
were also psychological factors. The background of the wagon
emigrants was normally uneven, tree-dotted country where the range
of vision was limited and objects were familiar and predictable.
Here everything was strange. The horizon seemingly radiated to
the edges of the world. Distant objects—which might be mountains
or sandhills, antelope or Indians or trees—were unfamiliar in the
first place, and there was nothing handy to judge their distance in
the second place. Even the general "levelness" was deceptive be-

cause nothing was actually level after all; there were rises and hollows, ridges and ravines, undulations of all kinds which might intervene between viewer and object, disrupting all estimates. In addition to this there were occasional phenomena of mirages, rainbows, sunglows or sundogs, and northern lights, all of which further distorted vision. Emigrants did not have the benefit of the mountain man's experience in readjusting their eyesight to Plains conditions. Neither did they have the benefit of the hindsight with which we are blessed today, coupled with ready-made visual scales that have been provided for us in the form of telephone poles, power lines, highway markers, and towns.

Although the emigrants had some experience with atmospheric deception along the South Platte, it was not until they reached the Court House that the phenomenon really went to work on them. Judging the distance of this Rock from the California Road was the first big test—and most flunked it. At right angles from the wagon road it would have been about six miles, or the same as the distance from Bridgeport. Of course the distance would be greater if the estimates were made at an acute angle farther east. In the journals the procedure is almost routine. The Court House (or Solitary Tower, etc.) is seen in the distance; approaching it, somebody decides to hike over to it, imagining that it will be a brief stroll, and then is amazed to find that he has grossly miscalculated, either giving up the attempt or dragging back late to the train, hungry, exhausted, and foot-sore. Many were fooled by the Court House:

> Encamped this evening within 1½ mile of the Solitary Castle, apparently, but upon examination it proved to be six miles. A party went to visit it after supper and were obliged to remain all night.— SNYDER, 1845

> It is from 8 to 10 miles from the road although it does not appear more than ¾ of a mile. Here more than any other place I ever saw it is more difficult to calculate distances or the size of objects. Several of our company turned off to view this rock and did not overtake us until long after noon. Faint and weary they took their dinner which we had kept waiting for several hours & complained bitterly of this foolish deception. Some said the rock was 20 miles from the road.— JAGGER, 1849

> Court-house Rock appeared only about two miles off, when in reality it was ten or twelve. Some of our men set out to walk to it, but as

they approached it appeared to recede, and after walking a couple of hours, some returned, while others who finally reached it did not return till nearly nine o'clock at night, having walked steadily for ten hours.—DELANO, 1849

We took our nooning nearly opposite the [Court House] which arose before us isolated and in bold relief out of the bosom of the plain. . . . It would be easy enough, to all appearance to step over to the Court House, cut across to the Chimney, and reach the train by camping time. . . . We were all afoot, but the distance appeared so trifling as to give us no concern. Well, the upshot of it was, that we did not reach the Court House until about sundown. We hurriedly carved our names upon its walls; viewed for a moment the strange landscape roundabout; and giving the Chimney an askance glance, were glad to bear away for camp, which we did not make till far in the night. . . .

The extreme transparency of the atmosphere in this section explains the illusory phenomenon. Objects appeared but a mile or two away when in reality they were often from five to ten. Even the stars seemed to steal down from their wonted depths, and look vastly nearer.—LEEPER, 1849

. . . 12 miles south of the road at its nearest point.—J. EVANS, 1850 ......

We encamped early and several of the company went to it & I was one of the number. We didn't suppose it to be more than one or two miles from the road   we went on foot but as we found it to be at least four miles our trip was not so easy as we supposed . . . but like all the rest we must see the Elephant & some of the party did see his back before they got to camp as some of them was out till 9 o'clock.—JOHN LEWIS, 1852

While nooning, some of the party set out to go the few hundred yards away as it appeared to be, but the distances here are so deceptive that it proved to be a long way.—CARPENTER, 1856

Distances are deceiving, 1 mile is 5.—WILKINSON, 1859

I cannot judge the dimensions of this wonderful piece of nature's handiwork.—BURGESS, 1866

I won't say how far. Guessing at distance is the most complete Horn-swoggling game that a man ever undertook.—WAYMAN, 1852

Birge and McBride, already quoted, were among the exclusive fraternity of those who made the famous climb to the summit of the Court House. Any agile person, irrespective of age or sex, can climb the Rock today. Obviously, this was not a feat in the same class with climbing the Matterhorn or the Grand Teton; but it was a supreme thrill for the emigrants who had toiled over the prairies and looked upon this isolated bluff as their introduction to the fabled Rocky Mountains. Their journals are replete with graphic accounts, not only of the "perilous" ascent, but also the multitude of names carved all over the Rock, particularly on the summit, and the vast panoramic view from that point. The opportunity to climb the Court House is still there and so is the view, but the emigrant names have long since eroded away.

. . . made our noon halt opposite Court House bluff after noon several of our party went over to take a look at it it I climbed to the top and engraved my name and such a view man seldom sees.—STAPLES, 1849

I took off my boots and climbed to the top of this wonderful rock.— HOWELL, 1849

. . . many hundreds of names carved. . . . Scene from the top one of sterile desolation, and seems entirely uninhabitable. . . . other rugged bluffs bordering the Platte present a more desolate appearance, resembling vast artificial structures carved in every conceivable shape by the furious storms that rage in these parts.—LINDSEY, 1849

I ascended partly by the ravines that had washed in it and partly by holes that had been dug in the rock for that purpose. It was not perpendicular on the side that we went up, for we frequently came to benches like, that we could walk some distance on before we came to a place that was perpendicular. In this way we arrived at the top.

The view was fine; in the immediate vicinity I had a view of the prairie and sand bank over which I had traveled and the horses that we rode, but they did not look larger than sheep. . . . on the south a most beautiful plain with several trees scattered about, and a creek that wound its way through the plain and came near the foot of the hill on which the rocks stand. The margins of the creek were covered with thornberry. On the west a deep ravine was near; at a distance a high mound with a round top and high bluffs; also the famous Chimney Rock. At the top the rock is small. Where you ascend it is not more than two or three feet wide; further west it is six or eight. . . . On the south side and end it is nearly perpendicular. To all appearances it is fast washing away and I believe in time will be mingled with the balance of the earth in the vicinity. Hundreds have inscribed their names upon it, and places of residence and date.

Two hundred yards east stands another monument. It resembles a wall about 80 feet long and 30 or 40 wide and 150 high. I could not get on it, but from the appearance the rock was similar. . . . It had not been injured so much by rains.—HALE, 1849

When we arrived at the rock we found quite a number of specimens there among them were 3 ladies one of which seemed to be rambling all over the rock. . . . there were steps cut in the rock so we ascended to its top where I with my pocket knife engraved my name in the stone where there are thousands of names. . . . We now made our way back to the road where we expected to find the train where they had halted to masticate their cold bit of grub.—CASTLEMAN, 1849

. . . the name of J J Astor, 1798, said to have been carved there, one of the American fur traders to cross the continent [an obvious hoax; Astor never came this way].—WEBSTER, 1849

At the summit it is about 20 by 10 feet broad and it is ascended by holes dug in the sides which other emigrants have made. . . .

We spent about an hour on the summit writing. Our heads became dizzy, we began to hunt the base and had a hard time to overtake our wagons which we could only see by the dust they raised; and being nearly fifteen miles off we travelled hard but did not overtake them until they camped for the night. We had left camp without a gun, pistol or knife, which we ought to have had as the wolves and bears became unusually thick before we got in.—PIGMAN, 1850

As the wagons left this morning, myself and Collins started horse back on a visit to Council Rock, a large and tall rock that stands isolated from all others, the largest and tallest I've seen since we left. It is quite a curiosity, it stands several miles off the road, and is visited constantly by passers-by. Many names are to be seen engraved on its walls, many of them dating back to '49 and '50. I left my name engraved on a high place near the top.—SAMUEL WORD, 1863

Captain [O'Brien] and I got up early and with a couple of lariat-ropes started out to ascend Court House Rock. We both succeeded in getting to the top of the precipice. It had a covering of stone, not very hard, on which there were several names carved; we took a few minutes to add our names to the number. It was a great deal of a task to get to the top and one equally difficult to get down. [Ware may have ascended the south face].—EUGENE WARE, 1864

The rock itself is mainly composed of sand, hard pan and clay, so that it is easily chopped with the hatchet, and thus steps are made for those who have the nerve and patience to climb to its top, nearly

600 feet above the water of the creek. A few of our party accomplished the feat, Adjutant Phisterer taking the lead. The ascent is quite easy, but peculiar. The notches receive the toes and about half of the foot, and the hands grasp the gaps above to support the body and keep its gravity within the line of danger. The return trip is not so pleasant, as the heels take the place of the toes and the back rests upon the bluff itself. . . . Centuries of exposure have evidently wrought their changes upon the great face of Court-house Rock, and constant waste is now so rapidly changing its proportions that, even in 1867, it had lost some of that boldness of definition which in 1866, and for years before, had made it such a noted landmark.—M. CARRINGTON, 1866

The Court House did not sit for a photographic portrait until the twentieth century, as far as has been discovered. It did, however, become the subject of several artists' sketches during migration days. Many emigrants mention sketches they made which do not seem to have survived, nor is there record of what became of illustrations known to have been made by Mr. Preuss of Fremont's expedition, the anonymous friend of Capt. Gove of the Utah Expedition, and Richard Burton in 1860. A few commendable artistic efforts have survived, however, some published in connection with the journals, others still buried in archives with their accompanying manuscripts. Accounted for are at least ten contemporary Court House Rock pictures to date, the work of these travelers: Dr. Charles Parke, D. Jagger, J. Goldsborough Bruff, and James F. Wilkins, 1849; Seth Lewelling, 1850; W. Wadsworth, 1852; Cornelius Conway, 1857; Eugene Ware, 1864; Margaret Carrington and William H. Jackson, 1866.

Many emigrants, on arriving at Court House Rock, began to experience the euphoria that came from the invigorating atmosphere at 4,000 feet above sea level, coupled with self-congratulation at having arrived at another great milestone. However, cholera and accidents with firearms continued to take their toll. Although the grave of Amanda Lamin on Pumpkin Creek is the only one now identified, documentary evidence is found of at least thirty emigrant burials within the Court House encampment area (say Pumpkin Creek to the Chimney Rock rise), of which at least a dozen are identified by the journalists.

There are four 1849 witnesses, the first being Castleman. When he returned from his ascent of the Rock he was informed of the cholera death of Preston Moore, a wagonmate who had complained

the day before of "diarea," an all too common symptom. Moore
was seized with cramps at 10 A.M. and died at 4 P.M., "the sixth man
we have lost of this dread disease." Castleman tells of two other
fatalities here:

> A sad accident happened to a company that has encamped near
> us this evening two of their men were riding along the road when
> one observed to the other they would ride a little faster as the moske-
> toes were very bad so they rode on a fast lope for a few rods when
> one of their guns fired and the ball past through the others body
> which proved to be a mortal wound of which he died before night
> there was a train that past here about this time and two of their men
> came to the tent where the wounded man was lying one of them
> took sick and fainted and after he recovered of this he was taken
> [by] the cholera which terminated in his death before morning this
> being three men that I know of that died within two miles of this place
> in less than 12 hours.

On the following day Castleman himself became feverish, feeling
"quite unwell," but he survived to reach California. Joseph Sedgley
names Jno. Campbell as the man who was accidentally shot while
riding. He mentions also the nearby graves of J. P. Towle of
Missouri and Reuben Scroggin of Kentucky, age eighteen years.
To judge from Castleman's estimated encampment, these graves
would have been in the general vicinity of present Bridgeport.

About halfway between the trail and the Court House, on June
19, 1849, one of Jagger's companions found "the skeleton of a man
with a ball hole through his skull but whether of a white man or
Indian he could not say." If this was a case of murder, it could
have been a Forty-Niner, since the wolves and buzzards made fast
work of any unburied remains.

On July 3, 1849, J. G. Bruff reports the grave of N. T. Phillips of
"Bristol age 35, June 11, of cholera." This was on "Dry Ford, a
small marshy stream near Court House Rock," which must have
been Pumpkin Creek, the original Dry Creek, or Lawrence Fork.
The erratic and branching character of the California Trail is
evident from the fact that Bruff apparently missed the three graves
described by Castleman and Sedgley. However, on July 4, camping
several miles east of Chimney Rock, Bruff tells of three graves by a
spring and "left of 2 sandhills," which suggests the vicinity of the
modern Bridgeport cemetery. Buried here were Sam. P. Judson, a
Mason; E. Moore, aged thirty years; and Ellis Russell. These same

three are probably described on July 2 by Dewolf: "We passed today 9 graves, three were in one place and all from one Co. in Indiana."

On May 24, 1850, one emigrant passed eight graves between Pumpkin Creek and "camp near Chimney Rock." On June 30 Micajah Littleton camped opposite, or directly north of, the Court House, reporting that in the course of a twenty-mile journey, "we have already passed six graves today," all west of Pumpkin Creek. Four of these were Missourians: "N. Campbell June 16th age 21 of Mo. Saml. Hinch June 17th age 33 yrs & 4 days old of Saline Co. Mo. Calvin Green June 12 age 23. Howard Co. Mo. Amanda Lamme June 23 age 28 Boon Co. Mo. B. E. Davis June 17th age 26, Wm. Dalton June 17th age 24 Jones Co. Iowa."

In 1852 Caroline Richardson counted five new graves along the road west of the Court House. That same season Jno. H. Clark, encamped here, says that he "met 3 men returning, the only 3 men left out of company of 17 who had left Ash Hollow a few days ago for California. Their misfortune commenced soon after leaving the Hollow and by the time they reached Fort Laramie 14 of their number had died. The remaining three now concluded to return. The road has been thickly strewn with graves today."

Except for the epic passage of emigrants, no historical events of great moment occurred in the neighborhood of the Court House. The small but lively Battle of Mud Springs in 1865 between Sioux and U.S. Cavalry occurred several miles to the north. The advent of the Sidney-Deadwood Trail, the Camp Clarke bridge, and the hordes of homesteaders falls beyond our time range. There are a few legends and incidents, however, which deserve brief recitation— not including Jim Bridger's yarn, related by Eugene Ware, that "Court House Rock had grown up from a stone which he threw at a jack-rabbit."

Previously noted here has been the alleged murder in about 1833 of a trapper named Gonneville or Lawrence, or both. Likewise, the fable of "Pumpkinseed Creek." Shumway has two other legends, upon which he elaborates in great detail and which probably have some element of truth, though not very much, since the Pawnee Indians did at one time hunt buffalo in western Nebraska but were forced by the Sioux to retreat to the Lower Platte by the time of the westward migration. At any rate, both of these Pawnee legends are centered around Court House Rock, which we are informed was the habitat of "Ti-wa-ra, the god of Court House Rock."

One is a tale of a young brave, his grandmother, and a supernatural horse, a tale climaxed by a fierce battle between Pawnee and Sioux "at a point nearly opposite the opening in the hills now known as Round House or Reddington Gap." In this particular battle the Pawnee emerge victorious, but "about the year 1835" their luck ran out and they were finally chased out of the country by the Sioux. The Sioux-Pawnee donnybrook at Ash Hollow, referred to by Sage, was apparently part of this episode. But the one that concerns the Court House is the part about a small band of Pawnees who formed a rear guard

> to keep the Sioux engaged while the main village was moving. And these were attacked by the Sioux with such fierceness of purpose that they were driven to the top of Court House Rock for refuge. About the base of the rock camped a number of the Sioux, with the evident intention of starving them to come down, or to their death. . . .
>
> Meanwhile [after the Ash Hollow struggle] the young chief left with the braves to the defense of the rear were marooned on the top of Court House Rock. . . . He went out alone at night and plead with the god Ti-wa-ra to show him some avenue of escape, and the answer came. He went near the edge of the rock and found one of the perforations that extended downward into darkness. He tied his lariat and the lariats of others together, and fastened the upper end to a jutting rock point, and let himself down into the hole or "well" as it is called. At its bottom he found an opening large enough for a man to crawl through, and it was unguarded. He climbed back up the rope to await the following night. When the darkness came over the land he called his men together, and told them of his plan for escape, and they all crawled to the edge where the perforation in the brule rocks made the well. One by one they went down the rope, and crawled out through the hole at the bottom, and away in the darkness. And the last to go was the young chief.

John Bratt is responsible for another story, which has to be classed as rumor rather than legend since it seems to have no wider currency: "It is claimed that a band of outlaws were followed from the Gallatin valley mines by Captain Bailey's company of mountaineers, were overtaken, tried and found guilty and twelve of them shot to death on the top of Court House Rock, hence its name." Bratt fails to explain just what it is the outlaws were guilty of; also, he ignores the fact that this rock was so named as early as 1841, over twenty years before gold was discovered in Montana.

More substantial than legend or rumor were two unusual incidents which occurred in the forties, both principals, like the mysterious Gonneville, being of French-Canadian ancestry. In 1843 while William Sublette was leading a hunting expedition up the Platte, young Cyprian Menard, apparently frightened by Indians, disappeared from the camp at Ash Hollow. The party continued westward, reassured of Menard's survival because of messages found on buffalo skulls. When abreast of the Court House, they found Menard, "cooking 4 terrapins. He had taken us for Indians on the afternoon of his loss, then lost his horse in the night, cached his saddle the next day, and travelled on, subsisting on roots and birds, which latter he killed with pebbles. . . . Menard looking dreadful—his eyes staring wide, and his cheeks hollow, but with a heart firm as a lion. He slept last night by the side of the Church."

The Menard story appears in Matt Field's *Prairie and Mountain Sketches.* Francis Parkman's 1846 journals contain a reference to an American Fur Company winter cache which would have been someplace in the Court House vicinity: "Rode to Lawrence Fork and nooned. Passed on, saw in the distance a half-subterranean house which Frederic had made to winter in, in charge of some furs to be sent down in the spring. What a devil of a solitary time!" Frederic was, of course, an employee of the company at Fort Laramie. The only reason for storing furs here would have been that there was an unscheduled stoppage of the fur shipments by boat the previous autumn, and the company was waiting for the spring rise to get floating again.

This history of the Court House may be concluded with certain incidents of the mid-1860s associated with the passage of military caravans up the Julesburg Road to and from Fort Laramie. The first episode is recounted in Ware's *Indian War of 1864*:

> There came word [at Fort Laramie] that an empty Mormon train with quite a lot of extra men, and seventeen wagons drawn by mules, was coming down, bound for Omaha. . . . These Mormons traveled through the Indian country more safely than if they had been Indians themselves. I suggested that as the Mormon train was traveling light, they be impressed into service, and that I be permitted to load them near Court House Rock with pine timber for building purposes at Julesburg. This seemed to meet approval, and Colonel Collins took

it up over the telegraph with General Mitchell, commanding at Fort Kearney, who approved the plan. The train came along; we equipped it with axes, a few picks and shovels to make roads with, a small supply of provisions, and . . . it went on down the road. I expected to overtake them on the route, which I did at Mud Springs. . . .

At Mud Springs, on the evening of October 31, 1864, we found the Mormon train camped, together with eight wagons drawn by nineteen yoke of oxen belonging to Alexander Noble. . . . Noble's wagons were in bad condition, and so were his oxen. I pressed them all in. . . . It had snowed and hailed all day, the wind was blowing hard, skits of snow were coming all night, and the weather was growing colder. On the morning of November 1st we made a road and got the wagons and stock several miles up to where the trees were, and as we had plenty of help we cut the trees as long as the wagons could hold them . . . and let the wagons start down to Mud Springs. We cut only small, straight trees that were easily handled. No sign of Indians was seen anywhere.

On November 2 . . . we finished the loading of the wagons and sent them all . . . on down to Mud Springs. My squad of men was camped on the north side of Lawrence's Fork, in a very nice little grove that stood about forty feet above the stream and formed a sort of shelf, above which, back of us, rose the high ragged edges of the plateau. It was a beautiful little camping-place, and was up three or four miles above Court House Rock. All this time it had been snowing. And as the snow fell upon the plateau the wind blew it down onto our camp, and it began to get deeper and deeper. We had run out of provisions.

Ware and his men were trapped by the drifting snow in the pine grove, where it stacked up ten and twenty feet high from "all the snow that fell upon the plateau for miles." During their two-day ordeal they were able to survive, thanks to a wealth of firewood and the lucky kill of curious deer and antelope.

In the same vicinity Holliday and his company of volunteer cavalry camped in the summer of 1865. After their ascent of the Court House, mentioned above, they were subject to dangers of a different sort:

That night we caught hundred of small fish from a brooklet which flowed at the foot of this great rock, and all night long we listened to the whooping of Indians several miles north of us who seemed to be having a war dance. Then to add to the gloom a pack of hungry white wolves set up a wail of woe and we had to abandon the thought of sleep and take our places among our ponies in order to prevent a stampede and protect our ponies from the gang of ravenous wolves.

In June of 1866, Col. Carrington and the Eighteenth Regiment of Infantry, bound for Fort Laramie and the Bozeman Trail, camped on Pumpkin Creek at the foot of the great rock. Two army wives remembered the experience most vividly. Frances Grummond (Carrington) recalls: "After partaking of supper, and the tin cups and pans had been washed in the clear water of the creek, and campfires were burning low, I proposed to take a saunter to the great rock. The idea was at once ridiculed as it was actually five miles distant." But Margaret Carrington and others did hike over and make the climb, as we have seen. Then, "the mounted infantry pitched their tents in the basin of the cañon, a short distance from the beautiful grove of cottonwood that lies at the very base of the rock." Of her accompanying sketch, Margaret Carrington writes, "The above sketch will preserve its outline and present character; but, like all other odd and wild things in that region, it will soon become the prey of innovation and the mastery of Time."

XII

Chimney Rock, Eighth Wonder Of the World

"CHIMNEY ROCKS" ARE COMMONPLACE on topographic maps of the United States. Easily the most illustrious of all these natural chimneys, however, is the one on the south side of the North Platte River, which was a landmark for travelers on the Great Platte River Road. This was no ordinary landmark. More enthusiasm and more diary space was devoted to this particular landmark than to any other of the covered wagon migration.

Blasé travelers in high-speed automobiles are less given to keeping diaries, and less apt to go into raptures over North Platte valley scenery than their ancestors traveling by means of ox-drawn covered wagons. Nevertheless, Chimney Rock is still a striking phenomenon, eliciting much comment.

In covered wagon days this was the ultimate in natural curiosities, the zenith of sight-seeing goals. To emigrants, Chimney Rock was indeed the eighth wonder of the world. Recognition of its unique historic role has been given today by the establishment of Chimney Rock as a National Historic Site through cooperative agreement between the Nebraska State Historical Society, which holds title to the property, and the United States Department of the Interior.

This honored landmark lies in the southwest quarter of Sec. 17, Twp. 20 N., Rge. 52 W. sixth principal meridian near the western edge of Morrill County, Nebraska, about three and a half miles southwest of Bayard and about twenty miles east of Scotts Bluff

National Monument. In emigrant days a more common reckoning was 12 or 14 miles west of Court House Rock, about 75 miles above Ash Hollow, or about 550 miles from St. Joe. It can be seen today to best advantage in the manner of most California emigrants, by approaching it along the south side of the river via U.S. 26 and thence by State Highway 92 directly past the Chimney and on toward Scotts Bluff National Monument. It may also be seen on a clear day from the north side of the river where U.S. 26 goes some distance north of the original Mormon Trail, or Council Bluffs Road, before turning west; but from the north side it is apt to be missed by the uninformed because it blends into the background bluffs.

State Highway 92 is only a few hundred feet south of surviving remains of the California Road, which hugged the river. Accordingly, the modern highway traveler still finds himself over two miles away from the Chimney at the nearest highway point, but there is a turn-off provided by the Nebraska State Highway Department and an aluminum information marker provided by the Nebraska Historical Land Mark Council. If he wants to view the landmark at closer range but still stay in his car, he can reach the dead-end of section line roads approaching from the north and east. Those who want to hike to the base of Chimney Rock, or ascend its cone to the base of its unclimbable spire, must first hike a good mile or more over rough terrain to get there, but this is an unforgettable experience. With the great Chimney preserved in its primitive glory (except for the inevitable toll of erosion), such a hike is like a pilgrimage into the past.

The pedestrian approaches to Chimney Rock are gashed with badlands and ravines, and the hiker must crawl over, through, or under barbed wire fence which encloses the eighty acres which comprise the Historic Site. At the foot of the Rock, on the south side, he will find the only other addition, a memorial of cast concrete with a bronze plaque recording the gift of this property to the public by the Frank Durnal family.

Chimney Rock is a slender column upon a broad conical base or mound, standing apart from the principal ridge which bounds the North Platte valley on the south bank. The Camp Clark Quadrangle of the U.S. Geological Survey, based on a survey of 1895, shows its summit to be 4,242 feet above sea level. A resurvey in 1965 shows an elevation of 4,225 feet, the loss of 17 feet being accounted for by disintegration of the spire during the past seventy years. The tip of the Rock today is 325 feet above the base of the cone, or about 470 feet above the North Platte River. The vertical spire alone measures 120 feet. An analysis of descriptions and sketches, 1837 to 1867, suggests that the spire may then have towered 50 to 100 feet higher.

A history of Chimney Rock in terms of special historical events which occurred there would not be worth recording. There were no special events which shook the world. This history pertains primarily to *psychological* events. The significant thing about Chimney Rock was the powerful impact of this strange and spectacular phenomenon on the mind and emotions of the traveler. Ash Hollow had created some excitement, with its "perpendicular descent" and its oasis-like canyon. Court House Rock had elicited admiration for its solitary grandeur and its mirage-like qualities. But Chimney Rock was the great scenic climax, a spectacle of such rarity that it seemed, like Niagara Falls, to rival the Seven Wonders of the ancient world.

Chimney Rock was the most famous of all the landmarks on the Great Platte River Road. This is not idle rhetoric. That it was the greatest and most memorable of landmarks can be proven with something approaching scientific accuracy. Again, as in the case of Fort Kearny, it is assumed that the journalists and letter-writers of record (at the approximate ratio of one to every 500 travelers) reflect the views of the non-journalists. The writer once made a tabulation of the principal landmarks along the North Platte valley trunkline of the trail, coming up with eight in number—Ash Hollow, Court House Rock, Chimney Rock, Scott's Bluffs, Laramie Peak, Independence Rock, Devil's Gate, and South Pass—then listed 100 of the best known journals and guidebooks, representing the period 1830–1866 on both sides of the Platte, and compared the frequency rate of the respective landmarks. The results of this tabulation are convincing. Chimney Rock is mentioned or described in 97 per cent of these sources. The nearest competitor is Scott's Bluffs, with a figure of 77 per cent. Then comes Independence Rock with 65 per cent, South Pass, 51 per cent; the Court House, 46 per cent; and Ash Hollow, 44 per cent.

In a more recent analysis of over 350 documents which report travel up the North Platte, it was found that 330, or 95 per cent, include a Chimney Rock reference. Thus, on a mathematical basis alone, Chimney Rock was unique in the overland migrations. Adjectives like "famous," "noted," "notorious," "grand," "splendid," and "celebrated," are commonplace, as are phrases like "a great natural curiosity," "a mighty landmark," "noble monument," and "a singular freak of nature." These encomiums might be discounted, but many others are more specific in placing this landmark among scenic attractions of the first magnitude:

. . . the most remarkable thing I ever saw.—M. CRAWFORD, 1842

. . . one of the greatest curiosities I have ever seen in the West.—NESMITH, 1843

. . . one of the greatest curiosities—perhaps the greatest—in the whole valley of the Mississippi.—CARLETON, 1845

. . . most splendid and grand sight.—ROBINSON, 1849

. . . most remarkable object that I ever saw and if situated in the states would be visited by persons from all parts of the world.—HACKNEY, 1849

. . . one of the most grand and splendid objects I ever saw.—SHOMBRE, 1849

. . . well worth a visit across the Plains to see . . . in the dizziness of distance, and towering to the heavens.—GELWICKS, 1849

. . . one of the great curiosities of the Western plains.—PARKE. 1849

. . . this wonderful rock and its strange shape, apparently sculptured by a giant architect, towered before their eyes at last.—NOAH BROOKS, n.d.

. . . presents the finest view for an artist to display his talents of any place I ever beheld. It is grand beyond description.—ATHEARN, 1849

Truly it is a wonder.—EBEY, 1854

. . . the greatest thing that I have ever yet seen.—GAGE, 1852

. . . the most remarkable landmark we have seen since leaving the Missouri River.—BRACKETT, 1862

. . . a great monument of nature.—BURGESS, 1866

In emigration days it was standard practice to rave about Chimney Rock, and this effusion was not limited to personal diaries and letters hidden away in trunks. Aside from the guidebooks, many personal journals (like Bryant, 1846) and government reports (like those of Frémont, 1845, and Stansbury, 1851) were published soon enough to be familiar to travelers before their journey, and of course trail lore was part of the equipment of every wagon train pilot. So everyone looked eagerly ahead to get a glimpse of this marvel. While most were duly impressed and jotted down their observations, a few travelers became a bit jaded by all the fuss. Thus, Benjamin Ferris could write, "This curiosity has been well described. I will not inflict another upon the reader." In reverse fashion, this is one of the finest tributes to the historical primacy of Chimney Rock. It had become such an important fixture of the western landscape that its image was in danger of becoming stereotyped as a mere symbol. Indeed, if a symbol were needed, Chimney Rock would be to the Oregon-California Trail what Old Faithful, for example, is to Yellowstone Park.

All the evidence is that during the Rocky Mountain fur trade this was "the Chimney," and it did not metamorphose into Chimney Rock until the 1840s. Although Bonneville's account of his 1832 journey, published by Irving in 1836, became the first printed reference to "the Chimney," the name was evidently in use as early as 1827 when, according to Shumway, Joshua Pilcher took forty-five trappers up the Platte to the Bear Lake rendezvous. The first use of "Chimney Rock" appears in Preuss' official journal of 1842, published by Fremont in 1845.

While the Court House was also the Solitary Tower, the Church, the Castle, and various other things, the name Chimney Rock was surprisingly stable and was used uniformly by the great majority. Sometimes during the migrations it re-emerges as "The Chimney." Once in a great while it is misspelled as "Chimley" (Sponsler), or "Chimly" (J. Campbell), but that's the way it was probably pronounced, too. And there are a few innocent variations, such as Rock Chimney (Thomasson), Chimney Cliff (Leonard), Chimney Rockhouse (Anon.), Chimney Tower (Scott), and Chimney Mountain (Newby), while Shepherd says it *ought* to be called Chimney Mound. The writer has been able to find only six instances among hundreds of journals where an English name other than Chimney (or its variants) is used. In 1830 the fur trader Warren Ferris called it Nose Mountain. Thomas Eastin, a Forty-Niner, invented the name Tower Rock, while Alfred Lambourne referred to the Chimney as the Half-Way-Post.

Three other journalists, all early fur traders, share a common effort to convey by circumlocution the vulgar Indian name for this phenomenon. Zenas Leonard tells us it was known among the natives as Elk Peak. Nathaniel Wyeth refers to "Elk Brick the Indian name," while William Anderson's narrative reads, "E.P., or Chimney Rock, a solitary shaft." The exact spelling of this anatomical reference may be found in the French translation which is written on an A. J. Miller water color sketch of fur traders "Returning from Hunting, near the Puine du Cerf," in the Joslyn Art Museum in Omaha. There is no evidence whatever to support Grant Shumway's assertion that the Indian name for Chimney Rock was Tipi or Wigwam. The fur traders had a much better understanding of native symbolism.

To appreciate the force exerted by Chimney Rock on the imagination of nineteenth century travelers, it is necessary to delve into their written records. Before examining different facets of what might be called "the Chimney Rock experience," it seems appropriate to look at a chronological cross section of the literature of the pre-Gold Rush period. As noted, the first written record of which there is knowledge is that of Warren A. Ferris of the American Fur Company, who in 1830 was one of the real pioneers of the north side or Council Bluffs Road:

> We reached on the following day the "Nose Mountain," or as it is more commonly called, the "Chimney," a singular mound, which has the form of an inverted funnel, is half a mile in circumference at the base, and arises to the height of three hundred feet. It is situated on the southern margin of the North Fork of the Platte, in the vicinity of several high bluffs, to which it was evidently once attached; is on all sides inaccessible, and appears at the distance of fifty miles shooting up from the prairie in solitary grandeur, like the limbless trunk of a gigantic tree. It is 500 miles west from the Council Bluffs.

As noted, Chimney Rock first came to public attention with the publication of *The Adventures of Captain Bonneville* in 1836, reporting events of 1832:

> Opposite to the camp at this place was a singular phenomenon, which is among the curiosities of the country. It is called the Chimney. The lower part is a conical mound, rising out of the naked plain; from the summit shoots up a shaft or column, about 120 feet in height, from which it derives its name. The height of the whole, according to Captain Bonneville, is 175 yards. It is composed of indurated clay,

with alternate layers of red and white sandstone, and may be seen at the distance of upwards of thirty miles.

Among the fur traders who followed the south bank, which would become the main emigrant road, was Nathaniel Wyeth, who found that "this singular object looks like a Monument about 200 feet high." He was the first man to formulate a theory as to how the Chimney was formed: "[It] is composed of layers of sand and lime stone. . . . the sand blowing out lets the lime rock fall down and this action has in time reduced what was once a hill to a spire of nearly the same dimensions at top and bottom." In 1833 Charles Larpenteur, also en route to a Rocky Mountain rendezvous, regarded the Chimney as "the only curiosity of note" this side of South Fork and marveled that "it is seen in clear weather for the distance of three or four days travel." In 1837 A. J. Miller, artist in company with fur traders, made these notes to accompany his sketch of the Chimney, probably the first one ever made:

> The curious formation here presented is situated some 8 or 900 miles west of the Mississippi, near the Platte River. It forms one of the great land-marks on the journey to the mountains and when we saw it was probably 150 or 200 feet in height. It is composed of clay with strata of rock at intervals. In its neighborhood are other formations taking their names from familiar buildings in cities from their fancied resemblance, such for instance as Court House, the Cathedral, etc.

Two distinguished visitors in 1835 were the Presbyterian missionaries to Oregon, Marcus Whitman and Samuel Parker, who viewed the spectacle from the north bank. In his notebook Whitman wrote, "Passed the beacon hill called chimney from a spindle which surmounts the base." Parker's published account of 1838 is more elaborate:

> Encamped at noon of the 22nd, near another of nature's wonders. It has been called the chimney; but I should say, it ought to be called beacon hill, from its resemblance to what was beacon hill in Boston. Being anxious to have a near view, although in a land of dangers, I concluded to take an assistant and pass over the river to it. The river where we crossed was about a mile wide, shallow and full of quicksand, but we passed it without any difficulties. We rode about three miles over a level plain, and came to the base. The distance from the other side of the river did not appear more than a mile, so deceptive are distances over plains without any landmarks.

This beacon hill has a conical formed base of about half a mile in circumference, and is 150 feet in height; and above this is a perpendicular column, twelve feet square, and eighty feet high; making the whole height about 230 feet. We left our horses at the base, and ascended to the perpendicular. It is formed of indurated clay or marl, and in some parts is petrified. It is of a light chocolate, or rufous color, in some parts white. Near the top were handsome stalactites, at which my assistant shot, and broke off some pieces, of which I have taken a small specimen.

The Belgian priest Father DeSmet passed by in 1840, camping near "one of the most remarkable curiosities of this savage region. . . . A cone-shaped eminence of not far from a league's circumference. . . . From the summit rises a square shaft, 30 to 40 feet through by 150 in height." DeSmet had evidently read Bonneville, for he also describes the total height as 175 yards. "A few years more," he predicts, "and this great natural curiosity will crumble away and make only a little heap upon the plain; for when it is examined near at hand, an enormous crack appears in its top." The good Father thought its name was "rather unworthy of this wonder of nature." He thought, like Ferris, that it more nearly resembled an inverted funnel.

Another 1841 commentator was the keenly observant Rufus Sage:

Oct. 26. Raising camp at daylight we resumed our way, and soon afterwards arrived opposite the "Chimney," an extraordinary natural curiosity that had continued in view and excited our admiration for some four days past.

This singular formation surmounts a conical eminence which rises, isolated and lonely, in the open prairie, reaching a height of 300 feet. It is composed of terrene limestone and marl, quadrangularly shaped, like the spire of some church, six feet by ten at its base, with an altitude of more than 200 feet,—making, together with the mound, an elevation of 500 feet. A grand an imposing spectacle, truly;—a wonderful display of the eccentricity of Nature!

In July, 1842, Capt. Fremont's surveyor Charles Preuss came in sight of the celebrated Rock, looking "at this distance of about thirty miles, like what it is called—the long chimney of a steamfactory establishment, or a shot-tower in Baltimore." Since Preuss drew a picture, the second oldest of record, he refrained from more detailed description except to note: "It consists of marl and earthy limestone, and the weather is rapidly diminishing its height, which is now not more than 200 feet above the river. Travellers who visited it some years since place its height at upwards of 500 feet."

When Col. Kearny's Dragoons came through in 1845, Capt. Cooke was poetically inspired. At first glimpse, from a distance of thirty miles, he thought the Chimney had merely "the appearance of a tall post seen a mile off." At close range, however, the adjacent bluffs became "Hudson Palisades" while "right in front stood the lofty white Chimney Rock, like the pharos of a prairie sea." As noted above, his fellow officer Lt. Carleton was tremendously impressed. He was highly critical of Preuss' drawing, which he considered entirely inadequate to portray a structure of such beauty and magnitude. Carleton was in entire agreement, however, with Father DeSmet that this lovely object was doomed, "as the materials of which it is formed are decomposing very fast, and in a few years it will have worn entirely away. The shaft is already rent from top to bottom, and one would suppose that the first high wind would topple it down."

A worthy representative of the Oregon migration is Virgil Pringle, who wrote in 1846: "June 19—Passed the chimney in the forepart of the day and the formation of the bluffs have a tendency to fill the mind with awe and grandeur. The chimney might pass for one of the foundries in St. Louis were it blackened by burning stone coal." In 1847 William Clayton of the Mormon Pioneers first sighted the Chimney from an elevation near Crab Creek, opposite and a little above Ash Hollow. As he approached he wrote:

> Saturday 22nd [May] . . . At the distance I should judge of about twenty miles, I could see Chimney Rock very plainly with the naked eye, which from here very much resembles the large factory chimneys in England. . . .
>
> Chimney Rock [later in the day] shows very plain and appears not more than two miles distance but is no doubt five miles distance or over. . . . Elder Orson Pratt is taking an observation to ascertain the height of Chimney Rock. . . .
>
> Wednesday 26th. . . . we arrived at a point directly north of Chimney Rock which we ascertained by compass, having traveled since it was first discovered 41½ miles. . . . Elder Pratt found that Chimney Rock is 260 feet high from its base to its summit and the distance from our road at the nearest point three miles.

Two of the best known published accounts of 1849 are those

of non-emigrants, Capt. Stansbury of the Topographical Engineers and the English journalist William Kelly. It is regrettable that Stansbury failed to sketch "the celebrated Chimney Rock . . . a point on this route so well known and so often described." He is among the first to note that there were attractions here other than the scenery: "Its vicinity has long been a favorite camping ground for the emigrants, as there are springs of water near and the grass is tolerably good." Kelly, less concerned with prosaic things, gives a glowing description:

> There was now observable through the mist high up in the clouds a pointed object, that looked like the top of some monumental erection, becoming more and more distinctly defined as we proceeded. With its base still enveloped in fog, we camped parallel with it. . . . We headed toward this tapering rock, called by roamers of the prairie "Chimney Rock," though, to my eye, there is not a single lineament in its outline to warrant the christening. The Wellington Testimonial, in the Phoenix Park, elevated on a Danish Fort, would give a much more correct idea of its configuration, though not of its proportions. It is, I should say, 500 feet high. . . . It appears to be fast chipping and crumbling away, and I have no doubt that, ere half century elapses, "Troja fuit" will apply to Chimney Rock. After surveying it on every side, and adorning its base with some hieroglyphics, we went about gathering our firewood; and while ransacking the ravines I was quite astonished to find considerable deposits of that fine black sand which most generally indicates the presence of gold.

To our knowledge none among some 25,000 Forty-Niners took Kelly's hint and searched for gold at the foot of Chimney Rock, but many of them became equally fascinated by the landmark. Among dozens of excited 1849 witnesses, we quote in some detail from five who are relatively unknown, but whose manuscript journals are highly illuminating:

> 12 miles west of [the Court House] you come to what is called chimney rock, the greatest natural curiosity we saw   it could be seen 20 miles and at first it looks like an old tree with the limbs all off but when you get to it it appears like a crater or a chimney of a volcano   it is about 360 feet high from the base   it stands on a rise of about 2 acres of land on hard clay and as it goes up grows harder till as hard as chalk whare thare are hundreds of names cut in it with dates & my name with the rest   and then it is composed of rotten rock 20 feet

by 40 & runs to a great height   it appears as if it had ben higher for their is tons of rocks at the bottom.—DAVID COSAD, May 26

. . . at 10 o'clock saw Chimney Rock 25 miles off like a speck or cloud in the horizon.

Thursday 29   From camp Chimney Rock appears 4 miles off Drove 5 miles & started for and found it [still] some 4 miles distant   approached it on level plain.   Rock surrounded with deep Ravines   going into one my horse fell, jumped off and led him   some hundreds of yards off are dreary bluffs & hills of great height with clumps of cedar. . . . Chimney Rock stands alone with a base covering several acres receding all around to a cone 150 ft high on which rests a sandy column of Rock 100 ft higher & will soon crumble.   I ascended about 150 ft by a winding step path   many names cut in sand rock. Inscribed mine.   Fired one of my holster pistols & echoed greatly. Scenery unlimited in extent.—PETER DECKER, May 28

Chimney Rock looked like a shot tower at a great distance. . . . nooned nearly opposite. . . . I thought it was not over two miles from us and started to go to it . . . but found that it was four. . . . It is a very singular pile.   The base is very steep so much so that it would be impossible to climb on some sides. . . . The Chimney is rough and looks as if it would not stand a week.   The whole hill and rock is composed of a very hard clay or soft stone and some rock.   I climbed up to the base of the Chimney and cut my name among some thousand others   probably it will be cut away in a short time to make room for another.—FRANKLIN STARR, June 6

. . . 1 of the most grand and splendid objects I ever saw   it [is] 10040 steps round the base   600 ft high   the first 250 are like a large shapeless mound   then a spar of hard sand extends almost to the clouds   it can be ascended to the monument, which is inaccessible by the power of man. . . . the monument appears to be split all the way down.—HENRY SHOMBRE, June 15

. . . at 12 camped opposite to & about 1 mile from Chimney Rock.   I had some curiosity to see this as I had noticed a plate of the same in Fremont's work & it far exceeded my expectations.   The plate spoken of does not do it justice.   Imagine a pyramid standing alone though surrounded by rocky precipices some 150 feet high & at its base 20 feet through & then compare with Fremont's picture and his will look like a pile of stones on a hill.   No conception can be formed of the magnitude of this grand work of nature till you stand at its base & look up.   If a man does not feel like an insect then I don't know when he should.—ELISHA PERKINS, June 27

It may be seen that by 1849, when the Great Migration was just beginning to hit its stride, Chimney Rock loomed gigantic, not only against the western horizon, but also in the minds of travelers through the Nebraska wilderness. From these early journals, which represent only a fair sampling, there clearly emerges the characteristic features of a trail phenomenon which might be described as the Chimney Rock syndrome:

1. The startling visual phenomenon of Chimney Rock, viewed at first from distances up to forty miles from the east on either side of the river, and then viewed at close range with all the strangeness of something on the moon.

2. The wide range of images conjured up by Chimney Rock, from the romantic and sublime to the prosaic and ridiculous.

3. The many efforts at scientific description and measurement, with a wide variety and conflict of data.

4. The usual assortment of geological theories, from legendary to accurate; and along with this, dire predictions of the Chimney's early disintegration into dust.

5. The big adventure of climbing up the Chimney as high as possible, engraving your name for posterity, and drinking in the intoxicating scenery.

By exploring the hundreds of other journals which pay homage to Chimney Rock, this syndrome can be examined in greater detail. First to be considered, since it affected all others, is the matter of hallucinations, or what might be called "the Chimney Rock optical illusion." There had been some preparation for this in the optical tricks of Court House Rock, but there was a difference. The Court House was, after all, solid and blocky, undoubtedly there, even though it tripped up all estimates of distance. The Chimney was of such strange and slender configuration that it was often debatable whether it actually existed or not, and when its existence was confirmed, it seemed to assume all manner of shapes and sizes, as well as having a knack of moving away as if it were on wheels.

The needle-like object became visible to emigrants on the California Road in the vicinity of Rush Creek, where they first also glimpsed the Court House, or Solitary Tower. This is about thirty-three miles to the east. Those on the Council Bluffs Road first discerned it at or near Ancient Bluff Ruins, some forty miles away. At this distance the chimney, only a few feet in diameter, is a faint pencil line against the sky. Only the most eagle-eyed of scouts would have spotted it at these distances but for the fact that Chimney Rock had good publicity in advance and everyone was on the lookout for the first sight of it, in a spirit of competition, much as the mariners of old, aloft in the crow's nests of their sailing vessels, vied to see who would be the first to spot the whale. Many travelers claimed the limit of Chimney Rock visibility at fifty miles or more; with powerful glasses that might have been the case, but with the naked eye thirty or forty miles seems to have been the limit in 1849. In 1850 Davis says that it rose to so great a height in the air that it may be seen from nearly 100 miles away! This is a patent exaggeration; but it has this germ of truth: at one time, when the Chimney was even higher than in emigrant days (as fur traders indicated it was), it is reasonable to suppose that it could have been seen at longer distances. Thus, Rufus Sage in 1841: "Formerly the Chimney was much higher than at present, and could be distinctly seen in a clear day as far as Ash Creek," and again in 1849 McCoy quotes "some old plainsmen" to this same effect, by which was meant the observer would have had to be on the heights above Ash Hollow, about seventy-five miles distant.

In any event most writers, particularly those on the north side, agree that Chimney Rock was within view for several days' travel, say from Ancient Bluff Ruins to Scott's Bluffs, which would represent a stretch of nearly 100 miles when the Rock was within sight, or roughly forty or fifty miles maximum from extreme east or west viewing points. It is small wonder that this persistent "natural curiosity" engraved itself so deeply on the emigrant mind.

Lt. Carleton thought that the visibility of the Chimney at thirty or more miles must be due to the effect of mirage which "brought it so completely above the horizon that its general outline and comparative height could be determined." John Minto in 1844 also thought that he was beholding "the subtle transformation of the mirage" when he could see Chimney Rock far up the valley, its top seemingly "suspended in the sky, as the light seems to join between the top and base." But if the actual elevation of the Chimney at this time was 550 feet or more above the Platte River (most emigrants underestimated), no mirage was required to lift it above the horizon to counteract the earth's curvature. If the sun was shining and eyesight was good enough, it could be seen because it was there!

What did help, undoubtedly, was the clarity of the High Plains atmosphere, which might be considered as having a magnifying effect at horizon distance. Thus, Wolcott in 1850 exclaims that he was "never more deceived by the distance of an object," which he supposed due to "superior cleanness and transparency of the sun's rays" in this region. Alvah Davis discovered that what had "seemed 10 was really 50 miles." At close range the effects of magnification were such, according to Gilbert Cole, that, "When several miles distant we could see the rock and men who looked like ants as they crept or crawled up its sides." In like vein, Cartwright testifies that in this neighborhood, "A man at a distance of 3 miles would seem to be 10 or 12 feet tall," and further that "when yet 25 or 30 miles of the Chimney Rocks [?] we could distinctly see them, and could also trace the outline of trees as they stood against them."

Magnification seems to be the factor also to account for the phenomenon that Chimney Rock seemed to violate the laws of physics. Rev. Wyllis Alden studied it from the north bank: "We travelled abreast of it four or five days, but it never seemed to change position." Wm. Lorton, on the south side, observed just the opposite effect. He calls it "the most deceiving thing in the world as for distance. It seems to recede as you approach," a phenomenon which "calls forth wonder and amazement." This is the same puzzlement which caused the hunter hereabouts to miss his target, as Wistar explains: "Distances are much misunderstood in these wide level bottoms, and when hunting, it requires both experience and calculation to avoid shooting under." Dougherty thought that this difficulty was caused, not only by magnification, but by the fact of "no intervening objects to assist the eye." In the account of his 1846 travels J. Quinn Thornton devotes three pages to an effort to explain the Chimney Rock illusion, finally falling back on the mirage theory: "These effects result from a partial alteration in the density of the atmosphere." Thornton saw similarities between this illusion and a famous phenomenon of the Swiss Alps: "The Spector of the Brocken, which for so many years was the terror of the superstitious, and the wonder of the scientific, is a phenomenon of the same general character."

When the emigrants finally made camp near the Chimney, they were still fooled, never being as near as they thought they were (a fact which their experience at the Court House should have taught them). The trail at its nearest point was about two and a half miles from the Rock, and camps might be as much as five miles away. If it was decided to stroll over to the base of the Chimney, it was found to be a considerable hike. The journals are replete with instances of disillusionment. Wistar's party found that camp was three miles away instead of the estimated half mile. Similarly, Sage thought it 800 yards but learned from the experience of another that it was six times that distance: "'One fellow offered to bet $5. he could run to it in 15 minutes. The banter was promptly accepted, and the greenhorn doffing his coat and hat, started in full expectation of winning the wager. But instead of 15 it took 45 minutes to reach the spot." Many, like the companions of Dr. T., became disgusted and abandoned the effort: "Some of our men started on foot across the bottom to examine the chimney rock. . . . They supposed they would reach it in two miles, but after travelling seven miles, some abandoned the trip, declaring it as far from them when they turned back as when they left the waggons."

One of the favorite pastimes of our migrant ancestors was a guessing game which might be called "What does Chimney Rock look like?" As the following quotations illustrate, a fair number took the view that it was well-named; it was indeed a chimney!

. . . old dilapidated chimney.—FERGUSON, 1849

. . . resembling an old chimney stack.—CRAMER, 1859

It resembles precizely a chimney.—LARPENTEUR, 1833

. . . truly named for it stands looking like the smoke stack of a furnace.—FLINT, 1853

. . . by a slight stretch of the imagination may be said to resemble a chimney.—McCOY, 1849

. . . chimney of a great factory.—SHAW, 1849

. . . a mammoth chimney to a steam mill.—SNODGRASS, 1852

. . . a huge chimney such as seen at a steam factory.—FARNHAM, 1849

. . . chimney of a sugar refinery.—GRAY, 1849

. . . chimney of a chemical works.—JAGGER, 1849

. . . tall column like the flue of an iron foundry.—BERRIEN, 1849

. . . chimney of a glass-house furnace.—DELANO, 1849

At least three others agreed with Steele that the landmark had the forlorn resemblance of "the lone chimney sometimes seen after a building has been destroyed by fire." Benjamin Ferris in 1852 was impressed by the "justly celebrated Chimney Rock, pointing its solitary column to the sky," and thought "you every moment expect to see issuing smoke or jets of steam from the fancied furnace beneath." In 1860 English globetrotter Richard Burton felt that "the name is not, as is that of the Court-house, a misnomer; one might almost expect to see smoke or steam jetting from the summit." Mary Fish, en route that same year, went Burton one better, thinking that "the clouds had the appearance of smoke rising from the side of the rock."

In many cases the Chimney was transformed by distance into something else—and vice versa. J. M. Stewart thought that it looked more like a chimney from a distance than it did when passing near it. Caroline Richardson was in agreement. To her at a great distance it was a high factory chimney, "but as you approach it assumes the appearance of a strong fortification." Foster saw "a large building with a tall chimney at a distance of 44 miles," but when opposite it became "a large pyramid or castle with a dome in the middle." But others saw it the other way around. J. E. Brown saw a shot tower in the distance "but on approaching it the chimney form is quite perceptible." From afar Duniway saw a "tall spire in the blue distance, pointing toward the heavens," but this Byronesque image became, after all, only "a chimney, extending high above a dome-shaped building."

In 1841 Bidwell notes that the name was given by the "mountaineers" and the name stuck, but in most of the emigrant journals the dull image of a plain old chimney usually gave way to something else. "The Chimney," says Bidwell, "was seen towering like a huge column at the distance of thirty miles." And in 1865, to Sgt. George Holliday of the U.S. Army, the "old furnace stack" became a great monumental obelisk. In fact, many journal-keepers didn't accept the chimney idea at all and saw something quite different. To many it was a great geometrical figure:

. . . single shaft or column rising from the summit of a conical hill. hill.—BRYANT, 1853

. . . spiral column.—TATE, 1849

. . . oblong column on a cone.—PATTERSON, 1859

. . . slim perpendicular column on top of a cone-shaped hill.—STIM-
SON, 1850

. . . a gigantic pillar rising from the prairie.—CHAMBERS, 1855

. . . a column of immense height, round and perfect, as though built
by human hands.—SHAW, 1850

. . . cone-shaped base, pyramidal top.—WISLIZENUS, 1839

. . . solitary shaft of sand rock.—DICKSON, 1864

To others the Chimney was more like a heroic monument of
some kind, often resembling something they had seen back home or
in their textbook on ancient history:

. . . time-chiselled monument.—MAXWELL, 1857

. . . nearly opeset it looks like a Monument.—FULLER, 1849

. . . in distant horizon . . . looming up like the Monument of some
departed hero.—DUNLAP, 1864

. . . looks like the drawing of Cleopatra's needle in Egypt.—BACON,
1851

. . . has loomed up steadily, reminding us of pictures often seen of
the great Egyptian obelisks, towering high above vast deserts.—JOHNS-
TON, 1849

. . . an isolated bluff, in the shape of a pyramid.—WOOD, 1850

. . . about as high as Bunker Hill Monument, and looks very much
like it.—INGALLS, 1850

. . . not unlike Bunker Hill Monument.—WOOLLEY, 1849

. . . looms up like Bunker Hill Monument.—STUART, 1849

. . . a high natural sandstone monument . . . almost precisely like
. . . Bunker Hill Monument.—BACHELDER, 1849

. . . strikingly like the contemplated Washington Monument.—WHITE,
1842

It is of interest to note that the Washington Monument in
Washington, D.C., and the Bunker Hill Monument in Boston are
both obelisks patterned after an Egyptian original, so that all such

references assign a square-tapered effect to the Chimney. Both of these famous American monuments still stand, of course. The Boston monument, commemorating the Battle of Bunker Hill in 1776, rises to a height of 220 feet. The Washington Monument, a much publicized project but not actually under construction when Elijah White wrote in 1842, now pierces the sky at 555 feet.

The resemblance most commonly suggested is that of a shot-tower, and this may be attributed to the influence of Preuss' well-known description in Fremont's report. Thus, Starr's "shot-tower at a great distance," Johnson's "splendid shot-tower," and Bailey's "shot-tower in St. Louis." Crane couldn't decide between "a shot-tower or an Egyptian pillar." Kirk Anderson came up with the idea that Chimney Rock itself "would make a splendid shot-tower for some enterprising gentleman in the lead business, if the bluffs or prairies would only yield the raw materials." A shot-tower is a rare sight today; in pre–Civil War days it was a familiar kind of industrial structure, a tall cylindrical tower which provided a facility for dropping red-hot lead into cold water, resulting in lead balls or ammunition of specified sizes.

The tall, slim column against the sky conjured up other images. Ebey saw a Liberty Pole. Dinwiddie and W. Lee both thought they saw here a lighthouse and, according to the latter, "You can easily imagine the broad level prairie [as] water." Like Warren Ferris in 1830, Nesmith in 1843 saw "the trunk of a tree standing erect." Wistar noted in 1849, "It is in sight far off over the plain before one can distinguish what it is, looking like the dead trunk of a gigantic tree, though in a country where to all appearances, no tree ever existed." The ardent churchgoers among the emigrants were apt to discern the likeness of a church steeple or spire:

. . . appearance of a tall spire.—WOLCOTT, 1850

Chimney Rock shot up like a spire in the heavens, its top gilded by the setting sun, looking like its crest was burnished with gold.—ANDERSON, 1858

. . . stands out in bold relief against the western horizon, & looks like a church steeple in the distance, no larger than a Man's body.—EASTIN, 1849

. . . like a huge steeple placed atop of some mighty ruins.—D. CARR, 1850

. . . spire of a cathedral, rising with a beauty of finish and symmetry of shape unsurpassed by art.—WOODWARD, 1850

. . . like Trinity Church steeple in New York City.—McKEEBY, 1850

. . . something similar to the steeple on the First Presbyterian Church of old Dr. Smith's.—R. HICKMAN, 1852

A few writers show a high degree of originality in their Chimney Rock imaginings, producing metaphors which are unclassifiable:

At . . . 30 miles it rises perpendicular and alone like an old dry stump not larger in appearance than your finger. . . . [Later it] changed . . . & Shewed like a large conicle fort with a Tremendous large & high flag staff.—CLYMAN, 1844

. . . towering like a huge cloud.—HARRITT, 1845

. . . like the neck of an ostrich.—GELWICKS, 1849

. . . a glass funnel inverted or a huge gourd cut across, leaving one third on the stem and set down with the stem up.—LORD, 1849

. . . a huge Demijon . . . the nozzle rising.—CAGWIN, 1850

. . . like some vast giant leaning against the distant clouds, standing sentinal at the entrance to an enchanted fairyland.—BLOOM, 1850

. . . very much like a round cupelow with the litning rod running above the Senter.—THOMASSON, 1850

. . . minaret of a mosque, or smoke-pipe of a steamer.—LANGWORTHY, 1850

. . . ancient stupendous castle now deserted.—GORGAS, 1850

Finally in this catalog of resemblances there is the school of thought that Chimney Rock is not a thing of beauty or inspiration, but something rather plain and ordinary:

. . . a funnel reversed.—NESMITH, 1843

. . . resembles precisely a funnel set upon the large end.—SQUIRES, 1849

. . . funnel-shaped mass of clay.—TAYLOR, 1853

. . . in outline resembling an immense funnel.—COLE, 1852

. . . sugar-loaf shaped hill of sand and mud rock. . . . on this rises the chimney proper . . . at least 100 feet above the sugar loaf.—McBRIDE, 1850

. . . pole set in the Prairie.—EDMUNDSON, 1850

. . . like a pole.—KETCHAM, 1853

. . . a high mound, about the shape of a potato-hole.—LOOMIS, 1850

. . . haystack with a pole stuck in the top.—CRAWFORD, 1851

. . . haystack with a long pole sticking in the top—PARKE, 1849

. . . some big hay stack with an awful big stick stuck on top of it. —McCOWEN, 1854

. . . immense hay stack with a long pole in the center.—WARD, 1853

. . . haystack with a pipe on it.—CRANSTONE, 1851

. . . another vast heap of sand blown up to a height of 250 feet in the shape of a haystack with a spire.—LAMPTON, 1850

. . . what remains of a sand bluff.—GOULD, 1849

So much for general impressions, from the heroic to the anticlimactic. Now it is in order to consider briefly those travelers who were not content to say simply what Chimney Rock looked like, but were anxious to give their readers a more precise description or exact measurements.

Its height today measures 325 feet above the base of the mound, 470 feet above the river. It is instructive to compare these figures with those estimated by the emigrants, bearing in mind that while the other data probably haven't changed much over the past 125 years the spire has probably eroded some 50 to 100 feet in that time.

As might be expected, there are wide variations in estimates, which may be blamed on the optical problems mentioned. While most citizens of that day were experienced estimators, they were used to estimating the height of trees or haystacks nearby, not some weird rock in a strange country full of distortions. Some pretty wild extremes in guesses were made about the height of the Chimney, ranging from the (apparently) nearsighted Hamilton Scott, who, in 1862, peering over from the north side, tells us that "this rock stands on a sand bar and is 30 feet high," to the imaginative mind of the Italian traveler Cipriani, who believed in 1853 that this "calcareous peak rises 1,000 metres above the level of the plains," (the upper part being a mere 300 meters). Since a meter is thirty-nine inches, this would make the Rock pierce the clouds at something like 3,500 feet above the Platte, including a 1,000 foot spire!

More sober estimates of the Chimney alone range from 50 to 200 feet, while those of the mound plus the chimney fall within a spread of 250 to 500 feet, with an occasional daring suggestion of 600 to 800 feet.

The estimates of 500 feet or more given by Bonneville, Wislizenus, and Sage seem more dependable for the earlier period (to judge from the awesome Chimney shown in A. J. Miller's sketch) than most others, who tend to underestimate. Miller's notebook figure of 200 feet in 1837 clearly belies his own art work. In the case of those not scientifically trained, such distortion is understandable. On the other hand, Charles Preuss of Frémont's expedition in 1842 was a trained cartographer, and it is a puzzle why he, too, judged Chimney Rock to be "not more than two-hundred feet above the river."

Of all the quarter million or more emigrants who passed the Chimney, wondered at it, and speculated about it, there is evidence of only two who made any really scientific effort to ascertain the exact height of the Chimney, and it is somewhat disconcerting to find these two still 100 feet apart! One, of course, was Orson Pratt of the Mormon Pioneers, mentioned by Clayton. By the use of instruments he came up with the conservative finding that "Chimney Rock is 260 feet high from its base to its summit." Compare this with the remarkably accurate measurement of David Cosad, employing a geometric device discovered by the ancient Greeks: "The way we assertained the height [Chimney] Rock Mr. A. was 5 feet and nine inches high, and I measured his shadow and paced the shadow of the rock and made it 360 feet from the base to the top."

Since Cosad's higher calculation was in 1849, two years after Orson Pratt's reading of instruments, the difference cannot be explained away by a theory that sometime in between the Rock suffered a partial collapse. Of the two figures, that of Cosad seems to be the most nearly correct for that time; but the difference between the figures of Cosad and Bonneville (360 vs. 500 plus) *could* have been a true difference resulting from a radical reduction in the Chimney sometime between 1832 and 1849.

The educated guesses of Decker, Shombre, and other Forty-Niners have been noted. It may be enlightening to make note of some other stabs at measurements, all dependent on estimates by eye:

. . . 400 feet above the level of the Prairy.—KENNERLY, 1843

. . . rising from a mountain 200 feet high and 800 yards in circumference, a shaft or column 15 feet deep and 175 feet high—READING, 1843

. . . towering to a height of 250 feet. It rises in a gradual slope 150 feet, then making a perpendicular peak of 100 feet and is about 30 feet in diameter.—HARRITT, 1845

Its elevation is said to be between 250 & 300 feet. . . . Its shape is simply a round nole or mound thrown up to a great hight with benches or Storys—and from the center this chimney runs up from 75 to 100 feet above the main boddy. When you are clost to it, its shap is a Squair.—PRITCHARD, 1849

The bottom or bass of the rock is in the form of a hay stack & on top of the bacement part stands a purpendiculr rock 100 feet high about as large at the top as it is at the bottom. . . . the whole stack bacement and all is about 250 ft.—TINKER, 1849

The rock is about ½ mile in circumference at the base & about 500 feet high. . . . at about 250 feet from the base there is quite an ofset the base of which is 100 feet in diameter & 50 feet high, the which then rises in the center of its base & is 200 feet high, 20 feet wide and 8 thick.—DEWOLF, 1849

The base of this wonderful object is conical, about 1 mile in circumference. . . . Its height we judged to be about 150 feet. From the summit of this cone, the column or Chimney extends upward to an equal height with the cone. Its diameter though, when seen at a distance . . . appears to be not over a few feet, yet when measured proves to be some fifty feet.—SEARLS, 1849

The base is formed in the shape of a moune . . . up to the higth of 100 feet. . . . then comes on the Chimney which is in surcumferance one way 10 feet and about 20 feet the other way and ascends as near as we can estimate it 90 feet.—LEWIS, 1849

The Rock from the road presents the appearance of a mound of conical shape about 100 feet high whose base is 300 feet in circ. This is about the same size as its whole length. These measurements are only guessed at and that to from a distance of 2 miles.—DR. T., 1850

. . . 300 feet; some say 5 to 800 feet.—SMITH, 1850

The whole thing was at least 200 feet in height, the chimney part starting in about midway, was about 50 feet square; its top sloped off like the roof of a shanty. Beginning at the top, there was a split down one quarters of its length.—COLE, 1852

The basement covers about 6 acres of ground.—HICKMAN, 1852

. . . 600 feet high.—PRICHET, 1849

Chimney rock is about, from its base to its apex, 400 feet high, consisting of a low and second platform. Upon the latter is the chimney or shaft . . . nearly 100 feet high.—LOBENSTINE, 1851

Above the bace is a cap piece about 30 feet squair & 50 feet high the spiral chimney then rises to the highth of 60 to 80 feet it is about 50 feet in circumference at the bace and gradually tapors to the top. —BIRD, 1854

. . . 150 to 250 feet high . . . chimney only 4 feet across.—CARPENTER, 1856

It consists of a large, square column of clay and sand . . . with a base of conical form . . . and appears as if the column had been set up and the sand heaped around it to sustain in. It is said to be 500 feet high but doubt it.—ADAMS, 1852

. . . perhaps 170 feet high, of really fine shape, & its center being a shaft probably 60 feet high and seemingly not more than 4 feet in diamter. They are both entirely naked of vegetation.—TAYLOR, 1853

. . . situated upon a base of low sand hills covering about ten acres on which there rises a regular cone of about 100 feet in height and about 2 or 300 in diameter at the base. . . . Crowning this there is a cubical block of sides squaring 30 or 40 feet; upon which rises the round column from which the rock takes its name . . . to the height of 50 feet.—CRAMER, 1859

. . . three divisions or stories, the last or top about 15 feet square, 50 feet high.—BURGESS, 1866

. . . circular base 150 feet high, above this a column 30 to 40 feet square, rises another 125 or more.—BUTTERFIELD, 1861

. . . pyramidal base 125 feet surmounted by a column 100 feet high. —TOMPKINS, 1850

. . . oblong column 200 feet high, standing on a cone same height. —PATTERSON, 1859

. . . 320 feet high [plus] chimney 150 feet high.—LEE, 1858

. . . Cituated 30 rods from the river, Base 60 rods Diameter, tapers up 90 feet, forming a handsome space for a walk or Promenade around it; another gradual taper 60 feet, and a second offset; up 30 feet, another jog and offset; [then] dome or chimney 15 feet diameter, up 60 feet.—KILGORE, 1850

In the matter of accurate description, special commendation should be given to six writers—Cramer, Lobenstine, Burgess, Bird, Dewolf, and Kilgore—for noting an important detail not mentioned by others. This is the actual existence of three geometric parts to the Chimney. Where others make note of only a cone and a chimney spire, these six were keen enough observers to discern a third or intermediate section between cone and spire, the distinctly separate base of the chimney, resembling a massive tree trunk base and spreading roots, which is probably more pronounced today than it was then.

All of the above followed the south side (California Trail, or St. Joe Road), and it is interesting to note that this group, combined with the five Forty-Niners quoted in full above, come up with a conservative but not too inaccurate average height of 320 feet of Chimney Rock from the base of the cone. In contrast are the following five, who, viewing the Chimney from the north side (or Council Bluffs Road), are just as far off as H. Scott in 1862 in their consistent underestimates:

. . . a mound 40 or 50 feet, the chimney standing more than 60 feet above the mound.—WEST, 1853

. . . camped in the meridian of chimney rock . . . it is situated on a large mound 50 feet high.—DENNIS, 1850

It is a sandstone shaft, say 50 feet high, standing on a conical shaped mound about twice as high.—FLINT, 1853

The whole appears to be 60 feet high.—HEWITT, 1862

. . . pyramid-shaped pile of earth and rock about 50 feet high & in the center is a rock resembling an old chimney 40 feet higher.—Fox, 1866

The geology of the Chimney Rock formation, as presently conceived, is simple. Like its adjoining bluff and neighboring isolates, it is an erosional remnant. What is left today is composed entirely of Brule clay of Oligocene age, with interspersed layers of volcanic ash. Although there is no rational accounting for its unique "inverted funnel" form, it may safely be assumed that the principal factor in its survival was an earlier top stratum of Arickaree sandstone, probably with a concentration of limestone accretion layers.

To judge from the A. J. Miller sketch, this protective cap had disappeared as early as 1837, and erosion or fracturing would thence-
forth be rapid. The Arickaree sandstone is abundantly present, of
course, in the loftier Court House and Scott's Bluffs.

Some of the emigrants, attempting to account for the Chimney's durability, supposed that it was composed of granite (Ivins,
Scheller). Buffum says, "The lower part is cemented stone, the
tower is basalt," while Mrs. Vogdes says, "I think the formation
shale." But most writers, without benefit of modern geological
knowledge, came to the intelligent conclusion that this was a most
perishable material of some sort, rapidly deteriorating, although
none could explain how this soft stuff happened to be standing
way up there in the air like that in the first place (and that is what
made the Chimney such a miracle). Again emulating Fremont,
many called this "marl and earthy limestone." Other terms used
include "sand bluff" (Gould), "soft rock and sand" (J. E. Brown),
"conglomerate of earth and pebble" (Chandless), "a kind of clay
easily broken" (Martha Moore), "indurated clay" (Robe), "soft
sandstone or very hard clay" (Butterfield), "a kind of soapstone"
(Curtis), "chalk rock" (Wilkinson), "cemented sand" (Ingersoll),
and "hard baked dirt instead of rock" (Farnham). Keller found it
"nearly as soft as magnesian limestone, though not so white." Disappointed, Sponsler exclaims, "It is cald rock but is nothing but
sand and dirt!"

Rev. Parker in 1835 spoke of a light chocolate color. Among
the very few others who manage to convey something of the delicate
hue of the Brule clay is Mrs. Vogdes: " a formation of sand forming
a high tower, with a strong looking foundation, of cream colored
earth. . . . The bluffs along the road are a light yellow color."

Several were observant enough to recognize that the Chimney
was a geological first cousin of the Court House and other formations. Thus, Riley Root in 1848: "the same material as Babel
Tower, fast crumbling down;" and Caroline Richardson speaks of
"the same material as lonely tower." In 1849 Castleman writes:
"It is composed of the same material as the Castle Rock being of a
sandy nature showing many different stratas of different collores
in which we found many fragments of shells and other things which
shows that it has been thrown up by watter in the course of time."
Another notes that Chimney Rock "stands in front of some bluffs
of about its own height" and supposes that it "might have once

been one of them but is now disconnected." Lewis Dougherty also recognizes this as a remnant of the adjoining bluff: "This is not a rock but a part of the hills south of the river, cut off the main hill by wind, water and time. The space between it and the main hill is near 300 yards. . . . Twenty feet from the top is a white clay rock completely exposed and corresponding to a similar ledge in the main hill, confirming the supposition that the hill and Chimney Rock were once the same."

Brackett is one of the few, along with Castleman and Dougherty, who noted varying geological strata: "It is composed of hardened clay, with alternate layers of red and white sandstone," by which he presumably refers to the whitish volcanic ash layers which delicately interlay the Brule clay (normally a pale yellow or buff color, but reddish brown when wet). Castleman is almost alone in suggesting the sedimentary character of the formation. Strangely enough, despite the existence of volcanic ash in the Rock, no emigrant seems to have come up with a theory about a volcanic upheaval, such as was invoked by several to account for Ash Hollow.

The action of erosion was well understood by many emigrants, who logically supposed that, high as it was in the mid–nineteenth century ("towering to the heavens," as several say), it must have been higher still a few years before, an impression reinforced by the recollections of wagon train guides and old fur traders:

> It is likely the earth has mouldered away from around these towers, and left them to be wondered at by man.—Scott, 1849

> It is about 200 feet in height and some years ago was calculated at double that—but that is doubtful.—Gray, 1849

> Its summit is about 150 feet above the plain, but it was at one time much higher, early travellers say 500 feet. . . . the ground around its base is covered with pieces which have fallen from the summit. . . . rain and wind . . . have worn away its softer constituents and left a column standing.—Kenderdine, 1858

> As the mountains are continually crumbling and falling down I suppose this must have been a column of the mountain . . . & this being a solid column, it has endured while all around has fallen from it. —Kerns, 1852

> The top of the column is somewhat crumbling and for that reason I should think it had once stood much higher in the world than at present.—Jno. Clark, 1852

. . . not more than 200 feet above the Platte. It is said when first visited to have been 500 feet high.—McGLASHAN, 1850

It is said by the French traders to have been much higher than at present but is wearing away every year by the action of the elements. —INGALLS, 1850

The entire height is said to be 180 feet, and within memory to have been thirty feet higher.—CHANDLESS, 1855

. . . circular shaped . . . then carrying its size to the top which is said to have been 200 feet but of late part of the top fell off.—HARTER, 1864

Our guide informs me that when first visited by him its height was much greater than at present, and that when this region was first visited by whites it was discernible from the bluff near Ash Hollow. —SEARLS, 1849

. . . . found that it had been a very large rock and that the teeth of time had been gnawing on it until in the distance it looked like a chimney. There was a massive pile of rock at the foot. . . . a mere stem was left standing.—CRAWFORD, 1851

Within the memory of men there may have been forces at work other than simple weathering, something catastrophic. "It was the opinion of Mr. Bridger," reports Capt. Stansbury in 1849, "that it was reduced to its present height by lightning, or some other catastrophe, as he found it broken on his return from one of his trips to St. Louis, though he had passed it uninjured on his way down." Buffum thought that the Chimney "appeared to have been struck by lightning." An old-timer in Leeper's train confirmed that "a few years ago lightning hurled some thirty feet of the chimney or spire to the ground." In 1858 Kirk Anderson got another version from

an old mountaineer, who lives way up in the mountains. [He] says that when he first saw it, forty years ago, it was a great deal taller than it is now, but that about that time, in a severe storm, lightning struck it and knocked it off about two miles—rather improbable, it is true.

Conway, who was also a visitor in the late 1850s, embroidered the tale further, with a supernatural twist:

Some years ago lightning is supposed to have struck this hill, whereby about one-half of it was dissevered. The Indians and mountaineers who beheld this catastrophe aver that masses of rock and earth were hurled to the distance of two or three miles . . . and the remarks here of the Indians and others who saw this event may not be uninteresting. One declared half the hills were swallowed up; another, that the rocks were bent in two; but the most ridiculous opinion is one from the Indians, who positiviely asserted that the rock grew to such a height above the surface of the prairie that the moon once came in the shape of a powder horn—caught the top—and broke it asunder in the middle!

A more practical explanation is offered by A. J. Dickson in 1864: "We were told that some years earlier a company of soldiers in target practice had trained a small cannon upon it, breaking off about thirty feet of its top."

In covered wagon days Chimney Rock, whether viewed as "one of Nature's freaks" or as a delicate finger pointing heavenward, was to most everyone a marvel to behold, the more marvelous because it had once been an even more incredible, cloud-piercing spire. The obverse side of this image was the Chimney Rock of the future, toppled by time, only a memory. So to make more poignant and precious their own experience, the emigrants freely predicted the early collapse of the Chimney. Their journals sound like the tolling of funeral bells:

The pillar has from its top a fissure extending forty feet, threatening destruction. I have no doubt in a few years it will be destroyed.— READING, 1843

. . . split at the top & looks so now it might fall apart.—FARNHAM, 1849

It appeared to be cracking and decaying away.—BENSON, 1849

It is wasting away very fast and I dare say in a few years this old and weather beaten rock will entirely waste away.—CASTLEMAN, 1849

It is quite likely the chimney will be broken off in time, leaving nothing but its cone to gratify the curiosity of future travelers.—DELANO, 1849

The chimney has a large crevice running through the middle, which will eventually cause it to split asunder and tumble down. Large detached masses of it were laying around its base, which had tumbled down from the top.—McBRIDE, 1850

It is fast mouldering to ruins and if you don't look sharp, my friends, you will never see it.—WOOD, 1850

The rain, that has caused the remarkable shape, is now rapidly lessening and destroying the object.—CHANDLESS, 1855

Every year washes away some of its glory. . . . the Chimney is cracked
at present . . . in a few years this part of the rock will fall.—BIRD, 1855

It appears to be decaying very fast as it is falling off in great scales.
Ere long the great conical shaft will disappear from the gaze of man.
—DINWIDDIE, 1863

At least two reminiscing emigrants announced the end of the
Chimney. Butterfield recollects that in 1861 the famous Rock
"seemed to be dissolving quite fast, and doubtless ere this it has
all gone down." G. M. West, recalling the tottering Chimney Rock
of 1853 in his own old age, confides to his readers, "It has since
fallen down!" These requiems were premature, for the Rock has
survived for over 100 years, at least, confounding the prophets of
doom. Almost alone among emigrants in recognizing its durable
qualities is Cramer, writing in 1859: "Such structures as these
would not last in the moist climate of the Eastern States a single
lifetime, I suppose, but in this region they may be of a very remote
period."

There is no possible way to chart the actual reduction of Chimney Rock in historical times. Comparison of the strange formation
in A. J. Miller's painting of 1837 with the Rock of 1967 suggests, as
Shakespeare put it, "What a falling off was here!" Because of the
wide variations in measurements, scientific or otherwise, which
were offered a century ago, it is not even safe to venture a guess as
to how much higher the Chimney Rock of 1849 really was above
the base of the cone compared with the 325-foot altitude measurable
today. From the several references to a collapse of the chimney top,
together with fallen chunks at the base, it seems probable that there
was a cataclysm sometime between Miller's visit of 1837 and the
Gold Rush of 1849. Another collapse can be predicted between
1859, when Cramer makes the last mention of the giant crack or
fissure, and 1864, when Harter reports that "of late part of the top
fell off." Also, the crack is missing in the W. H. Jackson sketch of
1866. Photographs made in the early 1900s show a rock somewhat
higher than in 1938, when there was a sharp spike like a finger
pointing to the heavens. This landmark is such a venerated object
in western Nebraska that in recent years every time the tip of the
spire crumbles noticeably, it makes headlines in the regional daily,
the Scottsbluff *Star-Herald*.

Even with all these recurring calamities, there was so much

chimney to Chimney Rock to begin with that it still looms up impressively against the western sky and still rivets the attention of the traveler. There is something seemingly supernatural about this old Oregon Trail landmark. It erodes and falls away; and yet it continues to rise up, like human hope, eternal.

Viewing the Chimney, dim against the far horizon or looming like a cathedral spire at close range, was a memorable experience. But the supreme thrill was to hike over to the Rock, scramble up the forty-five degree elevation of the cone, carve your name on the perpendicular chimney somewhere—the higher the better—and get one of the most inspiring views on the North American continent. To judge from the number of self-confessed climbers and carvers, the Chimney was a veritable mecca, and its worshipers were legion:

> . . . visited the 'chimney' . . . crossed enormous gulleys and saw a flock of mountain sheep looking like birds upon the ledge [of the nearby bluff?] . . . ascended the chimney half way . . . Father Hoecken getting to heaven on his knees . . . swallows like bumble bees up the chimney.—FIELD, 1843

> Some men ascended the perpendicular shaft, none could get further. —STUART, 1849

> Had an extensive view of it with the glass and saw several persons about its base.—GRAY, 1849

> The base is very steep so much so that it would be impossible to climb on some sides. . . . I climbed up to the base of the Chimney and cut my name among some thousand others. . . . probably it will be cut away in a short time to make room for another.—STARR, 1849

> It is composed of sandstone, and thousands of names are written on it, or rather cut with knives. Several of us climbed high as we could and cut our names.—WOOD, 1850

> Encamped for noon opposite Chimney Rock on the south side of Platte River. . . . I had but little difficulty in crossing the river though the current is very swift and I had to swim a considerable way. . . . I saw hundreds of names out in the rock some at a dizzy height. . . . I wrote mine above all except two and theirs were about 8 feet higher than mine.—TUTTLE, 1850

> On getting within a quarter of a mile of it I took a drawing of that wonderful natural monument. After which I clambered up the Chimney on the south side to the first and only bench above the top of the base or cone, which was as high as any mortal could climb it,

for the stem of the Chimney runs perpendicularly about 200 feet higher. There I engraved my name and the name of my wife. There were several Ladies and Gentlemen on the rock with me; and after I had completed my name I looked to my left and there stood a young lady who had cut foot and handholes in the soft rock busily engaged in inscribing her name about 2 feet higher than my own!—EVANS, 1850

Part of this ascent was made with difficulty being as steep as a house roof & if one had got a start from it he could not have stopped till he would have rolled head long to the bottom. . . . On this rock as on the Court House many pioneered in the way of name carving, had been before us, and used all the eligible locations, so that I did not place my name on this Rock.—MCBRIDE, 1850

. . . is visited by a great deal of pilgrims. . . . Many names and old dates are to be seen carved high on its precipitous walls.—WORD, 1863

When we reached the towering column we all fell to deciphering the names and dates cut on almost every portion of its surface that could be reached by even the most agile climbers.—ARNOLD, 1863

Since Chimney Rock was such a great milestone and offered excellent camping facilities, the Chimney Rock climb became rather standard procedure on any excursion up the Great Platte River Road. Because of its closer proximity to the wagon road as well as its weird beckoning contours, Chimney Rock was undoubtedly much more frequently visited or climbed than the Court House. But not everyone made it, discouraged either by the "optical shift" or just plain fatigue. Pigman said he did not ascend the Chimney, his curiosity being satisfied by the Court House experience. Berrien claimed blisters, while Delano pleaded exhaustion after a tough day. Helen Carpenter said that her object was to get to California, and she "had no time for natural curiosities." Breyfogle made an honest effort to climb the Chimney but was defeated by storms which made the clay slippery.

But these were exceptions to a Chimney-climbing impulse so strong that it inspired many travelers up the north bank to make a wet and dangerous side trip across the North Platte. Charles Tuttle, quoted above, is a typical case. Turnbull wanted to cross over to the Rock, which seemed no more than "¼ mile from the St. Joe Road" but changed his mind when informed (mistakenly) that "it is over 10 miles away." William Earnshaw started to cross but was warned "that we would drown." There is only one recorded instance of an entire wagon train crossing the river at this point, north to south; this was the Reuben Miller train of 1849, composed of Mormons bound for Salt Lake City. The motive for this unusual crossing is not given. Sight-seeing hardly seems to justify the effort, which was made safely "with the exception of the breaking of a wheel or two and some light injuries." Orson Hyde, who measured Chimney Rock with a sextant in 1847, is identified as the captain of this maverick train.

There is plentiful evidence that the base of Chimney Rock was once festooned with emigrant carvings, probably the usual assortment of names, initials, dates, and places of origin. Perhaps there was also a fair quota of heart-shaped messages of love and the names of wives or sweethearts back in the states. One emigrant says that here in the desert, in the "Indians' Enchanted Ground," he carved the name of his betrothed on this, the highest pinnacle to be found along the North Platte. Today all names of covered wagon origin have vanished, along with several layers of soft Brule clay.

As noted, some of the names were fading in 1849, almost as soon as they were written. The last reference to Chimney Rock carving is Samuel Word's in 1863, noted above. In 1850 Seth Lewelling says that many names were those of old fur traders. In 1849 Geiger remarked on the survival of the name of Captain Smith, his wagon train boss, carved in 1845. While most names were carved with knives, Geiger found "at least 1000 more painted upon the Chimney." Solomon Gorgas in 1850 refers to "thousands of names cut and written with lead pencil."

The journals cited indicate that there was great competition to carve one's name higher than anyone else, and this led to some daring efforts to scale the Chimney shaft. In 1850, says John Carr, "as far up the shaft as could be reached were the names of hundreds of adventurers," while McGlashan that same year reports "thousands of names . . . each one trying to cut his name higher than his predecessors. . . . from the height of some of those names I witnessed, it must have required good nerve to climb."

What methods were used to scale the Chimney spire? It can be imagined the men stood on each others' shoulders, possibly even forming human pyramids in efforts to set new altitude records. Dr. Thomasson, also of 1850, suggests the principal climbing device used and further suggests what may have been the maximum climbing height safely attained—forty-five feet!

I went up it about 4 hundred feet then it became so step that they was feet holts cut in so we could clime up about 25 feet further then we could see where some had cut noches and drove little sticks to clime about 20 feet further but did not venture up that I suppose that thare is not less than 2 thousand names riten in difrin plases.

Did anyone ever manage to exceed the height to which Dr. Thomasson testifies? Did anyone ever reach the summit of Chimney Rock? In 1856 William Pleasants says, "I attempted to climb to the top but could not do so by at least 100 feet." In 1859 Martha Moore says that she could get no higher than "to where the Chimney sets off, but the boys went up the shaft. They looked like mere doll babies up so far." That sounds like "the boys" got pretty high up there. John Wood reports a rumor that "when Col. Fremont came to this rock he stopped his company for several days, trying to ascend to the top, but could not." (There is nothing in Fremont's journal to support this.) The only man who ever reached the top of Chimney Rock, apparently, was a nameless Sioux Indian whose sensational (but probably apocryphal) feat is described by George Holliday in 1865:

> It was told us that at one time a band of Sioux passing there, an offer was made by the Chief, of a pony to the young brave who would climb to the pinnacle and stand upon it. Several fruitless attempts were made but finally a daring young buck succeeded by cutting niches with his tomahawk in reaching its dizzy height, but just as he was in the act of standing on top, his moccasin slipped and down he came. Had he found a soft place upon which to light he would have won the broncho and perhaps been made a chief and then married the old chief's daughter and all that, but he struck the ground too hard, and so he gave up the ghost—and the pony too. But the old chief did the next best thing he could. He erected a scaffold, wrapped the dead Indian up in all his available assets, and wythed him fast on top of the scaffold, then he killed the pony which the poor fellow had lost his life in winning, and placed its carcass under the scaffold for the dead warrior to ride on his hunts in the happy hunting grounds. We looked about for the scaffold and thought we found evidence of it in the shape of rotten wood and small bits of hides.

Assuming that no one in his right mind today would attempt to emulate the Sioux brave and invite suicide by scaling the Chimney, what of the view from the top of the conical base? In 1849 Ferguson says he "climbed to the top" and from there "men looked like toddling children, and horses no more than one foot high." In 1863 Redman carved his name on this "queer looking rock," then turned around and was amazed to see that covered wagons looked no larger than baby buggies. Today, from the Chimney cone, cars on the paved highway, which follows the old California Road, look no larger than ants, and railroad trains which pass daily up both sides of the North Platte look like caterpillars.

But these are things nearby. The ultimate reward of a Chimney Rock climb is the vast panorama which sweeps the horizon, east to west, with the North Platte glistening snake-like in its continental journey and the bluffs from the Court House to Scott's Bluffs describing a series of giant amphitheaters with formations as fantastic as the surface of the moon.

Before moving westward, it is in order to examine certain neighboring topographic features, graves, incidents, and stations— all dwarfed in importance by the famous Rock itself, but all of vital interest to covered wagon emigrants.

Not everyone lived to see the glorious sunrise at Chimney Rock. Although no identifiable emigrant graves survive today, the Chimney Rock vicinity had its quota of emigrants dead from cholera and accident. The Asiatic plague was diminishing at this elevation. Chimney Rock was not the mass grave marker that some popular writers would have us believe, but there were certainly fatalities enough, beginning in 1849. The plague was carried to this point in June. Later that month David Staples reported seven new graves east of the Chimney; Joseph Sedgley found three just below and identified these as Wm. Ray of Missouri, G. S. Ferguson, and Dr. G. Macbeth of Buffalo. Dr. Macbeth's grave must have been among the most prominent along the trail, for it also attracted the notice of Dr. Lord, Castleman, and Bruff. The latter reports the grave of "G. McBeth, M.D., June 21" as two miles below the Rock, on the left of the trail. Nearby was the grave of "Wm. K. Colly of Ray Co., Mo., died of cholera, June 18, aged 49 years." The burial of "Mr. Colley" on that date is reported by Howell. (It seems probable that Sedgley's "Wm. Ray of Mo." was in fact Wm. Colly.)

On the "N.W. side of Chimney Rock," Bruff found the graves of M. Dade and J. Griffith, both of Buffalo, N.Y. One mile below the Rock, on the left, was "Wm. Witt of Mackin [Macon?] Co., Mo., June 21, age 29." About five miles west of the Rock were the graves of two more Missourians, P. W. Tolle of Morin [Morgan?] County (cholera), and Jno. Campbell of Lafayette County, who "came to his death by the accidental discharge of his gun, while riding with a friend, June 21, Age 18." One more casualty of 1849 is noted by Thurber: "Young man by the name of Shead, died with cholera. He was buried with one of his blankets around him, also a canvas hammock."

In 1850 Micajah Littleton passed eight graves in a twenty-mile stretch divided by the Chimney: "F. Masher, June 11; W. P. Temple, June 24 age 35, Carroll Ct., Ark.; Cissero H. Morrow June 15th Ozark, Green Co., Mo.; Thos. Price, June 28th aged 26 T. A. Mo.; Nancy Jane Smith, June 28th, age 18 of Franklin Co., Mo.; Wm. Finell, June 16th age 47, Howard Co., Mo.; Oliver Sutton, June 20th aged 16 of Saline Co., Mo." (John Steele's account of the 1850 grudge fight which resulted in two deaths here was reported in Chapter III).

In 1852 Caroline Richardson reports four fresh graves here, while Hampton counted ten, new and old. In a notation in his copy of the Frizzell diary, E. E. Ayer says that this year "a man named Dunn who was father's partner" died here of cholera. E. S. Carter remembers that it was here a young man buried a companion, and then turned his team back to St. Joe. He was the only survivor of a party of four.

Two more Chimney Rock burials are noted, and these were military. In October, 1857, Col. Cooke (who first saw this landmark eleven years before) reported, "Pvt. Whitney, Co. G, died in camp near Chimney Rock of lockjaw. He was buried on the bluff, with the honors of war, next morning at sunrise." In August, 1858, Patrick Laughnahan, a teamster with an army supply train, died here of "fever and ague." His burial, according to Sgt. Percival Lowe, was attended by complications. A band of Indians under Little Thunder (presumably the same who was defeated near Ash Hollow three years before) appeared, begging for food. A mischievous soldier frightened the Indians by telling them that the man had died of smallpox. It took a lot of diplomacy on Lowe's part to calm Little Thunder, who thought he had been tricked into exposure to a fatal disease. "Taking my knife," says Lowe, "I ripped open the cover and removed the handkerchief, revealing the pale, smooth face, and succeeded in inducing all of them to come close and look carefully. I explained to them as best I could the cause of the man's death. The man who had lied to them kept hidden; he was more scared than were the Indians."

The high bluffs to the south, forming the backdrop of the Chimney, in 1852 caught the attention of Cecelia Adams, who was reminded of "an Illinois straw stable." Dr. Parke thought that these bluffs were more arresting than the Chimney, and some of the contemporary artists did a fair job of representing them. Of more immediate concern to travelers, however, were camping facilities. It may be fairly judged that the Chimney Rock neighborhood was a major campground, and indeed several diarists describe the large concentration of wagon corrals here.

Wood was a scarce commodity all the way from Ash Hollow to Scott's Bluffs and any wood found in this neighborhood was apt to be a chunk of the mysterious dead cedar found on the valley floor or scrub pine or cedar from a distant hill. While the Chimney formation itself was as barren as a billiard ball, a few campers mention scattered timber on the adjacent bluffs. But the big surprise was the number of springs here, where according to the guidebooks, no springs were supposed to be. These were modest springs, nothing more than trickles in comparison with the famous and bountiful springs at Ash Hollow and Scott's Bluffs, and in some seasons they may have evaporated; but they were much in evidence in June when the migrations crested here. Modern ranching practices and possible changes in drainage patterns make it nearly impossible to pinpoint the location of these historical springs today, but they are suggested by these emigrants:

> One-fourth of a mile from the chimney is a fountain of pure water, situated in what is called Chimney Rock Ravine, and the spring is known as Chimney Rock Spring. It is 100 yards up the bluff, in a stone formation, which is soft and smooth as marble. It is hollowed out as if by art. Hundreds of names are carved on this rock.—SEDGLEY, 1849

> Here we found a spring not spoken of by any of our guides.—PIGMAN, 1850

> About half a mile from Chimney Rock to the southeast in a cedar ravine is an excellent spring.—EVANS, 1850

> . . . drove up to the fine spring near CR.—J. E. BROWN, 1849

> . . . spring near the Rock coming out of a clay bluff, cold and reviving.—STAPLES, 1849

. . . three first rate springs here, three miles from Chimney Rock. —HAMPTON, 1852

. . . camp four miles from CR, near several springs of water . . . [also] good springs in the bluff near it.—LOTTS, 1849

There are several good springs about a mile and a half or two miles before you get to Chimney Rock.—LITTLETON, 1850

Descending from the rock we struck off in an easterly direction to our encampment situated about ¾ mile, near which was a spring bubbling from the bottom of the ravine, among a few starved cedars.—SEARLS, 1849

About 100 yards away is a cold spring.—BENSON, 1849

The concentration of springs to the east seems to correspond with those known today as Facus Springs. The smaller ones nearer the Chimney are difficult to find today. Also mentioned by travelers in this area were soda flats and alkali beds. It was hard to keep the cattle from drinking alkali water, which gave them cramps. The earth near the chimney is still "strong with lye," as Elizabeth Geer wrote in 1847, and "here thrive hostile plants, sage, greasewood, prickly pear." In 1849 Amos Bachelder observed that this "water would make good soap by boiling with plenty of grease, it was so strongly impregnated with alkali. . . . If we had plenty of acid we might have set up a soda fountain."

After a heavy rain the alkali beds became shallow lakes, and the trail which passed between the Chimney and the river became boggy. Several writers complain of this. In 1849 Amos Josselyn's wagons came to a dead stop with mud up to the axles, and it took "18 yoke of oxen to pull our wagon out, a mile through the musky ground." That same season J. H. Johnson here passed sixty government mule teams stuck in the mud, many with wagon tongues broken.

Except for the rather dubious Indian legends reported above by Conway and Holliday, Chimney Rock does not seem to have figured prominently in Sioux Indian lore. This is rather strange, considering the impact such a strange object must have had on primitive minds. Nor was this vicinity the scene of any notable episodes in the history of Indian warfare. There are a few stray references to Sioux encampments here, but they seem to have preferred the territory between Ash Hollow and the Court House. In

1858 Sgt. Lowe, in advance of his supply train, was hunting ducks in a bayou of the Platte east of the Chimney when he was accosted by a band of Sioux warriors. Instead of lifting his scalp, however, they merely begged for food, and when his wagon train came up, he allowed them each a soldier's ration.

There is fleeting evidence of some kind of a skirmish between soldiers and Indians near here in 1865. In August of that year Jake Pennock wrote: "Hear our troop had a fight west of Chimney Rock. Killed two Indians and wounded one." Burgess, a freighter heading for Montana, reported: "A little above Chimney Rock there were signs of the soldier fight with the Indians. We found one grave outside the breast works." A search of old army records fails to throw light on this engagement.

In 1854, while camped near Chimney Rock, Patrick Murphy mentioned "two trading posts here, also a blacksmith shop." Since there seems to be no further reference to such an establishment here, it is concluded that these were portable tepees or Indian village trading posts rather than any permanent structures.

Allen's guide mentions a mail station at Chimney Rock in 1859. That same year, Martha Moore says she "camped two miles above the stage station," which would probably be at the same place. The location of this structure is suggested by Ada Millington in 1862: "After dinner we went on till we came to a stage station and were then just between the Rock and the river. The former did not look to be more than a quarter of a mile but the station keeper said it was two miles away."

In October, 1861, the new telegraph line up the Platte went into operation. Beginning in 1863, Indian war bands began to burn the poles and tear down the lines; in 1864 the U.S. Army, with district headquarters at Fort Laramie, set up a series of telegraph stations and military guards. From 1864 to 1868 there was a telegraph station here, sandwiched between the stations at Mud Springs and Scott's Bluffs. Apparently also there was a detachment of soldiers here to guard this installation, and these troops were lodged in a new adobe structure, probably fortified. Several references to the Chimney Rock Station throw dim light on this forgotten site.

In 1861 Oscar Collister, age nineteen, was one of a group of four young telegraph operators sent out by stage to man stations "in the western wild." Collister was sent to Deer Creek, Wyoming, but one of the other three, unidentified, was left at Chimney Rock. Like everyone else, Collister was deceived by the distance of the Chimney from the stage road.

In 1860 Capt. Albert Tracy stopped overnight at this stage station en route to Salt Lake City. He slept on the dirt floor of the "dobie hut" and was billed $2.50 for the privilege. At this date he writes, "Chimney Rock stands boldly up to greet us . . . & in the distant glow in the renewed sunlight a long and castellated line indicates the Bluffs of Scott. But we move mercilessly away, glad soon to put behind us the whole locality—landlord of hut inclusive."

In 1865 Holliday, en route with troops from Julesburg to Fort Laramie, says he passed Fort Mitchell at the foot of Scott's Bluffs, then "camped the next night at Chimney Rock, which stands back three miles from the river at the foot of the sand bluff. At this point on the Platte was another blockhouse called Chimney Rock Station, and guarded by twenty-five men of the Third U.S. Infantry. Viewing the rock from the station it resembled an old furnace stack standing alone like a giant obelisk. Its height is 170 feet." Then he tells the story of the Indian who ascended the pinnacle, given above. Scott's Bluffs and Fort Mitchell would have been visited *after* Chimney Rock and not before on this march. Holliday is confused in his recollections, but his account of Chimney Rock Station seems trustworthy.

The latest reference to this station is to be found in the manuscript journal of Ada Vogdes, who accompanied her officer husband to Fort Laramie in 1868. All she has to say is this: "We are encamped three miles from Chimney Rock Station immediately above a high piece of ground that ends at the river bank." This does not constitute proof that this station was still occupied at this late date; it seems probable that it would have been abandoned in 1867, the same year which marked the end of Fort Mitchell and other outposts of Fort Laramie.

As might be expected of a landmark which in its day was such a world wonder, Chimney Rock was often the subject for artists. Research to date has disclosed that no less than thirty-five artistically inclined travelers did make sketches of the Rock and vicinity between 1837 and 1874. Sketches reportedly made by Eastin in 1849, J. Evans in 1850, and Gove in 1857 are missing. This leaves thirty-two contemporary artists whose efforts have survived, to our knowledge. These are listed in the accompanying table.

Surprisingly enough, all have seen publication in one form or

CHECKLIST OF KNOWN CHIMNEY ROCK SKETCHES:

Artist	Date of Sketch	Date of Pub.	Author and Title of Publication, or Name of Repository
A. J. Miller	1837	1947	DeVoto, *Across the Wide Missouri*
Nicholas Point	1841	1952	McDermott, *Nebraska History,* March, 1952
Charles Preuss	1842	1845	Fremont, *Report of Explorations*
J. Quinn Thornton	1846	1849	Thornton, *Oregon & California*
Howard Egan	1847	1917	Egan, *Pioneering the West*
James F. Wilkins	1849	1968	McDermott, *Artist on the Overland Trail*
J. G. Bruff	1849	1944	Bruff, *Gold Rush*
D. Jagger	1849	–	California Historical Society
Dr. Charles Parke	1849	–	Huntington Library
William Lorton	1849	–	Bancroft Library
Joseph A. Stuart	1849	1896?	Stuart, *My Roving Life*
Seth Lewelling	1850	–	California State Library
Franklin Street	1850	1851	Street, *California in 1850*
Cyrenius Hall	1852	–	Wyoming State Archives
W. Wadsworth	1852	1858	Wadsworth, *National Wagon Road*
Geo. H. Baker	1853	?	*Hutchings Panoramic Scenes*
Frederick Piercy	1853	1855	Linforth, *Route from Liverpool*
J. Robert Brown	1856	–	Newberry Library
William A. Maxwell	1857	1915	Maxwell, *Crossing the Plains*
Cornelius Conway	1857	1858	Conway, *Utah Expedition*
T. S. Kenderine	1858	1888	Kenderine, *A California Tramp*
Albert Bierstadt	1859	1866	*Ladies' Repository* (Ewers)
Albert Bierstadt	1859	–	Joslyn Art Museum
Randolph Marcy	?	1859	Marcy, *Prairie Traveller*
Alfred Lambourne	?	–	Union Pacific Museum
Alfred Lambourne	?	1892	Lambourne, *The Old Journey*
Richard Burton	1860	1861	Burton, *City of the Saints*
George Simons	1861	–	Joslyn Art Museum
George M. Ottinger	1861	1867	*Harper's Weekly,* November 2, 1867
Eugene Ware	1864	1911	Ware, *Indian War of 1864*
Geo. H. Holliday	1865	1883	Holliday, *On the Plains in '65*
Margaret Carrington	1866	1879	Carrington, *Ab-sa-ra-ka*
Wm. H. Jackson	1866	–	Scotts Bluff National Monument
Wm. H. Jackson	1866	1942	Driggs, *Westward America*
Wm. H. Jackson	1866	1958	C. Jackson, *Pageant of Pioneers*
George M. Ottinger	1873	–	Franz Stenzel Collection, Portland
Jules Tavernier	1874	1953	Taft, *Artists and Illustrators*

another with these exceptions: sketches by Jagger, Parke, Lewelling, Lorton, Hall and Simons and oil paintings by Ottinger and Bierstadt. Some, like those of Preuss, Piercy, and Burton, are long famous, having appeared in these frontier classics: Fremont's *Explorations*, Linforth's *Route from Liverpool to Great Salt Lake Valley*, and Burton's *City of the Saints*. Others, like those of A. J. Miller, J. G. Bruff, and William H. Jackson, are now well known to the public. Miller's Chimney Rock was introduced by DeVoto in *Across the Wide Missouri*, Bruff's in his magnificent Gold Rush journals edited by Read and Gaines. Two of the Jackson versions have been published, in Driggs' *Westward America* and Clarence Jackson's *Pageant of the Pioneers*. His original pencil sketch is on display at the Oregon Trail Museum, Scott's Bluff National Monument. Albert Bierstadt, who later achieved fame for his mountain landscapes, accompanied Gen. Lander westward in 1859. He is credited with two paintings of Chimney Rock, a small conventional sketch and a romanticized version with an Indian encampment in the foreground, both in the Joslyn Art Museum, Omaha. An engraving by S. V. Hunt in the *Ladies' Repository*, January, 1866, and also reproduced in John Ewers' *Artists of the Old West*, is an acknowledged copy of the second Bierstadt.

Four of the sketches, as indicated, are to be found only in manuscript originals. The others mainly appear in contemporary guidebooks or autobiographies that are now exceedingly rare. Guidebook versions include Street, Wadsworth, and Marcy; of course Preuss (with Fremont) and Thornton were travel classics that saw service as guidebooks. Sketches associated with military personnel, in addition to Fremont and Marcy, are those of Conway, Holliday, Eugene Ware, and Margaret Carrington. Father Point is the only missionary among the Chimney Rock artists, while Burton was a gentleman adventurer and T. S. Kenderdine and W. H. Jackson were bullwhackers. James Wilkins was a professional artist making pictorial notes for a planned panoramic public exhibition. All the others are covered wagon emigrants, including Mormons Piercy, Egan, Lambourne, and Ottinger.

From the standpoint of artistic merit, four works are outstanding: the versions of A. J. Miller and W. H. Jackson, at either end of the time span; the Ottinger oil version in the Stenzel Collection; and the Alfred Lambourne sketch which hangs in the Union Pacific Museum in Omaha, all four of which are in color. Miller's 1837 rendering, now in the Walters Art Gallery in Baltimore, is of out-standing historical value, for it shows the Rock in its primitive form, so to speak, at maximum height and with a great cleft at its peak, before the disintegration so often referred to. Jackson's two panoramic water color sketches showing the relationship of the Chimney to other landmarks are classics, although the Indian attack on covered wagon emigrants depicted in one of these is purely imaginary. The original field sketch, in pencil at close range, may be considered as documentary. While the date of Lambourne's crossing is not known, it appears that he followed the south bank sometime in the 1850s. His hitherto unpublished original sketch, while idealized, conveys the great psychological impact of Chimney Rock on the emigrants. His own published sketch of this subject, and a poor copy of this same sketch in Maxwell, are uninspired but obvious imitations of the original. George Ottinger's field sketch of 1861 was later transformed by him into an oil painting of power-ful impact, with a Pony Express rider in the foreground.

The Point, Preuss, Thornton, Burton, and Carrington sketches are reasonably accurate but uninspired. Thornton's seems to be a rough copy of Preuss, and Egan seems to copy Piercy. The Marcy sketch is among the more interesting, showing a dome-shaped rather than a cone-shaped effect for the base, and a quite exaggerated chimney; one wonders if Marcy actually saw the landmark. Kender-dine seems to be a pirated copy of Marcy.

The Preuss sketch, which appeared in Fremont's journal, was criticized by many emigrants, as well as by Burton, who wrote: "The old sketches of this curious needle now necessarily appear exag-gerated; moreover, those best known represent it as a column rising from a confused heap of boulders, thus conveying a completely false idea." To Burton, "Nothing could be more picturesque than this lone pillar of pale rock lying against a huge black cloud, with forked lightning playing over its devoted head." But Burton somehow fails to convey any of this grandeur in his own sketch.

Other guidebook versions by Street and Conway are stylized and inaccurate. Wadsworth is better, however. He shows a spiral around the cone which might be the "winding pathway" mentioned by Peter Decker in 1849, although no other reference to such a thing is known. Sketches by Parke, Lorton, and Lewelling are crudely diagrammatic, all showing the chimney shaft at a climber's vantage point. The two Bruff sketches, both chimney close-ups also, are far superior, showing skill in draftsmanship and scaled with ant-like human figures.

Jagger's sketch, while amateurish, is commendable for its accurate proportions and faithful delineation of the bluffs in the background. Ware's sketch is a simple silhouette but an accurate one, showing the relationship in cross section. James Wilkins' sketch, though less imaginative, is comparable to the Jackson sketch in showing the Chimney in relationship to other landmarks. The stylized, exaggerated, and totally unreal spire in Street is echoed by the artist who illustrated for Holliday and showed an Indian brave toppling off the summit.

In various sketches giving general views, the Chimney is projected from almost all angles. Some of the most admirable are those of Miller, Ware, Jackson, and Burton, looking to the west. Lambourne and Tavernier portray the Rock eastward, with wagon trains approaching. Father Point is unique in sketching from the bluffs, looking north toward the Platte. Most are views to the south from various vantage points along the trail, showing the high bluff background.

One picture poses a real puzzle and that is the Tavernier sketch of 1874, the original of which hangs in the Bohemian Club, San Francisco. It is a spectacular picture, showing Indians lurking in ambush next to a crude bridge in the foreground and the trail extending into the distance at the foot of enormous bluffs. This bears the title, "Attack by Indians near Chimney Rock, Nebraska." The problem here is that there is almost nothing in the picture that is recognizable as Chimney Rock, and the trail runs along the immediate base of the bluffs, unlike the actual situation at the Chimney, where the trail was three miles distant. It is entirely possible that the editor of *Artists and Illustrators*, Robert Taft, is in error about the location; or it may be a sketch so idealized for journalistic effect that the Chimney spire has become an unrecognizable mass. In any event, the picture cannot be ignored. One feels that this romanticized version of the giant landmark accurately portrays the typical emigrant impression, if not the photographic reality.

XIII

Mr. Scott's Bluffs and
Mr. Robidoux's Pass

BETWEEN CHIMNEY ROCK and Scott's Bluffs is a succession of curious mounds and buttes. Several emigrants, including Bachelder, Hale, and Littleton, described five or six of these intermediate mounds, which correspond to Castle, Table, Steamboat, Coyote, and Smokestack rocks, and possibly the Round Top and Twin Sisters, which are named on the U.S.G.S. Quadrangle. The largest and best known of these is Castle Rock near Melbeta (not to be confused with the Castle Rock west of Ash Hollow), which was also called Capitol Rock, Roman Castle (John Clark), and Alcohol Butte (Eugene Ware). But these curiosities were only the prelude to scenic marvels that were beginning to loom ahead, the assemblage of rock formations that came under the general designation of Scott's Bluffs. While the towering Chimney Rock was perhaps more wondrous because of its incredible isolated spire, the Scott's Bluffs scenery generally was considered the most magnificent the emigrants had seen.

It is a little difficult for the jaded traveler of today, to whom the scenic wonders of the western United States have become commonplace, to put himself in the position of the typical emigrant, who had been over a month on the trail plodding over the monotonous prairie toward its endless horizons, coming upon this succession of seemingly spectacular heights. Admittedly, there were some contemporaries who were not impressed. Overton Johnson in 1843 spoke only of "a range of high Sand Hills," while Calvin West in

421

1853 exclaimed, "What mammoth heaps of sand!" An anonymous contributor to the *Missouri Republican* dismissed the whole idea in a sentence: "Conceive a line of sand hills about as high as a three or four story house, composed of sand and gravel, to be washed by the rain in a few shapes tending to the perpendicular, and you have a first rate idea of Platte scenery." But these unimaginative cynics were a minority. Most covered wagon emigrants fell in love with Scott's Bluffs. If they had been delighted with Ash Hollow and dazzled with Chimney Rock, they were held in thrall for at least two days' travel by the magic quality and infinite variety of these "hanging gardens."

Beset by the exhaustion of their labors, most had time for only a line or two of appreciation. Myra Eells, wife of an 1838 missionary, commented on the "grand scenery." Oregon emigrant Medorem Crawford in 1842 thought the bluffs "presented the most romantic scenery I ever saw." Dr. T. considered this "the most grand, sublime and magnificent scenery that can possibly be imagined." Franklin Street called it "one of the most delightful places that nature ever formed," while Celinda Hines thought "the scenery was most enchanting, entirely surpassing in loveliness and originality anything I had ever beheld." To Thomas Woodward, "Every place seems like a fairy vision. It is no use trying to describe [it] for language cannot do it."

But several emigrants tried anyhow. To P. Castleman these bluffs were "fascinating . . . lofty peaks reminiscent of some large city, or an old fort, or ruins of an ancient city as pictured by Byron or Shakespeare." Rev. Hinds was "perfectly enchanted by the prospect" of high bluffs resembling "the walled towers of Europe." To James Evans the bluffs took on "the appearance of a vast city, composed of high castles and wide streets," which were "inhabited by a race of giants." In 1852 Caroline Richardson felt that Scott's Bluffs had been undersold by the guidebooks: "This picturesque place deserves more attention than the renowned Courthouse or Chimney Rock."

Some writers had time to become more poetic on the subject. These romantic descriptions of Scott's Bluffs are typical:

> They encamped amidst high and beetling cliffs of indurated clay and sandstone, bearing the semblance of towers, castles, churches and fortified cities. At a distance it was scarcely possible to persuade one's

self that the works of art were not mingled with those fantastic freaks of nature.—CAPT. BONNEVILLE, 1832

All about were rocks piled up by Nature in merry mood, giving full scope to fancy in the variety of their shapes. Some were perfect cones; others flat tops; others, owing to their crenelated projections, resembled fortresses; others old castles, porticos, etc. The scenery has obvious resemblance to several places in Switzerland.—DR. WISLIZENUS, 1839

The spectacle was grand and imposing beyond description. It seemed as if Nature, in mere sportiveness, had thought to excel the noblest works of art, and rear up a mimic city as the grand metropolis of her empire.

No higher encomium could be passed upon it than by employing the homely phrase of one of our voyageurs. In speaking of the varied enchantments of its scenery at that season, he said: "I could die here . . . certain of being not far from heaven."—RUFUS SAGE, 1841

That immense and celebrated pile . . . advances across the plain nearly to the water's edge. If one could increase the size of the Alhambra of Grenada, or the Castle of Heidelberg, which Professor Longfellow has so poetically and graphically described . . . he could form some idea of the magnitude and splendor of this *chef d'oeuvre* of Nature at Palace-Building. . . . it constitutes a Mausoleum which the mightiest of earth might covet.—J. HENRY CARLETON, 1845

Looming afar over river and plain was "Scott's Bluff," a Nebraska Gibraltar; surmounted by a colossal fortress and a royal castle, it jutted on the water. . . .
This morning marched three miles still nearer to that mysterious mountain—and, without being disenchanted of its colossal ruins and phantom occupants, turned toward the left, and ascended the wild sandy hills.—PHILIP ST. GEORGE COOKE, 1845

The Tower of Babel, if its builders had been permitted to proceed in their ambitious undertaking would have been but a feeble imitation of these stupendous structures of nature. While surveying this scenery . . . the traveller . . . imagines himself in the midst of the desolate and deserted ruins of vast cities, to which Nineveh, Thebes and Babylon were pigmies in grandeur and magnificence.—EDWIN BRYANT, 1846

The silence of death reigned over a once populous city. . . . It was a Tadmor of the Desert, in ruins. No signs of life were visible; a whole people were extinct. . . . The city had fallen into the hands of a beleaguering and sanguinary foe . . . the day of . . . slaughter and outpouring of blood, was one which the ascending fire made terribly sublime. . . .

It being reported by . . . my ox driver, that one of the wheels of my wagon was making a most terrible groaning for grease, I was brought down from my celestial aerie with such force, upon vulgar realities as . . . broke both wings of my imagination, and, indeed, every bone in them.—J. QUINN THORNTON, 1846

How can I describe the scene that now bursts upon us? Scotts bluffs lay to the North. Another range of high hills extends along the south side of this valley. Tower, bastion, dome and battlement vie in all their majesty before us. . . . A dark cloud is rising in the Northwest. The sun is just sinking behind the western range of the hills, fringing the cloud hills, tower and dome with golden hue. A more beautiful or majestic scene cannot be conceived. How wonderful, how great, how sublime are Thy works, O God!—THOMAS EASTIN, 1849

The bluffs, as we first sighted them, treated us to a magnificent optical illusion—a striking instance of the mirage. The Platte seemed to be lifted high from its bed and swollen to a mighty flood sweeping the entire valley. Out of this apparent expanse of rushing waters the rugged form of the bluffs loomed up in blunted and exaggerated outline, a hazy, dreamy, tremulous atmosphere the while lending its weird-like effect to the scene.—D. R. LEEPER, 1849

It seemed as if the wand of a magician had passed over a city, and like that in the Arabian Nights, had converted all living things to stone. Here you saw the minarets of a castle; there, the loop-holes of a fort; again, the frescoes of a huge temple . . . while at other points Chinese temples, dilapidated by time, broken chimney rocks in miniature, made it appear as if by some supernatural cause we had been dropped in the suburbs of a mighty city.—ALONZO DELANO, 1849

The whole country seems overspread by the ruins of some of the loftiest and most magnificent palaces the imagination of man can reach in its most extravagant conceptions. Here lays the ruins of a lofty Pyramid, there a splendid castle. On the one hand is the citadel, on the other the grand hall of legislation. Yonder is the facsimile of our nation's capitol at Washington and there again is the City Hall at N. Y., only enlarged perhaps a dozen times or more. . . .

On all sides lay the ruins of more grandeur than man has ever had a conception of. Even the ruins of Rome, Athens, Bagdad and Petra fall into perfect insignificance.—DR. TOMPKINS, 1850

Scott's Bluffs, situated 285 miles from Fort Kearny and 51 from Laramie, was the last of the great marl formations which we saw on this

line, and was of all by far the most curious. In the dull uniformity
of the prairies, it is a striking and attractive object, far excelling the
castled crag of Drachenfels or any of the beauties of the romantic
Rhine. From a distance of a day's march it appears in the shape of a
large blue mound, distinguished only by its dimensions from the
detached fragments of hill around. As you approach within four or
five miles, a massive medieval city gradually defines itself, clustering,
with a wonderful fullness of detail, round a colossal fortress, and
crowned with a royal castle. Buttress and barbican, bastion, demilune
and guardhouse, tower, turrent and donjon-keep, all are there; on
one place parapets and battlements still stand upon the crumbling wall
of a fortalise like the giant ruins of Chateau Gaillard. . . . Quaint
figures develop themselves; guards and sentinels in dark armor keep
watch and ward upon the slopes, the lion of Bastia crouches unmistakably overlooking the road. . . . Travellers have compared the
glory of the mauvaises terres to Gibraltar, to the Capitol at Washington, to Stirling Castle. I could not think of anything in its presence
but the Arab's "City of Brass," that mysterious abode of bewitching
infidels, which often appears at a distance to the wayfarer toiling under
the buning sun, but ever eludes his nearer approach.—RICHARD BURTON,
1860

This Scotts Bluff is grand beyond description. . . . It looks exactly
like a splendid old Fort all in thorough order, equipped and manned
& ready for service, at a moment's notice. It is covered all over . . .
with little pines, & these, when a few miles off reminds one of soldiers
scattered around.—MRS. VOGDES, 1868

These fanciful and impassioned descriptions of Scott's Bluffs
were written by those who followed the south bank, or Oregon-
California Trail, and actually penetrated the bluffs. But those
who came on the Mormon Trail, or Council Bluffs Road, were
equally impressed. It is from the north side, that is, from the city of
Scottsbluff today, that the main bluff probably presents its most
magnificent front, towering massively above the river badlands.
William Clayton was the official scribe for the Mormon Pioneers of
1847. "I consider our view this morning more sublime than any
other," he wrote. "Scott's Bluffs looks majestic and sublime."
Shortly after passing "the meridian of the northernmost peak," the
Mormons paused for some inspiration by one of Brigham Young's
fiery sermons. In 1848 another Mormon, O. B. Huntington, noted
the bluffs had the "actual appearance of mammoth cities," containing "every order of architecture." In 1850 Leander V. Loomis

encamped "nearly opposite what is called Scotts Bluffs, a high range of mountains," and was impressed by a "clowd" that floated around its summit, creating the illusion of a gigantic theater. That same year Henry Coke thought the huge bluffs across the river were "fortified citadels with perfect deceptions of turrets and buttresses," and the cedars were "warriors moving athwart the sky." In 1851 John Zieber thought that this landmark was "a far more magnificent work of Nature" than Ancient Bluff Ruins or Chimney Rock. In 1853 the artist James Linforth noted: "Scott's Bluffs were in view all day. They were certainly the most remarkable sight I had seen since I left England. Viewed from the distance at which I sketched them the shadows were of an intense blue, while the rock illuminated by the setting sun partook of its gold, making a beautiful harmony of color." In 1864 Mary Warner also "sketched the bluffs," thinking she had "seen nothing so beautifull on my journey."

THE TRAGEDY OF SCOTT'S BLUFFS

The North Platte valley was first traversed in 1812 by Robert Stuart and others bound from Fort Astoria, at the mouth of Columbia River, to St. Louis. "The hills on the south," wrote Stuart, "have lately approached the river, are remarkably rugged and Bluffy, and possess a few Cedars." The future Oregon Trail was rediscovered in 1824 by Thomas Fitzpatrick and James Clyman, taking beaver pelts from the Sweetwater near South Pass to Fort Atkinson near Omaha; after that time, fur trade caravans moved past here annually, taking supplies to the mountain rendezvous points and returning to St. Louis wth beaver pelts. A tragedy here befell one of the mountain traders, and that is how Scott's Bluffs got their name.

At least sixty travelers on the Platte River Road, a respectable percentage of the 200 who described or mentioned Scott's Bluffs, have volunteered their own hearsay version of how it happened. Most agree that there was a fur trader named Scott who died tragically at an early date in this neighborhood after being abandoned by companions and that his remains were later found here. But beyond these few points of agreement there is every variation imaginable, with no two versions the same. From this body of folklore we can take our choice. Scott was "a young man;" he was "an old mountaineer." He worked for the American Fur Company;

he worked for the Rocky Mountain Fur Company; he was an unemployed hermit. He died from wounds inflicted by Indians; he died from a mysterious malady; or he died of starvation or from various other causes. Whatever his problem, he was afflicted with it at the Black Hills, at Laramie's Fork, or at Scott's Bluffs, or somewhere in between; and, of course, he either walked or crawled 10, 60, or 100 miles; or he was transported in a canoe; or he moved just a short distance, or he never moved an inch in the first place. His skeleton was found in the badlands, either at the foot or on the summit of Scott's Bluffs, at Robidoux Pass, or indeed almost anywhere else. He was abandoned by the main party of fur traders; he was abandoned by two companions; he was left briefly, but when his rescuers returned he had died; he was not really abandoned at all, since he wanted to be left to die in peace; he urged his rescuers to save themselves. He didn't die at all, but just elected to live in this scenic spot. At least no one claims to have seen Scott's ghost, which is about the only story no one thought of.

There is no doubt that Scott's memory has been very well preserved through his identification with the great bluff. And the Scott legend, with all its kaleidoscopic variety, has been well perpetuated. A catalog of all known versions would fill a book; it will be sufficient to examine here briefly a cross section of this literature. The three earliest versions ever penned, being closest to the event, might be considered to have some elements of truth. These are the writings of Warren A. Ferris, who traveled up the north side of the Platte in 1830; Washington Irving's redaction of Capt. Bonneville's journal of 1832; and the story given by Jason Lee, a missionary to Oregon in company with Nathaniel Wyeth in 1834:

> We encamped opposite to "Scott's Bluffs," so called in respect to the memory of a young man who was left here alone to die a few years previous. He was a clerk in a company returning from the mountains, the leader of which found it necessary to leave him behind at a place some distance above this point, in consequence of a severe illness which rendered him unable to ride. He was consequently placed in a bullhide boat, in charge of two men, who had orders to convey him by water down to these bluffs, where the leader of the party promised to await their coming. After a weary and hazardous voyage, they reached the appointed rendezvous, and found to their surprise and bitter disappointment, that the company had continued on down the river without stopping for them to overtake and join it.

Left thus in the heart of a wide wilderness, hundreds of miles from any point where assistance or succour could be obtained, and surrounded by predatory bands of savages thirsting for blood and plunder, could any condition be deemed more hopeless or deplorable? They had, moreover, in descending the river, met with some accident, either the loss of the means of procuring subsistence or defending their lives in case of discovery and attack. This unhappy circumstance, added to the fact that the river was filled with innumerable shoals and sand-bars, by which its navigation was rendered almost impracticable, determined them to forsake their charge and boat together, and push on night and day until they should overtake the company, which they did on the second or third day afterward.

The reason given by the leader of the company for not fulfilling his promise, was that his men were starving, no game could be found, and he was compelled to proceed in quest of buffalo.

Poor Scott! We will not attempt to picture what his thoughts must have been after his cruel abandonment, nor harrow up the feelings of the reader, by a recital of what agonies he must have suffered before death put an end to his misery.

The bones of a human being were found the spring following, on the opposite side of the river, which were supposed to be the remains of Scott. It was conjectured that in the energy of despair, he had found strength to carry him across the stream, and then staggered about the prairie, till God in pity took him to himself.

Such are the sad chances to which the life of the Rocky Mountain adventurer is exposed.—WARREN FERRIS, 1830

On the 21st (June) they encamped amid high and beetling cliffs of indurated clay and sandstone, bearing the semblance of towers, castles, churches and fortified cities. At a distance it was scarcely possible to persuade one's self that the works of art were not mingled with those fantastic freaks of nature. They have received the name of Scott's Bluffs from a melancholy circumstance. A number of years since, a party were descending the upper part of the river in canoes, when their frail barks were overturned and all their powder spoiled. Their rifles being thus rendered useless, they were unable to procure food by hunting and had to depend upon roots and wild fruits for subsistence. After suffering extremely from hunger, they arrived at Laramie's Fork, a small tributary of the north branch of the Nebraska, about sixty miles above the cliffs just mentioned. Here one of the party, by the name of Scott, was taken ill; and his companions came to a halt, until he should recover health and strength sufficient to proceed. While they were searching round in quest of edible roots

Court House Rock today, showing approach road provided by citizens of Bridgeport, Nebraska.

—Photo by Merrill J. Mattes

Court House Rock or Solitary Tower, as crudely depicted in Wadsworth's National Wagon Road Guide.

—Newberry Library

—Charles Preuss, 1842
　　Nebraska State Historical Society

—W. Wadsworth, 1852
　　Nebraska State Historical Society

As demonstrated by the heavy preponderance of references in emigrant journals, and the remarkable number of contemporary sketches, Chimney Rock (opposite present Bayard, Nebraska) was the most celebrated trailside phenomenon between the Missouri River and South Pass.

—Frederick Piercy, 1853
　　Nebraska State Historical Society

—Randolph B. Marcy, 1859
　　Nebraska State Historical Society

No other emigrant artist equalled the accuracy and draftmanship of J. Goldsborough Bruff, from Washington, D.C., 1849. This sketch, a more finished product than the field sketches reproduced on pp. 29 and 374 of Bruff's published Gold Rush journals, shows the scale and configuration of the Chimney in 1849, as well as the vista of other landmarks to westward. Collection HM 8044 (23).

—The Huntington Library, San Marino, California

Photo of Chimney Rock today, from approximately the same distance away (300 yards) as the Bruff sketch, above, reveals the extent of spire collapse and general erosion over the past century.

—Photo by Merrill J. Mattes

In 1837 Alfred J. Miller made the earliest known sketch of Scott's Bluffs while en route from St. Louis to the annual fur trade rendezvous at Green River, with his employer Sir William Drummond Stewart. Eighteen years earlier the 1837 caravan leader, William Sublette, had discovered the remains of Hiram Scott in this vicinity.

Scott's Bluffs, sketch by George Simons, probably late 1850's. Although the drawing is crude compared to Miller's, it is a fairly accurate portrayal of the main features— Dome Rock, South Bluff, Mitchell Pass, and the main bluff—now comprising Scotts Bluff National Monument.

Topographically, the historic Scott's Bluffs curved around like a shepherd's crook, with bluffs and badlands reaching the North Platte, and forming a barricade with only two passes. The longer Robidoux Pass route was used mainly through 1850; Mitchell Pass, used mainly thereafter, was shorter but notorious for its dangers. William H. Jackson, a young bull-whacker who lived long enough to dedicate the Oregon Trail Museum in 1936, made this notebook sketch in 1866.

—Oregon Trail Museum,
Scotts Bluff National Monument

West of Mitchell Pass the deep trough of the Great Platte River Road, gouged out of the rugged terrain by countless thousands of hooves and wagon wheels, is well preserved by the National Park Service.

—Photo by Charles Humberger

Joseph Robidoux, patriarch of St. Joseph, Missouri, was the licensee and proprietor of Robidoux's trading post, at the earlier pass through Scott's Bluffs. Various brothers, sons and nephews were also involved. No contemporary sketch of the 1849–1850 post exists, apparently. But in 1851 the German traveller Mollhausen made this sketch of the second Robidoux post, in a nearby secluded spot today called Carter Canyon.

—from copy at Kansas Historical Society of original at Staatliches Museum, Für Volkerkunde, Berlin

In 1864 Captain Eugene Ware found the 11th Ohio Cavalry putting up an adobe-stockade called Fort Mitchell, a satellite of Fort Laramie. Here, at a sharp bend of the North Platte, was an earlier trading post of the American Fur Company. The short-lived military post, 2½ miles northwest of Mitchell Pass, is here depicted by an artist who presumably accompanied Professor F. V. Hayden on a geological survey of Nebraska and Wyoming in 1867.

—Nebraska State Historical Society

Fort Laramie

"*Fort Laramie, purchased by our Government, from the American Fur Company, is an extensive rectangular structure of adobie . . . Heavy portals and watch tower, and square bastions at 2 angles, enfilading the faces of the main walls. It has suffered much from time and neglect.*" So wrote J. Goldsborough Bruff on July 11, 1849. The lack of activity in Bruff's finished sketch is due to the lateness of the season. HM 8044 (38)

—The Huntington Library, San Marino, California

The earliest known photograph of Fort Laramie, made by C. C. Mills, a member of an Army engineer party in 1858 (See William Lee and William Seville journals), is likewise evidence of much historic value. At left are the crumbling ruins of the 1849 trading post purchased by Lieutenant Woodbury and sketched by Bruff. Of the several new structures, two remain today in restored condition—two-story Old Bedlam (center) and the adobe sutler's store (2nd to right of flagpole). ,

—Collections of the Library of Congress

A recent view of partially restored Fort Laramie, now a National Historic Site, shows the Laramie River and, left to right, the following main structures: officers quarters, 1870; Old Bedlam, 1849–1850; officers quarters, 1874 and 1886; ruins of the administration building, 1886; the old guardhouse, 1866; new guardhouse, 1884; commissary warehouse, 1883 and old bakery, 1876.

—Photo by Merrill J. Mattes

Aerial perspective of Fort Kearny State Park today (wooded square in foreground) and the main Platte River. All traces of the Oregon-California Trail (between the fort and the river) and the old Council Bluffs Road (across the river) have apparently vanished beneath modern roads and farms.

—Nebraska Game and Parks Commission

they discovered a fresh trail of white men, who had evidently but recently preceded them. What was to be done? By a forced march they might overtake this party, and thus be able to reach the settlements in safety. Should they linger they might all perish of famine and exhaustion. Scott, however, was incapable of moving; they were too feeble to aid him forward, and dreaded that such a clog would prevent their coming up with the advance party. They determined, therefore, to abandon him to his fate. Accordingly, under pretense of seeking food, and such simples as might be efficacious in his malady, they deserted him and hastened forward upon the trail. They succeeded in overtaking the party of which they were in quest, but concealed their faithless desertion of Scott; alleging that he had died of disease.

On the ensuing summer, these very individuals visiting these parts in company with others, came suddenly upon the bleached bones and grinning skull of a human skeleton, which by certain signs they recognized for the remains of Scott. This was sixty long miles from the place where they had abandoned him; and it appeared that the wretched man had crawled that immense distance before death put an end to his miseries. The wild and picturesque bluffs in the neighborhood of his lonely grave have ever since borne his name.—CAPT. BONNEVILLE, 1832

A Mr. Scott superintendent of General Ashley's Fur Company, was taken delirious in the Black Hills but at lucid intervals expressed a great desire to go home to die and the[y] thought it best to make a boat of skins and send him down the Platte some distance by water where the Com. if they arrived first were to await their arrival. Two men were sent with him but they were upset in rapids and narrowly escaped being drowned and lost their guns and everything but one knife and a horn of powder. The leader of the Com. did not stop for them and it was with the greatest difficulty that the men could find enough to subsist on until they overtook the Com. Their report was that he died and they buried him but his bones and blanket were found . . . 100 mi. from the place they said he had died and near the Bluff.—JASON LEE, 1834

John Townsend, another early visitor, offers a simpler version: "The unfortunate trader . . . perished here from disease and hunger." In 1841 Rufus B. Sage, in company with fur traders to Fort Platte, became quite poetic in his portrayal of Scott as simply a lonely wanderer:

[He was] attracted by the enchanting beauty of the place, and the

great abundance of game the vicinity afforded. . . . he wandered
hither alone and made it his temporary residence. While thus enjoying
the varied sweets of solitude, he became the prey to sickness and
gasped his life away;—none were there to watch over him, but the
sun by day and the stars by night; or fan his fevered brow, save the
kindly breezes; or bemoan his hapless fate, other than the gurgling
stream that sighed its passing sympathy beside the couch of death!

The Scott legend made good campfire material during the
Oregon migration. Overton Johnson of 1843 relates "the melancholy circumstances." In his version Indians threatened the party
and Scott was taken sick. His companions carried him to these
bluffs, "and supposing that he could not recover, they left him." In
1845 Joel Palmer had the Scott party "robbed of their peltries and
food" by hostile savages. Scott "fell sick and could not travel. The
others remained with him until the sufferer, despairing of ever
beholding his home, prevailed on his companions to abandon him,"
but after this heroic act of resignation Scott managed to crawl
"several miles." In 1847 Isaac Pettijohn understood that "a trapper
by the name of Scott was murdered here some twenty years ago."
Edwin Bryant identifies the American Fur Company as the outfit
in question:

> [It was] under the command of a man—a noted mountaineer—named
> Scott. They attempted to perform the journey in boats, down the
> Platte. The current of the river became so shallow that they could
> not navigate it. Scott was seized with a disease, which rendered him
> helpless. The men with him left him in the boat, and when they
> returned to their employers, reported that Scott had died on the
> journey, and that they had buried him on the banks of the Platte.
> The next year a party of hunters, in traversing this region, discovered
> a human skeleton wrapped in blankets which from the clothing and
> papers found upon it, was immediately recognized as being the remains
> of Scott. He had been deserted by his men, but afterwards recovering
> his strength sufficiently to leave the boat, he had wandered into the
> bluffs where he died, where his bones were found, and which now
> bear his name.

The Scott story was in full bloom when the Forty-Niners arrived.
Isaac Wistar dwells on "the tragic death from starvation of a man
who was deserted by his companions on Laramie Fork." Elijah
Farnham also leaves out the Indians and gives no motives for the
crime: "These bluffs are so called from the fact of a party of fur

traders headed by a man of the name of Scott. . . . [They] set him out on the bank of the river and left him to his fate. . . . The next spring his body was found high on the bluffs by another party of traders and by his clothing was identified." John McCoy reported that "Scott's skeleton was found later nearly forty miles from where he was deserted, he by some shift having made his way hither until death relieved him of his sufferings." One of the most imaginative of the 1849 versions is that of Joseph Stuart, who has the party starting out in a canoe which had a tendency to capsize: "One of their number was taken sick, and thinking he could not recover, and that by lightening the canoe of their weight it might go safely over the shoals and he might thus get through if at all, they left him in the canoe to float down with the current. They reached their destination on foot, but saw no more of Scott. A party of trappers found his skeleton at the foot of this bluff and recognized his rifle that still lay at his side." Concludes J. Hamelin: "Speaking of fame, what an immortality has Scott made of himself by having a pile of rock to bear his name, on account of there breathing out his last. Great consolation to his widow and children, if he left any!"

In 1850, James Abbey says "'the noted mountaineer" was seized with disease here and "buried on the bluff." Dr. J. S. Shepherd heard, on the contrary, that these bluffs were named for a trapper "left at their base . . . not by the savage Indians, but by his remorseless companions, calling themselves civilized men." Franklin Langworthy also refers to "the immense castle, lacking only artillery to render it a grand fortification," being named for one "whose mortal remains lie entombed at its base," but he does not share Dr. Shepherd's moral indignation, for the way he heard it, Scott's party left him "at his own request."

Through the fifties there were endless variations on the same theme. In the shadow of the "beautiful bluffs," Francis Sawyer grieved for him "who perished under them for want of food. The story of his death is a pitiful one." John Kerns likewise has Scott "buried at the foot or base of the river bluff." Eliza McAulay gets him out of the fur trade altogether: "A company returning from Oregon in '46 had got this far when one of their number a Mr. Scott was unable to travel further and they being short of provisions he begged them to go on and leave him which they were reluctantly compelled to do." W. Wadsworth is unique among early travelers in offering two brand-new versions of the tragedy:

A party of trappers had been detained in the Indian country too late in the season to insure their safe return, if attended by the least impediment. . . . One of their number . . . having wounded himself by an accidental discharge of his gun . . . insisted, and prevailed upon his companions to leave him . . . to his fate, and save, if possible, their own lives. His skeleton was found the next year, under a shelving portion of the bluff near the river, where they had left him.

Another version is, that of a party of hunters returning from the mountains, Scott became diseased from his own imprudence, and unable to proceed; was abandoned by his party, and probably soon died; that his bones were found scattered about, doubtless by wolves; but recognized by his blankets, hunting knife, and tobacco box.

Celinda Hines, Rebecca Ketcham, and Abigail Duniway, all of the 1853 migration, heartily agree with the part that the dying Scott prevailed on his companions to abandon him and save themselves. This version was more palatable to the emigrant ladies, apparently. In 1854 Edwin Bird tells of the Rocky Mountain trapper who "died here with starvation," referring to the version in *The Prairie Flower*, a popular paperback novel of the period by Emerson Bennett. An interesting variation of 1856 is that of J. R. Brown, who claims that Scott was "a mountaineer who was shot by the Indians and crawled here to save his scalp and died on these bluffs." Another twist is given in 1859 by J. A. Wilkinson: "[Scott] was pursued by Indians and hid in a cave and starved to death rather than be taken." In 1860, however, Wm. Earnshaw says the Indians did find him and killed him according to plan.

The story of the unhappy fur trader continues to crop up in the journals of the sixties. Julius Birge gives a fairly conventional resume of the basic Bonneville version, but the others show a trend toward more and more erratic imaginings. Richard Burton has Scott "put on shore in the olden time by his boat's crew, who had a grudge against him; the wretch in mortal sickness crawled upon the mount to die." W. S. Brackett provides a new angle by having the Scott expedition going up river toward South Pass instead of the usual descent toward St. Louis. Lewis B. Dougherty has Scott "frozen to death." Robert Campbell, a fur trade contemporary, is more plausible in stating that Scott was "devoured by wolves." A tradition of Scott family descendants, according to Hiram Daniel Scott, is that he was mangled by a grizzly bear. An echo of the Indian pursuit theory is given by Ben Arnold of the U.S. Volunteers, who in 1863 said that he was told by scout Jim Bridger that "a man named Scott had saved his life from pursuing Indians by taking refuge in the eroding cliffs of the bluff." Since Bridger knew Scott personally and must have known the facts about his death, this lends weight to the idea that Indians were somehow involved. Furthermore, Bridger's failure to mention Scott's subsequent death suggests an element of guilt on his part. Although proof, of course, is beyond reach, Jim Bridger could well have been one of Scott's actual traveling companions.

These are the emigrants' concepts of the tragedy. What are the documentable facts? Results of research by the writer may be summarized briefly. This man was Hiram Scott, one of Gen. William Ashley's one hundred "enterprising young men" recruited in St. Louis in 1822 for his Rocky Mountain Fur Company. Meager records in the Missouri Historical Society and vague family tradition establish Scott's identity. He was born about 1805 in St. Charles County, Missouri, and is reported to have grown into a tall and handsome young man. In 1823 he was one of Ashley's most able and trusted lieutenants. In a joint campaign of fur traders and the U.S. Army under Col. Leavenworth against Arikara Indians on the Upper Missouri, Hiram Scott is identified as one of the two captains designated to lead Ashley's volunteers, called "The Missouri Legion." His role with the company in its exploration of the Rocky Mountains is unknown, but he presumably trapped and traded on the Upper Green River and was involved in Ashley's first rendezvous at Great Salt Lake in 1826.

Scott next emerges clearly with James B. Bruffee as a co-leader of Ashley's supply caravan to the Bear Lake rendezvous, which included a four-pounder cannon drawn by two mules, the first wheeled vehicle on the Oregon Trail. Scott appears as a clerk or field commander in this enterprise. The two associates delivered over $20,000 worth of beaver pelts to Ashley in October; that same month Ashley sent them back to the mountains, where they gathered more beaver and fought blizzards and Indians. There was a battle with the Blackfeet Indians during the 1828 rendezvous at Bear Lake; all of these experiences with the elements, plus the fighting, might provide a clue to Scott's difficulties (pneumonia, arrow wounds?). It must have been on the return of the company from the 1828 rendezvous that Scott came to grief, because he was alive and on the company payroll in 1827, and he is heard of no more after 1828.

The Ferris and Lee versions are more accurate than Bonneville's, to judge from the New Orleans *Picayune* account of Matthew Field, who in 1843 went on a trip to the mountains with William Sublette. Sublette and others had taken over Ashley's company at the 1826 rendezvous, but Ashley continued to act as supplier. Thus, Sublette would be expected to have personal knowledge of Scott; this is probably as close as we will ever get to knowing the truth:

"Scott's Bluffs" were named from the following melancholy circumstance. . . . In 1828, Scott and Bruffee went out to the mountains with an equipment for a trading firm then in existence, known as Smith, Jackson & Sublette. . . . Scott became oppressed with some bodily infirmity on his way out, and was a helpless invalid by the time he reached the Green River rendezvous. In this condition he was compelled to start for home, his partner, Bruffee, having already commenced his return travel in advance, agreeing to pause some time at the bluffs and await the arrival of Scott. At a point known as "Lebonte's Cabin," on the Sweetwater, poor Scott grew so much worse that he could no longer sustain himself in the saddle, and a "bull-boat" was made, in which he was transported safely enough until it was upset and broken among the rapids in the Black Hills. Here guns, ammunition, everything was lost, and the two men attending upon Scott barely made out to get their sick charge in safety to shore. From this place they were nine days in reaching these bluffs on the Platte, the two men getting their burden along as well as they could, and the whole three lingering upon the very brink of starvation all the way. Their guns were gone, and they could get no game, being left to pick up a little miserable sustenance by visiting old camping grounds of their own and other parties, and getting the marrow from bones yet unbroken by the wolves.

Exhausted and feeble, they at length reached the Bluffs. No sign of Bruffee could be found. It was clear Scott could linger but a few hours longer, and it seemed nearly as evident that the other two would become helpless in the same space of time. They could carry the unfortunate trader no farther. To stay with him would be to starve with him, and to save him was beyond the reach of human hope. In this frightful predicament, there was but one cruel alternative, and the two men took it. Leaving their gasping charge in the grass, with a gourd of water beside him, they hurried away, without daring to say farewell, to make what use they yet could of their remaining strength in getting on their way homeward. There Scott was left, and there *he died alone!* under the bluffs that have since borne his name. The scattered remnants of his bones were sought after, found, gathered and buried the next summer by Wm. L. Sublette, and there lies poor Scott, with a mournful fate and magnificent monument.

In his 1834 diary William Anderson condemns the heartless inhumanity of the caravan leader who failed to keep his promise and wait at the bluffs. "I know the name of the soulless villain, and so does God and the devil!" exclaims Anderson. Although he doesn't reveal the name, it would seem to be the "Bruffee" above, who appears as James B. Bruffee in Ashley records. This still leaves the identity of the two desperate "companions" a complete puzzle.

THE TWO PASSES AT SCOTT'S BLUFFS

The distinction between "Scotts Bluff" and "Scott's Bluffs" is both geographic and historical. Today "Scotts Bluff" is understood to mean the large bluff which is the dominant feature of Scotts Bluff National Monument. It extends north–south between the river badlands and Mitchell Pass, which separates it from a ridge extending westward at a right angle; about ten miles south of the river, parallel to this ridge, lie the Wildcat Hills, which extend for over twenty-five miles from Chimney Rock to Robidoux Pass. Because the modern usage is in the singular, many historians have misunderstood the emigrant diaries, failing to realize that in Trail days the plural form was commonly used, and this referred not just to the one bluff, but all of these bluffs, including the Wildcat Hills. True, Fremont describes "Scotts Bluff" as "an escarpment on the river of about 900 yards in length," and Cooke and Burton, quoted above, are among others who seem to identify Scott's Bluffs primarily as *the* Scotts Bluff of today; but most emigrants clearly relate it to the whole U-shaped range. Forty-Niner William Kelly showed remarkable topographic skill in likening the outline of Scott's Bluffs to a shepherd's crook, with the present Wildcat Hills as the straight staff and present Scotts Bluff as the flare at the end of the crook.

Similarly, there has been great confusion over the identity of "Scott's Bluffs Pass" as the result of failure to recognize that there were actually two passes by that name. The first, which would be at the bow of Kelly's shepherd's crook, is now called Robidoux Pass, and this was the one mainly used during the period up to and including 1850. The second, the gap known today as Mitchell Pass (inside the National Monument), was used by occasional pack-trains in early years, but it was not until 1851 that it became the principal route, and Robidoux Pass declined in importance. These alternate routes split near present Melbeta and were reunited east of Horse Creek. Either way was about twenty-five miles, although earlier travelers thought they were making a long detour because they were out of sight of the North Platte. The splitting of the Oregon-California Trail here was caused by the fact that the main bluff (today's Scotts Bluff) sprawls like a giant whale across the valley floor, blocking the way, with impenetrable badlands between it and the river; and Mitchell Pass could not be used by wagons until it was made passable by some pick and shovel work. (See Chapter XIV.) The balance of this chapter will concern itself with the earlier route.

Robidoux Pass, though seldom visited today, can nevertheless claim to be one of the great milestones on the emigrant road. As Ash Hollow was famous for its treacherous hill and bubbling spring, and Chimney Rock was notable for its weird contours, Robidoux Pass had seven memorable features which crop up frequently in the journals: (1) a beautiful valley (today's Gering Valley), with scenery already alluded to; (2) evidence of locally torrential rains and flooding of the enclosed valley floor, in the form of accumulated cedar driftwood (Fremont, Clyman, Thornton); (3) a dry run but an exceptionally fine roadway through the valley, followed by a long tough pull to the crest of the pass, described by Maj. Cross as "the first real hill [uphill] since leaving Leavenworth"; (4) from the summit, a spectacular view twenty-five miles back toward Chimney Rock and westward over 100 miles toward Laramie Peak, often referred to as the Black Hills or "the first view of the Rocky Mountains;" (5) at the Pass, the first good supply of wood since leaving Ash Hollow; (6) fine, dependable cold springs, described by several guidebooks as among the best springs on the California Trail; and (7) beginning in 1849, the remarkable Mr. Robidoux himself, complete with Indian family and relatives, and an expandable and movable trading post and blacksmith shop, which ranked almost with Chimney Rock as one of the curiosities of the Trail.

The pre-Robidoux period is well documented. One of the earliest accounts is that of Dr. Wislizenus in 1839:

> We travelled somewhat away from the river toward the left, and enjoyed a picturesque landscape. . . . at noon we halted in a little valley where rocks from either side confronted each other at a distance

of half a mile. A fresh spring meanders through the valley. We encamped on the hill from which the spring flows. . . . from the top of
the hill one enjoyed a wide prospect. On the one side the Chimney
and the whole chain of rocks we had passed showed themselves; on
the other side, fresh hills. Before us lay the Platte.

John Brown in 1849 noted: "14 miles from Chimney Rock the
road leaves the river . . . through one of the finest valleys I ever saw
and is decidedly the best twenty miles of road we have travelled."
The heavy majority of pre-1851 travelers are similarly specific about
making the left-hand turn away from the river to pass through a
picturesque valley; at the head of which was the pass bounded by
confronting cliffs, an excellent campground with plentiful wood
and water, and the grand panoramic view. There is ecstatic praise
for this "enchanted valley," which is today's Gering Valley filled
with prosperous farms. On T. J. Jefferson's "Map of the Emigrant
Road" this valley is called Karante Valley. The origin of this name
is obscure.

One feature of the scenery missed by most emigrants was the
mountain sheep, plentiful in 1832 according to Irving: "Amidst
this wild and striking scenery, Captain Bonneville, for the first time,
beheld flocks of the . . . bighorn, an animal which frequents these
cliffs in great numbers. They accord with the nature of such
scenery . . . bounding like goats from crag to crag, often trooping
along the lofty shelves of the mountains, under the guidance of
some venerable patriarch, with horns twisted lower than his muzzle,
and sometimes peering over the edge of a precipice." Father DeSmet
in 1840 and John Bidwell in 1841 mention the grosse-corne, or
bighorn; they were still to be seen in 1849, to judge from the
journal of David Dewolf: "We saw about 30 mt. goats they
climbed the sides with a fleetness that seemed . . . incredible." A
catalog of game animals at Scott's Bluffs is given by James Clyman,
who wrote in 1844: "These hills are finely stored with game Such as
Black tailed deer antelope mountain Sheep & some times Buffaloe
Elk & Grisled Bear." In 1845, Carleton wrote that the Scott's Bluffs
ravines were "famous for grizzly bears when the cherries are ripe!"
The skulls of these ferocious animals have been found at Robidoux
Pass, but there is no record of an actual encounter with them by an
emigrant here.

Two events of the forties seem prophetic. In 1845 at the point
where the Robidoux Valley road diverged from the river, the U.S.

Dragoons under Col. Kearny paused while the guide Fitzpatrick parleyed with a large and colorful warrior band of the Brule Sioux, who were the legal residents of this part of the world. This meeting was peaceful enough, but the Indians must have had some foreboding about the future. In 1846 the young historian Francis Parkman "camped by the spring at Scott Bluff" amid its "singular and fantastic formations." Camping with him was a fellow named "Roubideau," who had been guiding some emigrants and was heading for Fort Laramie. Perhaps it was on this occasion that this Robidoux conceived the idea of a trading post in the vicinity.

ROBIDOUX'S TRADING POST AT SCOTT'S BLUFFS

The name Robidoux is a challenge, for, with three wobbly French vowels, it is spelled every conceivable way. Among variations to be found in emigrant journals are Roubeaudeau, Rubado, Roubadoe, Rubideaux, Roubido, Rubidou, Roubaudu, Ribidoux, and such forthright specimens as Rubydoo, Rubidoo, and Roubydouse! Then there is also quite an assortment of quaint, even whimsical spellings, like Rubidone, Rouberdean, Rubidness, Rubadove, Roughbedughs, Rubidere, Roby, and even Troubadore and Thibbadoux!

One would suppose that Robidoux himself knew how to spell his own name, as witness the "A. Rubidue" sign at the trading post reported by Gibbs in 1849. Or one might give credence to Robidoux's friend, Thomas Cramer, of the 1959 migration, who speaks of "my old friend Robideau." This spelling, which is used also by Parkman, is getting warm. The undeniably correct spelling is "Robidoux," as recorded in family legal documents, church records, licenses issued by the Indian service, and authoritative histories of St. Louis and St. Joseph. It is a matter of congratulation that at least one fur trader (Ferris) and four emigrants (Abbey, Boyle, Buffum, and Howell) managed to get it straight, probably by pure coincidence. So did those two distinguished European globetrotters, Sir Richard Burton and Prince Paul of Wurttemberg; but considering that one of the time-honored prerogatives of early travelers is "freedom of spelling," it is not surprising that Prince Paul's companion, Mollhausen, labeled his sketch of Robidoux's trading post "Fort Roupideau"! It *is* surprising that the U.S. Geological Survey has attempted, on its topographic maps, to perpetuate the erroneous spelling as "Roubideaux." One can only hope that eventually genealogy will triumph over geology. Similarly, the "Roubedeau" spelling used in the largely authoritative *Nebraska Place-Names* is in error.

It is clear that the famous trading post and blacksmith shop was located in 1849 in the immediate vicinity of the famous springs, halfway up the hill to the summit. But there are actually two major springs, perhaps half a mile apart. One of these, the first one encountered by the emigrants, came out of the rocks at the foot of the south bluff (to the left of westbound emigrants), at the head of the north-bearing ravine around which the wagons had to detour. The other spring was in the main ravine bearing west to east, heading at the crest of the Pass, flowing as an intermittent rivulet, and draining the Pass. The first spring almost everyone saw because they went right by it; the second would be missed by many because it was somewhat to the north of the road.

A bronze plaque on the granite marker near the first spring, left of the county road, claims that it stands on the site of "Roubedeau's blacksmith shop" and that here sundry artifacts were found. But the plaque appears to be in error. An examination of surface evidence today, coupled with analysis of emigrant journals, leads to the conclusion that this post was, instead, some 300 yards north of the alleged site, at the intersection of the main ravine with the rivulet spring and the northward ravine draining the rock spring.

There are at least eighty journalists of the 1849–1850 migrations who mention the blacksmith shop setup here, and small wonder, since this was indeed a phenomenon, the first white man's habitation for over 300 miles west of Fort Kearny. But there is an almost equal number of emigrants at this time who do *not* mention Robidoux at this place, and this is even more remarkable. If this post had been at the marker site, almost squarely on the main trail, it is hard to see how any could have avoided either seeing it or mentioning it. But at the other location, at the intersection of the two ravines, Robidoux would have been several hundred yards north of the trail. In this location he could easily have escaped notice by those emigrants doggedly continuing their climb toward the crest of the Pass, particularly if the intervening ground was covered—as it would have been much of the time—by emigrant campsites.

To our knowledge, no eyewitness ever drew a map of the layout.

Most of those who do mention the famous blacksmith are vague as
to his exact whereabouts. But, fortunately, confirming the meager
archeological evidence is the illuminating testimony of at least five
travelers. By describing the two different springs in two different
ravines, they locate Robidoux with geographic precision:

> June 15, 1849 . . . road lay for 8 miles along a valley south of the
> bluffs when it commenced a gradual ascent to the Ridge. . . . near the
> sumit is a small spring of cold water S. of Road ½ mile further on is
> a splendid spring North of Road down a deep ravine 300 yards from
> Road over hung with Cedar Here is found a man by the name of
> [?] working at Blacksmithing.—Simon Doyle

> June 23, 1849 . . . Passed the head of a deep ravine where is some
> poor stock water. 1½ miles at the left at the base of the mountain in
> a deep ravine are some good springs. . . . Half a mile north of the
> spring lives a gentleman with a Squav. lady love. He has a store of
> goods for Indian trade.—Dr. Lord

> June 25, 1849 . . . The trail leaves the bluffs to the right and,
> after passing over a succession of long levels and gradual swells, we
> approached the Bluff on the left and crossed a precipitate ravine, in
> the bottom of which gushed forth an abundant supply of pure water.
> Passing on one-half a mile we encamped near another ravine close by
> another equally good spring. . . . Near this is the house of a Mr.
> Rubidone, a Canadian Frenchman, who has a native wife.—Niles
> Searls

> June 28, 1849 . . . at 2 PM started left of the River again and
> went in behind the bluffs and began the ascent of a long steep hill or
> a succession of ascents altogether some two miles in length. About
> half way up came to a spring of water coming out of the mountain.
> . . . below the spring in the ravine a Frenchman has established him-
> self in a log cabin.—Elisha Perkins

> July 1, 1849 . . . A mile from the road, across a deep ravine in
> which there are several springs, a man has a blacksmith's shop, and
> keeps certain supplies for emigrants. In the ravine the largest cedars
> I ever saw flourish.—James Pratt

Now that we have the location nailed down, just what did
Robidoux's trading post consist of? Almost all emigrants who
mention anything at all identify a blacksmith shop. Mark Manlove
writes, "The first settlement we came to was Rubedeaux's trading
post. . . . A blacksmith shop constituted the town." Shoeing animals

and repairing wagon gear was undoubtedly the heaviest part of the operation, as might be expected when Robidoux's "covered wagon garage" was the only place to service vehicles between Fort Kearny and Fort Laramie, a distance of 300 miles. The terms next most common are store and trading post. David Cosad refers to "a kind of traiding post and blacksmith shop called *The Ceders* on account a large grove of ceders." Gelwicks refers to "a miniature store." Other branches of the business mentioned include "house of entertainment" (Gelwicks), "tinware" (Gibbs) or "tin shop" (Hackney), "grog shop" (Stansbury), "gun smith" (Lord), and "emigrant swap shop" (Staples). Elisha Perkins says the proprietor was "jack of all trades—blacksmith, stove-maker, tailor, etc." who "keeps a large stock of groceries, hardware, etc."

Actually, it develops that all of these functions took place under one roof. Robidoux's many-faceted trading post of 1849, undoubtedly western Nebraska's first shopping center, was a single log cabin in conjunction with a few Indian tipis (Bruff). The tepees sheltered the French trader, his family, and a goodly number of relatives. Business was transacted in the log cabin, and, while its dimensions are not known, its character may be judged from certain references. Leeper called it "a temporary shop," but conceded that "even this makeshift of a habitation had a refreshing effect on our spirits." Maj. Cross reports, "Here is a blacksmith shop and trading-house built in the true log cabin style, which made us all feel as if we were in reality approaching once more a civilized race." George Gibbs was astonished to find in the wilderness a log cabin which "turned out to be the 'fort' of an Indian trader." J. Hamelin said he "passed a log cabin inhabited by a Robideaux, who divides his time between shoeing horses and selling what he calls whiskey (a composition of alcohol, ipecac & tartar emitic) at $1. pt." But perhaps the clearest picture of the whole operation is given by Capt. Howard Stansbury on July 9, 1849: "There is a temporary blacksmith's shop here, established for the benefit of emigrants, but especially for that of the owner who lives in an Indian lodge, and had erected a log shanty by the roadside, on one end of which was the blacksmith's forge and in the other a grog-shop and sort of grocery." From this it may be judged that in 1849 the trading post, store, saloon, tinshop, and what-have-you were all one and the same department store in one room occupying roughly half of the structure, while the blacksmith shop occupied the other half.

According to another entry in Stansbury, which could only reflect a conversation with the proprietor, "Robideaux's post is to be removed to a creek south, and over the bluffs." Such a move was made eventually, but certainly not in 1849 or the first half of 1850, because in the latter year, which saw the heaviest California migration on record, the French trader was in business at the same old stand. The same location, that is, but with a bigger emporium or larger set of shops, which either replaced or were added to the original 1849 cabin. This expansion, evident enough from the 1850 descriptions, is happily verified in the 1849 journal of Reuben G. Miller, who was in a Mormon train bound for Salt Lake that turned up several weeks after the main migration wave had passed. On July 29 Miller's train, on the Council Bluffs Road north of the Platte, took the unheard-of step of crossing to the south side five miles above Chimney Rock. On the thirtieth they traveled another twenty miles, or a total of twenty-five miles from Chimney Rock, and "camped for the night in Scotts Bluffs," which by mileage reckoning would be in Robidoux Pass: "At this place we found from 500 to 1000 Indians (Sioux) with a great number of ponies. During the travel of today some of the men in camp took up 21 head of oxen and brought them on to this place. When we arrived here they were all claimed by some French traders located at this point, and *about to build a large trading establishment.*"

Accordingly, during the 1850 migration season "Rubadoe's trading post" (Lewelling) or "Rubidou's Station" (McBride) emerges as huts or cabins, in the plural, but still with a complement of Indian lodges. As Thomasson says on May 26, "Scots bluff is a small trading post seroundid by bluffs except the pass we come in at   thare is 1 store 2 blacksmith shops sevrel wigwams some 3 or 4 smaller seder cabins." Wolcott describes "2 or 3 low cabins made of cedar and mud—many Indian lodges around." And James Bennett, on June 22, "found here an encampment of near a hundred Sioux Indians. The village contained 13 lodges and a row of rudely constructed huts." In October, 1850, Stansbury, returning from his Salt Lake exploration, clearly describes the post and its relationship to the two springs: "Scott's Bluffs—at a small rivulet, row of old deserted houses. A spring at the foot of Sandstone Bluffs, where the road crosses the ridge."

In the autumn of 1850 or the spring of 1851 Robidoux built a new post "south and over the bluff." That there was a second post

there is abundantly clear from surface examination of the site in
present Carter Canyon, as well as the conclusive proof of the sketch
of "Fort Roupideau," made in 1851 by Heinrich Mollhausen, companion of Prince Paul of Wurttemberg. In his account Prince Paul
mentions only his stay at the trading post of "my friends of thirty
years standing, the Brothers Robidoux," and the repair of a broken
axle at the Robidoux shop. It is certain that Mollhausen visited
the Carter Canyon site, since the sketch vividly depicts bluffs which
have their counterpart in that location. The U-shaped group of log
cabins with associated tepees in the foreground were perhaps, archi-
tecturally, duplicates of the original structures in Robidoux Pass.

How long did Robidoux's cabins survive in the Pass? One
would suppose that, since they were "deserted" in October, 1850,
since a new post had been constructed in Carter Canyon, and since
the Mitchell Pass route opened in 1851, that would be the end of
Robidoux Pass. The year 1851 was a slack year for emigration
anyhow, and business must have been poor; yet there is clear evidence that Robidoux's post in the Pass was again in business in
1851. Witness P. V. Crawford on June 2: "[We] reached the Bluffs
at 9 O'clock at night. . . . Here we found a trading post belonging
to Rubedo, a Frenchman," and on June 11 Robert Robe "passed
Robedory trading post." Also in 1851, Cranstone mentions a blacksmith shop at "scotts bluffs and springs in a romantic place, in a
hollow where there was a small stream and high bluffs nearly surrounding us." Post No. 2 (in Carter Canyon) was a mile south of
the California Road and would have required a lengthy and
pointless side trip for an emigrant; so it is concluded that it was
designed primarily for the Indian trade. At least if any emigrant
visited there it is not a matter of record. It is concluded, also, that
Robidoux kept the two posts going in 1851 for the benefit of Indians
and emigrants, respectively. While Prince Paul clearly visited No.
2, one can only guess which places were meant by the missionary
Father DeSmet on his return to St. Louis from the Horse Creek
Treaty Council of September, 1851: "I directed my course towards
the springs about 14 miles distant in the vicinity of the Roubideaux
trading house, for Colonel Mitchell had named this as the rendezvous for all those who proposed going directly to the United
States. . . . I visited on my way two trading houses, in order to
baptize 5 half-blooded children." There were three posts "at Scott's
Bluffs" in 1851, the two Robidoux posts and Fort John, described

in Chapter XIV. Robidoux's Post No. 2 and Fort John seem the most likely places visited by Father DeSmet.

After 1851 no more is heard of an occupied trading post in the location known as Robidoux Pass, so it is safely concluded that it was finally abandoned. Neither is there any evidence of how long Post No. 2 was occupied. That it may have been short-lived is evidenced by other trading posts associated with the Robidoux name which begin to appear in late 1851 at two other locations nearby, one at the east fork in the road near Melbeta, the other at the point where the two branches rejoined at Horse Creek. Both are described in 1851 by Lobenstine and in 1852 by Caroline Richardson and William Hampton. Susan Bordeaux Bettelyoun confirms that Robidoux "ran a blacksmith shop on the Oregon Trail on a branch of Horse Creek." Capt. Gove says that the approach to Horse Creek was called Robideaux Sloughs. Association of the Robidoux name with the trading post at the east junction, near Melbeta, is given by several travelers, including J. R. Brown in 1856 and Chillson in 1859. In 1860 Burton refers to the east junction post as "Robidoux Fort, from the well-known trader of that name."

The ruins of the Robidoux post in the Pass are described by several travelers. In 1853 Celinda E. Hines found "several log buildings connected together. In them were remnants of wagons and other things which the emigrants would want. In one had been a blacksmith shop. The whole was now deserted. Near by was one of the most beautiful springs I have ever seen." That same season J. Hamelin "breakfasted near Robidoux's old trading house. . . . appropriated a large portion of the latter to our own use." In 1856, according to J. R. Brown, the old trading post was still there, but "now in ruins."

The Robidoux route itself was not entirely abandoned. Mrs. Bettelyoun said: "All the men dealing in the fur trade moved to the Platte, when most of the travelling was done along the river road. At other times when the roads were bad, the travelling went on higher ground, back of Scotts Bluff by Rubideaux's place." Helen Carpenter in '56 and T. S. Kenderdine in '58 both confirm that the old route was the best, but that the river road "directly over the summit" of the bluffs (Mitchell Pass) was usually taken because it was thought to be shorter. Capt. Gove and William Carter indicate that troops of the Utah Expedition in 1857 took the Robidoux route, and Capt. Luther North indicates it was still in occasional use during the Indian campaigns of the sixties.

The mortality rate among emigrants at Robidoux Pass was not as high as might be expected from the large concentration of campers there. The Asiatic cholera, which plagued emigrants along the main Platte valley and up the North Platte as far as Chimney Rock, was diminishing at this elevation; and before reaching this point, after thirty days or more out of the border towns, the accident-prone had been pretty well weeded out. Even so, there were casualties.

Several diarists (including Boyle, Decker, and Gelwicks) in late May, 1849, mention Mormons who showed up at the trading post from the west, in desperate condition, having been robbed and beaten by Crow Indians. At this same time Breyfogle tells of a drinking spree at Robidoux's tavern which resulted in two men gunning each other down. One was reported dying when the emigrant train departed. Whether these acts of violence resulted in funeral services is not a matter of record, but in the month of June, 1849, five deaths from cholera are known.

One of the few known emigrant graves in this neighborhood is that of a Mr. Dunn just west of the first spring. His funeral was well recorded. C. G. Hinman, writing from Fort Laramie, tells of his tribulations at Robidoux Pass: "Have turned our Waggon over once and broke 3 bows, 2 Stakes and my Rifle. It was close by an Indian traders and Black smith shop, and it hapened one of our company was taken with the cholera at the same time, which caused us to camp, and during the afternoon we had everything in repair. The man Died about 10 oclock the same night [June 13]. We buried him at 8 oclock the next morning with as much decency as if he had been in the States, put a sand stone up with his name, Age, etc cut on it, and left him. He was a young man and left a wife and one child in Indian town, Ill. His name was Dunn." On June 14 Edwin Banks reports: "As we were ascending Scott's Bluffs we saw a funeral. A Mr. Dunn of Illinois died of cholera after ten hours' illness." On that same date Dunn's brand-new grave was noted by Charles Parke.

On the twentieth Howell tells of the death of a soldier of Company I, Mounted Riflemen, eight miles east of Robidoux's, in the vicinity of Dome Rock, Scotts Bluff National Monument. On the twenty-third, writes Dr. Lord, "At noon just before reaching the spring was called to see a cholera patient, a woman. Stayed an hour and left her very comfortable. Two others had cholera. One will die certainly, perhaps all 3." In July, Bruff identifies the fallen soldier near Dome Rock "in the heart of Scotts Bluffs, right of Trail" as James Roby, age twenty, of Ohio. In the Pass he records "3 Graves near the Spring: Jesse Galen, Independence, Mo., Joseph Blake, F. Dunn, age 26."

At the end of May, 1850, Abbey and McBride both record the accidental shooting of Mr. Jamieson, a Methodist preacher from Kentucky: "This man on stooping over let a loaded pistol fall from a breast pocket, which discharged and carried away a part of his under jaw. Subsequently erysipelas set in and destroyed his life. . . . His wife and children pursued their journey to California."

On July 2, while encamped two miles west of "the gap," Littleton wrote that he had recorded nine fresh graves between Chimney Rock and Robidoux's. His list includes Rev. Jamieson, "age 49, of Mo." Since this man is third on Littleton's list and Littleton was camped only a short distance from the Pass, it seems probable that these six on his list were also buried in this vicinity, all victims of the 1850 cholera: "John McCarty, June 5, age 25, of Mo.; M. W. Murray, June 19, age 25, Poole Ct., Indiana; I. M. McKay, June 20, age 37 of Maples, Iowa; Francis M. Bradley, June 21, age 23, Howard C., Mo.," and "2 no names."

Five emigrant graves are identifiable today in the Robidoux Pass area, that of Dunn (recorded by U.S. Government surveyors in 1878) west of the rock springs, and four nameless graves, halfway between the two springs and marked by a bronze and granite memorial.

Robidoux Pass was a Sioux Indian graveyard as well. "Immediately above the watercourse," wrote Gelwicks in 1849, "on a large cedar tree, an Indian was buried." Elisha Lewis describes this "burial" method as utilizing a basket made of buckskin with hoops or ribs as in a canoe, and "the corps is then fixed permanent in the top of a tree with cord fasting to the limbs." In 1850 Reuben Knox here saw "an Indian buried in a sitting position in his basket," also "two graves of Indians . . . hung up in a scaffold formed of lodge poles. . . . Sad to relate the last two mentioned were killed in a drunken frolic . . . having been furnished with the fire and Death water by some emigrants who took this way to get their ponies." Robidoux gave Charles Darwin some insight into

Sioux burial customs: "He says they change occasionally the bones of the dead from tree to tree & even the bones of a little girl who had been dead ten years had lately been moved near his house."

THE MYSTERY OF MR. ROBIDOUX

Some journals afford tantalizing glimpses of private enterprise in action at Scott's Bluffs, 1849–1850. The primary business of the Robidoux clan was to trade with the Indians. In 1850 Solomon Gorgas said that "Mr. Roubedou . . . buys and trades a great deal of Furs for the Indians and sends them to the Missouri River." As previously noted, the Robidoux eastbound caravans were often observed by emigrants; Howell was told by Robidoux that it was 602 miles from this place to St. Joe. Indians continued to bring in buffalo robes, beaver skins, and other wares and exchange them for tinware, guns, gewgaws, and whiskey; and here, also, they came to get sharp iron arrows made from abandoned wagon rims. But the passage over the California Road of at least 75,000 people in these two hectic seasons certainly was not to be ignored by a shrewd businessman; so Robidoux made a big pitch also for the emigrant trade and, being the only entrepreneur around for over 300 miles, he prospered. As James Pratt put it on July 1, 1849: "The man has an Indian wife and family, and seems much at his ease, making money plentifully." The dual character of his operation is put concisely by Castleman: "Rubado was trading with the Indians. He had a blacksmith shop here and was doing a great deal of work for the Emigration."

Horses, mules, and oxen, getting thin and hoof-sore, had to be shod. Robidoux had a fine monopoly going for him, and prices proved to be very elastic. One of the earliest Forty-Niners, Col. Jarrott, on May 26, 1849, raced to the shop for repairs, says Berrien, "for he was fearful that some of the waggons behind us might get ahead of him." While at the shop, "nearly forty waggons passed us on the way to the diggings. As I brought shoes for my mules with me, I had them nailed on . . . 25¢ for each shoe." Prices climbed sharply. On June 12 Wakeman Bryarly complained, "For goods of every description he charges the most exorbitant prices, & for work, truly extortionate. For instance if an emigrant finds the mule shoes, nailes &c, & puts the shoes on, he has to pay $1. per pair and everything in proportion." On June 28, observed Perkins, shoeing mules was $2 per shoe and sugar 40¢ a pound. "Some of his prices was amusing enough to us," says Perkins, "but not so to the unfortunate traveller whose misfortunes compelled him to refit here." By July 4, said James D. Lyon, business was slacking off: "He shoes horses for one dollar a shoe and setts the tires on the wagon for 18. He sells flour at eight and Bacon at $10 per hundred."

Toward the end of the 1849 season, on July 9 according to Stansbury, blacksmithing was again on a do-it-yourself basis, with shop facilities renting for the modest price of 75¢ an hour, "but it was not until waiting for several hours that I could get the privilege of shoeing two of the horses, even at that price, the forge having been in constant use by the emigrants."

In 1850 profiteering soared. On June 18 Sponsler paid $4 to shoe a horse; on June 23 Greenville's correspondent paid $8 for the privilege! Whiskey, apparently the principal commodity, commanded 50¢ a jigger and $5 to $8 a gallon (Steck), which perhaps does not seem exorbitant, by today's standards, but doubtless was then, particularly in view of the manner in which the vile stuff, imported in kegs from St. Louis, was watered down by the traders.

Gorgas thought that Robidoux "has a neat assortment of dry goods," but there was grousing, not only about prices, but about the merchandise generally. McGlashan felt that he was "poorly supplied" with the necessities of life. He had no fresh meat, and "mockasons were of an inferior quality." Buffalo robes of Sioux manufacture were also available to emigrants, but these were in light demand because of the added weight.

Although he had some St. Louis merchandise (whiskey, tinware, guns, trade goods, and cloth), Robidoux's stock was largely on a revolving basis. As Staples put it, "He bought his goods of emigrants who find they have too much and most of them do. . . . We sold him a bag of coffee . . . Pork he would not take as a gift." He was the clearinghouse, the stock exchange of the migration.

Who was this Robidoux, this frontier tycoon, this jack-of-all-trades, this squaw man of Scott's Bluffs? From the emigrant journals one may glean a few facts, some of them confusing and contradictory. According to various informants he had been in this territory from ten to sixteen years. Most agree that he lived with one or two Sioux squaws (Tompkins says there were three), but beyond this there are wide discrepancies in the testimony.

The main Mrs. Robidoux, according to William Kelly, was a

"perfect queen of the wilderness." Here, said Bruff, "You can buy whiskey and look at the *beautiful* squaws of the traders" (plural, and the emphasis is Bruff's). Dr. Lord refers to a Frenchman and his "squaw lady love," surrounded by cliffs, which makes it sound romantic. Solomon Gorgas, whom Robidoux invited into his quarters to see his squaw about moccasins, describes her as "rather a better-looking woman than most Squaws—but hard enough." Charles Darwin says, "This man has two wives who look pretty well." But when we turn to Madison Moorman, the image is shattered: "His squaw was the most uncomely in appearance I had seen—and how he managed to *love* just such a human being is past my divination. Their lodge was the most indifferent and unclenly in the village." To make his point, Moorman adds, "Many [others] of the Sioux are fine looking."

Ugly or beautiful, Mrs. Robidoux was the mother of what one writer called "numerous progeny." The unusually observant Gorgas found "no papoucies" around, but the youngsters must have been off playing in the canyon, because many observers mention an indefinite number of half-breed children. At least two emigrants, Lindsey and Hackney, specify three children in 1849, but Darwin says there were four, at least one of whom was "a beautiful boy."

If anything is clear, it is that the Robidoux clan was prolific. Besides the Joseph of Blacksnake Hills, who founded St. Joseph, Missouri, there were many brothers, sons, nephews. But which Robidoux was this? The heavy majority of observers simply say Robidoux (or one of its variants) and let it go at that. Bruff, for example, speaks only of "one of the Rubideaus of St. Jo."

There is plenty of evidence that there was not just one Robidoux here; the whole family was involved. Although most observers speak of only one Frenchman at the blacksmith shop, there is occasional reference to more than one. In 1850 James Bennett speaks of "two Frenchmen with Indian wives and children." Thomasson helpfully contributes "6 or 8 Frenchmen with squaws." Of course, not all Frenchmen at Scott's Bluffs were necessarily Robidouxs. In 1849, for example, Wm. Johnston speaks of inhabitants named Palliday and Bordeau. There are emigrant references to anonymous "mechanics and Canadian blacksmiths." Mrs. Bettelyoun explains that "Rubideau was pretty well to do. He had five or six hired white men." But the unavoidable conclusion is that in 1849–1850 the Scott's Bluffs trading post was the headquarters for not just one

Robidoux but the whole Robidoux family, probably including Joseph Robidoux, the old patriarch of St. Joe.

Travelers who met "Robidoux" on the Trail actually met all kinds of them, sometimes singly, sometimes in quantity, but rarely with first names. They seemed to be part of the Platte River scenery. As early as 1830 Warren Ferris of the American Fur Company had a Robidoux (oldest son Joseph?) with him up the north bank. The Bidwell expedition of 1841 was inspired by "a Frenchman named Roubideaux who said he had been to California." This was doubtless "Antoine Robidoux of the Spanish country," whom Jacob Snyder met on the Oregon Trail in 1845. In 1846 the Aram train had a Robidoux as guide. This was possibly Joseph, Jr., again, the same who joined Francis Parkman at Scott's Bluffs and told him he had been among the Navaho near Santa Fe. In 1847 Clayton relates how the Mormons shared buffalo meat with a "Rubidoos" opposite Chimney Rock. In April, 1849, Capt. Ruff at Fort Kearny reports Francois, "a brother of Old Man Robidoux," among "a party of mountain men en route Fort Laramie to St. Joe." As we have seen, the Robidoux caravan appears in several 1849 emigrant journals, but usually without any given names. One exception to this is Elijah Howell, who says, "Here [at Plum Creek] we met Isadore Robidoux with four wagons loaded." Henry Page says one of the men in the caravan was Michael, "younger brother of the founder, gray-haired but still handsome," who may or may not have been the same whom Gelwicks described as Col. Jarrott's schoolmate. (See Chapter V.) The Kanesville *Frontier Guardian* for June 26, 1850, contains an interview with "the Messrs. Robidoux's who have a trading post near Fort Laramie."

The official Robidoux biography by O. M. Robidoux is quite hazy on this aspect of the family tree, but the identity of those engaged in trade is clearly defined in the licenses issued by the Bureau of Indian Affairs, records of which were found by the writer in the National Archives. All such licenses were issued in the name of Joseph Robidoux, who is incontestably the founder of St. Joe. Among associates named in the 1849 license to trade with "Sioux, Cheyenne and Arapahoes" are four Robidouxs—identified only as F., J., N., and S. On the register for 1850 are five Robidouxs, M., E., F., J. E., and A. In 1851 the record is more specific. In this year Joseph Robidoux lists among his employees the following: "Michael Robidoux, Isadore Robidoux, as assistant traders, Joseph

E. and Antoine Robidoux as clerks." There is substantiating evidence that the latter two were the regular proprietors of the Scott's Bluffs trading post.

This Antoine (not the famous brother but a nephew of Joseph, Sr., and thus first cousin of Joseph E.) seems to be the prime candidate because of the "A. Rubidue, Tinware" sign mentioned by Gibbs and the convincing testimony of Charles Darwin, both in 1849:

> Here is a Blacksmiths shop by A. Roubideaux & a trading post—55 from Laramie. . . .
>
> And Antoine Robidoux is a gentleman. He taught me much of the Sioux. . . . He procured my reading of some medicinal directions which were in French as he could not read. . . . I read too for him a letter from his Uncle Joseph Robidoux of St. Joseph in which he insisted on his not going to California but staying to make *beaucoup d'argent.* He invited me to take dinner with him. . . . It consisted of pork, fried batter cake & milkless coffee. We sat on a cedar stool made of slabs & ate off a similar table with our fingers for forks. . . . Never did I look on so beautiful a spot as the valley of his residence.

But there is also positive identification of Joseph, who could only be Joseph E. (Joseph, Jr.), the oldest son of the original Joseph of St. Joe. In 1859 Thomas Cramer camped here and penned:

> Here in 1854 my old friend Joe Robideau (who was for many years a trader among the Ioway, Pawnee and Sioux Indians) was located. . . . He is now among his early friends the Ioways and has taken a wife and land among them. Joe is a curious specimen of our race. He has resided so long among the savages that he more resembles them in his habits and tastes than the people to whom he originally belonged.

Joseph E. is identified by the family biographer O. M. Robidoux as one who lived among the Sioux for many years before returning (about 1857) to live on the Nemaha (Kansas) Reservation. This ties in with the Robidoux whom Robert Robe met in 1851 who had two daughters in Rev. Hamilton's school on the Kansas Reservation. Joseph and his family are also named by Susan Bordeaux (interviewed in 1936 as Mrs. Bettelyoun), whose father was James Bordeaux of Fort Laramie fame:

> Joseph Silko [Sellico?] Rubideaux built the first log houses at St. Joseph, Mo. He was married to a Yantony Sioux woman. He had two sons from the widow of John Baptiste Bordeau. . . . he ran a black-

smith shop on the Oregon Trail on a branch of Horse Creek. His place was a little southwest of Scottsbluff. It was near the creek with a good deal of timber.

Antoine (the son of Francois, according to Earl Harris and W. S. Wallace), would probably have been younger than his uncles Joseph, Sr., and Antoine and somewhat younger than his cousin Joseph; he probably fits into Gorgas' description of "a man of about 30." There are several references to an "old French trader," both at the trading post and on the Trail, and one might suppose that this would describe cousin Joseph, Jr. However, Prince Paul's reference to "my friends of thirty years standing, the Brothers Robidoux at Scotts bluff," definitely suggests Joseph, Sr. (whom Prince Paul met at Bellevue trading post in 1823), and old Antoine of southwestern fame. In 1850 McBride refers to "Old Robidoux of Castle Bluffs," while in 1851 the "Roubydouse" train met by J. L. Johnson west of Fort Kearny included an "old man who was entirely blind" and who had "wintered at Scott's Bluffs." This would probably be the elder Antoine, whose blindness is attested to in his brief biography by Wallace.

One final note, this on the cultural level of Robidoux's trading post. The emigrants were inclined to take a rather dim view of the trader, not only because of his sharp business practices, but also because of his moral turpitude. Shombre portrays him as a "renegade white," while Tompkins calls him a desperado. In 1850 observers describe a dog feast, which naturally appeared repugnant in their eyes and suggested the habits of barbarians. John Wood wrote: "They live on game and are not particular what kind. As we passed today they killed a large dog which was very fat. They made soup of him. It was held by the men while the women beat it to death with clubs." James Bennett observed: "They were having a dog feast. Near their camp fire was the head of a large mastiff; bleeding evidence of the fact." Moorman refers to "the savagized son of papal France and his little Indians going about with their tin cups of dog stew." Mary Bailey mentions Robidoux's Horse Creek post in 1852: "Passed a Frenchman's blacksmith shop. His wife, a squaw of the Sioux tribe, sat in the door of their hut rolled in a scarlet blanket. . . . Another squaw was on horseback, chasing a drove of horses and mules. She was only half dressed."

There is nothing here to suggest that Joseph Robidoux was

anything more or less than a typical mountain man or squaw man, Cramer's "curious specimen" who lived according to the native customs. According to Roy Coy, back in St. Joseph he was known as "Indian Joe" because of habits and native dress acquired from life on the Plains. Also, because of his irresponsible ways, his father was "forced to act as the younger Joseph's guardian." A few emigrants give insight to a different Robidoux of some learning or refinement. Gorgas pictures him as "a gentleman" with whom he shook hands upon departure. Dr. Boyle mentions a Robidoux here who was the owner of western Nebraska's first library: "Here 500 miles from any place I found Webster's Dictionary and other books to match, besides some French devotional and historical works!" Since Joseph E. was, apparently, an uncouth mountain man and young Antoine "could not read," according to Darwin, who was this scholarly Robidoux?

There are many Robidoux (usually spelled "Roubideaux") on the Pine Ridge and Rosebud Sioux reservations in South Dakota today, several of whom have informed the writer personally that their common ancestor was an 1849 resident of Scott's Bluffs, that his name was Joseph, and that he had two sons, Charles and Louis, from whom the Sioux Indian Roubideaux clans have descended. Indian family tradition has it that this ancestor was killed by a fractious mule and buried at Robidoux Pass. Mrs. Bettelyoun says that Joseph died on Horse Creek, but Cramer, Coy, and Messmore all affirm that he left western Nebraska and took up life with the Iowa tribe in northeastern Kansas, marrying an Oto woman. From this it is concluded (1) that Joseph E. abandoned his Indian family and the story of his death was invented to put a good face on things, and (2) that if a mule did actually kill a Robidoux, it was not Joseph E., but possibly the younger Antoine. In any event it must be conceded that knowledge of the various members of the Scott's Bluffs Robidoux clan is still incomplete. Like Hiram Scott, they seem to belong more to folklore than to definite history.

XIV

General Mitchell's Pass

The Three River Bluffs

ALTHOUGH THE "HILL ROAD" past Robidoux's trading post was the dominant one through 1850, the river road through Mitchell Pass (the second Scott's Bluffs Pass) was used by *some* early travelers. The Nathaniel Wyeth party of 1834 "passed through two high bluffs through a pretty good pass and avoided going between one of them and the river where there are bad ravines." John K. Townsend of Wyeth's party offers the first written description of Mitchell Pass:

> Here we diverged from the usual course, leaving the bank of the river, and entered a large and deep ravine between the enormous bluffs.
>
> The road was very uneven and difficult, winding from amongst innumerable mounds six to eight feet in height, the space between them frequently so narrow as scarcely to admit our horses, and some of our men rode for upwards of a mile kneeling upon their saddles. These mounds are of hard yellow clay.

In 1840 Father DeSmet's party "found a narrow passage . . . between two perpendicular cliffs 300 feet in height." A. J. Miller's sketch of 1837 shows the east elevation of the main bluff, which strongly suggests that the Sublette expedition he was with that year also used the nearby pass. That some emigrants prior to 1851 managed to negotiate this pass is suggested by Bennett Clark's 1849 reference to his "encampment within a semicircle of high bluffs, which rise abruptly from the river's edge and sweep around rainbow-like." It is not improbable that some wagons got through somehow, though the Pass was supposed to be barely negotiable by pack-trains.

The earliest clear-cut evidence of the use of the Mitchell Pass route by wagons is provided by Capt. Stansbury. In 1849 he had gone west through Robidoux Pass; in October, 1850, returning eastward, he found, west of Horse Creek, that "a road lies along the river, but it is not worn; said to be shorter than that by Scott's Bluffs [Robidoux Pass]." Official records are vague on this point, but there are several hints that somebody did use a pick and shovel to smooth the road and possibly straighten out a kink or two in the tortuous passage. Perry Burgess, for example, says the pass was "partly natural and partly artificial." It seems that soldiers out of Fort Laramie would be the only ones who would be sufficiently organized or motivated to accomplish this, although another possibility is that the American Fur Company made the improvement to divert traffic away from their arch-rival Robidoux and toward their new trading post on the Platte (see below). In any event, from 1851 on we find many references to the new road' splitting off east of the bluffs (near Melbeta) and clear descriptions of Mitchell Pass. Thus, in that year Wm. Lobenstine writes: "The rock itself is separated nearly at its middle, having a pass here fifty to sixty feet wide, ascending at both sides perpendicular to a height of three to four hundred feet. The passage through here was *only made possible* in 1851 and is now preferred by nearly all emigrants, cutting off a piece of eight miles from the old road."

Robidoux Pass was the primary route of the Oregon migration and the California-bound for 1849–1850, but Mitchell Pass became the main route for most California emigrants after 1850, as well as for the military and for stage, Pony Express, and telegraph lines. This later route through Mitchell Pass has left deep-cut ruts through the sandy soil, now covered with buffalo grass, and deeper troughs through the soft sandstone or Brule clay, which are vivid reminders of covered wagon days. Scotts Bluff National Monument now protects Mitchell Pass and the three most conspicuous of the formations which were once part of the "greater Scott's Bluffs." These are the main Scotts Bluff and the opposite South Bluff, with the V-shaped Mitchell Pass between them, and the huge, turret-shaped Dome Rock, the three together forming a semicircle or amphitheater. In 1853 Count Cipriani described "a semi-circular valley resembling an amphitheater with five enormous, almost regular steps of calcareous blocks, recalling Etruscan and Pelasgian constructions. The illusion was so perfect that only very close scrutiny could convince one that the steps were merely a caprice of Nature." The Alfred Lambourne sketch of this scene shows a vast covered wagon encampment here, and the Wilkinson journal of 1859 indicates use of the spring at the east base today called Scott's Spring. It seems that most emigrants, however, drove through the Pass and camped on the North Platte River beyond rather than within this amphitheater. Perhaps the existence of a spring here was not generally known, for in 1861 Butterfield reports, "No place for a camp on the road through the bluffs."

A state highway now bisects the Monument through Mitchell Pass and, for the benefit of tourists, there is an ingeniously engineered road to the summit of Scotts Bluff to afford panoramic views. At the foot of this bluff, near the Pass, is a building complex housing the Monument headquarters and the Oregon Trail Museum.

Several travelers are quite specific in describing the formations within the present Monument. G. A. Smith in 1852 says, "These bluffs are 2 in number, situated on either side of the road." Others understood, like Burton in 1860, that "Scott's Bluffs . . . are divided into three distinct masses, the largest 800 feet high . . . on the right and next to the river," then a "second castle" (South Bluff), and "an outwork, a huge detached cylinder" (Dome Rock). S. H. Taylor in 1853 said the bluff

> is nearly divided but encloses a fine green area like a court, around which, except on the east, rises what seems like an imposing pile of regal buildings in the style of the earlier days of monarchy. It appears as if two immense structures had been raised. . . . East . . . is a beautiful tower, apparently as perfect in its form as the hand of man could make it. . . . In the center . . . rises a noble perfect dome.

While on a journey with fur traders to Fort Platte in 1841 Rufus Sage wrote a description of Dome Rock and the main bluff which is remarkably accurate:

> Near this [South Bluff] stood a more singular formation than any previously noted. It described a complete circle, of one thousand feet in circumference, and attained an altitude of not more than four hundred feet. Its sides were of great regularity, and represented masses of solid mason-work, rising abruptly till within sixty or seventy feet

of the summit, where they accline in a blunt, cone-like manner, reducing the periphery to one third that of the base. At this point is reposed a semi-spherical form, regularly jutting with a gradual swell upon all sides—then tapering to an oval shape till near the apex, at which the whole mass is surmounted by a rude imitation of sculptured flame. . . .

Still further to the right, upon the river bank, is another immense pile, exceeding either of the before described in altitude. It is an oblong square and presents erect lateral walls on three sides, leaving upon a fourth a gradual acclivity which faces the river. Its summit expands into a beautiful terrace containing an area of several acres, which at the proper season is adorned with herbs, flowers, shrubbery and grass, like a pleasure garden upon some house-top, and commands a view of the whole country.

Dome Rock, with its remarkable bulk and symmetry, attracted much attention. Mrs. Ferris said this gigantic perpendicular rock in the form of a cylinder "looked like a vast mausoleum of some hero of a past race." Kilgore, viewing it from the north side of the river, remarked, "At the east end of [the ancient fort] stands a rock that has very mutch the appearance of a Lite house." Gray thought it resembled the famous Castle Garden on the Battery in New York City. D. B. Andrews called it Church Rock because of its stately design, while Martin Patterson called it Tower Rock. An excellent sketch is to be found in the notebook of Wm. Lorton.

The striking formations here resulted in some efforts to rename the whole group, but particularly the main bluff. The Hosea Horn guidebook called these the Capitol Hills, while W. Wadsworth suggested Convent Rock. Other ideas were Gibraltar, already noted, Mt. Ararat (Kelly), Scott's Rock (Mary Warner), and Mount Scott (Fancher Stimson). The use of "Scotch Bluffs" by Laub, Lobenstine, Lowe, Munger, and others is a simple phonetic error.

The Second Scott's Bluffs Pass

The name "Mitchell Pass" was not used in covered wagon days. Conway calls it Devil's Gap because of the winds which howled through it, and Ben Arnold named it Marshall Pass after one of his captains. But aside from becoming simply "the pass through Scott's Bluffs" or "The Gap," it really didn't have a name until early settlement days in Mitchell Valley and the town of Mitchell. These, of course, derived from old Fort Mitchell, in turn named for a commander of Indian-fighting Volunteers, Brig. Gen. Robert B. Mitchell. But first there must be an examination of this remarkable pass, which is one of the most striking pieces of scenery on the Great Plains. Through this tortuous, narrow gap moved countless thousands of covered wagons, hundreds of military expeditions, the shuttle of stagecoaches and Pony Express riders, and the first transcontinental telegraph line.

Rolling through the Pass today on the paved highway, it is not easy to imagine the difficulties of scrambling through it with a clumsy wagon drawn by several yoke of oxen. From the distance it looked like a modest little climb, and, indeed, some journals are misleading on this point. Gilbert Cole, for example, says that in its ancient history "nature's forces had cleft [the bluff] in two parts, making an avenue through its center at least 100 feet wide," while Ira Butterfield states that "the road through the bluffs has the appearance of a wide natural highway, cut through the white clay." The actual passage of the cut, however, was just as winding and rough as it looks today to anyone who gets out of his auto and hikes through. The rugged Pass, with its yawning cliffs, made for a memorable experience. Mary Bailey described the Pass as "crooked and rough," so twisted and sunken, in fact, that "you could not see the road unless in it." Ada Millington noted that "the road passed between two mountains and was so narrow we could not more than pass." Frances G. Carrington pointed out the S-shaped character of the turn west of the Pass to get around the head of ravines. She wrote that this was "so tortuous that the first wagon of a train making a turn, if you were near the center, would appear to be retracing the journey." George Beehrer's account is grossly exaggerated. He would have it believed that his freighting boss ordered a night trip through the Pass so the drivers wouldn't be scared by the spectacle of what he describes as a steep zigzag road down a precipice: "Suddenly it seemed as if we dropped out into space. . . . A single mis-step by any of us walking alongside our oxen would have meant certain death."

Nevertheless, the Pass was extraordinary enough to make a profound impression. Its tortuous up and down hill effect, the gaping cliffs, the incurable habit of emigrant name-carving, and the magnificent view to be gained on the west side are vividly expressed by these other travelers:

Reached scotts bluffs after coming through a deep ravine [the ravine north from Dome Rock, just inside the east boundary of the National Monument]. . . . the eastern view is grand. . . . each side of the road was covered with large pieces of rock which had fallen from the top on which was inscribed a great many names and some in flaming black letters. . . . the cenery was very wild and romantic. . . . on the western side is two large towering rocks resembling each other as we passed through several deep ravines.—CAROLINE RICHARDSON, 1852

We then went through a pass which one would almost believe was artificial. . . . it is very winding & is a good register containing many carved names. We then came out upon the west side where if possible it is still more grand. From this point the Platt can be seen to a great distance studded with numerous islands. . . . Taking the whole journey thus far it is by far the most magnifican sight we have looked upon.—EDWIN BIRD, 1854

The bluffs are of light colored sandy clay—and the road is cut down into it . . . in places, to the depth of six or eight feet, with little more than room for the wagon to pass through. It looks as though this cut had been made by a great body of water rushing through, making many curves and angles, and at such points, cutting out underneath, leaving overhanging walls. . . . under the overhanging places, many persons have left their names. . . . we went on record with the rest.—HELEN CARPENTER, 1856

[We were advised] to take the straight forward road leading through the chain of Bluffs and descending it by a nearer rout to the Platt again. This, we afterwards regretted as we got through the pass with great difficulty—we found a large freight stopped in the pass, the mud being very deep. The axle of one wagon was broken and a dying ox lying crippled in the road—the bellowing of the Ox which reverberated along the bluff—and the croaking of the thousands of ravens that were hovering over, had a gloomy and ominous sound. This pass is truly a wonder. The bluffs here form a semi-circle and on each side rise up into huge towers which make the head dizzy to look up at. The passage through is level, but has been cut into deep ravines by the torrents which run down the sides of the Bluffs.—WILLIAM A. CARTER, 1857

The ascent was easy and gradual, until we came to a deep gorge, which intersected our road at the foot of the main bluff [the ravine north from Dome Rock]. Crossing this at the imminent risk of being run over by the teams as they plunged headlong to the bottom, we came to a series of steep hills and narrow, deep and sandy defiles, through which there was barely room for a wagon to pass. So squarely hewn were some of these passes, that one could hardly believe that art had not a hand in their formation. After a vast deal of exertion we at last reached the summit, where we commenced the still more danger-ous descent. Tumbling pell-mell down narrow passages, slowly crawling over abrupt ascents, we at length reached the bottom, and in two miles struck the river.—T. S. KENDERDINE, 1858

The route [by mail wagon] lay between the right-hand fortress and the outwork, through a degraded bed of softer marl. . . . The sharp, sudden torrents which pour from the heights on both sides, and the draughty winds—Scott's Bluffs are the permanent headquarters of hur-ricanes—have cut up the ground into a labyritch of jagged gulches steeply walled in. We dashed down the drains and pitchholes with a violence which shook the nave-bands from our sturdy wheels. Ascend-ing, the driver showed a place where the skeleton of an "elephant" had been lately discovered. . . . The descent was abrupt, with sudden turns round the head of earth-cracks. . . . one place showed the remains of a wagon and team which had lately come to grief.—RICHARD BURTON, 1860

The Pass is only wide enough to admit one wagon to go through at a time & when we reached the entrance to it, we all got out & walked through, as the road was steep and winding & we were afraid to trust ourselves in the wagon. We all walked through the Pass at noon time, in the midst of a hot broiling sun. . . . I could not but admire [the pass] even in the midst of this great heat. . . . the color is of a yellowish cream. . . . In this pass were to be seen the most beautiful blue flowers and sun flowers. . . . On this sand, which is as hard as bristol brick, we saw the greatest number of names cut.—MRS. VOGDES, 1868

In 1866 the Eighteenth U.S. Infantry regiment, the largest con-centration of military strength to that date, marched through the Pass. Margaret Carrington, the colonel's wife, observed that the bluffs were "of mixed clay and sand, plentifully supplied with fossils, and throw a spur across the Platte basin so as to compel the traveler to leave the river and make a long detour to the south, or to pass through the bluffs themselves. This passage is by a tortuous gorge where wagons can seldom pass each other; and at times the drifting snows or sands almost obscure the high walls and battlements that rise several hundred feet on either side." Wagonmaster Wm. Murphy, with the supply train, said that a bull team stampeded downhill with parts and equipment for a sawmill, with disastrous results. That same year young bullwhacker Wm. H. Jackson reports:

> We drove up to & into the pass. . . . We had one of the steepest and worst gulches to drive through that we have yet had. [Here Jackson is talking, again, about the ravine north from Dome Rock, east of the Pass.] Got through [the Pass] safely. Had quite a time getting supper. When we got the keg out for water to make the coffee & bread we found that the precious liquid was minus. The nearest water was some 3 miles away [the North Platte River; further proof that "Scott's Spring" was ignored]. After much swearing and damning around by all hands some of the boys started off with buckets for some. . . . Our camp is right in one of the narrowest places of the pass & the walls rise up perpendicularly on either hand.

In 1938 the ninety-five-year-old Jackson showed the writer and others of the Oregon Trail Memorial Association the exact location of his 1866 campsite (now marked within the National Monument) as well as the point from which he made his famous pencil sketch of Mitchell Pass. The William H. Jackson Memorial Room of the Oregon Trail Museum now houses this and most other original Jackson sketches of Trail scenes and landmarks.

A. J. Miller, in 1837, and W. H. Jackson, in 1866, are the best known Scott's Bluffs artists. Other travelers whose published journals include sketches of the bluff and pass include George Simons, Joseph Stuart, David Leeper, Benjamin Ferris, Cornelius Conway, W. Wadsworth, T. S. Kenderdine, Richard Burton, and Alfred Lambourne. A remarkable sketch of "The Gorge, Scott's Bluff" was made by Gen. Grenville M. Dodge while on a survey for the Union Pacific Railroad in 1864 and appears in Perkins' *Trails, Rails and War.* Undoubtedly the earliest photograph of Scott's Bluffs was taken in 1858 by the Corps of Topographical Engineers, as reported by William Lee: "The photographers were out today taking the pass through High Bluff."

On his return trip in September, 1859, Lee reports: "At the bluff we found some very large fossilized bones of species of the Mastodon. They were dug out carefully and packed in the wagons. Also found some large fossilized turtles." The highly fossiliferous character of the Scott's Bluffs badlands was noted by Overton Johnson in 1843. In 1866 Julius Birge noted great quantities of fossil remains, which he later reported to Prof. Powell of the U.S. Geological Survey. In 1870 the first scientific expedition to explore the famed Scott's Bluffs fossil quarries was led by Dr. O. C. Marsh of Yale University (see below). Specimens from the Scott's Bluffs badlands are to be found today in the Oregon Trail Museum and in several natural history museums throughout the United States.

It would not be supposed that anyone toiling up the Platte valley would have either the time or inclination to climb Scott's Bluff. Before modern trails were constructed it was not unclimbable, but the sheer parapet walls did make it a real challenge. At least one Forty-Niner, Joseph Stuart did make it to the top. "Ascended a portion of this bluff at our noon halt," he said, "and had a fine view of the surrounding country. . . . Found the bleached skeleton of a buffalo upon the very top. We capsized an eagle's nest on a narrow shelf." In 1858 Kirk Anderson climbed "one of the highest points." "Far as the vision could strain itself," he continues, he could see the Platte, "resembling in the sunlight a silver thread stretched across the plain and dividing centre of the valley." In 1862 Burlingame, after several unsuccessful attempts, was able to find a route to the summit: "The scene that greeted my astonished vision defies description. Mighty, ragged, rocky crests, silent sentinels, kept watch and ward over the vast solitude." Witnessing the passage of a thunderstorm in the valley below, he wrote: "The scene there beheld was one seldom vouchsafed to mortals." In 1866 the main bluff was climbed by two people, each of whom left a detailed account of his breathless and hair-raising adventures. These remarkable stories, by Julius Birge, first to report to scientists about the fossils, and by drummer boy Alson B. Ostrander of the Eighteenth U.S. Infantry, are too involved to be related here; both got themselves trapped on the high cliffs and knife ridges and narrowly escaped with their lives.

One would expect that Mitchell Pass would make an ideal place for an Indian ambush. No documented account is to be found, but Grant Shumway reports two such events based on "old-timer" interviews. Pony Express rider Charles Cliff is supposed to have been attacked by Indians in Mitchell Gap, "and when he arrived at Scott's Bluff Station he had three bullets in his body and twenty-seven in his clothes." Then there is the story of "The Battle of Scottsbluff Mountain Pass" in 1866, on which occasion a combination emigrant and freighting outfit was allegedly attacked by Indians, which resulted in "thirty-eight dead."

Another tale of gunplay is offered by George Holliday in 1865.

He says that Scott's Bluffs was the hiding place for "Green River, the road agent," a stagecoach bandit who waylaid returning Californians and robbed them of their hard-earned gold dust. Holliday heard also that "not long before a paymaster was forced to hand out $60,000 of Uncle Sam's money to a band of Indians who spoke plain English" and who were led by this same young desperado. There might be some substance to this yarn, for in 1868 Mrs. Vogdes wrote in her journal: "Scotts Pass where we had such a time getting through this A.M. was some five years ago a scene of great terror. The overland mail coach party were all murdered, & not one man left to tell the story. They found only their bones."

As previously noted, the first paleontologists to study the ancient turtles and three-toed horses of this vicinity were led by Dr. Marsh in an 1870 expedition based at Cheyenne and escorted by soldiers from Fort D. A. Russell. Dr. Marsh's notes on this expedition reveal the bad reputation, deserved or not, which then lingered over the Mitchell Pass vicinity:

> On reaching the North Platte we followed the old California emigrant trail, in whose deep-worn ruts the grass is now growing. The column left us at an extensive fossil locality; and so absorbing is the practical study of paleontology that sunset surprised us still at work. Here we were found by some soldiers, who had been sent back to guide us through a labyrinth of shale and sandstone known as Scott's Bluff. It was pitch-dark when we began to pick our way through these narrow and rugged defiles. . . . Fitted by nature for ambush and surprise, this had been the Indians' favorite spot to fall upon the emigrants; and those dim bluffs, that towered so gray and ghostly silent, could tell many a tale of lurking savages, of desperate fights and massacres. Guards were posted to watch the borders of the river, and many an anxious glance was cast across into the Sioux reservation.

THE AMERICAN FUR COMPANY AT SCOTT'S BLUFFS

Before considering the history of Fort Mitchell military post (on the North Platte, about two miles northwest of Mitchell Pass), the evidence that this neighborhood was first occupied by a trading post of the American Fur Company, which was later coincident with a U.S. Mail and Pony Express Station, must be examined. As with so many other aspects of Scott's Bluffs, there is a mystery here, in this case concerning just who built exactly what, when, and where.

But the situation in outline seems to be that, when the American Fur Company sold Fort Laramie (Fort John) to the U.S. Government in 1849, they then moved to Scott's Bluffs, and in the process of trying to outwit the rival Robidouxs, they moved their trading post three different times. Location number one was at the bend of the North Platte fifty-five miles east of Fort Laramie, that is, at or near the later Fort Mitchell site. This was a makeshift post occupied for expediency late in 1849 but abandoned in the spring of 1850 for location number two, a more substantial post at a place called Helvas Canyon, about eight miles due south of Mitchell Pass (in Gering Valley). Location number three was back on the bank of the North Platte again, presumably near, but not necessarily coincident with, location number one, and this final move was made late in 1851. The second move was probably made to take advantage of the main travel route in 1850 up Gering Valley through Robidoux Pass, while the third move was intended to catch up with the new trend through Mitchell Pass that began in 1851. Of these three American Fur Company posts at Scott's Bluffs, the second one in Helvas Canyon is the only one that has been identified on the ground; this was the "Fort John, Scott's Bluffs" which is the principal one referred to in fur trade correspondence.

There is no known basis for the undocumented assertion by Grant Shumway in his *History of Western Nebraska* that the post on the river bank (either No. 1 or No. 3) was called Fontenelle's Post. There was a Fort Mitchell trading post at the mouth of the Niobrara River in northeastern Nebraska, which has also caused some confusion.

Aside from the meager evidence of travelers' journals, some insight into the operation of the American Fur Company in the Scott's Bluffs area is to be found in contemporary newspapers, as well as correspondence preserved at the Missouri Historical Society and the Bancroft Library, principally involving Andrew S. Drips at the Platte River posts, Honore Picotte and Alexander Culbertson of the Upper Missouri outfit at Fort Pierre on the Missouri River, and Pierre Chouteau, Jr., at St. Louis. First, it must be clarified that the correct legal name of the American Fur Company at this period was Pierre Chouteau, Jr. & Company. Second, the correct legal name for the original trading post at Fort Laramie was Fort John, and the name Fort John was transferred to the new trading post at Scott's Bluffs.

In August, 1848, Andrew Drips was named manager of the first Fort John on the Laramie. In his absence from the post, Bruce Husband acted for him in June, 1849, when the U.S. Army purchased adobe-walled Fort John for $4,000. Wanting to take advantage of the plentiful water and timber there, the company decided to move to Scott's Bluffs, first wintering "at the bend of the North Platte." Since the Robidouxs were entrenched in the pass then in use by the emigration, the company decided to set up its 1850 post in the valley further east, which theoretically would enable them to get first chance at the emigrant trade. The man primarily identified with the new "Fort John, Scott's Bluffs" with Major Andrew S. Drips (sometimes spelled Dripps).

The luckless Hiram Scott and the enigmatic Robidouxs are the only ones who have a greater claim to identification with the famous bluffs than the enterprising Drips. Born in Pennsylvania in 1789, he became an employee of the Missouri Fur Company with Joshua Pilcher in 1820; in 1822 he was in charge of transporting furs down the Missouri. In 1824 he was with the American Fur Company at Bellevue, where he married an Oto woman who bore him four children. He commanded fur brigades in the Rocky Mountains, later guiding missionaries and emigrant trains over the Oregon Trail. In 1842 President Tyler appointed him Indian Agent for all the tribes of the Upper Missouri, including those camped along the Platte and congregated at Fort Laramie; he is credited with a firm hand in suppressing the odious whiskey trade. He once more became associated with the American Fur Company (Pierre Chouteau, Jr.) in 1848 and conducted the business of the trade until 1860. In that year he died at Westport, Missouri, where he had acquired property as early as 1838. He is eulogized in the Westport *Border Star* of September 8, 1860, as a man of "probity of character and noble qualities of heart."

One of his daughters, Mrs. William Mulkey, who died in Kansas City in 1904, was born at the Pierre's Hole rendezvous of 1832 on the day of the famous battle there between trappers and Blackfeet Indians. Another daughter was married to F. M. Barnes, a licensed Indian trader at Oto Agency under Maj. A. L. Green. Maj. Green's son, the late T. L. Green of Scottsbluff, did the primary research on Andrew Drips and discovered the site of the second Fort John in Helvas Canyon. No systematic digging has been undertaken, but the site is plainly identified by charcoal, burnt wood, the usual trade goods and hardware fused by fire, and the outlines of an uneven six-sided structure roughly 100 feet across. The evidence of the post's destruction by fire is compatible with the hearsay testimony of earliest residents "that the Indians got drunk and burned it down." Green's collection of gun parts, lead bars, buttons, implements, trade goods (bells, beads, rings, etc.), clay pipes, and prized Roman Catholic medallions and crucifixes has been donated to the Oregon Trail Museum.

In 1850 evidence of the company post is given by at least two westering emigrants. On June 22 James Bennett wrote: "Today at 9 O'clock we arrived at Scotts Bluffs. The road leaves the river at this point and goes by a circuitous route for 30 miles. We met an Indian Trader here who pointed out to us an excellent spring, 7 or 8 miles ahead. He also stated that there was a regularly established trading post 3 miles to our left, where we could see a herd of cattle grazing." Similarly, on June 19 Seth Lewelling "took a left hand cutoff, travelled without water, over butiful Prairie with high peaks rising on each side of the Road. Thence to Dribbs trading post. . . . There are three good log cabbins at this post & several Indian tents." His testimony clearly distinguishes between the rival Drips and Robidoux outfits, for he continues, "thence to Rubadoes trading post. Here is a blacksmith shop & Several cabbins besides a number of Indian tents & a fine spring." He gives the distance between "Dribbs and Rubadoes" as eight miles.

That the 1850 season at Helvas Canyon was reasonably successful is indicated in Culbertson's letter of August 31 to the effect that "Maj. Drips also done well for us on the Platte having made about $3500. clear (after taking inventory) in fine horses & Gold." The general plan of operation was the shipment of goods by steamer some 1,200 miles from St. Louis to Fort Pierre (in central South Dakota), then their transportation some 500 miles overland to Scott's Bluffs. In retrospect this seems like an extremely roundabout way of transporting merchandise, but apparently the much lower cost of steamboating made it feasible; furthermore, Fort Pierre was the general distribution point for goods throughout the Northwest.

To judge from evidence left by emigrants themselves, Fort John was little visited by them in comparison with the Robidoux establishment. Since the location required a considerable detour from the emigrant road, in contrast to Robidoux's choice location, and emigrant references are scarce, it is probable that trade with them was not considered a primary objective. Emigrants needed services such as blacksmithing, and they were especially anxious to purchase corn for their stock and groceries to augment their dwindling provisions; in exchange for these items, lacking cash, they would trade in their lame stock and defective wagons, which Drips could restore or repair to advantage. The emigrants had little use for buffalo robes and salted tongues, offered at $4 each and 50¢ respectively. Most of the items stocked by the trader were Indian goods, to judge from inventories and archeological remains, and the main objective was the accumulation of furs for shipment by caravan to Kansas or Westport Landing. An 1851 inventory of goods includes the following items suggestive of the character of the trade:

white blankets	gun flints
scarlet ditto	hawk bells
blue ditto	spanish saddle
green ditto	pipes
blue cloth	red cock feather
scarlet ditto	tobacco
cotton rugs	chewing tobacco
blue drilling	spanish tobacco
sheeting	syrup
bed tick	salt
plaid linsey	coffee
calico shirts	bacon
blanket coat	molasses
vests	pilot bread
fur seal caps	Navy bread
linen thread	clarified sugar
Henry rifles	brandy
brass kettles	rhubarb
hoop iron	laudanum
assorted butcher knives	calomel
caps	peppermint
fry pans	opium
gorgets	shaving soap
hair pipe wampum	fish hooks
sleigh bells	axe handles
gun tubes	scythes

No emigrants of record speak of the Drips outfit in 1851, but the correspondence indicates continued occupancy of the fort, though with some apprehension about prospects for trade, partly from a lull in the migration, partly from aggressive competition by Robidoux and Bordeaux. However, Drips had several visitors in connection with the Horse Creek Treaty Council held west of Scott's Bluffs in September. He had as his guests two of the commissioners, David D. Mitchell and Father DeSmet (quoted above in connection with Robidoux). En route to the council with the U.S. Dragoons, Sergeant Lowe noted: "Having crossed to the east side of Scotts Bluffs . . . we turned south and camped near a trading post belonging to Major Dripps, who was or had been an Indian agent." Also visiting at this time was Prince Paul Wilhelm of Wurttemberg:

> I arrived at Scott's Bluffs on October 1. Nearby is Fort John, one of the trading posts of the American Fur Company. Here I was most cordially welcomed by my old friend, Major Tripp, who is in sole charge of this important establishment. I was also overjoyed at meeting again my beloved and reverend old friend, the missionary Pere de Smet.
>
> There were a great number of leather tents close by, along a little brook that issues from a gorge some distance back from the establishment. These sheltered a body of Ogalalas, a tribe related to the Sioux nation. . . .
>
> On October 3 we left the hospitable roof of Major Tripp and travelled up the La Platte along the California route. The valley is honey-combed with prairie-dog holes.

T. L. Green discovered Pierre D. Papin's grave at Fort John. This was apparently the same Papin, or Pappan, whose relatives ran the ferry at Unionville on the Kansas River and who was frequently encountered by emigrants (Gelwicks, Hale) on the trail hauling buffalo hides from Fort Laramie to market. The exact date and circumstances of his death are not revealed.

A letter of December 4, 1851, from Fort Pierre to Pierre Chouteau, Jr. & Company reveals that Maj. Drips "was engaged in moving his Fort, and calculated to be in comfortable quarters before the cold weather." The reasons for the move could only have been a decline in trade and hopes to improve it in a handier location. Conclusive documentary evidence that Drips moved his post to the Fort Mitchell neighborhood during the winter of 1851–1852 is lacking, but the correspondence indicates that he did move *some-*

where else, and no other location quite fits the bill. It may be that he started construction at the new site in late autumn of 1851 but did not close out the old Fort John site until May, 1852, at which time he advised Picotte that his winter trade "is now at a close. I have 380 pack Buffalo Robes . . . 500 Buffalo tongues . . . castorum . . . Wolf skins, etc. I will start the wagons in a few days for the states." Two weeks later Stephen Gage reported he met "10 teams from Scotts Bluffs with buffalo skins." Having shipped off his hides, Drips would now be free to move to new quarters.

At least two emigrant journals of the 1852 season describe a new trading post setup west of Mitchell Pass. Jay Green went through the gap, "which is very windy and difficult," got a supply of "seeder wood" from the slopes, and then, "after passing the bluffs two miles I find a trading post." Wm. Hampton stopped at the new Robidoux post ten miles *east* of Scott's Bluffs [near Melbeta] to have blacksmithing done, then on June 19 he went through "some deep ravines, steep banks, very long hill to descend to get to the bottom again. Here are some of the highest rocks I have ever seen. . . . splendid view of Laramie Peak. . . . There is a U.S. Mail Station and a blacksmith shop here, also some French traders and Indians. . . . Campt near the river." This station handled mail on contract for the overland service inaugurated in 1850 between Independence and Salt Lake City. It is not clear if mail contractor Samuel H. Woodson rented quarters from the American Fur Company or actually built a separate station nearby.

In 1853 Abraham Hite "passed through Scotts Bluffs in the evening in sight of another smithshop, and there I got two screws made and camped." Bradway describes the setup this year as "three or four shanties" in a setting of twenty-five Indian lodges. He also mentions "a small shanty at the entrance of the bluff and a bridge," which sounds like an effort to collect toll for the privilege of going through Mitchell Pass. Bradway says his wagons didn't use the bridge, and this collection must have failed, for we find no further reference to it.

Also in 1853, Rebecca Ketcham found Capt. Drips "8 miles the other side of Laramie River," which would be the Ward and Guerrier post near Sand Point, or Register Cliff; presumably he was only visiting there. On this occasion her leader, the missionary Mr. Gray, recalled Drips' piloting of his train in 1838. She adds, "He is quite a pleasant spoken man. . . . He spends his summers on the prairies and mountains and his winters in some of the villages on the border; he has done so for over 30 years. . . . Mr. Gray presumes he is worth $100,000." After 1852 Drips seems to have been associated with various company enterprises in the Fort Laramie neighborhood, apparently not confining himself to the third Scott's Bluffs post. An article in the Kansas City *Journal of Commerce* mentions his "trading post near Fort Laramie" in 1858, which might be the "Maj. Dripps' trading house 19 miles below [Fort] Laramie [in the vicinity of Torrington]" referred to by Lowe in 1857. His last trip, to Fort Laramie from Westport, occurred in 1860 just before his death.

After 1853 and prior to 1860, we have several clear-cut references to the trading post and mail station on the west side of Scott's Bluffs, and the earliest of these gives important evidence of ownership. In 1856 J. R. Brown camped here "at an old Frenchman, Jean Baitan's [?] trading post. It is now in ruins, the Indians having driven him away." More significant is an entry under "Remarks" in the 1857 odometer record of the advance engineering party for the survey of a Pacific wagon road under William Magraw:

> Road . . . passes through to Scotts Bluffs in gap. . . . Road was bad, but was improved after passing gap. . . . Road bears to river on a gradual descent. . . . Sand stone and Cedar in bluffs. Camp left of Road ¾ miles from River. . . . grass poor and thin, water good, cottonwood on islands in River and fuel in old houses, once mail station and trading post of the American Fur Co.

No other observers speak of this place as if it were abandoned, but we know there was a disruption in the contract overland mail service at this time partly because of government difficulties with Brigham Young, leading to the U.S. Army expedition to Utah. That year the mail contract with the Mormon Hiram Kimball was cancelled. In 1858 mail service was revived and Wm. Lee reports: "Pass a mail station shortly after leaving the bluff and camped within a half mile of it." Marcy's guide, based on observations of this same period, notes: "In seven miles the road passes through Scott's Bluffs. . . . The road then descends the mountain, at the foot of which is the Platte and a mail station." In 1859 Allen's *Guidebook* has "U.S. Mail Station No. 23 a distance of three miles west of the point where the road runs between two bluffs [Mitchell Pass]." At this time the station would have been operated by mail contractor John M. Hockaday. Finally, in 1859 emigrant J. A. Wilkinson writes, "Beyond the bluffs we come to an Indian village on the Platte and a trading post kept by an old Frenchman with a squaw for a wife." Thus, it seems clear that, despite the apparent disruption in 1856–1857, this place was active in 1858–1859, combining the functions of trading post and mail station right up to the more dramatic period of stagecoach and Pony Express.

THE PONY EXPRESS ROUTE UP THE NORTH PLATTE

Chapter VIII identified Pony Express and stage stations as far as Julesburg. Since the famed "Pony" went through Mitchell Pass, it is logical here to complete a rundown of Pony Express stations from Julesburg on the South Platte across the prairie to the North Platte at Court House Rock, then westward past Chimney Rock and Scott's Bluffs into Wyoming.

Nine Mile Station: Two miles southeast of Chappell, Nebraska.

Pole Creek Station No. 2: Site unidentified, vicinity of Lodgepole, Nebraska. The route was along Lodgepole Creek, future route of the Union Pacific Railroad into Cheyenne.

Pole Creek Station No. 3: On the north side of Lodgepole Creek, on the old St. George cattle ranch three and one-half miles east of Sidney. Old maps identify this as the stage ranch of Rouliette and Pringle, a well-fortified dugout of sod and logs. This is where the route crossed to the north side of the Lodgepole. Here the Pony Express, following the Fort Laramie Road from Julesburg, turned north. Later a new stage road would head due west toward future Cheyenne and to a junction with the stage road out of Denver near Elk Mountain. Richard Burton's description of the station here would characterize most such specimens:

> The hovel fronting the creek was built like an Irish shanty, or a Beloch hut, against a hill side, to save one wall, and it presented a fresh phase of squalor and wretchedness. The mud walls were partly papered with 'Harper's Magazine,' 'Frank Leslie,' and the 'New York Illustrated News;' the ceiling was a fine festoon-work of soot, and the floor was much like the ground outside, only not nearly so clean. In a corner stood the usual bunk, a mass of mingled rags and buffalo robes; the centre of the room was occupied by a ricketty table, and boxes, turned up on their sides, acted as chairs. The unescapable stove

was there, filling the interior with the aroma of meat. As usual, the materials for ablution, a dipper or cup, a dingy tin skillet of scanty size, a bit of coarse gritty soap, and a public towel like a rag of gunny bag, were deposited upon a ricketty settle outside.

Government Well: Within the present Sioux Ordnance Depot area, it is about three miles south and one mile west of Gurley on U.S. 385. Dennis Ferrell later established a ranch in this vicinity.

Mud Springs Station: About twelve miles southeast of Bridgeport in Morrill County, it is now within a one-acre state park. This was a home station. Surface indications conform to the Collins plan of the fortification in 1864. The 1865 Battle of Mud Springs is mentioned below. There were alternate routes from Mud Springs to the North Platte. The Pony Express riders used the left fork to Pumpkinseed Crossing, going southwest of Court House Rock. The main trail used by covered wagons and later stagecoaches passed the landmark to the north.

Court House Rock Station: Remains have been identified five miles south and one mile west of Bridgeport.

Chimney Rock Station: The station was somewhere between the landmark and the river but remains unidentified. See discussion in Chapter XII.

Ficklin's Springs Station: Contrary to Shumway's assertion, this was not the Scott's Bluff Station, but was the first station *east* of Scott's Bluff. This was named for Benjamin F. Ficklin, general superintendent of Pony Express field operations. The site, with visible surface remains, is marked on State Highway 92 one mile west of Melbeta in Scotts Bluff County. In 1871, according to Shumway, the sod structure was used by Mark Coad for his cattle ranch headquarters. Foundation stones are still in evidence.

Scott's Bluffs Station: When men of the Eleventh Ohio Cavalry from Fort Laramie built Fort Mitchell in 1864, they were not aware, apparently, that in this immediate neighborhood there had been an American Fur Company trading post and a contract mail station. At least to judge from Ware's account it looked like a virgin site; but the old structures, or their leveled remains, could not have been far distant, because they were very much erect and in use just a few years before, in 1859. Presumably the men responsible for providing Pony Express stations made arrangements with the American Fur Company, or the mail contractor, or "the old Frenchman," or somebody, to utilize the old buildings. It is also assumed that the Scott's Bluffs station was a home station, being roughly halfway between Mud Springs and Fort Laramie, both believed to be home stations also (the usual distance between such stations being forty-five or fifty miles).

Horse Creek Station: This was on the west bank of Horse Creek about two miles northeast of Lyman, and it possibly coincides with Robidoux's later trading post. Again Richard Burton provides a peek into the past:

> Presently we dashed over the Little Kiowa Creek, forded the Horse Creek, and, enveloped in a cloud of villainous mosquitoes, entered at 8:30 P.M. the station in which we were to pass the night. It was tenanted by one Reynal, a French creole—the son of an old soldier of the Grand Armee, who had settled at St. Louis—a companionable man, but an extortionate; he charged us a florin for every "drink" of his well-watered whiskey. The house boasted of the usual squaw, a wrinkled old dame, who at once began to prepare the supper. . . . These hard-working but sorely ill-favoured beings, are accused of various horrors in cookery. . . .
>
> Our breakfast was prepared in the usual prairie style. First the coffee—three parts burnt beans—was placed on the stove to simmer until every noxious principle was duly extracted from it. Then the rusty bacon, cut into thick slices, was thrown into the fry-pan. Thirdly, antelope steak, cut off a corpse suspended for the benefit of flies.

Cold Springs Station: Believed to be about two miles southeast of Torrington.

Verdling's Ranch Station: This was probably the old Bordeaux Trading Post near the Grattan Massacre site. It is eight miles from Fort Laramie or about two miles west of Lingle.

Fort Laramie Station: The military post itself, with its post office in the sutler's store, was not a station. As in the case of Fort Kearny, the Pony Express and stage station which served Fort Laramie was at an undetermined point west thereof. Richard Burton indicates that, as a mail passenger in 1860, he was granted "a few minutes of grumbling delay" to pause at the fort for supplies and then was "hurried on to some distant wretched ranch."

FORT MITCHELL, SCOTT'S BLUFFS, NEBRASKA TERRITORY

In the mid-sixties Fort Mitchell of Scott's Bluffs was an exciting place, complete with clashing soldiers and Indians, desperate characters, frontier notables, and officers' charming wives. A fortified adobe stockade with the majestic bluffs in the background, it would have delighted the heart of a television script writer. Today all trace of the fort has vanished under the plow; there are no reminders of its fleeting glory except granite markers and a few obscure documents, books, and museum objects.

Fort Mitchell was located on the right bank (Oregon Trail side) of the North Platte River, on an elevation just west of the present highway bridge over the North Platte three miles west of the city of Scottsbluff. This was at the foot of the long slope from Mitchell Pass. It was short-lived (1864–1867) and would not compare in importance with Fort Kearny, Fort Laramie, or Fort McPherson, but it was a classic example of a frontier military outpost and witnessed all manner of alarms, excursions, and sinister events.

Fort Mitchell cannot be understood without reference to the overland communications picture following the Pony Express. After 1862 there was only intermittent stagecoach service up the North Platte, the main line having been diverted from Julesburg westward up Lodgepole Creek (the future Union Pacific line), but there was a continuing, vital need to protect telegraph lines and overland mail service which went through Scott's Bluffs, Fort Laramie, and South Pass to California. When the Sioux and Cheyenne went on the warpath in 1864, Fort Mitchell was born.

In 1864 the Army District of Nebraska (under Gen. Samuel R. Curtis of the Department of Kansas, Fort Leavenworth) was commanded by Gen. Robert B. Mitchell, a Kansan who had distinguished himself in the Civil War, described by Capt. Eugene Ware as a tall, handsome man with a full, dark brown, curly beard and mustache and a dignified bearing. Early in 1864 Gen. Mitchell held a series of councils with the Sioux at Fort Cottonwood on the Platte, but could get no promise of peace. He then proceeded up the Platte River Road with 160 men of the Seventh Iowa Cavalry, reaching Fort Laramie on July 27. This was garrisoned by the Eleventh Ohio Volunteer Regiment. Realizing that the Platte River Road was gravely threatened, he determined to set up new military posts at Julesburg, Mud Springs, Ficklin's Springs, and Scott's Bluffs. Capt. J. S. Shuman of the Eleventh Ohio was ordered to build the fort at the bluffs. On September 1, 1864, Ware left Fort Laramie with Gen. Mitchell en route to Julesburg. He writes:

On our road down we passed Camp Shuman. The men were busy building solid quarters with adobe trimmings on the North Platte River bank, south side, three miles west of the gap at Scott's Bluffs. Captain Shuman had just received a box marked "Saint Croix Rum Punch" and he opened a bottle in our honor. He introduced us to his first Lieutenant named Ellsworth, and showed us the outline of the proposed walls which they were hurrying to build before cold weather set in.

When Ware revisited Camp Shuman on October 30, its name had been changed to Camp Mitchell, but in 1865 it appears in official correspondence as Fort Mitchell. During its brief career it was under the general direction of a succession of post commanders at Fort Laramie, most conspicuously Col. William O. Collins of the Eleventh Ohio Volunteer Regiment. Capt. Shuman was in command until August, 1865; thereafter the succession of officers in charge for significant periods were Lt. William Ellsworth, Capt. W. R. Beymer, and Capt. Robert P. Hughes. Beginning in September, 1865, all of Nebraska and Wyoming fell under the new Department of the Platte, with headquarters in Omaha. Although Fort Mitchell correspondence places it variously in Dakota and Idaho territories (along with its parent, Fort Laramie), it was actually always within Nebraska Territory.

Most of the military action around Fort Mitchell occurred in 1865. For patroling his entire district, Col. Collins had not more than 500 men, thinly scattered at stations for several hundred miles up and down the Platte. Fort Mitchell was manned originally by Co. H, Eleventh Ohio, which never exceeded a component of sixty men. The nature of the trouble then brewing appears in a report from Gen. Mitchell to Gen. Curtis, written from Fort Kearny on August 15, 1864: "I find the Indians at war with us the entire District . . . from South Pass to the Blue, a distance of 800 miles or more, and have laid waste the country . . . and murdered men, women and children." A brief truce was shattered on November 29, when hundreds of Cheyenne and Arapaho were massacred at Sand Creek, Colorado, by Volunteers under Col. Chivington. Enraged, a large band of Cheyenne and Sioux in January, 1865, converged on Julesburg and sacked it. When they advanced on Mud Springs in early February, word was telegraphed to Fort Laramie, 105 miles west. Col. Collins ordered Lt. Ellsworth to proceed there with the Fort Mitchell company. Marching all night, he reached Mud Springs at daybreak with thirty-six men. Col.

Collins, with 120 men, traveled that same night from Fort Laramie to Fort Mitchell, where he was compelled to leave part of his men who were suffering from frostbite, and the next day he advanced to Mud Springs. The Indians attacked on February 5. Though they had the advantage of overwhelming numbers, they were successfully repulsed by skillful sharpshooting. The troops trailed the Indians up the Platte, skirmishing with them again at Rush Creek near Chimney Rock, but the Indians finally fled north across the river with their Julesburg loot and disappeared. The regimental report on "the celebrated Indian fights at Mud Springs and Rush Creek" indicates that 150 men under Collins fought 1,500 to 2,000 of the Indian warriors. "Since that time," the report continues, "this Company has carried the Mail from Julesburg to Laramie. This has been heavy and laborious duty, yet they have never flinched but have had the Mail through in good time. Beside this the company has built one Mail Station, near the noted Land Mark Chimney Rock, besides repairing the one at Mud Springs."

Fort Mitchell figures in another Indian battle of 1865, described by George Bird Grinnell, John J. Pattison, and official reports by Capt. Wilcox and Col. Moonlight in the annual report of the U.S. Secretary of War for 1865. About 1,500 Sioux (185 lodges) who had remained friendly were encamped at Fort Laramie. With exceedingly poor judgment, the army decided to send them to Fort Kearny to remove them from hostile influences, and apparently women and children were roughly handled. On June 11 the Indians were headed east with an armed escort of 135 enlisted men under Capt. W. D. Fouts of the Seventh Iowa Cavalry and four other officers. The cavalcade proceeded slowly, with suspicious smoke signals appearing on the north side of the Platte. On the morning of June 14, after leaving the encampment at Horse Creek, the Indians made a concerted break for the north side of the river, killing Capt. Fouts. In the subsequent fighting, directed by Capt. Wilcox, three enlisted men were killed and four wounded. Capt. Shuman arrived from Fort Mitchell with reinforcements, but was too late to take up the pursuit of the Indians, who had now safely crossed the river. Col. Moonlight attempted to track down the Indians from Fort Laramie; he succeeded only in having his horses stolen.

Emigrant H. D. Barton, bound for Idaho, says that he "passed Scott's Bluff" right after the battle and then "came to where the soldiers had a fight with the Indians. . . . found some ponies of which one had two arrows in its back. . . . some saddles were also picked up." In August enlisted man Jake Pennock passed "the spot where Capt. Folks and his men were attacked . . . and killed by Indians. . . . Several dead bodies of Indians found at Horse Creek by our men." According to the official report by Wilcox, the three soldier victims were buried at the battlefield; Capt. Fouts was buried at the Fort Mitchell cemetery and later reinterred at Fort McPherson.

Geo. Holliday of the West Virginia Volunteers trooped past Fort Mitchell later in the year: "We heard much of this post and the 11th Ohio boys who held the fort. Nestled away down in a horseshoe curve of the North Platte, we can see the smoke coming up from a half-dozen chimneys, and see the long rows of port holes in the sides of the low dismal walls." He said a rumor was current that the masked Mitchell Pass bandits aforementioned were actually some of the Fort Mitchell garrison seeking to relieve their boredom and make some extra money. Holliday protested the libel: "Notwithstanding the tales we had heard of how these boys plundered everybody who passed . . . we left next morning with a good opinion of them, and feeling assured that they had been lied upon."

There were several 1866 visitors. Bullwhacker Thomas Creigh noted that the sod fort was "the best fort we have yet passed." At the post sutler's he had a chance to read the Chicago *Tribune* and was informed that a party had left Fort Laramie to prospect for gold in the Black Hills (eight years before its official "discovery" in 1874). When the Eighteenth U.S. Regiment of Infantry marched through here under Col. Carrington, Capt. Hughes was detached to command here. Margaret Carrington describes the post:

> After the gorge is passed, we find Fort Mitchell. This is a sub-post of Fort Laramie of peculiar style and compactness. The walls of the quarters are also the outlines of the fort itself, and the four sides of the rectangle are respectively the quarters of officers, soldiers and horses, and the warehouse of supplies. Windows open into the little court or parade-ground; and bed-rooms, as well as other apartments, are loop-holed for defense.

Later in the year Frances Carrington (then Mrs.. Grummond) thought Fort Mitchell "peculiar and compact, unlike any fort I have ever seen." Her party enjoyed the hospitality of Capt. Hughes, as did Col. Carrington's family when they returned eastward in

1867. After his clamber to the summit of the bluffs and the discovery of fossils, Julius Birge traveled on, giving Fort Mitchell only a passing glance, but it was noted with keen interest by John Bratt, who was bullwhacking for a freighting outfit:

> We finally wended our way, through a crooked, narrow pass, through Scotts Bluff. Two miles west, of these bluffs, standing on the south bank of the North Platte River, was Fort Mitchell, a two-company adobe post. Directly south of this, across the overland trail, stood the Mitchell Road ranch and stage station kept at this time by John Sibson.

Bratt's destination was Fort Phil Kearny on the Bozeman Trail. He returned from there to Fort Mitchell late in December. He was instructed by his employers to remain and assist Sibson in the operation of the road ranch. He remained until September, 1867, and his adventures here, which he relates in some detail in his autobiography, *Trails of Yesterday,* provides exciting glimpses of life at the Fort Mitchell road ranch:

> Jack Gibson kept a Sioux squaw . . . to do the cooking, with which . . . I often helped, especially when the stage coaches came in filled with passengers. . . . The road ranch was large, built of cedar logs, and had seven fair-sized rooms besides the store. It had dirt floors and roof. It had a large corral built of cedar logs. . . . We milked a number of cows. . . . There were also a good-sized bunch of ponies and some work cattle and horses. These were kept for trading purposes.
>
> There were several tepees pitched outside but near the corrals. . . . The fort across the road was garrisoned by two companies of the 8th Infantry under Captain Hughes. One company had been mounted. His garrison was kept busy protecting the stage coaches, road ranches between Fort Laramie and Pole Creek . . . freight and emigrant trains, and keeping up the overland telegraph line. . . .
>
> The store carried the usual stock of a ranch—clothing, provisions, including canned goods, and plenty of whiskey . . . buffalo robes, elk and deer skins, harness, saddles, guns, revolvers. . . .
>
> The beds, made on the dirt floors, consisted of buffalo, elk and bear skins, with whatever could be found for a pillow. . . .
>
> I remember Brigham Young's sharing my bed for two nights. He was on his way to Salt Lake by stage coach and awaited the arrival of a Mormon train. . . .
>
> When the telegraph lines were not working . . . and stage coaches were not making their usual trips, I was often called upon to carry dispatches. . . . My trip to Fort Laramie . . . was usually made in

eight or nine hours, either day or night, the latter being preferable. . . . On the night Mr. Gilman and Mr. Kountz lost their 28 four-mule teams while camped within a quarter of a mile of our ranch . . . the stage coach coming from Laramie or Reynold's stage station was chased the last five miles of the road up to the door of the ranch by a large bunch of Indians, said to be Big Mouth's band of Sioux. One dead passenger was in this coach.

It is not known exactly how long Fort Mitchell remained in business after the Carringtons' return visit of February, 1867. It was apparently still operating in the summer of 1867 when Dr. Ferdinand V. Hayden of the U.S. Geological Survey went through on an exploring tour. We only know for certain that it was deserted in July, 1868, when Mrs. Vogdes went by with her officer husband, reporting to Fort Laramie. She writes: "We are now encamped on the North Platte at the foot of Scotts Bluff, near Ft. Mitchell, a dreary, deserted old Post that only a few months before had been garrisoned by one company. . . . a dreadful looking place, & I am thankful that it has been abandoned for we might have been sent out there, some time."

Three contemporary sketches of old Fort Mitchell survive. These are a rather crude drawing by bugler C. Moellman, Co. G, Eleventh Ohio, reproduced in Hebard and Brininstool's *Bozeman Trail*; the sketch by William H. Jackson, also made on his 1866 trip and now preserved at Scotts Bluff National Monument; and a published sketch of "Fort Mitchell—Scott's Bluff" by Nichols, published in F. V. Hayden's *Preliminary Report of the U.S. Geological Survey of Wyoming*. All show a rectangular adobe fort, portholed for defense with a sentinel tower at one corner, the log corral next to the river, and the trail from the Pass. The Nichols sketch also shows the road ranch and telegraph line. The archeological remains, which have now disappeared in a plowed field, were observed and measured in 1910 by Robert Harvey. Col. Collins' ground plan of this post, showing overall dimensions of 100 x 180 feet, survives in the collections of Colorado State University, Fort Collins, Colorado.

XV

Fort Laramie and the Forty-Niners

ONE OF THE MOST historic spots in the trans-Mississippi West lies on the tongue of land formed by the junction of the Laramie and North Platte rivers in eastern Wyoming. Here, at Fort Laramie National Historic Site, are the impressive remains of a military post which, for over forty years, represented the might of the United States Government on the Great Plains frontier. The post was born in 1849, the year of the epic gold rush to California, within the walls of an old adobe stockade, the event being witnessed by a motley horde of emigrants, Indians, and squaw men. Fort Laramie's star ascended amid the exciting and violent scenes of the migrations, the Mormon Rebellion, and the Sioux-Cheyenne wars, declined with the advent of the Union Pacific Railroad, the Black Hills stage line, and the open-range cattle industry, and died tranquilly when the first wave of homesteaders reached Wyoming.

Laramie Fork was historic ground long before soldiers were stationed there. Before the Fort Laramie military post, there were the trading posts of Fort John, Fort Platte, and Fort William. Before these, even, were many camps, trading sessions, and councils. The very name of "Laramie" harks back to a tradition of uncertain date that an early Canadian trapper, one Jacques LaRamee, was killed by Indians and his body thrown in this stream. The natural attractions of Laramie Fork were noted as early as 1812 by Robert Stuart: "Tuesday, 22nd—Soon after leaving Camp the Country opened greatly to [the] Eastward, and a well wooded stream appar-

480

ently of considerable magnitude came in from the South West."
They were noted also by Warren A. Ferris, fur trapper with the
American Fur Company in 1830: " We crossed the Platte in bull-
hide canoes, on the second of June, and encamped a short distance
above the mouth of Laramie's Fork, at the foot of the Black Hills."

Laramie Fork drained a rich trapping territory, and many
licenses were issued "to trade at Laremais' Point." Zenas Leonard's
journal of 1832 paints a graphic picture of a trapper's conclave here,
preliminary to a general movement toward the Pierre's Hole
rendezvous in the mountains, while Charles Larpenteur in 1833
records another encampment: "On approaching La Ramie's River
we discovered three large buffaloes lying dead close together. . . .
the animals had been killed by lightning during a storm we had the
previous day. . . . we were ordered to dismount and go to work
making a boat out of the hides of the buffalo . . . and the party
with all the goods were crossed over by sunset. . . . On the arrival of
the trappers and hunters a big drunken spree took place."

THE TRADING POSTS ON THE LARAMIE

The strategic and commercial advantages of the location on
Laramie's Fork, at the intersection of the Great Platte route to the
mountains and the Trappers Trail south to Taos, were at once
apparent to William Sublette and Robert Campbell in 1834, when
they paused here en route to the trappers' rendezvous at Ham's
Fork of the Green River to launch the construction of stockaded
Fort William. The event is simply recorded by William Anderson:

> [May] 31st.—This evening we arrived at the mouth of Laramie's
> Fork, where Capt. (William L.) Sublette intends to erect a trader's
> fort.
> June 1st 1834—This day laid the foundation log of a fort, on
> Laramee's Fork. A friendly dispute arose . . . as to the name. . . .
> William Patton offered a compromise which was accepted, and the foam
> flew, in honor of Fort William, which contained the triad prenames
> of clerk, leader and friend. Leaving Patton and fourteen men to
> finish the job we started upwards.

In 1835 the enterprising partners sold their interest in Fort William
to James Bridger, Thomas Fitzpatrick, and others, who in turn
released it to the western department of the American Fur Company
(after 1838, Pierre Chouteau, Jr., & Company).

In July, 1835, Samuel Parker, one of the first missionaries up the Trail, arrived in the company of fur traders at "the fort of the Black Hills." He writes: "At this place the caravan halted, and according to immemorial usage, the men are allowed a 'day of indulgence,' as it is called, in which they drink ardent spirits as much as they please, and conduct as they choose. Not unfrequently, the day terminates with a catastrophe of some kind. . . . Today one of the company shot another." At this time a horde of Oglala Sioux came into the fort to trade. Parker and his aide, Marcus Whitman, met in council with the chiefs and then were treated to a buffalo dance. Continues Parker, "I cannot say I was much amused to see how well they imitate brute beasts, while ignorant of God and salvation. . . . what will become of their immortal spirits?"

In 1836 the wives of Marcus Whitman and Rev. H. H. Spalding, the first white women to follow the Oregon Trail, accepted the meager hospitality of the fort. Particularly noteworthy were the chairs with buffalo skin bottoms, a welcome contrast to the inflexible saddles and wagon-boxes.

The only known pictures of Fort William were made in 1837 by A. J. Miller, an artist in the entourage of Sir William Drummond Stewart. Here, in Miller's own notes, is the traditional log post,

> of a quadrangular form, with block houses at diagonal corners. . . . over the front entrance is a large block house in which is placed a cannon. . . . The Indians encamp in great numbers here 3 or 4 times a year, bringing peltries to be exchanged for dry goods, tobacco, beads and alcohol.
>
> The Indians have a mortal horror of the "big gun" which rests in the block house, as they have had experience of its prowess and witnessed the havoc produced by its loud "talk." They conceive it to be only asleep and have a wholesome dread of its being waked up.

In 1840 the illustrious Father DeSmet paused at this "Fort la Ramee," where he found some forty lodges of the Cheyenne, "polite, cleanly and decent in their manners. . . . The head chiefs of this village invited me to feast, and put me through all the ceremonies of the calumet."

In the fall of that year or the spring of the following, a rival establishment appeared on the nearby banks of the North Platte. This was adobe-walled Fort Platte, built by Lancaster P. Lupton, veteran of the South Platte trade, and taken over in 1842 by Sybille, Adams and Company. This development, coupled with the rotting condition of Fort William, prompted the Chouteau interests to build a new adobe fort in 1841, officially christened Fort John (after John B. Sarpy) but more commonly called Fort Laramie. The exact site of adobe Fort John, on the plateau at the bend of the Laramie River, adjoining the later parade ground, is known from early military ground-plans. There are no maps of the Fort William period, and archeology has failed to reveal the exact site of Fort William. Some scholars have supposed that it was at or quite near Fort John, but the writer believes that this original establishment was literally "at the mouth of Laramie's Fork," as stated by William Anderson, and on low ground as suggested by the A. J. Miller sketches. The rotting condition of the log pickets could have been hastened by the seasonal overflows of the Laramie; and the Company would have been prompted to build on higher ground, a mile upstream. The preacher, Joseph Williams, is the prime source for the new construction date of 1841. That summer, he writes, his party crossed the Laramie, and then "went up to a new fort that they were building, called Fort Johns."

The decade of the 1840s was characterized by bitter rivalry among the trading companies, the coming of the first emigrants to Oregon and Utah, and the appearance of many notable travelers.

The open traffic in firewater characterized the degenerate condition of the fur trade at this time. Reports Rufus B. Sage in November, 1841:

> The night of our arrival at Fort Platte was the signal for a grand jollification to all hands . . . who soon got most gloriously drunk. . . . Yelling, screeching, firing, shouting, fighting, swearing, drinking and such like interesting performances, were kept up without intermission. . . . The scene was prolonged till near sundown the next, and several made their egress from this beastly carousal, minus shirts and coats—with swollen eyes, bloody noses, and empty pockets. . . . liquor, in this country, is sold for four dollars per pint.

Coincident with the construction of the rival forts in 1841 came the pioneers of the Bidwell expedition, usually conceded to be the first bona fide covered wagon emigrants. In July, 1842, Fort John was visited by Lt. John C. Fremont on his first exploring expedition to the Rocky Mountains. Of this post he writes:

> This was a large post, having more the air of military construction than the fort at the mouth of the river. It is on the left bank, on a

rising ground some twenty-five feet above the water; and its lofty walls, whitewashed and picketed, with large bastions at the angles, gave it quite an imposing appearance in the uncertain light of evening. . . .

I walked up to visit our friends at the fort, which is a quadrangular structure, built of clay, after the fashion of the Mexicans, who are generally employed in building them. The walls are about fifteen feet high, surmounted with a wooden palisade, and form a portion of ranges of houses, which entirely surround a yard of about one hundred and thirty feet square. There are two entrances. Over the great entrance is a square tower with loopholes . . . built of earth.

The "cow column," the first migration to Oregon, consisting of near 1,000 persons, passed by in 1843. Thereafter, the white-topped emigrant wagons became a familiar sight in May and June of each year. Many travelers have left their impression of the clear, swift Laramie River, the neat walled fort, and the frequent Indian tepee villages nearby. In 1843, writes Overton Johnson: "The occupants of the fort, who have been long there, being mostly French and having married wives of the Sioux, do not now apprehend any danger." In 1844 John Minto records: "We had a beautiful camp on the bank of the Laramie, and both weather and scene were delightful. The moon, I think, must have been near the full. . . . at all events we leveled off a space and one man played the fiddle and we danced into the night."

The year 1845 was a banner one for Oregon-bound emigrants, who numbered upward of 3,000. The classic account of that year is Joel Palmer's journal, which vividly describes the two rival posts at the junction of the Platte and the Laramie and a great feast given by the emigrants on behalf of the multitude of Sioux Indians there assembled. Brotherly love also prevailed later that same year when five heavily armed companies of the First Dragoons, led by Col. Stephen W. Kearny, arrived and encamped in the vicinity. At a formal council the savages were diplomatically reminded of the might and beneficence of the Great White Father.

Francis Parkman, in his famous book, *The Oregon Trail*, has left an indelible impression of the situation at Fort Laramie in 1846, whence he traveled in the role of historian and ethnologist, sojourning that summer in the region in company with Oglala Sioux. Less well known than the book is his published journal, in which he notes the passing of Fort Platte and the appearance of the ill-starred Donner party:

Rode towards the fort. Laramie Mt., Sybil & Adams's deserted fort, and finally Laramie appeared, as the prospect opened among the hills. Rode past the fort, reconnoitred from the walls, and passing the highest ford of Laramie Fork, were received at the gate by Boudeau, the burgeois. Leading our horses into the area, we found Inds.—men, women and children—standing around, voyageours and trappers—the surrounding apartments occupied by squaws and children of the traders. . . . They gave us a large apartment, where we spread our blankets on the floor. From a sort of balcony we saw our horses and carts brought in, and witnessed a picturesque frontier scene. . . .

The emigrants' party passed, the upper ford, and a troop of women came into the fort, invading our room without scruple or reserve. Yankee curiosity and questioning is nothing to those of these people. . . . Most of them are from Missouri.

In 1847 the Mormon Pioneers, who had been traveling the north bank (the Mormon Trail, or Council Bluffs Road), crossed here en route to the Promised Land. They investigated the place thoroughly, making detailed measurements of Fort Laramie and the abandoned Fort Platte.

In 1848 James Marshall discovered gold at the millrace near Sutter's Fort on the Sacramento River. As the year 1849 dawned, the California craze was beginning to sweep the country. There were not a fraction enough ships to provide passage for all those who wanted to get to the mines by way of Cape Horn. Thousands converged on the Missouri border towns, aiming to get to the mines via the Great Platte River Road. It was clear that something was about to happen to "the Great American Desert" and the adobe-walled trading post on the Laramie.

The U.S. Army Moves on Fort Laramie

Even before the gold fever, with increasing numbers of its citizens migrating westward across the hostile plains, it was perhaps inevitable that the federal government would set up a chain of military posts along the Great Platte route, and the idea had been broached at various times by such respected authorities as Fremont, Parkman, and Fitzpatrick. It was officially set in motion by President Polk in a message to Congress in 1845, which resulted in the enactment, on May 19, 1846, of "an act to provide for raising a regiment of Mounted Riflemen, and for establishing military sta-

tions on the route to Oregon." The Mexican War delayed action
until 1848, when Fort Kearny, the first military post on the Trail,
was established on the Lower Platte. Then destiny pointed its
finger at "Fort John on the Laramie." This fated structure was to
provide the picturesque backdrop for a colorful pageant soon to
be enacted. From yellowing documents in the War Department
Records, National Archives, the epic of 1849 unfolds:

> March 23, Washington, Adj. Gen. R. Jones to Bvt. Maj. Gen.
> D. E. Twiggs, at St. Louis:
> To carry out the provisions of . . . the Act of May 19, 1846, relative
> to establishing the military posts on the Oregon route, and to afford
> protection to emigrants to that country and California, known to be
> numerous, it now becomes necessary to establish the second station,
> as directed by the Secretary of War, June 1, 1847, at or near Fort
> Laramie, a trading station belonging to the American Fur Company.
> You are desired to authorize [Lt. Woodbury of the Corps of
> Engineers] to purchase the buildings of Fort Laramie, the second
> station, should he deem it necessary to do so.

> April 9: Orders by Gen. Twiggs:
> There will be a post established at or near Fort Laramie. Its
> garrison will consist of companies A and E, Mounted Riflemen, and
> Company G, 6th Infantry, under the command of Maj. W. F. Sander-
> son, Mounted Riflemen. . . . Major Sanderson will leave Fort Leaven-
> worth by the 10th of May, with Company E . . . and will proceed to
> locate a post in the vicinity of Fort Laramie. . . . The remainder of the
> garrison for this post will follow on the 1st of June, with the years
> supplies . . . ordered for the post.

> April 19, St. Louis, Asst. Adj. Gen. D. C. Buell to Maj. Sanderson:
> A copy of the original instructions of the Secretary of War . . .
> is herewith respectfully enclosed. . . . A thorough reconnoissance should
> be made of the country in the vicinity of Fort Laramie, before deciding
> upon a locality.
> It is believed that Fort Laramie is not the most suitable position
> for the post, and the momentary advantage of finding there, at once,
> temporary shelter, of course will not of itself decide you in favor of
> that point. Nevertheless, authority will be given to the Engineer
> Officer to purchase it, if necessary.

> April 20, at St. Louis, Buell to Woodbury:
> Should the position of the Indian Station of Fort Laramie be found
> the most eligible for the military post to be established in the vicinity,

you are authorized to purchase the station of its owners; provided it can be done at a reasonable price, say not to exceed two thousand dollars.

April 23, at St. Louis, Bvt. Maj. Gen. D. E. Twiggs to Gen. R. Jones: The expense of supplying the posts at Fort Laramie and Salt Lake will be very great. . . . Should it be impracticable to supply those posts from the cultivation of the lands about them, I am convinced that the withdrawal to the frontier of the Mounted portion of the garrisons during the winter, will be found the best plan that can be adopted; the posts being held during that time by the Infantry.

THE MIGRATION WAVE HITS FORT LARAMIE

While the Mounted Riflemen were still making preparations for their strenuous assignment, the first wave of emigrants was rolling westward from the border settlements. Endless columns of white-topped wagons crawled like gigantic ants along both sides of the river Platte, jockeying for position, milling and piling up at the dangerous fords. The advance guard of a multitude was spear-heading the advance upon Fort Laramie.

According to eastbound Mormon observers, the first Argonauts reached Laramie Fork by May 22, 1849. Among the first identified travelers to reach the trading post, about May 28, was William Kelly, and he was not impressed:

My glowing fancy vanished before the wreched reality a miserable, cracked, dilapidated, adobe, quadrangular enclosure, with a wall about twelve feet high, three sides of which were shedded down as stores and workshops, the fourth, or front, having a two-story erection, with a projecting balcony, for hurling projectiles or hot water on the foe, propped all around on the outside with beams of timber, which an enemy had only to kick away and down would come the whole structure.

Bruce Husband, who was to figure in the sale of Fort Laramie, had been left in charge by Maj. Andrew Drips, who had gone in the spring to take his buffalo robes to St. Louis. Little is known of Husband, but we may infer that he was a full-blown mountain man of the old-time trade who viewed with distaste the manner in which events were rushing toward him. In a postscript to a letter of May 24 at "Fort John" to Andrew Drips, he prophesied: "I don't think I shall go back to St. Louis or even to the states again."

William Johnston's company on May 29 found the Laramie
River low enough to ford comfortably, then camped at the forks
and walked up to the stockade, which Johnston describes with more
fervor than Kelly:

> Besides a private entrance, there was a large one with a gate which
> faced toward the angles of the rivers. Over the entrance was a tower
> with loopholes, and at two of the angles, diagonally opposite each
> other, were bastions, also perforated with loopholes, through which
> all sides of the fort could be defended. Two brass swivels were
> mounted at the entrance. . . . Fort Laramie is the principal trading
> post of the American Fur Company. . . . It is soon, however, to pass
> into possession of the United States. . . .
>
> It seems to be a custom of emigrants on arriving here to lighten
> up, and Fort Laramie is made a dumping place for all that can be
> spared. . . .
>
> We observed quite a number of Indian women, the wives of traders
> and trappers, and their children, lounging [in] the fort or sitting in the
> doorways. . . . We could not escape the conviction that soap and water
> were scarce . . . or . . . greatly neglected.

By June 12 the Laramie was running high and causing trouble.
In George P. Burrall's diary is this entry: "A good many teams
crossing here. Had to raise our wagon boxes to keep the water
from running in. Stopped at the fort one hour. No troops there.
One trader and a blacksmith shop. Good many wagons repairing
here and some thrown away." Alonzo Delano, who also appeared
on the scene on June 12, was a more useful observer:

> A drive of seven miles from our encampment brought us to Laramie
> River, where we found a multitude of teams, waiting their turn to
> cross a swift and not safe current. It became necessary to raise our
> wagon boxes about six inches, in order to prevent the water flowing
> in and wetting our provisions. . . . Fort Laramie is simply a trading
> post, standing about a mile above the ford. . . . Its neat whitewashed
> walls presented a welcome sight to us . . . and the motley crowd of
> emigrants, with their array of wagons, cattle, horses and mules, gave
> a pleasant appearance of life and animation. . . .
>
> Around the fort were many wagons, which had been sold or
> abandoned. . . . Here was a deposit for letters to be sent to the States
> . . . on which the writers paid twenty-five cents.

On the following day, June 13, Joseph Hackney found the river
still up and very swift: "went 4 miles to larime river   we had to

raise our wagon beds up and put block under them to raise them above the water. . . . [some] teams got into deep water and wet all of their load. . . . fort larime is one mile from the river   it is built after the fashion of the mexican's ranch   theiere is no troops hear yet but they expect them in a few days."

Two valuable informants appear on June 14 to reflect the crescendo of the migration. Both mention the difficult ford and the deserted Fort Platte. Joseph Wood writes:

> Found the water in Laramie's Fk so deep as to cover the fore wheels of our Wagon. . . . On our right from here was the bare mud walls of an old deserted fort and on our left & one mile up Laramie's fork was the Fort of that name. It present quite an imposing appearance as you approach it & was surrounded with emigrants, who were gratifying their long pent up curiosity. . . . The fort was nearly deserted by those who properly belong to it . . . they being gone to the States with hides and furs. Emigrants were throwing away freight which they had retained with the hope of selling here to advantage. . . . I went to view a spot where an Indian corpse had been pulled down from a tree.

Vincent Geiger found Husband still head man at the fort. He continues, "Several Indian squaws with half breed children were found there, and a number of Mexicans. There is nothing enticing or pleasing about the place. They were destitute of all articles of trade except jerked buffalo meat. We found a young emigrant who had been accidentally shot in the thigh. . . . There were no Indians about, they having gone to war with the Crows."

On June 15 Isaac Wistar and a companion, scouting in advance of their train, attempted to elude Indians on the prowl for stray scalps. Writes Wistar: "We hoped to put Laramie's Fork between us and those undesirable acquaintances, but on reaching it, found it swelled to a turbulent river . . . cold as ice and with a rushing current full of slippery, round boulders. . . . We both stripped for swimming, and securely fastened clothes and arms to the saddles, tying the ammunition on our heads. . . . I jumped my horse off the vertical bank, found swimming water almost immediately, and quartering down stream, made the opposite bank some 100 yards below." Walking up to the adobe fort, "a rough and primitive-looking place," Wistar found countless dilapidated wagons standing about, some broken up for material for pack saddles. Its inhabitants consisted of a "clerk" and six or eight others, all French or half-

breeds. He continues: "We lounged round the fort, looking at
the trading and store rooms, fur presses and other arrangements
novel to us . . . when, being assured . . . that Indians would not
molest us in the sight of the fort . . . we moved across the level
plain to the Platte . . . and had an opportune success in killing a
young antelope." Wistar is one of the last recorded eyewitness of
the adobe fort in its role as a sleepy trading post. The next day,
June 16, Sanderson and his company of Mounted Riflemen arrived
on the scene. Wistar's journal continues:

> A man and several head of stock were drowned last night from a
> large emigrant train, while crossing Laramie's Fork. Tonight our own
> train came rolling with men and teams well battered by . . . forced
> marches. . . . The Fork having gone down very much, all hands went
> right to work blocking up wagon beds, doubling teams, lashing fast
> cargoes, etc. and, after some hard work, crossed everything without
> loss. Later a U.S. Government train of one company of dragoons under
> Major Saunders, with wagons, stock and belongings, arrived and
> crossed, the stream having still further fallen. Their business is to take
> charge of the fort for a government post.

E. B. Farnham was another eyewitness of events on this crucial
day:

> Started at sunrise. Came to Larimie creek, one mile from the fort,
> that we had to ford. . . . Other trains that had gotten there earlier had
> to take their turn, and there was quite a number. Our hearts were
> light in anticipation of getting to the fort. Here among this multitude
> all was excitement to get across. Something was ahead, it seemed like
> a gala day, as a convention. . . . Then the sound of the cannon, that was
> fired to greet the arrival of Major Sanderson, came booming from the
> fort. . . .
> We found [Fort Laramie] to be a place of no very imposing structure
> and appearance. . . . The inhabitants of this fort consist at this time
> of about 18 or 20 traders and trappers, regular old "hosses" as they
> term themselves. Some of these have squaw wives living here at the
> fort and are a rough, outlandish, whisky drinking, looking set. . . .
> Major Sanderson is to take possession.

Company E, now on the scene, included fifty-eight enlisted men,
five officers. Besides Sanderson and Woodbury, these were Maj.
S. P. Moore, surgeon; Capt. Thomas Duncan; and Capt. George
McLane, adjutant and quartermaster.

The emigrants who have testified thus far all followed the south bank of the Platte. A respectable number, however, jumped off from Council Bluffs and thence followed the north bank of the Platte as far as Fort Laramie, where they finally crossed. The Platte was, of course, a much more formidable stream than the Laramie and during flood stage could not be crossed here except by a precarious ferryboat, apparently rigged up and operated by the traders. Isaac Foster was among those who pulled up on the fifteenth on the left bank:

One man was drowned, they advised us not to attempt to swim the river, which is 200 yards in width; saw an Indian; young one, in the top of a tree, buried, being wrapped in a blanket and skin.

Saturday, 16th—Crossed the Platte over to Fort Laramie. . . . we paid $1.00 per wagon for the use of the boat to ferry us over. . . . there seems to be about 50 persons residing [at the fort], and provisions without money and without price; as you pass along you see piles of bacon and hard bread thrown by the side of the road; about 50 wagons left here, and many burned and the irons left; trunks, clothes, boots and shoes, left by the hundred, spades, picks, guns and all other fixings for a California trip. . . . here in the junction of the roads hundreds of teams are coming together. . . . here came up a company of U.S dragoons, two companies having passed on before, and a company of infantry behind the troops for the protection of the emigrants; I learned that one company is to be stationed hereabouts; here we enter the Black Hills.

Lt. Woodbury wasted no time in getting down to brass tacks with the fur company management. Although formal arrangements were not concluded for another ten days, and although none of the principals have recorded the event, it seems clear that Woodbury and Husband talked things over right away and a deal was agreed upon, for, writes eyewitness Wistar, on June 17, "The stars and stripes went up on the fort this morning, receiving our hearty cheers." The alacrity of the company at the prospect of a cash offer is testimonial enough to the decrepit state of the fur trade in 1849.

The significance of Fort Laramie as a "shakedown" point for the emigrants is further reported by Wistar:

Since we can get no more animals and there is no other inhabited place nearer than Fort Hall, many hundred miles distant, it is evident we must carry our wagons through, or do worse; so we conclude to

nurse our failing teams and make the best of it . . . and we still farther
reduced our [load] to the estimated weight of about 200 pounds per
man. This work, with washing, mending, reloading and cooking for
some days ahead, occupied all hands today, and tomorrow bright and
early, away we go.

Farnham's train also laid over on the seventeenth:

> This day we lay by and while we were here we had the tires to our
> wagons cut and re-set. . . . One of our men took a faint spell while
> walking around the fort. . . . [I] took him into the avenue of the fort
> where there was a shade and he soon recovered. The weather was sultry
> hot. I saw a man that was wounded by a comrade . . . the man that
> shot him deserted him and . . . stole one of his blankets. . . . Another
> man that was sick and reduced to a mere living frame, was lying in a
> wagon near the fort. His entire company had deserted him. However,
> they left him the wagon to lay in and provisions of two barrels of
> liquor; these they could not take along with them.

Fort Laramie marked the end of the High Plains, the beginning
of the long upgrade haul to the Rocky Mountains. It was the end
of the line for the sick, the tired, the downhearted. Tempers, frayed
by weeks of mud, dust, sunglare, and Indian alarms, snapped. Amos
Steck on June 19 tried to buy shoes for his oxen and was asked an
exorbitant price by the traders, "though there was a blacksmith
shop there and a copious abundance of iron. Such imposition we
could not stand. Camped one mile beyond." Sterling Clark was
among those who, fed up with a clumsy, temperamental wagon,
discarded it and the bulk of his earthly possessions at this point
and pinned his faith on a pack mule. Packing problems, coupled
with diarrhea, continued to plague him. Another kind of annoyance cropped up to bother Lucius Fairchild of the Madison (Wisconsin) Star Company. This was the advent of a contingent of
Mounted Riflemen under Col. William Loring headed for Oregon.
He writes, "The U.S. Train has been near us ever since they struck
this road and always in the way, in fact they were the most perfect
nusance on the whole road." Fairchild made it to the fort just
ahead of the Riflemen, pausing only long enough to observe: "Fort
Laramie is built of mud & stone in the form of a Hollow square."
Later at Green River, his luck ran out and he was "taken with the
Mountain Fever . . . and lay nearly 2 weeks in the wagon being
draged over a most awful road."

The arrival of the regiment of Mounted Riflemen at Laramie Creek at 2 P.M. on June 22 has been officially and duly recorded by Maj. Osborne Cross, quartermaster:

> It was excessively warm and dusty. . . .
>
> There are no trees about the fort to protect it from the rays of the sun, which are reflected from the surrounding hills. It is by no means a handsome location. . . . The hunting at this place has generally been very good and is its only attraction. Even this has been greatly diminished since the emigrants have made it the great thoroughfare to Oregon and California. . . .
>
> This was to be a resting place for us for a few days. . . .
>
> From the first of June our journey was made very unpleasant by constant rains which made the roads very heavy and the hauling extremely hard. Wood is not to be procured from the time you leave Fort Kearny until you arrive at this place. Nothing is to be seen but the naked valley and boundless prairies in whatever direction the eye is turned. There is a little more variety after arriving on the North Platte river.

Much less stiff and stilted, and more informative, is the journal of Pvt. George Gibbs:

> Marched sixteen and one-half miles, reaching Fort Laramie. Finding the grass destroyed by the emigrants in its immediate vicinity [we] camped a mile or two above on the bank of Laramie's river without crossing. We found Major Sanderson's command, consisting at present of Company E only, already arrived, and encamped on this side of the creek opposite the trading-fort. Major S[anderson], with [Lieutenant Daniel P.] Woodbury of the engineers, had proceeded some forty or fifty miles up the Platte to select the site of the new fort but we were most hospitably welcomed by Captains Duncan and McLane. The situation of this trading-post is well known from Fremont's report. Hardly anything could be more forlorn and destitute of interest. The regiment, however, found excellent grass on the river in a pleasant spot fringed with trees where the facilities for bathing and washing our clothes were equally welcome. In the afternoon we had an amusing scene at the lower encampment.

Here follows an account of a drumhead court-martial staged by the enlisted men for the benefit of an emigrant found in possession of army horses. Just as the terror-stricken culprit supposed he was about to be hanged, an officer intervened and told him to run for his life, which he did "amidst a volley of balls fired in every other

direction but his, and ran for the hills with the speed of a grey-
hound." Gibbs resumes, on June 24, "Orders had been given out to
cut and dry a quantity of grass in anticipation of scarcity on the
route, but Major Sanderson had returned with information that
abundance exists for a distance of seventy-five miles above here. . . .
The only change in the disposition of the command is that Captain
Rhett remains here and Captain [Mc]Lane proceeds with us." And
on June 25: "The regiment has crossed the creek and is under way.
This letter goes by special express sent by Major Sanderson under
charge of Captain Perry. A charge of two cents a letter is made to
defray expenses."

FORT LARAMIE BECOMES AN ARMY POST

The following day marks officially the transition from trading
post to military post. The purchase transaction is fully recorded
in the deed, dated June 28, 1851, at St. Louis, signed by Pierre
Chouteau, Jr., John B. Sarpy, Joseph A. Sire, and John F. A.
Sandford:

> On the 26th day of June 1849 it was agreed by and between Bruce
> Husband acting as agent and attorney for Pierre Chouteau Jr. &
> Company . . . and D. P. Woodbury, Lieut. of Corps of Engineers act-
> ing for and on behalf of the United States: that Pierre Chouteau Jr.
> & Co. should release and transfer to the United States all the houses,
> buildings and improvements by them at any time held or occupied as
> a trading post at Fort John, commonly called Fort Laramie . . . includ-
> ing all permanent buildings . . . situated within ten miles of the
> junction . . . of said Laramie Fork with said Platte river, including
> also, all the rights and claims of said Pierre Chouteau Jr. & Co. to
> trade with Indians and others.
>   Said D. P. Woodbury did on the 26th day of June A. D. 1849, for
> and on behalf of the United States, pay to the said Co. the full amount
> of said sum of Four thousand dollars.

On the following day Maj. Sanderson reported to Adj. Gen. Jones
that, since his arrival at the site on June 16, he and Woodbury
made a thorough reconnaissance of the country in the neighborhood of this place, going at least seventy-five miles up the Platte:

> This was found to be the most eligible for a military post, and
> was purchased at my request. . . .
>   Pine timber suitable for all building purposes is found in abund-
> ance within twelve miles, on the north side of the Platte.

The best of limestone is also found about the same distance, on the south side of the same river.

The Laramie is a rapid and beautiful stream, and will furnish an abundance of good water for the command.

There is plenty of grass for making hay within convenient distance of the post.

Good dry wood is found in abundance and easily to be obtained.

The entire command . . . are already employed in cutting and hauling timber, burning lime and coal, cutting and making hay. The saw-mill will soon be in active operation.

The official transition of the post, of momentous consequence for the years to come, was hardly noticed by the emigrants at flood tide. The case of John E. Brown is typical. At Fort Laramie, where Brown arrived June 28, one of his messmates was turned over to the army surgeon with one leg full of buckshot, received accidentally; another, simply fed up, turned around and started for home. The party then cast off their heavy wagon, attached six mules to the small one, and prepared to set forth when an officer of the post accosted them and appropriated one mule with the "U.S." stamp. The pages of Brown's diary now smolder with a sense of outrage: "The protection afforded to emigrants by the chain of Military Posts is only another name for robbery. . . . In consequence of this high-handed piece of villainy we struck our tent and drove four miles." The very next day two delegates, sent to the fort to expostulate with the commander, returned in triumph with the sorely needed beast, and the deserter also returned, "having taken a second thought about the difficulties in reaching home." The Brown diary now takes a different tack: "Major Sanderson . . . conducts himself with much credit. Especially in this affair. He is a Gentleman in every sense of the word, and will be of infinite service to the emigrants."

Sunday, July 1, was hot with a dense overcast reports Joseph Sedgley:

Musquitoes and gnats about in any quantity. Some of the men are badly poisoned, and we are obliged to wear veils for protection from these troublesome pests. . . . Met soldiers with the mail, bound for the States. At nine, we came to the Laramie River. . . . It took us two hours to ford. Two men . . . were drowned here. There are about seventy-five soldiers here, under Maj. Sanderson. Here we found a great variety of articles which California-bound travelers have been

obliged to leave behind. . . . we, following their example, again lighted
our load of about five hundred pounds . . . and camped at the Black
Hills.

On July 4 Oliver Goldsmith's train celebrated patriotically near
the fort, and he complains that

general hilarity prevailed. . . . Two good days were thus lost, which
only Captain Potts and myself seemed to realize might be very valuable
before our journey's end was reached. . . .

On the fifth of July we arrived at Fort Laramie, at the foot of the
Rocky Mountains. . . . There were stationed at the fort about fifty
men. . . . There were several camps of mountaineers, trappers and
Indians just outside the fort. . . .

These people all thought we were rather late in our journey, and
advised us to keep moving as rapidly as possible. When we reached
this altitude the cholera left us, but we were never without some draw-
back. From good roads, plenty of feed for our stock and drinkable
water we were now to experience the trials, discomforts, and, finally,
the horrors of journeying through a country lacking all three.

On July 9 the Washington City and California Mining Association
rolled up to the Laramie, blocked up the wagon beds, and forded.
The J. G. Bruff journal gives a most vivid picture of the situation
at that time:

Several hundred yards back from the river's bank, on the right, stood
the old adobe walls of Fort Platte, the original post of the fur traders,
now in ruin; and looks like an old Castle. . . .

After crossing, I directed the train to continue on to the left, on
the trail to Ft. Laramie a couple of miles off, and camp in the bottom
close by: (Tolerable grass) and proceeded to the right to a Camp of
American Fur trade[r]s and Indians. [The temporary camp set up after
Fort John was turned over to the military]. Here I was welcomed
very kindly and most courteously by Mr. Husband. . . . [He] informed
me that he had a letter for me, but which some 10 days ago, he had
turned over to the Officer at the Fort, who was acting as Post Master.
. . .

July 10: . . . I spent the forenoon at the Fort. Maj. Simons
[Sanderson] treated me most kindly; and on enquiry for the letter, Mr.
Husband said was there for me, found that some days ago, a man belonging to a Company from Tennessee or Kentucky, had enquired for
and obtained it! Had to send the mules up the Laramie river, 5 miles,
under a guard, to graze.

July 11: . . . Dined at the Fort, with the Major. Had the pleasure of seeing Lt. Woodbury of the Engineers. Sketched the fort. . . .

Fort Laramie is an extensive rectangular structure of adobe. It forms an open area within—houses and balconies against the walls. Heavy portals and watch tower, and square bastions at 2 angles, enfilading the faces of the main walls. It has suffered much from time and neglect. . . . After bidding my kind friends farewell, I shouldered my gun, to walk over the hills alone, to reach the camp of my company. A few hundred yards from the fort, after rising a sand hill, the trail passes through a burial ground of the Traders, and mountaineers. . . . Laramie Peak stood up boldly on my left.

The next day, July 12, the establishment was honored by the arrival of Capt. Howard Stansbury and Lt. J. W. Gunnison of the Corps of Topographical Engineers, commissioned to explore and survey the valley of the Great Salt Lake of Utah and to report on the state of affairs in that new Mormon community. Stansbury's manuscript journal, found in the National Archives, is illuminating:

Thursday, July 12 . . . after a march of 13 miles crossed Laramie fork and drove up to this Fort. Called upon Major Sanderson and paid respects. Dined at the mess. Lt. Woodbury and Captain Rhett the QrMr were absent hunting. Encamped just above the fort. Below us is a company of mounted rifles. . . The Laramie river is quite a rapid stream about 3 feet deep where the wagons crossed which was just opposite and old adobe Fort now abandoned. The American Fur Companys peo[pl]e are encamped on the left bank having sold out Ft. Laramie to the Govt. for $4,000.

Friday, July 13 . . . Engaged all day in repacking the wagons, overhauling provisions and making arrangements for the march to Fort Hall. . . . Lt. Woodbury called. . . .

Saturday, July 14. Morning bright and pleasant. . . . Engaged in writing to Dept. . . . Arranging the loading a new, dividing the provisions into messes &c &c. Opened the two barometers belonging to the Smithsonian Institution and found them to be in perfect order and very correct. . . . Sent it up to the Fort in care of Lieut. Woodbury. . . . Lt. Gunnison engaged in making observations for time and for latitude. . . . Singing in the evening.

By this date the emigrant flood had fallen off sharply. Latecomers were taking the desperate gamble that the Reed-Donner party had taken—and lost—of beating the snow in the Sierra Nevadas. Joaquin, correspondent of the Kanesville *Frontier Guardian*, wrote from Fort Laramie on July 21: "According to statistics kept by an intelligent gentleman . . . 5,500 wagons with 3½ people per wagon passed; number of deaths from the Missouri river to this point, one and a half per mile a low estimate." On August 1 an anonymous emigrant wrote to the *Frontier Guardian* about a significant change: "The old fort is now used for store-houses, stables, &c, and after the completion of the new one, which is to be erected in the immediate vicinity, will doubtless be used for stables solely." This taxpayer was critical of the plan of pre-tentious fixed forts, claiming that Kearny and Laramie had already cost over a million dollars. Since there were only 3,000 Indians in the country, he continued, it would be much more feasible to send out squadrons of mounted troops from Fort Leavenworth each spring, foraging off the country. As it was, he noted, "Each post is supplied with eight heavy 12-pound howitzers and ammunition enough to send all the red men of the Western Prairies to their happy hunting grounds forthwith."

On July 26 the small garrison was augmented by the appearance of Co. C, Mounted Riflemen, composed of two officers and sixty men, under the command of Capt. Benjamin S. Roberts and First Lt. Washington L. Elliott. Capt. Stewart Van Vliet, accompanying Roberts, replaced Rhett as acting quartermaster. On August 12 Co. G, Sixth Infantry, composed of two officers and thirty-three men, brought in a train of wagons from Fort Leavenworth. This outfit remained, completing the Fort Laramie garrison of 1849. However, the most important newcomer at the time was Col. Aeneas Mackay, sent by the high command to inspect the new post. His reports to Thomas Jesup, quartermaster general, are found in a communique of July 31; he describes the adobe work:

> It is a good deal in decay and needs repairs. Those the Engineers are employed in making and in addition have commenced the con-struction of quarters outside the walls, a part of which they expect to complete this fall and by crowding to shelter the whole command this winter. They have already a saw mill in operation, which begins to produce lumber very rapidly. . . .
>
> Since my arrival here I have been much more favorably impressed with the advantages of this station than I had ever expected to be. Indeed the prejudices which appear to have existed in the mind of everybody in regard to it, have unjustly deprived it of the credit of many recommendations to which it is entitled. In comparison with Fort Kearny, it goes far beyond it in respect to almost every requisite;

and under the care of the perservering and discreet officer who now
has the command, I have no doubt that it will become a most comfortable and desirable station. . . .

Having arrived at the Termination of our Route, to take all the advantage possible of our retrograde movement, I have ordered Captain
Easton with a portion of our party to return to Ft. Leav by the way
of Republican Fork and Kansas River . . . to make a critical examination of it. . . . For myself I prefer to return by the way of Ft.
Pierre and the Missouri River to Ft. Leavenworth.

Col. Mackay proceeded without incident to Fort Pierre on
the Missouri. He was accompanied by an escort of ten Mounted
Riflemen commanded by Capt. Van Vliet, "to keep the Sioux and
other red gentlemen of the prairies from molesting his scalp," to
use the language of an anonymous member of the escort. The
captain, in his report of September 20, submitted a map of the Fort
Pierre route, well known to the fur traders, and deplored the lack
of scientific instruments. He also was vastly annoyed by the
resultant delay in getting the command under cover before winter
set in. However, a much more ominous situation confronted late
emigrants. He reports:

> Persons just in from the Mormon settlement of Salt Lake represent
> that the great majority of the California emigrants cannot reach the
> gold country this year and will therefore be obliged to winter in the
> Valley. It is supposed that about three fourths of the whole emigration,
> that is, over 17,000 souls, will thus be thrown upon the Mormon popu-
> lation. Should such be the case great will be the suffering as the
> Mormons have barely sufficient to carry their own population through
> the winter—Many of the emigrants before they reached Salt Lake were
> carrying their all on their backs. Their teams died. [This] was caused
> by the leading Companies . . . burning the country beyond that point
> so as to render it impossible to find feed for animals.

Undoubtedly many emigrants were thrown upon the mercy of the
Mormons, just as certainly as many of them likewise were forced
to hibernate at Fort Laramie. Writes one soldier in April, 1850:
"The emigrants who passed the winter here—may Heaven never
send us any more— . . . will [soon] be on the road to California."
The rumor that "thousands" were stranded seems, however, to have
been an exaggeration. A letter of September 18 by an unidentified
soldier, published in the *Missouri Republican* also reflects this
rumor and supplements Capt. Van Vliet's report in other respects:

All hands are driving away at our new buildings, and strong hopes are entertained that before the mercury is at zero we shall be round our new hearths.

We were visited, a few days since, by about two hundred Cheyennes and Sioux, who danced a little, stole a little, ate a great deal, and finally went on their way rejoicing. These Platte Sioux, by the way, are the best Indians on the prairies. Look at their conduct during the past summer. Of the vast emigration, which rolled through their country this year, not a person was molested, not an article stolen. Such good conduct deserves reward.

In mid-November a party of Mormon missionaries, traveling east from Salt Lake City to Kanesville, reached the post and reported: "On our arrival at Fort Laramie we obtained supplies. . . . Those of our number who had passed this fort the present summer were astonished at the great improvements which have been made here in a few months' time. There is an air of quietness and contentment, of neatness and taste, which in connection with the kind of reception given by the polite and gentlemanly commander, Major Sanderson, made us feel as if we had found an oasis in the desert." In Maj. Sanderson's report of September 18, 1849, is the prediction: "The troops at this post will all be in good permanent quarters by the middle of November. One company will be quartered in the old building at present occupied by the officers and permanent quarters for the other two companies are at this time being erected and will be finished in time for the approaching winter. The building intended for the officers quarters is well under way, and will soon be finished." The Chief Engineer, in his annual report for 1849, seems equally optimistic: "The old adobe work called Fort Laramie has been purchased which has obviated the necessity of wasting time on temporary buildings. . . . The buildings now under way, and which are expected to be ready for use before winter, are, a two-story block of officers' quarters, containing 16 rooms; a block of soldiers' quarters, intended for one company, but which will be occupied by two during the coming winter; a permanent bakery, and two stables for one company each." Later evidence suggests that none of the buildings listed were entirely completed before the onslaught of winter, but it is supposed that the partly finished structures, together with the ailing old adobe fort, provided passable shelter for the garrison.

XVI

Fort Laramie, Gateway
To the Mountains

UNTIL THE BIRTH OF CHEYENNE in 1867, incidental to construction
of the Union Pacific Railroad, Fort Laramie was the undisputed
capital of the vast territory between Santa Fe and Denver to the
south and the chain of Missouri River posts to the north, as well
as the last significant outpost of civilization on the Great Platte
River Road from Fort Kearny to South Pass. From 1867 to its
demise in 1890 it continued to be a key military installation on the
Northern Plains. The previous chapter dealt with events of the
fateful year 1849; it would take several volumes to do equal
justice to the rest of Fort Laramie's history. This chapter sketches
only that aspect which relates most vitally to the Great Platte River
Road, that is, Fort Laramie as it is revealed by covered wagon
emigrants and other travelers from 1850 to 1866.

The image of Fort Laramie as a symbolic gateway, through
which one departed from the level Plains and entered the mountain
country, was recognized by Cornelius Conway: "Here comes the
ascent to the Rocky Mountains," and John Udell: "From here
we travel in the mountains all the way to California." It is a
topographic fact that the Trail west of Fort Laramie immediately
became more rugged and bifurcated because of hills, canyons, and
a more tortuous North Platte, a condition which would worsen
toward South Pass and beyond. But the visible sign and symbol of
the new challenge was Laramie Peak, looming in the sunset some
forty miles away. Usually mantled in snow in the spring months,
this provided an awesome and majestic setting for the isolated fort.

501

Lonely as it was, Fort Laramie was an authentic reminder of the familiar United States. Here were substantially designed houses with unmistakably civilized inhabitants, the only such between Fort Kearny and Salt Lake City. In 1848 Bruce Cornwall found at Fort Laramie and Fort Hall the only houses he saw between Council Bluffs and the Cascades of the Columbia River. In their first enthusiasm many emigrants forgot that this was a military post and spoke instead of a village or town or settlement.

"Who can describe his feelings on arrival at this place inhabited by white people 500 miles from the States?" asked G. A. Smith. Joy at beholding the long-awaited fort was soon tempered by realization of what lay ahead. To leave Fort Laramie was to cast off all ties with civilization. To "The General" it seemed like "parting anew from all that was hallowed on earth." It was an alien land. Says Dr. Shepherd, "We proceeded (westward from Fort Laramie) and encamped outside the boundaries of Uncle Sam."

Fort Laramie was about an even one-third of the 2,000 mile distance from St. Joe to Sacramento—665 miles according to J. H. Clark, and during the 37 days it took him to travel this he tabulated also 248 graves and 35 abandoned wagons. Wadsworth computed 618 miles from St. Joe, or 337 from Fort Kearny, while Dr. Dalton guessed 700 miles from Independence. Far more variation is to be found in the emigrants' conception of how to spell the place: Larmie, Larama, Larimi, Laremy, Learima, Learamey, etc. The name of the original legendary Jacques LaRamee like that of his fellow French-Canadian, Joseph Robidoux, could be spelled or pronounced an infinite variety of ways.

Of greater moment than any hair-splitting over mileages and spelling is the historical fact of the Fort Laramie emigrant register, which, like the Fort Kearny register, has since mysteriously dissolved into thin air but for which there is solid documentary evidence in the journals.

There is no actual evidence of a register in 1849. In 1850, however, the registration of emigrants seems to have been a very important ceremony. John Wood reports, "Here Captain Robinson gave a list of the number of men, cattle and wagons in our company . . . a customary thing with all companies." At least eight other emigrants of 1850 (including Trowbridge, Scheller, Bloom, Wolcott, and Mason, as well as correspondents of St. Louis newspapers) cite figures noted in the register. The most complete set of figures (as of July 5, 1850) is given by Henry Stine: 37,171 men, 803 women, 1,094 children, 7,472 mules, 30,616 oxen, 22,742 horses, 8,998 wagons, 5,270 cows, 257 deaths (presumably deaths enroute, although this figure is surprisingly low). He also suggests that "doubtless a great number have passed up registering their names." He looked for a friend's name, "but from the number of names it was too big a job." John Carr says his name was "number 53,232" (May 24). The number itself is an unexplained discrepancy, since it is patently too high to represent either an 1850 total or a combined 1849–1850 total at Fort Laramie up to that date.

Oddly enough, in 1852 no statistics are reflected in researched journals, although Bloemker says, "They stop every wagon, and check up on the number of oxen, horses, wagons and men in each." A St. Louis news item reports the Fort Laramie count as of mid-August, 1853: some 15,000 people, over 100,000 cattle, and 48,000 sheep. While the emigration count was lower, livestock were sharply higher; trail herds and flocks were now being driven to California for speculative sale. According to Edwin Bird, in 1854 the register, "containing the names of thousands of emigrants," was kept in a store, evidently the famous sutler's store.

From the scattered notations in emigrant journals, what inferences may be drawn about the famous Fort Laramie register? This was evidently a ledger of a standard type procured by the army from a contract supplier, large enough to contain at least the nine columns referred to by Stine: (1) men, (2) women, (3) children, (4) mules, (5) oxen, (6) horses, (7) wagons, (8) cows, and (9) deaths. The St. Louis news item suggests that there may have been another column to register sheep. It is fairly evident that these were the numerical tally columns; that is, each would have a double entry, one for the numbers of the party reporting and beside it another for the cumulative total to that date. The date would have required another column, making a total of eleven columns. Thus a typical entry for a given date might have read: "Date, June 15; Men, 10 [in the party] (12,214) [to date]; Women, 1 (611); Children, 13 (860); Mules, 80 (6,505)," etc.

From the evidence, there was also another type of entry— individual emigrant *names* together with cumulative totals, as clearly shown by Stine and Carr. This might have read: "June 15, #34,165, John Miller, Columbus, Ohio; #34,166, Matthew Jones, Columbus, Ohio; #34,167, Rebecca Brown, Liberty, Missouri," etc.

It is not really clear if the checklist of names represented another column in the above-mentioned register or if there was in fact a separate register for names only, with cumulative totals and possibly places of origin. Because of the disparity in the data, we may hypothesize the probability of two separate record books, one with the ten to twelve double tabular columns indicated and one for emigrant names in numerical sequence. We are also free to speculate that there were not one or two but a whole series of registers in sequence through the period of the California Gold Rush.

Further tantalizing speculation dwells on the process of the actual registration. Did the emigrants enter the records themselves, or was there a soldier scribe? This latter seems more likely. Assuming that a soldier interrogated the emigrants and then made the appropriate entries in the tabular book, did the emigrants then sign their own names in a second book? At the peak of the migrations, one can imagine lines of impatient emigrants forming for this purpose. Also, despite Bird's assertion that in 1854 the register was housed in the sutler's store, it would seem more likely that during the climax years this official record would have been kept at the post adjutant's office or even at some point of interception along the emigrant route, since it is evident that all emigrants did not elect to visit the fort. Whatever the actuality, what a historical treasure for posterity this would have been if it, or they, had somehow been miraculously preserved.

Emigration statistics for Fort Laramie through 1858 would of course correspond closely with the general statistics suggested in Chapter II. Beginning in 1859 with the Colorado Gold Rush, most of the emigrant traffic was siphoned off at Julesburg down the South Platte and the Overland Trail through southern Wyoming. Thereafter the road up the North Platte became more exclusively a military road. However, during the initial phase of the Montana gold rush of the mid-sixties there was a brief revival of civilian traffic up the North Platte.

THE TWO RIVER CROSSINGS

While California gold was (hopefully) at the end of the continental rainbow, it could only be reached step by painful step, and Fort Laramie was the most important mile-stone to date. If you made it to Laramie you were already entitled to spit in the

Elephant's eye; to reach Laramie was like crossing the equator on an ocean voyage. Accordingly, you approached the fabled spot with some ceremony. Whereas in crossing the equator you were splashed by Father Neptune, to attain Fort Laramie you were baptized, so to speak, in the waters of the Laramie or the North Platte.

The fifty miles, more or less, from Scott's Bluffs were not in themselves memorable. It only required moving the wheels up the sandy valley floor past Horse Creek, past the invisible line that would one day separate Nebraska and Wyoming, past many Sioux encampments and scaffold burials, and (after 1850) past various transitory trading posts offering chiefly the solace of whiskey. Fort Laramie, the primary goal, was not to be attained without first crossing either the treacherous North Platte (if traveling up the Council Bluffs Road) or the Laramie River, the largest Platte tributary above the Loup, which in spring flood could be just as difficult and deadly as the North Platte. (Grindell, Hickman, and others speak of the Laramie, not as a tributary, but as "the Middle Fork of the Platte River.") Although both rivers today have been tamed somewhat by the Bureau of Reclamation, in covered wagon days they were wildly unfettered, cascading with melted snow from Laramie Peak and the more distant Rockies.

Fort Laramie reposes on an elevated triangular plateau between the Laramie, flowing from the southwest, and the North Platte, flowing from west-by-northwest. To be more precise, it is on the west bank of the Laramie, about one and a half miles above its mouth. The North Platte crossing was within a range of 200 yards of the present highway bridge. The Laramie crossing shifted more drastically. In the fur-trading 1830s, when Fort William apparently stood on the flood plain near its mouth, the crossing was here likewise. This crossing remained to serve later Fort Platte; but in 1841 when adobe-walled Fort John was built, the main crossing moved well upstream to a point just above the new fort, as described by Francis Parkman in 1846. In 1849 the gold-rushers divided, some crossing opposite the fort, some at the river mouth. In 1850 the military discouraged any more traversing of the new parade ground or camping nearby, so the main crossing was again near the mouth (Cagwin, Grindell).

Most emigrants arrived at this point in late May or June; in 1850 the Laramie was on a rampage, estimates of its width varying up to 100 yards and, according to Thomasson, "the swiftist stream

I ever saw." While its depth may not have exceeded four feet, this was a dangerous ford, the scene of uncounted drownings. The common practice was to raise wagon boxes several inches before driving in (Trowbridge, Lampton). At best one might expect a soaked cargo; at worst, the unbalanced wagon might tip over, sweeping man and beast to their doom (Frink). Solomon Gorgas rated this crossing as "swollen, barely fordable."

In 1852 the emigrants were greeted by a new toll bridge installed by an army contractor, but it failed to come up to expectations. The rates were so exorbitant (from $2 to $3 per team) that most travelers continued to take their chances on fording and drowning. Furthermore, it was a jerry-built affair (Gage, M. Bailey) which indeed collapsed in the spring rise of 1853. This year the crossing moved again upstream to a point opposite the adobe fort (Bradway, Flint), where a crude ferry was available at $2 a wagon (Graham, A. Stewart). Finally, in 1854 the army had a good solid bridge built *above* the fort (Murphy) and instituted a modest toll of 25¢ per wagon, which proved satisfactory for some years. In 1859, because of the increase in army traffic, a yet bigger and more permanent bridge was built, this time again near the mouth of the Laramie. H. D. Williams and H. M. Chillson mention an inflationary toll of $2.50. In later years, the army provided other substantial bridges opposite the fort.

Meanwhile, those on the Council Bluffs Road, north side, had arrived at the point where the guidebooks said to cross the North Platte and were appalled to find a wild river of even greater magnitude than the Laramie. According to Franklin Langworthy, the 1850 rise measured forty rods (about 200 yards) wide, sixteen feet deep, and raced along at twenty miles per hour. A bridge here was out of the question; at any rate none was built by the army until 1876, far too late to be helpful to the emigrants. When the Platte subsided it too could be forded, but those bound for California could not wait. The alternatives left to them, therefore, were: (1) use the precarious public ferry, when it was operating; (2) ferry yourself over, if you could; or (3) stay on the north side.

Until 1868, when Alexander Gardner recorded it in photographs, not much is known of this erratic facility. In 1850, according to Thissell and Ingalls, for a while at least there was a crude contraption sponsored by officers of the fort "to make money out of the emigrants for a library." Thissell complained that they charged

$25 per wagon (did he mean $2.50?); McKeeby and Dennis paid $2 and $1, respectively, and crossed safely and with satisfaction. A Mormon party waited for forty teams to cross ahead of them, then "paid $1. per load, & had to do the work [themselves]" (Loomis). Jerome Dutton reported that the boat was sunk "by some Californians who went on a spree." Kilgore's party got dunked in the river by the capsizing ferry but scrambled to safety. Through mechanical failures, carelessness, laziness, or whatever cause, the ferry was frequently out of action. A few trains brought boats along for the occasion (McKinstry), but most emigrants who had to fall back on their own resources improvised ferries out of wagon-boxes (Hinds). No one kept tally on the number of emigrants drowned and swept down the river, but Langworthy heard of six in one day. Carlisle Abbott, swimming horses across, almost went under but was fished out by companions who left him in an Indian tepee to recover.

Today large cottonwoods and other trees are dense along the Platte and the Laramie; this is because the river has been stabilized for irrigation purposes. In emigrant days, no such timber existed or much difficulty in crossing would have been eliminated by the construction of rafts or pontoons. By the same token, the fort was much more visible from across the two rivers than it is now. Modern conditions make it difficult to recapture the scene.

If the option of staying on the north side was exercised, it was not to twiddle the thumbs, but to continue up the north side of the North Platte, a route which in 1850 was reputed to be dangerously beset by Indians and wild beasts, if not impassable because of high cliffs and other dangers. The notion that the north side beyond Fort Laramie was hardly passable was ingrained in early guidebooks and further nurtured by the soldiers who stood to profit from the ferry (Abbott). But in 1850 the Wheeler and McKinstry parties, "more afraid of cholery than Indians," joined others in blazing a north side trail; and in 1852 continuing on the north side had become the accepted thing to do (Foster). Many like Cornwall and McAulay swam over to "see the town" but returned to the north side. From 1859 to 1868 no mention is made of a ferry, as such, but only skiffs and canoes, sometimes operated by Indians for a fee (Case, Gould, Earnshaw). Mostly these were sidetrips to get mail and supplies, and the wagons stayed on the north side.

The U.S. Army Establishment

Most of the surviving buildings and ruins at Fort Laramie today, comprised of lime-concrete, were constructed in the 1870s and 1880s. However, the present parade ground is the same one outlined by Capt. Woodbury in 1849, and four buildings survive from the 1849–1866 period: the imposing two-story officers' quarters called Old Bedlam, the adobe and stone portion of the sutler's store, the stone magazine, and the 1866 stone guardhouse. The archeological remains of other buildings, notably the 1850 guardhouse and two-story soldiers' barracks, are much in evidence. The quadrangular adobe trading post, which was bought by the army in 1849 and had limited use until its demolition about 1860, stood at the south end of the parade ground on the river's edge, its place now usurped by an 1870 officers' quarters. Thus, because of the army's later construction program, the Fort Laramie described by emigrants little resembles the restored version of today, except for the identical location and the four buildings mentioned. For this very reason emigrant impressions of the early military post have special historical value:

A beautiful location for a fort, a far better looking place than Fort Kearny.—John Wood, 1850

This is quite a place . . . several fine buildings nestled here among the hills, it looks like a rose in the wilderness.—Lodisa Frizzell, 1852

Frame houses and barracks of dried brick, a post office, a bakery, and a saw-mill drawn by 16 horses.—Hagelstein, 1854

It is of Spanish brick . . . also, most of the buildings connected with it. . . . there are a few framed buildings under construction.—George Wheeler, 1850

Fort Laramie & Fort John [the adobe fort] are situated 1½ miles from the river [crossing] in a beautiful bottom in plain view of the Laramie Peak of the Rocky Mountains in sight of perpetual snow. It consists of a trading establishment and a small garrison of U.S. troops. The old fort is built of adobes or spanish brick containing about 15 or 16 houses, enclosed by a wall eleven feet high. . . . Upon the whole it is a beautiful and handsome location.—Letter to Greenville, 1850

It is a very miserable apology for a fort being a quadrangular structure of sun dried bricks about 10 feet high and perhaps 40 by 120 feet square. The walls vary from 8 to 10 inches in thickness. This is called the Old Fort.

A fine plain containing perhaps 6 acres extends to the east of this cobhouse fortification. On the south side of this plain or yard is a long row of Stables in which the horses of the officers and the fragments of 3 companies of Dragoon are duly cared for.

On the east and southeast are numerous shanties for the lodgement of the fag ends of three companies of infantry, sundry blacksmith's shops, carpenters shops, a bakery, etc. On the north or rather northeast may be seen the Sutler's store where evil filth in the name of whiskey is sold for $8. per gallon.

A kind of enclosure [a fence?] nearly 4 miles in extent appeared designed for surrounding this mockery of a military post, stationed here for the purpose of overawing the Indians whenever they threaten to become refractory. It would seem that a company of squaws could sack the whole concern in half an hour. . . . Its walls are actually propped up by sticks of timber.—DR. TOMPKINS, 1850

The old Fort is used as a soldiers' quarters and quite a number of new adobe buildings have been added outside the old fortification for the same purpose . . . and 2 two story wooden houses for the commissioned officers. . . . There is here a store quite well supplied with a great variety of goods, most of which are sold at reasonable prices.—ADDISON CRANE, 1852

Found Larmie to be quite a pretty place. The buildings belong to the government. It contains one hotel for the accomadation of the Offacers [Old Bedlam], one store, one government blacksmith shop, & a few other buildings beside store houses for the army.—CHARLES CUMMINGS, 1859

The road does not lie through the fort, so we can not get a very good view of it, yet, what we saw was very pretty and the stars and stripes were majestically floating over it—ADA MILLINGTON, 1862

Real houses with siding painted white . . . a stone church . . . a village in the wilderness—ELISHA BROOKS, 1866

The best record of Fort Laramie and its structural evolution over the decades is to be found in army ground plans, a few random sketches by inhabitants, and a series of panoramic views taken by various photographers over the decades. For the early 1850s reliance must be mainly on ground plans; a sketch by Frederick Piercy in 1853 stands alone for the pictorial record. In 1858 C. C. Mills of the U.S. Topographical Engineers made the first photographic record; here the old adobe trading post is still visible, but only as ruined walls. The next known photograph is dated 1867. During the interim the layout is recorded mainly by army draftsmen and in the sketches of two or three artistically inclined enlisted men.

It was not until 1868 that a real building boom got underway at Fort Laramie. The earlier period, with which we are concerned, was a primitive one as far as post facilities were concerned; and these can be summarized thus: one decrepit adobe fort which by 1862 had disappeared altogether, one two-story frame officers' quarters (Old Bedlam), one two-story frame infantry barracks, several adobe officers' quarters, several stables and warehouses, two successive stone guardhouses, the magazine, and the sutler's store.

There is evidence of entrenchments of sorts following the Indian troubles of 1854, but there was never a stockade enclosing the whole group of buildings. The adobe stockade (Fort John), which was a ruin by 1858, and a fortified adobe corral built in 1867 both had the look of classic forts. But these were incidental; Fort Laramie after 1849 was never a fortified post, and had no need to be, apparently, since it never suffered armed assault by the Indians. Except for the uniformed soldiers themselves and the lofty flagpole (from spliced Laramie Peak timbers), the only distinctly military objects in evidence were the wheeled artillery, principally the famed mountain howitzers. In 1850 Loomis observed, "In the [adobe] fort were plassed 2 Brass cannon . . . about 9 pounders." In 1853 Cipriani noted "four exceedingly well-kept field guns" and four mounted cannon. In the soldier sketches of the sixties these guns are conspicuous on the parade ground. Though seldom resorted to for defense, these guns saw much ceremonial use. Isaiah Bryant didn't visit the fort, but wrote, "The roar of the cannons could be plainly heard as we were passing by."

Until the Utah War of 1858, the Fort Laramie garrison was not of impressive strength, apparently ranging from 60 (Cipriani) to 200 soldiers (Wolcott), these statistics being borne out by the regimental returns. During the Civil War it was again reduced to skeleton strength despite the Sioux uprisings. The Mounted Riflemen and the Sixth Infantry in the early years, and the Eleventh Ohio Volunteer Cavalry during the early sixties, were the units of most historical interest stationed here. Maj. Sanderson and Capt. Ketchum were the most prominent officers during the peak migration years, 1850–1852. Col. William O. Collins was the notable commander of the Ohioans. These and other officers were frequently praised by emigrants for their courtesies to travelers ("Cheyenne,"

Day, Mrs. Ferris). Sometimes official hospitality went so far as to extend to the wayfarer an invitation to a dinner of buffalo meat or Laramie trout (Pigman, Coke).

While the officers in their resplendent uniforms interested some, the common soldiers were more of a curiosity. They were often scolded by the diarists, such as Wolcott, who saw "200 soldiers with nothing to do!" and Dr. Tompkins, who complained of provisions reserved for "government pets." Katherine Dunlap in 1864 asserted that "soldiers were insolent to emigrants. . . . They all have their squaws and white men have been imprisoned for insulting Indians." However, these peevish judgments were scarcely warranted. The frontier enlisted man was probably the most underpaid and abused soldier in our national history, a fact recognized by some of the more discerning writers, like G. A. Smith: "We found the soldiers very friendly as they only see white men once a year. They lead a hard life." Rev. Alden reports: "We went over to watch the artillery drill and amuse ourselves watching some prisoners trying to bathe in the river, with ball and chain attached to their ankles." Other instances of harsh treatment (Wilkinson), and a glimpse today of the solitary confinement cells in the surviving guardhouses, are convincing. And in addition to the usual monotony and frequent frustrations of their daily life, the Fort Laramie soldiers occasionally had to fight Indians, sometimes getting scalped or wounded in the process. It is not to be wondered at that they frequently deserted with government horses and headed for the gold fields.

Sometimes curious emigrants shared the excitement of the evening retreat ceremony, with lowering flag and sound of bugle. "We heard the drums beat the roll call at the Fort last evening," writes Larkin, "so know we are almost there." Leander Loomis remembers, "It happened that day we passed they were Drilling the soldiers, we saw them all dressed in uniform, and marched on the parade ground. . . . They looked splended, I tell you, neat as new pins."

In addition to military spectacles, there was an occasional celebrity at the fort to give the emigrants an extra thrill. Most noted of these, probably, was the celebrated Kit Carson. In 1850 this fabled ex-mountain man put in some time at the fort, apparently involved in arranging for Mexican laborers from Taos and in trading horses before making up an expedition for Santa Fe and California. William Frush, D. A. Shaw, James Evans, and Dr. Knox were among those who saw and conversed with him. In 1859 the famed newspaperman Horace Greeley stopped at the fort, fresh from the Colorado mines, and lectured to a gaping audience about the advantages of getting rich quick. Charles M. Tuttle says, "He [Greeley] gave a very flattering account of the diggings." Tuttle later "saw about 15 waggons head for Pike's Peak on account of what he said." Martin Patterson's diary shows that he was one of those so moved. It should be noted that, like most others, he later went back home broke. Mark Twain, bound for the Nevada silver mines in 1861, unfortunately went through during the night by stage. Jim Bridger, Brigham Young, Chief Red Cloud, Gen. W. T. Sherman, and Buffalo Bill Cody were among the passing celebrities of later years.

Somewhat more prosaic than military show was the evidence of agriculture, or rather its failure, at Fort Laramie. The Government Farm was located above the fort as early as 1850 (McKinstry). In 1853 the *Missouri Republican* reported the onion crop a success, but for the most part scant rainfall prevented satisfactory results. In 1854 Edwin Bird reported: "They are trying to grow a few vegetables [at the farm] but so far without success." For sustenance Fort Laramie depended upon provisions freighted from Fort Leavenworth, plus wild meat which might be brought in by hunters. In consequence symptoms of scurvy were often the badge of a Fort Laramie soldier. Farming never proved feasible here in army days, except for natural bottomland hay crops harvested by contractors. A few sickly trees were nursed around the perimeter of the parade ground in the 1880s, but that was the extent of it. Thomas Cramer predicted in 1859: "As for settlement, there is not now, nor ever will be any." The sparseness of Wyoming's population 100 years later, even with irrigation and other aids, suggests that his prophecy was only half wrong.

Although the soldiers' bodies sometimes suffered from malnutrition and harsh discipline, it is worth noting that their immortal souls were not neglected. In 1850 Rev. Vaux arrived to serve as chaplain (an occurrence noted by Gershom Day), and in addition to rites for the deceased, he conducted Sunday services regularly. G. A. Smith and Dr. Tompkins were among emigrants who availed themselves of the opportunity to go to church services for a change. Where the stone church mentioned by an emigrant in 1866 was located, or just what constituted the church in earlier years, is not known. What *is* known is the location of the post cemetery. Before 1868, when this adjunct of all civilized communities was moved farther away, the cemetery was on the hilltop now occupied by the ruins of the 1883 hospital. In 1852 Caroline Richardson "saw a person entered into the graveyard." This plot of ground was well filled, not only by earlier fur traders and many soldier victims of scurvy and Sioux arrows, but by the considerable number of civilian employees and emigrants who, according to the journals, died here from "colery" or other diseases, accident, murder, or old age (including Harlow Thompson's little old lady who brought along her own coffin).

The fort medical and hospital facilities were made available in extreme cases to the emigrants, particularly those who had to be left behind by impatient Argonauts. Keller's party left a Mr. Sturgis here on account of acute rheumatism. The correspondent "Cheyenne" speaks of several sick emigrants "in charge of the Surgeon of the post," as well as "a man brought in today with one of his legs broken." Woodward was grateful for prompt surgical aid for a gashed foot. Besides first aid, hospital, and cemetery facilities, Fort Laramie also served as a place for recuperation, provisioning, and streamlining of mobile equipment.

After 1849 it was next to impossible to camp in the immediate vicinity of the fort because all grass and foliage had been eaten off by the vast number of animals (Wheeler). In an effort to restore the grass, the army, as at Fort Kearny, first prohibited camping "in the valley" (Ingalls, 1850) and later extended the ban to a radius of "two miles of the fort" (Murphy, 1854). Whether this was enforced effectively is doubtful; all the evidence is that Fort Laramie and vicinity remained treeless and grassless until the 1880s. But this did compel many emigrants to bypass the fort without stopping even for a glimpse (like Helen Carpenter), while others had to camp at a distance and hike several miles to get to the fort. And most of them felt obliged to get there to buy, sell, or swap things, to obtain services (surgery, blacksmithing, etc.), or to stop at the post office. After all, here was the only "shopping center" of consequence for the 800 miles between Fort Kearny and Salt Lake City.

Because of the hauling difficulties up to this point, which promised to become more severe, many emigrants felt obliged to revamp their equipment here, and there was a great to-do about reducing overloads, cutting wagons down in size, and replacing worn-out stock. This resulted in a surplus of beans, bacon, hardware, chests, clothes, and many other items littering the fort area. ("Cheyenne" reported far fewer items of heavy equipment—"gold washers, saw mills or steamboats"—in 1850 than 1849; some lessons had been learned). Thus, the first thing necessary to do at the fort was to sell surplus items or swap for something else if possible. Some were successful in this, but naturally the fort traders had all the advantage. The G. A. Smith party sold wagons, converting to "one horse apiece to carry our baggage," and Byron McKinstry found that "they will pay 4 or 5 dollars for a good wagon sometimes," but most wagons simply had to be abandoned. Thomasson counted thirty-five such derelicts on the premises, and noted also "a great many horses sold at the fort for little or nothing." J. M. Stewart managed to exchange one heavy wagon for a pack horse, while Dr. Knox had to pay an exorbitant price for horses "to replace jaded mules." In 1852 Cartwright found a man whose business it was to exchange cattle with travelers, and "two days out we saw an immense drove of cattle," presumably the range herd made up from worn-out emigrant stock.

Blacksmithing services (shoeing horses and oxen, setting wagon tires, and repairing gear) could be obtained at the fort. In 1854 McCowen paid $2 to shoe one ox and $4 for one horse; nine years later, Col. Word still paid $1 per hoof for horses and $2 a wheel for setting tires. The location of the fort blacksmith would have been near the parade ground. In 1852 Snodgrass found a new blacksmith shop opposite the fort, east of the Laramie River crossing. This establishment is noted also by Ebey in 1854 and it shows up likewise on a map drawn by Cummings in 1859.

The purchase of supplies generally was either through the post trader (sutler) or the army quartermaster, and it isn't always possible to tell which. The army was not normally in the business of selling supplies, but this was done at the commander's discretion in desperate cases or when official policy in Washington so dictated. In 1852 Capt. Ketchum told Crane that he had orders to sell to the emigrants for cost plus transportation: "Flour could be had for 10½ cwt., hams and bacon 15¢, dried fruit 12½¢ per bushel, etc." But such bargains at the commissary were exceptional; most emigrants dealt with the post sutler, paid through the nose, and complained to their diaries. Witness Col. Word: "[I] paid very high prices for everything. . . . 12 to 20 cents for bacon; $12. to $18.

per hundred for flour, smoking tobacco $1. a pound, whiskey $1. a pint, mean at that." Although there is no other hint that the sutler ran a restaurant, Dr. Dalton says he "took dinner on buffalo meat, Bread and Butter, Coffee etc. at 50 cents."

A Fort Laramie postmarked letter in existence today is worth a small fortune to collectors. This was the last chance to mail anything this side of California without detouring to Salt Lake City, and the emigrants made the most of it, often swimming the North Platte for the privilege. The post office was not a separate building; it was a part of the sutler's store. In 1850 Lewelling says that letters there cost "10¢ each to the States," while in 1854 McCowen "had to pay 5¢ over and above postage." Woodson, Magraw, and Hockaday, the regular mail carriers from Salt Lake City to the Missouri River, took turns at attempting to run monthly mails, though frequently interrupted by weather and Indians. Sometimes emigrant mail was accepted for delivery by army messengers. Dr. Knox writes that, through the courtesy of an officer, "It is a mere accident that I have the privilege of sending you this hasty note as a government express starts in half an hour directly to Fort Leavenworth. . . . it will reach you in about a month in advance of the regular mail." Sgt. Leodegar Schnyder did extra duty as postmaster for many years. Apparently his methods were highly informal. In 1859 Wilkinson found that the general delivery system for the benefit of emigrants inquiring for their mail consisted of a bushel basket. Everyone was free to paw through its contents looking for chance letters from home.

Although the mail normally ran in just two directions, east and west along the Platte, Fort Laramie also served briefly as the mail contact point for two distant gold rush communities, south and north. In 1858–1859, before more direct routes were established, mail for the Denver area was routed to the states through Fort Laramie; and for a few years beginning in 1876 Fort Laramie was a major stage and mail route on the Cheyenne-Deadwood Trail to the Black Hills of South Dakota.

THE FORT LARAMIE INDIANS

During early emigrant years assemblages of Indian tepee villages in the neighborhood of Fort Laramie were standard fixtures. Mary Jane Guill reported: "The town [is] full of Indians, their wigwams all through the town except on Main Street." The Indians benefited financially by the regular trade in buffalo robes and other skins and by begging or swapping with the emigrants. Also, they were gregarious; they liked the pageantry that was being enacted at the fort. Emigrant reaction to the natives was mixed. Rev. Crawford in 1851, for example, noted with repugnance that "the Indians seated themselves on the ground and commenced to pick lice from each others' heads and crack them between their teeth as though they were precious morsels. There was more filth than I expect to see among human beings." On the other hand Crane in 1852 reports that "the Indians which I saw at the Ft. impressed me very favourably. They are a well formed race—tidy and neat in their dress, and of pleasing expression of countenance." Most felt that, one way or another, the Indians ranked high on the list of curiosities seen on their journey, whether they were lounging around the trading post, giving ceremonial dances, feasting on boiled puppies, or en route in travois columns. Just as fascinating as the live Indians, perhaps, were the dead ones, wrapped in red blankets and placed in trees or, more often, on crude scaffolds, "reared up toward heaven as high as they could get" (Sutton).

Except to cope with the Indians' insistent begging and occasional pilfering, most emigrants never thought of them as hostile. Hugo Hoppe gives a hearsay account of a scalping and train-burning episode in 1851, but until the 1860s there are almost no documented cases of Indians attacking a civilian wagon train, and even then they were rare. Nevertheless, despite their primitive ways and stoic mien, the Indians viewed with consternation the great wagon train phenomenon of 1849 and thereafter, and this gradually became smoldering resentment which broke out into sporadic clashes and finally into open warfare.

The unrest among the tribes camped along the North Platte and elsewhere led to the Great Fort Laramie Treaty Council of 1851, unique in western annals because of its immense size and the number of different tribes from all over the Northern Plains— including hereditary enemies such as Cheyenne and Shoshoni, Sioux and Crow—who attended in an unaccustomed spirit of peace and brotherly love. Indian agent Thomas Fitzpatrick, Superintendent of Indian Affairs D. D. Mitchell, Jim Bridger (with the Shoshoni), and the Catholic missionary Father DeSmet (with a delegation of Mandan, Gros Ventres, and other tribesmen from the Upper

Missouri) were among the white notables present at the conference. The dearth of grass around Fort Laramie compelled a removal of the council to the vicinity of Horse Creek near Scott's Bluffs, where there was much feasting and ceremony. At the time, the colorful gathering of some 10,000 tribesmen was accounted a diplomatic success. In the treaty, tribal territories were roughly delineated and, in exchange for their good behavior along the emigrant road, the Indians were promised that their tribal rights would be respected. In addition, and more to the point, they would receive $50,000 in annuity goods for fifty years. Before accepting the treaty, the U.S. Congress reduced this to ten years.

The Great Council was recorded by several witnesses, including Father DeSmet, Sgt. Lowe, and Col. Chambers, editor of the *Missouri Republican*, who was one of the commissioners. Hugo Hoppe's party arrived at the fort while "the government was negotiating their first treaty with the Indians whereby they promised the Indians annuities if they would give the emigrants a right of way through their lands, and there were thousands of Indians around the fort. Their tepees stood in rows facing one another to make a street with a road in between, the whole forming a village." However, there were no other emigrant witnesses of record to any part of the proceedings; the council occurred in September, well after the main migration of that year had passed by.

During the large migration of 1852 all went smoothly, but a serious incident occurred in mid-June of 1853. When the North Platte ferryman, busy with emigrants, refused to transport a party of young Sioux, they "took the skiff by force." It was recaptured by a detail of soldiers from the fort, but when the Indians fired on them, the commander, Richard B. Garnett, sent Lt. Fleming and twenty-three men to arrest the culprits. In the ensuing exchange of gunfire three Indians were killed and two taken prisoners; thus were planted the seeds of disaster. Basil Longsworth appeared on the scene the next day, and his journal confirms the official account. Because of the affair, he reports, "400 warriors were encamped near the river . . . determined to murder every emigrant on the road." The emigrants huddled together until 50 wagons and over 100 men had been assembled, then "mustered all our arms and resolved to clear the road of every obstacle, and marched forward." After passing the fort safely, continues Longsworth, "We posted a strong guard and commended our lives to God."

The big blowup occurred in August, 1854, near Bordeaux's trading post, eight miles east of the fort. Over 1,000 hungry Sioux were camped there waiting for their annuities when one of their number killed and butchered a cow strayed from a Mormon train. Upon the complaint of the aggrieved owner, Fleming sent Lt. Grattan, Sixth Infantry, with a French-Canadian interpreter and twenty-eight men to arrest the offender. Handicapped by a profound ignorance of Indian psychology, as well as his interpreter's drunkenness, Grattan gave peremptory orders to fire, resulting in the death of Chief Conquering Bear (a signer of the 1851 treaty) and the retaliatory massacre of Grattan, his interpreter, and his entire command. The maddened Indians killed no one else, but broke into Bordeaux's storehouses and threatened what was left of the Fort Laramie garrison. Thus, in a few bloody minutes the harmony of 1851 was destroyed and a twenty-five year period of intermittent warfare was inaugurated.

Bordeaux and other traders, and certain Sioux chiefs, all eye-witnesses of the Grattan tragedy, testified for the government. Post sutler Lewis B. Dougherty described the frightened reaction of those left at the fort, who sought sanctuary in decrepit old Fort John. History does not record if the owner of the ill-starred cow remained in the vicinity long enough to learn of the disastrous consequences of his complaint. A few weeks later another Mormon traveler, Thomas Sutherland, found the soldiers' graves "close by the road." The graves were so shallow that "some of the men's heads are not even covered." In 1856 William Pleasants found the "victims buried in one large grave." That same year J. Hamelin reported a stone monument at the site (rough and without inscription) and near by several platforms of Indian dead. He concluded that these were the remains of those slain by Grattan's men, "the ornaments worn at the time of the death still waving in the breeze from the boxes which enclosed what once was human. Here was a place for a Hamlet soliloquy." In 1859 H. Williams described the monument as "a pile of stones four feet high upon their grave." In 1910 the victims of the Grattan Massacre were reburied in the Fort McPherson cemetery near North Platte, Nebraska.

In mid-November, 1854, Spotted Tail and other Sioux, thirsting for white blood, assaulted the Salt Lake mail stage below Fort Laramie, killing the three employees, wounding a passenger, and making off with $10,000 in gold. In 1857 M. Long of the Pacific

Wagon Road Surveys identified the site as a good twenty-five miles east of Fort Laramie, a few miles from Maj. Drips' stone trading house (south of present Torrington, Wyoming). He refers to this site as "Jamieson's Bluffs, so named after one of a party of four mail men who were killed there three years ago by the Sioux. . . . Their bodies are buried by the roadside where they fell."

The punitive campaign of 1855 under Gen. Harney was the subject of Chapter X. At Fort Laramie the second half of the 1850s was preoccupied with the Mormon Rebellion, or Utah War (in which it played a pivotal role), campaigns against the Cheyenne Indians, and the rise of the great freighting business on the Plains dominated by the firm of Russell, Majors & Waddell. While some military and freighting figures (Lowe, Kenderdine) provide some Fort Laramie insights, eyewitness accounts of these events by emigrants are scarce.

The exciting episodes of the Pony Express, the transcontinental telegraph, and the overland stage in this area, beginning in the 1860s, as well as the Sioux Wars of 1862–1866, are revealed primarily in official records and by direct participants, and thus fall largely beyond the primary scope of the migration story. With the exception of the terror inspired by the Grattan Massacre, the years during the Civil War were the most harrowing in the fort's history. The scanty forces of the Eleventh Ohio Volunteer Cavalry under Col. Collins, spread out for several hundred miles at outposts from Mud Springs to South Pass to protect the new telegraph line, had repeated conflicts with the Sioux. In 1866, while peace commissioners were dickering with the Sioux at the fort, Col. Carrington showed up with the Eighteenth U.S. Regiment of Infantry to install regulars at Fort Laramie and set up a chain of forts along the new Bozeman Trail to Montana north via the Bighorn Mountains.

Although civilian emigrant wagon traffic westward up the North Platte in the sixties was considerable, it was seldom molested by the Sioux and Cheyenne, whose main quarrel was with the military. Thus, the emigrant view of the Sioux troubles was limited. In 1860 Lavinia Porter was told by the soldiers that Indians had attacked and destroyed a train ahead of them, killing eight men (an event not confirmed elsewhere). Because of the alleged danger, the Porter train was required to wait for other trains in order to make up a larger party for strong defense. This policy, similar to that at Fort Kearny during the same period, is mentioned also by H. D. Barton, but it could not have been followed very consistently, for other such references are lacking. Two other emigrants witnessed the events of 1866 when Indians, peace commissioners, and troops all converged on the fort. Julius Birge and Margaret Carrington describe the colorful spectacle of Indians swarming into the sutler's store on this occasion. Sarah Wisner's party was urged by Col. Carrington to leave the fort "with all possible speed, as Red Cloud was getting ready for the war path, as he was jerking his beef & packing it on ponies."

Col. Carrington's surmise was correct. When Carrington proceeded with the construction of forts along the Bozeman Trail to Montana—Reno, Phil Kearny, and C. F. Smith—Red Cloud declared war and there were many casualties. In 1868 there was a second Fort Laramie Treaty Council, which led to an uneasy peace on the Plains until the discovery of gold in the Black Hills, 1874–1875. During the Sioux campaign of 1876–1877 Fort Laramie again played a central role. The following decade was anticlimactic; in 1890 Fort Laramie was abandoned, and the buildings were sold at auction.

In contrast with the unhappy case of Fort Kearny, where all buildings and appurtenances disappeared during settlement days, many of the Fort Laramie structures—including the most historic—survived. Soon after the auction many buildings were razed or moved, leaving only archeological remains or naked, standing, grout walls. Three purchasers, however, each for different reasons, preserved a substantial part of the old fort. John Hunton, the last post sutler, had a great sentimental regard for the historic post, and through his efforts most of "officers' row," including Old Bedlam, two officers' quarters, and the sutler's store, were saved. A man named Hart decided to convert the cavalry barracks to a hotel and the nearby commissary warehouse and the old bakery to barns. A Mr. Sandercock, who had worked at the fort, decided to keep right on living there and so preserved an officers' quarters of 1870, plus the 1866 guardhouse. Thus, ten principal buildings were still intact, though in extremely dilapidated condition, when in 1938 the National Park Service received this property from the State of Wyoming and began the process of converting it to a National Historic Site. Since 1950 there has been a continuing program of stabilization and restoration of these old structures, including interior furnishings.

One can visit Fort Laramie today and relive the days of the frontier army post. In the sutler's store, hybrid relic of 1849–1852– 1883 construction periods, is the store and post office, officers' club and enlisted men's bar, with everything in place for business. Old Bedlam is once more the impressive structure conceived by Lt. Woodbury, complete with commanding officer's headquarters and residence and quarters for bachelor officers. Two concrete officers' quarters look like they are still inhabited by the families of frontier soldiers. The old bakery, guardhouse, magazine, commissary, and cavalry barracks, as well as the 1876 bridge across the North Platte, have been restored to their original condition. The flag flies over the parade ground, helping to reinforce the illusion of a military post revived. True, the hospital, administration building, several officers' quarters and other structures are only shells, and the adobe-walled quadrangle purchased from the American Fur Company in 1849 is called to mind only by a sign overlooking the Laramie. But the historical setting is still the same. There is the little valley formed by the confluence of the North Platte and the Laramie. Nearby are the low brown hills, while Laramie Peak looms starkly against the western sky. And approaching the fort are miraculously preserved sections of the Oregon-California Trail, deep troughs cut into the land by the passage of thousands of hooves and wagon wheels.

Here at old Fort Laramie, as at Ash Hollow and Scott's Bluffs, if one looks and listens and ponders, he can hear the creak of harness, the crack of bullwhips, the bellowing of oxen, the shouts of drivers, the rustling of wagon covers in the wind. Here, some 600 miles from the jumping-off places, is the gateway to the Rocky Mountains and South Pass, key to the crossing of a continent. At this same place, above all others, he can also hear the Indian tom-toms, the jingling of cavalry spurs, and the sweet-sad music of emigrants on their epic journey, the deep heartbeat of the Great Platte River Road.

Bibliography

A. OVERLAND NARRATIVES AND OTHER PRIMARY SOURCES*

*Asterisks indicate cross-references in Bibliography B.

Abbey, James. *California: A Trip Across the Plains in the Spring of 1850.* New Albany, Ind.: n.d.   1850[1]   NL[2]

Abbott, Carlisle S. *Recollections of a California Pioneer.* New York: 1917.   1850   NL

Ables, T. J. Letter of October 12, 1857, from Petaluma, Calif., typescript.   1857   NL

Ackley, Mary E. *Crossing the Plains—Early Days in California.* San Francisco: 1928.   1852   BL

Ackley, Richard Thomas. "Across the Plains in 1858," *Utah Historical Quarterly*, IX, (July, October, 1941), 190–228.   1858   NSHS

Adair, Sarah D. "Pioneer of 1843," *Transactions, Oregon Pioneer Association* (1900), 65–82.   1843   OHS

Adam, George. *Dreadful Sufferings and Thrilling Adventures*, ed. Wm. Beschke. St. Louis: 1850.   1846   NL

Adams, Cecelia E. M. "Crossing the Plains," *Transactions, Oregon Pioneer Association* (1904), 288–329.   1852   OHS

Agatz, Cora Wilson. "A Journey Across the Plains in 1866," *Pacific Northwest Quarterly*, XXVII (April, 1936), 170–74.   1866   NSHS

Akin, James. *Journal . . .* , ed. E. E. Dale. University of Oklahoma *Bulletin*, No. 9 (June 1, 1919).   1852   NL

---

[1] Year of overland passage or period of interest.

[2] Location of material used by the author. See page 566 for key.

Alden, Rev. Wyllis. Journal, in H. C. Fielding, *Ancestors and Descendants of Isaac Alden*. n.p.: 1903.   1851   NPS

Allen, A. J. *Thrilling Adventures, Travels & Explorations of Dr. Elijah White* . . . . New York: 1859.   1842   NL

Allen, O. *Allen's Guide Book & Map to the Gold Fields of Kansas and Nebraska*. Washington, D.C.: 1859.   1859   HC

Allyn, Henry. "Journal of 1853," *Transactions, Oregon Pioneer Association* (1921), 372–435.   1853   OHS

Anderson, Chas. L. "Across the Plains, 1862–1863," photostat of ms.   1862   BL

Anderson, David. "Early Settlements of Platte Valley," *Collections of the Nebraska State Historical Society*, XVI (1911), 193–204.   1867   NSHS

Anderson, Kirk. "Trip to Utah, 1858," *Missouri Historical Society Bulletin*, XVIII (October, 1961), 3–15.   1858   NSHS

Anderson, William Marshall. "Narrative of a Ride," in A. J. Partoll (ed.), *Frontier Omnibus*. Helena: 1962.   1834   NPS

———. *The Rocky Mountain Journals of William Marshall Anderson*, eds. Dale L. Morgan and Eleanor T. Harris. San Marino, Calif.: 1967.   1834   HL

Andrews, D. B. "Overland Journal, 1852," microfilm of typescript at Yale University.   1852   WU

Angell, Susan P. "Sketch of a Pioneer," *Transactions, Oregon Pioneer Association* (1928), 55–56.   1852   OHS

Applegate, Jesse. "A Day with the Cow Column," *Oregon Historical Quarterly*, I (December, 1900), 371–83.   1843   OHS

Aram, Capt. Joseph. "Reminiscences. . . ," *Journal of American History*, I (1907), 617–32.   1846   NSHS

Armstrong, J. Eliza. "Diary," in H. L. Scamehorn (ed.), *Buckeye Rovers in the Gold Rush*. Athens, O.: 1965.   1849   NPS

Arnold, Ben (or Monroe or Connor). *Rekindling Campfires: The Exploits of Ben Arnold*, ed. Lewis F. Crawford. Bismarck, N.D.: 1926.   1862   NSHS

Arthur, John. "Pioneer of 1843," *Transactions, Oregon Pioneer Association* (1887), 96–104.   1843   OHS

Ashley, Algeline J. "Diary, Crossing the Plains," typescript of ms. in San Diego Public Library.   1852   HL

Ashley, Delos R. "Records . . . California Association from Monroe, Michigan," ms. book.   1849   BL

Athearn, P. A. "Logbook," *Pacific Historian*, II (May, 1958), 6–7; (August, 1958), 9–12; (November, 1958), 13–16.   1849   NSHS

Austin, Henry. "Diary," microfilm copy of ms. in private possession.   1849   BL

Ayer, Edward E. "Trip Across the Plains," typescript.   1860   HL

Babcock, Leonard. "Recollections . . . ," ms.   1849   BL

Bachelder, Amos. "Journal of a Trip," ms.   1849   BL

Bacon, Daniel. Photostat of letters in private possession.   1851   NPS

Bailey, Mary S. "Journal, Ohio to California," ms.   1852   HL

Bailey, Washington. *A Trip to California*. n.p.: 1915.   1853   HL

Bakcr, Gco. H. Illustrations. See *Hutching's Panoramic Scenes.*   1853

Baker, William B. Diary, typescript.   1852   CSL

Ball, John. "Across the Continent Seventy Years Ago," *Oregon Historical Quarterly*, III (March, 1902), 82–101.   1832   OHS

Bandel, Eugene. *Frontier Life in the Army, 1854–1861.* Glendale: 1932.   1855   NSHS

Banks, Edwin. Journal, in T. L. Scamehorn (ed.), *Buckeye Rovers in the Gold Rush.* Athens, O.: 1965.   1849   NPS

Barker, Amselm H. . . . *Diary of 1858 from Plattsmouth to Cherry Creek.* Denver: 1859.   1858   NSHS

Barrows, William. *"The General"; or Twelve Nights in the Hunter's Camp.* Boston: 1870.   1850   HL

Barry, J. Neilson. "On the Plains in 1852," *Oregon Historical Quarterly*, XXIX (June, 1928), 209–10. (Quoting anonymous emigrant.)   1852   OHS

Bartholomew, Jacob. "Overland diary," ms.   1850   InS

Barton, H. D. Diary, typescript.   1865   CSL

Beehrer, George W. "Freighting Across the Plains," *Montana Magazine of History*, XII (October, 1962), 2–17.   1858   MHS

Belshaw, George. "Journal from Indiana to Oregon," typescript.   1853   HL

Belshaw, Maria P. "Diary. . . ," ed. J. W. Ellison. *Oregon Historical Quarterly*, XXXIII (December, 1932), 318–33.   1853   OHS

Bennett, James. *Overland Journey to California.* New
Harmony, Ind.: 1906.　　　　　　　　　　　　　1850　NL

Benson, John H. "From St. Joseph to Sacramento,"
typescript.　　　　　　　　　　　　　　　　　1849　NSHS

Bermingham, Twiss. Journal, in Eliza M. Wakefield,
The Handcart Trail. Carlsbad, N.M.: 1949.　　　1856　UHS

Berrien, Joseph W. "Overland from St. Louis," ed.
T. and C. Hinckley. *Indiana Magazine of History,*
LVI (December, 1960), 273–352.　　　　　　　　1849　NPS

Bettelyoun, Susan Bordeaux. Ms., interviews by Mrs.
Josephine Waggoner, ca. 1936–1937.　　1857–1866　NSHS

Biddle, B. R. Letters of May 13, 20, and 24 and June
17, 1849, in the Springfield *Illinois State Journal,* n.d.　1849　ISL

Bidlack, Russell E. *Letters Home: The Story of Ann
Arbor's Forty-Niners.* Ann Arbor, Mich.: 1960.　1849　NSHS

Bidwell, John. *A Journey to California,* ed. Herbert I.
Priestly. San Francisco: 1937.　　　　　　　　　1841　NL

Bird, Edwin R. Journal, ms.　　　　　　　　　　1854　NL

Birge, Julius C. *The Awakening of the Desert.* Boston:
1912.　　　　　　　　　　　　　　　　　　　　1866　DPL

Blackwood, Dr. Thomas. *See* Bidlack.　　　　　1849

Blake, Winslow. Diary, ms.　　　　　　　　　　1852　WHS

Bloemker, Bernard. Letter of June 29, 1852, from Fort
Laramie, photostat.　　　　　　　　　　　　　1852　MiHS

Blood, James A. "Diary . . . Peoria to Sacramento," typescript.　　　　　　　　　　　　　　　　　　　1850　NL

Bloom, Henry S. "Tales . . . ," typescript from the
Kankakee, Ill., *Daily Republican,* May 27 to July
3, 1931.　　　　　　　　　　　　　　　　　　1850　CSL

Boardman, John. "Journal of John Boardman," *Utah
Historical Quarterly,* II (October, 1929), 99–121.　1843　UHS

Boggs, John. "Diary of John Boggs," photostat of ms.　1849　BL

Boggs, W. M. Ms. No. 21, "Sketches of California
Pioneers."　　　　　　　　　　　　　　　　　1846　BL

Bond, Jesse W. Letters, photostat.　　　　　　　1852　WHS

Bonner, John H. "Daily Journal Across the Plains,"
microfilm of ms. in private possession.　　　　1861　BL

Bonneville, Capt. B. L. E. *See* Irving.　　　　　1832

Bonney, Benjamin F. "Recollections," ed. Fred Lockley *Oregon Historical Quarterly*, XXIV (March, 1923), 36–55.   1845   OHS

"Boone Emigrant." Letter to the St. Louis (?) *Missouri Statesman*, in Wyman (ed.), *California Emigrant Letters*.   1850   NPS

Bowen, James E. "Diary Crossing the Plains," microfilm copy of ms.   1851   BL

Bowles, Samuel. *Across the Continent*. Springfield, Mass.: 1865.   1865   NSHS

Bowman, E. L. Journal, in Page, *Wagons West*.   1849   NPS

Boyle, Dr. Charles E. Diary, in the Columbus, O., *Dispatch*, October 2 to 28, 1849.   1849   OHS

Brackett, W. S. "Bonneville and Bridger," *Contributions to the Historical Society of Montana*, III (1900), 175–200.   1862   MHS

Bradley, Henry. Journal, microfilm of ms. at Yale University   1852   WU

Bradway, J. R. "Diary of a Journey, Wisconsin to California," typescript.   1853   WHS

Brady, Charles C. "From Hannibal to the Gold Fields," *Pacific Historian*, IV (November, 1960), 145–52.   1849   NSHS

Bratt, John. *Trails of Yesterday*. Chicago: 1921.   1866   NSHS

Bray, Edmund. Ms. No. 44 in "Sketches of California Pioneers."   1844   BL

Breyfogle, Joshua D. Overland journal, ms.   1849   DC

Brooks, Elisha. *Pioneer Mother of California*. San Francisco: 1922.   1852   BL

Brooks, Noah. *The Boy Emigrants*. New York: 1885.   n.d.   NL

Brooks, Quincy Adams. Letter, of November 7, 1851, *Oregon Historical Quarterly*, XV (September, 1914), 210–15.   1851   OHS

Brown, J. Robert. Journal, photostat of ms.   1856   NL

Brown, Jno. E. *Memoirs of a Forty-Niner*, ed. Katie E. Blood. New Haven: 1907.   1849   NL

Brown, Joseph H. "Trip Across the Plains in Winter," ms. in Oregon Miscellanies.   1848   BL

Bruff, J. Goldsborough. *Gold Rush: [His] Journals, Drawings, and Other Papers*, ed. Georgia Willis Read and Ruth Gaines. New York: 1944.   1849–1851   HL

Bryan, Charles W. "Marthasville to Marysville," *Bulletin of Missouri Historical Society*, XIX (January, 1963), 115–26. 1850 MiHS

Bryan, Lt. F. T. "Report . . . on a . . . Road Between Fort Riley and Bridger's Pass," *Annals of Wyoming*, XVII (January, 1945), 24–55. 1856 NSHS

Bryant, Edwin. *What I Saw in California*. New York: 1849. 1846 NPS

Bryant, Isaiah W. Diary, typescript copy of ms. in private possession. 1853 NPS

Bryarly, Wakeman. *See* Geiger. 1849

Buck, Mrs. W. W. "Reminiscences," *Transactions, Oregon Pioneer Association* (1894), 67–69. 1845 OHS

"Buckskin Mose." *See* Rosenberg. 1855

Buffum, Jos. C. "Diary . . . Pittsburgh to Sacramento," typescript. 1849 CSL

Burch, John C. "Missouri to California," microfilm of ms. at Yale University. 1850 WU

Burgess, Perry A. "Diary . . . Illinois to Montana," *Pacific Northwest Quarterly*, XLI (January, 1950), 43–65. 1866 NSHS

Burlingame, —— (Mr. and Mrs.), Journals in Mrs. C. V. Waite, *Adventures in the Far West*. 1862 NSHS

Burnett, Finn. *See* David. 1866

Burnett, Peter H. *Recollections & Opinions of an Old Pioneer*. New York: 1880. 1843 NL

Burrall, George P. "Trip Across the Plains," typescript. 1849 NL

Burris, Davis. "Narrative," ms. No. 13, "Sketches of California Pioneers." 1849 BL

Burt, Andrew and Elizabeth. *See* Mattes, *Indians, Infants and Infantry*.* 1866

Burton, Richard F. *City of the Saints*. New York: 1862. 1860 NPS

Butscher, Louis C. (ed.). "A Brief Biography of Prince Paul Wilhelm of Wurttemberg," *New Mexico Historical Review*, XVII (July, 1942), 181–215. 1851 DPL

Butterfield, Ira H., Jr. "Michigan to California in 1861," *Michigan History Magazine*, XI (July, 1927), 392–423. 1861 NSHS

Butterfield, Thomas. "Interesting Account," ed. Mrs. E. O. Thompkins. *Grizzly Bear* (January, 1908), 42. 1853 CSL

Byers, William N. "Overland Journal," in the Denver, Colo., *Overland News*, May and June, 1958. 1852 NSHS

Byers, Wm. N., and Jno. H. Kellom. *Handbook to the Gold Fields of Nebraska and Kansas.* New York: 1859.   1859   HC

Cagwin, N. A. Diary, typescript.   1850   CSL

Caldwell, Dr. ——. "Diary," in Bruff, *Gold Rush.* . . .   1849   HL

"California." Letters from St. Joe and Independence to the St. Louis *Missouri Republican. See also* Wyman.   1849   MiHS

Campbell, James. Diary, microfilm of ms.   1850   BL

Campbell, Robert. Dictated ms.   1827   MiHS

——."News from the Plains," in the Kanesville, Ia., *Frontier Guardian,* July 24, 1850.   1850   MC

Caples, Mrs. James. "Overland to California," ms.   1849   CSL

Carleton, J. Henry. *The Prairie Logbooks,* ed. Louis Pelzer. Chicago: 1943.   1845   NL

Carpenter, Helen. "A Trip Across the Plains," ms.   1856   HL

Carr, Dabney T. "Platte River near Chimney Rock." Letter of May 31, 1850.   1850   MiHS

Carr, John. *Pioneer Days in California.* Eureka, Calif.: 1891.   1850   NL

Carriger, Nicholas. "Autobiography," ms. No. 6, "Sketches of California Pioneers."   1846   BL

Carrington, Frances C. *My Army Life.* Philadelphia: 1911.   1866   NPS

Carrington, Col. Henry. Map of Platte River Ford, in *Publications of the Nebraska State Historical Society,* XXI, (1930).   n.d.   NSHS

Carrington, Margaret I. *Ab-sa-ra-ka, Land of Massacre.* Philadelphia: 1879.   1866   NPS

Carter, E. S. *Life and Adventures.* . . . St. Joseph: 1896.   1852   NL

Carter, Judge William A. "Diary . . . 1857," *Annals of Wyoming,* XI (April, 1939), 75–110.   1857   WHS

Cartwright, David W. "A Tramp to California," in *Natural History of Western Wild Animals.* n.p.: n.d.   1852   LC

Case, Hamet, H. "Laramie to Oregon," ms.   n.d.   BL

Case, William M. "Reminiscences," *Oregon Historical Quarterly,* I (September, 1900), 269–77.   1844   OHS

Castleman, P. F. "Diary While Crossing the Plains," microfilm of ms.   1849   BL

Chadwick, Samuel. Diary, ms.   1852   WHS

Chalmers, Robert. "Journal. . . ," *Utah Historical Quarterly*, XX (January, 1952), 31–55.   1850   UHS

Chamberlain, Wm. E. "Iowa to Sutter's Fort," typescript.   1849   CSL

Chambers, Margaret. *Reminiscences.* n.p.: 1903.   1851   HL

Chambers, William and Robert (eds.). "Journey from New Orleans to California." Excerpt from *Chamber's Journal.* London (?)   1855   NL

Chandless, William. *A Visit to Salt Lake.* London: 1857.   1859   NL

Chapman, William W. Diary, ms.   1849   HL

"Cheyenne." Letters to the St. Louis *Missouri Republican*, in Wyman (ed.), *California Emigrant Letters.*   1850   NPS

Child, Andrew. *New Guide for the Overland Route to California.* Milwaukee: 1852.   1850   NL

Chillson, H. M. Diary, ms. notebook.   1859   HL

Cipriani, Count Leonetto. *California and Overland Diaries*, ed. Ernest Falbo. Portland: 1962.   1853   NPS

Clark, Bennett C. ". . . Missouri to California in 1849," ed. Ralph P. Bieber. *Missouri Historical Review*, XXIII (October, 1928), 3–43.   1849   HSM

Clark, C. M. *A Trip to Pike's Peak*, ed. R. Greenwood. San Jose: 1958.   1860   DPL

Clark, John (of Virginia). "The California Guide," microfilm of typescript at Yale University.   1852   WU

Clark, John Hawkins. "Overland to the Gold Fields . . . ," ed. Louise Barry. *Kansas Historical Quarterly*, XI (August, 1942), 227–96.   1852   NSHS

Clark, Dr. Jonathan. "Across the Plains," in the San Francisco *Argonaut*, August 1, 8, and 15, 1925.   1849   DPL

Clark, Jno. H. "Notes of a Trip," typescript.   1852   NL

Clark, Sterling B. F. *How Many Miles from St. Joe?* San Francisco: 1929.   1849   NL

Clark, William. "A Trip Across the Plains in 1857," *Iowa Journal of History and Politics*, XX (April, 1922), 163–223.   1857   NSHS

Clayton, William. *Journal, A Daily Record* . . . . Salt Lake City: 1921.   1847   NL

Clemens, Samuel (Mark Twain). *Roughing It.* Hartford: 1872.   1861   NSHS

Clifton, John. "Journal," in Ritter, *More Than Gold in California.*   1852   BL

Clinkinbeard, Anna Dell. *Across the Plains in '64.* New York: 1953.   1864   NSHS

Clyman, James. *James Clyman . . . Frontiersman,* ed. C. L. Camp. Portland: 1960.   1844   NPS

Coke, Hon. Henry J. *A Ride over the Rocky Mountains.* London: 1852.   1850   NL

Cole, Cornelius. *Memoirs of Cornelius Cole.* New York: 1908.   1849   HL

Cole, Gilbert L. *In the Early Days.* Kansas City: 1905.   1852   NPS

Collins, Catherine Wever. "An Army Wife Comes West," *Colorado Magazine,* XXXI (October, 1954), 241–73.   1863   NSHS

Collins, John S. *Across the Plains in '64.* Omaha: 1904.   1864   NSHS

Collins, Martha Elizabeth Gilliam. "Reminiscences . . . ," *Oregon Historical Quarterly,* XVII (December, 1916), 358–72.   1844   OHS

Collins' Emigrant Guide to the Gold Mines of the Rocky Mountains, in the Council Bluffs, Ia., *Daily Telegraph,* April 9, 1861. Photostat.   1861   MC

Collister, Oscar. "Life of (a) Wyoming Pioneer . . . ," *Annals of Wyoming,* VII (July, 1930), 343–61; (October, 1930), 370–78.   1861   NSHS

Colvig, William M. "Annual Address . . . ," *Transactions, Oregon Pioneer Association* (1916), 333–50.   1851   OHS

Cone, Anson S. "Reminiscences," *Oregon Historical Quarterly,* IV (September, 1903), 251–59.   n.d.   OHS

Conway, Cornelius. *The Utah Expedition.* Cincinnati: 1858.   1857   NL

Conyers, E. W. "Diary," *Transactions, Oregon Pioneer Association* (1905), 423–512.   1852   OHS

Cooke, Lucy R. *Crossing the Plains.* Modesto, Calif.: 1923.   1852   BL

Cooke, Lt. Col. Philip St. George. "March of the 2d Dragoons . . . ," ed. Hamilton Gardner. *Annals of Wyoming,* XXVII (April, 1955), 43–60.   1857   NSHS

———. Report on the Battle of Blue Water. Senate Executive Documents, 34th Congress, 3d Session, Vol. 8, Doc. 58.   1855   LC

———. *Scenes and Adventures in the Army.* Philadelphia: 1859.   1845   NL

Cornwall, Bruce. *Life Sketch of Pierre Barlow Cornwall.* San Francisco: 1906.   1848   HL

Cornwall, Pierre Barlow. *See* Bruce Cornwall.   1848

Cosad, David. "Journal," microfilm of original ms. at California Historical Society.   1849   BL

Cosgrove, Hugh. "Reminiscences," *Oregon Historical Quarterly*, I (September, 1900), 253–69.   1847   OHS

Coy, Owen C. *The Great Trek.* Los Angeles: 1931. (Diaries of Dr. E. A. Tompkins and Lemuel C. McKeeby.)   1850   NSHS

Cramer, Thomas. "Kansas to California," microfilm from typescript at Yale University.   1859   WU

Crandall, Elaphalet. "Diary, Plattsmouth to Sacramento," ms.   1859   MC

Crane, Addison M. Journal, ms.   1852   HL

Cranstone, Susan. Diary, ms.   1851   BL

Crawford, C. H. *Scenes of Earlier Days, Etc.* Petaluma, Calif.: 1898.   1851   NL

Crawford, Medorem. *Journal (Sources of the History of Oregon*, Vol. I.) Portland: 1900.   1842   OHS

Crawford, P. V. "Journal of a Trip. . . ," *Oregon Historical Quarterly*, XXV (June, 1924), 136–69.   1851   OHS

Creigh, Thomas R. "From Nebraska to Montana," ed. James C. Olson. *Nebraska History*, XXIX (September, 1948), 208–37.   1866   NSHS

Crosby, Jesse W. "History and Journal. . . ," *Annals of Wyoming*, XI (July, 1939), 145–219.   1847   NSHS

Cross, Maj. Osborne. Journal, in Settle (ed.), *March of the Mounted Riflemen.*   1849   NSHS

Cummings, Charles J. Journal, microfilm from typescript at Yale University.   1859   WU

Cummins, Sarah J. *Autobiography and Reminiscences.* La Grande, Ore.: 1914.   1845   NPS

Curry, Col. Geo. B. ". . . A Pioneer of 1853," *Transactions, Oregon Pioneer Association* (1916), 333–50.   1853   OHS

Curtis, Waters. Letters of May 27 and June 8, 1849, in the Springfield *Illinois Daily Journal*, August 8, 1849.   1849   IHS

Cutting, A. Howard. Journal, ms.   1863   HL

Dalton, John E. Diary, typescript.   1852   WHS

Darby ——, and —— Miller. *History of California*. Auburn,
N.Y.: 1850. Typescript.   1850   HC

Darling, Lucia. "Crossing the Prairies in a Covered
Wagon," typescript.   1863   MC

Darwin, Charles B. Journal, 3 vols., ms.   1849   HL

Davidson, John N. Letters of June 13 and 16, 1850.   1850   WHS

Davis, Alvah Isaiah. "Diary . . . ," *Transactions, Oregon
Pioneer Association* (1909), 355–81.   1852   OHS

Davis, Rev. Henry T. *Solitary Places Made Glad*. Cincinnati: 1890.   1850   CSL

Day, Gershom and Elizabeth. *See* Trowbridge.   1849

Deady, Mrs. M. P. "Crossing the Plains . . . ," *Transactions, Oregon Pioneer Association* (1928), 57–64.   1846   OHS

Dean, F. S. Letter of June 10, 1849, in the Springfield
Illinois State Journal, August 7, 1849.   1849   IHS

Decker, Peter. *Diaries of Peter Decker*, ed. Helen S.
Giffen. Georgetown, Calif.: 1966.   1849   SCP

——. Diary, microfilm of original ms. at Society of
California Pioneers.   1849   BL

Delano, Alonzo. *Across the Plains and Among the Diggings*. New York: 1936.   1849   NSHS

Dennis, Bryan. Diary, typescript of ms. in private
possession.   1850   NPS

DeSmet, Father Pierre J. *Life, Letters and Travels*, ed.
H. M. Chittenden. 4 vols. Cleveland: 1905.   1840–1851   NSHS

Dewolf, Capt. David. "Diary . . . and Letters," *Transactions, Illinois State Historical Society* (1925),
183–222.   1849   ISL

"Diary of an Unknown Scout," photostat copy of ms. in
private possession.   1854   BL

Dickson, Albert Jerome. *Covered Wagon Days*, ed.
Arthur Jerome Dickson. Cleveland: 1929.   1864   NSHS

Dinwiddie, ——. "Dinwiddie Journal," ed. Margaret
Booth, in A. J. Partoll (ed.), *Frontier Omnibus*.
Helena: 1962.   1853   NPS

Dodge, Gen. Grenville M. Journal. *See also* J. R.
Perkins.   1865   NPS

Dougherty, Lewis B. "Experiences . . . on the Oregon
Trail," ed. Ethel M. Withers. *Missouri Historical
Review*, XXIV (April, 1930), 359–78; (July, 1930),

550–67; (October, 1930), 102–15; (January, 1931), 306–21; (April, 1931), 474–89.   1849   NSHS

Douglas, James A. Letter in the St. Louis (?) *Missouri Statesman*, n.d. *See* Wyman.   1849   NPS

Downer, D. C. *See* Bidlack.   1849

Doyle, Simon. Journal, microfilm of ms. at Yale University.   1849–1854   WU

Draper, Elias J. *Autobiography of . . . a Pioneer of California*. Fresno: 1904.   1853   NL

Drips, Andrew. Collection, ms.   1843–1851   BL

———. Papers, ms.   1844–1860   MiHS

Drum, Gen. Richard D. "Reminiscences of . . . Ash Hollow," *Collections of the Nebraska State Historical Society*, XVI (1911), 143–51.   1855   NSHS

Dundass, Samuel R. *Journal of Samuel R. Dundass*. Steubenville.: 1857.   1849   LC

Duniway, Abigail J. *Captain Gray's Company*, Portland: 1859.   1852   HL

Dunlap, Katherine. Journal, photocopy of typescript.   1864   BL

Dutton, Jerome. "Across the Plains," *Annals of Iowa*, IX (1909–1911), 447–83.   1850   NSHS

Earnshaw, William. "Across the Plains," typescript copy of reprint in the Waterford, Wis., *Post*, June 5 to September 4, 1897.   1860   NL

Eastin, Thomas. ". . . Henderson, Ky. to . . . California," copy of ms. at Filson Club, Louisville, Ky.   1849   NPS

Ebey, Scott W. "Record of Travel," ms.   1854   BL

Eccles, Mrs. David. Interview by Maurice Howe, in A. J. Partoll (ed.), *Frontier Omnibus*. Helena: 1962.   1867   NPS

Edmundson, William. "Diary," *Annals of Iowa*, VIII (1907–1908), 516–35.   1850   NSHS

Edwards, P. L. *Sketch of Oregon Territory, or Emigrant's Guide*. Liberty, Mo.: 1842. (Reprint.)   1841   NPS

Eells, Rev. M. "Rev. H. H. Spaulding," *Transactions, Oregon Pioneer Association* (1897), 106–11.   1838   OHS

Eells, Myra. "Diary, April–September, 1838," in Drury (ed.), *First White Women Over the Rockies*,* 71–89.   1838   NPS,

Egan, Howard. *Pioneering the West, 1846–1878*. Richmond, Utah: 1917.   1847   NL

Ellenbecker, John G. *Jayhawkers of Death Valley.* Marysville, Kan.: 1938.   1849 NL

Enos, James E. "Recollections of the Plains," typescript.   1855 NL

Evans, B. W. "Diary . . . Missouri to California," microfilm of ms. in private possession.   1849 BL

Evans, James W. "Journal of a Trip to California," ms.   1850 BL

Ewers, Anton. "Reminiscences," bound typescript, D.A.R. Pioneer Records.   1854 CSL

Fairchild, Lucius. *California Letters*, ed. Joseph Shafer (*Wisconsin History Collections*, Vol. XXXI). Madison: 1931.   1849 WHS

Farnham, Elijah Bryan. "From Ohio to California . . . ," eds. Merrill J. Mattes and Esley J. Kirk. *Indiana Magazine of History*, XLVI (September, 1950), 297–318; (December, 1950), 403–20.   1849 NSHS

Ferguson, Charles D. *Experiences of a Forty-Niner. . .* Cleveland: 1888.   1849 NL

Ferrell, Dennis. "Adventures on the Plains. . . ," *Collections of the Nebraska State Historical Society*, XVII (1913), 247–58.   1865 NSHS

Ferris, Benjamin G. *Utah and the Mormons.* New York: 1854.   1854 NSHS

Ferris, Mrs. Benjamin G. *The Mormons at Home. . . .* New York: 1856.   1854 HL

Ferris, Warren A. *Life in the Rocky Mountains*, ed. Paul C. Phillips. Denver: 1940.   1830 DPL

Field, Matthew C. *Prairie and Mountain Sketches*, ed. Kate L. Gregg. Norman: 1957.   1843 NPS

Findley, Mrs. Jane L. "Sketch of Pioneer Days," *Transactions, Oregon Pioneer Association* (1926), 23–25.   1847 OHS

Fish, Juliette G. "Crossing the Plains," photostat of original ms. in private possession.   1862 HL

Fish, Mary C. "Daily Journal," ms.   1860 BL

Flint, Thomas. *Diary . . . California to Maine and Return.* Los Angeles: 1923.   1851–1855 NSHS

Forsdick, Stephen. "On the Oregon Trail to Zion," *Denver Westerners Brand Book*, IX (1953), 33–55.   1853 NPS

Fort Kearney, South Pass and Honey Lake Wagon Road Company. Journals and field notes including data by

William Magraw, Frederick Lander, M. M. Long, O. H. O'Neill, W. H. Wagner, R. L. Poor, J. F. Mallowney, and Charles H. Miller. 1857–1859 NatA

Foster, Rev. Isaac. *The Foster Family, California Pioneers,* ed. Lucy Foster Sexton. Santa Barbara: 1925. 1849–1852 NL

Fouts, William. "Diary . . . Overland to Oregon. . . ," typescript. 1850 NL

Fox, George W. "Diary. . . ," *Annals of Wyoming,* VIII (January, 1932), 580–601. 1866 NSHS

Fox, Jared. "Memorandum of a Trip . . . Wisconsin to California," typescript. 1852 CSL

Francl, Joseph. "The Story of Joseph Francl," tr. Fred Francl, ed. Rose Rosicky. *Bratrsky Vestnick:* n.d. 1854 NL

Frear, Harry James. Diary, typescript from ms. in private possession. 1852 HC

Fremont, Lt. Charles C. *Report of the Exploring Expedition to the Rocky Mountains. . . .* Washington, D.C.: 1845. 1842–1844 NPS

Frink, Margaret A. *Journal . . . of a Party of California Gold Seekers. . . .* Oakland: 1897. 1850 NL

Frizzell, Lodisa. *Across the Plains to California.* New York: 1915. 1852 NL

Frontier Guardian (Kanesville, Ia.). Intermittent issues, April 4, 1849, to July 24, 1850, with migration news and notices. . Photostat copies. 1849–1850 MC

Frost, Mary P. "Experiences of a Pioneer," *Washington Historical Quarterly,* VII (April, 1916), 123–25. n.d. NSHS

Frush, William H. Diary, microfilm of ms. at Yale University. 1850 WU

Fulkerth, William L. "Diary . . . Iowa to California," photostat of ms. 1863 BL

Fuller, Randall. "Journal. . . ," copy of ms. in private possession. 1849 NPS

Gage, Stephen T. Diary typescript. 1852 CSL

Garrison, Rev. A. E. *Life and Labours of Rev. A. E. Garrison* n.p.: 1887. 1846 HL

Gatton, Benjamin J. Letter of July 1, 1849, in the Springfield *Illinois Daily Journal,* September 28, 1849. 1849 ISL

Gaylord, Orange. "Diary to California and Oregon. . . ,"
Transactions, Oregon Pioneer Association (1917),
394–439.   1850–1853   NSHS

Geer, Elizabeth D. Smith. "Diary. . . ," *Transactions,
Oregon Pioneer Association* (1907), 153–85.   1847   OHS

Geiger, Vincent, and Bryarly Wakeman. *Trail to California*, ed. David M. Potter. New Haven: 1945.   1849   NPS

Gelwicks, Daniel W. "Diary . . . Belleville, Illinois to
South Pass," ms.   1849   ISL

"The General." *See* Barrows.   1850

Gibbs, George. Journal, in Settle (ed.), *March of the
Mounted Riflemen.*   1849   NSHS

Gibson, J. W. *Recollection of a Pioneer.* St. Joseph:
1912.   1849–1852   NPS

Gilbert, William W. Diary, typescript.   1850   NL

Gilfry, Henry H. "Annual Address. . . ," *Transactions,
Oregon Pioneer Association* (1903), 202–20.   1852   OHS

Gill, Thomas. "Across the Plains," in the Sonora (?)
Calif., *Stanislaus Weekly News*, August 14, 1903. 1853   CSL

Gilliam, Washington S. "Reminiscences. . . ," *Transactions, Oregon Pioneer Association* (1905), 411–23. 1844   OHS

Gilmore, Alexander. "The Gilmore Story," typescript. n.d.   CSL

Glasscock, C. B. *Lucky Baldwin.* Indianapolis: 1933. n.d.   HL

Goldsmith, Oliver. *Overland in Forty-Nine.* Detroit:
1896.   1849   NL

Goodyear, Andrew. Letters, in Charles Kelly, *Miles
Goodyear.*   1847   BL

Goodyear, Miles. *See* Charles Kelly.   1832   BL

Gorgas, Solomon C. "Diary . . . St. Joseph to Placerville,"
ms. notebook.   1850   HL

Goughnor, E. *Across the Plains in '49.* n.p.: n.d. 1849   LC

Gould, Charles. "Diary . . . Boston and Newton Joint
Stock Association," typescript.   1849   NL

Gove, Jesse A. *The Utah Expedition.* Concord, N.H.:
1928.   1857–1858   NPS

Graham, Calvin. "Journal . . . Pennsylvania to California," typescript.   1853   KHS

Gratiot, Henry. Journal, ms.   1859   MiHS

Gray, Charles G. "Journal of an Overland Passage from
Independence to San Francisco" 2 vols. ms.   1849   HL

Gray, W. H. *A History of Oregon.* Portland: 1870.   1836   NPS

———. "Journal of 1838," ed. C. M. Drury. *Pacific Northwest Quarterly*, XXIX (July, 1938), 227–82.   1838   NSHS

Greeley, Horace. *An Overland Journey, New York to
San Francisco.* New York: 1860.   1859   HL

Green, Caleb. "A Visit to Great Salt Lake," ms. journal
book.   1856–1857   MiHS

Green, Jay. *Diary . . . Duncan's Ferry to Hangtown . . . .*
Stockton, Calif.: 1955.   1852   CSL

Green, Joseph. Letter of July 24, 1850, to Mrs. Nancy
Johnson, Plymouth, Vt., *re* Sanford Johnson.   1850   HC

Grindell, John. Diary, typescript.   1850   WHS

"Guide to the Gold Mines—Table of Distances from
Omaha to Denver," Council Bluffs, Ia., *Daily Telegraph*, April 19, 1861.   1861   MC

Guill, Mary Jane. Diary, typescript.   1860   CSL

Gunnison, John Williams. Letters, June 2 to August 4,
1849.   1849   HL

Haas, John B. "Autobiography," Placerville, Calif., *Pony
Express Courier* (June-July, 1939).   1858   NSHS

Hackney, Joseph. Diary, in Elizabeth Page, *Wagons
West.*   1849   NPS

Hadley, Mrs. E. A. Diary, typescript from ms. in private
possession.   1851   HC

Hagelstein, Georg M. Diary, mimeograph.   1854   CSL

Hale, Edward Everett. *Kanzas and Nebraska.* Boston:
1854.   1854   LC

Hale, Israel. "Diary of a Trip to California," *Quarterly,
Society of California Pioneers*, II, 2 (1925), 61–134.   1849   HL

Hall, Cyrenius. Checklist of sketches in the Wyoming
State Archives and Historical Department. *See also*
Neal E. Miller.   1852–1853   WSA

Hall, O. J. Diary, typescript.   1849   BL

Hambly, David W. "Autobiography," ms.   1852   BL

Hamelin, J. P., Jr. Diaries and microfilm from mss. at
Yale University.   1849–1856   WU

Hampton, William H. *Diary* . . . . Reproduction by California Department of Natural Resources. n.p.: 1958.   1852   CSL

Hancock, Samuel. *Narrative of Samuel Hancock.* New York: 1927.   1845   NSHS

Harker, George M. "Morgan Street to Old Dry Diggings," *Glimpses of the Past,* VI (April-June, 1939), 35–76.   1849   MiHS

Harlan, A. W. "Journal . . . While Crossing the Plains," *Annals of Iowa,* XI (1913–1915), 32–62.   1850   NSHS

Harmon, Appleton Milo. *Appleton Milo Harmon Goes West,* ed. M. H. Anderson. Berkeley: 1946.   1847   NSHS

Harney, Gen. William S. Report of September 5, 1855, in *Annual Report of the Secretary of War.* Washington, D.C.: 1856.   1855   NSHS

Harritt, Jesse. "Diary. . . ," *Transactions, Oregon Pioneer Association* (1911), 206–26.   1845   OHS

Harter, George. Diary, ms.   1864   CSL

Harvey, August F. "A New Map of the Principal Routes to the Gold Regions of Colorado Territory."   1862   NSHS

Harvey, Isaac J. "To California in 1850," typescript.   1850   BL

Hastings, Lansford W. *Emigrant's Guide to Oregon and California.* Princeton: 1932.   1842   NPS

Hastings, Loren B. "Diary of . . . a Pioneer. . . ," *Transactions, Oregon Pioneer Association* (1923), 12–26.   1847   OHS

Haun, Catherine M. "A Woman's Trip Across the Plains," ms.   1849   HL

Hayden, Mary Jane. *Pioneer Days.* San Jose, Calif.: 1915.   1852   BL

Hazlip, John B. Letter of July 8, 1849, at Great Salt Lake. Reprinted in Dale L. Morgan, "Letters by Forty-Niners."   1849   UHS

Hearst, George. *Autobiography,* part 3. ("Grandpa Hearst Strikes It Rich," ed. William Randolph Hearst, Jr.) San Francisco *Sunday Examiner,* August 28, 1966.   1852   CSL

Hedges, William H. *Pike's Peak . . . or Busted!,* ed. Herbert O. Brayer. Evanston: 1954.   1860   NPS

Helmick, Sarah. "Recollections . . . ," *Oregon Historical Quarterly,* XXVI (December, 1925), 444–47.   1845   OHS

Henderson, Paul. Notes on data concerning claims filed by mail contractors, from U.S. House Executive Documents, 32nd, 33rd, 34th, and 35th Congresses. 1852–1858 HC

Herndon, Sarah R. *Days on the Road* . . . . New York: 1902. 1865 HL

Hester, Sallie. "Diary of a Pioneer Girl," San Francisco *Argonaut*, Vols. 96A–97 (1925). 1849 DPL

Hewitt, Randall H. *Notes by the Way* . . . *Dundee, Illinois, Olympia, Washington.* n.p.: n.d. 1862 BL

———. *Across the Plains and Over the Divide.* New York: 1906. 1862 HL

Hickman, Peter. Diary, typescript. 1852 CSL

Hickman, Richard O. "An Overland Journey," ed. Catherine White, in A. J. Partoll (ed.), *Frontier Omnibus.* Helena: 1962. 1852 NPS

Hinds, Rev. T. W. "Crossing the Plains. . . . ," photocopy of typescript. 1850 BL

Hines, Celinda E. "Diary . . . ," *Transactions, Oregon Pioneer Association* (1918), 69–125. 1853 OHS

Hinman, Alanson. "Reminiscences," ed. James R. Robertson, *Oregon Historical Quarterly*, II (September, 1901), 266–86. n.d. OHS

Hinman, Charles G. Diary, ms. 1849 CHS

———. *A Pretty Fair View of the Elephant*, ed. Colton Storm. Chicago: 1960. 1849 MC

Hite, Abraham. "Diary. . . ," typescript, with diary of Mary F. Hite Sanford. 1853 CSL

Hixson, I. M. Letter of May 20, 1849, from Camp No. 19. 1849 MiHS

Hodder, Mrs. Halie R. "Crossing the Plains in War Time," *Colorado Magazine*, X (July, 1933), 131–36. 1864 CHS

Hoffman, Benjamin. "West Virginia Forty-Niners," ed. C. H. Ambler. *West Virginia History*, III (October, 1941), 59–73. 1849 NPS

Holliday, George H. *On the Plains in '65.* n.p.: 1883. 1865 HL

Holt, James. "Reminiscences . . . ," part 2, ed. Dale L. Morgan. *Utah Historical Quarterly*, XXIII (April, 1955), 151–75. 1846 UHS

Hoppe, Hugo. *See* McPherren. 1851

Hopper, Silas L. "Diary by Silas Hopper," *Annals of Wyoming*, III (October, 1925), 117–26.   1863   NSHS

Horn, Hosea B. *Horn's Overland Guide* . . . . New York: 1853.   1850   NL

Horton, Emily M. *Our Family* . . . . n.p.: 1922.   1856   NL

Hoth, Hans P. E. Diary, photostat of German original and typed translation.   1854   BL

Howard, Mary E. S. "After Lapse of 50 Years," photostat of typescript in private possession.   n.d.   CSL

Howell, Elijah P. Diary, ms.   1849   HSM

Howell, John E. "Diary of an Emigrant . . . ," *Washington Historical Quarterly*, I (April, 1907), 138–58.   1845   NSHS

Hubbell, W. W. "Notes on Desert Life," *Meigs County Telegraph*, series, 1855–1856.   1850   OhHS

Hull, Lewis Byram. "Soldiering on the High Plains . . . 1864–1866," *Kansas Historical Quarterly*, VII (February, 1938), 3–53.   1864   KHS

Huntington, O. B. "Pioneer Journal," ms.   1848   BYU

Hutcheson, Austin E. "Overland in 1852: The McGuirk Diary," *Pacific Historical Review*, XIII (December, 1944), 426–32.   1852   BL

Hutchings, James M. Diary, ms.   1849   LC

Hutchings Panoramic Scenes—Crossing the Plains. Composite photoplate: "Views Drawn from Nature in 1853," by George H. Baker, mounted on reverse side of original letter written by Edwin R. Bird, August 13, 1855. Placerville, Calif.: n.d. (Published by J. H. Hutchings.)   1853   NL

Ingalls, E. S. *Journal of a Trip to California.* Waukegan, Ill.: 1852.   1850   NL

Ingersoll, Chester. *Overland to California*, ed. Douglas McMurtie. Chicago: 1937.   1847   NL

Inman, Mrs. Margaret W. "My Arrival in Washington," *Washington Historical Quarterly*, XVIII (October, 1957), 254–60.   1852   NSHS

Irving, Washington. *Adventures of Captain Bonneville, U.S.A.*, ed. Edgeley W. Todd. Norman: 1961.   1832   NPS

Ivins, Virginia W. *Pen Pictures of Early Western Days.* n.p.: 1905.   1853   NL

Jackman, Levi. Journal, typescript.   1847   BYU

Jackson, William H. *The Diaries of William H. Jackson,*
ed. LeRoy R. Hafen. Glendale: 1959.   1866   NSHS

Jacob, Norton. Journal, typescript.   1847   BYU

Jagger, D. Diary, ms.   1849   CaHS

Jefferson, T. H. "Map of the Emigrant Road from Independence, Missouri to San Francisco, California," in
Dale L. Morgan (ed.), *Overland in 1846,* Vol. I.   1846–1849   NSHS

Jensen, Andrew. *Day by Day with the Utah Pioneers.*
n.p.: n.d.   1847   UHS

Jewett, George E. Diary, microfilm from ms. at San
Mateo County Historical Society.   1849   BL

"Joaquin." Correspondence in the Kanesville, Ia., *Frontier Guardian* in Watkins (ed.), *Publication of the
Nebraska State Historical Society.* XX, 208–209.   1849   NSHS

Johnson, J. L. Diary, microfilm from ms. at Yale University.   1851   WU

Johnson, Joseph H. "Diary of Joseph H. Johnson," ms.   1849   HL

Johnson, Overton, and Wm. H. Winter. *Route Across
the Rocky Mountains.* Princeton: 1932.   1843   NSHS

Johnston, Wm. G. *Experiences of a Forty-Niner.* Pittsburgh: 1892.   1849   NL

Jones, Mary A. "'Story of My Life," typescript in California Pioneer Collection.   1846   BL

Jory, James. "Recollections," ed. H. S. Lyman. *Oregon
Historical Quarterly,* III (September, 1902), 271–86.   n.d.   OHS

Josselyn, Amos P. Letter of July 15, 1849, in Dale L.
Morgan (ed.), "Letters by Forty-Niners."   1849   UHS

———. ". . . Zanesville to Sacramento," ms.   1849   CSL

"Journal of Overland Trip," ms. book. (Monroe, [Mich-
igan] Company with Delos Ashley.)   1849   BL

Judson, Phoebe G. *A Pioneer's Search for an Ideal
Home.* Bellingham, Wash.: 1925.   1853   NL

Keegan, Elizabeth. Letters, D.A.R. Pioneer Records.   1852   CSL

Keil, William. "Letters from . . . Missouri to Oregon,"
Missouri Historical Review, XLVIII (October, 1953),
23–41.   1855   HSM

Keller, Geo. *A Trip Across the Plains. . . .* Massilon,
O.: 1851.   1850   NL

Kellogg, Jane D. "Memories of 1852," *Transactions,
Oregon Pioneer Association* (1913), 86–94.   1852   OHS

Kelly, Charles. *Miles Goodyear.* Salt Lake City: 1937. BL

Kelly, Rev. Clinton. "Pioneer of 1848," *Transactions, Oregon Pioneer Association* (1887), 52–63. 1848 OHS

Kelly, William. *An Excursion to California.* . . . London: 1851. 1849 NPS

Kenderdine, T. S. *A California Tramp.* . . . Newton, Penn.: 1888. 1858 NL

Kennerly, William C. *Persimmon Hill.* Norman: 1938. 1843 NPS

Kerns, John T. "Journal . . . ," *Transactions, Oregon Pioneer Association* (1914), 148–93. 1852 OHS

Ketcham, Rebecca. "From Ithaca to Clatsop Plains," *Oregon Historical Quarterly,* LXII (September, 1961), 237–87; (December, 1961), 337–402. 1853 OHS

Keyes, Elizabeth. "Across the Plains. . . ," *Colorado Magazine,* X (March, 1933), 71–78. n.d. CHS

Kilgore, William T. *The Kilgore Journal.* New York: 1949. 1850 NSHS

King, John. Letters, in King Family Papers. 1849 ISL

Kingman, Henry. *Three-Fourths of a Century* . . . . Delevan, Kan.: 1917. n.d. HL

Kingman, Romanzo. "Pike's Peak Journal," *Iowa Journal of History,* XLVIII (January, 1950), 55–85. 1859 NSHS

Kingsbury, Joseph. "Pike's Peak Rush," *Colorado Magazine,* IV (January, 1927), 1–6. 1859 CHS

Kirkpatrick, Charles A. Journal, ms. 1849 BL

Kiser, Joseph C. Diary, ms. 1850 WHS

Knapp, Cornelius. Letter of May 31, 1850, from Fort Laramie. Typescript copy, original in private possession. 1850 NPS

Knight, Mrs. Amelia S. "Diary," *Transactions, Oregon Pioneer Association* (1928), 38–53. 1853 OHS

Knight, Thomas. Ms. in "Sketches of California Pioneers." 1845 BL

Knight, William H. "An Emigrant's Trip . . . ," *Publications of the Historical Society of Southern California,* XII, 3 (1923), 32–41. 1859 HL

Knox, Reuben. ". . . Letters, 1849–1851," ed. Charles W. Turner. *North Carolina Historical Review,* XXXVII (January, 1960), 66–93; (April, 1960), 243–70; (July, 1960), 397–418. 1850 NPS

Krepps, Bolivar G. Journal, ms.   1849   CHS

Lambourne, Alfred. *The Old Journey.* n.p.: 1897.   n.d.   NPS

———. *The Pioneer Trail.* Salt Lake City: 1913.   n.d.   NL

Lampton, Wm. "Diary of a Trip . . . ," typescript.   1850   MiHS

Lander, William. *See* Fort Kearney, South Pass and Honey Lake Wagon Road Company.   1857–1859

Lane, S. A. "Diary of a Trip . . . ," photocopy.   1850   BL

Langworthy, Franklin. *Scenery of the Plains . . . ,* ed. Paul C. Phillips. Princeton: 1932.   1850   NPS

Larkin, William. Letter of June 27, 1864, *Pacific Historian,* II (February, 1958), 2–4.   1864   NSHS

Larpenteur, Charles. *Forty Years a Fur Trader . . . ,* ed. Elliott Coues. New York: 1898.   1833   NPS

Latter Day Saints' Millenial Star, Vols. XI and XII. Council Bluffs (?): n.d.   1849–1850   NSHS

Laub, George. "Pioneer Journal," ms.   1852   BYU

Lee, D., and J. H. Frost. *Ten Years in Oregon.* New York: 1844.   1834   NL

Lee, Jason. "Diary of 1834," *Oregon Historical Quarterly,* VII (September, 1906), 225–33; XVII (June, 1916), 116–46; (September, 1916), 240–66; (December, 1916), 397–430.   1834   OHS

Lee, John D. *Journals of John D. Lee* (1846–1847 and 1859), ed. Charles Kelly. Salt Lake City: 1938.   1846–1859   LC

Lee, William. "Notes . . . on a Journey . . . Washington to Genoa, Carson Valley, Utah," ms.   1858–1859   LC

Leeper, David R. *The Argonauts of Forty-Nine . . . .* South Bend, Ind.: 1894.   1849   NL

Leonard, Zenas. *Adventures of Zenas Leonard,* ed. W. F. Wagner. Cleveland: 1904.   1831–1834   NSHS

Lester, Gurdon P. "A Round Trip to the Montana Mines . . . ," ed. Charles W. Martin. *Nebraska History* XLVI (December, 1965), 273–314.   1866   NSHS

Letter, in the Kanesville, Ia., *Frontier Guardian,* in Watkins, ed. *Publication of the Nebraska State Historical Society.* XX, 207–208.   1849   NSHS

Letter, September 27, 1850, from Sacramento. Microfilm from ms. at Yale University.   1850   WU

Lewelling, Seth. Journal, typescript.   1850   CSL

Lewis, Elisha B. Diary, typescript.   1849   WHS

Lewis, John N. "Diary, Indiana to Oregon," ms.   1852   BL

Lienhard, Heinrich. *From St. Louis to Sutter's Fort,* ed. E. G. and E. K. Gudde. Norman: 1961.   1846   NPS

Lindsey, Tipton. "The Plains and Deserts of North America," ms.   1849   BL

Linforth, James (ed.). *Route from Liverpool to Great Salt Lake Valley.* Liverpool: 1855.   1853   NL

Little, James A. *From Kirtland to Salt Lake City.* Salt Lake City: 1890.   1848   NSHS

Littleton, Micajah. "Journal of a Trip," typescript.   1850   CSL

Lobenstine, William C. *Extracts from the Diary of William C. Lobenstine.* n.p.: 1920.   1851   NPS

Long, M. N. *See* Fort Kearney, South Pass and Honey Lake Wagon Road Company.   1857–1859

Long, Margaret. *Shadow of the Arrow.* Caldwell, Ida.: 1941.   1849   BL

Long, Stephen H. "Travels," in Edwin James, *Account of an Expedition from Pittsburgh to the Rocky Mountains. (Early Western Travels,* ed. R. G. Thwaites, Vols. XIV–XVIII.) Cleveland: 1905.   1819–1820   NPS

Longmire, James. "Narrative of a Pioneer," *Washington Historical Quarterly,* XXIII (January, 1932), 47–60.   1853   NSHS

Longsworth, Basil N. *Diary of Basil N. Longworth [sic] Oregon Pioneer.* Transcribed by the Historical Records Survey, WPA. Portland: 1938.   1853   NSHS

Loomis, Leander V. *Journal of the Birmingham Emigrating Company.* Salt Lake City: 1928.   1850   NPS

Lord, Brackett. "Letter of June 17 from Fort Kearny," *Collections of the Nebraska State Historical Society,* XVII (1913), 124–26.   1849   NSHS

Lord, Dr. Israel S. P. Journal (incomplete), with mounted excerpts from the Elgin, Ill., *Western Christian.*   1849   HL

Lorton, William B. Letters, in the New York *Sun.* Letter of May 9, 1849, in June 8 issue; letter of June 30, 1849, in September 7 issue.   1849   BL

———. Diary notebooks, ms.   1849   BL

Lotts, Judge Charles. Diary, typescript.   1849   CSL

Love, Alexander. Journal typescript, microfilm from ms. at Yale University.   1849   WU

Lovejoy, Asa L. "Lovejoy's Pioneer Narrative, 1842–48,"
ed. Henry E. Reed. *Oregon Historical Quarterly*,
XXXI (September, 1930), 237–60.   1842   OHS

Loveland, Cyrus C. *California Trail Herd . . . ,* ed.
Richard H. Dillon. Los Gatos, Calif.: 1961.   1850   BL

Lowe, Percival G. *Five Years a Dragoon.* Kansas City:
1906.   1851–1857   NPS

Lowry, James L. Diary, typescript.   1860   WHS

Ludlow, Fitz Hugh. *Heart of the Continent.* New York:
1870.   1863   NSHS

Lyman, Amasa. Journal, ms.   1847   BYU

Lyon, James D. Letters in the Detroit *Daily Advertiser.*
Letter of July 4, 1849, in September 10 issue; letter
of December 24, 1849, in the February 2, 1850, issue. 1849 MnHS

"M. M." Letters to the St. Louis *Missouri Republican*, in
Wyman (ed.), *California Emigrant Letters.*   1849   NPS

"M. M. G." Letter to the St. Louis *Missouri Republican*,
in Wyman (ed.), *California Emigrant Letters.*   1849   NPS

McAllister, Rev. John. "Diary . . . ," *Transactions, Oregon Pioneer Association* (1922), 471–508.   1852   OHS

McAulay, Eliza. "Overland Trip to California," typescript copy from ms. in private possession.   1852   NPS

McBride, W. "Journey to California," journal. ms.   1850   HL

McCollum, Dr. T. *See* Bidlack.   1849

McCowen, George. "Notes of a Journey," typescript. 1854   NL

McCoy, John. *Pioneering on the Plains.* n.p.: 1924. 1849   HL

McDermott, John Francis. *See* Wilkins.   1850   HL

McFarlane, Andrews. "Letter of a Gold Rusher of 1850,"
ed. A. R. Mortensen, *Utah Historical Quarterly*, XXII
(January, 1954), 57–61.   1850   UHS

McGlashan, John M. Overland journal, typescript.   1850   ChHS

McIlhany, Edward W. *Recollections of a '49er.* Kansas
City: 1908.   1849   NSHS

McKeeby, Lemuel C. "Memoirs of Lemuel McKeeby,"
California Historical Society Quarterly, III (March,
1924), 45–72. *See also* Coy.   1850   HL

McKinstry, Byron Nathan. Diary, typescript copy.   1850   BL

McKinstry, George. "Diary," in Dale L. Morgan (ed.),
Overland in 1846.   1846   NSHS

McPherren, Ida. *Imprints on Pioneer Trails*. Boston: 1950. (Hugo Hoppe's adventures.)   1851   HL

Magraw, Col. William. *See* Fort Kearney, South Pass and Honey Lake Wagon Road Company.   1857–1859   NatA

Mallory, Samuel. "Overland to Pike's Peak with a Gold Mill," *Colorado Magazine*, VIII (May, 1931), 108–14.   1859   CHS

Mallowney, J. F. *See* Fort Kearney, South Pass and Honey Lake Wagon Road Company.   1857–1859   NatA

Maltby, Charles. Letter of May 24, 1849, at Fort Kearny, in the Springfield *Illinois Daily Journal*, June 25, 1849.   1849   ISL

Manlove, Mark D. Diary, typescript, in Pioneer Letters Collection.   1849   CSL

Mapel, Eli B. Diary, ms.   1852   CSL

Marcy, Randolph. *The Prairie Traveller*. n.p.: 1859.   1857   NPS

Marsh, Dr. O. C. *See* Schuckert and Levene.*   1870   NPS

Marshall, Philip C. "The Newark Overland Company," *Proceedings of the New Jersey Historical Society*, LXX (July, 1952), 173–87.   1849   NPS

Mason, James. "Diary . . . Ohio to California," ed. James C. Olson. *Nebraska History*, XXXIII (June, 1952), 103–21.   1850   NSHS

Matthieu, F. X. 'Reminiscences," ed. H. S. Lyman. *Oregon Historical Quarterly*, I (March, 1900), 73–104.   n.d.   NSHS

Maxwell, William A. *Crossing the Plains* . . . . San Francisco: 1915.   1857   NPS

Maynard, Dr. David S. "Diary . . . ," *Washington Historical Quarterly*, I (October, 1906), 50–62.   1850   NSHS

Meeker, Ezra, and Howard Driggs. *Covered Wagon Centennial and Ox Team Days*. New York: 1932.   1852   NSHS

Meline, James F. *Two Thousand Miles on Horseback* . . . . New York: 1867.   1866   NSHS

Mengarini, Gregory. "Narrative of the Rockies . . . ," in A. J. Partoll (ed.), *Frontier Omnibus*. Helena: 1962.   1841   NPS

Merrill, Joseph Henry. Diary, typescript.   1849   HSM

Mersman, Joseph I. Journal, ms. in Oregon Envelope.   1847   MiHS

Michael, Howard. "Reminiscences," *Annals of Wyoming*, V (October, 1927), 79–89.   1861   NSHS

Miller, Alfred Jacob. Sketches and captions. *See also*
Devoto and Ross.*   1837   NPS

Miller, Charles H. *See* Fort Kearney, South Pass and
Honey Lake Wagon Road Company.   1857–1869   NatA

Miller, Hiram O. "Diary," in Dale L. Morgan (ed.),
Overland in 1846.   1846   NSHS

Miller, J. D. "Early Oregon Scenes," *Oregon Historical
Quarterly*, XXXI (March, 1930), 55–68.   1848   OHS

Miller, Neal E. Letter of December 18, 1967, *re* Cyrenius
Hall.   1852–1853 NPS

Miller, Reuben G. Journal, photostat of typescript.   1849   HL

Miller, S. V. "Letter from Salem, Oregon, November 24,"
Wyoming Historical Society Miscellanies (1919), 31–40. 1852   NSHS

Millington, Ada. "Journal Kept While Crossing the
Plains," photostat of ms. in private possession.   1862   BL

Milner, John T. "Trip to California," *Alabama Historical Quarterly*, XX, 3 (1858), 523–56. (Letters.)   1849   NPS

Minto, John. "Reminiscences . . . ," *Oregon Historical
Quarterly*, II (une, 1901), 119–67.   1844   OHS

Mitchell, Lyman. Journal, microfilm of ms. in private
possession.   1849   BL

Mollhausen, Heinrich B. *Diary of a Journey from the
Mississippi to the Coasts of the Pacific.* London:
1858.   1851   NL

Moore, Martha Missouri. Journal, typescript.   1859   MiHS

Moorman, Madison B. *Journal of Madison B. Moorman,*
ed. Irene D. Paden. San Francisco: 1948.   1850   NPS

Montgomery, William. Notebook, ms.   1850   HL

Moreland, J. C. "Annual Address. . . ," *Transactions,
Oregon Pioneer Association* (1900), 26–34.   1852   OHS

Morgan, Dale L. (ed.). "Letters by Forty-Niners, Written
from Great Salt Lake City," *Western Humanities Review*, (April, 1949), 98–116.   1849   UHS

———. (ed.). *Overland in 1846: Diaries and Letters of
the California-Oregon Trail.* 2 vols. Georgetown,
Calif.: 1963.   1846   NSHS

Morgan, Martha M. *A Trip Across the Plains. . . .* San
Francisco: 1864.   1849   HL

Morris, Maurice O'Connor. *Rambles in the Rocky Mountains. . . .* London: 1864.   1863   NPS

Morrison, Robert Wilson. "Biography of . . . ," ed. John
Minto. *Transactions, Oregon Pioneer Association*
(1894), 53–57.   1845   OHS

Moses, Israel. "Odometer Record," in Settle, *March of
the Mounted Riflemen.*   1849   NSHS

Moss, William C. "Overland to California . . . ," *Pony
Express Courier,* V (November, 1938), 6–14.   1861   NSHS

Mowry, Sylvester. Letters, photostats.   1854   BL

Munger, Asahel. "Diary . . . ," *Oregon Historical Quar-
terly,* VIII (December, 1907), 387–415.   1839   OHS

Murphy, Patrick H. "Across the Plains," typescript.   1854   CSL

Murphy, William. "The Forgotten Battalion," *Annals
of Wyoming,* VII (October, 1930), 383–401; (January,
1931), 441–42.   1865–1866   NSHS

Nash, Marie. Diary, typescript.   1861   CSL

"Nebraska," correspondent of the St. Louis *Missouri
Republican.* Watkins, ed. *Publications of the Nebraska State Historical Society,* XX (1922), 180–88,
214–16.   1849   NSHS

Nesmith, James W. "Diary of the Emigration," *Oregon
Historical Quarterly,* VII (December, 1906), 329–59.   1843   OHS

Newby, William T. "Diary of the Emigration," *Oregon
Historical Quarterly,* XL (September, 1939), 219–42.   1843   OHS

Newcomb, Silas. Journal, photostat from original ms.
in Yale University.   1850   NL

Nobles, Wm., and Mary Ellen. "Memoirs of Pioneer
Life," typescript in California Pioneer Collection.   1853   BL

Norton, Col. L. A. *Life and Adventures.* Oakland: 1887.   n.d.   BL

Nott, Manfred A. *Across the Plains in '54.* n.p.: n.d.   1854   HL

Nusbaumer, Louis. Diary, photostat of ms.   1849   BL

O'Brien, Maj. Geo. M. Letter of January 10, 1865, to
Capt. George Price, in Holmes, *Fort McPherson.*   1865   NSHS

Oglesby, Richard J. Letter of August 12, 1849, in the
Springfield *Illinois State Journal,* October 23, 1849.   1849   ISL

"Old Boone." Letters to the St. Louis (?) *Missouri
Statesman,* in Wyman (ed.), *California Emigrant
Letters.*   1849–1850   NPS

"Old Oregon Trail." Hearings with overland journal
excerpts, before the Committee on Roads, H. R.,
68th Congress, 2nd Session.   1847–1850   NSHS

Olson, Rev. Jonas W. Journal, in "Historical Notes,"
Journal of the Illinois State Historical Society,
XLVIII (Winter, 1955), 466–69. 1850 ISL

O'Neill, O. H. *See* Fort Kearney, South Pass and Honey
Lake Wagon Road Company. 1857–1859 NatA

Ormsby, Dr. Caleb. *See* Bidlack. 1849

Ottinger, George M. *See* Stenzel.

Pacific Wagon Road Surveys. *See* Fort Kearney, South
Pass and Honey Lake Wagon Road Company. 1857–1859 NatA

Packard, Maj. Wellman. *Early Emigration to California.*
Bloomington, Ill.: 1928. 1849 NL

Packwood, William. "Reminiscences," *Oregon Historical
Quarterly*, XVI (March, 1915), 33–54. 1849 OHS

Page, Elizabeth. *Wagons West.* New York: 1930. 1849 NPS

Page, Henry. Journal, in Elizabeth Page, *Wagons West.* 1849 NPS

Palmer, Joel. *Journal of Travels to the Rocky Mountains.* Cincinnati: 1847. 1845–1846 NL

Parke, Dr. Charles R. "California Notes," ms. 1849 HL

Parker, Inez E. A. "Early Recollections," *Transactions,
Oregon Pioneer Association* (1928), 17–35. 1848 OHS

Parker, Rev. Samuel. *Journal of an Exploring Tour Beyond the Rocky Mountains.* Ithaca, N.Y.: 1944. 1835 NPS

Parkman, Francis. *Journals of Francis Parkman*, ed.
Mason Wade. 2 vols. New York: 1947. 1846 NPS

———. *The Oregon Trail.* New York: 1950. 1846 NSHS

Parkinson, John B. *Memories of Early Wisconsin and
the Gold Mines.* n.p.: n.d. 1852 WHS

Parr, Dick. *See* Louise L. Parr. 1855

Parr, Louise L. "Sketch of the Life of Dick Parr,"
Annals of Wyoming, IX (July, 1932), 649–65. 1855 NSHS

Parrish, Edward E. "Crossing the Plains," *Transactions,
Oregon Pioneer Association* (1888), 82–121. 1844 OHS

Parry, Henry C. "Letters from the Frontier, 1867,"
Annals of Wyoming, XXX (October, 1958), 126–44. 1867 NSHS

Patterson, Martin. "Trip to Pike's Peak," typescript
copy of ms. in private possession. 1858–1859 Author

Pattison, Jno. J. "With the U.S. Army Along the Oregon
Trail, 1863–66," *Nebraska History*, XV (June, 1834),
79–93. (Diary.) 1863 NSHS

Pattison, Nathan. Typescript of letter in private possession. 1849 HC

Paul Wilhelm, Duke of Wurttemberg. *See* Butscher.

"Pawnee." Letters to the St. Louis *Missouri Republican,* in Wyman (ed.), *California Emigrant Letters.* 1849 NPS

Peabody, Francis C. "Across the Plains DeLuxe in 1865," *Colorado Magazine,* XVIII (March, 1941), 71–76. 1865 CHS

Pearce, William E. Letter of May 12, 1851. 1851 HL

Pearson, G. C. *Overland in 1849, from Missouri to California.* Los Angeles: 1961. 1849 NPS

Pease, David E. Diary, typescript. 1849 NSHS

Pennock, Jake. "Diary . . . ," *Annals of Wyoming,* XXIII (July, 1951), 4–29. 1865 NSHS

Pennock, Taylor. "Recollections . . . ," *Annals of Wyoming,* VI (July–October, 1929), 199–212. 1865 NSHS

Penter, Samuel. "Recollections of an Oregon Pioneer," *Oregon Historical Quarterly,* VII (March, 1906), 56–61. 1843 OHS

Perkins, Elisha Douglas. *Gold Rush Diary,* ed. Thomas D. Clark. Lexington: 1967. (Ms. diary in Huntington Library.) 1849 HL

Perkins, J. R. *Trails, Rails and War.* Indianapolis: 1929. 1865 NPS

Pettijohn, Isaac. "Overland Journey . . . Missouri to Oregon," ms. 1847 BL

Piercy, Frederick H. *See* Linforth. 1853 NL

Pigman, Walter G. *Journal of Walter G. Pigman,* ed. U. S. Fowkes. Mexico, Mo.: 1942. 1850 NL

Platt, P. L., and N. Slater. *Traveler's Guide Across the Plains upon the Overland Route to California.* San Francisco: 1963. (Reprint of 1852 edition.) n.d. BL

Pleasants, William J. *Twice Across the Plains.* San Francisco: 1906. 1849–1856 BL

Point, Father Nicholas. *See* McDermott.* 1841 NSHS

Poor, R. L. *See* Fort Kearney, South Pass and Honey Lake Wagon Road Company. 1857–1859 NatA

Porter, Lavinia. *By Ox Team to California.* Oakland: 1910. 1860 BL

Porter, Lt. Chas. F. "Report from Fort Kearny" (August, 14, 1864), in the Omaha *Nebraskan,* August 17, 1864. 1864 MC

"Postmaster General's Order Relating to Route of the Overland Mail Company, March 12, 1861," ms. copy. 1861 HC

Potter, Theodore Edgar. *Autobiography . . . 1832–1910.* Concord, N.H.: 1913. 1852 NL

Powell, M. "Overland Journey to California," *Littell's Living Age*, XXIII (1849), 155–58. 1846 CSL

Pratt, James. Letters, March 10 to June 10, 1849, in the Marshall, Mich., *Statesman*, April 4 to July 18, 1849. 1849 MU

Pratt, Orson. Journal, *Latter-Day Saints' Millenial Star*, XI (1849), 362–70; XII (1850), 1–180. Council Bluffs (?): n.d. 1846–1849 NSHS

Preston, Leander S. Diary, ms. 1860 HL

Preuss, Charles. Exploring with Fremont, tr. and ed. E. G. and E. K. Gudde. Norman: 1958. 1842 NPS

Price, Joseph. "The Road to California: Letters of Joseph Price," ed. Thomas Marshall. *Mississippi Valley Historical Review*, XI (September, 1924), 237–57. 1850 NSHS

Prichet, John. Diary, typescript. 1849 InS

Pringle, Virgil K. "Diary . . . ," *Transactions, Oregon Pioneer Association* (1920), 281–300. 1846 OHS

Pritchard, James A. *The Overland Diary of James A. Pritchard, Kentucky to California*, ed. Dale L. Morgan. Denver: 1959. 1849 NSHS

Pulsipher, John. "Pioneer Journal of John Pulsipher," ms. 1848 BYU

Purcell, Polly Jane. *Autobiography & Reminiscences of a Pioneer.* n.p.: n.d. (Leaflet.) 1846 HL

Radford, Sarah B. F. "A Sketch of Pioneer Days," *Transactions, Oregon Pioneer Association* (1926), 23–29. n.d. OHS

Rahm, Louise M. Diary, photocopy. 1862 BL

Ramsay, Alexander. ". . . Gold Rush Diary of 1849," ed. Merrill J. Mattes. *Pacific Historical Review*, XVIII (November, 1949), 437–68. 1849 NSHS

Ramsdell, T. M. "Reminiscences . . . ," *Transactions, Oregon Pioneer Association* (1896), 108–12. 1844 OHS

Randall, J. D. Typescript of ms. in private possession. 1852 MC

Rea, Mrs. Thomas. "Diary While Crossing the Plains," typescript, in California Pioneer Collection. 1853 BL

Read, George Willis. *A Pioneer of 1850.* Boston: 1927. 1850 NPS

Reading, Pierson Barton. "Journal . . . 123 Days from
Westport to Monterey," *Quarterly, Society of Cali-*
fornia Pioneers, VI, 3 (1930), 148–98. 1843 HL

Redman, T. J. "Reminiscences . . . ," typescript. 1863 NL

Reed, James Frazier. Letter of June 16, 1846, in Dale L.
Morgan (ed.), *Overland in 1846.* 1846 NSHS

Rhodes, Joseph. "Joseph Rhodes and the California
Gold Rush," ed. Merrill J. Mattes. *Annals of Wyo-*
ming, XXIII (January, 1951), 52–71. 1850 NSHS

Rice, Philip D. ". . . Overland Trip," excerpt from the
San Francisco *Chronicle,* July 21, 1907. 1849 CSL

Richardson, Alpheus. Journal, microfilm of typescript. 1852 BL

Richardson, Caroline L. Journal, ms. 1852 BL

Richey, Stuart and Caleb. "Letters," *Transactions, Ore-*
gon Pioneer Association (1912), 586–662. 1852 OHS

Ritter, Mary Bennett. *More Than Gold in California.*
Berkeley: 1913. 1852 BL

Robe, Robert. ". . . Diary While Crossing the Plains in
1851," *Washington Historical Quarterly,* XIX (January, 1928), 52–63. 1851 NSHS

Roberts, James. "Notes on Overland Journey, Wisconsin
to Idaho," typescript. 1864 WHS

Robidoux, Antoine. *See* Wallace.*

Robidoux, Joseph. Licences to trade in the Indian country, in "Register, Bureau of Indian Affairs," ms.
See also Mattes, "Robidoux."* 1848–1854 NatA

Robinson, Zirkle D. Typescript copy of ms. diary at
Prairie Press, Iowa City, Ia. 1849 NPS

Rockafellow, Capt. B. F. Diary, in *Powder River Cam-*
paign and Sawyer Expedition of 1865 (Far West and
the Rockies, eds. LeRoy R. and Ann W. Hafen. Vol.
XII.) Glendale: 1961. 1865 NSHS

Root, Frank A., and William Connelley. *Overland*
Stage to California. Topeka: 1901. 1863–1865 NSHS

Root, Riley. *Journal of Travels from St. Joseph to*
Oregon. Oakland: 1955. 1848 CSL

Rose, Rachel. Diary, typescript. 1852 CSL

Rosenberg, C. G. (ed.). *Buckskin Mose, or Life from the*
Lakes to the Pacific. New York: 1873. 1855 NL

Rowe, William R. "California Experiences," typescript
from the Waterford, Wis., *Post*, 1905.   1852   WHS

Royce, Sarah. *A Frontier Lady* . . . . ed. Ralph H.
Gabriel. New Haven: 1932.   1849   NL

Rueger, John. "Account of Hardships . . . ," typescript
from the Benecia, Calif., *Herald*, June 1, 8, and
15, 1923.   1850   BL

Ruff, Charles and Annie. Correspondence, 1842–1854.
Typescript copy of mss. in private possession.   1849   Author

Ruggles, Daniel. "Letters," ed. Mary Ruggles, typescript. 1865   WHS

Russell, F. T. Letter to the St. Louis (?) *Missouri Statesman* in Wyman (ed.), *California Emigrant Letters*.   1850   NPS

Sage, Rufus B. *Rocky Mountain Life*. Boston: 1857.   1841   NPS

Sandoz, Mari, letter of May 14, 1953 to Dr. John Lêer-
machers (copy), *re* Ash Hollow.   n.d.   HC

Sanford, Mary F. Hite. "Diary . . . ," typescript, with
diary of Abraham Hite.   1853   CSL

Sawyer, Mrs. Francis H. "Overland to California," typescript.   1852   NL

Sawyer, Lorenzo. *Way Sketches . . . St. Joseph to California*, ed. E. Eberstadt. New York: 1926.   1850   NSHS

Schallenberger, Moses. *Opening of the California Trail*,
ed. G. R. Stewart. Berkeley: 1953.   1844   NSHS

Scharman, H. B. *Overland Journey to California*, tr.
Zimmerman. n.p.: 1918.   1849   HL

Scheller, J. J. "Extracts from Autobiography . . . ,"
typescript. Translated from the German.   1850   CSL

Scott, Charles A. ". . . Diary of the Utah Expedition,
1857–1861," ed. Robert E. Stowers and John M. Ellis.
Utah Historical Quarterly, XXVIII (April, 1960), 155;
(October, 1960), 389–402.   1857   UHS

Scott, Hamilton. Journal, typescript, with notes by Alvin
Zaring.   1862   MC

Scott, Hiram Daniel. "The Scott Family Story as Remembered by Hiram Daniel Scott, Great Nephew and
Namesake of Hiram Scott, the Fur Trader." Ms. copy
loaned by Earl Harris, historian, Scotts Bluff National
Monument.   1828   NPS

Scott, John A. Letter of June 22, 1849.   1849   HL

Searls,, Niles. *Diary of a Pioneer . . . Independence to California.* San Francisco: 1940.   1849   CSL

Sedgley, Joseph. *Overland to California.* Oakland: 1877.   1849   NL

Senter, Riley. *Crossing the Continent to the California Gold Fields* (reprint from the Exeter, Calif., *Sun,* 1938).   1849   CSL

Settle, Raymond W. (ed.). *March of the Mounted Riflemen.* Glendale: 1940.   1840   NSHS

Seville, William P. *Narrative of the March of Co. A, Engineers, Fort Leavenworth to Fort Bridger & Return.* 1858 Washington, D.C.: 1912.   1858   NPS

Sexton, Lucy Foster (ed.). *The Foster Family, California Pioneers.* Santa Barbara: 1925.   1849   NL

Sharp, Cornelia A. "Crossing the Plains . . . ," *Transactions, Oregon Pioneer Association* (1903), 171–88.   1852   OHS

Sharp, Joe A. "Crossing the Plains . . . ," *Transactions, Oregon Pioneer Association* (1895), 91–95.   1852   OHS

Sharp, John. "Brief notes . . . ," ms.   1850   CSL

Shaw, Hon. D. A. *Eldorado, or California As Seen by a Pioneer.* Los Angeles: 1900.   1850   HL

Shaw, R. C. *Across the Plains in Forty-Nine.* Farmland, Ind.: 1896.   1849   HL

Shepherd, Dr. J. S. *Journal of Travel.* Racine, Wis.: 1851.   1850   NPS

Sherrod, James M. "Sketches from the Life . . . ." *Annals of Wyoming,* IV (January, 1927), 325–53.   1852   NSHS

Shields, R. M. "Crossing the Plains, Railroading with Ox Teams . . . ," in the Sacramento *Daily Record-Union,* May 22 and June 19, 1886.   1852   CSL

Shinn, John E. "Crossing the Plains . . . ," photocopy of ms.   1850   BL

Shires, William. Typescript journal, original in private possession.   1862   NPS

Shively, J. M. *Route and Distances to Oregon and California.* Washington, D.C.: 1846.   1845   LC

Shombre, Henry. Diary, ms.   1849   KHS

Short, George W. Diary, typescript.   1852   WHS

Shottenkirk, D. G. "Diary . . . ," fragment from the Mount Carroll, Ill., *Tribune,* in Langworthy, *Scenery of the Plains.*   1850   NPS

Simons, George. "Diary," in *Thirtieth Anniversary Bulletin*, Joslyn Art Museum, Omaha (1961).   1861   Author

Sitgreaves, Lorenzo. Maps of posts along the Platte and Little Blue rivers.   1864   NatA

Sloan, William K. "Autobiography," *Annals of Wyoming*, IV (July, 1926), 235–64.   1853–1854   NSHS

Smedley, William. *Across the Plains in '62*. Denver: 1916.   1862   HL

Smith, C. W. *Journal of a Trip to California*, ed. R. Vail. New York: n.d.   1850   NPS

Smith, E. Willard. Journal, in LeRoy R. Hafen (ed.), *To the Rockies and Oregon*. Glendale: 1955.   1839–1840   NSHS

Smith, G. A. "Journal . . . St. Joseph . . . to California," ms.   1852   MiHS

Smith, George Albert. Letters of December 3, 1936, and January 29, 1937, with excerpts from the journal of his grandfather, George Albert Smith.   1847   Author

Smith, Jedediah, David Jackson, and W. L. Sublette. Letter of October 29, 1830, from St. Louis to Hon. John H. Eaton, Secretary of War. Senate Documents, 21st Congress, 2nd Session, Doc. 39.   1830   LC

Smith, John. "Memorandum . . . to Oregon . . . from Indiana," ms. journal book.   1853   HL

Snodgrass, R. H. P. "Journal . . . Piqua, Ohio to Sacramento," microfilm from typescript in Yale University.   1852   WU

Snow, Taylor N. "Diary of . . . Hoosier Fifty Niner." ed. Arthur Homer Hays. *Indiana Magazine of History*. XXVIII (September, 1932), 193–208.   1859   NSHS

Snow, William. Diary, typescript.   1850   HC

Snyder, Jacob R. "Diary . . . ," *Quarterly, Society of California Pioneers*, VIII, 4 (1930), 224–60.   1845   HL

Somers, Mrs. Belle Redman. "Crossing the Plains . . . ," in the San Francisco *Argonaut*, Vol. 96A–97 (1925), 3.   1849   DPL

Sortore, Abraham. *Biography and Early Life Sketch*. Alexandria, Mo.: 1909.   1850   NPS

Spalding, Eliza Hart. Diary in Drury (ed.), *First White Women Over the Rockies*.* 188–192.   1836   NSHS

Spalding, Mrs. H. H. "Diary . . . ," in Eliza Spalding Warren, *Memoirs of the West*.   1836   BL

Spencer, Lafayette. "Journal of the Oregon Trail . . . ,"
Annals of Iowa, VIII (January, 1908), 304–10.   1852   NSHS

Spencer, Lucinda. "Pioneer of 1847," *Transactions,*
Oregon Pioneer Association (1887), 74–78.   1847   OHS

Sponsler, A. C. "An 1850 Gold Rush Letter," ed.
D. Heib. *Nebraska History*, XXXII (June, 1951),
130–39.   1850   NSHS

Squire, James E. Letter of July 18, 1849, from City
of Great Salt Lake, in Dale L. Morgan (ed.), "Letters
by Forty-Niners."   1849   UHS

Stabaek, T. K. "Account of a journey . . . ," tr.
E. I. Haugen. *Norwegian-American Historical Asso-*
ciation Studies and Records (Northfield, Minn.), IV,
92–124.   1852   CSL

Stansbury, Capt. Howard. *Exploration and Survey of*
the Valley of the Great Salt Lake . . . . Washington,
D.C.: 1853.   1849–1850   NSHS

———. Journal, ms.   1849–1850   NatA

Staples, David Jackson. "The Journal . . . ," *Cali-*
fornia Historical Society Quarterly, XXII (June,
1943), 119–50.   1849   HL

Starley, James. "Journal . . . ," *Utah Historical Quar-*
terly, IX (July, October, 1941), 169–78.   1854   UHS

Starr, Franklin. Diary, ms.   1849   ISL

Steck, Amos. Diary, photostat of ms.   1849   CHS

Steele, Edward D. *Diary of His Journey . . . Wisconsin*
to Colorado, ed. N. Mumey. Boulder: 1960.   1859   NSHS

Steele, John. *Across the Plains . . . ,*" ed. Joseph Schafer.
Chicago: 1930.   1850   NPS

———. *The Traveler's Companion Through the Great*
Interior. Galena, Ill.: 1854.   1850   HL

Stenzel, Dr. Franz. Letter of October 24, 1967, *re* George
M. Ottinger.   1861–1867   Author

Stephens, L. Dow. *Life Sketches of a Jayhawker of '49.*
n.p.: 1916.   1849   NL

Stevens, Charles. "Letters . . . ," ed. E. Ruth Lockwood.
Oregon Historical Quarterly, XXXVII (June, 1936),
137–59.   1852   OHS

Stewart, Agnes. "The Journey to Oregon . . . ," ed.
C. W. Churchhill, *Oregon Historical Quarterly*, XXIX
(March, 1928), 77–98.   1853   OHS

Stewart, J. M. "Overland Trip to California," *Publications, Historical Society of Southern California*, V
(1901), 176–85.   1850   HL

Stewart, Sir William Drummond. Travels, in DeVoto,
Across the Wide Missouri.*   1833–1841   NPS

Stimson, Fancher. "Overland Trip to California by
Platte River and South Pass," typescript.   1850   HL

Stine, Henry A. "Letters and Journals of Henry A.
Stine," typescript of original in private possession.   1850   CSL

Stobie, Charles S. "Crossing the Plains to Colorado in
1865," *Colorado Magazine*, X (November, 1933),
201–12.   1865   CHS

Stockman, Lawson. "Recollection of 1859," ed. B. F.
Manring. *Oregon Historical Quarterly*, XI (June,
1910), 162–76.   1859   OHS

Stott, Edwin. "Journal," *Utah Historical Quarterly*,
IX (July–October, 1941), 185–89.   1849–1864 UHS

Stoughton, John A. "Passing of an Emigrant of 1843,"
ed. J. Orin Oliphant. *Washington Historical Quar-
terly*, XV (July, 1924), 205–10.   1843   NSHS

Stout, Hosea. Journal, ms.   1848   HL

Street, Franklin. *California in 1850 . . . Also, a Concise
Description of the Overland Route.* Cincinnati: 1851.   1850   NL

Stuart, Granville. *Forty Years on the Frontier.* Cleveland: 1925.   1852   NPS

Stuart, Joseph A. *My Roving Life.* 2 vols. Auburn,
Calif.: 1895.   1849   HL

Stuart, Robert. *The Discovery of the Oregon Trail
. . . Narratives of His Trip*, ed. P. A. Rollins.
New York: 1935.   1812–1813 NSHS

Suckley, George. "The 1859 . . . Journal of Naturalist
George Suckley," ed. R. G. Beildleman, *Annals of
Wyoming*, XXVIII (April, 1956), 68–79.   1859   NSHS

Sullivan, W. W. "Crossing the Plains," typescript.   1862   HL

Sutherland, Thomas. Journal, in Hafen and Young,
Fort Laramie and the Pageant of the West.* 230.   1854   NSHS

Sutton, Sarah. Diary, typescript of ms. in private possession. 1854 NPS

Swain, William. Thirty letters, copies of originals at Yale University. 1849 MiHS

Swan, Chauncey. "Letters of a Forty-Niner," ed. Mildred Thone. *Iowa Journal of History*, XLVII (January, 1949), 63–77. 1849 NSHS

Swasey, W. F. *Early Days and Men of California.* Oakland: 1891. 1843 NL

Sweetland, Louisa M. "Reminiscences," typescript in D.A.R. Pioneer Records. 1863 CSL

Swingley, Upton. "A Brief Chronicle of My Life," in "Historical Notes," *Journal, Illinois Historical Society*, XVII (December, 1949), 457 62. n.d. IHS

Switzler, Simeon. Letter to the St. Louis (?) *Missouri Statesman*, in Wyman (ed.), *California Emigrant Letters.* 1849 NPS

Sydenham, Moses H. "Freighting Across the Plains . . . ," *Proceedings and Collections, Nebraska State Historical Society*, I (1894–1895), 164–84. 1856 NSHS

T., Dr. ———. Journal, ms. 1849 BL

Talbot, Theodore. *Journals, 1843 and 1849–52*, ed. Charles H. Carey. Portland: 1931. 1843 NPS

Tappan, Henry. "Diary," ed. E. Walters. *Annals of Wyoming*, XXV (July, 1953), 113–39. 1849 NSHS

Tate, Col. James. Diary, typescript. 1849 MiHS

Taylor, Calvin. "Journal . . . Overland to the Gold Fields," ed. Burton J. Williams. *Nebraska History*, L (July, 1969), 125–130. 1850 NSHS

Taylor, Emerson Gifford. *Gouverneur Kemble Warren . . . 1830–1882.* Boston: 1932. 1855 LC

Taylor, S. H. "Oregon Bound: Letters to the Watertown Chronicle," *Oregon Historical Quarterly*, XXII (June, 1921), 117–60. 1853 OHS

Taylor, William E. "Diary," in Dale L. Morgan (ed.), *Overland in 1846.* 1846 NSHS

Teeter, Charles N. "Four Years of My Life . . . ," *Thirteenth Biennial Report . . . of the State Historical Society of Idaho* (1932), 25–126. 1862 HL

Thissell, G. W. *Crossing the Plains in '49.* Oakland: 1903.   1849   NPS

Thomas, Robert. "Buckeye Argonauts," *Ohio State Archeological and Historical Quarterly*, LIX (July, 1950), 256–69.   1849   NSHS

Thomasson, Dr. A. H. Journal, typescript.   1850   CSL

Thompson, Harlow C. "Across the Continent on Foot," typescript recollections.   1859   HL

Thompson, William. *Reminiscences of a Pioneer.* San Francisco: 1912.   n.d.   NL

Thornton, J. Quinn. *Oregon and California in 1848.* New York: 1849.   1846   NPS

Thurber, Albert King. "Journal," typescript recollections.   1849   BL

Tinker, Charles. ". . . Journal . . . ," ed. E. H. Roseboom. *Ohio Archeological and Historical Quarterly*, LXI (January, 1952), 64–85.   1849   NSHS

Todd, Capt. John B. S. "The Harney Expedition Against the Sioux," ed. Ray H. Mattison. *Nebraska History*, XLIII (June, 1962), 89–130.   1855   NSHS

Tompkins, Dr. E. A. "Expedition to California," photostat of ms. *See also* Coy.   1850   HL

Tourtillot, Jane A. Journal, microfilm of ms.   1862   BL

Townsend, John K. *Narrative of a Journey Across the Rocky Mountains . . . .* (*Early Western Travels*, ed. R. G. Thwaites. Vol. XXI.) Cleveland: 1905.   1832   NPS

Tracy, Capt. Albert. "Journal of Capt. Albert Tracy," *Utah Historical Quarterly*, XIII (January–October, 1945), 1–117.   1860   UHS

Trowbridge, M. E. D. *Pioneer Days, the Life Story of Gershom and Elizabeth Day.* Philadelphia: 1895.   1849   NL

Tuller, Mrs. Miriam A. "Crossing the Plains," *Transactions, Oregon Pioneer Association* (1895), 87–90.   1845   OHS

Turnbull, Thomas. "Travels from the United States Across the Plains to California," *Proceedings of the State Historical Society of Wisconsin*, Separate 158 (1913), 151–225.   1852   NL

Turner, Henry S. "S. W. Kearny's March from California to Fort Leavenworth," photostat from National Archives.   1847   MiHS

Turner, William. Diary, typescript. 1850 WHS

Tuttle, Charles A. Letters, ms. 1849 BL

Tuttle, Charles M. "California Diary . . . ," *Wisconsin Magazine of History*, XV (September, 1931), 69–85; (December, 1931), 219–33. 1859 NSHS

Tuttle, Ziba Smith. Typescript letters, April 23 and May 25, 1850. Originals in private possession. 1850 MC

Twain, Mark. *See* Clemens. 1861

Twiss, Thomas. Correspondence, in U.S. Bureau of Indian Affairs. Records. 1851–1856 NatA

U.S. Bureau of Indian Affairs. Annual reports of the Commissioner. 1851–1866 NSHS

———. Records of the Upper Platte Indian Agency. 1851–1866 NatA

U.S. War Department. Annual reports of the Secretary of War. 1846–1866 LC

———. Records relating to old Fort Kearny, new Fort Kearny, Fort Laramie, and Fort Mitchell. 1846–1866 NatA

———. Records relating to the Sioux Expedition, including orders, Harney's report of September 5, 1855, and Warren's report of September 4, 1855. 1855 NatA

———. Report, 1866. "Distances on Road Between Fort Kearney, Nebraska Territory, and Junction Station, Colorado Territory," ms. 1866 NatA

Udell, John. *Incidents of Travel*. Jefferson, O.: 1856. NL

Vanderburgh, Philura. *See* Clinkinbeard. 1864 NSHS

Variel, Wm. J. "A Romance of the Plains," *Grizzly Bear* (July, 1907), 30–32; (August, 1907), 62–64; (September, 1907), 74–76. 1852 DPL

Vogdes, Ada. Journal, ms. 1868 HL

"W. R. R.," Letter to the St. Louis (?) *Missouri Statesman*, in Wyman, (ed.), *California Emigrant Letters*. 1850 NPS

Wadsworth, W. *The National Wagon Road*. San Francisco: 1858. 1852 NL

Waggoner, George A. *Stories of Old Oregon*. Salem, Ore.: 1905. 1852 HL

Wagner, W. H. *See* Fort Kearney, South Pass and Honey Lake Wagon Road Company. 1857–1869 NatA

Waite, Mrs. C. V. *Adventures in the Far West*. Chicago: 1882. 1862 NSHS

Walker, Mary. "Diary . . . ," in Drury (ed.), *First White Women Over the Rockies.** 1838 NSHS

Walters, Archer. "England to Utah," typescript. 1856 BYU

War of the Rebellion: A Compilation of the Official Records of the Union and Confederate Armies. Washington, D.C.: 1880–1891. 1861–1866 NPS

Ward, Harriet S. *Prairie Schooner Lady* . . . . Los Angeles: 1859. 1853 NPS

Ware, Capt. Eugene F. *The Indian War of 1864*, ed. Clyde Walton. New York: 1960. 1864 NSHS

Ware, Joseph E. *Emigrant's Guide to California* (from 1849 edition), ed. John Caughey. Princeton: 1932. 1849 NPS

Warner, Mary Elizabeth. "Wagon Train to California," microfilm of typescript. 1864 BL

Warner, William. Letter, typescript. 1853 BL

Warren, Daniel K. "Narrative of a Pioneer," *Oregon Historical Quarterly*, III (December, 1902), 396–409. (Letter of Tallmadge B. Wood and Peter H. Burnett.) 1852 OHS

Warren, Eliza Spalding. *Memoirs of the West.* Portland: 1916 (?). 1936 HL

Warren, G. K. Diary, in Emmerson Gifford Taylor, *Gouverneur Kemble Warren.* 1855 LC

Waters, Lydia M. "Account of a Trip Across the Plains in 1855," *Quarterly, Society of California Pioneers*, VI (1929), 59–79. 1855 NL

Watkins, Albert (ed.). *Publications of the Nebraska State Historical Society*, XX (1922). Notes of the early history of the Nebraska country and excerpts from contemporary newspapers, including the St. Louis *Missouri Republican*, the Franklin *Missouri Intelligencer*, the Cincinnati *Gazette*, the Washington, D.C., *National Intelligencer*, and others. 1841–1860 NSHS

Watson, Benjamin A. Letters, in the Springfield *Illinois State Journal*, n.d. 1849 ISL

Wayman, Dr. John. Diary, photocopy of ms. 1852 BL

Webster, Kimball. *The Gold Seekers of '49.* Manchester, N.H.: 1917. 1849 NPS

Wechselberg, Johannes P. Seven letters in German, ms. 1850 WHS

Welch, Nancy Dickerson. "Narrative. . . ," *Transactions, Oregon Pioneer Association* (1897), 97–103. 1844 OHS

Wells, Epaphroditus. Twelve letters to his wife, 1849–1851, typescripts.   1849   MiHS

West, Calvin B. "Calvin B. West of the Umpqua," ed. Reginald R. and Grace D. Stuart. *Pacific Historian,* IV (May, 1960), 48–57.   1853   NSHS

West, G. M. "Memoirs . . . Butler Wagon Train," type-script.   1853   BL

Wheeler, George N. Diary, ms. notebook.   1850   HL

White, Daniel. Diary, ms. notebooks.   1855   HL

White, Dr. Elijah. *See* A. J. Allen.   1842

White, Stephen. Recollections of 1850–1851, typescript.   1850   MC

Whitman, Marcus. "Journal and Report. . . ," *Oregon Historical Quarterly,* XXVIII (September, 1927), 239–57.   1835   OHS

Whitman, Narcissa. Diary, in Drury (ed.), *First White Women Over the Rockies.** 40–59.   1836   NSHS

Whitney, William T. "Trip Across the Plains," photostat from the Waterloo, Ia., *Daily Courier,* n.d.   1859   CSL

Wilkins, James F. Diary and sketches, in John Francis McDermott (ed.), *Artist on the Overland Trail.* San Marino, Calif.: 1968.   1849   HL

Wilkinson, J. A. "Journal Across the Plains," ms.   1859   NL

Williams, H. D. Diary, microfilm from ms. at Yale University.   1859   WU

Williams, James Stevens and Frances Helen. Letters, Iowa to Oregon, typescript copy in private possession.   1852   Author

Williams, Joseph. *Narrative of a Tour . . . Indiana to Oregon Territory.* Cincinnati: 1843.   1841   NL

Williams, Velina A. "Diary of a Trip . . . ," *Transactions, Oregon Pioneer Association* (1919), 178–226.   1853   OHS

Wilson, Alfred H. Diary, typescript.   1848   MC

Winne, Peter. "Across the Plains. . . ," ed. Robert G. Athearn. *Iowa Journal of History,* XLI (July, 1951), 221–40.   1863   NSHS

Winslow, George. Letter of May 12, 1849, *Collections of the Nebraska State Historical Society,* XVII (1913), 120–24.   1849   NSHS

Winthrop, Theodore. *The Canoe and the Saddle.* Tacoma: 1913.   1852   LC

Wislizenus, F. A. *Journey to the Rocky Mountains.*
St. Louis: 1912. 　　　　　　　　　　　　　　1839　NPS

Wisner, M. L. Letter of June 6 at Fort Kearny, in
excerpt from the Elgin, Ill., *Western Christian.*
See also Dr. Israel Lord. 　　　　　　　　　　1849　HL

Wisner, Sarah A. "A Trip Across the Plains," typescript. 　1866　NL

Wistar, Isaac Jones. *Autobiography . . . 1827–1905.*
Philadelphia: 1937. 　　　　　　　　　　　　1849　NPS

Wolcott, Lucian M. Diary, ms. notebooks. 　　　　1850　HL

Wood, Elizabeth. "Journal of a Trip . . . ," *Oregon
Historical Quarterly*, XXVII (March, 1926), 192–203. 　1851　OHS

Wood, John. *Journal . . . Cincinnati to the Gold Diggings.* Columbus, O.: 1871. 　　　　　　　　1850　NSHS

Wood, Joseph Warren. Diary, ms. 　　　　　　　1849　HL

Wood, Tallmadge B. Letter from Willamette, *Oregon
Hstorical Quarterly*, III (December, 1902), 395–98. 　1844　OHS

Woods, John Riley. Letter of September 27, 1852, from
the Neosho, Mo., *Benton County Pioneer.* 　　　1852　CSL

Woodward, Thomas. "Diary . . . While Crossing the
Plains. . . ," *Wisconsin Magazine of History*, XVII
(March, 1934), 345–60. 　　　　　　　　　　1850　NSHS

Woolley, Lell Hawley. *California, 1849–1913.* Oakland:
1913. 　　　　　　　　　　　　　　　　　　1849　NL

Word, Samuel. "Diary . . . Trip Across the Plains. . . ,"
Contributions, Historical Society of Montana, VIII
(1917), 37–92. 　　　　　　　　　　　　　1863　NSHS

Wyeth, John B. *Oregon; or, a Short History of a Long
Journey . . . , (Early Western Travels*, ed. R. G.
Thwaites, Vol. XXI.) Cleveland: 1905. 　　　　1832　NPS

Wyeth, Capt. Nathaniel J. *Correspondence and Journals.*
Eugene, Ore.: 1899. 　　　　　　　　　　1832–1834　NPS

Wyman, Walker D. (ed.). *California Emigrant Letters.*
New York: 1952. 　　　　　　　　　　　1849–1850　NPS

Young, Charles E. *Dangers of the Trail.* Geneva, N.Y.:
1912. 　　　　　　　　　　　　　　　　　1865　NSHS

Young, Frank C. *Across the Plains in '65 . . . Gotham
to Pike's Peak.* Denver: 1905. 　　　　　　　1865　HL

Young, George C. "Diary . . . ," (reprint), in the Horse
Cave, Ky. *Hart County Herald*, August 29, 1940. 　1850　NPS

Young, Harry. *Hard Knocks.* Chicago: 1915. 　　1865　NL

Young, Lorenzo D. "Diary. . . ," *Utah Historical Quar-* 1847 UHS
terly, XIV (January–October, 1946), 133–70.

Young, Sheldon. *See* Margaret Long. 1849

Young, Will H. "Journals. . . ," *Annals of Wyoming,*
VII (October, 1930), 378–82. 1865 NSHS

Zieber, John S. "Diary. . . ," *Transactions, Oregon Pio-*
neer Association (1920), 301–35. 1851 OHS

Zilhart, William. "Diary . . . Mo. to California," microfilm copy of original in private possession. 1853 BL

Key to location of primary sources:

BL   Bancroft Library, University of California, Berkeley
BYU   Brigham Young University, Provo, Utah
CaHS   California Historical Society, San Francisco
ChHS   Chicago Historical Society
CHS   State Historical Society of Colorado, Denver
CSL   California State Library, Sacramento
DC   Dartmouth College Collection, Hanover, N.H.
DPL   Denver Public Library
HC   Paul Henderson Collection, Bridgeport, Nebr.
HL   Huntington Library, San Marino, Calif.
HSM   State Historical Society of Missouri, Columbia
InS   Indiana State Library, Bloomington
ISL   Illinois State Historical Library, Springfield
KHS   Kansas State Historical Society, Topeka
LC   Library of Congress, Washington, D.C.
MC   Charles W. Martin Collection, Omaha, Nebr.
MiHS   Missouri Historical Society, St. Louis
MnHS   Historical Society of Michigan, Lansing
MU   University of Michigan, Ann Arbor
NatA   National Archives, Washington, D.C.
NL   Ayer Collection, Newberry Library, Chicago
NPS   National Park Service, Omaha, Nebr.
NSHS   Nebraska State Historical Society, Lincoln
OhHS   Ohio Historical Society, Columbus
OHS   Oregon Historical Society, Portland
SCP   Society of California Pioneers, San Francisco
UHS   Utah State Historical Society
WHS   State Historical Society of Wisconsin, Madison
WSA   Wyoming State Archives, Cheyenne
WU   University of Wyoming, Laramie

B. SECONDARY SOURCES

Andreas, A. T. (compiler). *History of the State of Nebraska.* Chicago: 1882.

Babbitt, Charles H. *Early Days in Council Bluffs.* Washington, D.C.: 1916.

Bancroft, Hubert Howe. *History of Nevada, Colorado and Wyomng, 1540–1888.* San Francisco: 1890.

Barrett, James T. "Cholera in Missouri," *Missouri Historical Review,* LV (July, 1961), 344–54.

Beers, Henry P. "A History of the U.S. Topographical Engineers," *The Military Engineer* (June, 1952), 287–91; (July, 1952), 348–52.

Brand, Donald D. *The History of Scotts Bluff, Nebraska.* Berkeley: 1934. (Mimeograph booklet, National Park Service.)

Bushnell, David I. *Burials of the . . . Tribes West of the Mississippi (Bureau of American Ethnology Bulletin 83).* Washington, D.C.: 1927.

Chittenden, Hiram M. "The Oregon Trail," in *History of the American Fur Trade,* Vol. I. Stanford, Calif.: 1954. (Reprint of 1902 edition.)

Clarke, Dwight L. *Stephen Watts Kearny, Soldier of the West.* Norman: 1961.

Coutant, C. G. *History of Wyoming.* Laramie: 1899.

Coy, Roy E. "The Early Years," *Museum Graphic, XVII* (Spring, 1965), 9.

Dale, Harrison C. "Organization of the Oregon Emigrating Companies," *Oregon Historical Quarterly,* XVI (September, 1915), 205–27.

Danker, Donald F. "Nebraska Winter Quarters Company and Florence," *Nebraska History,* XXXVI (March, 1956), 27–50.

David, Robert Beebe. *Finn Burnett, Frontiersman.* Glendale: 1937.

Dawson, Charles. *Pioneer Tales of the Oregon Trail and Jefferson County.* Topeka: 1912.

DeVoto, Bernard. *Across the Wide Missouri.* Boston: 1947.

Dodge, Nathan P. "Early Emigration Through and to Council Bluffs," *Annals of Iowa,* XVIII (January, 1932), 163–79.

Driggs, Howard R. *The Old West Speaks,* with paintings by William H. Jackson. Englewood Cliffs, N.J.: 1956.

———. *Westward America,* with paintings by William H. Jackson. New York: 1942.

Drury, C. M. (ed.). *First White Women Over the Rockies.* Glendale: 1963.

Dunbar, Seymour. *History of Travel in America.* 4 vols. Indianapolis: 1915.

Ewers, John C. *Artists of the Old West.* New York: 1965.

Federal Writers' Project, W.P.A. *The Oregon Trail.* New York: 1939.

Fitzpatrick, Lilian L. *Nebraska Place-Names.* Lincoln, Nebr.: 1960.

Garraghan, Gilbert, J. *The Jesuits of the Middle United States.* New York: 1938.

Ghent, W. J. *The Road to Oregon.* New York: 1929.

Grange, Roger. "Digging at Fort Kearny," *Nebraska History,* XLIV (June, 1963), 101–22.

Green, T. L. "A Forgotten Fur Trade Post in Scotts Bluff County," *Nebraska History,* XV (March, 1934), 38–46.

———. "Scotts Bluffs, Fort John," *Nebraska History,* XIX (September, 1938), 175–90.

Grinnell, George Bird. *The Fighting Cheyennes.* Norman: 1956. (Reprint.)

Hafen, LeRoy R. *Handcarts to Zion.* Glendale: 1960.

———. *The Overland Mail.* Glendale: 1926.

Hafen, LeRoy R., and Francis M. Young. *Fort Laramie and the Pageant of the West.* Glendale: 1938.

Hagerty, L. W. "Indian Raids Along the Platte and Little Blue Rivers," *Nebraska History,* XXVIII (July–September, 1947), 176–86; (October–December, 1947), 239–60.

Hansen, Geo. W. "A Tragedy of the Oregon Trail," *Collections of the Nebraska State Historical Society,* XVII (1913), 110–26.

Harris, Earl. "Courthouse and Jail Rocks: Landmarks on the Oregon Trail," *Nebraska History,* XLIII (March, 1962), 29–51.

Hartman, Amos W. "The California and Oregon Trail, 1849–1860," *Oregon Historical Quarterly,* XXV (March, 1924), 1–35.

Harvey, Robert. "The Battle Ground of Ash Hollow," *Collections of the Nebraska State Historical Society,* XVI (1911), 152–64.

Helvey, Frank. "Ranches and Stations on the Oregon Trail," in Dawson, *Pioneer Tales . . . .*

Henderson, Paul. *Landmarks on the Oregon Trail.* New York: 1953.

Henderson, Paul. "The Story of Mud Springs," *Nebraska History,* XXXII (June, 1951), 108–19.

Holmes, Louis A. *Fort McPherson, Nebraska.* Lincoln: 1963.

Howe, Octavius T. *Argonauts of '49 . . . .* Boston: 1923.

Hyde, George E. *Spotted Tail's Folk: A History of the Brule Sioux.* Norman: 1961.

Jackson, Clarence S. *Pageant of the Pioneers.* Minden, Nebr.: 1958.

Jackson, W. Turrentine. *Wagon Roads West.* Berkeley: 1952.

Kansas State Historical Society. *A Survey of Historic Sites and Structures in Kansas.* Topeka: 1957. (Booklet.)

Lavender, David. *Westward Vision: The Story of the Oregon Trail.* New York: 1963.

Long, Margaret. *The Oregon Trail: Following the Old Historic Trails on Modern Highways.* Denver: 1954.

McCann, Lloyd E. "The Grattan Massacre," *Nebraska History*, XXXVII (March, 1956), 1–26.

McDermott, John Francis. "De Smet's Illustrator: Father Nicholas Point," *Nebraska History*, XXXIII (March, 1952), 35–40.

Mantor, Lyle E. "Fort Kearny and the Western Movement," *Nebraska History*, XXIX (September, 1948), 175–207.

——. "Stage Coach and Freighting Days at Fort Kearny," *Nebraska History*, XXIX (December, 1948), 324–38.

Mattes, Merrill J. "Chimney Rock on the Oregon Trail," *Nebraska History*, XXXVI (March, 1955), 1–26.

——. *Fort Laramie and the Forty-Niners.* Estes Park, Colo.: 1949. (Monograph.)

——. "Fort Mitchell, Scott's Bluff, Nebraska Territory," *Nebraska History*, XXXIII (March, 1953), 1–34.

——. "Hiram Scott," in LeRoy R. Hafen (ed.), *The Mountain Men and the Fur Trade of the Far West*, Vol. I. Glendale: 1965.

——. "Hiram Scott, Fur Trader," *Nebraska History*, XXVI (July–September, 1945), 127–62.

——. "A History of Old Fort Mitchell," *Nebraska History*, XXIV (March, 1943), 71–82.

——. *Indians, Infants and Infantry: Andrew and Elizabeth Burt on the Frontier.* Denver: 1960.

——. "Robidoux's Trading Post at Scott's Bluffs and the California Gold Rush," *Nebraska History*, XXX (June, 1949), 95–138.

Mattes, Merrill J., and Paul Henderson. "The Pony Express . . . from St. Joseph to Fort Laramie," *Nebraska History*, XLI (March, 1960), 83–122.

Mattes, Merrill J. "The Jumping-Off Places on the Overland Trail," in John Francis McDermott, (ed.), *The Frontier Re-examined*, Urbana: 1967.

Morgan, Dale L. (ed.). *The West of William H. Ashley, 1822–1838.* Denver: 1964.

Morley, Thomas. "The Independence Road to Fort Laramie: by Aerial Photograph," *Plains Anthropologist*, VI (1961), 242–51.

Paden, Irene D. *The Wake of the Prairie Schooner.* New York: 1944.

Robidoux, Orral Messmore. *Memorial to the Robidoux Brothers.* Kansas City: 1924.

Ross, Marvin C. *The West of Alfred Jacob Miller.* Norman: 1965.

Schafer, Joseph. "Trailing a Trail Artist in 1849," *Wisconsin Magazine of History,* XII (September, 1928), 97–108.

Schuchert, Charles, and Clara Mae LeVene. *O. C. Marsh, Pioneer in Paleontology.* New Haven: 1940.

Shaffer, Leslie L. D. "Management of Organized Wagon Trains on the Overland Trail." *Missouri Historical Review,* LV (July, 1961), 355–65.

Shumway, E. W. "Winter Quarters, 1846–1848," *Nebraska History,* XXXV (June, 1954), 115–26; XXXVI (March, 1955), 43–54.

Shumway, Grant L. *History of Western Nebraska and Its People.* Lincoln: 1921.

Smith, Waddell F. (ed.). *The Story of the Pony Express.* San Francisco: 1960. (Centennial edition of original work by Glenn D. Bradley.)

Steele, Olga Sharp. "Geography of the Mormon Trail Across Nebraska." Unpublished master's thesis, University of Nebraska, 1933.

Stegner, Wallace. *The Gathering of Zion: The Story of the Mormon Trail.* New York: 1964.

Stewart, George R. *The California Trail.* New York: 1962.

Sweet, J. H. "Old Fort Kearny," *Nebraska History,* XXVII (October–December, 1946), 233–43.

Taft, Robert. *Artists and Illustrators of the Old West.* New York: 1953.

Thomas, Robert. "Buckeye Argonauts," *Ohio State Archeological and Historical Quarterly,* LIX (July, 1950), 256–69.

Troxel, Kathryn. "Food of the Oregon Emigrants," *Oregon Historical Quarterly,* LVI (March, 1955), 12–26.

Wagner, Henry R. *The Plains and the Rockies: A Bibliography of Original Narratives of Travel, 1800–1865,* ed. Charles L. Camp. Columbus, O.: 1953.

Wallace, William S. *Antoine Robidoux, 1794–1860.* Los Angeles: 1953.

Watkins, Albert. "History of Fort Kearny," *Collections of the Nebraska State Historical Society,* XVI (1911), 227–67.

Wedel, Waldo, R. *An Introduction to Pawnee Archeology (Bureau of American Ethnology Bulletin 112).* Washington, D.C.: 1936.

Weston, Queen of Steamboat Days. Weston, Mo.: 1964.

Willman, Lillian M. "The History of Fort Kearny," *Nebraska State Historical Society Collections*, XXI (1930), 211–318.

Wyman, Walker D. "Council Bluffs and the Westward Movement," *Iowa Journal of History*, XLVII (April, 1949), 99–118.

Young, F. G. "The Oregon Trail," *Oregon Historical Quarterly*, I (December, 1900), 339–70.

Young, Otis E. *The West of Philip St. George Cooke, 1809–1895*. Glendale: 1955.

Index

ABOUT THE AUTHOR

Merrill J. Mattes was a member of the Nebraska State Historical Society since he first arrived in Nebraska in 1935 as superintendent, Scotts Bluff National Monument. It was there that he became acquainted with overland journals and conceived the idea of writing a book on the Oregon Trail in western Nebraska. It was not until 1962, however, when he received a Nebraska Centennial research grant, that he began intensive research on the subject that had by then evolved into this comprehensive history of overland migrations from the various "jumping-off points" across the plains to Fort Laramie, "Gateway to the Mountains."

In 1946 Mr. Mattes was transferred to the Midwest Region of the National Park Service in Omaha, where for twenty years he served as Regional Historian. In 1966 he became Chief of History & Historic Architecture, Western Service Center, in San Francisco. In 1972 he was transferred to the Denver Service Center as Chief of Historic Preservation.

In addition to a lengthy list of publications in western history, including four books and many articles in periodicals and reference works, Mr. Mattes won several notable honors. In 1958, as Regional Historian for the National Park Service in Omaha, he was named Nebraska's Civil Servant of the Year. In 1959 he received the Distinguished Service Award of the U.S. Department of the Interior. He was a charter member of the Omaha Westerners, and served as Sheriff for both the San Francisco and Denver Westerners. He was also a cofounder of the Douglas County Historical Society (Omaha) and the Oregon-California Trails Association.